Pastor Christina Hosler
129 Steubenville Pike
Burgettstown, PA 15021
(724)729-3526

A HISTORY

OF

THE REFORMATION

BY

THOMAS M. LINDSAY, D.D., LL.D.

PRINCIPAL, THE UNITED FREE CHURCH
COLLEGE, GLASGOW

II

THE REFORMATION IN SWITZERLAND, FRANCE
THE NETHERLANDS, SCOTLAND AND ENGLAND
THE ANABAPTIST AND SOCINIAN MOVEMENTS
THE COUNTER-REFORMATION

Wipf and Stock Publishers
150 West Broadway • Eugene OR 97401

1999

Printed in the United States of America

A History of the Reformation

By Lindsay, Thomas M.

ISBN: 1-57910-283-2

Reprinted by *Wipf and Stock Publishers* 1999
150 West Broadway • Eugene OR 97401

Previously Published by Charles Scribner's Sons, 1906

PREFACE.

—✦—

In this volume I have endeavoured to fulfil the promise made in the former one to describe the Reformed Churches, the Anabaptist and Socinian movements and the Counter-reformation in the sixteenth century.

It has been based on a careful study of contemporary sources of information, and no important fact has been recorded for which there is not contemporary evidence. Full use has been made of work done by predecessors in the same field. The sources and the later books consulted have been named at the beginning of each chapter; but special reference is due to the writings of Professor Pollard on the reigns of Henry VIII. and Edward VI., and to those of MM. Lemonier and Mariéjol for the history of Protestantism in France. The sources consulted are, for the most part, printed in Calendars of State Papers issued by the various Governments of Europe, or in the correspondence of prominent men and women of the sixteenth century, edited and published for Historical and Archæological Societies; but the Calendar of State Papers, Domestic, relating to the reigns of Edward VI., Mary, and Elizabeth, is little more than a brief account of the contents of the documents, and has to be supplemented by reference to the original documents in the Record Office.

The field covered in this volume is so extensive that

the accounts of the rise and progress of the Reformation in the various countries included had to be very much condensed. I have purposely given a larger space to the beginnings of each movement, believing them to be less known and more deserving of study. One omission must be noted. Nothing has been said directly about the Reformed Churches in Bohemia, Hungary, and the neighbouring lands. It would have been easy to devote a few pages to the subject; but such a brief description would have been misleading. The rise, continuance, and decline of these Churches are so inseparably connected with the peculiar social and political conditions of the countries, that no adequate or informing account of them could be given without largely exceeding the limits of space at my disposal.

After the volume had been fully printed, and addition or alteration was impossible, two important documents bearing on subjects discussed came into my hands too late for references in the text.

I have found that the Library of the Technical College in Glasgow contains a copy, probably unique, of the famous Hymn-book of the *Brethren* published at Ulm in 1538. It is entitled: *Ein hubsch neu Gesangbuch darinnen begrieffen die Kirchenordnung und Geseng die zür Lants Kron und Fulneck in Behem, von der Christlichen Bruderschafft den Piccarden, die bishero für Unchristen und Ketzer gehalten, gebraucht und teglich Gott zum Ehren gesungen werden.* Gedruckt zu Ulm bey Hans Varnier. An. MDXXXVIII. I know of a copy of much later date in Nürnberg; but of no perfect copy of this early impression. It is sufficient to say that the book confirms what I have said of the character of the religion of the *Brethren.*

Then in December 1906, Señor Henriques published at Lisbon the authentic records of the trial of

George Buchanan and two fellow professors in the Coimbra College before the Inquisition. These records show that the prosecution had not been instigated by the Jesuits, as was generally conjectured, but was due to the malice of a former Principal of the College. The statement made on p. 556 has therefore to be corrected.

The kindness of the publishers has provided an historical map, which I trust will be found useful. It gives, I think for the first time, a representation to the eye of the wide extent of the Anabaptist movement. The red bars denote districts where contemporary documents attest the existence of Anabaptist communities. At least four maps, representing successive periods, would be needed to show with exactness the shifting boundaries of the various confessions; one map can only give the general results.

My thanks are again due to my colleague, Dr. Denney, and to another friend, for the care they have taken in revising the proof sheets, and for many valuable suggestions.

THOMAS M. LINDSAY.

January, 1907.

CONTENTS

—+—

BOOK III.

THE REFORMED CHURCHES.

CHAPTER I.

INTRODUCTION.

CHAPTER II.

THE REFORMATION IN SWITZERLAND UNDER ZWINGLI.

xi

CHAPTER III.

THE REFORMATION IN GENEVA UNDER CALVIN.

CHAPTER IV.

THE REFORMATION IN FRANCE.

BOOK IV.

THE REFORMATION IN ENGLAND.

CHAPTER I.

THE CHURCH OF HENRY VIII.

CHAPTER II.

THE REFORMATION UNDER EDWARD VI.

CHAPTER III.

THE REACTION UNDER MARY.

CHAPTER IV.

THE SETTLEMENT UNDER ELIZABETH.

BOOK V.

ANABAPTISM AND SOCINIANISM.

CHAPTER I.

REVIVAL OF MEDIÆVAL ANTI-ECCLESIASTICAL MOVEMENTS.

CHAPTER II.

ANABAPTISM.

CHAPTER III.

SOCINIANISM.

BOOK VI.

THE COUNTER-REFORMATION.

CHAPTER I.

THE NECESSITY OF A REFORMATION OF SOME SORT UNIVERSALLY ADMITTED.

CHAPTER II.

THE SPANISH CONCEPTION OF A REFORMATION.

CHAPTER III.

ITALIAN LIBERAL ROMAN CATHOLICS AND THEIR CONCEPTION OF A REFORMATION.

CHAPTER IV.

IGNATIUS LOYOLA AND THE COMPANY OF JESUS.

CHAPTER V.

THE COUNCIL OF TRENT.

CHAPTER VI.

THE INQUISITION AND THE INDEX.

BOOK III.

THE REFORMED CHURCHES.

CHAPTER I.

INTRODUCTION.

§ 1. *The Limitations of the Peace of Augsburg.*

THE Religious Peace of Augsburg (1555) secured the legal recognition of the Reformation within the Holy Roman Empire, and consequently within European polity. Henceforward States, which declared through their responsible rulers that they meant to live after the religion described in the *Augsburg Confession*, were admitted to the comity of nations, and the Pope was legally and practically debarred from excommunicating them, from placing them under *interdict*, and from inviting obedient neighbouring potentates to conquer and dispossess their sovereigns. The Bishop of Rome could no longer, according to the recognised custom of the Holy Roman Empire, launch a Bull against a Lutheran prince and expect to have its execution enforced as in earlier days. The Popes were naturally slow to see this, and had to be reminded of the altered state of matters more than once.[1]

[1] The fierce old Pontiff, Paul IV., declared in a Bull (Feb. 15, 1559) that the mere fact of heresy in princes deprived them of all lawful power; but he named no one. When his successor proposed, in 1563, to excommunicate Elizabeth of England by name simply as a Protestant, he was taken to task sharply by the Emperor Ferdinand; and the Queen was finally excommunicated in 1570 as a partaker "in the atrocious mysteries of Calvinism," and as such outside the Peace of Augsburg.

I**

Of course, the exalted Romanist powers, civil and ecclesiastical, never meant this settlement to be lasting. They intrigued secretly among themselves, and fought openly, against it. The final determined effort to overthrow it was that hideous nightmare which goes by the name of the Thirty Years' War, mainly caused by the determination of the Jesuits that by the help of God *and* the devil, for that, as Carlyle has remarked, was the peculiarity of the plan, all Germany must be brought back to the obedience of Holy Stepmother Church, and to submission to the Supreme Headship of the Holy Roman Empire—the Supreme Headship becoming more and more shadowy as the years passed. The settlement lasted, however, and remains in general outline until the present.

But the Religious Peace of Augsburg did not end the revolt against Rome which was simmering in every land in Western Europe. It made no provision for the multitude of believers in the *Augsburg Confession*, whose princes, for conscience' sake or for worldly policy, remained steadfast to Rome, save that they were to be permitted to emigrate to territories where the rulers were of the same faith as theirs. These Lutherans were to be found in every part of Germany, and were very abundant in the Duchy of Austria. The statement of Faber, the Bishop of Vienna, that the only good Catholics in that city were himself and the Archduke Ferdinand, was, of course, rhetorical; but it is a proof of the numbers of the followers of Luther.[1]

It chained irrevocably to the Romanist creed, by the clause called the *ecclesiastical reservation*, not merely the people, but the rulers in the numerous ecclesiastical principalities scattered all over Germany. This provision secured that if an ecclesiastical prince adopted the Lutheran faith, he was to be deprived of his principality.

---

[1] In the *Atlas zur Kirchengeschichte* by Heussi and Mulert (Tübingen, 1905), there is an attempt to represent to the eye the presence of German Protestants outside the territories of the Lutheran princes ; Map x. *Zur Geschichte der deutschen Reformation und Gegenreformation.*

It is probable that this provision did more than anything else to secure for the Romanists the position they now have in Germany. It was partly due to the alarms excited by the fact that Albert of Brandenburg, Master of the Teutonic Knights, had secularised his land of East Prussia and had become a Lutheran, and by the narrow escape of the province of Köln from following in the same path, under its reforming archbishop, Hermann von Wied.

The Peace of Augsburg made no provision for any Protestants other than those who accepted the Augsburg Confession; and thousands in the Palatinate and all throughout South Germany preferred another type of Protestant faith. It is probable that, had Luther lived for ten or fifteen years longer, the great division between the Reformed or Calvinist and the Evangelical or Lutheran Churches would have been bridged over; but after his death his successors, intent to maintain, as they expressed it, the deposit of truth which Luther had left, actually ostracised Melanchthon for his endeavour to heal the breach. The consequence was that the Lutheran Church within Germany after 1555 lost large districts to the Reformed Church.

Under Elector Frederick III., surnamed the Pious, the territorial Church of the Palatinate separated from the circle of Lutheran Churches, and in 1563 the Heidelberg Catechism was published. This celebrated doctrinal formula at once became, and has remained, the distinctive creed of the various branches of the Reformed Church within Germany; and its influence extended even farther.

Bremen followed the example of the Palatinate in 1568. Its divines published a doctrinal *Declaration* in 1572, and a more lengthy *Consensus Bremenensis* in 1595. Anhalt, under its ruler John George (1587–1603), did away with the consistorial system of Church government, and abandoned the use of Luther's Catechism. Hesse-Cassel joined the circle of German Reformed Churches in 1605. These examples were followed in many smaller principalities, most of which, imitating all the Reformed Churches, published separate and distinctive confessions of faith, which were nevertheless supposed to contain the sum and substance of the common Reformed creed.[1]

These German principalities, rulers and inhabitants, placed themselves deliberately outside the protection of the Religious Peace of Augsburg. The fundamental principles of their faith were not very different from the Lutheran, but they were important enough to make them forego the protection which the treaty afforded. Setting aside minor differences and sentiments, perhaps more powerful than doctrines, their separation from neighbouring Protestants was based on their objection to the doctrine of *Ubiquity*, essential to the Lutheran theory of the Sacrament of the Supper, and to the consistorial system of ecclesi-

---

[1] The fullest account of these German Reformed confessions is to be found in Müller's *Die Bekenntnisschriften der reformirten Kirche* — the *Emden Catechism* (1554), pp. 1 and 666 ; the *Heidelberg Catechism* (1563), pp. 1, 682 ; the *Nassau Confession* of the Dillenburg Synod (1578), liii, 720 ; the *Bremen Consensus* (1595), liv, 739 ; the *Staffort Book* (1559) for Baden, liv, 797 ; the *Confession of the General Synod of Cassel*, lv and 817, and the *Hessian Catechism* (1607), 822 ; and the *Bentheim Confession* (1613), 833. All these German Reformed confessions followed Melanchthon in his endeavours to unite the Calvinist and the Lutheran doctrinal positions.

By far the most celebrated, and the only one which maintains its place as a doctrinal symbol down to the present day, is the *Heidelberg Catechism*. It was drafted at the suggestion of the Elector Frederick the Pious by two theologians, Caspar Olevianus and Zacharias Ursinus, who were able to express in a really remarkable degree the thoughts of German Protestants who could not accept the hard and fast Lutheranism of the opponents of Melanchthon. It speedily found favour in many parts of Germany, although its strongest supporters belonged to the Rhine provinces. It was in use both as a means of instruction and as a doctrinal symbol in most of the German Reformed Churches along with their own symbolical books. Its use spread to Holland and beyond it. Two separate translations appeared in Scotland. The earlier is contained in (Dunlop's) *Collection of Confessions of Faith. . . . of public authority in the Church of Scotland*, under the title, *A Catechism of the Christian Religion, composed by Zachary Ursin, approved by Frederick III. Elector Palatine, the Reformed Church in the Palatinate, and by other Reformed Churches in Germany ; and taught in their schools and churches : examined and approved, without any alteration, by the Synod of Dort, and appointed to be taught in the reformed churches and schools in the Netherlands : translated and printed Anno 1591 by public authority for the use of Scotland, with the arguments and use of the several doctrines therein contained, by Jeremias Bastingius ; sometimes printed with the Book of Common Order and Psalm Book.*

astical government. They repudiated the two portions of
the Lutheran system which were derived professedly from
the mediæval Church, and insisted on basing their exposition of doctrine and their scheme of ecclesiastical government more directly on the Word of God. They had come
in contact with another reformation movement, had
recognised its sturdier principles, and had become so
enamoured of them that they felt compelled to leave the
Lutheran Church for the Reformed.

Still confining ourselves to Germany, it is to be noticed
that the Augsburg Confession ostentatiously and over and
over again separated those who accepted it from protesters
against the mediæval Church, who were called Anabaptists.
It repudiated views supposed to be held by them on
Baptism, the Holy Scripture, the possibility of a life of
sinless perfection, and the relation of Christian men to the
magistracy. In some of the truces arranged between the
Emperor and the evangelical princes,—truces which anticipated the religious Peace of Augsburg,—attempts were
made to induce Lutherans and Romanists to unite in sup-
pressing those sectaries. It is needless to say that *they*
were not included in the settlement in 1555. Yet they
had spread all over Germany, endured with constancy
bloody persecutions, and from them have come the large
and influential Baptist Churches in Europe and America.
From beginning to end they were outside the Lutheran
Reformation.

§ 2. *The Reformation outside Germany.*

When we go beyond Germany and survey the other
countries of Western Europe, it is abundantly evident that
the story of the Lutheran movement from its beginning
down to its successful issue in the Religious Peace of
Augsburg is only a small part of the history of the Reformation. France, Great Britain, the Netherlands,
Bohemia, Hungary, even Italy, Spain, and Poland, throbbed
with the religious revival of the sixteenth century, and its

manifestations in these lands differed in many respects from that which belonged to Germany. All shared with Germany the common experiences, intellectual and religious, political and economic, of that period of transition which is called the Renaissance in the wider sense of the word—the transition from mediæval to modern life.[1] They had all come to the parting of the ways. They had all emerged from Mediævalism, and all saw the wider outlook which was the heritage of the time. All felt the same longing to shake themselves clear of the incubus of clericalism which weighed heavily on their national life, whether religious or political. Each land went forward, marching by its own path marked out for it by its past history, intellectual, religious, and civil. The movements in these various countries towards a freer and more real religious life cannot be described in the same general terms ; but if Italy and Spain be excepted, their attempts at a national reformation had one thing in common which definitely separated them from the Lutheran movement.

§ 3. *The Reformed type of Doctrine.*

If the type of doctrine professed by the Protestants in those countries be considered (confessedly a partial, one-sided, and imperfect standard), it may be said that they all refused to accept some of the distinctive Lutheran dogmatic conclusions, and that they all departed more widely from some of the conceptions of the Mediæval Church. Their national confessions in their final forms borrowed more from Zurich and Geneva than from Wittenberg, and they all belong to the Reformed as distinguished from the Lutheran or Evangelical circle of creeds.[2] It was perhaps natural

---

[1] Compare vol. i. pt. i. 42 *ff.*

[2] The most complete collection of those Reformed creeds is given in Müller, *Die Bekenntnisschriften der reformirten Kirche* (Leipzig, 1903). The most important are the following (the figures within brackets give the pages in Müller) :—

SWITZERLAND.—Zwingli's *Theses* of 1523 (xvi, 1) ; *First Helvetic Confession* of 1536 (xxvi, 101) ; *Geneva Confession* of 1536 (xxvi, 111) ; *Geneva*

that differences in the ritual and theory of the Holy Supper, the very apex and crown of Christian Public Worship, should be to the general eye the visible cleavage between rival forms of Christianity. In the earlier stages of the Reformation movement, the great popular distinction between the Romanists and Protestants was that the one refused and the other admitted the laity to partake of the Cup of Communion; and later, within an orthodox Protestantism, the thought of *ubiquity* was the dividing line. The Lutherans asserted and the Reformed denied or ignored the doctrine; and those confessions took the Reformed view.

§ 4. *The Reformed ideal of Ecclesiastical Government.*

This similarity of published creed was the one *positive* bond which united all those Churches; but it may also be said that all of them, with the doubtful exception of the Church of England,[1] would have nothing to do with the consistorial system of the Lutheran Churches, and that most of them accepted in theory at least Calvin's conception of ecclesiastical government. They strove to get away from the mediæval ideas of ecclesiastical rule, and to return to the principles which they believed to be laid down for them in the New Testament, illustrated by the conduct of the Church of the early centuries. The Church,

Catechism of 1545 [(xxviii, 117) translated in (Dunlop's) *Confessions*, etc., ii, 139].

ENGLAND.—Edwardine *Forty-two Articles* of 1553, *Thirty-eight Articles* of 1563, *Thirty-nine Articles* of 1571 (xlii, 505); *Lambeth Articles* of 1595 (xliv, 525); *Irish Articles* of 1615 (xliv, 526).

SCOTLAND.—*Scottish Confession* of 1560, *National Covenant* of 1581 [(xxxv, 249), (Dunlop's) *Confessions*, etc., ii. pp. 21 and 103].

FRANCE.—*Confessio Gallicana* of 1559 (xxxii, 221).

NETHERLANDS.—*Confessio Belgica* of 1561 (xxxiv, 233); *Netherlands Confession* of 1566 (xxxv, 935); *Frisian Confession* of 1528 (xxi, 930).

HUNGARY.—*Hungarian Confession* of 1562 (xxviii, 376).

BOHEMIA.—*Bohemian Confession* of 1609 (xxxix, 453).

[1] It has been suggested that the ecclesiastical jurisdiction which grew out of the Elizabethan settlement of religion in England borrowed not a few characteristics from the Lutheran consistorial courts.

according to Calvin, was a theocratic democracy, and the ultimate source of authority lay in the membership of the Christian community, inspired by the Presence of Christ promised to all His people. But in the sixteenth century this conception was confronted and largely qualified in practice, by the dread that it might lead to a return to the clerical tutelage of the mediæval Church from which they had just escaped. Presbyter might become priest writ large; and the leaders of the Reformation in many lands could see, as Zwingli did in Zurich and Cranmer in England, that the civil authorities might well represent the Christian democracy. Even Calvin in Geneva had to content himself with ecclesiastical ordinances which left the Church completely under the control of *les très honnorès seigneurs syndicques et conseil de Genève*; and the Scottish Church in 1572 had to recognise that the King was the " Supreme Governor of this realm as well in things temporal as in the conservation and purgation of religion." The nations and principalities in Western Europe which had adopted and supported the Reformation believed that manifold abuses had arisen in the past, directly and indirectly, through the exemption of the Church and its possessions from secular control, and they were determined not to permit the possibility of a return to such a state of things. The scholarship of the Renaissance had discovered the true text of the old Roman Civil Code, and one of the features of that time of transition—perhaps its most important and far-reaching feature, for law enters into every relation of human life—was the substitution of civil law based on the Codes of Justinian and Theodosius, for canon law based on the Decretum of Gratian. These old Roman codes taught the lawyers and statesmen of the sixteenth century to look upon the Church as a department of the State; and the thought that the Christian community had an independent life of its own, and that its guidance and discipline ought to be in the hands of office-bearers chosen by its membership, was everywhere confronted, modified, largely overthrown by the imperious claim of the civilian lawyers. Ecclesiastical leaders within the Reformed Churches might strive as they liked to draw the line between the possessions of the Church, which they willingly placed under the control of civil law, and its discipline in matters of faith and morals, which they declared to be the inalienable possession of the Church; but, as a rule, the State refused to perceive the distinction, and insisted in maintaining full control over the ecclesiastical jurisdiction. Hence it came about that in every land where the secular authorities were favourable to the Reformation, the Church became more or less subject to the State; and this resulted in a large variety of ecclesiastical organisations in communities all belonging to the Reformed Church. While it may be said with perfect truth that the churchly ideal in the minds of the leaders in most of the Reformed Churches was to restore the theocratic democracy of the early centuries, and that this was a strong point of contrast between them and Luther, who insisted that the *jus episcopale* belonged to the civil magistrate, in practice the secular authorities in Switzerland, the Netherlands, the Palatinate, etc., kept almost as tight a hold on the Reformed national Churches as did the Lutheran princes and municipalities. In one land only, France, the ecclesiastical ideal of Calvin had full liberty to embody itself in a constitution, and that only because the French Reformed Church struggled into existence under the civil rule of a Romanist State, and, like the Christian Church of the early centuries, maintained itself in spite of the opposition of the secular authorities which persecuted it.

§ 5. *The Influence of Humanism on the Reformed Churches.*

The portion of the Reformation which lay outside the Peace of Augsburg had another characteristic which distinguished it from the Lutheran Reformation included within the treaty—it owed much more to Humanism. Erasmus and what he represented had a greater share in its birth and early progress, and his influence appeared

amidst the most dissimilar surroundings. Henry VIII. and
Zwingli seem to stand at opposite poles; yet the English
autocrat and the Swiss democrat were alike in this, that
they owed much to Erasmus, and that the reformations
which they respectively led were largely prompted by the
impulse of Humanism. One has only to compare the
Bishops' Book and the *King's Book* of the Henrican period
in England with the many statements Erasmus has made
about the kind of reformation he desired to see, to recognise
that they were meant to serve for a reformation in life
and morals which would leave untouched the fundamental
doctrinal system of the mediæval Church and its organisation in accordance with the principles laid down by the
great Humanist. The Bible, the Apostles', Nicene, and
Athanasian Creeds, with the doctrinal decisions of the first
four Œcumenical Councils, were recognised as the standards
of orthodoxy in the *Ten Articles*; and the Scholastic Theology, so derided by Erasmus, was contemptuously ignored.
The accompanying *Injunctions* set little store by pilgrimages,
relics, and indulgences, and the other superstitions of the
popular religious life which the great Humanist had treated
sarcastically. The two books alluded to above are full
of instructions for leading a wholesome life. The whole
programme of reformation is laid down on lines borrowed
from Erasmus.

Zwingli was under the influence of Humanism from
his boyhood. His young intellect was fed on the master-
pieces of classical antiquity—Cicero, Homer, and Pindar.
His favourite teacher was Thomas Wyttenbach, who was
half a Reformer and half a pure follower of Erasmus. No
man influenced him more than the learned Dutchman. It
was his guidance and not the example of Luther which
made him study the Scriptures and the theologians of the
early Church, such as Origen, Jerome, and Chrysostom.
The influence and example of Erasmus can be seen even
in his attempts to create a rational theory of the Holy
Supper. His reformation, in its beginning more especially,
was much more an intellectual than a religious movement.

It aimed at a clearer understanding of the Holy Scriptures, at the purgation of the popular religious life from idolatry and superstition, and at a clearly reasoned out scheme of intellectual belief. The deeper religious impulse which drove Luther, step by step, in his path of revolt from the mediæval Church was lacking in Zwingli. He owed little to Wittenberg, much to Rotterdam. It was this connection with Erasmus that created the sympathy between Zwingli and such early Dutch Reformers as Christopher Hoen, and made the Swiss Reformer a power in the earlier stages of the Reformation in the Netherlands.

The beginnings of the Reformation movement in France, Italy, and Spain were even more closely allied to Humanism.

If the preparation for reformation to be found in the work and teaching of mediæval evangelical nonconformists like the *Picards* be set aside, the beginnings of the Reformation in France must be traced to the small group of Christian Humanists who surrounded Marguerite d'Angoulême and Briçonnet the Bishop of Meaux. Marguerite herself and Jacques Lefèvre d'Etaples, the real leader of the group of scholars and preachers, found solace for soul troubles in the Christian Platonism to which so many of the Humanists north and south of the Alps had given themselves. The aim of the little circle of enthusiasts was a reformation of the Church and of society on the lines laid down by Erasmus. They looked to reform without " tumult," to a reformation of the Church by the Church and within the Church, brought about by a study of the Scriptures, and especially of the Epistles of St. Paul, by individual Christians weaning themselves from the world while they remained in society, and by slowly leavening the people with the enlightenment which the New Learning was sure to bring. They cared little for theology, much for intimacy with Christ; little for external changes in institutions, much for personal piety. Their efforts had little visible effect, and their *via media* between the stubborn defenders of Scholasticism on the

one hand and more thorough Reformers on the other, was
found to be an impossible path to persevere in; but it
must not be forgotten that they did much to prepare
France for the Reformation movement which they really
inaugurated; nor that William Farel, the precursor of
Calvin himself in Geneva, belonged to the "group of
Meaux."

If Humanism influenced the "group of Meaux," who
were the advance guard of the French Reformation, it
manifested itself no less powerfully in the training of
Calvin, who in 1536 unconsciously became the leader of
the movement. He was one of the earliest and most
enthusiastic students of the band of "royal lecturers"
appointed by Francis I. to give France the benefits of the
New Learning. He had intimate personal relations with
Budé and Cop, who were allied to the "group of Meaux,"
and were leaders among the Humanists in the University.
His earliest book, a Commentary on the *De Clementia* of
Seneca, shows how wide and minute was his knowledge of
the Greek and Latin classical authors. Like Erasmus,
he does not seem to have been much influenced by the
mystical combination of Platonism and Christianity which
entranced the Christian Humanists of Italy and filled the
minds of the "group of Meaux"; and like him he broke
through the narrow circle of elegant trifling within which
most of the Italian scholars were confined, and used the
New Learning for modern purposes. Humanism taught
him to think imperially in the best fashion of ancient
Rome, to see that great moral ideas ought to rule in the
government of men. It filled him with a generous
indignation at the evils which flowed from an abuse of
absolute and arbitrary power. The young scholar (he
was only three-and-twenty) attacked the governmental
abuses of the times with a boldness which revived the best
traditions of Roman statesmanship. He denounced venal
judges who made "justice a public merchandise." He
declared that princes who slew their people or subjected
them to wholesale persecution were not legitimate rulers,

but brigands, and that brigands were the enemies of the whole human race. At a time when persecution was prevalent everywhere, the Commentary of the young Humanist pleaded for tolerance in language as lofty as Milton employed in his *Areopagitica*. He was not blind to the defects of the stoical morality displayed in the book he commented upon. He contrasted the stoical indifference with Christian sympathy, and stoical individualism with the thought of Christian society; but he seized upon and made his own the loftier moral ideas in Stoicism, and applied them to public life. Luther was great, none greater, in holding up the liberty of the Christian man; but there he halted, or advanced beyond it with very faltering step. Humanism taught Calvin the claims and the duties of the Christian society; he proclaimed them aloud, and his thoughts spread throughout that portion of the Reformation which followed his leadership and accepted his principles. The Holy Scriptures, St. Augustine, and the imperial ethics of the old Roman Stoicism coming through Humanism, were a trinity of influence on all the Reformed Churches.

The Reformation in Spain and Italy was only a brief episode; but in its shortlived existence in these lands, Humanism was one of the greatest forces supporting it and giving it strength. In both countries the young life was quenched in the blood of martyrs. So quickly did it pass, that it seems surprising to learn that Erasmus confidently expected that Spain would be the land to accomplish the Reformation without " tumult " which he so long looked forward to and expected; that the Scriptures were read throughout the Spanish peninsula, and that women vied with men in knowledge of their contents, during the earlier part of the sixteenth century.

§ 6. *What the Reformed Churches owed to Luther.*

There was, then, a Reformation movement which in its earliest beginnings and in its final outcome was quite distinct from that under the leadership of Luther; but it would be erroneous to say that it was altogether outside Luther's influence, and that it owed little or nothing to the great German Reformer. It is vain to speculate on what might have been, or to ask whether the undoubted movements making for reformation in lands outside Germany would have come to fruition had not Luther's trumpet-call sounded over Europe. It is enough to state what did actually occur. If it cannot be said that the beginnings of the Reformation in every land came from Luther, it can scarcely be denied that he gave to his contemporaries the inspiration of courage and of assured conviction. He delivered men from the fear of priest-craft; he taught men, in a way that no other did, that redemption was not a secret science practised by the priests within an institution called the Church; that all believers had the privilege of direct access to the very presence of God; and that the very thought of a priest-hood who alone could mediate between God and man was both superfluous and irreconcilable with the truest instincts of the Christian religion. His teaching had a sounding board of dramatic environment which compelled men to listen, to attend, to be impressed, to understand, and to follow.

He had been and was a deeply pious man, with the piety of the type most esteemed by his contemporaries, and therefore easily understood and sympathised with by the common man. His piety had driven him into the convent, as then seemed both natural and necessary. Inside the monastery he had lived the life of a " young saint "—so his fellow monks believed, when, in the fashion of the day and of their class, they boasted that they had among them one destined to revive again the best type of mediæval saintship. No coarse, vulgar sins of the flesh, common enough at the time and easily condoned, smirched his young life. When he attained to peace in believing, he had no doubt of his vocation; no sudden wrench tore him away from the approved religious life of his time; no intellectual doubt separated him from the beliefs of his Church. His very imperviousness to the intellectual liberalising tendencies of Humanism made him all the more fit to be a trusted religious leader. He went forward step by step with such a slow, sure foot-tread that the common man could see and follow. When he did come forward as a Reformer he did not run amuck at things in general. He felt compelled to attack the *one* portion of the popular religious life of the times which all men who gave the slightest thought to religion felt to be a gross abuse. The way he dealt with it revealed that he was the great religious genius of his age—an age which was imperatively if confusedly calling for reform within the sphere of religion.

If to be original means simply to be the first to see and make known a single truth or a fresh aspect of a truth, it is possible to contest the claim of Luther to be an original thinker. It would not be difficult to point out anticipations of almost every separate truth which he taught to his generation. To take two only— Wessel had denounced indulgences in language so similar to Luther's, that, when the Reformer read it long after the publication of the *Theses*, he could say that people might well imagine that he had simply borrowed from the old Dutch theologian; and Lefèvre d'Etaples had taught the doctrine of justification by faith before it had flashed on Luther's soul with all the force of a revelation. But if originality be the gift to seize, to combine into one organic whole, separate isolated truths, to see their bearing upon the practical religious life of all men, educated and ignorant, to use the new light to strip the common religious life of all paralysing excrescences, to simplify it and to make it clear that the sum and essence of Christianity is "unwavering trust of the heart in Him who has given Himself to us in Christ Jesus as our Father, personal assurance of faith because Christ with His work undertakes our cause," and to do all this with the tenderest sympathy for every true dumb religious instinct which had made men wander away from the simplicity which is in Christ Jesus, then Luther stands alone in his day and generation, unapproachable by any other.

Hence it was that to the common people in every land in Europe up till about 1540, when Calvin's individuality began to make itself felt, Luther represented the Reformation; and all who accepted the new teaching were known as Lutherans, whether in England, the Low Countries, France, or French speaking Switzerland.[1]

Ecclesiastical historians of the Reformed Church from the sixteenth century downward have often been inclined to share Luther's supremacy with Zwingli. The Swiss Reformer was gifted with many qualities which Luther lacked. He stood in freer relation to the doctrines and practices of the mediæval Church, and his scheme of theology was perhaps wider and truer than Luther's. He had a keener intellectual insight, and was quicker to discern the true doctrinal tendencies of their common religious verities. But the way in which he regarded indulgences, and his manner of protesting against them, showed his great inferiority to Luther as a religious guide.

" Oh the folly of it ! " said Zwingli with his master Erasmus,—" the crass, unmitigated stupidity of it all ! " and they scorned it, and laughed at it, and attacked it with the light keen shafts of raillery and derisive wit. " Oh the pity of it ! " said Luther; and he turned men travelling by the wrong road on their quest for pardon (a real quest for them) into the right path. Zwingli never seemed to see that under the purchase of indulgences, the tramping on pilgrimages from shrine to shrine, the kissing, reverencing, and adoring of relics, there was a real

---

[1] William Farel, a devoted Zwinglian, was called a " Lutheran preacher " by the authorities of Freiburg (Herminjard, *Correspondance*, ii. 205.n.), and the teaching of himself and his colleagues was denounced as the " Lutheran heresy." This was the *popular* view. Educated and reforming Frenchmen like Lefèvre discriminated : they had no great liking for Luther, and admired Zwingli (*ibid.* i. 209 n.).

inarticulate cry for pardon of sins felt if not vividly repented of. Luther knew it, and sympathised with it. He was a man of the people, not merely because he was a peasant's son and had studied at a burgher University, but because he had shared the religion of the common people. He had felt with them that the repeated visits of the plague, the new mysterious diseases, the dread of the Turks, were punishments sent by God because of the sins of the generation. He had gone through it all; plunged more deeply in the terror, writhed more hopelessly under the wrath of God, wandered farther on the wrong path in his quest for pardon, and at last had seen the "Beatific Vision." The deepest and truest sympathy with fellowmen and the vision of God are needed to make a Reformer of the first rank, and Luther had both as no other man had, during the first quarter of the sixteenth century.

So men listened to him all over Europe wherever there had been a stirring of the heart for reformation, and it would be hard to say where there had been none. Czechs, Hungarians, and Poles in the east; Spaniards, Englishmen, Frenchmen, Dutch, and Scots in the west; Swedes in the north, and Italians in the south—all welcomed, and read, and were moved by what Luther wrote. First the *Theses*, then sermons and tracts, then the trumpet call *To the Nobility of the German Nation* and the *Præludium to the Babylonian Captivity of the Church of Christ*, and, above all, his booklet *On the Liberty of a Christian Man*. As men read, what had been only a hopeful but troubled dream of the night became a vision in the light of day. They heard proclaimed aloud in clear unfaltering speech what they had scarcely dared to whisper to themselves. Fond and devout imaginations became religious certainties. They risked all to get possession of the sayings of this "man of God." Cautious, dour Scotch burghers ventured ship and cargo for the sake of the little quarto tracts hid in the bales of cloth which came to the ports of Dundee and Leith. Oxford and Cambridge students passed them

2**

from hand to hand in spite of Wolsey's proclamations and Warham's precautions. Luther's writings were eagerly studied in Paris by town and University as early as May 1519.[1] Spanish merchants bought Luther's books at the Frankfurt Fair, spent some of their hard won profits in getting them translated and printed in Spanish, and carried them over the Pyrenees on their pack mules. Under the influence of these writings the Reformation took shape, was something more than the devout imagination of a few pious thinkers, and became an endeavour to give expression to common religious certainties in change of creed, institutions, and worship. Thus Luther helped the Reformation in every land. The actual beginnings in England, France, the Netherlands, and elsewhere had come into existence years before Luther had become known; it is possible that the movements might have come to fruition apart from his efforts; but the influence of his writings was like that of the sun when it quickens and makes the seed sprout that has been "happed" in a tilled and sown field.

§ 7. *National Characteristics.*

It was not that the Reformation in any of these countries was to become Lutheran in the end, or had a Lutheran stage of development. The number of genuine Lutherans outside Germany and Scandinavia was very small. Here and there a stray one was to be found, like Dr. Barnes in England or Louis Berquin in France. One of the deepest principles of the great Reformer's teaching itself checked the idea of a purely Lutheran Reformation

---

[1] Peter Tschudi, writing to Beatus Rhenanus from Paris (May 17th, 1519) says: "Reliqui, quod equidem literis dignum censeam, nil superest, quam M. Lutheri opera ab universa eruditorum cohorte obviis ulnis excipi, etiam iis qui minimum sapiunt plausibilia" (Herminjard, *Correspondance des Réformateurs dans les pays de langue française*, 2nd ed. i. 46). In Nov. 1520, Glareanus wrote to Zwingli that Paris was excited over the Leipzig Disputation; and Bulæus shows that twenty copies of a pamphlet, entitled *Disputatio inter egregios viros et doctores Joa. Eckium et M. Lutherum,* arrived in Paris on Jan. 20th, 1520 (*ibid.* 62, 63 *n.*).

which would embrace the whole Reformation Church. He taught that the practical exercise of faith ought to manifest itself within the great institutions of human life which have their origin in God—in marriage, the family, the calling, and the State, in the ordinary life we lead with its environment. Nations have their character and characteristics as well as individual men, and they mould in natural ways the expression in creed and institution of the religious certainties shared by all. The Reformation in England was based on the same spiritual facts and forces which were at work in France, Germany, and the Netherlands, but each land had its own ways of embodying them. It is interesting to note how national habits, memories, and even prejudices compelled the external embodiment to take very varying shapes, and force the historian to describe the Reformation in each country as something by itself.

The new spiritual life in England took a shape distinctly marked out for it by the almost forgotten reformatory movement under Wiclif which had been native to the soil. Scotland might have been expected to follow the lead of England, and bring her ecclesiastical reconstruction into harmony with that of her new and powerful ally. The English alliance was the great political fact of the Scottish Reformation, and leading statesmen in both countries desired the still nearer approach which conformity in the organisation of the Churches could not fail to foster. But the memory of the old French alliance was too strong for Cecil and Lethington, and Scotland took her methods of Church government from France (not from Geneva), and drifted farther and farther away from the model of the English settlement. The fifteenth century War of the Public Weal repeated itself in the Wars of Religion in France; and in the Edict of Nantes the Reformed Church was offered and accepted guarantees for her independence such as a feudal prince might have demanded. The old political local independence which had characterised the Low Countries in the later Middle Ages reasserted itself in the ecclesiastical arrangements of the Netherlands. The civic republics of Switzerland demanded and received an ecclesiastical form of government which suited the needs of their social and political life.

Yet amidst all this diversity there was the prevailing sense of an underlying unity, and the knowledge that each national Church was part of the Catholic Church Reformed was keener than among the Lutheran Churches. Protestant England in the time of Edward VI. welcomed and supported refugees banished by the Augsburg Interim from Strassburg. Frankfurt received and provided for families who fled from the Marian persecutions in England. Geneva became a city of refuge for oppressed Protestants from every land, and these strangers frequently added quite a third to her population The feeling of fraternity was maintained, as in the days of the early Church, by constant interchange of letters and messengers, and correspondence gave a sense of unity which it was impossible to embody in external political organisation. The sense of a common danger was also a wonderful bond of kinship; and the feeling that Philip of Spain was always plotting their destruction, softened inter-ecclesiastical jealousies. The same sort of events occurred in all the Churches at almost the same times. The Colloquy of Westminster (1559) was separated from the Colloquy of Poissy (1561) by an interval of two years only, and the same questions were discussed at both. Queen Elizabeth openly declared herself a Protestant by partaking of the communion in both "kinds" at Easter, 1559; and on the same day Antoine de Bourbon, King of Navarre, made the same profession in the same way at Pau in the south of France. Mary of Guise resolved that the same festival should see the Scots united under the old faith, and thus started the overt rebellion which ended in Scotland becoming a Protestant nation.

The course of the Reformation in each country must be described separately, and yet it is the one story with differences due to the accidents of national temperaments, memories, and political institutions.

CHAPTER II.

THE REFORMATION IN SWITZERLAND UNDER ZWINGLI.

§ 1. *The political Condition of Switzerland.*[1]

SWITZERLAND in the sixteenth century was like no other country in Europe. It was as divided as Germany or Italy, and yet it had a unity which they could not boast. It was a confederation or little republic of communes and towns of the primitive Teutonic type, in which the executive power was vested in the community. The various cantons were all independent, but they were banded together in a common league, and they had a federal flag—a white cross on a red ground, which bore the motto, " Each for all, and all for each."

The separate members of the Federation had come into existence in a great variety of ways, and all retained the distinctive marks of their earlier history. The beginnings go back to the thirteenth century, when the three Forest cantons, Schwyz, Uri, and Unterwalden, having freed themselves from the dominion of their feudal lords, formed themselves into a *Perpetual League* (1291), in which they pledged themselves to help each other to maintain the liberty they had won. After the battle of Morgarten they renewed the League at Brunnen (1315), promising again to aid each other against all usurping lords. Hapsburg, the cradle of the Imperial House of Austria, lies on the south-

---

[1] A. Rilliet, *Les Origines de la Confédération Suisse: Histoire et Légende* (Geneva, 1869); J. Dierauer, *Geschichte der schweizerischen Eidgenossenschaft* (Gotha, 1890).

east bank of the river Aare, and the dread of this great feudal family strengthened the bonds of the League; while the victories of the independent peasants over the House of Austria, and later over the Duke of Burgundy, increased its reputation. The three cantons grew to be thirteen— Schwyz, Uri, Unterwalden, Luzern, Zurich, Bern, Glarus, Zug, Freiburg, Basel, Schaffhausen, Solothurn, and Appenzell. Other districts, without becoming members of the League, sought its protection, such as the Valais and the town and country under the Abbey of St. Gallen. Other leagues were formed on its model among the peasantry of the Rhætian Alps—in 1396 the *League of the House of God* (*Lia da Ca' Dè*)—at the head of which was the Church at Chur; in 1424 the *Graubünden* (*Lia Grischa* or *Gray League*); in 1436 the *League of the Ten Jurisdictions* (*Lia della desch Dretturas*). These three united in 1471 to make the *Three Perpetual Leagues of Rhætia.* They were in close alliance with the Swiss cantons from the fifteenth century, but did not become actual members of the Swiss Confederacy until 1803. The Confederacy also made some conquests, and the districts conquered were generally governed on forms of mutual agreement between several cantons—a complicated system which led to many bickerings, and intensified the quarrels which religion gave rise to in the sixteenth century.

Each of these thirteen cantons preserved its own independence and its own mode of government. Their political organisation was very varied, and dependent to a large extent on their past history. The Forest cantons were communes of peasant proprietors, dwelling in inaccessible valleys, and their Diet was an assembly of all the male heads of families. Zurich was a manufacturing and commercial town which had grown up under the protection of an old ecclesiastical settlement whose foundation went back to an age beyond that of Charles the Great. Bern was originally a hamlet, nestling under the fortified keep of an old feudal family. In Zurich the nobles made one of the "guilds" of the town, and the constitution was thoroughly

democratic.   Bern, on the other hand, was an aristocratic
republic.   But in all, the power in the last resort belonged
to the people, who were all freemen with full rights of
citizenship.

The Swiss had little experience of episcopal government.
Their relations with the Papacy had been entirely political
or commercial, the main article of commerce being soldiers
to form the Pope's bodyguard, and infantry for his Italian
wars, and the business had been transacted through Legates.
Most of the territory of Switzerland was ecclesiastically
divided between the archiepiscopal provinces of Mainz and
Besançon, and the river Aare was the boundary between
them.   The division went back to the beginning of Christianity in the land.   The part of Switzerland which lay towards France had been Christianised by Roman or Gallic
missionaries ; while the rest, which sloped towards Germany,
had been won to Christianity by Irish preachers ! Basel
and Lausanne figure as bishoprics under Besançon ; while
Constance, a bishopric under Mainz, asserted episcopal rights
over Zurich and the neighbourhood.   The rugged, mountainous part of the country was vaguely claimed for the province of Mainz without being definitely assigned to any
diocese.   This contributed to make the Swiss people singularly independent in all ecclesiastical matters, and taught
them to manage their Church affairs for themselves.

Even in Zurich, which acknowledged the ecclesiastical
jurisdiction of the Bishop of Constance, the Council
insisted on its right of supervising Church properties, and
convents were under State inspection.

In the beginning of the sixteenth century, intercourse
with their neighbours was changing the old simple manners
of the Swiss.   Their repeated victories over Charles the
Bold of Burgundy had led to the belief that the Swiss
infantry was the best in Europe, and nations at war with
each other were eager to hire Swiss troops.   The custom
had gradually grown up among the Swiss cantons of
hiring out soldiers to those who paid best for them.   These
mercenaries, demoralised by making merchandise of their

lives in quarrels not their own, and by spending their pay in riotous living when they returned to their native valleys, were corrupting the population of the Confederacy. The system was demoralising in another way. The two great Powers that trafficked in Swiss infantry were France and the Papacy; and the French king on the one hand, and the Pope on the other, not merely kept permanent agents in the various Swiss cantons, but gave pensions to leading citizens to induce them to persuade the canton to which they belonged to hire soldiers to the one side or the other. Zwingli, in his earlier days, believed that the Papacy was the only Power with which the Swiss ought to ally themselves, and received a papal pension for many years.

§ 2. *Zwingli's Youth and Education.*[1]

Huldreich (Ulrich) Zwingli, the Reformer of Switzerland, was born on January 1st, 1484 (fifty-two days after Luther), in the hamlet of Wildhaus (or Wildenhaus), lying in the upper part of the Toggenburg valley, raised so high above sea-level (3600 feet) that fruits refuse to ripen. It lies so exactly on the central watershed of

[1] SOURCES: O. Myconius, "Vita Huldrici Zwinglii" (in Neander's *Vitœ Quatuor Reformatorum*, Berlin, 1841); H. Bullinger, *Reformationsgeschichte* (Frauenfeld, 1838–40); Johann Salat, *Chronik der schweizerischen Reformation von deren Anfängen bis 1534* (vol. i. of *Archiv für schweizerische Reformationsgeschichte*, Solothurn, 1868); Kessler, *Sabbata* (ed. by Egli, St. Gall, 1902); Strickler, *Actensammlung zur schweizerischen Reformationsgeschichte in den Jahren 1521–32* (Zurich, 1877–84); Egli, *Actensammlung zur Geschichte der Züricher Reformation, 1519–33* (Zurich, 1879); W. Gisi, *Actenstücke zur Schweizergeschichte der Jahre 1521–22* (vol. xv. of *Archiv für die schweizer. Geschichte*), pp. 285–318; Herminjard, *Correspondance des Réformateurs dans les pays de langue française* (Geneva, 166–93); Stähelin *Briefe aus der Reformationszeit* (Basel, 1887).

LATER BOOKS: Stähelin, *Huldreich Zwingli: sein Leben und Wirken nach den Quellen dargestellt*, 2 vols. (Basel, 1895–97); Mörikofer, *Ulrich Zwingli nach den urkundlichen Quellen*, 2 vols. (Leipzig, 1867–69); S. M. Jackson, *Huldreich Zwingli, 1484–1531* (New York, 1901); *Cambridge Modern History*, II. x. (Cambridge, 1903); Ruchat, *Histoire de la Réformation de la Suisse*, ed. by Vulliemin, 7 vols. (Paris, 1835–38).

Europe, that the rain which falls on the one side of the ridge of the red-tiled church roof goes into a streamlet which feeds the Danube, and that which falls on the other finds its way to the Rhine. He came third in a large family of eight sons and two daughters. His father, also called Huldreich, was the headman of the commune, and his uncle, Bartholomew Zwingli, was the parish priest. His education was superintended by Bartholomew, who became Dean of Wesen in 1487, and took the small Huldreich with him to his new sphere of work. The boy was sent to the school in Wesen, where he made rapid progress. Bartholomew Zwingli was somewhat of a scholar himself. When he discovered that his nephew was a precocious boy, he determined to give him as good an education as was possible, and sent him to Basel (Klein-Basel, on the east bank of the Rhine) to a famous school taught, by the gentle scholar, Gregory Buenzli (1494–98).

In four years the lad had outgrown the teacher's powers of instruction, and young Zwingli was sent to Bern to a school taught by the Humanist Heinrich Wölflin (Lupulus), who was half a follower of Erasmus and half a Reformer. He was passionately fond of music, and lodged in one of the Dominican convents in the town which was famed for the care bestowed on musical education. Zwingli was so carried away by his zeal for the study, that he had some thoughts of becoming a monk merely to gratify his musical tastes. His family, who had no desire to see him enter a monastery, removed him from Bern and sent him to the University of Vienna, where he spent two years (1500–1502). There he had for friends and fellow-students, Joachim von Watt [1] (Vadianus), Heinrich Loriti [2]

---

[1] Joachim de Watt, a native of St. Gallen (b. 1484, December 30) was a distinguished scholar. He became successively physician, member of council, and burgomaster in his native town, and did much to establish the Reformation ; he was a well-known author, and wrote several theological works.

[2] Heinrich Loriti was the most distinguished of all the Swiss Humanists. He studied successively at Bern, Vienna, and Köln, and attained the barren honour of being made Court-poet to the Emperor Maximilian. At Basel,

of Glarus (Glareanus), Johann Heigerlin[1] of Leutkirch (Faber), and Johann Meyer of Eck, the most notable of all Luther's opponents. In 1502 he returned to Switzerland and matriculated in the University of Basel. He became B.A. in 1504 and M.A. in 1506, and in the same year became parish priest of Glarus.

The childhood and youth of Zwingli form a striking contrast to Luther's early years. He enjoyed the rude plenty of a well-to-do Swiss farmhouse, and led a joyous young life. He has told us how the family gathered in the *stube* in the long winter evenings, and how his grandmother kept the children entranced with her tales from the Bible and her wonderful stories of the saints. The family were all musical, and they sang patriotic folk-songs, recording in rude verse the glories of Morgarten, Sempach, and the victories over the tyrant of Burgundy. "When I was a child," says Zwingli, "if anyone said a word against our Fatherland, it put my back up at once." He was trained to be a patriot. "From boyhood I have shown so great, eager, and sincere a love for our honourable Confederacy that I trained myself diligently in every act and discipline to this end." His uncle Bartholomew was an admirer of the New Learning, and the boy was nurtured in everything that went to make a Humanist, with all its virtues and failings. He was educated, one might almost say, in the art of enjoying the present without discriminating much between what was good and evil in surrounding society. He was trained to take life as it came. No

---

where he first settled, he kept a boarding school for boys who wished to study the classics, and in 1517 he transferred himself and about twenty young Switzers, his pupils, to Paris. He modelled his school, he was pleased to think, on the lines of the Roman Republic, was Consul himself, had a Senate, a prætor, and meetings of Comitia. He remained a fast friend of Zwingli.

[1] Johann Heigerlin (Faber) remained a steadfast Romanist. He became vicar-general to the Bishop of Constance, and as such was an antagonist of Zwingli. He ended his days as Bishop of Vienna. He wrote much against Luther, and was known as the "hammer of the Lutherans." Along with Eck and Cochlæus, he was the distinguished champion of the Romanist cause in Germany.

great sense of sin troubled his youthful years. He never shuddered at the wrathful face of Jesus, the Judge, gazing at him from blazoned church window. If he was once tempted for a moment to become a monk, it was in order to enjoy musical society, not to quench the sin that was burning him within, and to win the pardon of an angry God. He took his ecclesiastical calling in a careless, professional way. He belonged to a family connected on both sides with the clergy, and he followed the family arrangement. Until far on in life the question of personal piety did not seem to trouble him much, and he never belonged, like Luther and Calvin, to the type of men who are the leaders in a revival of personal religion. He became a Reformer because he was a Humanist, with a liking for Augustinian theology; and his was such a frank, honest nature that he could not see cheats and shams done in the name of religion without denouncing them. To the end of his days he was led more by his intellect than by the promptings of the heart, and in his earlier years he was able to combine a deep sense of responsibility about most things with a careless laxity of moral life.

§ 3. At Glarus and Einsiedeln.

At Glarus he was able to follow his Humanist studies, guided by the influences which had surrounded him during his last year at Basel. Among these his friendship with Thomas Wyttenbach was the most lasting. Wyttenbach taught him, he tells us, to see the evils and abuses of indulgences, the supreme authority of the Bible, that the death of Christ was the sole price of the remission of sins, and that faith is the key which unlocks to the soul the treasury of remission. All these thoughts he had grasped intellectually, and made much of them in his sermons. He prized preaching highly, and resolved to cultivate the gift by training himself on the models of antiquity. He studied the Scriptures, joyfully welcomed the new Greek Testament of Erasmus, published by Froben of Basel in 1516, when he was at Einsiedeln, and copied out from it the whole of the Pauline Epistles. On the wide margins of his MS. he wrote annotations from Erasmus, Origen, Chrysostom, Ambrose, and Jerome. It was his constant companion.

At Glarus he was personally introduced to the system of mercenary war and of pensions in which Switzerland had engaged. He went to Italy twice as regimental chaplain with the Glarus contingent, and was present at the fight at Novara (1513), and on the fatal day at Marignano (1515).

His experiences in these campaigns convinced him of the harm in this system of hiring out the Swiss to fight in others' quarrels; and when he became convinced of the evils attending it, he denounced the practice. His outspoken language displeased many of his most influential parishioners, especially those who were partisans of the French, and Zwingli resolved to seek some other sphere of work.

The post of people's priest at Einsiedeln, the famous monastery and pilgrimage resort, was offered to him and accepted (April 14th, 1516). He retained his official connection with Glarus, and employed a curate to do his parish work. His fame as a preacher grew. His friends desired to see him in a larger sphere, and through their exertions he was appointed to be people's priest in the Minster at Zurich. An objection had been made to his selection on the ground that he had disgracefully wronged the daughter of a citizen of Einsiedeln; and his letter of vindication, while it exonerates him from the particular charge brought against him, shows that he was by no means clear of the laxity in private morals which characterised the Swiss clergy of the time. The stipend attached to his office in the Great Minster was very small, and on this ground Zwingli felt himself justified, unwarrantably, in retaining his papal pension.[1]

[1] For details about Zwingli's papal pension, cf. S. M. Jackson, *Huldreich Zwingli*, p. 114.

§ 4. *Zwingli in Zurich.*

Zurich, when Zwingli went to it, was an imperial city. It had grown up around the Great Minster and the Minster of Our Lady (the Little Minster), and had developed into a trading and manufacturing centre. Its citizens, probably owing to the ecclesiastical origin of the town, had long engaged in quarrels with the clergy, and had generally been successful. They took advantage of the rivalries between the heads of the two Minsters and the Emperor's bailiff to assert their independence, and had passed laws subordinating the ecclesiastical authorities to the secular rule. The taxes were levied on ecclesiastical as well as on secular property; all the convents were under civic control, and liable to State inspection. The popes, anxious to keep on good terms with the Swiss who furnished soldiers for their wars, had expressly permitted in Zurich what they would not have allowed elsewhere.

The town was ruled by a Council or Senate composed of the Masters of the thirteen " gilds " (twelve trades' gilds and one gild representing the patriciate). The Burgomaster, with large powers, presided. A great Council of 212 members was called together on special occasions.

The city of Zurich, with its thoroughly democratic constitution, was a very fitting sphere for a man like Zwingli. He had made a name for himself by this time. He had become a powerful preacher, able to stir and move the people by his eloquence; he was in intimate relations with the more distinguished German Humanists, introduced to them by his friend Heinrich Loriti of Glarus (known as Glareanus). He had already become the centre of an admiring circle of young men of liberal views. His place as people's preacher gave to a man of his popular gifts a commanding position in the most democratic town in Switzerland, where civic and European politics were eagerly discussed. He went there in December 1519.

His work as a Reformer began almost at once. Bernardin Samson or Sanson, a seller of indulgences for

Switzerland, came to Zurich to push his trade. Zwingli had already encountered him at Einsiedeln, and, prompted by the Bishop of Constance and his vicar-general, John Faber, both of whom disliked the indulgences, had preached against him. He now persuaded the Council of Zurich to forbid Samson's stay in the town.

The papal treatment of the Swiss Reformer was very different from what had been meted out to Luther. Samson received orders from Rome to give no trouble to the Zurichers, and to leave the city rather than quarrel with them. The difference, no doubt, arose from the desire of the *Curia* to do nothing to hinder the supply of Swiss soldiers for the papal wars; but it was also justified by the contrast in the treatment of the subject by the two Reformers. Luther struck at a great moral abuse, and his strokes cut deeply into the whole round of mediæval religious life, with its doctrine of a special priesthood; he made men see the profanity of any claim made by men to pardon sin, or to interfere between their fellow-men and God. Zwingli took the whole matter more lightly. His position was that of Erasmus and the Humanists. He could laugh at and ridicule the whole proceeding, and thought most of the way in which men allowed themselves to be gulled and duped by clever knaves. He never touched the deep practical religious question which Luther raised, and which made his challenge to the Papacy reverberate over Western Europe.

From the outset Zwingli became a prominent figure in Zurich. He announced to the astonished Chapter of the Great Minster, to whom he owed his appointment, that he meant to give a series of continuous expositions of the Gospel of St. Matthew; that he would not follow the scholastic interpretation of passages in the Gospel, but would endeavour to make Scripture its own interpreter. The populace crowded to hear sermons of this new kind. In order to reach the country people, Zwingli preached in the market-place on the Fridays, and his fame spread throughout the villages. The Franciscans, Dominicans, and Augustinian Eremites tried to arouse opposition, but unsuccessfully. In his sermons he denounced sins suggested in the passages expounded, and found occasion to deny the doctrines of Purgatory and the Intercession of Saints.

His strongest attack on the existing ecclesiastical system was made in a sermon on tithes, which, to the distress of the Provost of the Minster, he declared to be merely voluntary offerings. (He had been reading Hus' book *On the Church*.) He must have carried most of the Chapter with him in his schemes for improvement, for in June 1520 the Breviary used in the Minster was revised by Zwingli and stripped of some blemishes. In the following year (March 1521), some of the Zurichers who were known to be among Zwingli's warmest admirers, the printer Froschauer among them, asserted their convictions by eating flesh meat publicly in Lent. The affair made a great sensation, and the Reformers were brought before the Council of the city. They justified themselves by declaring that they had only followed the teaching of Zwingli, who had shown them that nothing was binding on the consciences of Christians which was not commanded in the Scriptures. Zwingli at once undertook their defence, and published his sermon, *Selection or Liberty concerning Foods ; an offence and scandal ; whether there is any Authority for forbidding Meat at certain times* (April 16th, 1522). He declared that in such matters the responsibility rests with the individual, who may use his freedom provided he avoids a public scandal.

The matter was felt to be serious, and the Council, after full debate, passed an ordinance which was meant to be a compromise. It was to the effect that although the New Testament makes no rule on the subject, fasting in Lent is a very ancient custom, and must not be set aside until dealt with by authority, and that the priests of the three parishes of Zurich were to dissuade the people from all violation of the ordinance.

The Bishop of Constance thereupon interfered, and sent

a Commission, consisting of his suffragan and two others, to investigate and report.   They met the Small Council, and in a long address insisted that the Church had authority in such matters, and that the usages it commanded must be obeyed.   Zwingli appeared before the Great Council, and, in spite of the efforts of the Commission to keep him silent, argued in defence of liberty of conscience.   In the end the Council resolved to abide by its compromise, but asked the Bishop of Constance to hold a Synod of his clergy and come to a resolution upon the matter which would be in accordance with the law of Christ.   This resolution of the Council really set aside the episcopal authority, and was a revolt against the Roman Church.

Political affairs favoured the rebellion.   At the Swiss Diet held at Luzern (May 1521), the cantons, in spite of the vehement remonstrances of Zurich, made a treaty with France, and allowed the French king to recruit a force of 16,000 Swiss mercenaries.   Zurich, true to its protest, refused to allow recruiting within its lands.   Its citizens chafed at the loss of money and the separation from the other cantons, and Zwingli became very unpopular.   He had now made up his mind that the whole system of pensions and mercenary service was wrong, and had resigned his own papal pension.   Just then the Pope asked Zurich, which supplied him with half of his body-guard, for a force of soldiers to be used in defence of his States, promising that they would not be used to fight the French, among whose troops were many Swiss mercenaries from other cantons.   The Council refused.   Nevertheless, six thousand Zurichers set out to join the papal army. The Council recalled them, and after some adventures, in one of which they narrowly escaped fighting with the Swiss mercenaries in the service of France, they returned home. This expedition, which brought neither money nor honour to the Zurichers, turned the tide of popular feeling, and the Council forbade all foreign service.   When the long con-nection between Zurich and the Papacy is considered, this decree was virtually a breach between the city and the

Pope. It made the path of the Reformation much easier
(Jan. 1522), and Zwingli's open break with the Papacy
was only a matter of time.

It came with the publication of the *Archeteles* (August
1522), a book hastily written, like all Zwingli's works,
which contained a defence of all that he had done,
and a programme, ecclesiastical and political, for the future.
The book increased the zeal of Zwingli's opponents. His
sermons were often interrupted by monks and others
instigated by them. The burgomaster was compelled to
interfere in order to maintain the peace of the town. He
issued an order on his own authority, without any appeal
to the Bishop of Constance, that the pure Word of God
was to be preached. At an assembly of the country
clergy of the canton, the same decision was reached; and
town and clergy were ready to move along the path of
reformation. Shortly before this (July 2nd), Zwingli
and ten other priests petitioned the bishop to permit his
clergy to contract legal marriages. The document had no
practical effect, save to show the gradual advance of ideas.
It disclosed the condition of things that sacerdotal celibacy
had produced in Switzerland.

§ 5. *The Public Disputations.*

In these circumstances, the Great Council, now definitely
on Zwingli's side, resolved to hold a Public Disputation
to settle the controversies in religion; and Zwingli drafted
sixty-seven theses to be discussed. These articles contain
a summary of his doctrinal teaching. They insist that the
Word of God, the only rule of faith, is to be received upon
its own authority and not on that of the Church. They
are very full of Christ, the only Saviour, the true Son of
God, who has redeemed us from eternal death and reconciled us to God. They attack the Primacy of the
Pope, the Mass, the Invocation of the Saints, the thought
that men can acquire merit by their good works, Fasts,
Pilgrimages, and Purgatory. Of sacerdotal celibacy he

3**

says, "*I know of no greater nor graver scandal than that which forbids lawful marriage to priests, and yet permits them on payment of money to have concubines and harlots. Fie for shame!*"[1] The theses consist of single short sentences.

The Disputation, the first of the four which marked the stages of the legal Reformation in Zurich, was held in the Town Hall of the city on January 29th, 1523. More than six hundred representative men gathered to hear it. All the clergy of the canton were present; Faber watched the proceedings on behalf of the Bishop of Constance; many distinguished divines from other parts of Switzerland were present. Faber seems to have contented himself with asking that the Disputation should be delayed until a General Council should meet, and Zwingli replied that competent scholars who were good Christians were as able as a Council to decide what was the meaning of the Holy Scriptures. The result of the Disputation was that the burgomaster declared that Zwingli had justified his teaching, and that he was no heretic. The canton of Zurich practically adopted Zwingli's views, and the Reformer was encouraged to proceed further.

His course of conduct was eminently prudent. He invariably took pains to educate the people up to further changes by explaining them carefully in sermons, and by publishing and circulating these discourses. He considered that it was his duty to teach, but that it belonged to the civic authorities to make the changes; and he himself made none until they were authorised. He had very strong views against the use of images in churches, and had preached vigorously against their presence. Some of his more ardent hearers began to deface the statues and pictures. The Great Council accordingly took the whole question into consideration, and decided that a

---

[1] Cf. Schaff, *Creeds of the Evangelical Protestant Churches* (London, 1877), p. 197; Niemeyer, *Collectio Confessionum in ecclesiis reformatis, publicatarum* (Leipzig, 1840), p. 3; Müller, *Die Bekenntnisschriften der reformierten Kirche: Zwinglis Theses von 1523*, Art. 49, p. 5.

second Public Disputation should be held, at which the matter might be publicly discussed. This discussion (October 1523) lasted for two days. More than eight hundred persons were present, of whom three hundred and fifty were clergy. On the first day, Zwingli set forth his views on the presence of images in churches, and wished their use forbidden. The Council decided that the statues and pictures should be removed from the churches, but without disturbance; the rioters were to be pardoned, but their leader was to be banished from the city for two years. The second day's subject of conference was the Mass. Zwingli pled that the Mass was not a sacrifice, but a memorial of the death of our Lord, and urged that the abuses surrounding the simple Christian rite should be swept away. The presence of Anabaptists at this conference, and their expressions in debate, warned the magistrates that they must proceed cautiously, and they contented themselves with appointing a commission of eight—two from the Council and six clergymen—to inquire and report. Meanwhile the clergy were to be informed how to act, and the letter of instruction was to be written by Zwingli. The authorities also deputed preachers to go to the outlying parts of the canton and explain the whole matter carefully to the people.

The letter which Zwingli addressed to the clergy of Zurich canton is a brief statement of Reformation principles. It is sometimes called the *Instruction*. Zwingli entitles it, *A brief Christian Introduction which the Honourable Council of the city of Zurich has sent to the pastors and preachers living in its cities, lands, and wherever its authority extends, so that they may henceforth in unison announce and preach the gospel.*[1] It describes sin, the law, God's way of salvation, and then goes on to speak of images. Zwingli's argument is that the presence of statues and pictures in churches has led to idolatry, and that they ought to be removed. The concluding section discusses the Mass.

---

[1] Müller, *Die Bekenntnisschriften der reformierten Kirche* (Leipzig, 1903), pp. xviii and 7. The *Instruction* is a lengthy document.

Here the author states very briefly what he elaborated afterwards, that the main thought in the Eucharist is not the repetition of the sacrifice of Christ, but its faithful remembrance, and that the Romish doctrine and ceremony of the Mass has been so corrupted to superstitious uses that it ought to be thoroughly reformed.

This letter had a marked effect. The village priests everywhere refused to say Mass according to the old ritual. But there was a section of the people, including members of the chapter of the Minster, who shrunk from changes in this central part of Christian worship. In deference to their feelings, the Council resolved that the Holy Supper should be meanwhile dispensed according to both the Reformed and the mediæval rite ; in the one celebration the cup was given to the laity, and in the other it was withheld. No change was made in the liturgy. Then came a third conference, and a fourth ; and at last the Mass was abolished. On April 13th, 1525, the first Evangelical communion service took place in the Great Minster, and the mediæval worship was at an end. Other changes had been made. The monasteries had been secularised, and the monks who did not wish to leave their calling were all gathered together in the Franciscan convent. An amicable arrangement was come to about other ecclesiastical foundations, and the money thus secured was mainly devoted to education.

From 1522, Zwingli had been living in " clerical " marriage with Anna Reinhard, the widow of a wealthy Zurich burgher. She was called his wife by his friends, although no legal marriage ceremony had been performed. It is perhaps difficult for us to judge the man and the times. The so-called " clerical " marriages were universal in Switzerland. Man and woman took each other for husband and wife, and were faithful. There was no public ceremony. All questions of marriage, divorce, succession, and so forth, were then adjudicated in the ecclesiastical and not in the civil courts ; and as the Canon Law had insisted that no clergyman could marry, all such "clerical" marriages were simple concubinage in the eye of the law, and the children were illegitimate. The offence against the vow of chastity was condoned by a fine paid to the bishop. As early as 1523, William Röubli, a Zurich priest, went through a public form of marriage, and his example was followed by others; but it may be questioned whether these marriages were recognised to be legal until Zurich passed its own laws about matrimonial cases in 1525.

Luther in his pure-hearted and solemnly sympathetic way had referred to these clerical marriages in his *Address to the Christian Nobility of the German Nation* (1520).

" We see," he says, " how the priesthood is fallen, and how many a poor priest is encumbered with a woman and children, and burdened in his conscience, and no man does anything to help him, though he might very well be helped. . . . I will not conceal my honest counsel, nor withhold comfort from that unhappy crowd, who now live in trouble with wife and children, and remain in shame, with a heavy conscience, hearing their wife called a priest's harlot and the children bastards. . . . I say that these two (who are minded in their hearts to live together always in conjugal fidelity) are surely married before God."

He had never succumbed to the temptations of the flesh, and had kept his body and soul pure; and for that very reason he could sympathise with and help by his sympathy those who had fallen. Zwingli, on the other hand, had deliberately contracted this illicit alliance after he had committed himself to the work of a Reformer. The action remains a permanent blot on his character, and places him on a different level from Luther and from Calvin. It has been already noted that Zwingli had always an intellectual rather than a spiritual appreciation of the need of reformation,—that he was much more of a Humanist than either Luther or Calvin,—but what is remarkable is that we have distinct evidence that the need of personal piety had impressed itself on him during these years, and that he passed through a religious crisis, slight compared with that of Luther, but real so far as it went. He fell ill of the plague (Sept.–Nov. 1519), and the vision of death and recovery drew from him some hymns of resignation and thanksgiving.[1] The death of his brother Andrew (Nov. 1520) seems to have been the real turning-point in his inward spiritual experience, and his letters and writings are evidence of its reality and permanence. Perhaps the judgment which a contemporary and friend, Martin Bucer, passed ought to content us :

" When I read your letter to Capito, that you had made public announcement of your marriage, I was almost beside myself in my satisfaction. For it was the one thing I desired for you. . . . I never believed you were unmarried after the time when you indicated to the Bishop of Constance in that tract that you desired this gift. But as I considered the fact that you were thought to be a fornicator by some, and by others held to have little faith in Christ, I could not understand why you concealed it so long, and that the fact was not declared openly, and with candour and diligence. I could not doubt that you were led into this course by considerations which could not be put aside by a conscientious man. However that may be, I triumph in the fact that now you have come up in all things to the apostolic definition."[2]

The Reformation was spreading beyond Zurich. Evangelical preachers had arisen in many of the other cantons, and were gaining adherents.

§ 6. *The Reformation outside Zurich.*

Basel, the seat of a famous university and a centre of German Humanism, contained many scholars who had come under the influence of Thomas Wyttenbach, Zwingli's teacher. Wolfgang Fabricius Capito, a disciple of Erasmus, a learned student of the Scriptures, had begun as early as

---

[1] Literal translations of these hymns are given in Professor Macauley Jackson's *Huldreich Zwingli, the Reformer of German Switzerland* (New York and London, 1903), pp. 133, 134.

[2] Stähelin, *Briefe aus der Reformationszeit*, pp. 15–19.

1512 to show how the ceremonies and many of the usages of the Church had no authority from the Bible. He worked in Basel from 1512 to 1520. Johannes Oecolampadius (Hussgen or Heusgen), who had been one of Luther's supporters in 1521, came to Basel in 1522 as Lecturer on the Holy Scriptures in the University. His lectures and his sermons to the townspeople caused such a movement that the bishop forbade their delivery. The citizens asked for a Public Disputation. Two held in the month of December 1524—the one conducted by a priest of the name of Stör against clerical celibacy, and the other led by William Farel [1]—raised the courage of the

---

[1] William Farel was born in 1489 at a village near Gap in the mountainous south-east corner of Dauphiné, on the border of Provence. He belonged to a noble family, and was devout from his earliest years. He describes a pilgrimage which he made as a child in his book *Du vray usage de la croix de Jésus-Christ* (pp. 223 *f.*). All through his adventurous life he preserved his rare uprightness of character, his fervent devotion, and his indignation at wrong-doing of all kinds. He persuaded his parents to allow him to go to Paris for education, and reached the capital about 1509. He probably spent twelve years there, partly as student and partly as professor in the college Le Moine. There he became the friend and devoted disciple of Jacques Lefèvre d'Etaples, and this friendship carried him safely through several religious crises in his life. He followed Lefèvre to Meaux, and was one of the celebrated "group" there. When persecution and the timidity or scruples of the bishop caused the dispersion of these preachers, Farel went back to Dauphiné and attempted to preach the Gospel in Gap. He was not allowed *parce qu'il n'estoit ne moine ne prestre*, and was banished from the district by bishop and people. He next tried to preach in Guyenne, where he was equally unsuccessful. Thinking that there was no place in France open to him, he took himself to Basel. There he asked the University to allow him to hold a public disputation on certain articles which he sent to them. The authorities refused. He then addressed himself to the Council of the city, who permitted the discussion. The thirteen articles or *Theses* defended by Farel are given in Herminjard, *Correspondance des Réformateurs dans les pays de langue française* (i. 194, 195). He gathered a little church of French refugees at Basel (the *ecclesiola* of his correspondence), but was too much the ardent and impetuous pioneer to remain quietly among them. By the end of July 1524 he was preaching at Montbéliard, some miles to the south of Belfort, and the riots which ensued caused Oecolampadius to beseech him to temper his courage with discretion (Herminjard, *Correspondance*, etc., i. 255). He went thence to Strassburg (April 1525), to Bern, attempted to preach in Neuchâtel, and finally (middle of November 1526) opened a school at Aigle, an outlying dependency of Bern, hoping to get opportunity

Evangelical party.   In February 1525 the Council of the town installed Oecolampadius as the preacher in St. Martin's Church, and authorised him to make such changes as the Word of God demanded.   This was the beginning. Oecolampadius became a firm friend of Zwingli's, and they worked together.

In Bern also the Reformation made progress.   Berthold Haller[1] and Sebastian Meyer[2] preached the Gospel with courage for several years, and were upheld by the painter Nicolaus Manuel, who had great influence with the citizens. The Council decided to permit freedom in preaching, if in accordance with the Word of God; but they refused to permit innovations in worship or ceremonies; and they forbade the introduction of heretical books into the town. The numbers of the Evangelical party increased rapidly, and in the beginning of 1527 they had a majority in both the great and the small Councils.   It was then decided to have a Public Disputation.

The occasion was one of the most momentous in the history of the Reformation in Switzerland.   Hitherto Zurich had stood alone; if Bern joined, the two most

to carry on his evangelistic work.   He was soon discovered, and attempts were made to prevent his preaching ; but the authorities of Bern insisted that he should be unmolested.   In the beginning of 1527 he was actively engaged at the great Disputation in Bern.   That same year he was made pastor of Aigle and put in possession of the parsonage and the stipend ; but such work was too tame for him.   He made long preaching tours ; we find him at Lausanne, Morat, Orbe, and other places, always protected by the authorities of Bern.   He began his work in Geneva in 1532.

[1] Berthold Haller was born at Aldingen (1492) ; studied at Rothweil and Pforzheim, where he made the acquaintance of Melanchthon.   He became a Bachelor of Theology of the University of Köln ; taught for some time at Rothweil, and then at Bern (1513–1518).   He was elected people's priest in the great church there in 1521.   His sympathetic character and his great eloquence made him a power in the city ; but his discouragements were so many and so great that he was often on the point of leaving.   Zwingli encouraged him to remain and persevere.

[2] Sebastian Meyer was a priest from Elsass who had been preaching in Bern since 1518 against the abuses of the Roman Church.   The notorious conduct of the Dominicans in Bern (1507–9), and the action of Samson, the Indulgence-seller, in 1518, had made the Bernese ready to listen to attacks against Rome.

powerful cantons in Switzerland would be able to hold
their own. There was need for union. The Forest cantons
had been uttering threats, and Zwingli's life was not
secure. Bern was fully alive to the importance of the
proposed discussion, and was resolved to make it as imposing as possible, and that the disputants on both sides
should receive fair play and feel themselves in perfect
freedom and safety. They sent special invitations to the
four bishops whose dioceses entered their territories—the
Bishops of Constance, Basel, Valais, and Lausanne; and
they did their best to assemble a sufficient number of
learned Romanist theologians.[1] They promised not only
safe-conducts, but the escort of a herald to and from the
canton.[2] It soon became evident, however, that the
Romanist partisans had no great desire to come to the
Disputation. None of the bishops invited appears to
have even thought of being present save the Bishop of
Lausanne, and he found reasons for declining.[3] The *Disputation* was viewed with anxiety by the Romanist partisans,
and in a letter sent from Speyer (December 28th) the
Emperor Charles v. strongly remonstrated with the
magistrates of Bern.[4] The Bernese were not to be
intimidated. They issued their invitations, and made
every arrangement to give éclat to the great Disputation.[5]
Berthold Haller, with the help of Zwingli, had drafted

---

[1] Herminjard, *Correspondance des Réformateurs dans les pays de langue française* (2nd ed.), ii. 55.

[2] *Ibid.* ii. 94, 95.   [3] *Ibid.* ii. 61, 74, 89, 94, 96.

[4] Ruchat, *Histoire de la Réformation de la Suisse,* i. 368.

[5] The invitation began : "Nous l'Advoyer, le petit et le grand Conseil de la cité de Berne, à tous et à chascun, spirituelz et séculiers, prélatz, abbés, prévostz, doyens, chanoynes, curés, sacrestains, vicaires prescheurs de la Parolle de Dieu, et à tous prebstres, séculiers ou réguliers, et à tous Noz advoyers, chastellains, prévostz, lieutenans, et tous autres officiers et à tous Noz chers, féaulx et aymés subjectz, et à tous manans et habitans de Nostre domaine et ségnorie aux quelz les presentes lètres viendront,—Salut, grâce et bénivolance !

"Sçavoir faisons, combien que Nous ayons fait beaucoup d'ordonnance et mandemens publiques, pour la dissension de nostre commune foy Chrestienne, à ce meuz et espoirans, que cela profiteroit à la paix et concorde Chrestienne, comme chose très utile," etc. ; Herminjard, ii. 54.

ten *Theses,* which were to be defended by himself and his colleague, Francis Kolb; Zwingli had translated them into Latin and Farel into French for the benefit of strangers; and they were sent out with the invitations. They were—(1) The Holy Catholic Church, of which Christ is the only Head, is born of the Word of God, abides therein, and does not hear the voice of a stranger.[1] (2) The Church of Christ makes no law nor statute apart from the Word of God, and consequently those human ordinances which are called the commandments of the Church do not bind our consciences unless they are founded on the Word of God and agreeable thereto. (3) Christ is our wisdom, righteousness, redemption, and price for the sins of the whole world; and all who think they can win salvation in any other way, or have other satisfaction for their sins, renounce Christ. (4) It is impossible to prove from Scripture that the Body and Blood of Christ are corporeally present in the bread of the Holy Supper. (5) The Mass, in which Christ is offered to God the Father for the sins of the living and the dead, is contrary to the Holy Scripture, is a gross affront to the Passion and Death of Christ, and is therefore an abomination before God. (6) Since Christ alone died for us, and since He is the only mediator and intercessor between God and believers, He only ought to be invoked; and all other mediators and advocates ought to be rejected, since they have no warrant in the Holy Scripture of the Bible. (7) There is no trace of Purgatory after death in the Bible; and therefore all services for the dead, such as vigils, Masses, and the like, are vain things. (8) To make pictures and adore them is contrary to the Old and New Testament, and they ought to be destroyed where there is the chance that they may be adored. (9) Marriage is not forbidden to any estate by the Holy Scripture, but wantonness and fornication are forbidden to everyone in whatever estate he may be. (10) The

---

[1] Cf. *Scots Confession* of 1560, Art. **xix.**: "The trew Kirk quhilk alwaies heares and obeyis the voice of her awin Spouse and Pastor."

fornicator is truly excommunicated by the Holy Scripture, and therefore wantonness and fornication are much more scandalous among the clergy than in the other estate.

These *Theses* represent in succinct fashion the preaching in the Reformed Church in Switzerland, and the fourth states in its earliest form what grew to be the Zwinglian doctrine of the Holy Supper.[1]

The Council of Bern had sent invitations to be present to the leading preachers in the Evangelical cities of Germany and Switzerland. Bucer and Capito came from Strassburg, Jacob Ausburger from Mühlhausen, Ambrose Blaarer from Constance, Sebastian Wagner,[2] surnamed Hofmeister (Œconomus), from Schaffhausen, Oecolampadius from Basel, and many others.[3] Zwingli's arrival was eagerly expected. The Zurichers were resolved not to trust their leader away from the city without a strong guard, and sent him to Bern with an escort of three hundred men-at-arms. A great crowd of citizens and strangers filled the arcades which line both sides of the main street, and every window in the many-storied houses had its sightseers to watch the Zurichers tramping up from gate to cathedral with their pastor safe in the centre of the troop.

Romanist theologians did not muster in anything like the same strength. The men of the four Forest cantons stood sullenly aloof; the authorities in French-speaking Switzerland had no liking for the Disputation, and the strongly Romanist canton of Freiburg did its best to prevent the theologians of Neuchâtel, Morat, and Grandson from appearing at Bern; but in spite of the hindrances

---

[1] The *Theses*, in the original German, are printed by Müller, *Bekenntnisschriften der reformierten Kirche* (Leipzig, 1903), pp. xviii, 30 ; and in French by Herminjard in *Correspondance des Réformateurs dans les pays de langue française* (2nd ed.), ii. 59, 60.

[2] Sebastian Wagner was born at Schaffhausen in 1476. He studied at Paris under Lascaris, taught theology in the Franciscan monastery at Zurich, then at Constance. He adopted the Reformation, and, returning to his native town, became its reformer.

[3] Herminjard, *Correspondance des Réformateurs*, etc. ii. 95 s.

placed in their way no less than three hundred and fifty ecclesiastics gathered to the Disputation. The conference was opened on January 15th (*le dimenche après la feste de la circuncision*),[1] and was continued in German till the 24th; on the 25th a second discussion, lasting two days, was begun, for the benefit of strangers, in Latin. " When *la Dispute des Welches* (strangers) was opened, a stranger doctor (of Paris) came forward along with some priests speaking the same language as himself. He attacked the *Ten Theses*, and William Farel, preacher at Aigle, answered him." [2] The more distinguished Romanist theologians who were present seem to have refrained from taking part in the discussion. The Bishop of Lausanne defended their silence on the grounds that they objected to discuss such weighty matters in the vulgar tongue; that no opportunity was given to them to speak in Latin; and that when the Emperor had interdicted the Disputation they were told by the authorities of Bern that they might leave the city if it so pleased them.[3]

The result of the Disputation was that the authorities and citizens of Bern were confirmed in their resolve to adopt the Reformation. The Disputation ended on the 26th of January (1528), and on the 7th of February the Mass was declared to be abolished, and a sermon took its place; images were removed from the churches; the monasteries were secularised, and the funds were used partly for education and partly to make up for the French and papal pensions, which were now definitely renounced, and declared to be illegal.

The two sermons which Zwingli preached in the cathedral during the Disputation made a powerful impression on the people of Bern. It was after one of them that M. de Watteville, the Advoyer or President of the Republic, declared himself to be convinced of the truth of the Evangelical faith, and with his whole family accepted the Reformation. His eldest son, a clergyman whose

---

[1] Herminjard, *Correspondance des Réformateurs*, etc. ii. 55.
[2] *Ibid.* ii. 99 n.   [3] *Ibid.* ii. 98 n.

family interest had procured for him no less than thirteen benefices, and who, it was commonly supposed, would be the next Bishop of Lausanne, renounced them all to live the life of a simple country gentleman.[1]

The republic of Bern for long regarded the *Ten Theses* as the charter of its religious faith. Not content with declaring the Reformation legally established within the city, the authorities of Bern sent despatches or delegates to all the cities and lands under their control, informing them of what they had done, and inviting them to follow their example. They insisted that preachers of the Gospel must be at liberty to deliver their message without interruption throughout all their territories. They promised that they would maintain the liberty of both cults until means had been taken to find out which the majority of the inhabitants preferred, and that the decision would be taken by vote in presence of commissioners sent down from Bern.[2]   When the majority of

---

[1] Nicholas de Watteville, born in 1492, was canon of St. Vincent in Bern, protonotary apostolic, prior of Montpreveyres, and provost of Lausanne. He visited Rome in 1517, and there received the Abbey of Montheron ; and the year following he was made a papal chamberlain to Pope Leo x.   He gave up all his benefices on December 1st, and soon afterwards married Clara May, a nun who had left the convent of Königsfeld.   He was always a great admirer of William Farel, and often interfered to protect the impetuous Reformer from the consequences of his own rashness.   His younger brother, J. J. de Watteville, became Advoyer or President of Bern, and was a notable figure in the history of the Reformation in Switzerland. The family of de Watteville is still represented among the citizens of Bern.

[2] As early as June 15th, 1523, the Council of Bern had issued an ordinance for the preachers throughout their territories, which enjoined them to preach publicly and without dissimulation the Holy Gospel and the doctrine of God, and to say nothing which they could not establish by true and Holy Scripture ; to leave entirely alone all other doctrines and discussions contrary to the Gospel, and in particular the distinctive doctrines of Luther.   Later (May 21st, 1526), at a conference held between members of the Council of Bern, deputies from the Bernese communes, and delegates from the seven Roman Catholic cantons, it was agreed to permit no innovation in matters of religion.   This agreement was not maintained long ; and the Bernese went back to their ordinance of June 1523.   It seems to have been practically interpreted to mean that preachers might attack the power of the Pope, and the doctrines of Purgatory and the Invocation of Saints, but that they were not to say anything against the current doctrine

the parishioners accepted the Reformation, the new doctrinal standard was the *Ten Theses*, and the Council of Bern sent directions for the method of dispensing the Sacraments of Baptism and the Lord's Supper, and for the solemnisation of marriages. The whole of the German-speaking portion of the canton proper and its dependences seem to have accepted the Reformation at once. Bern had, besides, some French-speaking districts under its own exclusive control, and others over which it ruled along with Freiburg. The progress of the new doctrines was slower in these district, but it may be said that they had all embraced the Reformation before the end of 1530. The history of the Reformation in French-speaking Switzerland belongs, however, to the next chapter, and the efforts of Bern to evangelise its subjects in these districts will be described there.

Not content with this, the Council of Bern constituted itself the patron and protector of persecuted Protestants outside their own lands, and the evangelisation of western Switzerland owed almost everything to its fostering care.[1]

Thus Bern in the west and Zurich in the east stood forth side by side pledged to the Reformation.

The cantonal authorities of Appenzell had declared, as early as 1524, that Gospel preaching was to have free course within their territories. Thomas Wyttenbach had been people's priest in Biel from 1507, and had leavened the town with his Evangelical preaching. In 1524 he courageously married. The ecclesiastical authorities were strong enough to get him deposed; but a year or two later the citizens compelled the cantonal Council to permit the free preaching of the Gospel. Sebastian Hofmeister preached in Schaffhausen, and induced its people to declare

of the sacraments. Cf. Decrees of the Council of Bern, quoted in Herminjard, *Correspondance des Réformateurs dans les pays de langue française*, (Geneva, 1878), i. 434 *n.*, ii. 23 *n.*, also 20.

[1] Herminjard, *Crorespondance*, etc., ii. 123, 138, 199, 225, etc. In Sept. 1530, Bern wrote to the Bishop of Basel, who had imprisoned Henri Pourcellet, one of Farel's preachers : "Nous ne pouvons d'ailleurs pas tolérer que ceux qui partagent notre foi chrétienne soient traités d'une telle manière," p. 277.

for the Reformation. St. Gallen was evangelised by the
Humanist Joachim von Watt (Vadianus), and by John
Kessler, who had studied at Wittenberg. In German
Switzerland only Luzern and the Forest cantons remained
completely and immovably attached to the Roman Church,
and refused to tolerate any Evangelical preaching within
their borders. The Swiss Confederacy was divided ecclesiastically into two opposite camps.

The strong religious differences could not but affect the
political cohesion of the Swiss Confederacy, linked together
as it was by ties comparatively slight. The wonder is that
they did not altogether destroy it.

As early as 1522, the Bishop of Constance had asked
the Swiss Federal Diet at their meeting at Baden to prohibit the preaching of the Reformation doctrines within the
Federation; and the next year the Diet, which met again
at Baden (Sept. 1523), issued a declaration that all who
practised religious innovations were worthy of punishment.
The deputies from Luzern were especially active in inducing
the Diet to pass this resolution. The attempt to use the
Federation for the purpose of religious persecution, therefore,
first came from the Romanist side. Nor did they content
themselves with declarations in the Diet. The Romanist
canton of Unterwalden, being informed that some of the
peasants in the Bernese Oberland had complained that the
Reformation had been forced upon them, crossed the
Bernese frontier and committed an act of war. Bern
smarted under the insult.

These endeavours on the part of his opponents led
Zwingli to meditate on plans for leaguing together for the
purposes of mutual defence all who had accepted the
Reformation. His plans from the first went beyond the
Swiss Confederacy.

The imperial city of Constance, the seat of the diocese
which claimed ecclesiastical authority over Zurich, had
been mightily moved by the preaching of Ambrose Blaarer,
and had come over to the Protestant faith. The bishop
retired to Meersburg and his chapter to Ueberlingen.

The city feared the attack of Austria, and craved protection
from the Swiss Protestants. Its alliance was valuable to
them, for, along with Lindau, it commanded the whole Lake
of Constance. Zurich thereupon asked that Constance be
admitted within the Swiss Federation. This was refused
by the Federal Diet (Nov. 1527). Zurich then entered
into a *Christian Civic League* (*das christliche Bürgerrecht*)
with Constance,—a league based on their common religious
beliefs,—promising to defend each other if attacked. The
example once set was soon followed, and the two following
years saw the League increasing rapidly. Bern joined in
June 1528, St. Gallen in Nov. 1528, Biel in January,
Mühlhausen in February, Basel in March, and Schaffhausen
in October, 1529. Strassburg was admitted in January
1530. Even Hesse and Würtemburg wished to join.
Bern and Zurich came to an agreement that Evangelical
preaching must be allowed in the Common Lands, and that
no one was to be punished for his religious opinions.

The combination looked so threatening and contained
such possibilities that Ferdinand of Austria proposed a
counter-league among the Romanist cantons; and a
Christian Union, in which Luzern, Zug, Schwyz, Uri, and
Unterwalden allied themselves with the Duchy of Austria,
was founded in 1529, having for its professed objects the
preservation of the mediæval religion, with some reforms
carried out under the guidance of the ecclesiastical authorities. The Confederates pledged themselves to secure for
each other the right to punish heretics. This League had
also its possibilities of extension. It was thought that
Bavaria and Salzburg might join. The canton of the
Valais had already leagued itself with Savoy against Geneva,
and brought its ally within the *Christian Union*. The
very formation of the Leagues threatened war, and occasions of hostilities were not lacking. Austria was eager
to attack Constance, and Bern longed to punish Unterwalden
for its unprovoked invasion of Bernese territory. The condition and protection of the Evangelical population in the
Common Lands and in the Free Bailiwicks demanded

settlement, more especially as the Romanist cantons had promised to support each other in asserting their right to punish heretics. War seemed to be inevitable. Schaff- hausen, Appenzell, and the Graubünden endeavoured to mediate; but as neither Zurich nor Bern would listen to any proposals which did not include the right of free preaching, their efforts were in vain. The situation, difficult enough, was made worse by the action of the canton of Schwyz, which, having caught a Zurich pastor named Kaiser on its territory, had him condemned and burnt as a heretic. This was the signal for war. It was agreed that the Zurichers should attack the Romanist cantons, while Bern defended the Common Lands, and, if need be, the territory of her sister canton. The plan of campaign was drafted by Zwingli himself, who also laid down the conditions of peace. His proposals were, that the Forest cantons must allow the free preaching of the Gospel within their lands; that they were to forswear pensions from any external Power, and that all who received them should be punished both corporeally and by fine; that the alliance with Austria should be given up; and that a war indemnity should be paid to Zurich and to Bern. While the armies were facing each other the Zurichers received a strong appeal from Hans Oebli, the Landammann of Glarus, to listen to the proposals of the enemy. The common soldiers disliked the internecine strife. They looked upon each other as brothers, and the outposts of both armies were fraternising. In these cir- cumstances the Zurich army (for it was the Swiss custom that the armies on the field concluded treaties) accepted the terms of peace offered by their opponents. The treaty is known as the First Peace of Kappel (June 1529). It pro- vided that the alliance between Austria and the Romanist cantons should be dissolved, and the treaties "pierced and slit" (the parchments were actually cut in pieces by the dagger in sight of all); that in the Common Lands no one was to be persecuted for his religious opinions; that the majority should decide whether the old faith was to be

4**

retained or not, and that bailiffs of moderate opinions
should be sent to rule them; that neither party should
attack the other because of religion ; that a war indemnity
should be paid by the Romanist cantons to Zurich and
Bern (the amount was fixed at 2500 Sonnenkronen); and
that the abolition of foreign pensions and mercenary service
should be recommended to Luzern and the Forest cantons.
The treaty contained the seeds of future war; for the
Zurichers believed that they had secured the right of free
preaching within the Romanist cantons, while these cantons
believed that they had been left to regulate their own
internal economy as they pleased. Zwingli would have
preferred a settlement after war, and the future justified
his apprehensions.

Three months after the First Peace of Kappel, Zwingli
was summoned to the Marburg Colloquy, and the Reformation in Switzerland became inevitably connected with the
wider sphere of German ecclesiastical politics. It may be
well, however, to reserve this until later, and finish the
internal history of the Swiss movement.

The First Peace of Kappel was only a truce, and
left both parties irritated with each other. The friction
was increased when the Protestants discovered that the
Romanist cantons would not admit free preaching within
their territories. They also shrewdly suspected that,
despite the tearing and burning of the documents, the
understanding with Austria was still maintained. An
event occurred which seemed to justify their suspicions.
An Italian condottiere, Giovanni Giacomo de' Medici, had
seized and held (1525—31) the strong position called the
Rocco di Musso on the Lake of Como, and from this
stronghold he dominated the whole lake. This ruffian
had murdered Martin Paul and his son, envoys from the
Graubünden to Milan, and had crossed the lake and
harried the fertile valley of the Adda, known as
the Val Tellina, which was then within the territories
of the Graubünden (Grisons). The Swiss Confederacy
were bound to defend their neighbours; but when appeal

was made, the Romanist cantons refused, and the hand
of Austria was seen behind the refusal. Besides, at the
Federal Diets the Romanist cantons had refused to listen
to any complaints of persecutions for religion within
their lands. At a meeting between Zurich and her allies,
it was resolved that the Romanist cantons should be
compelled to abolish the system of foreign pensions, and
permit free preaching within their territories. Zurich
was for open war, but the advice of Bern prevailed. It
was resolved that if the Romanist cantons would not
agree to these proposals, Zurich and her allies should
prevent wine, wheat, salt, and iron from passing through
their territories to the Forest cantons. The result was
that the Forest cantons declared war, invaded Zurich
while that canton was unprepared, fought and won the
battle of Kappel, at which Zwingli was slain. He had
accompanied the little army of Zurich as its chaplain.
The victory of the Romanists produced a Second Peace of
Kappel which reversed the conditions of the first. War
indemnities were exacted from most of the Protestant
cantons. It was settled that each canton was to be
left free to manage its own religious affairs; that the
Christian Civic League was to be dissolved; and a number
of particular provisions were made which practically
secured the rights of Romanist without corresponding
advantages to Protestant minorities. The territories of
Zurich were left untouched, but the city was compelled
by the charter of Kappel to grant rights to her rural
districts. She bound herself to consult them in all
important matters, and particularly not to make war or
peace without their consent.

As a result of this ruinous defeat, and of the death of
Zwingli which accompanied it, Zurich lost her place as
the leading Protestant canton, and the guidance of the
Reformation movement fell more and more into the hands
of Geneva, which was an ally but not a member of the
Confederation. Another and more important permanent
result of this Second Peace of Kappel was that it was

seen in Switzerland as in Germany that while the Reformation could not be destroyed, it could not win for itself the whole country, and that Roman Catholics and Protestants must divide the cantons and endeavour to live peaceably side by side.

The history of the Reformation in Switzerland after the death of Zwingli is so linked with the wider history of the movement in Germany and in Geneva, that it can scarcely be spoken about separately. It is also intimately related to the differences which separated Zwingli from Luther in the doctrine of the Sacrament of the Lord's Supper.

§ 7. *The Sacramental Controversy.*[1]

In the Bern Disputation of 1528, the fourth thesis said " it cannot be proved from the Scripture that the Body and Blood of Christ are substantially and corporeally received in the Eucharist," [2] and the statement became a distinctive watchword of the early Swiss Reformation. This thesis, a negative one, was perhaps the earliest official statement of a bold attempt to get rid of the priestly miracle in the Mass, which was the strongest theoretical and practical obstacle to the acceptance of the fundamental Protestant thought of the spiritual priesthood of all believers. The question had been seriously exercising the attention of all the leading theologians of the Reformation, and this very trenchant way of dismissing it had suggested itself simultaneously to theologians in the Low Countries, in the district of the Upper Rhine,

---

[1] SOURCES : E. F. K. Müller, *Die Bekenntnisschriften der reformierten Kirche* (Leipzig, 1903), pp. 1–100 ; Hospinian, *Historia Sacramentaria,* 2 vols. (Geneva, 1681).

LATER BOOKS : Ebrard, *Das Dogma vom heiligen Abendmahl und seine Geschichte* (Frankfurt a M. 1845–46), vol. ii. ; Schweizer, *Die protestantischen Centraldogmen in ihrer Entwickelung innerhalb der reformierten Kirche* (Zurich, 1854–56); Hundeshagen, *Die Konflikte des Zwinglianismus, Lutherthums, und Calvinismus in den Bernischen Landkirchen 1522–1558, nach meist ungedruckten Quellen dargestelt* (Bern, 1842) ; compare also vol. i. 352 ff.

[2] Müller, *Die Bekenntnissrhriften des reformierten Kirche,* p. 30.

and in many of the imperial cities. It had been proclaimed in all its naked simplicity by Andrew Bodenstein of Carlstadt, the theologian of the German democracy but it was Zwingli who worked at the subject carefully, and who had produced a reasonable if somewhat defective theory based on a rather shallow exegesis, in which the words of our Lord, "This *is* My Body," were declared to mean nothing but "This *signifies* My Body." Luther, always disposed to think harshly of anything that came from Carlstadt, inclined to exaggerate his influence with the German Protestant democracy, believing with his whole heart that in the Sacrament of the Holy Supper the elements Bread and Wine were more than the bare signs of the Body and Blood of the Lord, was vehemently moved to find such views concerning a central doctrine of Christianity spreading through his beloved Germany. He never paused to ask whether the opinions he saw adopted with eagerness in most of the imperial cities were really different from those of Carlstadt (for that is one of the sad facts in this deplorable controversy). He simply denounced them, and stormed against Zwingli, whose name was spread abroad as their author and propagator. Nürnberg was almost the only great city that remained faithful to him. It was the only city also which was governed by the ancient patriciate, and in which the democracy had little or no power. When van Hoen and Karl Stadt in the Netherlands, Hedio at Mainz, Conrad Sam at Ulm, when the preachers of Augsburg, Strassburg, Frankfurt, Reutlingen, and other cities accepted and taught Zwingli's doctrine of the Eucharist, Luther and his immediate circle saw a great deal more than a simple division in doctrine. It was something more than the meaning of the Holy Supper or the exegesis of a difficult text which rent Protestantism in two, and made Luther and Zwingli appear as the leaders of opposing parties in a movement where union was a supreme necessity after the decision at Speyer in 1529. The theological question was complicated by social and political ideas, which, if not acknowledged openly, were at least in the minds of the leaders who took sides in the dispute. On the one side were men whom Luther held to be in part responsible for the Peasants' War, who were the acknowledged leaders of that democracy which he had learnt to distrust if not to fear, who still wished to link the Reformation to vast political schemes, all of which tended to weaken the imperial power by means of French and other alliances, and who only added to their other iniquities a theological theory which, he honestly believed, would take away from believers their comforting assurance of union with their Lord in the Sacrament of the Holy Supper.

The real theological difference after all did not amount to so much as is generally said. Zwingli's doctrine of the Holy Supper was not the crude theory of Carlstadt; and Luther might have seen this if he had only fairly examined it. The opposed views were, in fact, complementary, and the pronounced ideas of each were implicitly, though not expressly, held by the other. Luther and Zwingli approached the subject from two different points of view, and in debate they neither understood nor were exactly facing each other.

The whole Christian Church, during all the centuries, has found three great ideas embodied in the Sacrament of the Holy Supper, and all three have express reference to the death of the Saviour on the Cross for His people. The thoughts are Proclamation, Commemoration, and Participation or Communion. In the Supper, believers proclaim the death and what it means; they commemorate the Sacrifice; and they partake in or have communion with the crucified Christ, who is also the Risen Saviour. The mediæval Church had insisted that this sacramental union with Christ was in the hands of the priesthood to give or to withhold. Duly ordained priests, and they alone, could bring the worshippers into such a relation with Christ as would make the Sacramental participation a possible thing; and out of this claim had grown the mediæval theory of Transubstantiation. It had also divided the Sacrament of the Supper into two distinct rites (the phrase is not too strong)—the Mass and the Eucharist—the one connecting itself instinctively with the commemoration and the other with the participation.

Protestants united in denying the special priestly miracle needed to bring Christ and His people together in the Sacrament; but it is easy to see that they might approach the subject by the two separate paths of Mass or Eucharist. Zwingli took the one road and Luther happened on the other.

Zwingli believed that the mediæval Church had displaced the scriptural thought of *commemoration,* and put the non-scriptural idea of *repetition* in its place. For the mediæval priest claimed that in virtue of the miraculous power given in ordination, he could really change the bread and wine into the actual physical Body of Jesus, and, when this was done, that he could reproduce over again the agony of the Cross by crushing it with his teeth. This idea seemed to Zwingli to be utterly profane; it dishonoured the One great Sacrifice; it was unscriptural; it depended on a priestly gift of working a miracle which did not exist. Then he believed that the sixth chapter of St. John's Gospel forbade all thought that spiritual benefits could come from a mere partaking with the mouth. It was the atonement worked out by Christ's death that was appropriated and commemorated in the Holy Supper; and the atonement is always received by faith. Thus the two principal thoughts in the theory of Zwingli are, that the mediæval doctrine must be purified by changing the idea of repetition of the death of Christ for commemoration of that death, and the thought of manducating with the teeth for that of faith which is the faculty by which spiritual benefits are received. But Zwingli believed that a living faith always brought with it the presence of Christ, for there can be no true faith without actual spiritual contact with the Saviour. Therefore Zwingli held that there was a Real Presence of Christ in the Holy Supper; but a spiritual presence brought by the faith of the believing communicant and not by the elements of Bread and Wine, which were only the signs *representing* a Body which was corporeally absent. The defect of this theory is that it does not make the Presence of Christ in the Sacrament in any way depend on the ordinance; there is no sacramental presence other than what there is in any act of faith. It was not until Zwingli had elaborated his theory that he sought for and found an explanation of the words of our Lord, and taught that *This is My Body*, must mean *This signifies My Body*. His theory was entirely different from that of Carlstadt, with which Luther always identified it.

Luther approached the whole subject by a different path. What repelled him in the mediæval docrine of the Holy Supper was the way in which he believed it to trample on the spiritual priesthood of all believers. He protested against Transubstantiation and private Masses, because they were the most flagrant instances of that contempt. When he first preached on the subject (1519) it was to demand the "cup" for the laity, and he makes use of an expression in his sermon which reveals how his thoughts were tending. He says that in the Sacrament of the Holy Supper "the communicant is so united to Christ *and His saints*, that Christ's life and sufferings *and the lives and sufferings of the saints* become his." No one held more strongly than Luther that the Atonement was made by our Lord, and by Him alone. Therefore he cannot be thinking of the Atonement when he speaks of union with the lives and the sufferings of the saints. He believes that the main thing in the Sacrament is that it gives such a companionship with Jesus as His disciples and saints have had. There was, of course, a reference to the death of Christ and to the Atonement, for apart from that death no companionship is possible; but the reference is indirect, and through the thought of the fellowship. In the Sacrament we touch Christ as His disciples might have touched Him when He lived on earth, and as His glorified saints touch Him now. This reference, therefore, clearly shows that Luther saw in the Sacrament of the Supper the presence of the glorified Body of our Lord, and that the primary use of the Sacrament was to bring the communicant into contact with that glorified Body. This required a presence (and Luther thought a presence extended in space) of the glorified Body of Christ in the Sacrament in order that the communicant might be in actual contact with it. But communion with the Living Christ implies the appropriation of the death of Christ, and of the Atonement won by His death. Thus the reference to the Crucified Christ which Zwingli reaches directly, Luther attains indirectly; and the reference to the Living Risen Christ which Zwingli reaches indirectly, Luther attains directly. Luther avoided the need of a priestly miracle to bring the Body extended in space into immediate connection with the elements Bread and Wine, by introducing a scholastic theory of what is meant by presence in Space. A body may be present in Space, said the Schoolmen, in two ways: it may be present in such a way that it excludes from the space it occupies any other body, or it may be present occupying the same space with another body. The Glorified Body of Christ can be present in the latter manner. It was so when our Lord after His Resurrection appeared suddenly among His disciples in a room when the doors were shut; for then at some moment of time it must have occupied the same space as a portion of the walls or of the door. Christ's glorified Body can therefore be naturally in the *elements* without any special miracle, for it is *ubiquitous*. It is in the table at which I write, said Luther; in the stone which I hurl through the air. It is in the *elements* in the Holy Supper in a perfectly natural way, and needs no priestly miracle to bring it there. This natural presence of the Body of Christ in the elements in the Supper is changed into a Sacramental Presence by the promise of God, which is attached to the reverent and believing partaking of the Holy Supper.

These were the two theories which ostensibly divided

the Protestants in 1529 into two parties, the one of which was led by Zwingli and the other by Luther. They were not so antagonistic that they could not be reconciled. Each theologian held implicitly what the other declared explicitly. Zwingli placed the relation to the Death of Christ in the foreground, but implicitly admitted the relation to the Risen Christ—going back to the view held in the Early Church. Luther put fellowship with the Risen Christ in the foreground, but admitted the reference to the Crucified Christ—accepting the mediæval way of looking at the matter. The one had recourse to a very shallow exegesis to help him, and the other to a scholastic theory of space; and naturally, but unfortunately, when controversy arose, the disputant attacked the weakest part of his opponent's theory—Luther, Zwingli's exegesis; and Zwingli, Luther's scholastic theory of spatial presence.

The attempt to bring about an understanding between Luther and Zwingli, made by Philip of Hesse, the confidant of Zwingli, and in sympathy with the Swiss Reformer's schemes of political combination, has already been mentioned, and its failure related.[1] It need not be discussed again. But for the history of the Reformation in Switzerland it is necessary to say something about the further progress of this Sacramental controversy. Calvin gradually won over the Swiss Protestants to his views; and his theory, which at one time seemed about to unite the divided Protestants, must be alluded to.

Calvin began his study of the doctrine of the Sacrament of the Holy Supper independently of both Luther and Zwingli. His position as the theologian of Switzerland, and his friendship with his colleague William Farel, who was a Zwinglian, made him adapt his theory to Zwinglian language; but he borrowed nothing from the Reformer of Zurich. He was quite willing to accept Zwingli's exegesis so far as the words went; but he gave another and altogether different meaning to Zwingli's phrase, *This signifies My Body*. He was willing to call

[1] Cf. vol. i. 352 ff.

the "elements" *signs* of the Body and Blood of the Lord; but while Zwingli called them signs which *represent* (*signa representativa*) what was *absent*, Calvin insisted on calling them signs which *exhibit* (*signa exhibitiva*) what was *present* —a distinction which is continually forgotten in describing his relation to the theories of Zwingli, and one which enabled him to convince Luther that he held that there was a Real Presence of Christ's Body in the Sacrament of the Holy Supper. To describe minutely Calvin's doctrine of the Holy Supper would require more space than can be given here, and a brief statement of the central thoughts is alone possible. His aim in common with all the Reformers was to construct a doctrine of the Sacrament of the Supper which would be at once scriptural, free from superstition and from the crass materialist associations which had gathered round the theory of transubstantiation, and which would clearly conserve the great Reformation proclamation of the spiritual priesthood of all believers. He went back to the mediæval idea of transubstantiation, and asked whether it gave a true conception of what was meant by *substance*. He decided that it did not, and believed that the root thought in *substance* was not dimensions in space, but power. The *substance* of a body consists in its *power*, active and passive, and the *presence* of the *substance* of anything consists in the immediate application of that power.[1] When Luther and Zwingli had spoken of the *substance* of the Body of Christ, they had always in their mind the thought of something extended in space; and the one affirmed while the other denied that this Body of Christ, something extended in space, could be and was present in the Sacrament of the Supper. Calvin's conception of *substance* enabled him to say that wherever anything acts there it is. He denied the crude "substantial" presence which Luther insisted on; and in this he sided with Zwingli. But he affirmed a real because active presence, and in this he sided with Luther.

Calvin's view had been accepted definitely by

[1] Leibnitz, *Pensées de Leibnitz*, 2nd ed. (Paris, 1803) p. 106.

Melanchthon, and somewhat indefinitely by Luther
The imperial cities, led by Strassburg, which was under
the influence of Bucer, who had thought out for himself
a doctrine not unlike that of Calvin, had been included in
the Wittenberg Concord (May 1536); but Luther would
have nothing to do with the Swiss. As it was vain to
hope that Switzerland would be included in any Lutheran
alliance, Calvin set himself to produce dogmatic harmony
in Switzerland. In conjunction with Bullinger, Zwingli's
son-in-law and successor in Zurich, he drafted the *Consensus
of Zurich* (*Consensus Tigurinus*) in 1549.[1] The document
is Calvinist in theology and largely Zwinglian in language.
It was accepted with some difficulty in Basel and in Bern,
and heartily in Biel, Schaffhausen, Mühlhausen, and St.
Gallen. It ended dogmatic disputes in Protestant Switzerland, which was thus united under the one creed.

This does not mean any increase of Protestantism within
Switzerland. The Romanist cantons drew more closely
together. Cardinal Carlo Borromeo of Milan took a deep
interest in the counter-Reformation in Switzerland. He
introduced the Jesuits into Luzern and the Forest cantons,
and after his death these cantons formed a league which
included Luzern, Uri, Schwyz, Zug, Unterwalden, Freiburg,
and Solothurn (1586). This League (*the Borromean League*)
pledged its members to maintain the Roman Catholic
faith. The lines of demarcation between Protestant and
Romanist cantons in Switzerland practically survive to
the present day.

[1] Müller, *Die Bekenntnisschriften der reformierten Kirche*, p. 159.

CHAPTER III.

THE REFORMATION IN GENEVA UNDER CALVIN.[1]

§ 1. *Geneva.*

GENEVA, which was to be the citadel of the Reformed faith in Europe, had a history which prepared it for the part it was destined to play.

The ancient constitution of the town, solemnly promulgated in 1387, recognised three different authorities within its walls: the Bishop, who was the sovereign or "Prince" of the city; the Count, who had possession of the citadel; and the Free Burghers. The first act of the

[1] SOURCES: *Mémoires et documents publiés par la Société d'histoire et d'archœologie de Genève* (especially vols. ii. v. ix. xv. xx.); Froment, *Les Actes et gestes marveilleux de la cité de Genève* (ed. of 1854 by G. Revillod); La Sœur Jeanne de Jussie, *Le levain du Calvinisme* (ed. of 1865); G. Farel, *Lettres certaines d'aucuns grandz troubles et tumultes advenuz à Genève, avec la disputation faicte l'an 1534* (Basel, 1588); *Registres du Conseil de Genève* (known to me only through the extracts given by Herminjard, Doumergue, and others); Herminjard, *Correspondance des Réformateurs dans les pays de langue française*, 9 vols. (Geneva, etc., vols. i. ii. in a 2nd edition, 1878, vols. iii.–ix. 1870–97); Calvin, *Opera omnia*, vols. xxix.–lxxxvii. of the *Corpus Reformatorum* (Brunswick and Berlin, 1869–97); Bonnet, *Lettres françaises de Jean Calvin* (Paris, 1854); Beza, *Vita Calvini* (vol. xlix. of the *Corpus Reformatorum*); Rilliet, *Le premier catéchisme de Calvin* (Paris, 1878).

LATER WORKS: Doumergue, *Jean Calvin, les hommes et les choses de son temps* (only three vols. published, Lausanne, 1899, 1902, 1905); Bungener, *Jean Calvin, sa vie, son œuvre et ses écrits* (Paris, 1862–63); Kampschulte, *Johann Calvin, seine Kirche und seine Stadt in Genf* (Leipzig, 1869–99); A. Roget, *Histoire du peuple de Genève depuis la Reforme jusqu'à l'escalade* (Geneva, 1870–83); Dunant, *Les relations politiques de Genève avec Berne et les Suisses de 1536–64* (Geneva, 1894); Ruchat, *Histoire de la Réformation de la Suisse*, ed. by Vulliemin (Paris and Lausanne, 1835–38).

Bishop on his nomination was to go to the Church of St.
Peter and swear on the Missal that he would maintain the
civic rights. The House of Savoy had succeeded to the
countship of Geneva, and they were represented within
the town by a viceroy, who was called the Count or
Vidomne. He was the supreme justiciary. The citizens
were democratically organised. They met once a year in a
recognised civic assembly to elect four Syndics to be their
rulers and representatives. It was the Syndics who in
their official capacity heard the oaths of the Bishop and of
the Vidomne to uphold the rights and privileges of the town.
They kept order within the walls from sunrise to sunset.

These three separate authorities were frequently in
conflict, and in the triangular duel the citizens and the
Bishop were generally in alliance against the House of
Savoy and its viceroy. The consequence was that few
mediæval cities under ecclesiastical rule were more loyal
than Geneva was to its Bishop, so long as he respected the
people's rights and stood by them against their feudal lords
when they attempted oppression.

In the years succeeding 1444 the hereditary loyalty
to their bishops had to stand severe tests. Count
Amadeus VIII. of Savoy, one of the most remarkable men
of the fifteenth century,—he ascended the papal throne
and resigned the Pontificate to become a hermit,—used
his pontifical power to possess himself of the bishopric.
From that date onwards the Bishop of Geneva was almost
always a member of the House of Savoy, and the rights
of the citizens were for the most part disregarded. The
bishopric became an appanage of Savoy, and boys (one of
ten years of age, another of seventeen) and bastards ruled
from the episcopal chair.

After long endurance a party formed itself among the
townspeople vowed to restore the old rights of the city.
They called themselves, or were named by others, the
Eidguenots (*Eidgenossen*); while the partisans of the Bishop
and of the House of Savoy were termed *Mamelukes*, because,
it was said, they had forsaken Christianity.

In their difficulties the Genevans turned to the Swiss cantons nearest them and asked to be allied with Freiburg and Bern. Freiburg consented, and an alliance was made in 1519; but Bern, an aristocratic republic, was unwilling to meddle in the struggle of a democracy in a town outside the Swiss Confederacy. The citizens of Bern, more sympathetic than their rulers, compelled them to make alliance with Geneva in 1526,—very half-heartedly on the part of the Bernese Council.

The Swiss cantons, Bern especially, could not in their own interest see the patriotic party in Geneva wholly crushed, and the "gate of Western Switzerland" left completely in possession of the House of Savoy. Therefore, when the Bishop assembled an army for the purpose of effectually crushing all opposition within the town, Bern and Freiburg collected their forces and routed the troops of Savoy. But the allies, instead of using to the full the advantage they had gained, were content with a compromise by which the Bishop remained the lord of Geneva, while the rights of the Vidomne were greatly curtailed, and the privileges of the townsmen were to be respected (Oct. 19th, 1530).

From this date onwards Geneva was governed by what was called *le Petit Conseil*, and was generally spoken of as the Council; then a *Council of Two Hundred*, framed on the model of those of Freiburg and Bern; lastly, by the *Conseil General*, or assembly of the citizens. All important transactions were first submitted to and deliberated on by the *Petit Conseil*, which handed them on with their opinion of what ought to be done to the *Council of the Two Hundred*. No change of situation—for example, the adoption of the Reformation—was finally adopted until submitted to the *General Council* of all the burghers.

It is possible that had there seemed to be any immediate prospects that Geneva would join the Reformation, Bern would have aided the patriots more effectually. Bern was the great Protestant Power in Western Switzerland. Its uniform policy, since 1528, had been to

constitute itself the protector of towns and districts where
a majority of the inhabitants were anxious to take the
side of the Reformation and were hindered by their overlords. It made alliances with the towns in the territories
of the Bishop of Basel, and enabled them to assert their
independence. In May (23rd) 1532 it warned the Duke
of Savoy that if he thought of persecuting the inhabitants
of Payerne because of their religion, it would make their
cause its own, and declared that its alliance with the town
was much more ancient than any existing between Bern
and the Duke.[1] But the case of Geneva was different.
Signs, indeed, were not lacking that many of the people
were inclined to the Reformation.[2] It is more than probable that some of the members of the Councils were
longing for a religious reform But however much in
earnest the reformers might be, they were in a minority,
and it was no part of the policy of Bern to interfere
without due call in the internal administration of the
city; still less to see the rise of a strong and independent
Roman Catholic city-republic on its own western border.

Suddenly, in the middle of 1532, Geneva was thrown
into a state of violent religious commotion. Pope Clement
VII. had published an Indulgence within the city on the
usual conditions. On the morning of June 9th, the
citizens found posted up on all the doors of the churches
great printed placards, announcing that "plenary pardon
would be granted to every one for all their sins on the
one condition of repentance, and a living faith in the

---

[1] Ruchat, *Histoire de la Réformation de la Suisse* (Paris, 1835-38),
iii. 138.

[2] We read of Luther's books being read in Geneva as early as May 1521,
and that their effect was to give several of the people heart to care little for
the threats of the Pope; in 1522, Cornelius Agrippa, writing to Capito
(June 17th), and Haller, writing to Zwingli (July 8th), speak of Francis
Lambert (*vir probus et diligens minister Verbi Dei*), who had preached in
Geneva, Lausanne, Freiburg, and Bern; and in 1527, Hofen, secretary to
the Council of Bern, writing to Zwingli (Jan. 15th), thinks that Geneva
could be won for the Reformation,—he had noticed that the people no longer
cared much for Indulgences or for the Mass (Herminjard, *Correspondance*, etc.
i. 101-3, 318 *n.*, ii. 9 f., 10 *n.*; cf. 6).

promises of Jesus Christ." The city was moved to its depths. Priests rushed to tear the placards down. "Lutherans" interfered. Tumults ensued; and one of the canons of the cathedral, Pierre Werly, was wounded in the arm.[1]

The Romanists, both inside and outside the town, were inclined to believe that the affair meant more than it really did. Freiburg had been very suspicious of the influence of the great Protestant canton of Bern, perhaps not without reason. In March (7th) 1532, the deputies of Geneva had been blamed by the inhabitants of Freiburg for being inclined to Lutheranism, and it is more than likely that the Evangelicals of Geneva had some private dealings with the Council of Bern, and had been told that the times were not ripe for any open action on the part of the Protestant canton. The affair of the placards, witnessing as it did the increased strength of the Evangelical party, reawakened suspicions and intensified alarms. A deputy from Freiburg appeared before the Council of Geneva, complaining of the placards,[2] and of the distribution of heretical literature in the city of Geneva (June 24th). The Papal Nuncio wrote from Chambèry (July 8th), asking if it were true, as was publicly reported, that the Lutheran heresy was openly professed and taught in the houses, churches, and even in the schools of Geneva.[3] The letter of the Nuncio was dismissed with a careless answer; but Freiburg had to be contented.

---

[1] J. A. Gautier, *Histoire de Genève* (Geneva, 1896), ii. 349. The nun, Sœur Jeanne de Jussie, in her *Levain du Calvinisme* (p. 46), says "Au mois de Juin, dimanche matin, le 9, certain nombre de mauvais garçons plantèrent grands placards en impression par toutes les portes des églises de Genève, esquels estoient contenus les principaux poincts de la secte perverse luthérienne"; and another contemporary chronicler says that the placards promised a "grand pardon général de Jesus Christ" (Herminjard, *Correspondance*, etc. ii. 422 n.).

[2] Their letter said that it was reported that "nonnullos ex Gebennensibus apposuisse certas cedulas inductorias ad novam legem, contra auctoritatem episcopalem, et quod habent libros et promulgant; quod est contra voluntatem D. Friburgensium" (*Ibid*. ii. 421 n.).

[3] *Ibid*. ii. 424.

5**

Two extracts from the Register of the Council quoted by Herminjard show their anxiety to satisfy Freiburg and yet bear evidence of a very moderate zeal for the Romanist religion. They decided (June 29th) that no schoolmaster was to be allowed to preach in the town unless specially licensed by the vicar or the Syndics; and (June 30th) they resolved to request the vicar to see that the Gospel and the Epistle of the day were read " truthfully without being mixed up with fables and other inventions of men "; they added that they meant to live as their fathers, without any innovations.[1]

The excitement had not died down when Farel arrived in the city in the autumn of 1532. He preached quietly in houses; but his coming was known, and led to some tumults. He and his companions, Saunier and Olivetan, were seized and sent out of the city. The Reformation had begun, and, in spite of many hindrances, was destined to be successful.

§ 2. *The Reformation in Western Switzerland.*

The conversion of Geneva to the Reformed faith was the crown of a work which had been promoted by the canton of Bern ever since its Council had decided, in 1528, to adopt the Reformation. Bern itself belonged to German-speaking Switzerland, but it had extensive possessions in the French-speaking districts. It was the only State strong enough to confront the Dukes of Savoy, and was looked upon as a natural protector against that House and other feudal principalities. Its position may be seen in its relations to the Pays de Vaud. The Pays de Vaud consisted of a confederacy of towns and small feudal estates owning fealty to the House of Savoy. The nobles, the towns, and in some instances the clergy, sent deputies to a Diet which met at Moudon under the presidency of the " governor and bailli de Vaud," who represented the Duke of Savoy A large portion of the country had

---

[1] Herminjard, *Correspondance*, ii. 425 n.

broken away from Savoy at different periods during the
fifteenth century. Lausanne and eight other smaller
towns and districts formed the patrimony of the Prince-
Bishop of Lausanne. The cantons of Freiburg and Bern
ruled jointly over Orbe, Grandson, and Morat. Bern had
become the sole ruler over what were called the four
commanderies of Aigle, Ormonts, Ollon, and Bex. These
four commanderies were outlying portions of Bern, and
were entirely under the rule of its Council. When Bern
had accepted the Reformation, it naturally wished its de-
pendencies to follow its example; and its policy was
always directed to induce other portions of the Pays de
Vaud to become Protestant also. Farel, the Apostle of
French-speaking Switzerland, might almost be called an
agent of the Council of Bern.

Its method of work may be best seen by taking the
examples of Aigle and Lausanne, the one its own possession and the other belonging to the Prince-Bishop, who
was its political ruler.

William Farel, once a member of the "group of
Meaux," whom we have already seen active at the
Disputation in Bern in the beginning of 1528, had settled
at Aigle in 1526, probably by the middle of November.[1]
He did so, he says in his memoir to the Council of Bern—

"With the intention of opening a school to instruct the
youth in virtue and learning, and in order to procure for
myself the necessities of life. Received at once with
brotherly good-will by some of the burghers of the place,
I was asked by them to preach the Word of God before
the Governor, who was then at Bern, had returned. I
acceded to their request. But as soon as the Governor
returned I asked his permission to keep the school, and by
acquaintances also asked him to permit me to preach. The
Governor acceded to their request, but on condition that I
preached nothing but the pure simple clear Word of God
according to the Old and New Testament, without any
addition contrary to the Word, and without attacking the
Holy Sacraments. . . . I promised to conform myself to the

[1] Cf. p. 39, *n.*

will of the Governor, and declared myself ready to submit to any punishment he pleased to inflict upon me if I disobeyed his orders or acted in any way recognised to be contrary to the Word of God."[1]

This was the beginning of a work which gradually spread over French-speaking Switzerland.

The Bishop of Sion, within whose diocese Aigle was situated, published an order forbidding all wandering preachers who had not his episcopal licence from preaching within the confines of his diocese; and this appears to have been used against Farel. Some representation must have been made to the Council of Bern, who indignantly declared that no one was permitted to publish citations, excommunications, interdicts, *ne autres fanfares* within their territories; but at the same time ordered Farel to cease preaching, because he had never been ordained a priest (February 22nd, 1527).[2] The interdict did not last very long; for a minute of Council (March 8th) says, "Farel is permitted to preach at Aigle until the Coadjutor sends another capable priest."[3] Troubles arose from priests and monks, but upon the whole the Council of Bern supported him; and Haller and others wrote from Bern privately, beseeching him to persevere.[4] He remained, and the number of those who accepted the Evangelical faith under his ministry increased gradually until they appear to have been the majority of the people.[5] He confessed himself that what hindered him most was his denunciation of the prevailing immoralities. At the Disputation in Bern, Farel was recognised to be one of the ablest theologians present, and to have contributed in no small degree to the success of the conference. The Council

---

[1] Herminjard, *Correspondance*, etc. ii. 22 *f.* Farel preached his first sermon at Aigle on Friday, Nov. 30th, 1526

[2] *Ibid.* ii. 14, 15.

[3] *Ibid.* ii. 15 *n.*

[4] *Ibid.* ii. 31 *n.*

[5] Farel seems to have asked his converts to submit to baptism; they were baptized in the presence of the congregation on making a solemn and public profession of their faith.—*Ibid.* 48 *n.*

of Bern saw in him the instrument best fitted for the evangelisation of their French-speaking population. He returned to Aigle under the protection of the Council, who sent a herald with him to ensure that he should be treated with all respect, and gave him besides an "open letter," ordering their officials to render him all assistance everywhere within their four commanderies.[1] He was recognised to be the evangelist of the Council of Bern. This did not prevent occasional disturbances, riots promoted by priests and monks, who set the bells a-ringing to drown the preacher's voice, and sometimes procured men to beat drums at the doors of the churches in which he was preaching. His success, however, was so great, that when the commissioners of Bern visited their four commanderies they found that three of them were ready by a majority of votes to adopt the Reformation (March 2nd, 1528). The adoption of the Reformation was signified by the removal of altars and images, and by the abolition of the Mass.

In the parishes where a majority of the people declared for the Reformation, the Council of Bern issued instructions about the order of public worship and other ecclesiastical rites. Thus we find them intimating to their Governor at Aigle that they expected the people to observe the same form of Baptism, of the Table of the Lord, and of the celebration of marriage, as was in use at Bern (April 25th, 1528).[2] The Bern Liturgy, obligatory in all the German-speaking districts of the canton, was not imposed on the Romance Churches until 1552. Then, in July (1528), the Governor is informed that—

"My Lords have resolved to allow to the preachers Farel and Simon 'pour leur prébende' two hundred florins of Savoy annually, and a house with a court, and a kitchen garden. But if they prefer to have the old revenues of the parish cures . . . my Lords are willing. If, on the contrary, they take the two hundred florins, you are to

[1] Herminjard, *Correspondance*, etc. ii. 105 *n.*
[2] *Ibid.* ii. 130, 131.

sell the ecclesiastical goods, and you are to collect the hundredths and the tithes, and out of all you are to pay the two hundred florins annually." [1]

The pastors preferred to take the place of the Romanist incumbents, and there is accordingly another minute sent to the Castellan, syndic, and parishioners of Aigle, ordering Farel to be placed in possession of the ecclesiastical possessions of the parish, " seeing that it is reasonable that the pastor should have his portion of the fruits of the sheep." [2]

The history of Aigle was repeated over and over again in other parts of western Switzerland. In the bailiwicks which Bern and Freiburg ruled jointly, Bern insisted on freedom of preaching, and on the right of the people to choose whether they would remain Romanists or become Protestants. Commissioners from the two cantons presided when the votes were given.

Farel was too valuable to be left as pastor of a small district like Aigle. We find him making wide preaching tours, always protected by Bern when protection was possible. It was the rooted belief of the Protestants that a public Disputation on matters of religion in presence of the people, the speakers using the language understood by the crowd, always resulted in spreading the Reformation and Bern continually tried to get such conferences in towns where the authorities were Romanist. Their first interference in the ecclesiastical affairs of Lausanne was of this kind. It seems that some of the priests of Lausanne had accused Farel of being a heretic; whereupon the Council of Bern demanded that Farel should be heard before the Bishop of Lausanne's tribunal, in order to prove that he was no heretic. The claim led to a long correspondence. The Bishop continually refused; while the Council and citizens seemed inclined to grant the request. Farel could not get a hearing before the episcopal tribunal, but he visited the town, and on the second occasion was permitted by the Council to preach to the people. This occurred again and again; and the result was that the

[1] Herminjard, *Correspondance*, etc. ii. 131 *n.*   [2] *Ibid.* ii. 137.

town became Protestant and disowned the authority of the Bishop. Bern assisted the inhabitants to drive the Bishop away, and to become a free municipality and Protestant.

Gradually Farel had become the leader of an organised band of missioners, who devoted themselves to the evangelisation of western or French-speaking Switzerland.[1] They had been carefully selected—young men for the most part well educated, of unbounded courage, willing to face all the risks of their dangerous work, daunted by no threat or peril, taking their lives in their hand. They were the forerunners of the young preachers, teachers, and colporteurs whom Calvin trained later in Geneva and sent forth by the hundred to evangelise France and the Low Countries. They were all picked men. No one was admitted to the little band without being well warned of the hazardous work before him, and some who were ready to take all the risks were rejected because the leader was not sure that they had the necessary powers of endurance.[2] These preachers were under the protection of the canton of Bern, whose authorities were resolute to maintain the freedom to preach the Word of God ; but they continually went where the Bernese had no power to assist them; nor could the protection of that powerful canton aid them in sudden emergencies when bitter Romanist partisans, infuriated by the invectives with which the preachers lashed the abuses of the Roman religion, or wrathful at their very presence, stirred up the mob against them. When their correspondence and that of their opponents—a correspondence collected and carefully edited by M. Herminjard —is read, it can be seen that they could always count on a certain amount of sympathy from the people of the towns and villages where they preached, but that the

---

[1] M. Herminjard gives a list of their names—Claud de Glantinis, Alexandre le Bel, Thomas ——, Henri Pourcellet, Jean Bosset, Antoine Froment, Antoine Marcourt, Eymer Beynon, Pierre Marmoud, Hugues Turtaz, and perhaps Jean Holard, Pierre Simonin or Symonier, Claude Bigothier, Jean de Bély, Jean Fathon.

[2] Cf. letter of Farel to Fortunat Andronicus, in Herminjard, *Correspondance*, etc. ii. 307.

authorities were for the most part hostile. If Bern insisted on their protection, Freiburg was as active in opposing them, and lost no opportunity of urging the local authorities to harass them in every way, to silence their preaching, and if possible to expel them from their territories.

Such men had the defects of their qualities. Their zeal often outran their discretion. When Farel and Froment, the most daring and devoted of his band, were preaching at a village in the vale of Vallingin, a priest began to chant the Mass beside them. As the priest elevated the Host, Froment seized it and, turning towards the people, said, " This is not the God to adore ; He is in the Heaven in the glory of the Father, not in the hands of the priests as you believe, and as they teach." There was a riot, of course, but the preachers escaped. Next day, however, as they were passing a solitary place, they were assailed by a crowd of men and women, stoned and beaten with clubs, then hurried away to a neighbouring castle whose chatelaine had instigated the attack. There they were thrust violently into the chapel, and the crowd tried to make Farel prostrate himself before an image of the Blessed Virgin. He resisted, admonishing them to adore the one God in spirit and in truth, not dumb images without sense or power. The crowd beat him to the effusion of blood, and the two preachers were dragged to a vault, where they were imprisoned until rescued by the authorities of Neuchâtel.[1]

These preachers were all Frenchmen or French-Swiss. They had the hot Celtic blood in their veins, and their hearers were their kith and kin—prompt to act, impetuous when their passions were stirred. Scenes occurred at their preaching which we seldom hear of among slower Germans, who generally waited until their authorities led. In western Switzerland the audiences were eager to get rid of the idolatries denounced. At Grandson, the people rushed to the church of the Cordeliers, and tore down the altars and images, while the crosses, altars, and images

[1] Herminjard, *Correspondance*, etc. ii. 270 *n*.

of the parish church were also destroyed.[1] Similar tumults took place at Orbe; and the authorities at Bern, who desired to see liberty for both Protestants and Romanists, had occasion to rebuke the zealous preachers.

But the dangers which the missioners ran were not always of their own provoking. Sometimes a crowd of women invaded the churches in which they preached, interrupted the services with shoutings, hustled and beat the preachers; sometimes when they addressed the people in the market-place the preachers and their audience were assailed with showers of stones; sometimes Farel and his companions were laid wait for and maltreated.[2] M. de Watteville, sent down by the authorities of Bern to report on disturbances, wrote to the Council of Bern that the faces of the preachers were so torn that it looked as if they had been fighting with cats, and that on one occasion the alarm-bell had been sounded against them, as was the custom for a wolf-hunt.[3]

No dangers daunted the missioners, and soon the whole of the outlying districts of Bern, Neuchâtel, Soleure, and other French-speaking portions of Switzerland declared for the Reformation. The cantonal authorities frequently sent down commissioners to ascertain the wishes of the people; and when the majority of the inhabitants voted for the Evangelical religion, the church, parsonage, and stipend were given to a Protestant pastor. Many of Farel's missioners were temporarily settled in these village churches; but they were for the most part better fitted for pioneer work than for a settled pastorate. In January (9–14th) 1532, a synod of these Protestant pastors was held at Bern to deliberate on some uniform ways of exercising their ministry to prevent disorders arising from individual caprice. Two hundred and thirty ministers were present, and Bucer was brought from Strassburg to give them guidance. His advice was greatly appreciated and

[1] Herminjard, *Correspondance*, etc. ii. 365 *n.*, 390.
[2] *Ibid.* ii. 347, 372.
[3] *Ibid.* ii. 362 *n.*

followed by the delegates of the churches and the Council of Bern. The Synod in the end issued an elaborate ordinance, which included a lengthy exposition of doctrine [1]

§ 3. *Farel in Geneva.*

It was after this consolidation of the Reformation in Bern and its outlying provinces that Farel found himself free to turn his attention to Geneva. He had evidently been thinking for months about the possibility of evangelising the town. He had little fear of the people themselves, and he wrote to Zwingli (Oct. 1st, 1531) that were it not for the dread of Freiburg, he believed that the Genevese would welcome the Gospel.[2] The affair of the " placards " seems to have decided him to begin his mission in the city. When he was driven out he was far from abandoning the enterprise. He turned to Froment, his most trusted assistant, and sent him into Geneva.

Antoine Froment, who has the honour along with Farel of being the Reformer of Geneva, was born at Tries, near Grenoble, about 1510. He was therefore, like Farel, a native of Dauphiné. Like him, also, he had gone to Paris for his education, and had become acquainted with Lefèvre, who seems to have introduced him to Marguerite d'Angoulême, the Queen of Navarre,[3] as he received from her a prebend in a canonry on one of her estates. How

---

[1] The ordinance was entitled, *Ordnung wie sich pfarrer und prediger zu Statt und Land Bern, in leer und leben, halten sollen, mit wyterem bericht von Christo, und den Sacramenten, beschlossen im Synodo daselbst versamlet am 9 tag Januarij—Anno 1532.* The doctrinal decisions of the Synod are to be found in Müller, *Bekenntnisschriften der reformierten Kirche* (Leipzig, 1903), pp. 31 *ff.*

[2] Herminjard, *Correspondance*, etc. ii. 364.

[3] Froment married (1529) Marie Dentière, who had been abbess of a convent in Tournay, and had been expelled for her Evangelical opinions. She was a learned lady, a friend of the Queen of Navarre, who sometimes preached, according to the nun Jeanne de Jussie, and made many converts. She wrote a piquant epistle to the Queen of Navarre, exposing the intrigues which drove Calvin, Farel, and Coraut from Geneva. A portion of this very rare *Epistle* is printed by Herminjard, *Correspondance*. etc. v. 295 *ff.*

he came to Switzerland is unknown. Once there and introduced to Farel, he became his most daring and enthusiastic disciple, and Farel prized him above all the others. They were Paul and Timothy. It was natural that Farel should entrust him with the difficult and dangerous task of preaching the Gospel in Geneva.

Farel's seizure and expulsion made it necessary to proceed with caution. Froment entered Geneva (Nov. 3rd, 1532), and began his work by intimating by public advertisement (*placard*) that he was ready to teach any one who wished to learn to read and write the French language, and that he would charge no fees if his pupils were not able to profit by his instructions. Scholars came.[1] He managed to mingle Evangelical instruction with his lessons,—" every day one or two sermons from the Holy Scripture," he says,—and soon made many converts, especially among the wives of influential citizens. Towards the end of 1532, the monks of one of the convents in Geneva had brought to the city a Dominican, Christopher Bocquet, to be their Advent preacher. His sermons seem to have been largely Evangelical, and had the effect of inducing many of the citizens to attend Froment's discourses in the hall where he kept his school.[2] This provoked threats on the part of the Romanists, and strongly worded sermons from the priests and Romanist orators. One citizen, convicted of having spoken disrespectfully of the Mass, was banished, and forbidden to return on pain of death. On this the Evangelicals of the town appealed to Bern. Their letter was promptly answered by a demand on the part of the Council of that canton that the Evangelicals must be left in peace, and if attacked publicly must be allowed to answer in as public a fashion.[3] When their letter was read in the Council of Geneva, it provoked

---

[1] Froment, *Les Actes et gestes marveilleux de la cité de Genève* (ed. of 1854 by G. Revillod), pp. 9 and 12–15.

[2] The authorities of Freiburg in a letter to Geneva actually called this Dominican monk a "Lutheran preacher"; cf. their letter given in Herminjard, *Correspondance*, iii. 15 *f*.

[3] *Ibid.* iii. 38 *f*.

some protests from the more ardently Romanist members, and the priests stirred up part of the population to riotous proceedings, in which the lives of the Evangelicals were threatened. The Syndics and Council had difficulty in preventing conflicts in the streets. They published a decree (March 30th, 1533), in which they practically proclaimed liberty of conscience, but forbade all insulting expressions, all attacks on the Sacraments or on the ecclesiastical fasts and ceremonies, and again ordered preachers to say nothing which could not be proved from Holy Scripture.[1]

The numbers of the Evangelicals increased daily; they became bolder, and on the 10th of April they met in a garden, under the presidency of Guérin Muète, a hosier, for the celebration of the Lord's Supper. This became known to the Romanists, and there was a renewal of the threats against the Evangelicals, which came to a head in the riot of the 5th of May—a riot which had important consequences.[2] It seems that while several citizens, known to belong to the Evangelical party, were walking in the square before the Cathedral of St. Peter, they were attacked by a band of armed priests, and three of them were severely wounded. The leader of the band, a turbulent priest named Pierre Werly, who belonged to an old family of Freiburg, and was a canon in the cathedral, followed by five or six others, rushed down to the broad street Molard, with loud shouts. Werly was armed with one of the huge Swiss swords. He and his companions attacked the Evangelicals; there was a sharp, short fight; several persons were wounded severely, and Werly, " the captain of the priests," was slain.[3] The affair made a great noise. The Romanists at once proclaimed Werly a martyr, and honoured him with a pompous funeral. Freiburg insisted that all the Evangelicals who

[1] The text of the decree is given in Herminjard, iii. 41 *n.*

[2] Jeanne de Jussie, *Le Levain du Calvinisme*, p. 53 ; Froment, *Actes et Gestes*, etc. 48–51.

[3] For the affair of Werly, see the letter of the Evangelicals of Geneva to the Council of Bern, given in Herminjard, *Correspondance*, etc., and the notes of the editor (iii. 46 *ff.*).

happened to be in the Molard should be arrested; and it was said that preparations were being made for a massacre of all the followers of the Reformation. In their extremity they again appealed to Bern, whose authorities again interfered for their protection.

During these troublesome times the position of the Council of Geneva was one of great difficulty. The Prince-Bishop of Geneva, Pierre de la Baume, was still nominally sovereign, secular as well as ecclesiastical ruler. His secular powers had been greatly curtailed, how much it is difficult to say, but certainly to the extent that the criminal administration of the city and the territory subject to it was in the hands of the Council and Syndics. Freiburg, one of the two protecting cantons, insisted that all the ecclesiastical authority was still in the hands of the Bishop, to be administered in his absence by his vicar.[1] The Councils, although they had passed decrees (June 30th, 1532, and March 30th, 1533) which had distinctly to do with ecclesiastical matters, acknowledged for the most part that the ecclesiastical jurisdiction did not belong to them. But the whole of the inhabitants were not contented with this diminution of the episcopal authority. Turbulent priests and the yet more violent canons,[2] the great body of monks and nuns, wished, and intrigued for the restoration of the rule of the Bishop and of the House of Savoy. The beginnings of a movement for Reformation had increased the difficulties of the Council; it brought a third party into the town. The Evangelicals were all strongly opposed to the rule of the Bishop and Savoy, and they were fast growing in strength; a powerful minority of Roman Catholics

[1] After the defeat of his party by the combined efforts of Freiburg and Bern, the Bishop had quitted Geneva on August 1st, 1527 ; he returned there on July 1st, 1533, but left again after a fortnight's residence (July 14th, 1533), disgusted, he said, at an act of iconoclasm.

[2] The priests of Geneva were notoriously turbulent. We read of at least five riots which they headed. The canons were worse. Pierre Werly had attempted the assassination of Farel on October 3rd, 1532 (Jeanne de Jussie, Le Levain du Calvinisme, p. 50) ; he had taken an active part in the riots caused by the placards in 1532.

were no less strongly in favour of a return to the old con·
dition. The majority of the Roman Catholic citizens,
opposed to the Bishop as a secular ruler, had no desire
for the triumph of the Reformation. As time went on, it
was seen that these moderate Romanists had to choose
between a return of the old disorderly rule of the Bishop,
or to acquiesce in the ecclesiastical as well as the secular
superiority of the Council, pressed by the Protestant canton
of Bern. The Savoyard party evidently believed that their
hatred of the Reformation would be stronger than their
dislike to the Savoyard and episcopal rule—a mistaken
belief, as events were to show.

The policy of Bern, wherever its influence prevailed in
western Switzerland, was exerted to secure toleration for all
Evangelicals, and to procure, if possible, a public discussion
on matters of religion between the Romanists and leading
Reformers. They pressed this over and over again on their
allies of Geneva. As early as April 1533, they had insisted that a monk who had offered to refute Farel should
be kept to his word, and that the Council of Geneva should
arrange for a Public Disputation.[1] Towards the close of
the year an event occurred which gave them a pretext for
decisive interference.

Guy Furbiti, a renowned Roman Catholic preacher, a
learned theologian, a doctor of the Sorbonne, had been
brought to Geneva to be Advent preacher. He used the
occasion to denounce vigorously the doctrines of the Evangelicals, supporting his statements, as he afterwards confessed,
not from Scripture, but from the Decretals and from the
writings of Thomas Aquinas. He ended his sermon (Dec.
2nd) with the words: "Where are those fine preachers of
the fireside, who say the opposite ? If they showed themselves here one could speak to them. Ha ! ha ! they are
well to hide themselves in corners to deceive poor women
and others who know nothing."

After the sermon, either in church or in the square
before the cathedral, Froment cried to the crowd, " Hear

[1] Herminjard, *Correspondance*, etc. iii. 38.

me! I am ready to give my life, and my body to be
burned, to maintain that what that man has said is nothing
but falsehood and the words of Antichrist." There was a
great commotion. Some shouted, "To the fire with him!
to the fire!" and tried to seize him. The chronicler nun,
Jeanne de Jussie, proud of her sex, relates that "les femmes
comme enragées sortirent après, de grande furie, luy jettant
force pierres."[1] He escaped from them. But Alexandre
Canus was banished, and forbidden to return under pain of
death; and Froment was hunted from house to house, until
he found a hiding-place in a hay-loft. Furbiti had permitted himself to attack with strong invectives the authorities of Bern, and the Evangelicals of Geneva in their appeal
for protection sent extracts from the sermons.[2] Bern had
at last the opportunity for which its Council had long
waited.

They wrote a dignified letter (Dec. 17th, 1533) to the
Council of Geneva, in which they complained that the
Genevese, their allies, had hitherto paid little attention to
their requests for a favourable treatment of the Evangelicals;
that they had expelled from the town "nostre serviteur
maistre Guillaume Farel"; not content with that, they had
recently misused their "servants" Froment and Alexandre
for protesting against the sermons of a Jacobin monk
(Furbiti) who "preached only lies, errors, and blasphemies
against God, the faith, and ourselves, wounding our honour,
calling us Jews, Turks, and dogs"; that the banishment
of Alexandre and the hunting of Froment touched them
(the Council of Bern), and that they would not suffer it.

---

[1] *Le Levain du Calvinisme*, pp. 74, 75, 247 (where Canus is called Alexander
de Molendino). Froment, who had been compelled to quit Geneva, had returned to the town along with Alexandre Canus immediately after the
departure of the Bishop on the 14th of July 1533.

[2] Furbiti permitted himself to use strong language. Even the Romanist
chronicler, the nun Jeanne de Jussie, records that Furbiti "touched to the
quick the Lutheran dogs," and said that "all those who belonged to that
cursed sect were licentious, gluttons, lascivious, ambitious, homicides, and
bandits, who loved nothing but sensuality, and lived as the brutes, reverencing neither God nor their superiors" (*Le Levain du Calvinisne*, p. 79).

They demanded the immediate arrest of the "*caffard*"[1] (Furbiti); and they said they were about to send an embassy to Geneva to vindicate publicly the honour of God and their own.[2]

As the Council of Bern meant to enforce a Public Disputation, they sent Farel to Geneva. He reached the city on the evening of December 20th.

The letter was read to the Council of Geneva upon Dec. 21st, and they at once gave orders to the vicar to prevent Furbiti leaving the town. But the vicar, who had resolved to try his strength against Bern, refused, and actually published two mandates (Dec. 31st, 1533, and Jan. 1st, 1534) denouncing the Genevese Syndics, forbidding any of the citizens to read the Holy Scriptures, and ordering all copies of translations of the Bible, whether in German or in French, to be seized and burnt.[3] The dispute between Syndics and vicar was signalised by riots promoted by the extreme Romanist party. The Council, anxious not to proceed to extremities, contented themselves with placing a guard to watch Furbiti; and the monk was attended continually, even when he went to and from the church, by a guard of three halberdiers.

The Bernese embassy arrived on the 4th of January, and had prolonged audience of the Council of Geneva on the 5th and 7th. They insisted on a fair treatment for the Evangelical party, which meant freedom of conscience and the right of public worship, and they demanded that Furbiti should be compelled to justify his charges against the Evangelicals in the presence of learned men who could speak for the Council of Bern. The Genevan authorities had no wish to break irrevocably with their Bishop, nor to coerce the ecclesiastical authorities; they pleaded that Furbiti was not under their jurisdiction, and they referred

---

[1] *Caffard* need not be taken to mean *hypocrite*: it was commonly used to denote a mendicant friar.

[2] The letter is given in Herminjard, *Correspondance*, etc. iii. 119 *f.*

[3] The MS. chronicle of Michel Roset is the source for the statement about the order to burn translations of the Scripture.

the Bernese deputies to the Bishop or his vicar. "We
have been ordered to apply to you," said the deputies from
Bern. "Your answer makes us see that you seek delay,
and that you are not treating us fairly ; that you think little
of the honour of the Council of Bern. Here is the treaty
of alliance (they produced the document), and we are about
to tear off the seals." This was the formal way among the
Swiss of cancelling a treaty. The Councillors of Geneva
then proposed that they should compel the monk to
appear before them and the deputies of Bern, when
explanations might be demanded from him. The deputies
accepted the offer, but on condition that there should be
a conference between the monk (Furbiti) and theologians
sent from Bern (Farel and Viret). Next day Furbiti was
taken from the episcopal palace and placed in the town's
prison (Jan. 8th), and on the morrow (Jan. 9th) he was
brought before the Council. There he refused to plead
before secular judges. The Council of Geneva tried in vain
to induce the vicar to nominate an ecclesiastical delegate
who was to sit in the Council and be present at the conference. Their negotiations with the vicar, carried on for
some days, were in vain. Then they attempted to induce
the Bernese to depart from their conditions. The Council
of Bern was immovable. It insisted on the immediate
payment by the Genevese of the debt due to Bern for the
war of deliverance and for the punishment of Furbiti (Jan.
25th, 1534). Driven to the wall, the Council of Geneva
resolved to override the ecclesiastical authority of the
Bishop and his vicar. Furbiti was compelled to appear
before the Council and the deputies of Bern, and to answer
to Farel and Viret on Jan. 27th and Feb. 3rd (1534).
On the afternoon of the latter day the partisans of the
Bishop got up another riot, in which one of them poniarded
an Evangelical, Nicolas Bergier. This riot seems to have
exhausted the patience of the peaceable citizens of Geneva,
whether Romanists or Evangelicals. A band of about five
hundred assembled armed before the Town Hall, informed
the Council that they would no longer tolerate riots caused
6**

by turbulent priests, and that they were ready to support civic authority and put down lawlessness with a strong hand. The Council thereupon acted energetically. That night the murderer, Claude Pennet, who had hid himself in the belfry of the cathedral, was dragged from his place of concealment, tried next day, and hanged on the day following (Feb. 5th). The houses of the principal rioters were searched, and letters discovered proving a plot to seize the town and deliver it into the hands of the Bishop. Pierre de la Baume had gone the length of nominating a member of the Council of Freiburg, M. Pavillard, to act as his deputy in secular affairs, and ordering him to massacre the Evangelicals within the city.

When the excitement had somewhat died down, the deputies of Bern pressed for a renewal of the proceedings against Furbiti. The monk was again brought before the Council, and confronted by Farel and Viret. He was forced to confess that he could not prove his assertions from the Holy Scriptures, but had based them on the Decretals and the writings of Thomas Aquinas, admitting that he had transgressed the regulations of the Council of Geneva. He promised that, if allowed to preach on the following Sunday (Feb. 15th), he would make public reparation to the Council of Bern. When Sunday came he refused to keep his promise, and was sent back to prison.[1]

Meanwhile the Evangelical community in Geneva was growing, and taking organised form. One of the most prominent of the Genevan Evangelicals, Jean Baudichon de la Maisonneuve, prepared a hall by removing a partition between two rooms in his magnificent house, situated in that part of the city which was the cradle of the Reforma-

---

[1] Furbiti was released in April 1536 at the request of Francis I. of France He was exchanged for Antoine Saunier, a Swiss Evangelical in prison in France. Such exchanges were not uncommon between the Protestant cantons and France.—Herminjard, *Correspondance*, etc. iii. 396 *f.*

A full account of the conferences between Farel and Furbiti is given in *Lettres certaines d'aucuns grandz troubles et tumultes nuz à Genève, avec la disputation faicte l'an 1534*, etc. (Basel, 1583). The booklet is very rare.

tion in Geneva. There Farel, Viret, and Froment preached to three or four hundred persons; and there the first baptism according to the Reformed rite was celebrated in Geneva (Feb. 22nd, 1533). The audiences soon increased beyond the capacity of the hall, and the Evangelicals, protected by the presence of the Bernese deputies, took possession of the large audience hall or church of the Convent of the Cordeliers in the same street (March 1st). The deputies from Bern frequently asked the Council of Geneva to grant the use of one of the churches of the town for the Evangelicals, but were continually answered that the Council had not the power, but that they would not object if the Evangelicals found a suitable place. This indirect authorisation enabled them to meet in the convent church, which held between four and five thousand people, and which was frequently filled. Thus the little band increased. Farel preached for the first time in St. Peter's on the 8th of August 1535. Services were held in other houses also.[1]

The Bishop of Geneva, foiled in his attempt to regain possession of the town by well-planned riots, united himself with the Duke of Savoy to conquer the city by force of arms. Their combined forces advanced against Geneva; they overran the country, seized and pillaged the country houses of the citizens, and subjected the town itself to a

---

[1] Adjoining the house of Baudichon, with one building between them, was a large mansion occupied by the Seigneur de Thorens, a strong partisan of the Reformation. He was a Savoyard, expelled from his country because of his religious principles. He acquired citizenship in Bern. The Bernese, on the eve of their embassy, which reached Geneva on Jan. 4th, had bought this house, and placed M. de Thorens therein, intending it to be a place where the Evangelicals could meet in safety under the protection of Bern. It is probable that in time of special danger the Evangelicals met there for public worship. When the Council of Freiburg objected to Farel's preaching, the Council of Geneva replied that the services were held in the house of the deputies of Bern. Cf. Herminjard, *Correspondance*, etc. ix. 459 *f.*, 489 *f.*; Jeanne de Jussie, *Le Levain du Calvinisme*, pp. 91, 106, 107 (where the poor nun describes the various ceremonies of the Reformed cult with all the venom and coarseness of sixteenth century Romanism); Baum, *Procès de Baudichon de la Maisonneuve accusé d'hérésie a Lyon, 1534* (Geneva, 1873), pp. 110, 111; Doumergue, *Jean Calvin*, ii. 126 *f.*, iii. 196-98.

close investment. The war was a grievous matter for the city, but it furthered the Reformation. The Bishop had leagued himself with the old enemy of Geneva; the priests, the monks, the nuns were eager for his success; he compelled patriotic Roman Catholics to choose between their religion and their country. It was also a means of displaying the heroism of the Protestant pastors. Farel and Froment were high-spirited Frenchmen, who scoffed at any danger lying in the path of duty. They had braved a thousand perils in their missionary work. Viret was not less courageous. The three worked on the fortifications with the citizens; they shared the watches of the defenders; they encouraged the citizens by word and deed. The Genevese were prepared for any sacrifices to preserve their liberties. Four faubourgs, which formed a second town almost as large as the first, were ordered to be demolished to strengthen the defence. The city was reduced to great straits, and the citizens of Bern seemed to be deaf to their cries for help.

Bern was doing its best by embassies to assist them; but it dared not attack the Pays de Vaud when Freiburg, angry at the process of the Reformation, threatened a counter attack. After the siege was raised, the strongholds in the surrounding country remained in the possession of the enemy, and the people belonging to Geneva were liable to be pillaged and maltreated.

Within the city the number of Evangelicals increased week by week. Then came a sensational event which brought about the ruin of the Roman Catholic party. A woman, Antoina Vax, cook in the house of Claude Bernard, with whom the three pastors dwelt, attempted to poison Viret, Farel, and Froment.[1] The confession of the prisoner,

---

[1] The poison was placed in some spinach soup, and the popular story was that Farel escaped because he did not like the food; that Froment had seated himself at table to take his share, when news was brought to him that his wife and children had arrived at Geneva—he rose from the table at once to go to meet them, and left the soup untasted. Poor Viret was the only one who took his share, and became very ill immediately afterwards. The prisoner's confession, lately exhumed from the Geneva archives, tells

combined with other circumstances, created the impression among the members of Council and the people of Geneva that the priests of the town had instigated the attempt, and a strong feeling in favour of the Protestant pastors swept over the city. The Council at once provided lodging for Viret and Farel in the Convent of the Cordeliers. When the guardian of that convent asked leave to hold public discussions on religious questions in the great church belonging to the convent, it was at once granted.

The Council itself made arrangements for the public Disputation. Five *Thèses évangéliques* were drafted by the Protestant pastors, and the Council invited discussion upon them from all and sundry.[1] Invitations were sent to the canons of the cathedral, and to all the priests and monks of Geneva; safe-conducts were promised to all foreign theologians who desired to take part;[2] a special attempt was made to induce a renowned Paris Roman Catholic champion, Pierre Cornu, a theologian trained at the Sorbonne, who happened to be at Grenoble, to defend the Romanist position by attacking the *Theses*. The *Theses* themselves were posted up in Geneva as early as the 1st of May (1535), and copies were sent to all the priests and convents within the territories of the Genevans.[3]

The Disputation was fixed to open on the 30th of May. The Council nominated eight commissioners, half of whom were Roman Catholics, to maintain order, and four secretaries to keep minutes of the proceedings.[4] Efforts were made to induce Roman Catholic theologians of repute for their learning to attend and attack the *Theses*. But the Bishop of Geneva had forbidden the Disputation, and the

---

another tale. The woman said that she stuffed a small bone with the poison, and placed it in Viret's bowl; but was afraid to do the same to Farel's because his soup was too clear. Cf. extracts quoted in Doumergue's *Jean Calvin*, etc. ii. 133, 134 *n*.

[1] The *Theses* are given in Ruchat, *Histoire de la Réformation de la Suisse*, iii. 357.

[2] Herminjard, *Correspondance*, etc. iii. 294, 295 *n*.

[3] *Le Levain du Calvinisme*, p. 118.

[4] Herminjard, *Correspondance*, etc. iii. 294 *n*.

Council were unable to prevail on any stranger to appear. When the opening day arrived, and the Council, commissioners, and secretaries were solemnly seated in their places in the great hall of the convent, no Romanist defender of the faith appeared to impugn the Evangelical *Theses.* Farel and Viret nevertheless expounded and defended. The Disputation continued at intervals during four weeks, till the 24th of June, Romanist champions accepted the Reformers' challenge—Jean Chapuis, prior of the Dominican convent at Plainpalais, near Geneva, and Jean Cachi, confessor to the Sisters of St. Clara in the city. But they were no match for men like Farel. Chapuis himself apologised for the absence of the Genevan priests and monks, by saying that even in his convent there was a lack of learned men. The weakness of the Romanist defence made a great impression on the people of Geneva. They went about saying to each other, " If all Christian princes permitted a free discussion like our MM. of Geneva, the affair would soon be settled without burnings, or slaughter, or murders ; but the Pope and his followers, the cardinals and the bishops and the priests, know well that if free discussion is permitted all is lost for them. So all these powers forbid any discussion or conversation save by fire and by sword." They knew that all throughout Romance Switzerland the Reformers, whether in a minority or in a majority, were eager for a public discussion.

When the Disputation was ended, Farel urged the Council to declare themselves on the side of the Reformation ; but they hesitated until popular tumults forced their hand. On July 23rd, Farel preached in the Church of the Madeleine. The Council made mild remonstrances. Then he preached in the Church of St. Gervais. Lastly, on the 8th of August, the people forced him to preach in the Cathedral, St. Peter's (Aug. 8th). In the afternoon the priests were at vespers as usual. As they chanted the Psalm—

> " Their idols are silver and gold,
> The work of men's hands.

They have mouths, but they speak not:
Eyes have they, but they see not;
They have ears, but they hear not;
Noses have they, but they smell not;
They have hands, but they handle not;
Feet have they, but they walk not;
Neither speak they through their throat,"

someone in the throng shouted, " You curse, as you chant, all who make graven images and trust in them. Why do you let them remain here ? " It was the signal for a tumult. The crowd rushed to throw to the ground and break in pieces the statues of the saints ; and the children pushing among the crowd picked up the fragments, and rushing to the doors, said, " We have the gods of the priests, would you like some ? "[1] Next day the riots were renewed in the parish and convent churches, and the images of the saints were defaced or destroyed.

The Council met on the 9th, and summoned Farel before them. The minutes state that he made an *oratio magna*, ending with the declaration that he and his fellow-preachers were willing to submit to death if it could be shown that they taught anything contrary to the Holy Scriptures. Then, falling on his knees, he poured forth one of those wonderful prayers which more than anything else exhibited the exalted enthusiasm of the great missionary. The religious question was discussed next day in the *Council of the Two Hundred,* when it was resolved to abolish the Mass provisionally, to summon the monks before the Council, and to ask them to give their reasons for maintaining the Mass and the worship of the saints. The two Councils resolved to inform the people of Bern about what they had done.[2]

It is evident that the two Councils had been hurried by the iconoclastic zeal of the people along a path they

---

[1] Froment, *Actes et gestes*, etc. pp. 144–146 : "Nous avons les dieux des Prebstres, en voullés vous ? et les iectoynt apres cielx " (p. 145).

[2] The minute is given in Herminjard, *Correspondance*, etc. iii. 424 ; and the letter of the two Councils written for the information of the Councils of Bern at p. 332.

had meant to tread in a much more leisurely fashion. The political position was full of uncertainties. Their enemies were still in the field against them. Bern seemed to be unable to assist them. They were ready to welcome the intervention of France. It was the fear of increasing their external troubles rather than any zeal for the Roman Catholic faith that had prevented the Council from espousing the Reformation immediately after the public Disputation. "If we abolish the Mass, image worship, and everything popish, for one enemy we have now we are sure to have an hundred," was their thought.[1]

The official representatives of the Roman Catholic religion did not appear to advantage at this crisis of their fate. They were in no haste to defend their worship before the Council. When they at last appeared (Nov. 29th, 1535), the monks in the forenoon and the secular clergy in the afternoon, there was a careless indifference in their answers. The Council seem to have referred them to Farel's summary of the matters discussed in the public Disputation which began on the 30th of May, and to have asked them what they had to say against its conclusions and in favour of the Mass and of the adoration of the saints.[2] The monks one after another (twelve of them appeared before the Council) answered monotonously that they were unlearned people, who lived as they had been taught by their fathers, and did not inquire further. The secular clergy, by their spokesman Roletus de Pane, said that they had nothing to do with the Disputation and what had been said there; that they had no desire to listen to more addresses from Farel; and that they meant to live as their predecessors.[3] This was the end. The two deputa-

[1] Froment, *Actes et gestes*, etc. pp. 142–144.

[2] The fullest contemporary account of these matters is to be found in *Un opuscule inédit de Farel ; Le Resumé des actes de la Dispute de Rive de 1535*, published in the 22nd vol. of the *Mémoires et Documents publiées par la Société d'Histoire et Archæologie de Genève*. It has been reprinted separately.

[3] The words used by the spokesman of the secular clergy, among whom were the canons of the cathedral, were : "*sua non esse sustinere talia, cum nec sint sufficientes nec sciant.*"

tions of monks and seculars were informed by the Council
that they must cease saying Mass until further orders were
given. The Reformation was legally established in Geneva,
and the city stood forth with Bern as altogether Protestant.[1]

The dark clouds on the political horizon were rising.
France seemed about to interfere in favour of Geneva, and
the fear of France in possession of the "gate of western
Switzerland" was stronger than reluctance to permit
Geneva to become a Protestant city. The Council of
Freiburg promised to allow the Bernese army to march
through their territory. Bern renounced its alliance with
Savoy on November 29th, 1535. War was declared on
January 16th. The army of Bern left its territories,
gathering reinforcements as it went; for towns like
Neuville, Neuchâtel, Lausanne, Payerne—oppressed Protestant communities in Romance Switzerland—felt that the
hour of their liberation was at hand, and their armed
burghers were eager to strike one good stroke at their
oppressors under the leadership of the proud republic.
There was little fighting. The greater part of the Pays de
Vaud was conquered without striking a blow, and the army
of the Duke of Savoy and the Bishop of Geneva was dispersed without a battle. A few sieges were needed to
complete the victory. The great republic, after its fashion,
had waited till the opportune moment, and then struck
once and for all. Its decisive victory brought deliverance
not only to Geneva, but to Lausanne and many other Protestant municipalities in Romance Switzerland (Aug. 7th,
1536). The democracy of Geneva was served heir to the
seignorial rights of the Bishop, and to the sovereign rights
of the Duke of Savoy over city and lands. Geneva became
an independent republic under the protectorate of Bern, and
to some extent dependent on that canton.

In the month of December 1535, the Syndics and
Council of Geneva had adopted the legend on the coat of
arms of the town, *Post tenebras lux*—a device which became

[1] The minute of Council is quoted in Doumergue, *Jean Calvin*, etc. ii.
147, 148.

very famous, and appeared on its coinage. The resolution of the Council of the Two Hundred to abolish the Mass and saint worship was officially confirmed by the citizens assembled, " as was the custom, by sound of bell and of trumpet " (May 21st, 1536).

Geneva had gained much. It had won political independence, for which it had been fighting for thirty years, modified by its relations to Bern,[1] but greater than it had ever before enjoyed. The Reformed religion had been established, although the fact remained that the Romanist partisans had still a good deal of hidden strength. But much was still to be done to make the town the citadel of the Reformation which it was to become. Its past history had demoralised its people. The rule of dissolute bishops and the example of a turbulent and immoral clergy had poisoned the morals of the city.[2] The liberty won might easily degenerate into licence, and ominous signs were not lacking that this was about to take place. " It is impossible to deny," says Kampschulte, the Roman Catholic biographer of Calvin, " that disorder and demoralisation had become threatening in Geneva ; it would have been almost a miracle had it not been so." Farel did what he could. He founded schools. He organised the hospitals. He strove to kindle moral life in the people of his adopted city. But his talents and his character fitted him much more for pioneer work than for the task which now lay before him.

---

[1] For these relations, cf. Durrant, *Les Relations politiques de Genève avec Berne et les Suisses, de 1536 à 1564* (1894).

[2] The devout Romanist, Sœur Jeanne de Jussie, testifies, with mediæval frankness, to the dissolute lives of the Romish clergy : " *Il est bien vray que les Prelats et gens d'Église pour ce temps ne gardoient pas bien leurs vœus et estat, mais gaudissoient dissolument des biens de l'Église tenant femmes en lubricité et adultère, et quasi tout le peuple estoit infect de cest abominable et de'estable péché : dont est à scavoir que les péchéz du monde abondoient en toutes sortes de gens, qui incitoient l'ire de Dieu à y mettre sa punition divine* " (*Le Levain du Calvinisme*, p. 35 ; cf. minutes of the Council of Geneva at p. 241). Even the nuns of Geneva, with the exception of the nuns of St. Clara, to whom Jeanne de Jussie belonged, were notorious for their conduct ; cf. Herminjard, *Correspondance*, etc. v. 349 n.

Farel was a chivalrous Frenchman, born among the mountains of Dauphiné, whose courage, amounting to reckless daring, won for him the passionate admiration of soldiers like Wildermuth,[1] and made him volunteer to lead any forlorn hope however desperate. He was sympathetic to soft-heartedness, yet utterly unable to restrain his tongue; in danger of his life one week because of his violent language, and the next almost adored, by those who would have slain him, for the reckless way in which he nursed the sick and dying during a visitation of the plague. He was the brilliant partisan leader, seeing only what lay before his eyes; incapable of self-restraint; a learned theologian, yet careless in his expression of doctrine, and continually liable to misapprehension. No one was better fitted to attack the enemy's strongholds, few less able to hold them when once possessed. He saw, without the faintest trace of jealousy—the man was too noble—others building on the foundations he had laid. It is almost pathetic to see that none of the Romance Swiss churches whose Apostle he had been, cared to retain him as their permanent leader. In the closing years of his life he went back to his beloved France, and ended as he had begun, a pioneer evangelist in Lyons, Metz, and elsewhere,—a leader of forlorn hopes, carrying within him a perpetual spring and the effervescing recklessness of youth. He had early seen that the pioneer life which he led was best lived without wife or children, and he remained unmarried until his sixty-ninth year. Then he met with a poor widow who had lost husband and property for religion's sake in Rouen, and had barely escaped with life. He married her because in no other way could he find for her a home and protection.

Geneva needed a man of altogether different mould of character to do the work that was now necessary. When Farel's anxieties and vexations were at their height, he

---

[1] Cf. Wildermuth's letter to the *Council of the Two Hundred* in Bern, telling that Farel was in prison at Payerne: "Would that I had twenty Bernese with me, and with the help of God we would not have permitted what has happened" (Herminjard, *Correspondance*, etc. ii. 344).

learned almost by accident that a distinguished young French scholar, journeying from Ferrara to Basel, driven out of his direct course by war, had arrived in Geneva, and was staying for a night in the town. This was Calvin.

§ 4. *Calvin : Youth and Education.*

Jean Cauvin (latinised into Calvinus) was born at Noyon in Picardy on the 10th of July 1509. He was the second son in a family of four sons and two daughters. His father, Gerard Cauvin, was a highly esteemed lawyer, the confidential legal adviser of the nobility and higher clergy of the district. His mother, Jeanne La France, a very beautiful woman, was noted for her devout piety and her motherly affection. Calvin, who says little about his childhood, relates how he was once taken by his mother on the festival of St. Anna to see a relic of the saint preserved in the Abbey of Ourscamp, near Noyon, and that he remembers kissing " part of the body of St. Anna, the mother of the Virgin Mary." [1]

The Cauvins belonged to what we should call the upper middle class in social standing, and the young Jean entered the house of the noble family of de Montmor to share the education of the children, his father paying for all his expenses. The young de Montmors were sent to College in Paris, and Jean Cauvin, then fourteen years of age, went with them. This early social training never left Calvin, who was always the reserved, polished French gentleman —a striking contrast to his great predecessor Luther.

Calvin was a Picard, and the characteristics of the province were seen in its greatest son. The Picards were always independent, frequently strongly anti-clerical, combining in a singular way fervent enthusiasm and a cold tenacity of purpose. No province in France had produced so many sympathisers with Wiclif and Hus, and " Picards " was a term met with as frequently on the books of Inquisitors as " Wiclifites," " Hussites," or " Waldenses "—

[1] Doumergue, *Jean Calvin*, etc. i. 42.

all the names denoting dissenters from the mediæval Church who accepted all the articles of the Apostles' Creed but were strongly anti-clerical. These " brethren " lingered in all the countries of Western Europe until the sixteenth century, and their influence made itself felt in the beginnings of the stirrings for reform.

Gerard Cauvin had early seen that his second son, Jean, was *de bon esprit, d'une prompte naturelle à concevoir, et inventif en l'estude des lettres humaines*,[1] and this induced him to give the boy as good an education as he could, and to destine him for the study of theology. His legal connection with the higher clergy of Noyon enabled him, in the fashion of the day, to procure for his son more than one benefice. The boy was tonsured, a portion of the revenue was used to pay for a curate who did the work, and the rest went to provide for the lad's education.

Young Calvin went with the three sons of the de Montmor family to the College de la Marche in Paris. It was not a famous one, but when Calvin studied there in the lowest class he had as his professor Mathurin Cordier, the ablest teacher of his generation.[2] His aim was to give his pupils a thorough knowledge of the French and Latin languages—a foundation on which they might afterwards build for themselves. He had a singularly sweet disposition, and a very open mind. He was brought to know the Gospel by Robert Estienne, and in 1536 his name was inscribed, along with those of Courat and Clement Marot, on the list of the principal heretics in Paris. Calvin was not permitted to remain long under this esteemed teacher. The atmosphere was probably judged to be too liberal for one who was destined to study theology. He was transferred to the more celebrated College de Montaigu. Calvin was again fortunate in his principal teachers. He became

---

[1] Doumergue, *Jean Calvin*, etc. i. 35.

[2] Cordier, Corderius, Cordery, was a well-known name in Scottish parish schools a century ago, where his exercises were used in almost every Latin class.   He became a convert of the Reformed faith, and did his best to spread Evangelical doctrines by means of the sentences to be turned into Latin.   He followed his great pupil to Geneva, and died there in his eighty-eighth year.

the pupil of Noël Béda and of Pierre Tempête, who taught him the art of formal disputation.

Calvin had come to Paris in his fourteenth year, and left it when he was nineteen—the years when a lad becomes a man, and his character is definitely formed. If we are to judge by his own future references, no one had more formative influence over him than Mathurin Cordier — short as had been the period of their familiar intercourse. Calvin had shown a singularly acute mind, and proved himself to be a scholar who invariably surpassed his fellow students. He was always surrounded by attached friends—the three brothers de Montmor, the younger members of the famous family of Cop, and many others. These student friends were devoted to him all his life. Many of them settled with him at Geneva.

Calvin left the College de Montaigu in 1528. Sometime during the same year another celebrated pupil entered it. This was Ignatius Loyola. Whether the two great leaders attended College together, whether they ever met, it is impossible to say—the dates are not precise enough.

"Perhaps they crossed each other in some street of Mount Sainte-Geneviève: the young Frenchman of eighteen on horseback as usual, and the Spaniard of six and thirty on foot, his purse furnished with some pieces of gold he owed to charity, shoving before him an ass burdened with his books, and carrying in his pocket a manuscript, entitled *Exercitia Spiritualia*." [1]

Calvin left Paris because his father had now resolved that his son should be a lawyer and not a theologian. Gerard Cauvin had quarrelled with the ecclesiastics of Noyon, and had even been excommunicated. He refused to render his accounts in two executry cases, and had remained obstinate. Why he was so, it is impossible to say. His children had no difficulty in arranging matters after his death. The quarrel ended the hopes of the father to provide well for his son in the Church, and he ordered

[1] Doumergue, *Jean Calvin*, etc. i. 126.

him to quit Paris for the great law school at Orleans. It is by no means improbable that the father's decision was very welcome to the son. Bèze tells us that Calvin had already got some idea of the true religion, had begun to study the Holy Scriptures, and to separate himself from the ceremonies of the Church; [1]—perhaps his friendship with Pierre Robert Olivétan, a relation, a native of Noyon, and the translator of the Bible into French, had brought this about. The young man went to Orleans in the early part of 1528 and remained there for a year, then went on to Bourges, in order to attend the lectures of the famous publicist, André Alciat, who was destined to be as great a reformer of the study of law as Calvin was of the study of theology. In Orleans with its Humanism, and in Bourges with its incipient Protestantism, Calvin was placed in a position favourable for the growth of ideas which had already taken root in his mind. At Bourges he studied Greek under Wolmar, a Lutheran in all but the name, and dedicated to him long afterwards his *Commentary on the Second Epistle to the Corinthians.* He seems to have lived in the house of Wolmar; another inmate was Theodore de Bèze, the future leader of the Protestants of France, then a boy of twelve.

The death of his father (May 26th, 1531) left Calvin his own master. He had obeyed the paternal wishes when he studied for the Church in Paris; he had obediently transferred himself to the study of law; he now resolved to follow the bent of his own mind, and, dedicating himself to study, to become a man of letters. He returned to Paris and entered the College Fortet, meaning to attend the lectures of the Humanist professors whom Francis I., under the guidance of Budé and Cop, was attracting to his capital. These "royal lecturers" and their courses of instruction were looked on with great suspicion by the Sorbonne, and Calvin's conduct in placing himself under their instruction showed that he had already emancipated himself from that strict devotion to the "superstitions of

[1] *Corpus Reformatorum.* xlix. p. 121.

the Papacy " to which he tells us that he was obstinately attached in his boyhood.   He soon became more than the pupil of Budé, Cop, and other Humanists.   He was a friend, admitted within the family circle.   He studied Greek with Pierre Danès and Hebrew under Vatable.   In due time (April 1532), when barely twenty-three years of age, he published at his own expense his first book, a learned commentary on the two books of Seneca's *De Clementia.*

The book is usually referred to as an example of precocious erudition.   The author shows that he knew as minutely as extensively the whole round of classical literature accessible to his times.   He quotes, and that aptly, from fifty-five separate Latin authors—from thirty-three separate works of Cicero, from all the works of Horace and Ovid, from five comedies of Terence, and from all the works of Virgil.   He quotes from twenty-two separate Greek authors—from five or six of the principal writings of Aristotle, and from four of the writings of Plato and of Plutarch.   Calvin does not quote Plautus, but his use of the phrase *remoram facere* makes it likely that he was well acquainted with that writer also.[1]   The future theologian was also acquainted with many of the Fathers —with Augustine, Lactantius, Jerome, Synesius, and Cyprian.   Erasmus had published an edition of Seneca, and had advised scholars to write commentaries, and young Calvin followed the advice of the Prince of Humanists. Did he imitate him in more ?   Did Calvin also disdain to use the New Learning merely to display scholarship, did he mean to put it to modern uses ?   Francis I. was busy with one of his sporadic persecutions of the Huguenots when the book was published, and learned conjectures have been made whether the two facts had any designed connection—An exhortation addressed to an emperor to exercise clemency, and a king engaging in persecuting his subjects.   Two things seem to show that

---

[1] I owe this inference to my brother, Professor Lindsay of St. Andrews ; he adds that Plautus was greatly studied in the time of Calvin's youth in France.

Calvin meant his book to be a protest against the persecution of the French Protestants.   His preface is a daring attack on the abuses which were connected with the administration of justice in the public courts, and he says distinctly that he hopes the Commentary will be of service to the public.[1]

It seems evident from Calvin's correspondence that he had joined the small band of Protestants in Paris, and that he was intimate with Gerard Roussel, the Evangelical preacher,[2] the friend of Marguerite of Navarre, of Lefèvre, of Farel, and a member of the "group of Meaux." The question occurs, When did his conversion take place? This has been keenly debated;[3] but the arguments concern words more than facts, and arise from the various meanings attached to the word "conversion" rather than from the difficulty of determining the time.   Calvin, who very rarely reveals the secrets of his own soul, tells in his preface to his *Commentary on the Psalms*, that God drew him from his obstinate attachment to the superstitions of the Papacy by a "sudden conversion," and that this took place after he had devoted himself to the study of law in obedience to the wishes of his father.   It does not appear to have been such a sudden and complete vision of divine graciousness as Luther received in the convent at Erfurt.   But it

---

[1] Cf. his letter to Francis Daniel, where he speaks about the publication of the Commentary ; says that he has issued it at his own expense ; that some of the Paris lecturers, to help its sale, had made it a book on which they lectured, and hopes *quod publico etiam bono forte cessurum sit* (Herminjard, *Correspondance,* etc. ii. 417).

[2] In a letter to Francis Daniel, of date Oct. 27th, 1553, Calvin calls Gerard "our Friend" ; and in another, written about the end of the same month, he describes with a minuteness of detail impossible for anyone who was not in the inner circle, the comedy acted by the students of the College of Navarre, which was a satire directed against Marguerite, the Queen of Navarre, and Gerard Roussel, and the affair of the connection of the University of Paris and the Queen's poem, entitled *le Miroir de l'âme pécheresse* ; cf. Herminjard, *Correspondance,* etc. iii. 103–11.

[3] Lang, *Die Bekehrung Johannes Calvins* (1897) ; Doumergue, *Jean Calvin,* etc. i. 344 *ff.* ; Müller, " Calvins Bekehrung " (*Nachrichten der Gött. Gel.* for 1905, pp. 206 *ff.*) ; Wernle, " Noch einmal die Bekehrung Calvins " (*Zeitschrift für Kirchengeschichte,* xxvii. 84 *ff.* (1906)).

7**

was a beginning. He received then some taste of true piety (*aliquo veræ pietatis gusto*). He was abashed to find, he goes on to relate, that barely a year afterwards, those who had a desire to learn what pure doctrine was gradually ranged themselves around him to learn from him who knew so little (*me novitium adhuc et tironem*). This was perhaps at Orleans, but it may have been at Bourges. When he returned to Paris to betake himself to Humanist studies, he was a Protestant, convinced intellectually as well as drawn by the pleadings of the heart. He joined the little band who had gathered round Estienne de la Forge, who met secretly in the house of that pious merchant, and listened to the addresses of Gerard Roussel. He was frequently called upon to expound the Scriptures in the little society; and a tradition, which there is no reason to doubt, declares that he invariably concluded his discourse with the words, " If God be for us, who can be against us ? "

He was suddenly compelled to flee from Paris. The theologians of the Sorbonne were vehemently opposed to the " royal lecturers " who represented the Humanism favoured by Margaret, the sister of Francis, and Queen of Navarre. In their wrath they had dared to attack Margaret's famous book, *Miroir de l'âme pécheresse*, and had in consequence displeased the Court. Nicolas Cop, the friend of Calvin, professor in the College of Sainte Barbe, was Rector of the University (1533). He assembled the four faculties, and the faculty of medicine disowned the proceedings of the theologians. It was the custom for the Rector to deliver an address before the University yearly during his term of office, and Cop asked his friend Calvin to compose the oration.[1] Calvin made use of the occasion to write on " Christian Philosophy," taking for his motto, "*Blessed are*

[1] For the history of this Discourse written by Calvin and pronounced by Cop, see E. Doumergue, *Jean Calvin ; Les hommes et les choses de son temps* (Lausanne, 1899), i. 331 *ff.* ; A. Lang, *Die Bekehrung J. Calvins* (Leipzig, 1897), p. 46 *ff.* For accounts of the attempts to arrest Nicolas Cop and Calvin, see the letter of Francis I. to the *Parlement* of Paris in Herminjard, *Correspondance,* etc. iii. 114–118, and the editor's notes, also p. 418.

the poor in spirit " (Matt. v. 3). The discourse was an eloquent defence of Evangelical truth, in which the author borrowed from Erasmus and from Luther, besides adding characteristic ideas of his own. The wrath of the Sorbonne may be imagined. Two monks were employed to accuse the author of heresy before *Parlement*, which responded willingly. It called the attention of the King to papal Bulls against the Lutheran heresy. Meanwhile people discovered that Calvin was the real author, and he had to flee from Paris. After wanderings throughout France he found refuge in Basel (1535).

It was there that he finished his *Christianæ Religionis Institutio*, which had for its preface the celebrated letter addressed to Francis I. King of France. The book was the strongest weapon Protestantism had yet forged against the Papacy, and the letter " a bold proclamation, solemnly made by a young man of six-and-twenty, who, more or less unconsciously, assumed the command of Protestantism against its enemies, calumniators, and persecutors." News had reached Basel that Francis, who was seeking the alliance of the German Lutheran Princes, and was posing as protector of the German Protestants, had resolved to purge his kingdom of the so-called heresy, and was persecuting his Protestant subjects. This double-dealing gave vigour to Calvin's pen. He says in his preface that he wrote the book with two distinct purposes. He meant it to prepare and qualify students of theology for reading the divine Word, that they may have an easy introduction to it, and be able to proceed in it without obstruction. He also meant it to be a vindication of the teaching of the Reformers against the calumnies of their enemies, who had urged the King of France to persecute them and drive them from France His dedication was : *To His Most Gracious Majesty, Francis, King of France and his sovereign, John Calvin wisheth peace and salvation in Christ.* Among other things he said :

" I exhibit my confession to you that you may know the nature of that doctrine which is the object of such unbounded rage to those madmen who are now disturbing your kingdom with fire and sword. For I shall not be afraid to acknowledge that this treatise contains a summary of that very doctrine which, according to their clamours, deserves to be punished with imprisonment, banishment, proscription, and flames, and to be exterminated from the face of the earth."

He meant to state in calm precise fashion what Protestants believed; and he made the statement in such a way as to challenge comparison between those beliefs and the teaching of the mediæval Church. He took the *Apostles' Creed*, the venerable symbol of Western Christendom, and proceeded to show that when tested by this standard the Protestants were truer Catholics than the Romanists. He took this *Apostles' Creed*, which had been recited or sung in the public worship of the Church of the West from the earliest times, which differed from other creeds in this, that it owed its authority to no Council, but sprang directly from the heart of the Church, and he made it the basis of his *Institutio*. For the *Institutio* is an expansion and exposition of the *Apostles' Creed*, and of the four sentences which it explains. Its basis is: *I believe in God the Father; and in His Son Jesus Christ; and in the Holy Ghost; and in the Holy Catholic Church.* The *Institutio* is divided into four parts, each part expounding one of these fundamental sentences. The first part describes God, the Creator, or, as the Creed says: "God, the Father Almighty, Maker of heaven and earth"; the second, God the Son, the Redeemer and His Redemption; the third, God the Holy Ghost and His Means of Grace; the fourth, the Holy Catholic Church, its nature and marks.

This division and arrangement, based on the *Apostles' Creed*, means that Calvin did not think he was expounding a new theology or had joined a new Church. The theology of the Reformation was the old teaching of the Church of Christ, and the doctrinal beliefs of the Reformers were those views of truth which were founded on the Word of God, and which had been known, or at least felt, by pious people all down the generations from the earliest centuries. He and his fellow Reformers believed and taught the old theology of the earliest creeds, made plain and freed from the superstitions which mediæval theologians had borrowed from pagan philosophy and practices.

The first edition of the *Institutio* was published in March 1536, in Latin. It was shorter and in many ways inferior to the carefully revised editions of 1539 and 1559. In the later editions the arrangement of topics was somewhat altered; but the fundamental doctrine remains unchanged; the author was not a man to publish a treatise on theology without carefully weighing all that had to be said. In 1541, Calvin printed a French edition, which he had translated himself "for the benefit of his countrymen."

After finishing his *Institutio* (the MS. was completed in August 1535, and the printing in March 1536), Calvin, under the assumed name of Charles d'Espeville, set forth on a short visit to Italy with a companion, Louis du Tillet, who called himself Louis de Haulmont. He intended to visit Renée, Duchess of Ferrara, daughter of Louis XII. of France, known for her piety and her inclination to the Reformed faith. He also wished to see something of Italy. After a short sojourn he was returning to Strassburg, with the intention of settling there and devoting himself to a life of quiet study, when he was accidentally compelled to visit Geneva, and his whole plan of life was changed. The story can best be told in his own words. He says in the preface to his *Commentary on the Psalms:*

" As the most direct route to Strassburg, to which I then intended to retire, was blocked by the wars, I had resolved to pass quickly by Geneva, without staying longer than a single night in that city. . . . A person (Louis du Tillet) who has now returned to the Papists discovered me and made me known to others. Upon this Farel, who burned with an extraordinary zeal to advance the Gospel, immediately strained every nerve to detain me. After having learnt that my heart was set upon devoting myself to private studies, for which I wished to keep myself free from other pursuits, and finding that he gained nothing by entreaties, he proceeded to utter an imprecation, that God would curse my retirement and the tranquillity of the studies which I sought, if I should withdraw and refuse assistance when the necessity was so urgent. By this imprecation I was so stricken with terror that I desisted from the journey which I had undertaken."

§ 5. *Calvin with Farel in Geneva.*

Calvin was twenty-seven years of age and Farel twenty years older when they began to work together in Geneva; and, notwithstanding the disparity in age and utter dissimilarity of character, the two men became strongly attached to each other. "We had one heart and one soul," Calvin says. Farel introduced him to the leading citizens, who were not much impressed by the reserved, frail young foreigner whose services their pastor was so anxious to secure. They did not even ask his name. The minute of the Council (Sept. 5th, 1536), giving him employment and promising him support, runs: "Master William Farel stated the need for the lecture begun by *this Frenchman* in St. Peter's."[1] Calvin had declined the pastorate; but he had agreed to act as "professor in sacred learning to the Church in Geneva (*Sacrarum literarum in ecclesia Genevensi professor*)." His power was of that quiet kind that is scarcely felt till it has gripped and holds.

He began his work by giving lectures daily in St. Peter's on the Epistles of St. Paul. They were soon felt to be both powerful and attractive. Calvin soon made a strong impression on the people of the city. An occasion

---

[1] "Magister Gulielmus Farellus proponit sicuti sit necessaria illa lectura quam initiavit *ille Gallus* in Sancto Petro. Supplicat advideri de illo retinendo et sibi alimentando. Super quo fuit advisum quod advideatur de ipsum substinendo" (Herminjard, *Correspondance*, etc. iv. 87 *n.*).

arose which revealed him in a way that his friends had never before known. Bern had conquered the greater part of the Pays de Vaud in the late war. Its Council was determined to instruct the people of its newly acquired territory in Evangelical principles by means of a public Disputation, to be held at Lausanne during the first week of October.[1] The three hundred and thirty-seven priests of the newly conquered lands, the inmates of the thirteen abbeys and convents, of the twenty-five priories, of the two chapters of canons, were invited to come to Lausanne to refute if they could the ten Evangelical *Theses* arranged by Farel and Viret.[2] The Council of Bern pledged itself that there would be the utmost freedom of debate, not only for its own subjects, but " for all comers, to whatever land they belonged." Farel insisted on this freedom in his own trenchant way : " You may speak here as boldly as you please ; *our* arguments are neither faggot, fire, nor sword, prison nor torture ; public executioners are not our doctors of divinity. . . . Truth is strong enough to out-weigh falsehood ; if you have it, bring it forward." The Romanists were by no means eager to accept the challenge. Out of the three hundred and thirty-seven priests invited, only one hundred and seventy-four appeared, and of these only four attempted to take part. Two who had promised to discuss did not show themselves. Only ten of the forty religious houses sent representatives, and only one of them ventured to meet the Evangelicals in argument.[3] As at Bern in 1528, as at Geneva in May 1535, so here at Lausanne in October 1536, the Romanists showed themselves unable to meet their opponents, and the policy of

---

[1] For the Disputation at Lausanne, see Herminjard, *Correspondance*, etc. iv. 86 *f.* (Letter from Calvin to F. Daniel, Oct. 13th, 1536) ; *Corpus Reformatorum*, xxxvii. p. 876 f. ; Ruchat, *Histoire de la Réformation de la Suisse*, vol. iv. ; Doumergue, *Jean Calvin*, ii. 214 *f.*

[2] The ten *Theses* are printed in the *Corpus Reformatorum*, xxxvii. 701.

[3] Their names were Jean Mimard, regent of the school in Vevey ; Jacques Drogy, vicar of Morges ; Jean Michod, dean of Vevey ; Jean Berilly, vicar of Prévessin ; and a Dominican monk, de Monbouson.

Bern in insisting on public Disputations was abundantly justified.

Farel and Viret were the Protestant champions. Farel preached the opening sermon in the cathedral on Oct. 1st, and closed the conference by another sermon on Oct. 8th. The discussion began on the Monday, when the huge cathedral was thronged by the inhabitants of the city and of the surrounding villages. In the middle of the church a space was reserved for the disputants. There sat the four secretaries, the two presidents, and five commissioners representing *les Princes Chretiens Messieurs de Berne*, distinguished by their black doublets and shoulder-knots faced with red, and by their broad-brimmed hats ornamented with great bunches of feathers,—hats kept stiffly on heads as befiting the representatives of such potent lords.

Calvin had not meant to speak; Farel and Viret were the orators; he was only there in attendance. But on the Thursday, when the question of the Real Presence was discussed, one of the Romanists read a carefully prepared paper, in the course of which he said that the Protestants despised and neglected the ancient Fathers, fearing their authority, which was against their views. Then Calvin rose. He began with the sarcastic remark that the people who reverenced the Fathers might spend some little time in turning over their pages before they spoke about them. He quoted from one Father after another,— " Cyprian, discussing the subject now under review in the third epistle of his second book of Epistles, says . . . Tertullian, refuting the error of Marcion, says . . . The author of some imperfect commentaries on St. Matthew, which some have attributed to St. John Chrysostom, in the 11th homily about the middle, says . . . St. Augustine, in his 23rd Epistle, near the end, says . . . Augustine, in one of his homilies on St. John's Gospel, the 8th or the 9th, I am not sure at this moment which, says . . ."; [1] and so on. He knew the ancient Fathers as no one else in the century. He had not taken their opinions second-hand from Peter

[1] *Corpus Reformatorum*, xxxvii. 879–81.

of Lombardy's *Sententiœ* as did most of the Schoolmen and contemporary Romanist theologians. It was the first time that he displayed, almost accidentally, his marvellous patristic knowledge,—a knowledge for which Melanchthon could never sufficiently admire him.

But in Geneva the need of the hour was organisation and familiar instruction, and Calvin set himself to work at once. He has told us how he felt. "When I came first to this church," he said, "there was almost nothing. Sermons were preached;[1] the idols had been sought out and burned, but there was no other reformation; everything was in disorder."[2] In the second week of January he had prepared a draft of the reforms he wished introduced. It was presented to the *Small Council* by Farel; the members had considered it, and were able to transmit it with their opinion to the *Council of the Two Hundred* on January 15th, 1537. It forms the basis of all Calvin's ecclesiastical work in Geneva, and deserves study.

The memorandum treats of four things, and four only —the Holy Supper of our Lord (*la Saincte Cène de Nostre Seigneur*), singing in public worship, the religious instruction of children, and marriage.

In every rightly ordered church, it is said, the Holy Supper ought to be celebrated frequently, and well attended. It ought to be dispensed every Lord's Day at least;[3] such was the practice in the Apostolic Church, and ought to be ours; the celebration is a great comfort to all believers, for in it they are made partakers of the Body and Blood of Jesus, of His death, of His life, of His

[1] Wherever Farel went he had instituted what was called the "congregation": once a week in church, members of the audience were invited to ask questions, which the preacher answered. These "congregations" were an institution all over Romance Switzerland. The custom prevailed in Geneva when Calvin came there, and it was continued.

[2] Bonnet, *Lettres françaises de Calvin*, ii. 574.

[3] "Il seroyt bien à désirer que la communication de la Saincte Cène de Jésuerist fust tous les dimenches pour le moins en usage, quant l'Église est assemblée en multitude" (*Corpus Reformatorum*, xxxviii. i. 7); cf. the first edition of the *Institutio* (1536): "Singulis, ad minimum, hebdomadibus proponenda erat christianorum cœtui mensa Domini"

Spirit, and of all His benefits. But the present weakness of the people makes it undesirable to introduce so sweeping a change, and therefore it is proposed that the Holy Supper be celebrated once each month " in one of the three places where sermons are now delivered—in the churches of St. Peter, St. Gervais, and de Rive." The celebration, however, ought to be for the whole Church of Geneva, and not simply for those living in the quarters of the town where these churches are. Thus every one will have the opportunity of monthly communion. But if unworthy partakers approach the Table of the Lord, the Holy Supper will be soiled and contaminated. To prevent this, the Lord has placed the *discipline de l'excommunication* within His Church in order to maintain its purity, and this ought to be used. Perhaps the best way of exercising it is to appoint men of known worth, dwelling in different quarters of the town, who ought to be trusted to watch and report to the ministers all in their neighbourhood who despise Christ Jesus by living in open sin. The ministers ought to warn all such persons not to come to the Holy Supper, and the discipline of excommunication only begins when such warnings are unheeded.

Congregational singing of Psalms ought to be part of the public worship of the Church of Christ; for Psalms sung in this way are really public prayers, and when they are sung hearts are moved and worshippers are incited to form similar prayers for themselves, and to render to God the like praises with the same loving loyalty. But as all this is unusual, and the people need to be trained, it may be well to select children, to teach them to sing in a clear and distinct fashion in the congregation, and if the people listen with all attention and follow " with the heart what is sung by the mouth," they will, " little by little, become accustomed to sing together " as a congregation.[1]

[1] Calvin says : "*C'est une chose bien expédiente à l'édification de l'esglise, de chanter aulcungs pseaumes en forme d'oraysons publicqs.*" The translations of the Psalms by Clement Marot, which were afterwards used in the

It is most important for the due preservation of purity of doctrine that children from their youth should be instructed how to give a reason for their faith, and therefore some simple catechism or confession of faith ought to be prepared and taught to the children. At "certain seasons of the year" the children ought to be brought before the pastors, who should examine them and expound the teachings of the catechism.

The ordinance of marriage has been disfigured by the evil and unscriptural laws of the Papacy, and it were well that the whole matter be carefully thought over and some simple rules laid down agreeable to the Word of God.

This memorandum, for it is scarcely more, was dignified with the name of the *Articles* (*Articuli de regimine ecclesiæ*). It was generally approved by the *Small Council* and the *Council of Two Hundred*, who made, besides, the definite regulations that the Holy Supper should be celebrated four times in the year, and that announcements of marriages should be made for three successive Sundays before celebration. But it is very doubtful whether the Council went beyond this general approval, or that they gave definite and deliberate consent to Calvin's proposals about "the discipline of excommunication."

These *Articles* were superseded by the famous *Ordonnances ecclésiastiques de l'Église de Genève*, adopted on Nov. 20th, 1541; but as they are the first instance in which Calvin publicly presented his special ideas about ecclesiastical government, it may be well to describe what these were. To understand them aright, to see the *new* thing which Calvin tried to introduce into the Church life of the sixteenth century, it is necessary to distinguish between two things which it must be confessed were

Church of Geneva, were not published till 1541, and the *pseaumes* may have been religious canticles such as were used in the Reformed Church of Neuchâtel from 1533; but it ought to be remembered that translations of the Psalms of David did exist in France before Marot's; cf. Herminjard, *Correspondance*, iv. 163 n.

practically entangled with each other in these days—the attempt to regulate the private life by laws municipal or national, and the endeavour to preserve the solemnity and purity of the celebration of the Holy Supper.

When historians, ecclesiastical or other, charge Calvin with attempting the former, they forget that there was no need for him to do so. Geneva, like every other mediæval town, had its laws which interfered with private life at every turn, and that in a way which to our modern minds seems the grossest tyranny, but which was then a commonplace of city life. Every mediæval town had its laws against extravagance in dress, in eating and in drinking, against cursing and swearing, against gaming, dances, and masquerades. They prescribed the number of guests to be invited to weddings, and dinners, and dances; when the pipers were to play, when they were to leave off, and what they were to be paid. It must be confessed that when one turns over the pages of town chronicles, or reads such a book as Baader's *Nürnberger Polizeiordnung*, the thought cannot help arising that the Civic Fathers, like some modern law-makers, were content to place stringent regulations on the statute-book, and then, exhausted by their moral endeavour, had no energy left to put them into practice. But every now and then a righteous fit seized them, and maid-servants were summoned before the Council for wearing silk aprons, or fathers for giving too luxurious wedding feasts, or citizens for working on a Church festival, or a mother for adorning her daughter too gaily for her marriage. The citizens of every mediæval town lived under a municipal discipline which we would pronounce to be vexatious and despotic. Every instance quoted by modern historians to prove, as they think, Calvin's despotic interference with the details of private life, can be paralleled by references to the police-books of mediæval towns in the fifteenth and sixteenth centuries. To make them ground of accusation against Calvin is simply to plead ignorance of the whole municipal police of the later Middle Ages. To

—

say that Calvin acquiesced in or approved of such legislation is simply to show that he belonged to the sixteenth century. When towns adopted the Reformation, the spirit of civic legislation did not change, but some old regulations were allowed to lapse, and fresh ones suggested by the new ideas took their place. There was nothing novel in the law which Bern made for the Pays de Vaud in 1536 (Dec. 24th), prohibiting dancing with the exception of "trois danses honêtes" at weddings; but it was a new regulation which prescribed that parents must bring their daughters to the marriage altar "le chiefz couvert." It was not a new thing when Basel in 1530 appointed three honourable men (one from the Council and two from the commonalty) to watch over the morals of the inhabitants of each parish, and report to the Council. It was new, but quite in the line of mediæval civic legislation, when Bern forbade scandalous persons from approaching the Lord's Table (1532).

Calvin's thought moved on another plane. He was distinguished among the Reformers for his zeal to restore again the conditions which had ruled in the Church of the first three centuries. This had been a favourite idea with Lefèvre,[1] who had taught it to Farel, Gerard Roussel, and the other members of the "group of Meaux." Calvin may have received it from Roussel; but there is no need to suppose that it did not come to him quite independently. He had studied the Fathers of the first three

---

[1] "Et comment ne souhaiterions-nous pas voir notre siècle ramené à l'image de cette église primitive, puisqu'alors Christ recevait un plus pur hommage, et que l'éclat de son nom était plus au loin répandu ? . . . Puisse cette extension de la foi, puisse cette pureté du culte, aujourd'hui que reparaît la lumière de l'Évangile, nous être aussi accordées par celui qui est béni au-dessus de toutes choses ! Aujourd'hui, je le répète, que reparait la lumière de l'Évangile, qui se répand enfin de nouveau dans le monde, et y éclaire de ses divins rayons un grand nombre d'esprits ; de telle sorte que, sans parler de bien d'autres avantages, depuis le temps de Constantine, où l'Église primitive peu à peu dégénérée perdit tout a fait son caracter, il n'y a eu dans aucune autre epoque plus de connaissance des langues. . . ."—Lefèvre d'Étaples, *aux Lecteurs chrétiens de Meaux* (Herminjard, *Correspondance*, etc. i. 93).

centuries more diligently than any of his contemporaries. He recognised as none of them did that the Holy Supper of the Lord was the centre of the religious life of the Church, and the apex and crown of her worship. He saw how careful the Church of the first three centuries had been to protect the sacredness of the simple yet profound rite; and that it had done so by preventing the approach of all unworthy communicants. Discipline was the nerve of the early Church, and excommunication was the nerve of discipline; and Calvin wished to introduce both. Moreover, he knew that in the early Church it belonged to the membership and to the ministry to exercise discipline and to pronounce excommunication. He desired to reintroduce all these distinctive features of the Church of the first three centuries —weekly communion, discipline and excommunication exercised by the pastorate and the members. He recognised that when the people had been accustomed to come to the Lord's Table only once or twice in the year, it was impossible to introduce weekly communion all at once. But he insisted that the warnings of St. Paul about unworthy communicants were so weighty that notorious sinners ought to be prevented from approaching the Holy Supper, and that the obstinately impenitent should be excommunicated. This and this alone was the distinctive thing about Calvin's proposals; this was the new conception which he introduced.

Calvin's mistake was that, while he believed that the membership and the pastorate should exercise discipline and excommunication, he also insisted that the secular power should enforce the censures of the Church. His ideas worked well in the French Church, a Church "under the cross," and in the same position as the Church of the early centuries. But the conception that the secular power ought to support with civil pains and penalties the disciplinary decisions of ecclesiastical Courts, must have produced a tyranny not unlike what had existed in the mediæval Church. Calvin's ideas, however, were never accepted save nominally in any of the Swiss Churches—not even in Geneva. The very thought of excommunication in the hands of the Church was eminently distasteful to the Protestants of the sixteenth century; they had suffered too much from it as exercised by the Roman Catholic Church. Nor did it agree with the conceptions which the magistrates of the Swiss republics had of their own dignity, that they should be the servants of the ministry to carry out their sentences.[1] The leading Reformers in German Switzerland almost universally held that excommunication, if it ever ought to be practised, should be in the hands of the civil authorities.

Zwingli did not think that the Church should exercise the right of excommunication. He declared that the example of the first three centuries was not to be followed, because in these days the " Church could have no assistance from the Emperors, who were pagans "; whereas in Zurich there was a Christian magistracy, who could relieve the Church of what must be in any case a disagreeable duty. His successor, Bullinger, the principal adviser of the divines of the English Reformation, went further. Writing to Leo Jud (1532), he declares that excommunication ought not to belong to the Church, and that he doubts whether it should be exercised even by the secular authorities; and in a letter to a Romance pastor (Nov. 24th, 1543) he expounds his views about excommunication, and states how he differs from his *optimos fratres Gallos* (Viret, Farel, and Calvin).[2] The German Swiss Reformers took the one side, and the French Swiss Reformers took the other; and the latter were all men who had learned to reverence the usages of the Church of the first three centuries, and desired to see its methods of ecclesiastical discipline restored.

The people invariably sided with the German-speaking

[1] The prevailing idea was that the Evangelical pastors were the servants of the community, and therefore of the Councils which represented it. J. J. Watteville, the celebrated Advoyer or President of Bern, and a strong and generous supporter of the Reformation, was accustomed to say : "Nothing prevents me dismissing a servant when he displeases me ; why should not a town send its pastor away if it likes?" (Herminjard, *Correspondance*, vii. 354 *n.*).

[2] Herminjard, *Correspondance*, etc. ix. 116.

Reformers.[1] Calvin managed, with great difficulty, to introduce excommunication into Geneva after his return from
exile, but not in a way conformable to his ideas. Farel
could not get it introduced into Neuchâtel. He believed,
founding on the New Testament,[2] that the membership of
each parish had the right to exclude from the Holy Supper
sinners who had resisted all admonitions. But the Council
and community of Neuchâtel would not tolerate the
"practice and usage of Excommunication," and did not
allow it to appear in their ecclesiastical ordinances of
1542 or of 1553. Oecolampadius induced the Council of
Basel to permit excommunication, and to inscribe the names
of the excommunicate on placards fixed on the doors of the
churches. Zwingli remonstrated vigorously, and the practice
was abandoned. Bern was willing to warn open sinners
from approaching the Lord's Table, but would not hear of
excommunication, and declared roundly that "ministers,
who were sinners themselves, being of flesh and blood,
should not attempt to penetrate into the individual consciences, whose secrets were known to God alone." Viret
tried to introduce a *discipline ecclésiastique* into the Pays de
Vaud, but was unable to induce magistrates or people to
accept it. The young Protestant Churches of Switzerland,
with the very doubtful exception of Geneva after 1541,
refused to allow the introduction of the disciplinary usages
of the primitive Church. They had no objection to discipline, however searching and vexatious, provided it was
simply an application of the old municipal legislation, to
which they had for generations been accustomed, to the
higher moral requirements of religion.[3] It was univers-

---

[1] Herminjard, *Correspondance*, etc. viii. 280, 281, ix. 117, vi. 183 ;
Ruchat, *Histoire de la Réformation de la Suisse*, ii. 520 *f.* ; Farel, *Summaire*,
edition of 1867, pp. 78 *ff*.

[2] Matt. xviii. 15-17.

[3] The action of the people of the four parishes which made the district
of Thiez illustrates a condition of mind not easily sympathised with by us,
and it shows what the commonalty of the sixteenth century thought of the
powers of the Councils which ruled their city republics. The district
belonged to Geneva, and was under the rule of the Council of that city.

ally recognised that the standard of moral living all over French Switzerland was very low, and that stringent measures were required to improve it.   No exception was taken to the severe reprimand which the Council of Bern addressed to the subject Council of Lausanne for their failure to correct the evil habits of the people of that old episcopal town;[1] but such discipline had to be exercised in the old mediæval way through the magistrates, and not in any new-fangled fashion borrowed from the primitive Church.   So far as Switzerland was concerned, Calvin's entreaties to model their ecclesiastical life on what he believed with Lefèvre to be the golden period of the Church's history, fell on heedless ears.   One must go to the French Church and in a lesser degree to the Church of Knox in Scotland, to see Calvin's ideas put in practice ; it is vain to look for this in Switzerland.

The *Catechism* for children was published in 1537, and was meant, according to the author, to give expression to a simple piety, rather than to exhibit a profound knowledge of

The inhabitants had been permitted to retain the Romanist religion.   They were, nevertheless, excommunicated by their Bishop for clinging to Geneva with loyalty.   They were honest Roman Catholics ; they could not bear the thought of living under excommunication, and longed for absolution ; the Bishop would not grant it ; so the *people applied to the Council of Geneva to absolve them,* which the Council did by a minute which runs as follows : "(April 4th, 1535) Sur ce qu'est proposé par nostre chastelain de Thiez, que ceux de Thiez font doubte soy présenter en l'esglise à ces Pasques prochaines (April 16th), à cause d'aucunes lettres d'excommuniement qui sont esté contre aucuns exécutées, par quoi volentier ils desirent avoir remède de absolution. . . . Est esté résolu que l'on escrive une patente aux vicaires du dict mandement (district), que nous les tenons pour absols."   This was enough.   The people went cheerfully to their Easter services (Herminjard, *Correspondance,* etc. iv. 26 *n.*).

[1] Cf. the letter of the Council of Bern to the Council of Lausanne : "(July 1541) : Concernant minas contra ministrum Verbi, lasciviam vitæ civium, bacchanalia, ebrietates, commessationes, contemptum Evangelii, rythmos impudicos, etc., ceux de Lausanne sont vertement réprimandés.   On leur remontre leur négligence à châtier les vices.   Il leur est ordonné de punir, dans le terme d'un mois, les bacchantes et aussi celui qui a menacé le prédicant et l'a interpellé dans la rue.   Il est également ordonné aux ambassadeurs qui seront envoyés pour les appels, de faire de sévères remonstrances devant le Conseil et les Bourgeois, et de les menacer en les exhortant à s'amender " (Herminjard, *Correspondance,* vii. 145).

8**

religious truth. But, as Calvin himself felt later, it was too theological for children, and was superseded by a second Catechism, published immediately after his return to Geneva in 1541. The first Catechism was entitled *Instruction and Confession of Faith for the use of the Church of Geneva.* It expounded successively the Ten Commandments, the Apostles' Creed, the Lord's Prayer, and the Sacraments. The duties of the pastorate and of the magistracy were stated in appendices.[1]

The *Confession of Faith* had for its full title, *Confession de la Foy laquelle tous bourgois et habitans de Genève et subjectz du pays doyvent jurer de garder et tenir extraicte de l'Instruction dont on use en l'Église de la dicte ville.*[2] It reproduced the contents of the *Instruction*, and was, like it, a condensed summary of the *Institutio.*

This Confession has often been attributed to Farel, but there can be little doubt that it came from the pen of Calvin.[3] It was submitted to the Council and approved by them, and they agreed that the people should be asked to swear to maintain it, the various divisions of the districts of the town appearing for the purpose before the secretary of the Council. The proposal was then sent down to the Council of the Two Hundred, where it was assented to, but not without opposition. The minutes show that some members remained faithful to the Romanist faith. They said that they ought not to be compelled to take an oath which was against their conscience. Others who professed themselves Protestants asserted that to swear to a Confession took from them their liberty.

---

[1] This first Catechism has been republished and edited under the title, *Le Catéchisme français de Calvin, publié en 1537, réimprimé pour la première fois d'après un exemplaire nouvellement retrouvé et suivi de la plus ancienne Confession de foi de l'Église de Genève, avec deux notices, l'une historique, l'autre bibliographique,* par Albert Rilliet et Théophile Dufour, 1878. The curious bibliographical history of the book is given in Doumergue, *Jean Calvin,* ii. p. 230 ; and at greater length in the preface to the reprint.

[2] Müller, *Die Bekenntnisschriften der reformierten Kirche,* p. 111.

[3] The question is carefully discussed by Rilliet in his *Le Catéchisme français de Calvin,* and by Doumergue, *Jean Calvin,* etc. ii. 237-39.

"We do not wish to be constrained," they said, "but to live in our liberty." But in the end it was resolved to do as the Council had recommended. So day by day the *dizenniers*, or captains of the divisions of the town, brought their people to the cathedral, where the secretary stood in the pulpit to receive the oath. The magistrates set the example, and the people were sworn in batches, raising their hands and taking the oath. But there were malcontents who stayed away, and there were beginnings of trouble which was to increase. Deputies from Bern, unmindful of the fact that their city had sworn in the same way to their creed, encouraged the dissentients by saying that no one could take such an oath without perjuring himself; and this opinion strengthened the opposition. But the Council of Bern disowned its deputies,[1] and refused any countenance to the malcontents, and the trouble passed. All Geneva was sworn to maintain the Confession.

Meanwhile the ministers of Geneva had been urging decision about the question of discipline and excommunication; and the murmurs against them grew stronger. The Council was believed to be too responsive to the pleadings of the pastors, and a stormy meeting of the General Council (Nov. 25th) revealed the smouldering discontent On the 4th of January (1538) the Councils of Geneva rejected entirely the proposals to institute a discipline which would protect the profanation of the Lord's Table, by resolving that the Holy Supper was to be refused to no person seeking to partake. On the 3rd of February, at the annual election of magistrates, four Syndics were chosen who were known to be the most resolute opponents of Calvin and of Farel. The new Council did not at first show itself hostile to the preachers : their earliest minutes are rather deferential. But a large part of the citizens were violently opposed to the preachers; the

[1] The letter from Bern (dated Nov. 28th) was read to the recalcitrants, who gave way and accepted the Confession on Jan. 4th, 1538 (Herminjard, *Correspondance*, iv. 340 *n.*).

Syndics were their enemies: collision was bound to come sooner or later.

It was at this stage that a proposal from Bern brought matters to a crisis.

The city contained many inhabitants who had been somewhat unwillingly dragged along the path of Reformation. Those who clung to the old faith were reinforced by others who had supported the Reformation simply as a means of freeing the city from the rule of the Prince Bishop, and who had no sympathy with the religious movement. The city had long been divided into two parties, and the old differences reappeared as soon as the city declared itself Protestant. The malcontents took advantage of everything that could assist them to stay the tide of Reformation and hamper the work of the ministers. They patronised the Anabaptists when they appeared in Geneva; they supported the accusation brought against Farel and Calvin by Pierre Caroli, that they were Arians because they refused to use the Athanasian Creed; above all, they declared that they stood for liberty, and called themselves Libertines. When Bern interfered, they hastened to support its ecclesiastical suggestions.

Bern had never been contented with the position in which it stood to Geneva after its conquest of the Pays de Vaud. When the war was ended, or rather before it was finished, and while the Bernese army of deliverance was occupying the town, the accompanying deputies of Bern had claimed for their city the rights over Geneva previously exercised by the Prince Bishop and the Vidomne or representative of the Duke of Savoy, whom their army had conquered. They claimed to be the overlords of Geneva, as they succeeded in making themselves masters of Lausanne and the Pays de Vaud. The people of Geneva resisted the demand. They declared, Froment tells us, that they had not struggled and fought for more than thirty years to assert their liberties, in order to make themselves the vassals of their allies or of anyone in the wide world.[1]

[1] *Actes et gestes marveilleux*, p. 215 f.

Bern threatened to renounce alliance; but Geneva stood firm ; there was always France to appeal to for aid. In the end Bern had to be content with much less than it had demanded.

Geneva became an independent republic, served heir to all the signorial rights of the Prince Bishop and to all his revenues, successor also to all the justiciary rights of the Vidomne or representative of the House of Savoy. It gained complete sovereignty within the city; it also retained the same sovereignty over the districts (*mande-ments*) of Penney, Jussy, and Thiez which had belonged to the Prince Bishop. On the other side, Bern received the district of Gaillard ; Geneva bound itself to make no alliance nor conclude any treaty without the consent of Bern; and to admit the Bernese at all times into their city. The lordship over one or two outlying districts was divided—Geneva being recognised as sovereign, and having the revenues, and Bern keeping the right to judge appeals, etc.

It seemed to be the policy of Bern to create a strong State by bringing under its strict control the greater portion of Romance Switzerland. Her subject territories, Lausanne, a large part of the Pays de Vaud, Gex, Chablais, Orbe, etc., surrounded Geneva on almost every side. If only Geneva were reduced to the condition of the other Prince Bishopric, Lausanne, Bern's dream of rule would be realised. The Reformed Church was a means of solidifying these conquests. Over all Romance territories subject to Bern the Bernese ecclesiastical arrangements were to rule. Her Council was invariably the last court of appeal. Her consistory was reproduced in all these French-speaking local Churches. Her religious usages and ceremonies spread all over this Romance Switzerland. The Church in Geneva was independent. Might it not be brought into nearer conformity, and might not conformity in ecclesiastical matters lead to the political incorporation which Bern so ardently desired? The evangelist of almost all these Romance Protestant

Churches had been Farel. Their ecclesiastical usages had grown up under his guidance. It would conduce to harmony in the attempt to introduce uniformity with Bern if the Church of Geneva joined. Such was the external political situation to be kept in view in considering the causes which led to the banishment of Calvin from Geneva.

In pursuance of its scheme of ecclesiastical conformity, the Council of Bern summoned a Synod, representing most of the Evangelical Churches in western Switzerland, and laid its proposals before them. No detailed account of the proceedings has been preserved. There were probably some dissentients, of whom Farel was most likely one, who pled that the Romance Churches might be left to preserve their own usages. But the general result was that Bern resolved to summon another Synod, representing the Romance Churches, to meet at Lausanne (March 30th, 1538). They asked (March 5th) the Council of Geneva to permit the attendance of Farel and Calvin.[1] The letter reached Geneva on March 11th, and on that day the Genevan magistrates, unsolicited by Bern and without consulting their ministers, resolved to introduce the Bernese ceremonies into the Genevan Church. Next day they sent the letter of Bern to Farel and Calvin, and at the same time warned the preachers that they would not be allowed to criticise the proceedings of the Council in the pulpit. Neither Farel nor Calvin made any remonstrance. They declared that they were willing to go to Lausanne, asked the Council if they had any orders to give, and said that they were ready to obey them; and this although a second letter (March 20th) had come from Bern saying that if the Genevan preachers would not accept the Bern proposals they would not be permitted to attend the Synod.

Farel and Calvin accordingly went to the Synod at Lausanne, and were parties to the decision arrived at, which

[1] Herminjard, *Correspondance*, etc. iv. 403, 404, 407 ; Doumergue, *Jean Calvin*, etc. ii. 278.

was to accept the usages of Bern—that all baptisms should be celebrated at stone fonts placed at the entrance of the churches; that unleavened bread should be used at the Holy Supper; and that four religious festivals should be observed annually, Christmas, New Year's Day, the Annunciation, and the Day of Ascension—with the stipulation that Bern should warn its officials not to be too hard on poor persons for working on these festival days.[1]

When the Council of Bern had got its ecclesiastical proposals duly adopted by the representatives of the various Churches interested, its Council wrote (April 15th) to the Council and to the ministers of Geneva asking them to confer together and arrange that the Church of Geneva should adopt these usages—the magistrates of Bern having evidently no knowledge of the hasty resolution of the Genevan Council already mentioned. The letter was discussed at a meeting of Council (April 19th, 1538), and several minutes, all relating to ecclesiastical matters, were passed. It was needless to come to any resolution about the Bern usages; they had been adopted already. The letter from Bern was to be shown to Farel and Calvin, and the preachers were to be asked and were to answer, yea or nay, would they at once introduce the Bern ceremonies? The preachers said that the usages could not be introduced at once. The third Genevan preacher, Élie Coraut, had spoken disrespectfully of the Council in the city, and was forbidden to preach, upon threat of imprisonment, until he had been examined about his words.[2] Lastly, it was resolved that the Holy Supper should be celebrated at once according to the Bern rites; and that if Farel and Calvin refused, the Council was to engage other preachers who would obey their orders.[3]

---

[1] Herminjard, *Correspondance*, etc. iv. 413.

[2] On April 8th it was reported that Coraut had said in a sermon that Geneva was a realm of tipplers, and that the town was governed by drunkards (from all accounts a true statement of fact, but scarcely suitable for a sermon), and had been brought before the Council in consequence.

[3] Herminjard, *Correspondance*, etc. iv. 413-16, 420-22.

Coraut, the blind preacher, preached as usual (April 20th). He was at once arrested and imprisoned. In the afternoon, Farel and Calvin, accompanied by several of the most eminent citizens of Geneva, appeared before the Council to protest against Coraut's imprisonment, and to demand his release—Farel speaking with his usual daring vehemence, and reminding the magistrates that but for his work in the city they would not be in the position they occupied. The request was refused, and the Council took advantage of the presence of the preachers to ask them whether they would at once introduce the Bern usages. They replied that they had no objection to the ceremonies, and would be glad to use them in worship provided they were properly adopted,[1] but not on a simple order from the Council. Farel and Calvin were then forbidden to preach. Next day the two pastors preached as usual—Calvin in St. Peter's and Farel in St. Gervaise. The Council met to consider this act of disobedience. Some were for sending the preachers to prison at once ; but it was resolved to summon the *Council of the Two Hundred* on the morrow (April 22nd) and the *General Council* on the 24th. The letters of Bern (March 5th, March 20th, April 15th) were read, and the Two Hundred resolved that they would "live according to the ceremonies of Bern." What then was to be done with Calvin and Farel ? Were they to be sent to the town's prison ? No ! Better to wait till the Council secured other preachers (it had been trying to do so and had failed), and then dismiss them. The General Council then met ;[2] resolved to "live according to the ceremonies of Bern," and to banish the three preachers from the town, giving them three days to collect their effects.[3]

---

[1] Calvin says that he wished the matter to be regularly brought before the people and discussed : " *Concio etiam a nobis habeatur de ceremoniarum libertate, deinde ad conformitatem populum adhortemur, propositis ejus rationibus. Demum liberum ecclesiæ judicium permittatur.*" Cf. the memorandum presented to the Synod of Zurich by Calvin and Farel, *ibid.* v. 3 ; *Corpus Reformatorum,* xxxviii. ii. 191.

[2] Herminjard, *Correspondence*, etc. iv. 423, 425, 426, 427, v. 3, 24.

[3] It is worth mentioning that while the three letters from Bern were

Calvin and Farel were sent into exile, and the magistrates made haste to seize the furniture which had been given them when they were settled as preachers.

Calvin long remembered the threats and dangers of these April days and nights. He was insulted in the streets. Bullies threatened to " throw him into the Rhone." Crowds of the baser sort gathered round his house. They sang ribald and obscene songs under his windows. They fired shots at night, more than fifty one night, before his door—" more than enough to astonish a poor scholar, timid as I am, and as I confess I have always been." [1]   It was the memory of these days that made him loathe the very thought of returning to Geneva.

The two Reformers, Calvin and Farel, left the town at once, determined to lay their case before the Council of Bern, and also before the Synod of Swiss Churches which was about to meet at Zurich (April 28th, 1538). The Councillors of Bern were both shocked and scandalised at the treatment the preachers had received from the Council of Geneva, and felt it all the more that their proposal of conformity had served as the occasion. They wrote at once to Geneva (April 27th), begging the Council to undo what they had done ; to remember that their proposal for uniformity had never been meant to serve as occasion for compulsion in matters which were after all indifferent.[2] Bern might be masterful, but it was almost always courteous. The secular authority might be the motive force in all ecclesiastical matters, but it was to be exercised through the

brought before the Council of the Two Hundred, the decisions of the Lausanne Synod were produced at the General Council. Did the Council wish to give their decision a semblance of ecclesiastical authority ?

[1] Bonnet, *Les Lettres françaises de Calvin,* ii. 575, 576.

[2] " A ceste cause, vous instantement, très-acertes et en fraternelle affection prions, admonestons et requérons que . . . la rigueur que tenés aux dits Farel et Calvin admodérer, pour l'amour de nous et pour éviter scandale, contemplans que ce qu'avons à vous et à eulx escript pour la conformité des cérimonies de l'Esglise, est procédé de bonne affection et par mode de requeste, et non pas pour vous, ne eulx, constraindre à ces choses, que sont indifferentes en l'Esglise, comme le pain de la Cène et aultres " (Hermnjard, *Correspondance,* etc. iv. 428).

machinery of the Church. The authorities of Bern had been careful to establish an ecclesiastical Court, the Consistory, of two pastors and three Councillors, who dealt with all ecclesiastical details. It encouraged the meeting of Synods all over its territories. Its proposals for uniformity had been addressed to both the pastors and the Council of Geneva, and had spoken of mutual consultation. They had no desire to seem even remotely responsible for the bludgeoning of the Genevan ministers. The Council of Geneva answered with a mixture of servility and veiled insolence [1] (April 30th). Nothing could be made of them.

From Bern, Farel and Calvin went to Zurich, and there addressed a memorandum to a Synod, which included representatives from Zurich, Bern, Basel, Schaffhausen, St. Gallen, Mühlhausen, Biel (Bienne), and the two banished ministers from Geneva. It was one of those General Assemblies which in Calvin's eyes represented the Church Catholic, to which all particular Churches owed deference, if not simple obedience. The Genevan pastors presented their statement with a proud humility. They were willing to accept the ceremonies of Bern, matters in themselves indifferent, but which might be useful in the sense of showing the harmony prevailing among the Reformed Churches; but they must be received by the Church of Geneva, and not imposed upon it by the mere fiat of the secular authority. They were quite willing to expound them to the people of Geneva and recommend them. But if they were to return to Geneva, they must be allowed to defend themselves against their calumniators; and their programme for the organisation of the Church of Geneva, which had already been accepted but had not been put in practice (January 16th, 1537),[2] must be introduced. It consisted of the following:—the establishment of an ecclesiastical discipline, that the Holy

[1] For the letter of Bern to Geneva, and the answer of Geneva, cf. Herminjard, *Correspondance*, etc. iv. 427–430.
[2] *Ibid.* iv. 165 *n.*

Supper might not be profaned; the division of the city into parishes, that each minister might be acquainted with his own flock; an increase in the number of ministers for the town; regular ordination of pastors by the laying on of hands; more frequent celebration of the Holy Supper, according to the practice of the primitive Church.[1] They confessed that perhaps they had been too severe; on this personal matter they were willing to be guided.[2] They listened with humility to the exhortations of some of the members of the Synod, who prayed them to use more gentleness in dealing with an undisciplined people. But on the question of principle and on the rights of the Church set over against the State, they were firm. It was probably the first time that the Erastians of eastern Switzerland had listened to such High Church doctrine; but they accepted it and made it their own for the time being at least. The Synod decided to write to the Council of Geneva and ask them to have patience with their preachers and receive them back again; and they asked the deputies from Bern to charge themselves with the affair, and do their best to see Farel and Calvin reinstated in Geneva.

The deputies of Bern accepted the commission, and the Geneva pastors went back to Bern to await the arrival of the Bern deputies from Zurich. They waited, full of anxiety, for nearly fourteen days. Then the Bern Council were ready to fulfil the request of the Synod.[3] Deputies were appointed, and, accompanied by Farel and Calvin, set out

---

[1] The memoir presented to the Synod of Zurich has been printed by Herminjard, *Correspondance*, etc. v. 3–6, and in the *Corpus Reformatorum*, xxxviii. ii. 190–192. The conclusion prays Bern to drive from their territory ribald and obscene songs and catches, that the people of Geneva may not cite their example as an excuse.

[2] " Wir habent ouch durch Etlich unsere vorordneten uffs ernstlichest mit ihnen reden lassen sich etlicher ungeschigter scherpffe zemaassen und sich by disem unerbuwenem volgk Cristenlicher sennffmütigkeit zu beflyssen " (*Corpus Reformatorum*, xxxviii. ii. 193).

[3] The minute of the Council of Bern says: " The Genevans had refused to receive Calvin and Farel. If my lords need preachers, they will keep them in mind " (Herminjard, *Correspondance*, v. 20 *n.*).

for Geneva. The two pastors waited on the frontier at Noyon or at Genthod while the deputies of Bern went on to Geneva. They had an audience of the Council (May 23rd), were told that the Council could not revoke what all three Councils had voted. The Council of the Two Hundred refused to recall the pastors. The Council General (May 26th) by a unanimous vote repeated the sentence of exile, and forbade the three pastors (Farel, Calvin, and Coraut) to set foot on Genevan territory.

Driven from Geneva, Calvin would fain have betaken himself to a quiet student life; but he was too well known and too much valued to be left in the obscurity he longed for. Strassburg claimed him to minister to the French refugees who had settled within its protecting walls. He was invited to attend the Protestant conference at Frankfurt; he was present at the union conferences at Hagenau, at Worms, and at Regensburg. There he met the more celebrated German Protestant divines, who welcomed him as they had done no one else from Switzerland. Calvin put himself right with them theologically by signing at once and without solicitation the Augsburg Confession, and aided thereby the feeling of union among all Protestants. He kindled in the breast of Melanchthon one of those romantic friendships which the frail Frenchman, with the pallid face, black hair, and piercing eyes, seemed to evoke so easily. Luther himself appreciated his theology even on his jealously guarded theory of the Sacrament of the Holy Supper.

Meanwhile things were not going well in Geneva. Outwardly, there was not much difference. Pastors ministered in the churches of the town, and the ordinary and ecclesiastical life went on as usual. The magistrates enforced the *Articles*; they condemned the Anabaptists, the Papists, all infringements of the sumptuary and disciplinary laws of the town. They compelled every householder to go to church. Still the old life seemed to be gone. The Council and the Syndics treated the new pastors as their servants, compelled them to render strict obedience to all their decisions in ecclesiastical matters, and considered religion as a political affair. It is undoubted that the morals of the town became worse,—so bad that the pastors of Bern wrote a letter of expostulation to the pastors in Geneva,[1]—and the Lord's Supper seems to have been neglected. The contests between parties within the city became almost scandalous, and the independent existence of Geneva was threatened.[2]

At the elections the Syndics failed to secure their re-election. Men of more moderate views were chosen, and from this date (Feb. 1539) the idea began to be mooted that Geneva must ask Calvin to return. Private overtures were made to him, but he refused. Then came letters from the Council, begging him to come back and state his terms. He kept silence. Lausanne and Neuchâtel joined their entreaties to those of Geneva. Calvin was not to be persuaded. His private letters reveal his whole mind. He shuddered at returning to the turbulent city. He was not sure that he was fit to take charge of the Church in Geneva. He was in peace at Strassburg, minister to a congregation of his own countrymen; and the pastoral tie once formed was not to be lightly broken; yet there was an undercurrent drawing him to the place where he first began the ministry of the Word. At length he wrote to the Council of Geneva, putting all his difficulties and his longings before them—neither accepting nor refusing. His immediate duty called him to the conference at Worms.

The people of Geneva were not discouraged. On the 19th October, the *Council of the Two Hundred* placed on their register a declaration that every means must be taken to secure the services of "Maystre Johan Calvinus," and on the 22nd a worthy burgher and member of the *Council of the Two Hundred*, Louis Dufour, was despatched to Strassburg with a letter from both the civic Councils, begging Calvin to return to his "old place" (*prestine plache*), "seeing

---

[1] Herminjard, *Correspondance*, etc. v. 139; *Corpus Reformatorum*. xxxviii. ii. 181.

[2] Doumergue, *Jean Calvin*, etc. ii. 681 ff.

our people desire you greatly," and promising that they would do what they could to content him.[1] Dufour got to Strassburg only to find that Calvin had gone to Worms He presented his letters to the Council of the town, who sent them on by an express (*eques celeri cursu*)[2] to Calvin (Nov. 6th, 1540). Far from being uplifted at the genuine desire to receive him back again to Geneva, Calvin was terribly distressed. He took counsel with his friends at Worms, and could scarcely place the case before them for his sobs.[3] The intolerable pain he had at the thought of going back to Geneva on the one hand, and the idea that Bucer might after all be right when he declared that Calvin's duty to the Church Universal clearly pointed to his return,[4] overmastered him completely. His friends, respecting his sufferings, advised him to postpone all decision until again in Strassburg. Others who were not near him kept urging him. Farel thundered at him (*consterné par tes foudres*).[5] The pastors of Zurich wrote (April 5th 1541).

" You know that Geneva lies on the confines of France, of Italy, and of Germany, and that there is great hope that the Gospel may spread from it to the neighbouring cities, and thus enlarge the ramparts (*les boulevards*) of the kingdom of Christ.—You know that the Apostle selected metropolitan cities for his preaching centres, that the Gospel might be spread throughout the surrounding towns." [6]

Calvin was overcome. He consented to return to Geneva, and entered the city still suffering from his repugnance to undertake work he was not at all sure that he was fitted to do. Historians speak of a triumphal entry There may have been, though nothing could have been more distasteful to Calvin at any time, and eminently so

---

[1] *Registres du Conseil*, xxxiv. f., 483, 485, 490 (quoted in Daumergue, *Jean Calvin*, ii. 700).

[2] Herminjard, *Correspondance des Réformateurs dans les pays de langue française* (Geneva, 1866–93), vi. 365.

[3] *Corpus Reformatorum*, xxxix. (xi.) 114.

[4] *Ibid.* p. 54.   [5] *Ibid.* p. 170.

[6] Herminjard, *Correspondance*, etc. vii. 77.

on this occasion, with the feelings he had. Contemporary
documents are silent. There is only the minute of the
Council, as formal as minutes usually are, relating that
" Maystre Johan Calvin, ministre evangelique," is again in
charge of the Church in Geneva (Sept. 13th, 1541).[1]

Calvin was in Geneva for the second time, dragged there
both times unwillingly, his dream of a quiet scholar's life
completely shattered. The work that lay before him proved
to be almost as hard as he had foreseen it would be. The
common idea that from this second entry Calvin was master
within the city, is quite erroneous. Fourteen years were
spent in a hard struggle (1541–55); and if the remaining nine years of his life can be called his period of triumph
over opponents (1555–64), it must be remembered that
he was never able to see his ideas of an ecclesiastical organisation wholly carried out in the city of his adoption. One
must go to the Protestant Church of France to see Calvin's
idea completely realised.[2]

On the day of his entry into Geneva (Sept. 13th,
1541) the Council resolved that a Constitution should be
given to the Church of the city, and a committee was formed,
consisting of Calvin, his colleagues in the ministry, and six
members of the Council, to prepare the draft. The work was
completed in twenty days, and ready for presentation. On
September 16th, however, it had been resolved that the
draft when prepared should be submitted for revision to
the *Smaller Council*, to the *Council of Sixty*, and finally to
the *Council of Two Hundred*. The old opposition at once
manifested itself within these Councils. There seem to
have been alterations, and at the last moment Calvin thought
that the Constitution would be made worthless for the purpose of discipline and orderly ecclesiastical rule. In the end,
however, the drafted ordinances were adopted unanimously
by the *Council of Two Hundred* without serious alteration.

[1] *Registres du Conseil*, xxxv. f., 824 (quoted in Doumergue, *Jean Calvin*,
etc. ii. 710).
[2] For the wonderful influence of Calvin on the French Reformation and
its causes, cf. below, pp. 153 ff.

The result was the famous *Ecclesiastical Ordinances of Geneva* in their first form. They did not assume their final form until 1561.[1]

When these *Ordinances* of 1541 are compared with the principles of ecclesiastical government laid down in the *Institutio*, with the *Articles* of 1537, and with the *Ordinances* of 1561, it can be seen that Calvin must have sacrificed a great deal in order to content the magistrates of Geneva.

He had contended for the self-government of the Church, especially in matters of discipline; the principle runs all through the chapters of the fourth book of the *Institutio*. The *Ordinances* give a certain show of autonomy, and yet the whole authority really rests with the Councils. The discipline was exercised by the *Consistory* or session of Elders (*Anciens*); but this Consistory was chosen by the *Smaller Council* on the advice of the ministers, and was to include two members of the *Smaller Council*, four from the *Council of Sixty*, and six from the *Council of Two Hundred*, and when they had been chosen they were to be presented to the *Council of Two Hundred* for approval. When the Consistory met, one of the four Syndics sat as president, holding his baton, the insignia of his magisterial office, in his hand, which, as the revised *Ordinances* of 1561 very truly said, "had more the appearance of civil authority than of spiritual rule." The revised *Ordinances* forbade the president to carry his baton when he presided in The Consistory, in order to render obedience to the distinction which is " clearly shown in Holy Scripture to exist between the magistrate's sword and authority and the superintendence which ought to be in the Church"; but the obedience to Holy Scripture does not seem to have gone further than laying aside the baton for the time. It appears also that the rule of consulting the ministers in the appointments made to the Consistory was not unfrequently omitted, and that it was

---

[1] *Articles* of 1537 in the *Corpus Reformatorum*, xxxviii. i. (x. i.) 5–14 ; *Ordinances* of 1541 ; *ibid.* pp. 15–30 ; *Ordinances* of 1561 ; *ibid.* pp. 91–124 ; *Institution*, IV. cc. i.–xii.

to all intents and purposes simply a committee of the Councils, and anything but submissive to the pastors.[1] The Consistory had no power to inflict civil punishments on delinquents. It could only admonish and warn. When it deemed that chastisements were necessary, it had to report to the Council, who sentenced. This was also done in order to maintain the separation between the civil and ecclesiastical power; but, in fact, it was a committee of the Council that reported to the Council, and the distinction was really illusory. This state of matters was quite repugnant to Calvin's cherished idea, not only as laid down in the *Institution*, but as seen at work in the Constitution of the French Protestant Church, which was mainly his authorship. "The magnificent, noble, and honourable Lords" of the Council (such was their title) of this small town of 13,000 inhabitants deferred in *words* to the teachings of Calvin about the distinction between the civil and the spiritual powers, but in *fact* they retained the whole power of rule or discipline in their own hands; and we ought to see in the disciplinary powers and punishments of the Consistory of Geneva, not an exhibition of the working of a Church organised on the principles of Calvin, but the ordinary procedure of the Town Council of a mediæval city. Their petty punishments and their minute interference with private life are only special instances of what was common to all municipal rule in the sixteenth century.

Through that century we find a protest against the mediæval intrusion of the ecclesiastical power into the realm of civil authority, with the inevitable reaction which made the ecclesiastical a mere department of national or civic administration. Zurich under Zwingli, although it is usually taken as the extreme type of this Erastian policy, as it came to be called later, went no further than Bern, Strassburg, or other places. The Council of Geneva had legal precedent when they insisted that the supreme ecclesiastical power belonged to them. The city had been an ecclesiastical principality.

---

[1] *Corpus Reformatorum*, xxxviii. i. 121, 122.

9**

ruled in civil as well as in ecclesiastical things by its Bishop, and the Council were legally the inheritors of the Bishop's authority. This meant, among other things, that the old laws against heresy, unless specially repealed, remained on the Statute Book, and errors in doctrine were reckoned to be of the nature of treasonable things; and this made heresies, or variations in religious opinion from what the Statute Book had declared to be the official view of truth, liable to civil pains and penalties.

"Castellio's doubts as to the canonicity of the Song of Songs and as to the received interpretation of Christ's descent into Hades, Bolsec's criticism of predestination, Gryet's suspected scepticism and possession of infidel books, Servetus' rationalism and anti-Trinitarian creed, were all opinions judged to be criminal. . . . The heretic may be a man of irreproachable character; but if heresy be treason against the State,"[1]

he was a criminal, and had to be punished for the crime on the Statute Book. To say that Calvin burnt Servetus, as is continually done, is to make one man responsible for a state of things which had lasted in western Europe ever since the Emperor Theodosius declared that all men were out of law who did not accept the Nicene Creed in the form issued by Damasus of Rome. On the other hand, to release Calvin from his share in that tragedy and crime by denying that he sat among the judges of the heretic, or to allege that Servetus was slain because he conspired against the liberties of the city, is equally unreasonable. Calvin certainly believed that the execution of the anti-Trinitarian was right. The Protestants of France and of Switzerland in 1903 (Nov. 1st) erected what they called a *monument expiatoire* to the victim of sixteenth century religious persecution, and placed on it an inscription in which they acknowledged their debt to the great Reformer, and at the same time

[1] *Cambridge Modern History*, ii. 375.

condemned his error, — surely the right attitude to assume.[1]

Calvin did three things for Geneva, all of which went far beyond its walls. He gave its Church a trained and tested ministry, its homes an educated people who could give a reason for their faith, and to the whole city an heroic soul which enabled the little town to stand forth as the Citadel and City of Refuge for the oppressed Protestants of Europe.

The earlier preachers of the Reformed faith had been stray scholars, converted priests and monks, pious artisans, and such like. They were for the most part heroic men who did their work nobly. But some of them had no real vocation for the position into which they had thrust themselves. They had been prompted by such ignoble motives as discontent with their condition, the desire to marry or to make legitimate irregular connections,[2] or dislike to all authority and wholesome restraints. They had brought neither change of heart nor of conduct into their new surroundings, and had become a source of danger and scandal to the small Protestant communities.

The first part of the *Ordinances* was meant to put an end to such a condition of things, and aimed at giving the Reformed Church a ministry more efficient than the old priesthood, without claiming any specially priestly character.

[1] On the one side of the stone is inscribed :

Le xxvii Octobre MDLIII
Mourut sur le bucher à Champel
MICHEL SERVET
de Villeneuve d'Aragon, né le xxix Septembre MDXI.

and on the other :

fils respectueux et reconnaissants de Calvin notre grand réformateur, mais condamnant une erreur qui fut celle de son siècle et fermement attachés à la liberté de conscience selon les vrais principes de la Reformation et de l'Évangile, nous avons élevé ce monument expiatoire. Le xxvii Octobre MCMIII.

[2] Like Jacques Bernard, the Franciscan monk, who was one of the pastors in Geneva after the banishment of Calvin and Farel, who, "cum esset inter Evangelii exordia, hostiliter repugnavit, donec Christum aliquando in uxoris forma contemplatus est."

The ministers were to be men who believed that they were called by the voice of God speaking to the individual soul, and this belief in a divine vocation was to be tested and tried in a threefold way—by a searching examination, by a call from their fellow-men in the Church, and by a solemn institution to office.

The examination, which is expressly stated to be the most important, was conducted by those who were already in the office of the ministry. It concerned, first, the knowledge which the candidate had of Holy Scripture, and of his ability to make use of it for the edification of the people; and, second, his walk and conversation in so far as they witnessed to his power to be an example as well as a teacher. The candidate was then presented to the *Smaller Council*. He was next required to preach before the people, who were invited to say whether his ministrations were likely to be for edification. These three tests passed, he was then to be solemnly set apart by the laying on of the hands of ministers, according to the usage of the ancient Church. His examination and testing did not end with his ordination. All the ministers of the city were commanded to meet once a week for the discussion of the Scriptures, and at these meetings it was the duty of every one, even the least important, to bring forward any cause of complaint he believed to exist against any of his brethren, whether of doctrine, or of morals, or of inefficient discharge of the duties entrusted to his care. The pastors who worked in the villages were ordered to attend as often as they could, and none of them were permitted to be absent beyond one month. If the meeting of ministers failed to agree on any matter brought before them, they were enjoined to call in the Elders to assist them; and a final appeal was always allowed to the Signory, or civil authority. The same rigid supervision was extended to the whole people, and in the visitations for this purpose Elders were always associated with ministers.[1] Every member of the

---

[1] *Corpus Reformatorum*, xxxviii. i. (x. i.) 17–20, 45–48, 55–58, 93–99 116–118.

little republic, surrounded by so many and powerful
enemies, was meant to be a soldier trained for spiritual as
for temporal warfare. Calvin added a spiritual side to
the military training which preserved the independence of
the little mediæval city republics.

He was unwearied in his exertions to make Geneva
an enlightened town. His educational policy adopted by
the Councils was stated in a series of famous regulations
for the management of the schools and College of the city.[1]
He sought out and presented to the Council the most
noted scholars he could attract to Geneva. Mathurin
Cordier, the ablest preceptor that France had produced in his
generation; Beza, its most illustrious Humanist; Castellio
and Saunier, were all teachers in the city. The fame of
its schools attracted almost as many as persecution drove
to take refuge within its walls. The religious instruction
of the young was carefully attended to. Calvin's earlier
Catechism was revised, and made more suitable for the
young; and the children were so well grounded that it
became a common saying that a boy of Geneva could give
an answer for his faith as ably as a "doctor of the
Sorbonne." But what Geneva excelled in was its training
for the ministry and other learned professions. Men with
the passion of learning in their blood came from all lands
—from Italy, Spain, England, Scotland, even from Russia,
and, above all, from France. Pastors educated in Geneva,
taught by the most distinguished scholars of the day, who
had gained the art of ruling others in having learned how
to command themselves, went forth from its schools to
become the ministers of the struggling Protestants in the
Netherlands, in England, in Scotland, in the Rhine
Provinces, and, above all, in France. They were wise, indefatigable, fearless, ready to give their lives for their work,
extorting praise from unwilling mouths, as modest, saintly,
"with the name of Jesus ever on their lips" and His Spirit
in their hearts. What they did for France and other
countries must be told elsewhere.

[1] *Corpus Reformatorum*, xxxviii. i. (x. i.) 65–90.

The once disorderly city, a prey to its own internal factions, became the citadel of the Reformation, defying the threats of Romanist France and Savoy, and opening its gates to the persecuted of all lands. It continued to be so for generations, and the victims of the *dragonnades* of Louis XIV. received the welcome and protection accorded to the sufferers under the Valois in the sixteenth century. What it did for them may be best told in the words of a refugee:

"On the next day, a Sunday, we reached a small village on a hill about a league from Geneva, from which we could see that city with a joy which could only be compared to the gladness with which the Israelites beheld the Land of Canaan. It was midday when we reached the village, and so great was our eagerness to be as soon as possible within the city which we looked on as our Jerusalem, that we did not wish to stay even for food. But our conductor informed us that on the Sunday the gates of Geneva were never opened until after divine service, that is, until after four o'clock. We had therefore to remain in the village until about that hour, when we mounted our horses again. When we drew near to the town we saw a large number of people coming out. Our guide was surprised, and the more so when, arriving at the Plain-Palais, a quarter of a league from the town, we saw coming to meet us, three carriages escorted by halberdiers and followed by an immense crowd of people of both sexes and of every age. As soon as we were seen, a servant of the Magistracy approached us and prayed us to dismount to salute respectfully 'Their Excellencies of Geneva,' who had come to meet us and to bid us welcome. We obeyed. The three carriages having drawn near, there alighted from each a magistrate and a minister, who embraced us with tears of joy and with praises of our constancy and endurance far greater than we merited. . . . Their Excellencies then permitted the people to approach, and there followed a spectacle more touching than imagination could picture. Several of the inhabitants of Geneva had relatives suffering in the French galleys (from which we had been delivered), and these good people did not know whether any of them might be among our company. So one heard a confused noise, 'My son so and so, my husband, my brother, are you there?' One can imagine what embracings welcomed any of our troop who could answer. All this crowd of people threw itself on our necks with inexpressible transports of joy, praising and magnifying the Lord for the manifestation of His grace in our favour; and when Their Excellencies asked us to get on horseback again to enter the city, we were scarcely able to obey, so impossible did it seem to detach ourselves from the arms of these pious and zealous brethren, who seemed afraid to lose sight of us. At last we remounted and followed Their Excellencies, who conducted us into the city as in triumph. A magnificent building had been erected in Geneva to lodge citizens who had fallen into poverty. It had just been finished and furnished, and no one had yet lived in it. Their Excellencies thought it could have no better dedication than to serve as our habitation. They conducted us there, and we were soon on foot in a spacious court. The crowd of people rushed in after us. Those who had found relatives in our company begged Their Excellencies to permit them to take them to their houses—a request willingly granted. M. Bosquet, one of us, had a mother and two sisters in Geneva, and they had come to claim him. As he was my intimate friend, he begged Their Excellencies to permit him to take me along with him, and they willingly granted his request. Fired by this example, all the burghers, men and women, asked Their Excellencies to allow them the same favour of lodging these dear brethren in their own houses. Their Excellencies having permitted some to do this, a holy jealousy took possession of the others, who lamented and bewailed themselves, saying that they could not be looked on as good and loyal citizens if they were refused the same favour; so Their Excellencies had to give way, and not one of us was left in the Maison Française, for so they had called the magnificent building." [1]

The narrative is that of a Protestant condemned to the galleys under Louis XIV.; but it may serve as a picture of how Geneva acted in the sixteenth century when the small city of 13,000 souls received and protected nearly 6000 refugees driven from many different lands for their religion.

[1] *Mémoires d'un protestant condamné aux galères de France pour cause de religion, écrits par lui-même* (1757, repub. 1865), pp. 404–407.

CHAPTER IV.

THE REFORMATION IN FRANCE.[1]

§ 1. *Marguerite d'Angoulême and the "group of Meaux."*

PERHAPS no one so thoroughly represents the sentiments which inspired the beginnings of the movement for Reformation in France as Marguerite d'Angoulême,[2] the sister of

[1] SOURCES: Theodore de Bèze (Beza), *Histoire Ecclésiastique des églises réformées au Royaume de France* (ed. by G. Baum and E. Cunitz, Paris, 1883–89); J. Crespin, *Histoire des martyrs persécutez et mis à mort pour la vérité* (ed. by Benoist, Toulouse, 1885–87); Herminjard, *Correspondance des Réformateurs dans les pays de langue française*, 9 vols. (Geneva, 1878–91); Calvin's *Letters, Corpus Reformatorum*, vols. XXXVIII. ii.–XLVIII. (Brunswick, 1872, etc.); Bonnet, *Lettres de Jean Calvin*, 2 vols. (Paris, 1854).
LATER BOOKS : E. Doumergue, *Jean Calvin*, 3 vols. (published Lausanne, 1899–1905); H. M. Baird, *History of the Rise of the Huguenots* (London, 1880), and *Theodore Beza* (New York, 1899); Lavisse, *Histoire de France*, v. i. pp. 339 ff. ; ii. 183 ff. ; VI. i. ii. ; Hamilton, "Paris under the Valois Kings" (*Eng. Hist. Review*, 1886, pp. 260–70).
[2] Marguerite was born at Angoulême on April 11th, 1492 ; married the feeble Duke of Alençon in 1509 ; was a widow in 1525 ; married Henri d'Albret, King of Navarre, in 1527 ; died in 1549. Her only child was Jeanne d'Albret, the heroic mother of Henry of Navarre, who became Henri IV. of France. When she was the Duchess of Alençon, her court at Bourges was a centre for the Humanists and Reformers of France ; when she became the Queen of Navarre, her castle at Nérac was a haven for all persecuted Protestants. The literature about Marguerite is very extensive : it is perhaps sufficient to mention—Génin, *Lettres de Marguerite d'Angoulême, reine de Navarre* (published by the *Société de l'Histoire de France*, 1841–42) ; *Les idées religieuses de Marguerite de Navarre, d'auprès son œuvre poétique* ; A. Lefranc, *Les dernieres poésies de Marguerite de Navarre* (Paris, 1896) ; Becker, " Marguerite de Navarre, duchesse d'Alençon et Guillaume Briçonnet, évêque de Meaux, d'aprés leur correspondance manuscrite, 1521–24 " (in the *Bulletin de la Société de l'Histoire du Protestantisme française*, XLIX. (Paris, 1890) ; Darmesteter, *Margaret of Angoulême, Queen of Navarre* (London,
136

King Francis I. A study of her letters and of her writings—the latter being for the most part in verse—is almost essential for a true knowledge of the aspirations of the noblest minds of her generation. Not that she possessed creative energy or was herself a thinker of any originality, but her soul, like some clear sensitive mirror, received and reflected the most tremulous throb of the intellectual and religious movements around her. She had, like many ladies of that age, devoted herself to the New Learning. She had mastered Latin, Italian, and Spanish in her girlhood, and later she acquired Greek and even Hebrew, in order to study the Scriptures in their original tongues. In her the French Renaissance of the end of the fifteenth was prolonged throughout the first half of the sixteenth century. She was all sentiment and affection, full of that gentle courage which soft feminine enthusiasm gives, and to her brother and more masculine mother (Louise of Savoy)[1] she was a being to be protected against the consequences of her own tender daring. Contemporary writers of all parties, save the more bitter defenders of the prevalent Scholastic Theology, have something good to say about the pure, bright, ecstatic Queen of Navarre. One calls her the "violet in the royal garden," and says that she unconsciously gathered around her all the better spirits in France, as the wild thyme attracts the bees.

Marsiglio Ficino had taught her to drink from the well of Christian Platonism;[2] and this mysticism, which had little to do with dogma, which allied itself naturally with the poetical sides of philosophy and morals which suggested great if indefinite thoughts about God,—*le Tout, le Seul Nécessaire, la Seule Bonté*,—the human soul and the

1886); Lavisse, *Histoire de France*, v. i. ; Herminjard, *Correspondance*, etc., vol. i., which contains sixteen letters written by her, and twelve addressed to her.

[1] Louise de Savoie, *Journal*, 1476-1522 (in Michaud et Poujoulat, *Collection*, etc. v.).

[2] Lefranc, "Marguerite de Navarre et le platonisme de la Renaissance" (vols. lviii. lix. *Bibliothèque de l'École des Chartes*, 1897-98).

intimate union between the two, was perhaps the abiding part of her ever-enlarging religious experience. Nicholas of Cusa, who tried to combine the old Scholastic with the new thoughts of the Renaissance, taught her much which she never unlearnt. She studied the Holy Scriptures carefully for herself, and was never weary of discussing with others the meaning of passages which seemed to be difficult. She listened eagerly to the preaching of Lefèvre and Roussel, and carried on a long private correspondence with Briçonnet, being passionately desirous, she said, to learn " the way of salvation." [1]   Both Luther and Calvin made a strong impression upon her, but their schemes of theology never attracted nor subjugated her intelligence. Her sympathies were drawn forth by their disdain of Scholastic Theology, by their denial of the supernatural powers of the priesthood, by their proclamation of the power and of the love of God, and by their conception that faith unites man with God—by all in their teaching which would assimilate with the Christian mysticism to which she had given herself with all her soul. When her religious poems are studied, it will be found that she dwells on the infinite power of God, the mystical absorption of the human life within the divine, and praises passionately self-sacrifice and disdain of all earthly pleasures. She extols the Lord as the one and only Saviour and Intercessor. She contrasts, as Luther was accustomed to do, the Law which searches, tries, and punishes, with the Gospel which pardons the sinner for the sake of Christ and of the work which He finished on the Cross. She looks forward with eager hope to a world redeemed and regenerated through the Evangel of Jesus Christ. She insists on justification by faith, on the impossibility of salvation by works, on predestination in the sense of absolute dependence on God in the last resort. Works are good, but no one is saved by works; salvation comes by grace, and "is the gift of the Most High God." She calls the Virgin the most blessed among women, because

[1] Herminjard, *Correspondance*, etc. i. 67.

she had been chosen to be the mother of the "Sovereign Saviour," but refused her any higher place; and in her devotions she introduced an invocation of Our Lord instead of the *Salve Regina.* This way of thinking about the Blessed Virgin, combined with her indifference to the Saints and to the Mass, and her undisguised contempt for the more superstitious ecclesiastical ceremonies, were the chief reasons for the strong attacks made on Marguerite by the Faculty of Theology (the Sorbonne) of Paris. She cannot be called a Protestant, but she had broken completely with mediæval modes of religious life and thought.

Marguerite's letters contain such graphic glimpses, that it is possible to see her daily life, whether at Bourges, where she held her Court as the Duchess of Alençon, or at Nérac, where she dwelt as the Queen of Navarre. Every hour was occupied, and was lived in the midst of company. Her *Contes* and her poetry were for the most part written in her litter when she was travelling from one place to another. Her "Household" was large even for the times. No less than one hundred and two persons—ladies, secretaries, almoners, physicians, etc.—made her Court; and frequently many visitors also were present. The whole "Household," with the visitors, met together every forenoon in one of the halls of the Palace, a room "well-paved and hung with tapestry," and there the Princess commonly proposed some text of Scripture for discussion. It was generally a passage which seemed obscure to Marguerite; for example, "The meek shall inherit the earth." All were invited to make suggestions about its meaning. The hostess was learned, and no one scrupled to quote the Scriptures in their original languages, or to adduce the opinions of such earlier Fathers as Augustine, Jerome, Chrysostom, or the Gregories. If it surprises us to find one or other of the twenty *valets de chambre,* who were not menials and were privileged to be present, familiar with theology, and able to quote Greek and even Hebrew, it must not be forgotten that Marguerite's *valets de chambre*

included distinguished Humanists and Reformers, to whom
she extended the protective privilege of being enrolled in
her "Household." When the weather permitted, the whole
company went for a stroll in the park after the discussion,
and then seated themselves near a "pleasant fountain" on
the turf, "so soft and delicate that they needed neither
carpet nor cushions."[1] There one of the ladies-in-waiting
(thirty *dames* or *demoiselles* belonged to the "Household")
read aloud a tale from the *Heptameron*, not forgetting the
improving conversation which concludes each story. This
gave rise to an animated talk, after which they returned to
the Palace. In the evening the "Household" assembled
again in a hall, fitted as a simple theatre, to witness one of
the Comedies or Pastorals which the Queen delighted to
write, and in which, through a medium as strange as the
Contes, she inculcated her mystical Christianity, and gave
expression to her longings for a reformation in the Church
and society. Her Court was the precursor of the *salons*
which in a later age exercised such a powerful influence on
French political, literary, and social life.

Marguerite is chiefly remembered as the author of the
Heptameron, which modern sentiment cannot help regarding
as a collection of scandalous, not to say licentious, tales.
The incongruity, as it appears to us, of making such tales
the vehicle of moral and even of evangelical instruction,
causes us frequently to forget the conversations which
follow the stories—conversations which generally inculcate
moral truths, and sometimes wander round the evangelical
thought that man's salvation and all the fruits of holy
living rest on the finished work of Christ, the only
Saviour. " *Voilà, Mesdames, comme la foy du bon Comte ne
fut vaincue par signes ne par miracles extérieurs, sachant très
bien que nous n'avons qu'un Sauveur, lequel en disant Con-
summatum est, a monstré qu'il ne laissoit point à un autre
successeur pour faire notre salut.*"[2] So different was the
sentiment of the sixteenth from that of the twentieth

[1] *Heptameron*, Preface.
[2] *Ibit*, Nouvelle xxxiii.

century, that Jeanne d'Albret, puritan as she undoubtedly was, took pains that a scrupulously exact edition of her mother's *Contes* should be printed and published, for all to read and profit by.

The Reformers with whom Marguerite was chiefly associated were called the "group of Meaux." Guillaume Briçonnet,[1] Bishop of Meaux, who earnestly desired reform but dreaded revolution, had gathered round him a band of scholars whose idea was a reformation of the Church by the Church, in the Church, and with the Church. They were the heirs of the aspirations of the great conciliar leaders of the fifteenth century, such as Gerson, deeply religious men, who longed for a genuine revival of faith and love. They hoped to reconcile the great truths of Christian dogma with the New Learning, and at once to enlarge the sphere of Christian intelligence, and to impregnate Humanism with Christian morality.

The man who inspired the movement and defined its aims—" to preach Christ from the sources "—was Jacques Lefèvre d'Étaples (Stapulensis).[2] He had been a distinguished Humanist, and in 1507 had resolved to consecrate his learning to a study of the Holy Scriptures. The first fruit of this resolve was a new Latin translation of the Epistles of St. Paul (1512), in which a revised version of the Vulgate was published along with the traditional text. In his notes he anticipated two of Luther's ideas—that works have no merit apart from the grace of God, and that while there is a Real Presence of Christ in the Sacrament of the Supper, there is no transubstantiation. The Reformers of Meaux believed that the Holy Scriptures

---

[1] Briçonnet belonged to an illustrious family. He was born in 1470, destined for the Church, was Archdeacon of Rheims, Bishop of Lodève in 1504, 1507 got the rich Abbey of St. Germain-des-Près at Paris, and became Bishop of Meaux in 1516. He at once began to reform his diocese ; compelled his curés to reside in their parishes ; divided the diocese into thirty-two districts, and sent to each of them a preacher for part of the year.

[2] Cf. K. H. Graf, "Jacobus Faber Stapulensis," in the *Zeitschrift für die historische theologie* for 1852, 1–86 ; Doumergue, *Jean Calvin*, i. 79-112 ; Herminjard, *Correspondance*, i. 3 *n*.

should be in the hands of the Christian people, and Lefèvre took Jean de Rély's version of the Bible,—itself a revision of an old thirteenth century French translation,—revised it, published the Gospels in June 1523, and the whole of the New Testament before the end of the year. The Old Testament followed in 1525. The book was eagerly welcomed by Marguerite, and became widely known and read throughout France. The Princess was able to write to Briçonnet that her brother and mother were interested in the spread of the Holy Scriptures, and in the hope of a reform of the Church.[1]

Neither Lefèvre nor Briçonnet was the man to lead a Reformation. The Bishop was timid, and feared the "tumult"; and Lefèvre, like Marguerite, was a Christian mystic,[2] with all the mystic's dislike to change in outward and fixed institutions. More radical ideas were entering France from without. The name of Luther was known as early as 1518, and by 1520, contemporary letters tell us that his books were selling by the hundred, and that all thinking men were studying his opinions.[3] The ideas of Zwingli were also known, and appeared more acceptable to the advanced thinkers in France. Some members of the group of Meaux began to reconsider their position. The Pope's Bull excommunicating Luther in 1520, the result of the Diet of Worms in 1521, and the declaration of the Faculty of Theology of the University of Paris (the Sorbonne) against the opinions of Luther, and their vindication of the authority of Aristotle and Scholastic Theology made it apparent that even modest reforms would not be tolerated by the Church as it then existed. The *Parlement*

---

[1] Herminjard, *Correspondance*, i. 78, 84, 85 n.

[2] It does not seem to be generally known that Lefèvre travelled to Germany in search of manuscripts of some of the earlier mystical writers, and that he published in 1513 the first printed edition of Hildegard of Bingen's *Liber Quoscivias* (Peltzer, *Deutsche Mystik und deutsche Kunst* (Strassburg, 1899), p. 35), under the title *Liber trium virorum et trium spiritualium virginum* (Paris, 1513).

[3] Herminjard, *Correspondance*, i. 37 n., 47, 48 n., 63 and n., 64 etc.

of Paris (August 1521) ordered Luther's books to be given up.[1]

Lefèvre did not falter. He remained what he had been—a man on the threshold of a new era who refused to enter it. One of his fellow-preachers retracted his opinions, and began to write against his leader. The young and fiery Guillaume Farel boldly adopted the views of the Swiss Reformers. Briçonnet temporised. He forbade the preaching of Lutheran doctrine within his diocese, and the circulation of the Reformer's writings; but he continued to protect Lefèvre, and remained true to his teaching.[2]

The energetic action of the Sorbonne and of the *Parlement* of Paris showed the obstacles which lay in the path of a peaceful Reformation. The library of Louis de Berquin was seized and condemned (June 16th, 1523), and several of his books burnt in front of Nôtre Dame by the order of *Parlement* (August 8th). Berquin himself was saved by the interposition of the King.[3] In March 1525, Jean Leclerc, a wool-carder, was whipt and branded in Paris; and six months later was burnt at Metz for alleged outrages on objects of reverence. The Government had to come to some decision about the religious question.

Marguerite could write that her mother and her brother were "more than ever well disposed towards the reformation of the Church";[4] but neither of them had her strong religious sentiment, and policy rather than conviction invariably swayed their action. The Reformation promoted by Lefèvre and believed in by Marguerite was at once too moderate and too exacting for Francis I. It could never be a basis for an alliance with the growing Protestantism of Germany, and it demanded a purity of individual life ill-suited either with the personal habits of

---

[1] *Journal d'un Bourgeois de Paris sous le règne de Francois I. 1515–1536* (Paris, 1854), p. 104.

[2] Herminjard, *Correspondance*, i. 153 *ff.*

[3] *Journal d'un Bourgeois*, etc. p. 169.

[4] Herminjard, *Correspondance*, i. 84, 105 ; cf. 85 n.

the King or with the manners of the French Court. It is therefore not to be wondered that the policy of the Government of Francis I. wavered between a negligent protection and a stern repression of the French Reformers.

§ 2. *Attempts to repress the Movement for Reform.*

The years 1523–26 were full of troubles for France. The Italian war had been unsuccessful. Provence had been invaded. Francis I. had been totally defeated and taken prisoner at Pavia. Dangers of various kinds within France had also confronted the Government. Bands of marauders—*les aventuriers* [1]—had pillaged numerous districts; and so many conflagrations had taken place that people believed they were caused by emissaries of the public enemies of France. Louise of Savoy, the Queen-Mother, and Regent during her son's captivity in Madrid, had found it necessary to conciliate the formidable powers of the *Parlement* of Paris and of the Sorbonne. Measures were taken to suppress the printing of Lutheran and heretical books, and the *Parlement* appointed a commission to discover, try, and punish heretics. The result was a somewhat ineffective persecution.[2] The preachers of Meaux had to take refuge in Strassburg, and Lefèvre's translation of the Scriptures was publicly burnt.

When the King returned from his imprisonment at Madrid (March 1525), he seemed to take the side of the Reformers. The Meaux preachers came back to France, and Lefèvre himself was made the tutor to the King's youngest son. In 1528–29 the great French Council of Sens met to consider the state of the Church. It reaffirmed most of the mediæval positions, and, in opposition to the teachings of Protestants, declared the unity, infallibility, and visibility of the Church, the authority of Councils,

---

[1] The depredations of those bands of brigands are frequently referred to in the *Journal d'un Bourgeois de Paris*, pp. 119, 159, 166, 176, 185, 201, 249, 257, 402, 196.

[2] Cf. *Journal d'un Bourgeois*, etc. p. 276.

the right of the Church to make canonical regulations, fasts, the celibacy of priests, the seven sacraments, the Mass, purgatory, the veneration of saints, the worship of images, and the Scholastic doctrines of free will and faith and works. It called on civil rulers to execute the censures of the Church on heretics and schismatics. It also published a series of reforms necessary—most of which were already contained in the canon law.

While the Council was sitting, the Romanists of France were startled with the news that a statue of the Blessed Virgin had been beheaded and otherwise mutilated. It was the first manifestation of the revolutionary spirit of the Reformation in France. The King was furious. He caused a new statue to be made in silver, and gave his sanction to the renewal of the persecutions (May 31st, 1528). Four years later his policy altered. He desired alliances with the English and German Protestants; one of the Reformers of Meaux preached in the Louvre during Lent (1533), and some doctors of the Sorbonne, who accused the King and Queen of Navarre of heresy, were banished from Paris. In spite of the ferment caused by the Evangelical address of Nicolas Cop, and the flight of Cop and of Calvin, the real author of the address, the King still seemed to favour reform. Evangelical sermons were again preached in the Louvre, and the King spoke of a conference on the state of religion within France.

The affair of the *Placards* caused another storm. On the morning of Oct. 18th, 1534, the citizens of Paris found that broadsides or *placards*, attacking in very strong language the ceremony of the Mass, had been affixed to the walls of the principal streets. These *placards* affirmed that the sacrifice of Christ upon the Cross was perfect and unique, and therefore could never be repeated; that it was sheer idolatry to say that the corporeal presence of Christ was enclosed within the wafer, "a man of twenty or thirty years in a morsel of paste"; that transubstantiation was a gross error; that the Mass had been perverted from its true meaning, which is to be a memorial of the sacrifice

10**

and death of our Lord; and that the solemn ceremony had become a time " of bell-ringings, shoutings, singing, waving of lamps and swinging of incense pots, after the fashion of sorcerers." The violence of language was extreme. " The Pope and all his vermin of cardinals, of bishops, of priests, of monks and other hypocrites, sayers of the Mass, and all those who consent thereto," were liars and blasphemers. The author of this broadside was a certain Antoine Marcourt, who had fled from France and taken refuge in Neuchâtel. The audacity of the men who had posted the *placards* in Paris and in other towns,—Orléans, Blois, Amboise,—and had even fixed one on the door of the King's bedchamber, helped to rouse the Romanists to frenzy. The *Parlement* and the University demanded loudly that extreme measures should be taken to crush the heretics;[1] and everywhere expiatory processions were formed to protest against the sacrilege. The King himself and the great nobles of the Court took part in one in January,[2] and during that month more than thirty-five Lutherans were arrested, tried, and burnt. Several well-known Frenchmen (seventy-three at least), among them Clement Marot and Mathurin Cordier, fled the country, and their possessions were confiscated.

After this outburst of persecution the King's policy again changed. He was once more anxious for an alliance with the Protestants of Germany. An amnesty was proclaimed for all save the " Sacramentarians," *i.e.* the followers of Zwingli. A few of the exiled Frenchmen returned, among them Clement Marot. The Chancellor of France, Antoine du Bourg, went the length of inviting the German theologians to come to France for the purpose of sharing in a religious conference, and adhered to his proposal in spite

[1] *Journal d'un Bourgeois*, etc.: " Fut sonné par deux trompettes et crié au Palays sur la pierre de marbre, que s'il y avoit personne qui sceut enseigner celuy ou ceulx qui avoient fisché les dictz placars, en révélant en certitude, il leur seroit donné cent escus par la cour" (p. 442).

[2] *Ibid.* pp. 442–444. The Dauphin, the Dukes of Orleans and Angoulême, and a young German, Prince de Vendôme, carried the four batons supporting "un beau ciel" over the Host.

of the protests of the Sorbonne. But nothing came of it. The German Protestant theologians refused to risk themselves on French soil; and the exiled Frenchmen mistrusted the King and his Chancellor. The amnesty, however, deserves remark, because it called forth the letter of Calvin to Francis I. which forms the " dedication " or preface to his *Christian Institution.*

The work of repression was resumed with increased severity. Royal edicts and mandates urging the extirpation of heresy followed each other in rapid succession— Edict to the *Parlement* of Toulouse (Dec. 16th, 1538), to the *Parlements* of Toulouse, Bordeaux, and Rouen (June 24th, 1539); a general edict issued from Fontainebleau (June 1st, 1540); an edict to the *Parlement* of Toulouse (Aug. 29th, 1542); *mandats* to the *Parlements* of Paris, Bordeaux, Dijon, Grenoble, and Rouen (Aug. 30th, 1542). The general Edict of Fontainebleau was one of exceptional severity. It was intended to introduce a more summary procedure in heresy trials, and enjoined officials to proceed against all persons tainted with heresy, even against ecclesiastics or those who had the " benefit of clergy "; the right of appeal was denied to those suspected; negligent judges were threatened with the King's displeasure; and the ecclesiastical courts were urged to show greater zeal, and to take advantage of the powers given to the civil courts. " Every loyal subject," the edict said, " must denounce heretics, and employ all means to root them out, just as all men are bound to run to help to extinguish a public conflagration." This edict, slightly modified by the *Parlement* of Paris (July 1543) by enlarging the powers of the ecclesiastical courts, remained in force in France for the nine following years. Yet in spite of its thoroughness, succeeding edicts and *mandats* declare that heresy was making rapid progress in France.

The Sorbonne and the *Parlements* (especially those of Paris and Aix) urged on the persecution of the " Lutherans." The former drafted a series of twenty-five articles (a refutation of the 1541 edition of Calvin's *Institution*), which were meant to assert concisely the dogma of the Church, and to deny whatever the Reformers taught prejudicial to the doctrines and practices of the mediæval Church. These articles were approved by the King and his Privy Council, who ordered them to be published throughout the whole kingdom, and gave instructions to deal with all who preached or taught anything contrary or repugnant to them. This ordinance was at once registered by the *Parlement* of Paris. Thus all the powers of the realm committed themselves to a struggle to extirpate the Reformed teaching, and were armed with a test which was at once clear and comprehensive. Not content with this, the Sorbonne began a list of prohibited books (1542–43)—a list containing the works of Calvin, Luther, Melanchthon, Clement Marot, and the translations of scripture edited by Robert Estienne, and the *Parlement* issued a severe ordinance against all Protestant propaganda by means of printing or the selling of books (July 1542).

These various ordinances for the extirpation of heresy were applied promptly and rigorously, and the fires of persecution were soon kindled all over France. The *place* Maubert was the scene of the martyrdoms in Paris. There were no great *auto-da-fés*, but continual mention is made of burning two or three martyrs at once. Two acts of persecution cast a dark stain on the last years of Francis I.—the slaughter of the Waldenses of the Durance in 1545, and the martyrdom of the "fourteen of Meaux."

A portion of Provence, skirting the Durance where that river is about to flow into the Rhone, had been almost depopulated in the fourteenth century, and the landowners had invited peasants from the Alps to settle within their territories. The incomers were Waldenses; their religion was guaranteed protection, and their industry and thrift soon covered the desolate region with fertile farms. When the Reformation movement had established itself in Germany and Switzerland, these villagers were greatly interested. They drew up a brief statement of what they believed, and sent it to the leading Reformers, accompanied by a number of questions on matters of religion. They received long answers from Bucer and from Oecolampadius, and, having met in conference (Sept. 1532) at Angrogne in Piedmont, they drafted a simple confession of faith based on the replies of the Reformers to their questions. It was natural that they should view the progress of the Reformation within France with interest, and that they should contribute 500 crowns to defray the expense of printing a new translation of the Scriptures into French by Robert Olivetan. Freedom to practise their religion had been granted for two centuries to the inhabitants of the thirty Waldensian villages, and they conceived that in exhibiting their sympathy with French Protestantism they were acting within their ancient rights. Jean de Roma, Inquisitor for Provence, thought otherwise. In 1532 he began to exhort the villagers to abjure their opinions; and, finding his entreaties without effect, he set on foot a severe persecution. The Waldenses appealed to the King, who sent a commission to inquire into the matter, with the result that Jean de Roma was compelled to flee the country.

The persecution was renewed in 1535 by the Archbishop and *Parlement* of Aix, who cited seventeen of the people of Merindol, one of the villages, before them on a charge of heresy. When they failed to appear, the *Parlement* published (Nov. 18th, 1540) the celebrated *Arrêt de Merindol*, which sentenced the seventeen to be burnt at the stake. The Waldenses again appealed to the King, who pardoned the seventeen on the condition that they should abjure their heresy within three months (Feb. 8th, 1541). There was a second appeal to the King, who again protected the Waldenses; but during the later months of 1541 the *Parlement* of Aix sent to His Majesty the false information that the people of Merindol were in open insurrection, and were threatening to sack the town of Marseilles. Upon this, Francis, urged thereto by Cardinal de Tournon, recalled his protection, and ordered all the Waldenses to be exterminated (Jan. 1st, 1545). An army was stealthily organised, and during seven weeks of slaughter, amid all the accompaniments of treachery and brutality, twenty-two of the thirty Waldensian villages were utterly destroyed, between three and four thousand men and women were slain, and seven hundred men sent to the galleys. Those who escaped took refuge in Switzerland.[1]

The persecution at Meaux (1546) was more limited in extent, but was accompanied by such tortures that it formed a fitting introduction to the severities of the reign of Henri II.

The Reformed at Meaux had organised themselves into a congregation modelled on that of the French refugees in Strassburg. They had chosen Pierre Leclerc to be their pastor, and one of their number, Étienne Mangin, gave his house for the meetings of the congregation. The authorities heard of the meetings, and on Sept. 8th, 1546, a sudden visit was made to the house, and sixty-one persons were arrested and brought before the *Parlement* of Paris. Their special crime was that they had engaged in the celebration of the Lord's Supper. The sentence of the Court declared that the Bishop of Meaux had shown culpable negligence in permitting such meetings; that the evidence indicated that there were numbers of "Lutherans" and heretics in Meaux besides those brought before it, and that all such were to be sought out; that all books in the town which concerned the Christian religion were to be deposited in the record-office within eight days; that special sermons were to be delivered and expiatory processions organised; and that the house of Étienne Mangin was to be razed to the ground, and a chapel in honour of the Holy Sacrament erected on the site. It condemned fourteen of the accused to be burnt alive, after having suffered the severest tortures which the law permitted; five to be hung up by the armpits to witness the execution, and then to be scourged and imprisoned; others to witness the execution with cords round their necks and with their heads bare, to ask pardon for their crime, to take part in an expiatory procession, and to listen

---

[1] *Bulletin de la Société de l'Histoire du Protestantisme français* for 1858, pp. 166 ff.

to a sermon on the adoration due to the Body of Christ present in the Holy Sacrament. A few, mostly women, were acquitted.[1]

Francis I. died in March 1547 The persistent persecution which had marked the later years of his reign had done little or nothing to quench the growing Protestantism of France. It had only succeeded in driving it beneath the surface.

Henry II. never indulged in the vacillating policy of his father. From the beginning of his reign he set himself resolutely to combat the Reformation. His favourite councillors—his all-powerful mistress, Diane of Poitiers ; his chief Minister, the Constable Montmorency, in high repute for his skill in the arts of war and of government; the Guises, a great family, originally belonging to Lorraine, who had risen to power in France—were all strong supporters of the Roman Catholic religion, and resolute to destroy the growing Protestantism of France. The declared policy of the King was to slay the Reformation by attacking it through every form of legal suppression that could be devised.

§ 3. Change in the Character of the Movement for Reform.

The task was harder than it had been during the reign of Francis. In spite of the persecutions, the adherents of the new faith had gone on increasing in a wonderful way. Many of the priests and monks had been converted to Evangelical doctrines. They taught them secretly and openly ; and they could expose in a telling way the corruptions of the Church, having known them from the inside. Schoolmasters, if one may judge from the arrêts of the Parlements, were continually blamed for dissuading their pupils from going to Mass, and for corrupting the youth by instructing them in the "false and pernicious doctrines of Geneva." Many Colleges were named as seed-beds of the Reformation —Angers, Bourges, Fontenay, La Rochelle, Loudun, Niort, Nimes, and Poitiers. The theatre itself became an agent

[1] H. M. Bower, *The Fourteen of Meaux* (London, 1894).

for reform when the corruptions of the Church and the
morals of the clergy were attacked in popular plays. The
refugees in Strassburg, Geneva, and Lausanne spared no
pains to send the Evangelical doctrines to their countrymen.
Ardent young Frenchmen, trained abroad, took their lives
in their hand, and crept quietly through the length and
breadth of France. They met converts and inquirers in
solitary suburbs, in cellars of houses, on highways, and by
the rivers. The records of the ecclesiastical police enable
us to trace the spread of the Reformation along the great
roads and waterways of France. The missioners changed
their names frequently to elude observation. Some, with
a daring beyond their fellows, did not hesitate to visit the
towns and preach almost openly to the people. The propaganda carried on by colporteurs was scarcely less successful
These were usually young men trained at Geneva or Strassburg. They carried their books in a pack on their backs,
and hawked them in village and town, describing their contents, and making little sermons for the listeners. Among
the notices of seizures we find such titles as the following :
—*Les Colloques* of Erasmus, *La Fontaine de Vie* (a selection
of scriptural passages translated into French), the *Livre de
vraye et parfaicte oraison* (a translation of extracts from
Luther's writings), the *Cinquante-deux psaumes*, the *Catéchisme
de Genève*, *Prières ecclésiastiques avec la manière d'administrer
les sacrements*, an *Alphabet chrétien*, and an *Instruction
chrétienne pour les petits enfants*. No edicts against printing
books which had not been submitted to the ecclesiastical
authorities were able to put an end to this secret
colportage.

In these several ways the Evangelical faith was spread
abroad, and before the death of Francis there was not a
district in France with the single exception of Brittany
which had not its secret Protestants, while many parts of
the country swarmed with them.

§ 4. *Calvin and his Influence in France.*

The Reformation in France had been rapidly changing its character since 1536, the year in which Lefèvre died, and in which Calvin's *Christian Institution* was published. It was no longer a Christian mysticism supplemented by a careful study of the Scriptures; it had advanced beyond the stage of individual followers of Luther or Zwingli; it had become united, presenting a solid phalanx to its foes; it had rallied round a manifesto which was at once a completed scheme of doctrine, a prescribed mode of worship, and a code of morals; it had found a leader who was both a master and a commander-in-chief. The publication of the *Christian Institution* had effected this. The young man whom the Town Council of Geneva could speak of as "a certain Frenchman" (*Gallus quidam*) soon took a foremost place among the leaders of the whole Reformation movement, and moulded in his plastic hands the Reformation in France.

Calvin's early life and his work in Geneva have already been described; but his special influence on France must not pass unnoticed.[1] He had an extraordinary power over his co-religionists in his native land.[2] He was a Frenchman—one of themselves; no foreigner speaking an unfamiliar tongue; no enemy of the Fatherland to follow whom might seem to be unpatriotic. It is true that his fixed abode lay beyond the confines of France; but distance, which gave him freedom of action, made him

---

[1] Cf. above, pp. 92 ff. What follows on Calvin's influence on the Reformation in France has been borrowed largely from M. Henri Lemonnier, *Histoire de France*, etc. (Paris, 1903–4) V. i. pp. 381–383, ii. pp. 183–187, etc.; only a Frenchman can describe it and him sympathetically.

[2] The Venetian Ambassador at the Court of France, writing in 1561 to the Doge, says, "Your Serenity will hardly believe the influence and the great power which the principal minister of Geneva, by name Calvin, a Frenchman and a native of Picardy, possesses in this kingdom. He is a man of extraordinary authority, who by his mode of life, his doctrines and his writings, rises superior to all the rest" (*Calendar of State Papers, Venetian, 1558–80*, p. 323).

the more esteemed. He was the apostle who wrote "to all that be in France, beloved of God, called to be saints."

While still a student, Calvin had shown that he possessed, besides a marvellous memory, an acute and penetrating intellect, with a great faculty for assimilating ideas and modes of thought; but he lacked what may be called artistic imagination,[1] and neither poetry nor art seemed to strike any responsive chord in his soul. His conduct was always straightforward, irreproachable, and dignified; he was by education and breeding, if not by descent, the polished French gentleman, and was most at home with men and women of noble birth. His character was serious, with little playfulness, little vivacity, but with a wonderful power of sympathy. He was reserved, somewhat shy, slow to make intimate friends, but once made the friendships lasted for life. At all periods of age, boy, student, man of letters, leader of a great party, he seems to have been a centre of attraction and of deferential trust. The effect of this mysterious charm was felt by others besides those of his own age. His professor, Mathurin Cordier, became his devoted disciple. Melanchthon wished that he might die with his head on Calvin's breast. Luther, in spite of his suspicion of everything that came from Switzerland, was won to love and trust him. And Knox, the most rugged and independent of men, acknowledged Calvin as his master, consulted him in every doubt and difficulty, and on all occasions save one meekly followed his counsels. He loved children, and had them at his house for Christmas trees; but (and this is characteristically French) always addressed them with ceremonious

---

[1] Calvin did not lack imagination. The sanctified imagination has never made grander or loftier flight than in the thought of the *Purpose of God* moving slowly down through the Ages, making for redemption and for the establishment of the Kingdom, which is the master-idea in the *Christian Institution*. It was de Bèze (Beza), not Calvin, who was the father of the seventeenth century doctrine of predestination, — a conception which differed from Calvin's as widely as the skeleton differs from the man instinct with life and action.

politeness, as if they were grown men and women deserving as much consideration as himself. It was this trait that captivated de Bèze when he was a boy of twelve.

Calvin was a democrat intellectually and by silent principle. This appears almost everywhere in his private writings, and was noted by such a keen observer as Tavannes. It was never more unconsciously displayed than in the preface or dedication of the *Christian Institution*.

"This preface, instead of pleading with the King on behalf of the Reformation, places the movement right before him, and makes him see it. Its tone throughout firm and dignified, calm and stately when Calvin addresses Francis I. directly, more bitter and sarcastic when he is speaking of theologians, *la pensée et la forme du style toutes vibrantes du ton biblique*, the very simplicity and perfect frankness of the address, give the impression of one who is speaking on equal terms with his peer. All suggest the Christian democrat without a trace of the revolutionary." [1]

The source of his power—logic impregnated by the passion of conviction—is so peculiarly French that perhaps only his countrymen can fully understand and appreciate it, and they have not been slow to do so.

All these characteristic traits appealed to them. His passion for equality, as strong as the Apostle Paul's, compelled him to take his followers into his confidence, to make them apprehend what he knew to the innermost thoughts of his heart. It forced him to exhibit the reasons for his faith to all who cared to know them, to arrange them in a logical order which would appeal to their understanding, and his passion of conviction assured him and them that what he taught was the very truth of God. Then he was a very great writer,[2] one of the founders

---

[1] Henri Lemonnier, *Histoire de France*, etc. (Paris, 1903) V. i. 383.

[2] "Calvin fut un très grand écrivain. Je dirais même que ce fut le plus grand écrivain du 16e siècle si j'estimais plus que je ne fais le *style* proprement dit. . . . Encore est-il qu'il me faut bien reconnaître que le style de Calvin est de tous les styles du 16e siècle celui qui a le plus de *style*. . . . Resta

of modern French prose, the most exquisite literary medium that exists, a man made to arrest the attention of the people. He wrote all his important works in French for his countrymen, as well as in Latin for the learned world. His language and style were fresh, clear, and simple; without affected elegance or pedantic display of erudition; full of vigour and verve; here, caustic wit which attracted; there, eloquence which spoke to the hearts of his readers because it throbbed with burning passion and strong emotion.

It is unlikely that all his disciples in France appreciated his doctrinal system in its details. The *Christian Institution* appealed to them as the strongest protest yet made against the abuses and scandals of the Roman Church, as containing a code of duties owed to God and man, as exhibiting an ideal of life pure and lofty, as promising everlasting blessedness for the called and chosen and faithful. "It satisfied at one and the same time the intellects which demanded logical proof and the souls which had need of enthusiasm."

It has been remarked that Calvin's theology was less original and effective than his legislation or policy.[1] The statement seems to overlook the peculiar service which was rendered to the Reformation movement by the *Institution*. The Reformation was a rebellion against the external authority of the mediæval Church; but every revolt, even that against the most flagrant abuses and the most corrupt rule, carries in it seeds of evil which must be slain if any real progress is to be made. For it instinctively tends to sweep away all restraints—those that are good and necessary as well as those that are bad and harmful. The leaders of every movement for reform have a harder

---

qu'il parle l'admirable prose, si claire, limpide et facile, du 15ᵉ siècle, avec ce quelque chose de plus ferme, de plus nourri et de plus viril que l'étude des classiques donne à ceux qui ne poussent pas jusqu'à l'imitation servile et à l'admirature des menus jolis détails. Reste qu'il parle la langue du 15ᵉ siècle avec quelques qualités déjà du 17ᵉ. C'est précisément ce qu'il a fait, et il est un des bons, sinon des sublimes, fondateurs de la prose française" (Emile Faguet, *Seizième Siècle: Études Littéraires*, pp. 188–89, Paris, 1898).

[1] *Cambridge Modern History*, ii. 366.

battle to fight against the revolutionaries in their following than against their avowed opponents. At the root of the Reformation of the sixteenth century lay an appeal from man to God—from the priest, granting or withholding absolution in the confessional, to God making the sinner, who turns from his sins and has faith in the person and work of Christ, know in his heart that he is pardoned ; from the decision of Popes and Councils to the decrees of God revealed in His Holy Word. This appeal was in the nature of the case from the seen to the unseen, and therein lay the difficulty ; for unless this unseen could be made visible to the eye of the intelligence to such a degree that the restraining authority which it possessed could impress itself on the will, there was risk of its proving to be no restraining authority whatsoever, and of men fancying that they had been left to be a law unto themselves. What the *Christian Institution* did for the sixteenth century was to make the unseen government and authority of God, to which all must bow, as visible to the intellectual eye of faith as the mechanism of the mediæval Church had been to the eye of sense. It proclaimed that the basis of all Christian faith was the Word of God revealed in the Holy Scriptures ; it taught the absolute dependence of all things on God Himself immediately and directly ; it declared that the sin of man was such that, apart from the working of the free grace of God, there could be neither pardon nor amendment, nor salvation ; and it wove all these thoughts into a logical unity which revealed to the intellectual eye of its generation the " House of God not made with hands, eternal in the heavens." Men as they gazed saw that they were in the immediate presence of the authority of God Himself, directly responsible to Him ; that they could test " the Pope's House " by this divine archetype ; that it was their duty to reform all human institutions, ecclesiastical or political, in order to bring them into harmony with the divine vision. It made men know that to separate themselves from the visible mediæval Church was neither to step outside the sphere of the purpose of

God making for their redemption, nor to free themselves from the duties which God requires of man.

The work which Calvin did for his co-religionists in France was immense. He carried on a constant correspondence with them ; he sustained their courage ; he gave their faith a sublime exaltation. When he heard of a French Romanist who had begun to hesitate, he wrote to him combining persuasion with instruction. He pleaded the cause of the Reformation with its nominal supporters. He encouraged the weak. He sent letters to the persecuted. He forwarded short theological treatises to assist those who had got into controversies concerning their faith. He advised the organisation of congregations. He recommended energetic pastors. He warned slothful ministers.

" We must not think," he says, " that our work is confined within such narrow limits that our task is ended when we have preached sermons . . . it is our part to maintain a vigilant oversight of those committed to our care, and take the greatest pains to guard from evil those whose blood will one day be demanded from us if they are lost through our negligence." [1]

He answered question after question about the difficulty of reconciling the demands of the Christian life with what was required by the world around—a matter which pressed hard on the consciences of men and women who belonged to a religious minority in a great Roman Catholic kingdom. He was no casuist. He wrote to Madame de Cany, the sister of the Duchess d'Étampes, that " no one, great or small, ought to believe themselves exempt from suffering for the sake of our sovereign King." He was listened to with reverence ; for he was not a counsellor who advised others to do what he was not prepared to do himself. He could say, " Be ye followers of me, as I am of the Lord Jesus Christ." Frenchmen and Frenchwomen knew that the master whom they obeyed, the director they consulted, to whom they whispered the secrets of their souls

[1] *La Catéchisme français*, p. 132. *Opera*, v. 319.

lived the hardest and most ascetic life of any man in Europe,—scarcely eating, drinking, or sleeping; that his frail body was kept alive by the energy of his indomitable soul.

Frenchmen of varying schools of thought have not been slow to recognise the secret of the power of their great countryman. Jules Michelet says:

"Among the martyrs, with whom Calvin constantly conversed in spirit, he became a martyr himself; he lived and felt like a man before whom the whole earth disappears, and who tunes his last Psalm his whole eye fixed upon the eye of God, because he knows that on the following morning he may have to ascend the pyre."

Ernest Renan is no less emphatic:

"It is surprising that a man who appears to us in his life and writings so unsympathetic should have been the centre of an immense movement in his generation, and that this harsh and severe tone should have exercised so great an influence on the minds of his contemporaries. How was it, for example, that one of the most distinguished women of her time, Renée of France, in her Court at Ferrara, surrounded by the flower of European wits, was captivated by that stern master, and by him drawn into a course that must have been so thickly strewn with thorns? This kind of austere seduction is exercised only by those who work with real conviction. Lacking that vivid, deep, sympathetic ardour which was one of the secrets of Luther's success, lacking the charm, the perilous, languishing tenderness of Francis de Sales, Calvin succeeded, in an age and in a country which called for a reaction towards Christianity, simply because *he was the most Christian man of his generation.*"

Thus it was that all those in France who felt the need of intimate fellowship with God, all to whom a religion, which was at once inflexible in matters of moral living and which appealed to their reasoning faculties, was a necessity, hailed the *Christian Institution* as the clearest manifesto of their faith, and grouped themselves round the young author (Calvin was barely twenty-six when he wrote it) as

their leader. Those also who suffered under the pressure
of a despotic government, and felt the evils of a society
constituted to uphold the privileges of an aristocracy,
learnt that in a neighbouring country there was a city
which had placed itself under the rule of the Word of
God; where everyone joined in a common worship attractive
from its severe simplicity; where the morals, public and
private, were pure; where the believers selected their
pastors and the people their rulers; where there were
neither masters nor subjects; where the ministers of
religion lived the lives of simple laymen, and were distinguished from them only by the exercise of their sacred
service. They indulged in the dream that all France
might be fashioned after the model of Geneva.

Many a Frenchman who was dissatisfied with the
condition of things in France, but had come to no personal
decision to leave the mediæval Church, could not help
contrasting what he saw around him with the life and
aspiration of those "of the religion,"[1] as the French
Protestants began to be called. They saw themselves
confronted by a religion full of mysteries inaccessible to
reason, expressing itself even in public worship in a
language unintelligible to most of the worshippers, full of
pomp, of luxury, of ceremonies whose symbolical meaning
had been forgotten. They saw a clergy commonplace and
ignorant, or aristocratic and indifferent; a nobility greedy
and restless; a Court whose luxurious display and scandals
were notorious; royal mistresses and faithless husbands
and wives. Almost everywhere we find a growing tendency
to contrast the purity of Protestantism and the corruption
of Roman Catholicism. It found outcome in the famous
scene in the *Parlement* of Paris (1559), when Antoine
de Bourg, son of a former Chancellor, advocated
the total suspension of the persecution against those
"who were called heretics," and enforced his opinion by
contrasting the blasphemies and scandals of the Court

---

[1] The term was adopted from the edicts, "ladite religion prétendue
réformée," with the qualifying adjectives left out.

with the morality and the purity of the lives of those who were being sent to the stake,—a speech for which he afterwards lost his life.[1]

It was this growing united Protestantism which Henry II. and his advisers had determined to crush by the action of the legislative authority.

§ 5. *Persecution under Henry II.*[2]

The repressive legal measures introduced by Francis I. were retained, and a new law against blasphemy (prepared, no doubt, during the last days of Francis) was published five days after the King's death (April 5th, 1547). But more was believed to be necessary. So a series of edicts, culminating in the Edict of Chateaubriand, were published, which aimed at uniting all

[1] Henri Lemonnier, *Histoire de France,* etc. (Paris, 1903) V. ii. 187.

[2] SOURCES in addition to those mentioned on p. 136 : *Lettres inédites de Diane de Poitiers, publiées avec une introduction et des notes par* G. Guiffrey (Paris, 1866) ; *Mémoires de Gaspard de Saulx-Tavannes,* 1530–73 (published in the *Collection* of *Michaud and Poujoulat,* viii.) ; *Mémoires de François de Guise* (in the same collection, vi.) ; *Lettres de Catherine de Médicis* and *Papiers d'État du Cardinal de Granvelle* (in the *Collection des Documents inédits de l'Histoire de France*) ; *Lettres d'Antoine de Bourbon et de Jeanne d'Albret* (in the publications of the *Société de l'Histoire de France*) ; *Les Œuvres complètes de Pierre de Bourdeille, Seigneur de Brantôme* (edit. by L. Lalanne for the *Société de l'Histoire de France,* important for the persons and morals of the times) ; C. Weiss, *La Chambre ardente, étude sur la liberté de Conscience en France, sous François I. et Henri II. 1540–50* (Paris, 1889). Layard, *Dispatches of Michele Suriano and Marcantonio Barbaro, Venetian Ambassadors at the Court of France* (Lymington, 1891, pub. by the *Huguenot Society of London*). Teulet, *Relations politique de la France et de l'Espagne avec l'Écosse* (Paris, 1862) ; and *Papiers dÉ'tat relatifs a l'Histoire de l'Écosse (Bannatyne Club,* Paris, 1851) ; *Correspondance du Cardinal de Granvelle* (Brussels, 1877–96) ; *Calendar of State Papers, Venetian, 1558–80* (London, 1890, etc.)

LATER BOOKS in addition to those mentioned on p. 136 : A. de Ruble, *Le Traité de Cateau-Cambrésis* (Paris, 1889) ; A. W. Whitehead, *Gaspard Coligny, Admiral of France* (London, 1905) ; the *Bulletin historique et littéraire de l'histoire du protestantisme français,* edited by Weiss, is a mine of information on all matters connected with the Reformation in France. A. de Ruble, *Antoine de Bourbon et Jeanne d'Albret* (Paris, 1881–82), and *Le Colloque de Poissy* (Paris, 1889) ; F. Decrue, *Anne de Montmorency* (Paris, 1885–89).

the forces of the kingdom to extirpate the Reformed faith.

On October 8th, 1547, a second criminal court was added to the *Parlement* of Paris, to deal solely with cases of heresy. This was the famous *Chambre Ardente*. It was ordered to sit continuously, even during the ordinary Parliamentary vacancies in August and September; and its first session lasted from Dec. 1547 to Jan. 1550, during which time it must have passed more than five hundred judgments. The clergy felt that this special court took from them one of their privileges, the right of trying all cases of heresy. They petitioned against it. A compromise was arranged (Edict of Nov. 19th, 1549), by which all cases of simple heresy (*cas communs*) were to be sent to the ecclesiastical courts, while cases of heresy accompanied by public scandal (*cas privilégiés*) were to be judged in the civil courts. In practice it usually happened that all cases of heresy went first before the ecclesiastical courts and, after judgment there, those which were believed to be attended by public scandal (the largest number) were sent on to the civil courts. These measures were not thought sufficient, and the Edict of Chateaubriand (June 27th, 1551) codified and extended all the various legal measures taken for the defence of the Roman Catholic faith.

The edict was lengthy, and began with a long preamble, which declared that in spite of all measures of repression, heresy was increasing; that it was a pestilence " so contagious that it had infected most of the inhabitants, men, women, and even little children, in many of the towns and districts of the kingdom," and asked every loyal subject to aid the Government in extirpating the plague. It provided that, as before, all cases of simple heresy should be judged in the ecclesiastical courts, and that heresy accompanied with public scandal should be sent to the civil courts of the *Parlements*. It issued stringent regulations about the publication and sale of books; forbidding the introduction into France of volumes from Protestant countries; forbidding the printing of books which had not passed the censor of the Faculty of Theology, and all books published anonymously; and ordering an examination of all printing houses and book-shops twice in the year. Private persons who did not inform against heretics were liable to be considered heretics themselves, and punished as such; and when they did denounce them they were to receive one-third of the possessions of the persons condemned. Parents were charged " by the pity, love, and charity which they owed to their children," not to engage any teachers who might be " suspect "; no one was permitted to teach in school or college who was not certified to be orthodox; and masters were made responsible for their servants. Intercourse with those who had taken refuge in Geneva was prohibited, and the goods of the refugees were confiscated. All Catholics, and more especially persons of rank and in authority, were required to give the earnest example of attending carefully to outward observances of religion, and in particular to kneel in adoration of the Host.

The edict was registered on Sept. 3rd, 1551, and immediately put in force. Six years later, the King had to confess that its stringent provisions had failed to arrest the spread of the Protestant faith. He proposed to establish the Inquisition in France, moved thereto by the Cardinal of Lorraine and Pope Paul IV.; and was prevented only by the strenuous opposition of his *Parlement*.[1] He had to content himself with issuing the Edict of Compiègne (1557), which, while nominally leaving trials for heresy in the hands of the ecclesiastical courts, practically handed

---

[1] The *Parlements* were the highest judicial courts in France. By far the most important was the *Parlement* of Paris, whose jurisdiction extended over Picardie, Champagne, l'Ile-de-France, l'Orléanais, Maine, Touraine, Anjou, Poitou, Aunis, Berri, La Bourbonnais, Auvergne, and La Marche— almost the half of France. The other *Parlements* in the time of Henry II. were those of Normandy, Brittany, Burgundy, Dauphiné, Provence, Languedoc, Guyenne, and, up to 1559, Chambery and Turin. The *Parlements* are frequently mentioned under the names of the towns in which they met; thus the *Parlement* of Normandy is called the *Parlement* of Rouen; that of Provence, the *Parlement* of Aix; that of Languedoc, the *Parlement* of Toulouse.

them over to the civil courts, where the judges were not allowed to inflict any lesser punishment than death. They were permitted to increase the penalty by inflicting torture, or to mitigate it by strangling the victims before burning them.

Armed with this legislation, the work of hunting out the Reformed was strenuously carried on. Certain prisons were specially reserved for the Protestant martyrs—the Conciergerie, which was part of the building of the Palace, and the Grand Châtelet, which faced it on the opposite bank of the Seine. They soon overflowed, and suspects were confined in the Bastille, in the Petit Châtelet, and in episcopal prisons. The cells of the Conciergerie were below the level of the river, and water oozed from the walls ; the Grand Châtelet was noted for its terrible dungeons, so small that the prisoner could neither stand upright nor lie at full length on the floor. Diseases decimated the victims ; the plague slew sixty who were waiting for trial in the Grand Châtelet in 1547. Few were acquitted ; almost all, once arrested, suffered death and torture.[1]

§ 6. *The Organisation of the French Protestant Church.*

It was during these years of terrible persecution that the Protestant Church of France organised itself—feeling the need for unity the better to sustain the conflict in which it was engaged, and to assist its weaker members. Calvin was unwearied in urging on this work of organisation. With the fire of a prophet and the foresight of a

---

[1] Weiss, *La Chambre ardente, étude sur la liberté de conscience en France, sous François I. et Henri II., 1540–50* (Paris, 1889), is very valuable from the collection of documents which it contains. Crespin's *Histoire des martyrs*, etc., when tested by the official documents now accessible, has been found to be almost invariably correct, and without exaggeration. Weiss, "Une Semaine de la Chambre ardente" (1–8 Oct. 1549), in the *Bulletin historique et littéraire de la société de l'histoire du protestantisme français* for 1899 ; and *Des cinq escoliers sortis de Lausanne brulez a Lyon* (Geneva, 1878).

statesman he insisted on the necessity of unity during the storm and strain of a time of persecution. He had already shown what form the ecclesiastical organisation ought to take.[1] He proposed to revive the simple three-fold ministry of the Church of the early centuries—a congregation ruled by a bishop or pastor, a session of elders, and a body of deacons. This was adopted by the French Protestants. A group of believers, a minister, a " consistory " of elders and deacons, regular preaching, and the sacraments duly administered, made a Church properly constituted. The minister was the chief; he preached; he administered the sacraments; he presided at the " consistory." The " consistory " was composed of elders charged with the spiritual oversight of the community, and of deacons who looked after the poor and the sick. The elders and the deacons were chosen by the members of the congregation; and the minister by the elders and the deacons. An organised Church did not come into existence all at once as a rule, and a distinction was drawn between an *église plantée*, and an *église dressée.* The former was in an embryonic state, with a pastor, it might be, but no consistory; or it might be only a group of people who welcomed the occasional services of a wandering missioner, or held simple services without any definite leader.

The year 1555 may be taken as the date when French Protestantism began to organise Churches. It is true that a few had been established earlier—at Meaux in 1546 and at Nimes in 1547, but the congregations had been dispersed by persecution. Before 1555 the Protestants of France had been for the most part solitary Bible students, or little companies meeting together for common worship without any organisation.

Paris set the example. A small company of believers had been accustomed to meet in the lodging of the Sieur de la Ferriere, near the Pré-aux-Clercs. The birth of a child hastened matters. The father explained that he

[1] *Institutio Christianæ Religionis,* IV. iii. iv.

could not go outside France to seek a pure baptism, and that his conscience would not permit his child to be baptized according to the rites of the Roman Church. After prayer the company resolved to constitute themselves into a Church. Jean le Maçon was called to be the minister or pastor; elders and deacons were chosen; and the organisation was complete.[1] It seemed as if all Protestant France had been waiting for the signal, and organised Churches sprang up everywhere.

Crespin names thirteen Churches, completely organised in the manner of the Church of Paris, founded between 1555 and 1557—Meaux, Poitiers, Angers, les Iles de Saintonge, Agen, Bourges, Issoudun, Aubigny, Blois, Tours, Lyon, Orléans, and Rouen. He adds that there were others. Documentary evidence now available enables us to give thirty-six more, all *dressées*, or completely organised, with a consistory or kirk-session, before 1560. One hundred and twenty pastors were sent to France from Geneva before 1567. The history of these congregations during the reign of Henry II. was full of tragic and dramatic incidents.[2] They existed in the midst of a population which was for the most part fanatically Romanist, easily excited by priests and monks, who poured forth violent addresses from the pulpits of neighbouring churches. Law-courts, whether in the capital or in the provinces, the public officials, all loyal subjects of the King, were invited, commanded by the Edict of Chateaubriand, to ferret out and hunt down those suspected of Protestant sympathies. To fail to make a reverence when passing a crucifix, to speak unguardedly against an ecclesiastical ceremony, to exhibit the slightest sympathy for a Protestant martyr, to be found in possession of a book printed in Geneva, was sufficient to provoke a

---

[1] Athanase Coquerel fils, *Précis de l'histoire de l'église réformée de Paris* (Paris, 1862) — valuable for the numerous official documents in the appendix.

[2] Antoine de Chandieu, *Histoire des persécutions et martyrs de l'Église de Paris, depuis l'an 1557* (Lyons, 1563).

denunciation, an arrest, a trial which must end in torture
and death. Protestants were compelled to worship in
cellars, to creep stealthily to their united devotions; like
the early Christians during the persecutions under Decius or
Diocletian, they had to meet at midnight; and these midnight assemblies gave rise to the same infamous reports
about their character which the Jews spread abroad
regarding the secret meetings of the Christians of the
first three centuries.[1] Every now and then they
were discovered, as in the incident of the Rue Saint-
Jacques in Paris, and wholesale arrests and martyrdoms
followed.

The organisation of the faithful into Churches had
done much for French Protestantism in bestowing upon
them the power which association gives; but more was
needed to weld them into one. In 1558, doctrinal differences arose in the congregation at Poitiers. The Church
in Paris was appealed to, and its minister, Antoine de
Chandieu, went to Poitiers to assist at the celebration of
the Holy Supper, and to heal the dispute. There, it is
said, the idea of a Confession of Faith for the whole
Church was suggested. Calvin was consulted, but did
not approve. Notwithstanding, on May 25th, 1559, a
number of ministers and elders, coming from all parts of
France, and representing, according to a contemporary
document whose authority is somewhat doubtful, sixty-six
Churches,[2] met in Paris for conference. Three days were
spent in deliberations, under the presidency of Morel, one
of the Parisian ministers. This was the *First National
Synod* of the French Protestant Church. It compiled a
Confession of Faith and a Book of Discipline.

---

[1] *Œuvres complètes de Pierre de Bourdeille, Seigneur de Brantôme,* edited
by L. Lalanne for the *Société de l'Histoire de France* (11 vols., Paris, 1864–
82), ix. 161–62.

[2] It is more probable that only twelve Churches were represented—Paris,
Saint-Lô, Rouen, Dieppe, Angers, Orléans, Tours, Poitiers, Saintes,
Marennes, Châtellerault, and Saint-Jean-d'Angely. H. Dieterlen, *La
Synode générale de Paris, 1559* (Montauban, 1873): this was published as a
thesis for the Theological Faculty (Protestant) of Montauban,

The Confession of Faith[1] (*Confession de Foi faite d'un commun accord par les François, qui desirent vivre selon la pureté de l'évangile de notre Seigneur Jésus Christ*) consists of forty articles. It was revised more than once by subsequent Synods, but may still be called the Confession of the French Protestant Church. It was based on a short Confession drafted by Calvin in 1557, and embodied in a letter to the King on behalf of his persecuted subjects. "It seemed useful," one of the members of the Synod wrote to Calvin, "to add some articles to your Confession, and to modify it slightly on some points." Probably out of deference to Calvin's objection to a creed for the whole Church, it was resolved to keep it secret for some time. The resolution was in vain. The Confession was in print, and known before the end of 1559.

The Book of Discipline (*Discipline ecclésiastique des églises réformées de France*) regulated the organisation and the discipline of the Churches. It was that kind of ecclesiastical polity which has become known as Presbyterian, but which might be better called Conciliar. A council called the *Consistory*, consisting of the minister or ministers, elders, and deacons, ruled the congregation. Congregations were formed into groups, over which was the *Colloquy*, composed of representatives from the Consistories; over the *Colloquies* were the *Provincial Synods*; and over all the *General* or *National Synod*. Rules were laid down about how discipline was to be exercised. It was stated clearly that no Church could claim a primacy over the others. All ministers were required to sign the Confession of Faith, and to acknowledge and submit to the ecclesiastical discipline.[2]

---

[1] The Confession will be found in Schaff, *The Creeds of the Evangelical Protestant Churches* (London, 1877), pp. 356 ff. ; Müller, *Die Bekenntnisschriften der reformierten Kirche* (1903), p. 221 ; the various texts are discussed at p. xxxiii.

[2] The Consistories sometimes condescended to details. In the calmer days after the Edict of Nantes, the pastor and Consistory of Montauban thought that the arrangement of Madame de Mornay's hair was *trop mondaine*: Madame argued with them in a spirited way ; cf. *Mémoires de*

It is interesting to see how in a country whose civil rule was becoming gradually more absolutist, this " Church under the Cross " framed for itself a government which reconciled, more thoroughly perhaps than has ever been done since, the two principles of popular rights and supreme central control. Its constitution has spread to Holland, Scotland, and to the great American Churches. Their ecclesiastical polity came much more from Paris than from Geneva.

§ 7. *Reaction against Persecution.*

An attentive study of the sources of the history of the period shows that the excessive severity of King and Court towards Protestants had excited a fairly widespread reaction in favour of the persecuted, and had also impelled the King to action which was felt by many to be unconstitutional. This sympathy with the persecuted and repugnance to the arbitrary exercise of kingship did much to mould the Huguenot movement which lay in the immediate future.

The protests against the institution of the *Chambre Ardente*, the refusal of the *Parlement* of Paris to register the edict establishing the Inquisition in France, and the hesitancy to put in execution extraordinary powers bestowed on French Cardinals for the punishing of heretics by the Bull of Pope Paul IV. (Feb. 26th, 1557), may all be ascribed to the jealousy with which the Courts, ecclesiastical and civil, viewed any interference with their privileged jurisdiction. But the Edict of Chateaubriand (1551), with its articles declaring the unwillingness or negligence shown by public officials in finding out and punishing heretics, making provisions against this, and ordaining that none but persons of well-known orthodoxy were to be appointed magistrates (Arts. 23, 28, 24), confessed that there were many even among those in office who disliked the policy of persecution.

Madame du Plessis-Mornay (Société de l'Histoire de France, Paris, 1868–69), i. 270–310.

Contemporary official documents confirm this unwillingness. We hear of municipal magistrates intervening to protect their Protestant fellow-citizens from punishment in the ecclesiastical courts; of town's police conniving at the escape of heretics; of a procurator at law who was suspended from office for a year for such connivance;[1] and of civil courts who could not be persuaded to pass sentences except merely nominal ones.

The growing discontent at the severe treatment of the persecuted Protestants made itself manifest, even within the *Parlement* of Paris, so long notorious for its persecuting zeal. This became evident when the criminal court of the *Parlement* (la Tournelle, 1559) commuted a sentence of death passed on three Protestants into one of banishment. The violent Romanists protested against this, and demanded a meeting of the whole *Parlement* to fix its mode of judicial action. At this meeting some of the members —Antoine Fumée, du Faur, Viole, and Antoine du Bourg (the son of a Chancellor in the days of Francis I.)—spoke strongly on behalf of the Protestants. They pleaded that a space of six months after trial should be given to the accused to reconsider their position, and that, if they resolve to stand fast in the faith, they should be allowed to withdraw from the kingdom. Their boldness encouraged others. The Cardinal Lorraine and the Constable Montmorency dreaded the consequences of prolonged discussion, and communicated their fears to the King. Henry, accompanied by the Cardinals of Lorraine and of Guise, the Constable, and Francis, Duke de Guise, entered the hall where *Parlement* sat, and ordered the discussion to be continued in his presence. The minority were not intimidated. Du Faur and Viole demanded a total cessation of the persecution pending the summoning of a Council. Du Bourg went further. He contrasted the pure lives and earnest piety of the persecuted with the scandals which disgraced the Roman Church and the Court. " It is no light matter," he said, " to condemn to the stake

[1] *Bulletin de la société de l'hist. du protestantisme français*, 1854, p. 24.

men who invoke the name of Jesus in the midst of the flames." The King was furious. He ordered the arrest of du Bourg and du Faur on the spot, and shortly afterwards Fumée and La Porte were also sent to the Bastile. This arbitrary seizure of members of the *Parlement* of Paris may be said to mark the time when the Protestants of France began to assume the form of a political as well as of a religious party. At this anxious juncture Henry II. met his death, on June 30th, by the accidental thrust of a lance at a tournament held in honour of the approaching marriage of his daughter Elizabeth with Philip of Spain. He lingered till July 10th, 1559.

§ 8. *The higher Aristocracy won for the Reformation.*

When the lists of Protestants who suffered for their faith in France or who were compelled to take refuge in Geneva and other Protestant towns are examined and analysed, as they have been by French archæologists, it is found that the great number of martyrs and refugees were artisans, tradesmen, farmers, and the like.[1] A few names of "notables"—a general, a member of the *Parlement* of Toulouse, a "gentleman" of Limousin—are found among the martyrs, and a much larger proportion among the fugitives. The names of members of noble houses of France are conspicuous by their absence. This does not necessarily mean that the new teaching had not found acceptance among men and women in the upper classes of French society. The noble of the sixteenth century, so long as he remained within his own territory and in his château, was almost independent. He was not subject to the provincial tribunals. Protestantism had been spreading among such. We hear of several high-born ladies present in the congregation of three or four hundred Protestants who were surrounded in a large house in the Rue St. Jacques (Sept. 4th, 1558), and who were released. Renée,

[1] Hauser, "La Réforme et les classes populaires en France au xvie siècle" in the *Revue d'hist. mod. et contemp.* i. (1899-1900).

daughter of Louis XII., Duchess of Ferrara, had declared
herself a Protestant, and had been visited by Calvin as
early as 1535.[1] Francis d'Andelot, the youngest of the
three Chatillons, became a convert during his imprisonment
at Melun (1551–56). His more celebrated brother, Gaspard
de Coligny, the Admiral of France, became a Protestant
during his imprisonment after the fall of St. Quentin
(1558).[2] De Bèze (Beza) tells us that as early as 1555,
Antoine de Bourbon, titular King of Navarre in right of
his wife Jeanne d'Albret, and next in succession to King
Henri II. and his sons, had the new faith preached in the
chapel at Nérac, and that he asked a minister to be sent
to him from Geneva. His brother Louis, Prince of Condé,
also declared himself on the Protestant side. The wives
of the brothers Bourbon, Jeanne d'Albret and Eléanore de
Roye, were more determined and consistent Protestants
than their husbands. The two brothers were among those
present at the assemblies in the Pré-aux-Clercs, where for
five successive evenings (May 13–17) more than five
thousand persons met to sing Clement Marot's Psalms.[3]
Calvin wrote energetically to all these great nobles, urging
them to declare openly on the side of the Gospel, and

[1] The best book on Renée is Rodocanchi, *Renée de France, duchesse de
Ferrare* (1896).

[2] For the Chatillon brothers, see Whitehead, *Gaspard de Coligny,
Admiral of France* (London, 1905).

[3] The singing of Clement Marot's version of the Psalms was not distinctively Protestant. The first edition of the translation, including thirty
Psalms, appeared in Paris in 1541 and in Geneva in 1542. The Geneva
edition had an appendix, entitled *La manière d'administrer les sacrements
selon la coutume de l'Église ancienne et comme on l'observe à Genève*, and was
undoubtedly a Protestant book ; but the Paris edition contained instead
rhymed versions of the Lord's Prayer, of the Apostles' Creed, and of the
angel's salutation to the Virgin. The book was a great favourite with
Francis I., who is said to have sung some of the Psalms on his deathbed. It
was very popular at the Court of Henri II., where it became fashionable for
the courtiers to select a favourite Psalm, which the King permitted them
to call "their own." Henri's "own" was Ps. xlii., *Comme un cerf altéré
brame après l'eau courante.* He was a great huntsman. Catherine de
Medici's was Ps. vi. The Psalm-singing at the Pré-aux-Clercs, however,
was regarded as a manifestation against the Court, and d'Andelot was imprisoned for his persistent attendance.

protect their brethren in the faith less able to defend themselves.

§ 9. *France ruled by the Guises.*[1]

The successor of Henry II. was his son Francis II., who was fifteen years of age, and therefore entitled by French law to rule in his own name. He was a youth feeble in mind and in body, and devotedly attached to his young and accomplished wife, Mary Queen of Scots. She believed naturally that her husband could not do better than entrust the government of the kingdom to her uncles, Charles the Cardinal of Lorraine, and Francis the Duke de Guise. The Cardinal had been Henry II.'s most trusted Minister; and his brother was esteemed to be the best soldier in France. When the *Parlement* of Paris, according to ancient custom, came to congratulate the King on his succession, and to ask to whom they were to apply in affairs of State, they were told by the King that they were to obey the Cardinal and the Duke "as himself." The Constable de Montmorency and the favourite, Diane de Poitiers, were sent from the Court, and the Queen-Mother, Catherine de' Medici, that "shopkeeper's daughter," as the young Queen called her, found herself as devoid of influence as she had been during the lifetime of her husband.

The Cardinal of Lorraine had been the chief adviser of that policy of extirpating the Protestants to which the late King had devoted himself, and it was soon apparent that

---

[1] The family of Guise, who played such a leading part in French history from the reign of Henry II. on to the downfall of the League, became French in the person of Claude, the fifth son of René, Duke of Lorraine, who inherited the lands of his father which were situated in France. Francis I. had loaded him with honours and lands. The family had always been devoted to the Papacy, and had profited by their devotion. The brother of Claude, Jean, had been made a Cardinal when he was twenty, and had accumulated in his own person an immense number of benefices. These descended to his nephews, Charles, who was first Cardinal of Guise and then Cardinal of Lorraine, and Louis, who was Cardinal of Guise. The accumulated benefices enjoyed by Charles amounted to over 300,000 livres. The Guises did not serve the Roman Church for nothing.

it would be continued by the new government. The process against Antoine du Bourg and his fellow-members of
the *Parlement* of Paris who had dared to remonstrate
against the persecution, was pushed forward with all speed.
They were condemned to the stake, and the only mitigation
of sentence was that Du Bourg was to be strangled before
he was burnt. His fate provoked much sympathy. As
he was led to the place of execution the crowd pleaded
with him to recant. His resolute, dignified bearing made
a great impression; and his dying speech, according to one
eye-witness, "did more harm to the Roman Church than a
hundred ministers could have done," and, according to
another, "made more converts among the French students
than all the books of Calvin." The persecutions of Protestants of lower rank increased rather than diminished.
Police made descents on the houses in the Rue de Marais-
Saint-Germain and neighbouring streets.[1] Spies were hired
to insinuate themselves into the confidence of the suspected
for the purpose of denouncing them. The *Parlement* of
Paris instituted four separate criminal courts for the sole
purpose of trying heretics brought before them. The
prisons were no sooner filled than they were emptied by
sentences which sent the condemned to the galleys or to
death. The government incited to persecution by new
declarations and edicts. It declared that houses in which
conventicles were held were to be razed to the ground
(Sept. 4th, 1559); that all who organised unlawful
assemblies were to be punished by death (Nov. 9th, 1559);
that nobles who had justiciary courts were to act according
to law in the matter of heresy, or to be deprived of their
justiciary rights (Feb. 1560). In spite of all this stern

---

[1] The street Marais-Saint-Germain was called *petite Genève*, because it was
supposed to be largely inhabited by Protestants. It was selected because
of its remoteness from the centre of Paris, and because it was partly under
the jurisdiction of the Abbey of Saint-Germain-des-Prés and of the University—two corporations excessively jealous of the infringements of their rights
of police. Cf. Athanase Cocquerel fils, "Histoire d'une rue de Paris," in the
*Bulletin historique et littéraire de la société de l'histoire du protestantisme
français* for 1866, pp. 185, 208.

repression, the numbers of the Protestants increased, and Calvin could declare that there were at least 300,000 in France.

The character of Protestantism in France had been changing. In the earlier years of the persecution they had submitted meekly without thought of revolt, resigned to their fate, rejoicing to suffer in the cause of Christ. But under this rule of the Guises the question of resistance was discussed. It could be said that revolt did not mean revenge for injuries done to themselves. A foreign family had overawed their King and imposed themselves on France. The Princes of the Blood, Antoine de Bourbon and his brother Louis de Condé, in whose veins ran the blood of Saint Louis, who were the natural leaders of the people, were flouted by the Guises. The inviolability of *Parlement* had been attacked in the execution of Antoine du Bourg, and the justiciary rights of great nobles were threatened simply in order to extirpate " those of the religion." They believed that France was full of men who had no good will to the tyranny of the " foreigners." They consulted their brethren in exile, and Calvin himself, on the lawfulness and expediency of an armed insurrection. The refugees favoured the plan. Calvin denounced it. " If one drop of blood is shed in such a revolt, rivers will flow ; it is better that we all perish than cause such a scandal to the cause of Christ and His Evangel." Some of the Protestants were not to be convinced. They only needed a leader. Their natural head was the King of Navarre ; but Antoine de Bourbon was too unstable. Louis de Condé, his brother, was sounded.[1] It is said that he promised to come forward if the enterprise was confined to the seizure of the Guises, and if it was successful in effecting this. A Protestant gentleman, Godefroy de Barry, Seigneur de la Renaudie, became temporary leader.

---

[1] *Les Mémoires du prince de Condé* (The Hague, 1743) ; Duc d'Aumale, *Histoire des Princes de Condé pendant les xvime et xviime siècles*, i. 57 (Paris, 1863-64 ; Eng. trans., London, 1872) ; Armstrong, *The French Wars of Religion* (London, 1892).

He had wrongs to avenge. He had been condemned by the *Parlement* of Dijon (Burgundy), had escaped to Geneva, and had been converted there; his brother-in-law, Gaspard de Heu, of Metz, had been strangled by the Guises in the castle of Vincennes without form of trial. A number of gentlemen and nobles promised their assistance. The conspirators swore to undertake nothing against the King; the enterprise was limited to the arrest of the Guises. News of the project began to leak out. Every information went to show that the Guises were the objects of attack. The Court was moved from Blois to Amboise, which was a fortified city. More precise information filtered to headquarters. The Duke of Guise captured some small bands of conspirators, and de la Renaudie himself was slain in a skirmish. The Guises took summary vengeance. Their prisoners were often slaughtered when caught; or were tied hand and foot and thrown into the Loire. Others were hurried through a form of trial. So many gallows were needed that there was not wood enough, and the prisoners were hung from the doors and battlements of the castle of Amboise. The young King and Queen, with their ladies, walked out after dinner to feast their eyes on the dead bodies.

Even before the Conspiracy of Amboise had run its length, members of the Court had begun to protest against the religious policy of the Guises. Catherine de' Medici had talked the matter over with the Admiral Coligny, had been told by him that the religious persecutions were at the bottom of the troubles in the kingdom, and had listened to his proposal that all such should be suspended until the meeting of a Council. The result was that government decided to pardon those accused of heresy if they would promise for the future to live as good Catholics. The brutalities of the methods by which the sharers in the foolishly planned and feebly executed Conspiracy of Amboise were punished increased the state of disorder in the kingdom, and the hatred against the Guises found vent in an *Epistle sent to the Tiger of France*, in which the

Duke is addressed as a "mad tiger, a venomous viper, a sepulchre of abominations."

Catherine de' Medici deemed the opportunity favourable for exercising her influence. She contrived to get Michel de l'Hôpital appointed as Chancellor, knowing that he was opposed to the sanguinary policy pursued. He was able to inspire the Edict of Romorantin (May 18th, 1560), which made the Bishops judges of the crime of heresy, imposed penalties on false accusers, and left the punishment to be bestowed on attendance at conventicles in the hands of the presidents of the tribunals. Then, with the help of the Chancellor, Catherine managed to get an *Assembly of the Notables* summoned to meet at Fountainebleau. There, many of the members advocated a cessation of the religious persecution. One Archbishop, Marillac of Vienne, and the Bishops of Orléans and Valence, asserted boldly that the religious disorders were really caused by the scandals in the Church; spoke against severe repression until a Council, national or general, had been held; and hinted that the services of the Guises were not indispensable. At the beginning of the second session Coligny spoke. He had the courage to make himself the representative of the Huguenots, as the Protestants now began to be nicknamed. He attacked boldly the religious policy of the Guises, charged them with standing between the King and loyal subjects, and declared that the persecuted were Christians who asked for nothing but to be allowed to worship God as the Gospel taught them. He presented a petition to the King from the Protestants asserting their loyalty, begging that the persecution should cease, and asking that "temples" might be assigned for their worship. The petition was unsigned, but Coligny declared that fifty thousand names could be obtained in Normandy alone. The Duke of Guise spoke with great violence, but the more politic Cardinal induced him to agree with the other members to call a meeting of the States General of France, to be held on the 10th of December 1560.

Shortly after the Notables had dispersed, word came

12**

of another conspiracy, in which not only the Bourbon Princes, but also the Constable Montmorency were said to be implicated. Disturbances broke out in Provence and Dauphiné. The Guises went back to their old policy of violence. The King of Navarre and the Prince of Condé were summoned by the King to appear before him to justify themselves. Although well warned of what might happen, they obeyed the summons, and presented themselves unattended by armed men. Condé was seized and imprisoned. He was condemned to death, and his execution was fixed for the 10th of December. The King of Navarre was left at liberty, but was closely watched; and more than one attempt was made to assassinate him. It was vaguely believed that the Cardinal of Lorraine had resolved to get rid of all the leaders of the Huguenots by death or imprisonment.

While these terrifying suggestions were being whispered, the young King fell ill, and died suddenly. This ended the rule of the Guises, and the French Protestants breathed freely again.

"Did you ever read or hear," said Calvin in a letter to Sturm, "of anything more opportune than the death of the King? The evils had reached an extremity for which there was no remedy, when suddenly God shows Himself from heaven. He who pierced the eye of the father has now stricken the ear of the son."

§ 10. *Catherine de' Medici becomes Regent.*

In the confusion which resulted, Catherine recognised that at last the time had come when she could gratify the one strong passion which possessed her—the passion to govern. Charles IX. was a boy of ten. A Regent was essential. Antoine de Bourbon, as the first Prince of the Blood, might have claimed the position; but Catherine first terrified him with what might be the fate of Condé, and then proposed that the Constable Montmorency and himself should be her principal advisers. The facile Antoine accepted the situation: the Constable was recalled to the Court; Louis de Condé was released from prison. His imprisonment had made a deep impression all over France. The Protestants believed that he had suffered for their sakes. Hymns of prayer had been sung during his captivity, and songs of thanksgiving greeted his release.[1]

> " Le pauvre Chrestien, qui endure
>   Prison, pour verité;
> Le Prince, en captivité dure
>   Sans l'avoir mérité
> Au plus fort de leurs peines entendent
>   Tes œuvres tous parfaits,
> Et gloire et louange te rendent
>   De tes merveilleux faits."

This was sung all over France during Condé's imprisonment; after his release the tone varied:

> " Resjouissez vous en Dieu
> Fidèles de chacun lieu ;
> Car Dieu pour nous a mandé (envoyé)
> Le bon prince de Condé;
>
> Et vous nobles protestans
> Princes, seigneurs attestans ;
> Car Dieu pour nous a mandé
> Le bon prince de Condé."

Catherine de' Medici was forty-one years of age when she became the Regent of France.[2] Her life had been hard. Born in 1519, the niece of Pope Clement VII., she was married to Henry of France in 1534. She had been a neglected wife all the days of her married life. For ten years she had been childless,[3] and her sonnets breathe the

---

[1] *Le Chansonnier Huguenot du xvi⁰ siècle* (Paris, 1871), pp. 204, 245.

[2] Buchot, *Catherine de Médicis* (Paris, 1899); Edith Sichel, *Catherine de' Medici and the French Reformation* (London, 1905).

[3] Catherine's children were—" Francis II., 1544-60 ; Elizabeth (married to Philip II. of Spain in 1559), 1545-68 ; Claude (m. to Charles III., Duke of Lorraine (1558), 1547-75 ; Louis, Duke of Orléans, 1548-50 ; Charles IX., 1550-74 ; Henri III. (first Duke of Orléans, then Duke of Anjou), 1551-89; Francis (Duke of Alençon, then Duke of Anjou), 1554-84 ; Marguerite

prayer of Rachel—Give me children, or else I die.   During Henry's absence with the army in 1552, he had grudgingly appointed her Regent, and she had shown both ability and patience in acquiring a knowledge of all the details of government.   After the defeat of Saint-Quentin she for once earned her husband's gratitude and praise by the way in which she had promptly persuaded the Parliament to grant a subsidy of 300,000 livres.   These incidents were her sole apprenticeship in the art of ruling.   She had always been a great eater, walker, and rider.[1]   Her protruding eyes and her bulging forehead recalled the features of her grand-uncle, Pope Leo x.   She had the taste of her family for art and display.   Her strongest intellectual force was a robust, hard, and narrow common sense which was responsible both for her success and for her failures.   She can scarcely be called immoral ; it seemed rather that she was utterly destitute of any moral sense whatsoever.

The difficulties which confronted the Regent were great, both at home and abroad.   The question of questions was the treatment to be given to her Protestant subjects.   She seems from the first to have been in favour of a measure of toleration ; but the fanatically Roman Catholic party was vigorous in France, especially in Paris, and was ably led by the Guises ; and Philip of Spain had made the suppression of the Reformation a matter of international policy.

Meanwhile Catherine had to face the States General, summoned by the late King in August 1560.   While the Guises were still in power, strict orders had been given to see that none but ardent Romanists should be elected ; but the excitement of the times could not be restrained by any management.   It was nearly half a century since a King of France had invited a declaration of the opinions of his

(married Henri iv.), 1552–1615 ; and twins who died in the year of their birth, Victorie and Jeanne, b. 1556.

[1] Some say that Catherine either invented or made fashionable the modern ladies' side-saddle ; during the Middle Ages ladies rode astride, or on pillion, or seated sideways on horseback with their feet on a board which was suspended from the front and rear of the saddle.

subjects; the last meeting of the States General had been in 1484.[1] Catherine watched the elections, and the expression of sentiments which they called forth. She saw that the Protestants were active. Calvinist ministers traversed the West and the South almost unhindered, encouraging the people to assert their liberties. They were even permitted to address some of the assemblies met to elect representatives. A minister, Charles Dalbiac, expounded the Confession of Faith to the meeting of the nobles at Angers, and showed how the Roman Church had enslaved and changed the whole of the Christian faith and practice. In other places it was said that Antoine de Bourbon had no right to allow Catherine to assume the Regency, and that he ought to be forced to take his proper place. The air seemed full of menaces against the Regent and in favour of the Princes of the Blood. Catherine hastened to place the King of Navarre in a position of greater dignity. She shared the Regency nominally with the premier Prince of the Blood, who was Lieutenant-General of France. If Antoine had been a man of resolution, he might have insisted on a large share in the government of the country, but his easy, careless disposition made him plastic in the hands of Catherine, and she could write to her daughter that he was very obedient, and issued no order without her permission.

The Estates met at Orléans on the 13th of December. The opening speech by the Chancellor, Michel d'Hopital, showed that the Regent and her councillors were at least inclined to a policy of tolerance. The three orders (Clergy, Nobles, and Third Estate), he said, had been summoned to find remedies for the divisions which existed within the kingdom; and these, he believed, were due to religion. He could not help recognising that religious beliefs, good or bad, tended to excite burning passions. He could not avoid seeing that a common religion was a stricter bond of unity than belonging to the same race or living under the same laws. Might they not all wait for the decision of a General Council? Might they not cease to use the irritating

[1] G. Picot, *Histoire des États Généraux*, ii. (Paris, 1872).

epithets of *Lutherans, Huguenots, Papists,* and remember that they were all good Christians. The spokesmen of the three orders were heard at the second sitting. Dr Quintin, one of the Regents of the University of Paris, voiced the Clergy. He enlarged against the proposals which were to be brought forward by the other two orders to despoil the revenues of the Church, to attempt its reform by the civil power, and to grant toleration and even liberty of worship to heretics. Coligny begged the Regent to note that Quintin had called subjects of the King heretics, and the spokesman of the Clergy apologised. Jacques de Silly, Baron de Rochefort, and Jean Lange, an advocate of Bordeaux, who spoke for the Nobles and for the Third Estate, declaimed against the abuses of ecclesiastical courts, and the avarice and ignorance of the clergy.

At the sitting on Jan. 1st, 1561, each of the three Estates presented a written list of grievances (*cahiers*). That of the Third Estate was a memorable and important document in three hundred and fifty-four articles, and reveals, as no other paper of the time does, the evils resulting from absolutist and aristocratic government in France. It asked for complete toleration in matters of religion, for a Reformation of the Church in the sense of giving a large extension of power to the laity, for uniformity in judicial procedure, for the abolition or curtailment of powers in signorial courts, for quinquennial meetings of the Estates General, and demanded that the day and place of the next meeting should be fixed before the end of the present sitting. The Nobles were divided on the question of toleration, and presented three separate papers. In the first, which came from central France, stern repression of the Protestant faith was demanded; in the second, coming from the nobles of the Western provinces, complete toleration was claimed; in the third it was asked that both parties should be made to keep the peace, and that only preachers and pastors be punished. The list presented by the Clergy, like those of the other two orders, insisted upon the reform of the Church but it took the line of urging the abolition of the Concordat, and a return to the provisions of the Pragmatic Sanction of Bourges.

The Government answered these lists of grievances presented by an edict and an ordinance. In the edict (Jan. 28th, 1561) the King ordered that all prosecutions for religion should cease, and that all prisoners should be released, with an admonition "to live in a catholic manner" for the future. The ordinance (dated Jan. 31st, but not completed till the following August), known as the *Ordinance of Orléans*, was a very elaborate document. It touched upon almost all questions brought forward in the lists of grievances, and enacted various reforms, both civil and ecclesiastic—all of which were for the most part evaded in practice. The Estates were adjourned until the 1st of May.

The Huguenots had gained a suspension of persecution, if not toleration, by the edict of Jan. 28th, and the disposition of the Government made them hope for still further assistance. Refugees came back in great numbers from Switzerland, Germany, England, and even from Italy. The number of Protestant congregations increased, and Geneva provided the pastors. The edict did not give liberty of worship, but the Protestants acted as if it did. This roused the wrath of the more fanatically disposed portion of the Roman Catholic population. Priests and monks fanned the flames of sectarian bitterness. The Government was denounced, and anti-Protestant riots disturbed the country. When the Huguenots of Paris attempted to revive the psalm-singings in the Pré-aux-Clercs, they were mobbed, and beaten with sticks by the populace. This led to reprisals in those parts of the country where the Huguenots were in a majority. In some towns the churches were invaded, the images torn down, and the relics burnt. The leaders strove to restrain their followers.[1] Calvin wrote energetically from Geneva against the lawlessness:

[1] Jeanne d'Albret wrote remonstrating strongly; cf. *Lettres d'Antoine de Bourbon et de Jeanne d'Albret*, pp. 233 *f.*

"God has never enjoined on any one to destroy idols, save on every man in his own house or on those placed in authority in public places. . . . Obedience is better than sacrifice; we must look to what it is lawful for us to do, and must keep ourselves within bounds."

At the Court at Fontainebleau, Renée, Duchess of Ferrara, and the Princess of Condé were permitted by the Regent to have worship in their rooms after the Reformed rite; and Coligny had in his household a minister from Geneva, Jean Raymond Merlin, to whose sermons outsiders were not only admitted but invited. These things gave great offence to the Constable Montmorency, who was a strong Romanist. He was still more displeased when Monluc, Bishop of Valence, preached in the State apartments before the boy King and the Queen Mother. He thought it was undignified for a Bishop to preach, and he believed that Monluc's sermons contained something very like Lutheran theology. He invited the Duke of Guise and Saint-André, both old enemies, to supper (April 16th, 1561), and the three pleged themselves to save the Romanism of France. This union was afterwards known as the Triumvirate.

Meanwhile religious disturbances were increasing. The Huguenots demanded the right to have "temples" granted to them or built at their own expense; and in many places they openly gathered for public worship and for the celebration of the Lord's Supper. They frequently met armed to protect themselves from attack. The Government at length interfered, and by an edict (July 1561) prohibited, under penalty of confiscation of property, all conventicles, public or private, whether the worshippers were armed or unarmed, where sermons were made and the sacraments celebrated in any other fashion than that of the Catholic Church. The edict declared, on the other hand, that magistrates were not to be too zealous; persons who laid false information were to be severely punished; and all attacks on houses were forbidden. It was evidently meant to conciliate both parties. Coligny did not discontinue the services in his apartments, and wrote to his co-religionists that they had nothing to fear so long as they worshipped in private houses. Jeanne d'Albret declared herself openly a Protestant; and as she travelled from Nérac to Fontainebleau she restored to the Huguenots churches which the magistrates had taken from them in obedience to the edict of July.

The prorogued meeting of the States General did not assemble until the 1st of August, and even then representatives of two orders only were present. An ecclesiastical synod was sitting at Poissy (opened July 28th), and the clerical representatives were there. It was the 27th of August before the three orders met together in presence of the King and the members of his Council at Saint-Germain. The meeting had been called for the purpose of discussing the question of national finance; but it was impossible to ignore the religious question.

In their *cahiers*, both the Nobles and the Third Estate advocated complete toleration and the summoning a National Council. The financial proposals of the Third Estate were thoroughgoing. After a statement of the national indebtedness, and a representation that taxation had reached its utmost limits, they proposed that money should be obtained from the superfluity of ecclesiastical wealth. In their *cahier* of Jan. 1st, the Third Estate had sketched a civil constitution for the French Church; they now went further, and proposed that all ecclesiastical revenues should be nationalised, and that the clergy should be paid by the State. They calculated that a surplus of seventy-two million livres would result, and proposed that forty-two millions should be set aside to liquidate the national debt.

This bold proposal was impracticable in the condition of the kingdom. The *Parlement* of Paris regarded it as a revolutionary attack on the rights of property, and it alienated them for ever from the Reformation movement; but it enabled the Government to wring from the alarmed

Churchmen a subsidy of sixteen million livres, to be paid
in six annual instalments.

§ 11. *The Conference at Poissy.*

It was scarcely possible, in view of the Pope and
Philip of Spain, to assemble a National Council, but the
Government had already conceived the idea of a meeting of
theologians, which would be such an assembly in all but
the name.   They had invited representatives of the Protestant ministers (July 25th) to attend the synod of the
clergy sitting at Poissy.   The invitation had been accepted,
and the Government intended to give an air of unusual
solemnity to the meeting.   The King, surrounded by his
mother, his brothers, and the Princes of the Blood, presided
as at a sitting of the States General.   The Chancellor, in
the King's name, opened the session with a remarkable
speech, in which he set forth the advantages to be gained
from religious union.   He addressed the assembled bishops
and Roman Catholic theologians, assuring them that they
ought to have no scruples in meeting the Protestant
divines.   The latter were not heretics like the old Mani-
cheans or Arians.   They accepted the Scriptures as the
Rule of Faith, the Apostles' Creed, the four principal
Councils and *their* Creeds (the symbols of Nicea, Constan-
tinople, and Chalcedon).   The main difference between
them was that the Protestants wished the Church to be
reformed according to the primitive pattern.   They had
given proof of their sincerity by being content to die for
their faith.

The Reformers were represented by twelve ministers,
among whom were Morel of Paris; Nicolas des Gallars.
minister of the French Protestant Church in London, and
by twenty laymen.   Their leader was Théodore de Bèze
(Beza), a man of noble birth, celebrated as a Humanist, a
brilliant writer and controversialist, whom Calvin, at the
request of Antoine de Bourbon, Catherine de' Medici, and
Coligny, had commissioned to represent him.   De Bèze

was privately presented to the King and the Regent by
the King of Navarre and by the Prince de Condé, and his
learning, presence, and stately courtesy made a great impression upon the Court. He had been born in the same
year as the Regent (1519), and had thrown away very
brilliant prospects to become a minister of the Reformed
Church.

The meeting was held in the refectory of the nuns of
Poissy.[1] The King and his suite were placed at one end
of the hall, and the Romanist bishops and theologians were
arranged by the walls on the two sides. After the Chancellor had finished his speech, the representatives of the
Protestants were introduced by the Duke of Guise, in
command of an escort of the King's archers. They were
placed in front of a barrier which separated them from the
Romanist divines. "There come the dogs of Geneva,"
said the Cardinal of Tournon as they entered the hall.

The speech of de Bèze, delivered on the first day (Sept.
7th) of the Colloquy, as it came to be called, made a great
impression. He expounded with clearness of thought and
precision of language the creed of his Church, showing
where it agreed and where it differed from that of the
Roman Catholic. The gravity and the charm of his
eloquence compelled attention, and it was not until he
began to criticise with frank severity the doctrine of transubstantiation that he provoked murmurs of dissent. The
speech must have disappointed Catherine. It had made
no attempt to attenuate the differences between the two
confessions, and held out no hopes of a reunion of the
Churches.

The Cardinal of Lorraine was charged to reply on behalf of the Roman Catholic party (Sept. 16th). His speech
was that of a strong partisan, and dealt principally with
the two points of the authority of the Church in matters
of faith and usage, and the doctrine of the Sacrament of

[1] For the Colloquy of Poissy, cf. Ruble, "Le Colloque de Poissy" (in
Mémoires de la Société de l'histoire de Paris et de l'Île de France), vol. xvi.,
Paris, 1889); Klipffel, *Le colloque de Poissy* (Paris and Metz, 1867).

the Holy Supper. There was no attempt at conciliation.

Three days after (Sept. 19th), Cardinal Ippolito d'Este
arrived at Saint-Germain, accompanied by a numerous suite,
among whom was Laynez, the General of the Society of
Jesus. He had been sent by the Pope, legate *a latere,* to
end, if possible, the conference at Poissy, and to secure the
goodwill of the French Government for the promulgation of
the decrees of the Council of Trent. He so far prevailed that
the last two sittings of the conference (Sept. 24th, 26th)
were with closed doors, and were scenes of perpetual recri-
minations. Laynez distinguished himself by his vitupera-
tive violence. The Protestant ministers were "wolves,"
"foxes," "serpents," "assassins." Catherine persevered.
She arranged a conference between five of the more liberal
Roman Catholic clergy and five Protestant ministers. It
met (Sept. 30th, Oct. 1st), and managed to draft a formula
about the Holy Supper which was at once rejected by the
Bishops of the French Church (Oct. 9th).

Out of this Colloquy of Poissy came the edict of January
17th, 1562, which provided that Protestants were to surrender all the churches and ecclesiastical buildings they
had seized, and prohibited them from meeting for public
worship, whether within a building or not, inside the walls
of any town. On the other hand, they were to have the
right to assemble for public worship anywhere outside
walled towns, and meetings in private houses within the
walls were not prohibited. Thus the Protestants of France
secured legal recognition for the first time, and enjoyed the
right to worship according to their conscience. They were
not satisfied—they could scarcely be, so long as they were
kept outside the walls; but their leaders insisted on their
accepting the edict as a reasonable compromise. " If the
liberty promised us in the edict lasts," Calvin wrote, " the
Papacy will fall to the ground of itself." Within one year
the Huguenots of France found themselves freed from persecution, and in the enjoyment of a measured liberty of
public worship. It can scarcely be doubted that they

owed this to Catherine de' Medici. She was a child of the Renaissance, and was naturally on the side of free thought; and she was, besides, at this time persuaded that the Huguenots had the future on their side. In the coming struggle they regarded this edict as their charter, and frequently demanded its restitution and enforcement.

Catherine de' Medici had shown both courage and constancy in her attempts at conciliation. To the remonstrances of Philip of Spain she had replied that she meant to be master in her own house; and when the Constable de Montmorency had threatened to leave the Court, he had been told that he might do as he pleased. But she was soon to be convinced that she had overestimated the strength of the Protestants, and that she could never count on the consistent support of their nominal leader, the vain and vacillating Antoine de Bourbon. Had Jeanne d'Albret been in her husband's place, things might have been different.

The edict of January 17th, 1562, had exasperated the Romanists without satisfying the mass of the Protestants. The marked increase in the numbers of Protestant congregations, and their not very strict observance of the limitations of the edict, had given rise to disturbances in many parts of the country. Everything seemed to tend towards civil war. The spark which kindled the conflagration was the Massacre of Vassy.[1]

§ 12. *The Massacre of Vassy.*

The Duke of Guise, travelling from Joinville to Paris, accompanied by his brother, the Cardinal of Guise, his children and his wife, and escorted by a large armed retinue, halted at Vassy (March 1st, 1562). It was a Sunday, and the Duke wished to hear Mass. Scarcely a gunshot from the church was a barn where the Protestants (in defiance of the edict, for Vassy was a walled town) were holding a

---

[1] Lavisse, "Le Massacre, fait à Vassy" in *Grandes Scènes historiques du xvie siècle* (Paris, 1886).

service. The congregation, barely a year old, was numerous and zealous. It was an eyesore to Antoinette de Bourbon, the mother of the Guises, who lived in the neighbouring château of Joinville, and saw her dependants attracted by the preaching at Vassy. The Duke was exasperated at seeing men whom he counted his subjects defying him in his presence. He sent some of his retainers to order the worshippers to quit the place. They were received by cries of " Papists ! idolaters !" When they attempted to force an entrance, stones began to fly, and the Duke was struck. The barn was rushed, the worshippers fusilladed, and before the Duke gave orders to cease firing, sixty-three of the six or seven hundred Protestants were slain, and over a hundred wounded.

The news of the massacre spread fast ; and while it exasperated the Huguenots, the Romanists hailed it as a victory. The Constable de Montmorency and the Marshal Saint André went out to meet the Duke, and the Guises entered Paris in triumph, escorted by more than three thousand armed men. The Protestants began arming themselves, and crowded to Paris to place themselves under the orders of the Prince of Condé. It was feared that the two factions would fight in the streets.

The Regent with the King retired to Fontainebleau. She was afraid of the Triumvirs (Montmorency, the Duke of Guise, and Marshal Saint-André), and she invited the Prince de Condé to protect her and her children. Condé lost this opportunity of placing himself and his co-religionists in the position of being the support of the throne. The Triumvirate, with Antoine de Bourbon, who now seemed to be their obedient servant, marched on Fontainebleau, and compelled the King and the Queen Mother to return to Paris. Catherine believed that the Protestants had abandoned her, and turned to the Romanists.

The example of massacre given at Vassy was followed in many places where the Romanists were in a majority. In Paris, Sens, Rouen, and elsewhere, the Protestant places of worship were attacked, and many of the worshippers slain. At Toulouse, the Protestants shut themselves up in the Capitol, and were besieged by the Romanists. They at last surrendered, trusting to a promise that they would be allowed to leave the town in safety. The promise was not kept, and three thousand men, women, and children were slain in cold blood. This slaughter, in violation of oath, was celebrated by the Roman Catholics of Toulouse in centenary festivals, which were held in 1662, in 1762, and would have been celebrated in 1862 had the Government of Napoleon III. not interfered to forbid it.

These massacres provoked reprisals. The Huguenots broke into the Romanist churches, tore down the images, defaced the altars, and destroyed the relics.

§ 13. *The Beginning of the Wars of Religion.*

Gradually the parties faced each other with the Duke of Guise and the Constable Montmorency at the head of the Romanists, and the Prince of Condé and Admiral Coligny at the head of the Huguenots. France became the scene of a civil conflict, where religious fanaticism added its cruelties to the ordinary barbarities of warfare.

The Venetian Ambassador, writing home to the chiefs of his State, was of opinion that this first war of religion prevented France from becoming Protestant. The cruelties of the Romanists had disgusted a large number of Frenchmen, who, though they had no great sympathy for the Protestant faith, would have gladly allied themselves with a policy of toleration. The Huguenot chiefs themselves saw that the desecration of churches did not serve the cause they had at heart. Calvin and de Bèze wrote, energetically urging their followers to refrain from attacks on churches, images, and relics. But it was all to no purpose. At Orléans, Coligny and Condé heard that their men were assaulting the Church of the Holy Spirit. They hastened there, and Condé saw a Huguenot soldier on the roof of the church about to cast an image to the ground. Seizing an arquebus, he pointed it at the man, and ordered him to desist and come down. The soldier did not stop his work for an instant. " Sire," he said, " have patience with me until I destroy this idol, and then let me die if it be your pleasure." When men were content to die rather than refrain from iconoclasm, it was in vain to expect to check it. Somehow the slaughter of men made less impression than the sack of churches, and moderate men came to the opinion that if the Huguenots prevailed, they would be as intolerant as the Romanists had been. The rising tide of sympathy for the persecuted Protestants was checked by these deeds of violence.

The progress of the war was upon the whole unfavourable to the Huguenots, and in the beginning of 1553 both parties were exhausted. The Constable Montmorency had been captured by the Huguenots, and the Prince de Condé by the Romanists. The Duke of Guise was shot from behind by a Huguenot, and died six days later (Feb. 24th, 1563). The Marshal Saint-André and Antoine de Bourbon had both died during the course of the war. Catherine de' Medici was everywhere recognised as the head of the Romanist party. She no longer needed the Protestants to counterbalance the Guises and the Constable. She could now pursue her own policy.

From this time forward she was decidedly hostile to the Huguenots. She had learned the resources and popularity of the Romanists. But she disliked fighting, and the religious war was ruining France. Her idea was that it would be necessary to tolerate the Protestants, but impossible to grant them common rights with the Romanists. She applied herself to win over the Prince de Condé, who was tired of his captivity. Negotiations were opened. Catherine, the Constable, Condé, and d'Andelot met at Orléans ; and, after discussion, terms were agreed upon (March 7th), and the Edict of Amboise incorporating them was published (March 18th, 1563).

Condé had asked for the restitution of the edict of Jan. 17th, 1561, and the strict enforcement of its terms.

This was refused. The terms of the new edict were as favourable for men of good birth, but not for others. Condé had to undergo the reproaches of Coligny, that he had secured rights for himself but had betrayed his poorer brethren in the faith; and that he had destroyed by his signature more churches than the united forces of Romanism had done in ten years. Calvin spoke of him as a poor Prince who had betrayed God for his own vanity.

The truce, for it was no more than a truce, concluded by the Edict of Amboise lasted nearly five years. It was broken by the Huguenots, who were suspicious that Catherine was plotting with the Duke of Alva against them. Alva was engaged in a merciless attempt to exterminate the Protestants of the Low Countries, and Catherine had been at pains to provide provisions for his troops. The Protestant leaders came to the desperate conclusion to imitate the Triumvirate in 1561, and seize upon the King's person. They failed, and their attempt began the Second War of Religion. The indecisive battle of Saint-Denis was fought on Nov. 10th, 1567, and the Constable Montmorency fell in the fight. Both parties were almost exhausted, and the terms of peace were the same as those in the Edict of Amboise.

The close of this Second War of Religion saw a determined attempt, mainly directed by the Jesuits, to inspire the masses of France with enthusiasm for the Roman Catholic Church. Eloquent preachers traversed the land, who insisted on the antiquity of the Roman and the novelty of the Protestant faith. Brotherhoods were formed, and enrolled men of all sorts and conditions of life sworn to bear arms against every kind of heresy. Outrages and assassinations of Protestants were common; and the Government appeared indifferent. It was, however, the events in the Low Countries which again alarmed the Protestants. The Duke of Alva, who had begun his rule there with an appearance of gentleness, had suddenly seized and executed the Counts Egmont and Horn. He

13**

had appointed a commission to judge the leaders and accomplices in the earlier rising—a commission which from its deeds gained for itself the name of the Tribunal of Blood. Huguenot soldiers hastened to enrol themselves in the levies which the Prince of Orange was raising for the deliverance of his countrymen. But the Huguenot leaders had other thoughts. Was Catherine meaning to treat them as Alva had treated Egmont and Horn? They found that they were watched. The suspicion and suspense became intolerable Coligny and Condé resolved to take refuge in La Rochelle. As they passed through the country they were joined by numbers of Huguenots, and soon became a small army. Their followers were eager to avenge the murders committed on those of their faith, and pillage and worse marked the track of the army. Condé and the Admiral punished some of their marauding followers by death ; and this, says the chronicler, " made the violence of the soldier more secret if not more rare."

D'Andelot had collected his Normans and Bretons. Jeanne d'Albret had roused her Gascons and the Provençals, and appeared with her son, Henry of Navarre, a boy of fifteen, at the head of her troops. She published a manifesto to justify her in taking up arms. In the camp at La Rochelle she was the soul of the party, fired their passions, and sustained their courage.[1]

In the war which followed, the Huguenots were unfortunate. At the battle of Jarnac, Condé's cavalry was broken by a charge on their flank made by the German mercenaries under Tavannes. He fought till he was surrounded and dismounted. After he had surrendered he was brutally shot in cold blood. The Huguenots soon rallied at Cognac, where the Queen of Navarre joined

---

[1] *Lettres d'Antoine de Bourbon et de Jeanne d'Albret* (Paris, 1877), pp. 305 *ff.* (Letter to Catherine de' Medici) ; pp. 322 *ff.* (letters to Protestants outside La Rochelle). In her letter to Catherine Jeanne demands for the Protestants liberty of worship and all the rights and privileges of ordinary citizens : if these are not granted there must be war.

:hem. She presented her son and her nephew, young Henry of Condé, to the troops, and was received with acclamations. Young Henry of Navarre was proclaimed head of the party, and his cousin, Henry of Condé, a boy of the same age, was associated with him. The war went on. The Battle of Moncontour ended in the most disastrous defeat the Huguenots had ever sustained. Catherine de' Medici thought that she had them at her mercy, and proposed terms of submission which would have left them liberty of conscience but denied the right to worship. The heroic Queen of Navarre declared that the names of Jeanne and Henry would never appear on a treaty containing these conditions; and Coligny, like his contemporary, William the Silent, was never more dangerous than after a defeat. The Huguenots announced themselves ready to fight to the last; and Catherine, to her astonishment, saw them stronger than ever. An armistice was arranged, and the Edict of Saint-Germain (Aug. 8th, 1570) published the terms of peace. It was more favourable to the Huguenots than any earlier one. They were guaranteed freedom of conscience throughout the whole kingdom. They had the liberty of public worship in all places where it had been practised before the war, in the suburbs of at least two towns in every government, and in the residences of the great nobles. Four strongly fortified towns—La Rochelle, Montauban, Cognac, and La Charité—were to be held by them as pledges for at least two years. The King withdrew himself from the Spanish alliance and the international policy of the suppression of the Protestants. William of Orange and Ludovic of Nassau were declared to be his friends, in spite of the fact that they were the rebel subjects of Philip of Spain and had assisted the Huguenots in the late war.

After the peace of Saint-Germain, Coligny, now the only great leader left to the Huguenots, lived far from the Court at La Rochelle, acting as the guardian of the two young Bourbon Princes, Henry of Navarre and Henry of Condé. He occupied himself in securing for the Reformed the advantages they had won in the recent treaty of peace.

Catherine de' Medici had begun to think of strengthening herself at home and abroad by matrimonial alliances. She wished one of her sons, whether the Duke of Anjou or the Duke of Alençon it mattered little to her, to marry Elizabeth of England, and her daughter Marguerite to espouse the young King of Navarre. Both designs meant that the Huguenots must be conciliated. They were in no hurry to respond to her advances. Both Coligny and Jeanne d'Albret kept themselves at a distance from the Court. Suddenly the young King, Charles IX., seemed to awaken to his royal position. He had been hitherto entirely submissive to his mother, expending his energies now in hunting, now in lock-making; but, if one can judge from what awakened him, cherishing a sullen grudge against Philip of Spain and his pretensions to guide the policy of Roman Catholic Europe.

Pope Pius v. had made Cosmo de' Medici, the ruler of Florence, a Grand Duke, and Philip of Spain and Maximilian of Austria had protested. Cosmo sent an agent to win the German Protestants to side with him against Maximilian, and to engage the Dutch Protestants to make trouble in the Netherlands. Charles saw the opportunity of gratifying his grudge, and entered eagerly into the scheme. His wishes did not for the time interfere with his mother's plans. If her marriage ideas were to succeed, she must break with Spain. Coligny saw the advantages which might come to his fellow-believers in the Netherlands—help in money from Italy and with troops from France. He resolved to make his peace with Catherine, respond to her advances, and betake himself to Court. He was graciously received, for Catherine wished to make use of him; was made a member of the Council, received a gift of one hundred and fifty thousand livres, and, although a heretic, was put into possession of an Abbey whose revenues amounted to twenty thousand livres a year. The Protestant chiefs were respectfully listened to when they stated grievances, and these were promptly put right, even at the risk of exasperating the Romanists. The somewhat unwilling consent of Jeanne d'Albret was won to the marriage of her son with Marguerite, and she herself came to Paris to settle the terms of contract. There she was seized with pleurisy, and died—an irreparable loss to the Protestant cause. Catherine's home policy had been successful.

But Elizabeth of England was not to be enticed either into a French marriage or a stable French alliance, and Catherine de' Medici saw that her son's scheme might lead to France being left to confront Spain alone; and the Spain of the sixteenth century played the part of Russia in the end of the nineteenth—fascinating the statesmen of the day with its gloomy, mysterious, incalculable power. She felt that she must detach Charles at whatever cost from his scheme of flouting Philip by giving assistance to the Protestants of the Low Countries. Coligny was in her way—recognised to be the greatest statesman in France, enthusiastically bent on sending French help to his struggling co-religionists, and encouraging Charles IX. Coligny must be removed. The Guises were at deadly feud with him, and would be useful in putting him out or the way. The Ambassador of Florence reported significantly conferences between Catherine and the Duchess de Nemours, the mother of the Guises (July 23rd, 1572). The Queen had secret interviews with Maureval, a professional bravo, who drew a pension as "tueur du Roy."

Nothing could be done until Henry, now King of Navarre by his mother's death, was safely married to Marguerite. The wedding took place on August 18th, 1572. On Friday (Aug. 22nd), between ten and eleven o'clock, Coligny left the Louvre to return to his lodging. The assassin was stationed in a house belonging to a retainer of the Guises, at a grated window concealed by a curtain. The Admiral was walking slowly, reading a letter

Suddenly a shot carried away the index finger of his right hand and wounded his left arm. He calmly pointed to the window from whence the shot had come; and some of his suite rushed to the house, but found nothing but a smoking arquebus. The news reached the King when he was playing tennis. He became pallid, threw down his racquet, and went to his rooms.

Catherine closeted herself with the Duke of Anjou to discuss a situation which was fraught with terror.[1]

§ 14. *The Massacre of St. Bartholomew.*

Paris was full of Huguenot gentlemen, drawn from all parts of the country for the wedding of their young chief with the Princess Marguerite. They rushed to the house in which Coligny lay. The young King of Navarre and his cousin, Henry de Condé, went to the King to demand justice, which Charles promised would be promptly rendered. Coligny asked to see the King, who proposed to go at once. Catherine feared to leave the two alone, and accompanied him, attended by a number of her most trusty adherents. Even the Duke of Guise was there. The King by Coligny's bedside swore again with a great oath that he would avenge the outrage in a way that it would never be forgotten. A commission was appointed to inquire into the affair, and they promptly discovered that retainers of the Guises were implicated. If the investigations were pursued in the King's temper, Guise would probably seek to save himself by revealing Catherine's share in the attempted assassination. She became more and more a prey to terror. The Huguenots grew more and more violent. At last Catherine, whether on her own initiative or prompted by others will never be known, believed that she could only save herself by a prompt and thorough

---

[1] For the attempted assassination of Coligny, cf. Whitehead, *Gaspard de Coligny, Admiral of France* (London, 1905), pp. 258 *ff.* ; *Bulletin de l'histoire du Protestantisme Français,* xxxvi. 105 ; *Bulletin de la Société de l'histoire de Paris,* etc. xiv. 38.

massacre of the Huguenots, gathered in unusual numbers in Paris.[1]

She summoned a council (Aug. 23rd), at which were present, so far as is known, the Duke of Anjou, her favourite son, afterwards Henry III., Marshal Tavannes, Nevers, Nemours (the stepfather of the Guises), Birago (Chancellor), the Count de Retz, and the Chevalier d'Angoulême—four of them Italians. They were unanimous in advising an instant massacre. Tavannes and Nevers, it is said, pled for and obtained the lives of the two young Bourbons, the King of Navarre and the Prince de Condé. The Count de Retz, who was a favourite with Charles, was engaged to win the King's consent by appealing to his fears, and by telling him that his mother and brother were as deeply implicated as Guise.

Night had come down before the final resolution was taken; but the fanatical and bloodthirsty mob of Paris might be depended upon. At the last moment, Tavannes (the son) tells us in his Memoirs, Catherine wished to draw back, but the others kept her firm. The Duke of Guise undertook to slay Coligny. The Admiral was run through with a pike, and the body tossed out of the window into the courtyard where Guise was waiting. At the Louvre the young Bourbon Princes were arrested, taken to the King, and given their choice between death and the Mass. The other Huguenot gentlemen who were in the Louvre were slain. In the morning the staircases, halls, and antichambers of the Palace were deeply stained with blood. When the murders had been done in the Louvre, the troops divided into parties and went to seek other victims. Almost all the Huguenot gentlemen on the north side of

---

[1] For the Massacre of St. Bartholomew, cf. Bonnardot, *Registres des Délibérations du Bureau de la Ville de Paris (1568-1572)*, vii. (Paris, 1893); *Mémoires de Madame du Plessis-Mornay*, publ. by the *Société de l'histoire de la France* (1868); *Mémoires et Correspondance de Du Plessis-Mornay* (1824), ii. ; Bordier, *Saint Barthélemy et la critique moderne*; Whitehead, *Gaspard de Coligny, Admiral of France* (London, 1905), pp. 253 ff. ; Froude, *History of England* (London, 1887), ix.-x. ; Mariéjol, *Histoire de France*, etc., vi. i. 114 ff.

the river were slain, and all in the Quartier Latin. But some who lodged on the south side (among them Montgomery, and Jean de Ferrières, the Vidame de Chartres) escaped.

Orders were sent to complete the massacre in the provinces. At Orléans the slaughter lasted five days, and Protestants were slain in numbers at Meaux, Troyes, Rouen, Lyons, Toulouse, Bordeaux, and in many other places. The total number of victims has been variously estimated. Sully, the Prime Minister of Henry IV., who had good means of knowing, says that seventy thousand perished. Several thousands were slain in Paris alone.

The news was variously received by Roman Catholic Europe. The German Romanists, including the Emperor, were not slow to express their disapprobation. But Rome was illuminated in honour of the event, a medal was struck to commemorate the *Hugonotorum Strages*,[1] and Cardinal Orsini was sent to convey to the King and Queen Mother the congratulations of the Pope and the College of Cardinals. Philip of Spain was delighted, and is said to have laughed outright for the first and last time in his life. He congratulated the son on having such a mother, and the mother on having such a son.

Catherine herself believed that the massacre had ended all her troubles. The Huguenots had been annihilated, she thought; and it is reported that when she saw Henry of Navarre bowing to the altar she burst out into a shrill laugh.

§ 15. *The Huguenot resistance after the Massacre.*

Catherine's difficulties were not ended. It was not so easy to exterminate the Huguenots. Most of the

---

[1] The existence of this medal has been unblushingly denied by some Roman Catholic controversialists. It is described and figured in the Jesuit Bonani's *Numismata Pontificum* (Rome, 1689), i. 336. Two commemorative medals were struck in France, and on the reverse of one of them Charles IX. is represented as Hercules with a club in the one hand and a torch in the other slaying the seven-headed Hydra. They are figured in the *Bulletin de la Société de l'histoire du Protestantisme Français* for 1855, pp. 139, 140.

leaders had perished, but the people remained, cowed for a time undoubtedly, but soon to regain their courage. The Protestants held the strongholds of La Rochelle and Sancerre, the one on the coast and the other in central France. The artisans and the small shopkeepers insisted that there should be no surrender. The sailors of La Rochelle fraternised with the Sea Beggars of Brill, and waged an implacable sea-war against the ships of Spain. Nimes and Montauban closed their gates against the soldiers of the King. Milhaud, Aubenas, Privas, Mirabel, Anduze, Sommières, and other towns of the Viverais and of the Cevennes became cities of refuge. All over France, the Huguenots, although they had lost their leaders, kept together, armed themselves, communicated with each other, maintained their religious services — though compelled generally to meet at night.

The attempt to capture these Protestant strongholds made the Fourth Religious War. La Rochelle was invested, beat back many assaults, was blockaded and endured famine, and in the end compelled its enemies to retire from its walls. Sancerre was less fortunate. After the failure of an attempt to take it by assault, La Châtre, the general of the besieging army, blockaded the town in the closest fashion. The citizens endured all the utmost horrors of famine. Five hundred adults and all the children under twelve years of age died of hunger. " Why weep," said a boy of ten, " to see me die of hunger ? I do not ask bread, mother : I know that you have none. Since God wills that I die, thus we must accept it cheerfully. Was not that good man Lazarus hungry ? Have I not so read in the Bible ? " The survivors surrendered ; their lives were spared ; and on payment of a ransom of forty thousand livres the town was not pillaged.

The war ended with the peace of Rochelle (July 1573), when liberty of conscience was accorded to all, but the right of public worship was permitted only to Rochelle, Nimes, Montauban, and in the houses of some of the principal Protestant nobles. These terms were hard in comparison with the rights which had been won before the Massacre of Saint Bartholomew; but the Huguenots had reason for rejoicing. Their cause was still alive. Neither war, nor massacre, nor frauds innumerable had made any impression on the great mass of the French Protestants.

The peace declared by the treaty of La Rochelle did not last long, and indeed was never universal. The Protestants of the South used it to prepare for a renewal of conflict. They remained under arms, perfecting their military organisation. They divided the districts which they controlled into regular governments, presided over by councils whose members were elected and were the military leaders of a Protestant nation for the time being separate from the kingdom of France. They imposed taxes on Romanists and Protestants, and confiscated the ecclesiastical revenues. They were able to stock their strongholds with provisions and munitions of war, and maintain a force of twenty thousand men ready for offensive action.

Their councils at Nimes and Montauban formulated the conditions under which they would submit to the French Government. Nimes sent a deputation to the King furnished with a series of written articles, in which they demanded the free exercise of their religion in every part of France, the maintenance at royal expense of Huguenot garrisons in all the strongholds held by them, and the cession of two strong posts to be cities of refuge in each of the provinces of France. The demands of the council of Montauban went further. They added that the King must condemn the Massacre of St Bartholomew, execute justice on those who had perpetrated it, reverse the sentences passed on all the victims, approve of the Huguenot resistance, and declare that he praised *la singulière et admirable bonté de Dieu* who had still preserved his Protestant subjects. They required also that the rights of the Protestant minority in France should be guaranteed by the Protestant States of Europe—by the German Protestant Princes, by Switzerland, England, and Scotland. They dated their document significantly August 24th—the anniversary of the Massacre of St. Bartholomew. The deputies refused to discuss these terms; they simply presented them. The King might accept them; he might refuse them. They were not to be modified.

Catherine was both furious and confounded at the audacity of these "rascals" (*ces misérables*), as she called them. She declared that Condé, if he had been at the head of twenty thousand cavalry and fifty thousand infantry, would never have asked for the half of what these articles demanded. The Queen Mother found herself face to face with men on whom she might practise all her arts in vain, very different from the *debonnaire* Huguenot princes whom she had been able to cajole with feminine graces and enervate with her "Flying Squadron." These farmers, citizens, artisans knew her and her Court, and called things by rude names. She herself was a "murderess," and her 'Flying Squadron" were "fallen women." She had cleared away the Huguenot aristocracy to find herself in presence of the Protestant democracy.

The worst of it was that she dared not allow the King to give them a decided answer. A new force had been rising in France since Saint Bartholomew's Day—the *Politiques*,[1] as they were called. They put France above religious parties, and were weary of the perpetual bloodshed; they said that "a man does not cease to be a citizen because he is excommunicated"; they declared that "with the men they had lost in the religious wars they could have driven Spain out of the Low Countries." They chafed under the rule of "foreigners," of the Queen Mother and her Italians, of the Guises and their Jesuits. They were prepared to unite with the Huguenots in order to give France peace. They only required leaders who could represent the two sides of the coalition. If the Duke of Alençon, the youngest brother of the King, and Henry of Navarre could escape from the Court and raise their standards together, they were prepared to join them.

Charles IX. died on Whitsunday 1574 of a disease

[1] La Ferrière, *Catherine de Médicis et les Politiques* (Paris, 1894).

which the tainted blood of the Valois and the Medicis induced. The memories of Saint Bartholomew also hastened his death. Private memoirs of courtiers tell us that in his last weeks of fever he had frightful dreams by day and by night. He saw himself surrounded by dead bodies; hideous faces covered with blood thrust themselves forward towards his. The crime had not been so much his as his mother's, but *he* had something of a conscience, and felt its burden. " Et ma Mère " was his last word— an appeal to his mother, whom he feared more than his God.

On Charles' death, Henry, Duke of Anjou, succeeded as Henry III.[1] He was in Poland—king of that distracted country. He abandoned his crown, evaded his subjects, and reached France in September 1574. His advent did not change matters much. Catherine still ruled in reality. The war went on with varying success in different parts of France. But the Duke of Anjou (the Duke of Alençon took this title on his brother's accession) succeeded in escaping from Court (Sept. 15th, 1575), and the King of Navarre also managed to elude his guardians (Feb. 3rd, 1576). Anjou joined the Prince of Condé, who was at the head of a mixed force of Huguenots and Politiques. Henry of Navarre went into Poitou and remained there. His first act was to attend the Protestant worship, and immediately afterwards he renounced his forced adhesion to Romanism. He did not join any of the parties in the field, but sent on his own demands to be forwarded to the King along with those of the confederates, adding to them the request that the King should aid him to recover the Spanish part of Navarre which had been forcibly annexed to Spain by Ferdinand of Aragon.

The escape of the two Princes led in the end to the " Peace of Monsieur," the terms of which were published in the Edict of Beaulieu (May 6th, 1576). The right of

---

[1] Pierre de l'Estoile, *Journal de Henri III*. (Paris, 1875–84) ; Michelet, *Histoire de France*, vols. xi. and xii ; Jackson, *The Last of the Valois* (London, 1888).

public worship was given to Protestants in all towns and places within the kingdom of France, Paris only and towns where the Court was residing being excepted. Protestants received eight strongholds, partly as cities of refuge and partly as guarantees. Chambers of Justice " mi-parties " (composed of both Protestants and Roman Catholics) were established in each Parliament. The King actually apologised for the Massacre of Saint Bartholomew, and declared that it had happened to his great regret; and all sentences pronounced on the victims were reversed. This edict was much more favourable to the Protestants than any that had gone before. Almost all the Huguenots' demands had been granted.

§ 16. *The beginnings of the League.*

Neither the King, who felt himself humiliated, nor the Romanists, who were indignant, were inclined to submit long to the terms of peace. Some of the Romanist leaders had long seen that the Huguenot enthusiasm and their organisation were enabling an actual minority to combat, on more than equal terms, a Romanist majority. Some of the provincial leaders had been able to inspire their followers with zeal, and to bind them together in an organisation by means of leagues. These provincial leagues suggested a universal organisation, which was fostered by Henry, Duke of Guise, and by Catherine de' Medici. This was the first form of that celebrated League which gave twenty years' life to the civil war in France. The Duke of Guise published a declaration in which he appealed to all France to associate together in defence of the Holy Church, Catholic and Roman, and of their King Henry III., whose authority and rights were being taken from him by rebels. All good Catholics were required to join the association, and to furnish arms for the accomplishment of its designs. Those who refused were to be accounted enemies. Neutrals were to be harassed with " toutes sortes d'offences et molestes "; open foes were to be fought strenuously.

Paris was easily won to the League, and agents were sent abroad throughout France to enrol recruits. Henry III. himself was enrolled, and led the movement.

The King had summoned the States General to meet at Blois and hold their first session there on Dec. 6th, 1576. The League had attended to the elections, and the Estates declared unanimously for unity of religion.   Upon this the King announced that the Edict of Beaulieu had been extracted from him by force, and that he did not intend to keep it.   Two of the Estates, the Clergy and the Nobles, were prepared to compel unity at any cost.   The Third Estate was divided.   A minority wished the unity brought about " by gentle and pacific ways "; the majority asked for the immediate and complete suppression of the public worship of the Protestants, and for the banishment of all ministers, elders, and deacons.

These decisions of the States General were taken by the Huguenots as a declaration of war, and they promptly began to arm themselves.   It was the first war of the League, and the sixth of Religion.   It ended with the Peace of Bergerac (Sept. 15th, 1578), in which the terms granted to the Huguenots were rather worse than those of the Edict of Beaulieu.   A seventh war ensued, terminated by the Peace of Fleix (Nov. 1580).

The Duke of Anjou died (June 10th, 1584), and the King had no son.   The heir to the throne, according to the Salic Law, which excluded females, was Henry of Navarre, a Protestant.   On the death of Anjou, Henry III. found himself face to face with this fact.   He knew and felt that he was the guardian of the dynastic rights of the French throne, and that his duty was to acknowledge Henry of Navarre as his successor.   He accordingly sent one of his favourites, Éperon, to prevail upon Henry of Navarre to become a Roman Catholic and come to Court.   Henry refused to do either.

§ 17. *The League becomes disloyal.*[1]

Meanwhile the Romanist nobles were taking their measures. Some of them met at Nancy towards the close of 1584 to reconstruct the League. They resolved to exclude the Protestant Bourbons from the throne, and proclaim the Cardinal Bourbon as the successor of Henry III. They hoped to obtain a Bull from the Pope authorising this selection; and they received the support of Philip of Spain in the Treaty of Joinville (Dec. 31st, 1584).

Paris did not wait for the sanction or recommendation of the nobles. A contemporary anonymous pamphlet, which is the principal source of our information, describes how four men, three of them ecclesiastics, met together to found the League of Paris. They discussed the names of suitable members, and, having selected a nucleus of trustworthy associates, they proceeded to elect a secret council of eight or nine who were to direct and control everything. The active work of recruiting was superintended by six associates, of whom one, the Sieur de la Rocheblond, was a member of the secret council. Soon all the most fanatical elements of the population of Paris belonged to this secret society, sworn to obey blindly the orders of the mysterious council who from a concealed background directed everything. The corporations of the various trades were won to the League; the butchers of Paris, for example, furnished a band of fifteen hundred resolute and dangerous men. Trusty

---

[1] *Dialogue d'entre le Maheustre et le Manant ; contenant les raisons de leurs débats et questions en ces présens troubles au royaume de France 1594 ;* this rare pamphlet is printed in the *Satyre Menippée, de la vertu du Catholicon d'Espagne,* Ratisbon (Amsterdam), 1709, iii. 367 *ff. Mémoires de la Ligue, contenant les événemens les plus remarquables depuis 1576 jusqu'à la paix accordée entre le roi de France et le roi d'Espagne en 1598* (Amsterdam, 1758); Pierre de l'Estoile, *Journal de Henri III.* (Paris, 1875–84), and *Journal du règne de Henri IV.* (The Hague, 1741); Robiquet, *Paris et la Ligue* (Paris, 1886); Victor de Chalambert, *Histoire de la Ligue* (Paris, 1854); Maury, "La Commune de Paris de 1588" (in *Rev. des Deux Mondes,* Sept. 1, 1871).

emissaries were sent to the large towns of France, and secret societies on the plan of the one in Paris were formed and affiliated with the mother-society in Paris, all bound to execute the orders of the secret council of the capital. The Sieur de la Rocheblond, whose brain had planned the whole organisation, was the medium of communication with the Romanist Princes; and through him Henry, Duke of Guise, le Balafré as he was called from a scar on his face, was placed in command of this new and formidable instrument, to be wielded as he thought best for the extirpation of the Protestantism of France.

The King had published an edict forbidding all armed assemblies, and this furnished the Leaguers with a pretext for sending forth their manifesto : *Déclaration des causes qui ont meu Monseigneur le Cardinal de Bourbon et les Pairs, Princes, Seigneurs, villes et communautez catholiques de ce royaume de France : De s'opposer à ceux qui par tous moyens s'efforcent de subvertir la religion catholique et l'Estat (30 Mars 1585).* It was a skilfully drafted document, setting forth the danger to religion in the foreground, but touching on all the evils and jealousies which had arisen from the favouritism of Henry III. Guise at once began to enrol troops and commence open hostilities ; and almost all the great towns of France and most of the provinces in the North and in the Centre declared for the League.

Henry III. was greatly alarmed. With the help of his mother he negotiated a treaty with the Leaguers, in which he promised to revoke all the earlier Edicts of Toleration, to prohibit the exercise of Protestant public worship throughout the kingdom, to banish the ministers, and to give all Protestants the choice between becoming Roman Catholics or leaving the realm within six months (Treaty of Nemours, July 7th, 1585). These terms were embodied in an edict dated July 18th, 1585. The Pope, Sixtus V., thereupon published a Bull, which declared that the King of Navarre and the Prince of Condé, being heretics, were incapable of succeeding to the throne of France, deprived them of their estates, and absolved all their vassals from allegiance. The King of Navarre replied to "Monsieur Sixtus, self-styled Pope, saving His Holiness," and promised to avenge the insult done to himself and to the *Parlements* of France.

"The war of the three Henrys," from Henry III., Henry of Guise, and Henry of Navarre, began in the later months of 1585. It was in some respects a triangular fight; for although the King and the Guises were both ostensibly combating the Huguenots, the Leaguers, headed by Guises, and the Loyalists, were by no means whole-hearted allies. It began unfavourably for the Protestants, but as it progressed the skilful generalship of the King of Navarre became more and more apparent—at Coutras (Oct. 20th, 1587) he almost annihilated the royalist army. The King made several ineffectual attempts to win the Protestant leader to his side. Navarre would never consent to abjure his faith, and Henry III. made that an absolute condition.

While the war was going on in the west and centre of France, the League was strengthening its organisation and perfecting its plans. It had become more and more hostile to Henry III., and had become a secret revolutionary society. It drafted a complete programme for the immediate future. The cities and districts of France which felt themselves specially threatened by the Huguenots were to beseech the King to raise levies for their protection. If he refused or procrastinated, they were to raise the troops themselves, to be commanded by officers in whom the League had confidence. They could then compel the King to place himself at the head of this army of the Leaguers, or show himself to be their open enemy by refusing. If the King died childless, the partisans of the League were to gather at Orléans and Paris, and were there to elect the Cardinal de Bourbon as the King of France. The Pope and the King of Spain were to be at once informed, when it had been arranged

14**

that His Holiness would send his benediction, and that His
Majesty would assist them with troops and supplies. A
new form of oath was imposed on all the associates of the
League. They were to swear allegiance to the King
so long as he should show himself to be a good Catholic
and refrained from favouring heretics. These instructions
were sent down from the mother-society in Paris to the
provinces, and the affiliated societies were recommended to
keep in constant communication with Paris. Madame de
Montpensier, sister to the Guises, at the same time
directed the work of a band of preachers whose business
it was to inflame the minds of the people in the capital
and the provinces against the King and the Huguenots.
She boasted that she did more work for the cause than
her brothers were doing by the sword.

The Guises, with this force behind them, tried to
force the King to make new concessions—to publish the
decisions of the Council of Trent in France (a thing that
had not been done); to establish the Inquisition in
France; to order the execution of all Huguenot prisoners
who would not promise to abjure their religion; and to
remove from the armies all officers of whom the League
did not approve. The mother-society in Paris prepared
for his refusal by organising a secret revolutionary government for the city. It was called "The Sixteen," being
one for each of the sixteen sections of Paris. This
government was under the orders of Guise, who communicated with them through an agent of his called
Mayneville. Plot after plot was made to get possession
of the King's person; and but for the activity and information of Nicholas Poulain, an officer of police who managed
to secure private information, they would have been
successful.

§ 18. *The Day of Barricades.*[1]

The King redoubled his guards, and ordered four thousand Swiss troops which he had stationed at Lagny into the suburbs of Paris. The Parisian Leaguers in alarm sent for the Duke of Guise; and Guise, in spite of a prohibitive order from the King, entered the city. When he was recognised he was received with acclamations by the Parisian crowd. The Queen-Mother induced the King to receive him, which he did rather ungraciously. Officers and men devoted to the League crowded into Paris. The King, having tried in vain to prevent the entry of all suspected persons, at last ordered the Swiss into Paris (May 12th, 1588). The citizens flew to arms, and converted Paris into a stronghold. It was " the day of Barricades." Chains were stretched across the streets, and behind them were piled beams, benches, carts, great barrels filled with stones or gravel. Houses were loopholed and windows protected. Behind these defences men were stationed with arquebuses; and the women and children were provided with heaps of stones. Guise had remained in his house, but his officers were to be seen moving through the crowds and directing the defence. The Swiss troops found themselves caught in a trap, and helpless. Henry III. was compelled to ask Guise to interfere in order to save his soldiers. The King had to undergo further humiliation. The citizens proposed to attack the Louvre and seize the King's person. Guise had to be appealed to again. He had an interview with the King on the 13th, at which Henry III. was forced to agree to all the demands of the League, and to leave the conduct of the war against the Huguenots in the hands of the leader of the League. After the interview the King was able to escape secretly from Paris.

The day of the " Barricades " had proved to Henry III. that the League was master in his capital. The meeting

[1] The scenes on the Day of the Barricades are described in a contemporary paper printed in *Satyre Menippée* (ed. of 1709), iii. 39 *ff.*

of the States General at Blois (Oct. 1588) was to show him
that the country had also turned against him.

The elections had been looked after by the Guises, and
had taken place while the impression produced by the
revolt of Paris was at its height.   The League commanded
an immense majority in all the three Estates.   The
business before them was grave.   The finances of the
kingdom were in disorder; favouritism had not been got
rid of; and no one could trust the King's word.   Above
all, the religious question was embittering every mind.
The Estates met under the influence of a religious
exaltation fanned by the priests.   On the 9th of Oct.
representatives of the three Estates went to Mass together.
During the communion the assistant clergy chanted the
well-known hymns,—*Pange lingua gloriosi, O salutaris Hostia,
Ave verum Corpus natum,*—and the excitement was immense.
The members of the Estates had never been so united.

Yet the King had a moment of unwonted courage.
He had resolved to denounce the League as the source
of the disorders in the kingdom.   He declared that he
would not allow a League to exist within the realm.   He
only succeeded in making the leaders furious.   His bravado
soon ceased.   The Cardinal de Bourbon compelled him to
omit from the published version of his speech the objectionable expressions.   The Estates forced him to swear that he
would not permit any religion within the kingdom but the
Roman.   This done, he was received with cries of *Vive le
Roi*, and was accompanied to his house with acclamations.
But he was compelled to see the Duke of Guise receive the
office of Lieutenant-General, which placed the army under
his command; and he felt that he would never be " master
in his own house " until that man had been removed from
his path.

The news of the completeness of the destruction of the
Armada had been filtering through France; the fear of
Spain was to some extent removed, and England might help
the King if he persisted in a policy of tolerating his Protestant subjects.   It is probable that he confided his project

of getting rid of Guise to some of his more intimate councillors, and that they assured him that it would be impossible to remove such a powerful subject by legal means.
The Duke and his brother the Cardinal of Guise were
summoned to a meeting of the Council. They had scarcely
taken their seats when they were asked to see the King in
his private apartments. There Guise was assassinated,
and the Cardinal arrested, and slain the next day.[1] The
Cardinal de Bourbon and the young Prince de Joinville
(now Duke of Guise by his father's death) were arrested
and imprisoned. Orders were given to arrest the Duchess
of Nemours (Guise's mother), the Duke and Duchess of
Elbœuf, the Count de Brissac, and other prominent
Leaguers. The King's guards invaded the sittings of the
States General to carry out these orders. The bodies of
the two Guises were burnt, and the ashes thrown into the
Loire.

The news of the assassination raised the wildest rage in
Paris. The League proclaimed itself a revolutionary society.
The city organised itself in its sections. A council was
appointed for each section to strengthen the hands of the
" Sixteen." Preachers caused their audiences to swear that
they would spend the last farthing in their purses and the
last drop of blood in their bodies to avenge the slaughtered
princes. The Sorbonne in solemn conclave declared that
the actions of Henry III. had absolved his subjects from their
allegiance. The " Sixteen " drove from *Parlement* all suspected persons; and, thus purged, the *Parlement* of Paris
ranged itself on the side of the revolution. The Duke of
Mayenne, the sole surviving brother of Henry of Guise, was
summoned to Paris. An assembly of the citizens of the
capital elected a *Council General of the Union of Catholics*
to manage the affairs of the State and to confer with all
the Catholic towns and provinces of France. Deputies sent
by these towns and provinces were to be members of the
Council. The Duke of Mayenne was appointed by the

---

[1] Brown, "The Assassination of the Guises as described by the Venetian
Ambassador" (*Eng. Hist. Review*, x. 304).

Council the *Lieutenant-General of the State and Crown of France.* The new Government had its seal—*the Seal of the Kingdom of France.* The larger number of the great towns of France adhered to this provisional and revolutionary Government.

In the midst of these tumults Catherine de' Medici died (Jan. 5th, 1589).

§ 19. *The King takes refuge with the Huguenots.*

The miserable King had no resource left but to throw himself upon the protection of the Protestants. He hesitated at first, fearing threatened papal excommunication. Henry of Navarre's bearing during these months of anxiety had been admirable. After the meeting of the States General at Blois, he had issued a stirring appeal to the nation, pleading for peace—the one thing needed for the distracted and fevered country. He now assured the King of his loyalty, and promised that he would never deny to Roman Catholics that liberty of conscience and worship which he claimed. A treaty was arranged, and the King of Navarre went to meet Henry III. at Tours. He arrived just in time. Mayenne at the head of an avenging army of Leaguers had started as soon as the provisional government had been established in Paris. He had taken by assault a suburb of the town, and was about to attack the city of Tours itself, when he found the Protestant vanguard guarding the bridge over the Loire, and had to retreat. He was slowly forced back towards Paris. The battle of Senlis, in which a much smaller force of Huguenots routed the Duke d'Aumale, who had been reinforced by the Parisian militia, opened the way to Paris. The King of Navarre pressed on. Town after town was taken, and the forces of the two kings, increased by fourteen thousand Swiss and Germans, were soon able to seize the bridge of St. Cloud and invest the capital on the south and west (July 29th, 1589). An assault was fixed for Aug. 2nd.

Since the murder of the Guises, Paris had been a caldron

of seething excitement. The whole population, " *avec dou-leur et gemissements bien grands*," had assisted at the funeral service for " the Martyrs," and the baptism of the posthumous son of the slaughtered Duke had been a civic ceremony. The Bull " monitory" of Pope Sixtus v., posted up in Rome on May 24th, which directed Henry III. on pain of excommunication to release the imprisoned prelates within ten days, and to appear either personally or by proxy within sixty days before the Curia to answer for the murder of a Prince of the Church, had fanned the excitement. Almost every day the Parisians saw processions of students, of women, of children, defiling through their streets. They marched from shrine to shrine, with naked feet, clad only in their shirts, defying the cold of winter. Parishioners dragged their priests out of bed to head nocturnal processions. The hatred of Henry III. became almost a madness. The Cordeliers decapitated his portraits. Parish priests made images of the King in wax, placed them on their altars, and practised on them magical incantations, in the hope of doing deadly harm to the living man. Bands of children carried lighted candles, which they extinguished to cries of, " *God extinguish thus the race of the Valois.*"

Among the most excited members of this fevered throng was a young Jacobin monk, Jacques Clément, by birth a peasant, of scanty intelligence, and rough, violent manners. His excitement grew with the perils of the city. He consulted a theologian in whom he had confidence, and got from him a guarded answer that it might be lawful to slay a tyrant. He prayed, fasted, went through a course of maceration of the body. He saw visions. He believed that he heard voices, and that he received definite orders to give his life in order to slay the King. He confided his purpose to friends, who approved of it and helped his preparations. He was able to leave the city, to pass through the beleaguering lines, and to get private audience of the King. He presented a letter, and while Henry was reading it stabbed him in the lower part of the body. The deed done, the monk raised himself to his full height, extended his arms to form himself into a crucifix, and received without flinching his deathblow from La Guesle and other attendants (Aug. 1st, 1589).[1]

The King lingered until the following morning, and then expired, commending Henry of Navarre to his companions as his legitimate successor.

The news of the assassination was received in Paris with wild delight. The Duchess de Nemours, the mother of the Guises, and the Duchess de Montpensier, their sister, went everywhere in the streets describing " the heroic act of Jacques Clément." The former mounted the steps of the High Altar in the church of the Cordeliers to proclaim the news to the people. The citizens, high and low, brought out their tables into the streets, and they drank, sang, shouted and danced in honour of the news. They swore that they would never accept a Protestant king [2] and the Cardinal de Bourbon, still a prisoner, was proclaimed as Charles x.

At Tours, on the other hand, the fact that the heir to the throne was a Protestant, threw the Roman Catholic nobles into a state of perplexity. They had no sympathy with the League, but many felt that they could not serve a Protestant king. They pressed round the new King, beseeching him to abjure his faith at once. Henry refused to do what would humiliate himself, and could not be accepted as an act of sincerity. On the other hand, the

---

[1] *Histoire de France depuis les origines jusqu'à la Revolution* (Paris, 1904), vi. i. 298 *f.*, by H. Mariéjol.

[2] They argued : "Je vous demande, voudriez-vous bailler une fille pudique, honneste, belle, verteuse et modeste, à un homme desbauché, et abandonné à tous vices, sous ombre qu'il vous diroit qu'il s'amenderoit, et qu'il n'y retournoit estant marié, que vous luy osteriez vostre fille ? Je crois que tout bon pere de famille ne se mettroit en ce hazard, ou feroit un tour d'homme sans cervelle. Or c'est l'Eglise Catholique, Apostolique et Romaine qui est une pucelle, belle et honneste en cette France qui n'a jamais eu pour Roy un hérétique, mais tous bons Catholiques et assidez à Jesus-Christ son espoux. Voudriez-vous donc bailler cette Eglise que les François ont tant fidélement servie et honourée sous leur Rois Catholiques, aujourd'huy la prostituer entre les mains d'un hérétique, relaps et excommunie !"—"Dialogue d'entre le Maheustre et le Manant" (*Satyre Menippée*, iii. 887).

nobles of Champagne, Picardy, and the Isle of France sent assurances of allegiance ; the Duke of Montpensier, the husband of the Leaguer Duchess, promised his support ; and the Swiss mercenaries declared that they would serve for two months without pay.

§ 20. *The Declaration of Henry IV.*[1]

Thus encouraged, Henry published his famous declaration (Aug. 4th, 1589). He promised that the Roman Catholic would remain the religion of the realm, and that he would attempt no innovations. He declared that he was willing to be instructed in its tenets, and that within six months, if it were possible, he would summon a National Council. The Roman Catholics would be retained in their governments and charges ; the Protestants would keep the strongholds which were at present in their hands ; but all fortified places when reduced would be entrusted to Roman Catholics and none other. This declaration was signed by two Princes of the Blood, the Prince of Conti and the Duke of Montpensier ; by three Dukes and Peers, Longueville, Luxembourg-Piney, and Rohan-Montbazon ; by two Marshals of France, Biron and d'Aumont ; and by several great officers. Notwithstanding, the defections were serious ; all the *Parlements* save that of Bordeaux thundered against the heretic King ; all the great towns save Tours, Bordeaux, Châlons, Langres, Compiègne, and Clermont declared for the League. The greater part of the kingdom

---

[1] SOURCES : *Recueil des Lettres Missives de Henri IV.* (*Collection de Documents inédits*, Paris, 1843–72), 8 vois. ; Alberi, *Relazioni degli Ambasciatori Veneti* (Florence, 1860, etc.) ; Charles, Duc de Mayenne, *Correspondance*, 2 vols. (Paris, 1860) ; Sir H. Upton, *Correspondence* (*Roxburgh Club*, London, 1847); Du Plessis-Mornay, *Mémoires*, 4 vols. (Amsterdam, 1624–52) ; Madame Du Plessis-Mornay, *Mémoires sur la Vie de Du Plessis-Mornay* (Paris, 1868–69, *Soc. Hist. de France*) ; Maréchal de Bassompierre, *Journal de ma vie 1579–1640*, 4 vols. (Paris, 1870–77, *Soc. Hist. de France*) ; *Satire Menipp'e*, 3 vols. (Ratisbon (Amsterdam), 1709) ; Bénoit, *Histoire de l'édit de Nantes.*

LATER BOOKS : Baird, *The Huguenots and Henry of Navarre* (London, 1887) ; Jackson, *The First of the Bourbons*, 2 vols. (London, 1890) ; Lavisse, *Histoire de France*, VI. i. ii. (Paris, 1904–5).

was in revolt. The royalist troops dwindled away. It was hopeless to think of attacking Paris, and Henry IV. marched for Normandy with scarcely seven thousand men. He wished to be on the sea coast in hope of succour from England.

The Duke of Mayenne followed him with an arm; of thirty thousand men. He had promised to the Parisians to throw the "Bearnese" into the sea, or to bring him in chains to Paris. But it was not so easy to catch the "Bearnese." In the series of marches, countermarches, and skirmishes which is known as the battle of Arques, the advantage was on the side of the King; and when Mayenne attempted to take Dieppe by assault, he was badly defeated (Sept. 24th, 1589). Then followed marches and countermarches; the King now threatening Paris and then retreating, until at last the royalist troops and the Leaguers met at Ivry. The King had two thousand cavalry and eight thousand infantry to meet eight thousand cavalry and twelve thousand infantry (including seventeen hundred Spanish troops sent by the Duke of Parma) under the command of Mayenne. The battle resulted in a surprising and decisive victory for the King. Mayenne and his cousin d'Aumale escaped only by the swiftness of their horses (March 14th, 1590).

It is needless to say much about the war or about the schemes of parties. Henry invested Paris, and had almost starved it into surrender, when it was revictualled by an army led from the Low Countries by the Duke of Parma. Henry took town after town, and gradually isolated the capital. In 1590 (May 10th) the old Cardinal Bourbon (Charles X.) died, and the Leaguers lost even the semblance of a legitimate king. The more fanatical members of the party, represented by the "Sixteen" of Paris, would have been content to place France under the dominion of Spain rather than see a heretic king. The Duke of Mayenne had long cherished dreams that the crown might come to him. But the great mass of the influential people of France who had not yet professed allegiance to Henry IV.

(and many who had) had an almost equal dread of Spanish domination and of a heretic ruler.

§ 21. *Henry IV. becomes a Roman Catholic.*

Henry at last resolved to conform to the Roman Catholic religion as the only means of giving peace to his distracted kingdom.   He informed the loyalist Archbishop of Bourges of his intention to be instructed in the Roman Catholic religion with a view to conversion.   The Archbishop was able to announce this at the conference of Suresnes, and the news spread instantly over France.   With his usual tact, Henry wrote with his own hand to several of the parish priests of Paris announcing his intention, and invited them to meet him at Mantes to give him instruction.   At least one of them had been a furious Leaguer, and was won to be an enthusiastic loyalist.

The ceremony of the reception of Henry IV. into the Roman Catholic Church took place at Saint Denis, about four and a half miles to the north of Paris.   The scene had all the appearance of some popular festival.   The ancient church in which the Kings of France had for generations been buried, in which Jeanne d'Arc had hung up her arms, was decked with splendid tapestries, and the streets leading to it festooned with flowers.   Multitudes of citizens had come from rebel Paris to swell the throng and to shout *Vive le Roi !* as Henry, escorted by a brilliant procession of nobles and guards, passed slowly to the church.   The clergy, headed by the Archbishop of Bourges, met him at the door.   The King dismounted, knelt, swore to live and die in the catholic apostolic and Roman religion, and renounced all the heresies which it condemned.   The Archbishop gave him absolution, took him by the hand and led him into the church.   There, kneeling before the High Altar, the King repeated his oath, confessed, and communicated.   France had now a Roman Catholic as well as a legitimate King.   Even if it be admitted that Henry IV. was not a man of any depth of religious feeling, the act of abjuration must have been a humiliation for the son of Jeanne d'Albret. He never was a man who wore his heart on his sleeve, and his well-known saying, that "Paris was well worth a Mass," had as much bitterness in it as gaiety. He had paled with suppressed passion at Tours (1589) when the Roman Catholic nobles had urged him to become a Romanist. Had the success which followed his arms up to the battle of Ivry continued unbroken, it is probable that the ceremony at Saint Denis would never have taken place. But Parma's invasion of France, which compelled the King to raise the siege of Paris, was the beginning of difficulties which seemed insurmountable. The dissensions of parties within the realm, and the presence of foreigners on the soil of France (Walloon, Spanish, Neapolitan, and Savoyard), were bringing France to the verge of dissolution. Henry believed that there was only one way to end the strife, and he sacrificed his convictions to his patriotism.

With Henry's change of religion the condition of things changed as if by magic. The League seemed to dissolve. Tenders of allegiance poured in from all sides, from nobles, provinces, and towns. Rheims was still in possession of the Guises, and the anointing and crowning took place at Chartres (Feb. 27th, 1594). The manifestations of loyalty increased.

On the evening of the day on which Henry had been received into the Roman Catholic Church at Saint Denis, he had recklessly ridden up to the crest of the height of Montmartre and looked down on Paris, which was still in the hands of the League. The feelings of the Parisians were also changing. The League was seamed with dissensions; Mayenne had quarrelled with the "Sixteen," and the partisans of these fanatics of the League had street brawls with the citizens of more moderate opinions. *Parlement* took courage and denounced the presence of Spanish soldiers within the capital. The loyalists opened the way for the royal troops, Henry entered Paris (March 22nd), and marched to Notre Dame, where the clergy chanted the *Te Deum*. From the cathedral he rode to the Loûvre through streets thronged with people, who pressed up to his very stirrups to see their King, and made the tall houses re-echo with their loyalist shoutings. Such a royal entry had not been seen for generations, and took everyone by surprise. Next day the foreign troops left the city. The King watched their departure from an open window in the Louvre, and as their chiefs passed he called out gaily, " My compliments to your Master. You need not come back."

With the return of Paris to fealty, almost all signs of disaffection departed; and the King's proclamation of amnesty for all past rebellions completed the conquest of his people. France was again united after thirty years of civil war.

§ 22. *The Edict of Nantes*

The union of all Frenchmen to accept **Henry IV.** as their King had not changed the legal position of the Protestants. The laws against them were still in force; they had nothing but the King's word promising protection to trust to. The war with Spain delayed matters, but when peace was made the time came for Henry to fulfil his pledges to his former companions. They had been chafing under the delay. At a General Assembly held at Mantes (October 1593–January 1594), the members had renewed their oath to live and to die true to their confession of faith, and year by year a General Assembly met to discuss their political disabilities as well as to conduct their ecclesiastical business. They had divided France into nine divisions under provincial synods, and had the appearance to men of that century of a kingdom within a kingdom. They demanded equal civic rights with their Roman Catholic fellow-subjects, and guarantees for their protection. At length, in 1597, four delegates were appointed with full powers to confer with the King. Out of these negotiations came the Edict of Nantes, the Charter of French Protestantism.

This celebrated edict was drawn up in ninety-five more general articles, which were signed on April 13th, and in fifty-six more particular articles which were signed on May 2nd (1598). Two *Brevets*, dated 13th and 30th of April, were added, dealing with the treatment of Protestant ministers, and with the strongholds given to the Protestants. The Articles were verified and registered by *Parlements*; the *Brevets* were guaranteed simply by the King's word.

The Edict of Nantes codified and enlarged the rights given to the Protestants of France by the Edict of Poitiers (1577), the Convention of Nérac (1578), the treaty of Fleix (1580), the Declaration of Saint-Cloud (1589), the Edict of Mantes (1591), the Articles of Mantes (1593), and the Edict of Saint-Germain (1594).

It secured complete liberty of conscience everywhere within the realm, to the extent that no one was to be persecuted or molested in any way because of his religion, nor be compelled to do anything contrary to its tenets; and this carried with it the right of private or secret worship. The full and free right of public worship was granted in all places in which it existed during the years 1596 and 1597, or where it had been granted by the Edict of Poitiers interpreted by the Convention of Nérac and the treaty of Fleix (some two hundred towns); and, in addition, in two places within every *bailliage* and *sénéchaussée* in the realm. It was also permitted in the principal castles of Protestant *seigneurs hauts justiciers* (some three thousand), whether the proprietor was in residence or not, and in their other castles, the proprietor being in residence; to nobles who were not *hauts justiciers*, provided the audience did not consist of more than thirty persons over and above relations of the family. Even at the Court the high officers of the Crown, the great nobles, all governors and lieutenants-general, and captains of the guards, had the liberty of worship in their apartments provided the doors were kept shut and there was no loud singing of psalms, noise, or open scandal.

Protestants were granted full civil rights and protection, entry into all universities, schools, and hospitals, and admission to all public offices. The *Parlement* of Paris admitted six Protestant councillors. And Protestant ministers were granted the exemptions from military service and such charges as the Romanist clergy enjoyed. Special Chambers (*Chambres d'Édit*) were established in the *Parlements* to try cases in which Protestants were interested. In the *Parlement* of Paris this Chamber consisted of six specially chosen Roman Catholics and one Protestant; in other *Parlements*, the Chambers were composed of equal numbers of Romanists and Protestants (*mi-parties*). The Protestants were permitted to hold their ecclesiastical assemblies—consistories, colloquies, and synods, national and provincial; they were even allowed to meet to discuss political questions, provided they first secured the permission of the King.

They remained in complete control of two hundred towns, including La Rochelle, Montauban, and Montpellier, strongholds of exceptional strength. They were to retain these places until 1607, but the right was prolonged for five years more. The State paid the expenses of the troops which garrisoned these Protestant fortified places; it paid the governors, who were always Protestants. When it is remembered that the royal army in time of peace did not exceed ten thousand men, and that the Huguenots could raise twenty-five thousand troops, it will be seen that Henry IV. did his utmost to provide guarantees against a return to a reign of intolerance.

Protected in this way, the Huguenot Church of France speedily took a foremost place among the Protestant Churches of Europe. Theological colleges were established at Sedan, Montauban, and Saumur. Learning and piety flourished, and French theology was always a counterpoise to the narrow Reformed Scholastic of Switzerland and of Holland.

CHAPTER V.

THE REFORMATION IN THE NETHERLANDS.[1]

§ 1. *The Political Situation.*

IT was not until **1581** that the *United Provinces* took rank as a Protestant nation, notwithstanding the fact that the Netherlands furnished the first martyrs of the Reformation in the persons of Henry Voes and John Esch, Augustinian monks, who were burnt at Antwerp (July 31st, 1523).

' As they were led to the stake they cried with a loud voice that they were Christians ; and when they were fastened to it, and the fire was kindled, they rehearsed the twelve articles of the Creed, and after that the hymn *Te Deum laudamus,* which each of them sang verse by verse alternately until the flames deprived them both of voice and life." [2]

[1] SOURCES : Brandt, *The History of the Reformation and other ecclesiastical transactions in and about the Low-Countries* (English translation in 4 vols. fol., London, 1720 : the original in Dutch was published in 1671) ; Brieger, *Aleander und Luther* (Gotha, 1894) ; Kalkoff, *Die Despatchen des nuntius Aleander* (Halle, 1897) ; Poullet Piot, *Correspondance du Cardinal Granvelle,* 12 vols. (Brussels, 1878–97) ; Weiss, *Papiers d'État du Cardinal Granvelle,* 9 vols. (Paris, 1841–52) ; Gachard, *Correspondance de Philippe II. sur les affaires des Pays Bas,* 5 vols. (Brussels, 1848–79) ; *Correspondance de Marguerite d'Autriche avec Philippe II., 1554–68* (Brussels, 1867–87) ; *Correspondance de Guillaume le Taciturne, Prince d'Orange,* 6 vols. (Brussels, 1847–57) ; van Prinsterer, *Archives ou correspondance inédite de la Maison d'Orange-Nassau,* in two series, 9 and 5 vols. (Utrecht, 1841–61) ; Renon de France, *Histoire des troubles des Pays-Bas,* 3 vols. (Brussels, 1886–92) ; *Mémoires anonymes sur les troubles des Pays-Bas, 1565–80* (in the *Collection des Mémoires sur l'histoire de Belgique*).

LATER BOOKS : Armstrong, *Charles V.* (London, 1902) ; Motley, *The Rise of the Dutch Republic* (London, 1865) ; Putnam, *William the Silent* (New York, 1895) ; Harrison, *William the Silent* (London, 1897) ; *Cambridge Modern History,* III. vi. vii. (Cambridge, 1904).

[2] Brandt, *The History of the Reformation,* etc. i. **49 ; cf.** *Journal d'un Bourgeois de Paris,* p. 185.

The struggle for religious liberty, combined latterly
with one for national independence from Spain, lasted
therefore for almost sixty years.

When the lifelong duel between Charles the Bold of
Burgundy and Louis XI. of France ended with the death
of the former on the battlefield under the walls of Nancy
(January 4th, 1477), Louis was able to annex to France a
large portion of the heterogeneous possessions of the Dukes
of Burgundy, and Mary of Burgundy carried the remainder
as her marriage portion (May 1477) to Maximilian of
Austria, the future Emperor. Speaking roughly, and not
quite accurately, those portions of the Burgundian lands
which had been *fiefs* of France went to Louis, while Mary
and Maximilian retained those which were *fiefs* of the
Empire. The son of Maximilian and Mary, Philip the
Handsome, married Juana (August 1496), the second
daughter and ultimate heiress of Isabella and Ferdinand
of Spain, and their son was Charles V., Emperor of Germany
(b. February 24th, 1500), who inherited the Netherlands
from his father and Spain from his mother, and thus
linked the Netherlands to Spain. Philip died in 1506,
leaving Charles, a boy of six years of age, the ruler of the
Netherlands. His paternal aunt, Margaret, the daughter
of the Emperor Maximilian, governed in the Netherlands
during his minority, and, owing to Juana's illness (an
illness ending in madness), mothered her brother's
children. Margaret's regency ended in 1515, and the
earlier history of the Reformation in the Netherlands
belongs either to the period of the personal rule of Charles
or to that of the Regents whom he appointed to act for
him.

The land, a delta of great rivers liable to overflow
their banks, or a coast-line on which the sea made continual encroachment, produced a people hardy, strenuous,
and independent. Their struggles with nature had braced
their faculties. Municipal life had struck its roots deeply
into the soil of the Netherlands, and its cities could vie
with those of Italy in industry and intelligence. The

15**

southern provinces were the home of the Trouvères.[1] Jan
van-Ruysbroec, the most heart-searching of speculative
Mystics, had been a curate of St. Gudule's in Brussels.
His pupil, Gerard Groot, had founded the lay-community
of the Brethren of the Common Lot for the purpose of
spreading Christian education among the laity ; and the
schools and convents of the Brethren had spread through
the Netherlands and central Germany. Thomas à Kempis,
the author of the *Imitatio Christi*, had lived most of his
long life of ninety years in a small convent at Zwolle,
within the territories of Utrecht. Men who have been
called " Reformers before the Reformation," John Pupper
of Goch and John Wessel, both belonged to the Netherlands. Art flourished there in the fifteenth century in the
persons of Hubert and Jan van Eyck and of Hans Memling.
The Chambers of Oratory (*Rederijkers*) to begin with
probably unions for the performance of miracle plays or
moralities, became confraternities not unlike the societies
of *meistersänger* in Germany, and gradually acquired the
character of literary associations, which diffused not merely
culture, but also habits of independent thinking among the
people.

Intellectual life had become less exuberant in the end
of the fifteenth century ; but the Netherlands, nevertheless,
produced Alexander Hegius, the greatest educational
reformer of his time, and Erasmus the prince of the
Humanists. Nor can the influence of the Chambers of
Oratory have died out, for they had a great effect on
the Reformation movement.[2]

When Charles assumed the government of the
Netherlands, he found himself at the head of a group
of duchies, lordships, counties, and municipalities which
had little appearance of a compact principality, and he
applied himself, like other princes of his time in the same

---

[1] A collection of their *chansons d'amour, jeux-partis, pastourelles,* and
fabliaux will be found in Scheler's *Trouvères Belges* (Bruxelles, 1876).

[2] *Correspondance de Philippe II. sur les affaires des Pays-Bas,* i. 321, 327,
379 ; *Correspondance de Guillaume le Taciturne,* ii. 161, 168.

situation, to give them a unity both political and territorial. He was so successful that he was able to hand over to his son, Philip II. of Spain, an almost thoroughly organised State. The divisions which Charles largely overcame reappeared to some extent in the revolt against Philip and Romanism, and therefore in a measure concern the history of the Reformation. How Charles made his scattered Netherland inheritance territorially compact need not be told in detail. Friesland was secured (1515); the acquisition of temporal sovereignty over the ecclesiastical province of Utrecht (1527) united Holland with Friesland ; Gronningen and the lands ruled by that turbulent city placed themselves under the government of Charles (1536) ; and the death of Charles of Egmont (1538), Count of Gueldres, completed the unification of the northern and central districts. The vague hold which France kept in some of the southern portions of the country was gradually loosened. Charles failed in the south-east. The inde· pendent principality of Lorraine lay between Luxemburg and Franche-Comté, and the Netherland Government could not seize it by purchase, treaty, or conquest. One and the same system of law regulated the rights and the duties of the whole population ; and all the provinces were united into one principality by the reorganisation of a States General, which met almost annually, and which had a real if vaguely defined power to regulate the taxation of the country.

But although political and geographical difficulties might be more or less overcome, others remained which were not so easily disposed of. One set arose from the fact that the seventeen provinces were divided by race and by language. The Dutchmen in the north were different in interests and in sentiment from the Flemings in the centre ; and both had little in common with the French-speaking provinces in the south. The other was due to the differing boundaries of the ecclesiastical and civil jurisdictions. When Charles began to rule in 1515, the only territorial see was Arras. Tournai, Utrecht, and Cambrai became territorial before the abdication of Charles. But the confusion between civil and ecclesiastical jurisdiction may be seen at a glance when it is remembered that a great part of the Frisian lands were subject to the German Sees of Münster, Minden, Paderborn, and Osnabrück; and that no less than six bishops, none of them belonging to the Netherlands, divided the ecclesiastical rule over Luxemburg. Charles' proposals to establish six new bishoprics, plans invariably thwarted by the Roman Curia, were meant to give the Low Countries a national episcopate.

§ 2. *The beginnings of the Reformation*

The people of the Netherlands had been singularly prepared for the great religious revival of the sixteenth century by the work of the *Brethren of the Common Lot* and their schools. It was the aim of Gerard Groot, their founder, and also of Florentius Radevynszoon, his great educational assistant, to see "that the root of study and the mirror of life must, in the first place, be the Gospel of Christ." Their pupils were taught to read the Bible in Latin, and the Brethren contended publicly for translations of the Scriptures in the vulgar tongues. There is evidence to show that the Vulgate was well known in the Netherlands in the end of the fifteenth century, and a translation of the Bible into Dutch was published at Delft in 1477[1]. Small tracts against Indulgences, founded probably on the reasonings of Pupper and Wessel, had been in circulation before Luther had nailed his *Theses* to the door of All Saints' church in Wittenberg. Hendrik of Zutphen, Prior of the Augustinian Eremite convent at Antwerp, had been a pupil of Staupitz, a fellow student with Luther, and had spread Evangelical teaching not only among his order, but throughout the town.[2] It need be no matter

---

[1] Van der Meersch, *Recherches sur la vie et les travaux des imprimeurs belges et hollandais*, pp. 142–144; cf. Walther, *Die deutsche Bibelübersetzungen des Mittelalters*, p. 652.

[2] Aleander, writing to the Cardinal de' Medici (Sept. 8th, 1520),

for surprise, then, that Luther's writings were widely circulated in the Netherlands, and that between 1513 and 1531 no fewer than twenty-five translations of the Bible or of the New Testament had appeared in Dutch, Flemish, and French.

When Aleander was in the Netherlands, before attending the Diet of Worms he secured the burning of eighty Lutheran and other books at Louvain;[1] and when he came back ten months later, he had regular literary *auto-da-fés*. On Charles' return from the Diet of Worms, he issued a proclamation to all his subjects in the Netherlands against Luther, his books and his followers, and Aleander made full use of the powers it gave. Four hundred Lutheran books were burnt at Antwerp, three hundred of them seized by the police in the stalls of the booksellers, and one hundred handed over by the owners; three hundred were burnt at Ghent, " part of them printed here and part in Germany," says the Legate; and he adds that " many of them were very well bound, and one gorgeously in velvet." About a month later he is forced to confess that these burnings had not made as much impression as he had hoped, and that he wishes the Emperor would " burn alive half a dozen Lutherans and confiscate their property." Such a proceeding would make all see him to be the really Christian prince that he is.[2]

Next year (1522) Charles established the Inquisition within the seventeen provinces. It was a distinctively civil institution, and this was perhaps due to the fact that there was little correspondence between the civil and ecclesiastical jurisdictions in the Netherlands; but it must not be forgotten that the Kings of Spain had used the Holy Office for the purpose of stamping out political

attributes the spread of Lutheranism in the Netherlands to the teaching of Erasmus and of the Prior of the Augustinians at Antwerp.—Brieger, *Aleander und Luther, 1521 ; Die vervollständigten Aleander-Depeschen* (Gotha, 1884), p. 249.

[1] Kalkoff, *Die Depeschen des nuntius Aleander* (Halle a S. 1897), p. 20.

[2] Brieger, *Aleander und Luther ; Die vervollständigten Aleander Depeschen*, pp. 249, 252, 262.

and local opposition, and also that the civil courts were usually more energetic and more severe than the ecclesiastical. The man appointed was unworthy of any place of important trust. Francis van de Hulst, although he had been the Prince's counsellor in Brabant, was a man accused both of bigamy and murder, and was hopelessly devoid of tact. He quarrelled violently with the High Court of Holland; and the Regent, Margaret of Austria, who had resumed her functions, found herself constantly compromised by his continual defiance of local privileges. He was a "wonderful enemy to learning," says Erasmus. His colleague, Nicolas van Egmont, a Carmelite monk, is described by the same scholar as "a madman with a sword put into his hand who hates me worse than he does Luther." The two men discredited the Inquisition from its beginning. Erasmus affected to believe that the Emperor could not know what they were doing.

The first victim was Cornelius Graphæus, town clerk of Antwerp, a poet and Humanist, a friend of Erasmus; and his offence was that he had published an edition of John Pupper of Goch's book, entitled the *Liberty of the Christian Religion*, with a preface of his own. The unfortunate man was set on a scaffold in Brussels, compelled to retract certain propositions which were said to be contained in the preface, and obliged to throw the preface itself into a fire kindled on the scaffold for the purpose. He was dismissed from his office, declared incapable of receiving any other employment, compelled to repeat his recantation at Antwerp, imprisoned for two years, and finally banished.[1]

The earliest deaths were those of Henry Voes and John Esch, who have already been mentioned. Their Prior, Hendrik of Zutphen, escaped from the dungeon in which he had been confined. Luther commemorated them in a long hymn, entitled *A New Song of the two*

---

[1] Graphæus' appeal to the Chancellor of the Court of Brabant is printed in full in Brandt's *History of the Reformation . . . in the Low Countries* (London, 1720), i. 42.

Martyrs of Christ burnt at Brussels by the Sophists of Louvain :

" Der erst recht wol Johannes heyst,
  So reych an Gottes hulden
Seyn Bruder Henrch nach dem geyst,
  Eyn rechter Christ on schulden :
    Vonn dysser welt gescheyden synd,
  Sye hand die kron erworben,
  Recht wie die frumen gottes kind
Fur seyn wort synd gestorben,
  Sein Marter synd sye worden." [1]

Charles issued proclamation after proclamation, each of increasing severity. It was forbidden to print any books unless they had been first examined and approved by the censors (April 1st, 1524). " All open and secret meetings in order to read and preach the Gospel, the Epistles of St. Paul, and other spiritual writings," were forbidden (Sept. 25th, 1525), as also to discuss the Holy Faith, the Sacraments, the Power of the Pope and Councils, "in private houses and at meals." This was repeated on March 14th, 1526, and on July 17th there was issued a long edict, said to have been carefully drafted by the Emperor himself, forbidding all meetings to read or preach about the Gospel or other holy writings in Latin, Flemish, or Walloon. In the preamble it is said that ignorant persons have begun to expound Scripture, that even regular and secular clergy have presumed to teach the "errors and sinister doctrines of Luther and his adherents," and that heresies are increasing in the land. Then followed edicts against unlicensed books, and against monks who had left their cloisters (Jan. 28th, 1528); against the possession of Lutheran books, commanding them upon pain of death to be delivered up (Oct. 14th, 1529); against printing unlicensed books—the penalties being a public whipping on the scaffold, branding with a red-iron, or the loss of an eye or a hand, at the discretion

[1] Wackernagel, *Das deutsche Kirchenlied von der ältesten Zeit bis an zu Anfang des xvii. Jahrhunderts,* iii. §

of the judge (Dec. 7th, 1530); against heretics "who are more numerous than ever," against certain books of which a long list is given, and against certain hymns which increase the zeal of the heretics (Sept. 22nd, 1540); against printing and distributing unlicensed books in the Italian, Spanish, or English languages (Dec. 18th, 1544); warning all schoolmasters about the use of unlicensed books in their schools, and giving a list of those only which are permitted (July 31st, 1546). The edict of 1546 was followed by a long list of prohibited books, among which are eleven editions of the Vulgate printed by Protestant firms, six editions of the Bible and three of the New Testament in Dutch, two editions of the Bible in French, and many others. Lastly, an edict of April 29th, 1550, confirmed all the previous edicts against heresy and its spread, and intimated that the Inquisitors would proceed against heretics "notwithstanding any privileges to the contrary, which are abrogated and annulled by this edict." This was a clear threat that the terrible Spanish Inquisition was to be established in the Netherlands, and provoked such remonstrances that the edict was modified twice (Sept. 25th, Nov. 5th) before it was finally accepted as legal within the seventeen provinces.

All these edicts were directed against the Lutheran or kindred teaching. They had nothing to do with the Anabaptist movement, which called forth a special and different set of edicts. It seems against all evidence to say that the persecution of the Lutherans had almost ceased during the last years of Charles' rule in the Netherlands, and Philip II. could declare with almost perfect truth that his edicts were only his father's re-issued.

The continuous repetition and increasing severity of the edicts revealed not merely that persecution did not hinder the spread of the Reformed faith, but that the edicts themselves were found difficult to enforce. What Charles would have done had he been able to govern the country himself it is impossible to say. He became harder and more intolerant of differences in matters of doctrine as years went on, and in his latest days is said to have regretted that he had allowed Luther to leave Worms alive; and he might have dealt with the Protestants of the seventeen provinces as his son afterwards did. His aunt, Margaret of Austria, who was Regent till 1530, had no desire to drive matters to an extremity; and his sister Mary, who ruled from 1530 till the abdication of Charles in 1555, was suspected in early life of being a Lutheran herself. She never openly joined the Lutheran Church as did her sister the Queen of Denmark, but she confessed her sympathies to Charles, and gave them as a reason for reluctance to undertake the regency of the Netherlands. It may therefore be presumed that the severe edicts were not enforced with undue stringency by either Margaret of Austria or by the widowed Queen of Hungary. There is also evidence to show that these proclamations denouncing and menacing the unfortunate Protestants of the Netherlands were not looked on with much favour by large sections of the population. Officials were dilatory, magistrates were known to have warned suspected persons to escape before the police came to arrest them; even to have given them facilities for escape after sentence had been delivered. Passive resistance on the part of the inferior authorities frequently interposed itself between the Emperor and the execution of his bloodthirsty proclamations. Yet the number of Protestant martyrs was large, and women as well as men suffered torture and death rather than deny their faith.

The edicts against conventicles deterred neither preachers nor audience. The earliest missioners were priests and monks who had become convinced of the errors of Romanism. Later, preachers were trained in the south German cities and in Geneva, that nursery of daring agents of the Reformed propaganda. But if trained teachers were lacking, members of the congregation took their place at the peril of their lives. Brandt relates how numbers of people were accustomed to meet for service in a shipwright's yard at Antwerp to hear a monk who had been " proclaimed ":

" The teacher, by some chance or other, could not appear, and one of the company named Nicolas, a person well versed in Scripture, thought it a shame that such a congregation, hungering after the food of the Word, should depart without a little spiritual nourishment; wherefore, climbing the mast of a ship, he taught the people according to his capacity; and on that account, and for the sake of the reward that was set upon the preacher, he was seized by two butchers and delivered to the magistrates, who caused him to be put into a sack and thrown into the river, where he was drowned."[1]

§ 3. *The Anabaptists.*

The severest persecutions, however, before the rule of Philip II., were reserved for those people who are called the Anabaptists.[2] We find several edicts directed against them solely. In February 1532 it was forbidden to harbour Anabaptists, and a price of 12 guilders was offered to informants. Later in the same year an edict was published which declared " that all who had been re-baptized, were sorry for their fault, and, in token of their repentance, had gone to confession, would be admitted to mercy for that time only, provided they brought a certificate from their confessor within twenty-four days of the date of the edict; those who continued obdurate were to be treated with the utmost rigour of the laws " (Feb. 1533). Ana-baptists who had abjured were ordered to remain near their dwelling-places for the space of a year, " unless those who were engaged in the herring fishery " (June 1534). In 1535 the severest edict against the sect was published.

---

[1] Brandt, *History of the Reformation in the Low Countries* (London, 1720), p. 51.

[2] The history of the struggle with the Anabaptists of the Netherlands is related at length by S. Blaupot ten Cate in *Geschiedenis der Doopgezinden in Friesland* (Leeuwarden, 1839) ; *Geschiedenis der Doopgezinden in Groningen* (Oberijssel, 1842) ; *Geschiedeniss der Doopgezinden in Holland en Gelderland* (Amsterdam, 1847). A summary of the history of the Anabaptists is given in Heath's *Anabaptism* (London, 1895), which is much more accurate than the usual accounts.

All who had "seduced or perverted any to this sect, or had rebaptized them," were to suffer death by fire; all who had suffered themselves to be rebaptized, or who had harboured Anabaptists, and who recanted, were to be favoured by being put to death by the sword; women were "only to be buried alive." [1]

To understand sympathetically that multiform movement which was called in the sixteenth century *Anabaptism*, it is necessary to remember that it was not created by the Reformation, although it certainly received an impetus from the inspiration of the age. Its roots can be traced back for some centuries, and its pedigree has at least two stems which are essentially distinct, and were only occasionally combined. The one stem is the successions of the *Brethren*, a mediæval, anti-clerical body of Christians whose history is written only in the records of Inquisitors of the mediæval Church, where they appear under a variety of names, but are universally said to prize the Scriptures and to accept the Apostles' Creed. [2] The other existed in the continuous uprisings of the poor — peasants in rural districts and the lower classes in the towns — against the rich, which were a feature of the later Middle Ages. [3]

So far as the Netherlands are concerned, these popular outbreaks had been much more frequent among the towns' population than in the rural districts. The city patriciate ordinarily controlled the magistracy; but when flagrant cases of oppression arose, all the judicial, financial, and other functions of government were sure to be swept out of their hands in an outburst of popular fury. So much was this the case, that the real holders of power in the towns in the Netherlands during the first half of the sixteenth century were the artisans, strong in their trade organisations. They had long known their power, and had been accustomed to exert it. The blood of a turbulent

---

[1] Cf. *Letters and Papers, Foreign and Domestic, of the Reign of Henry VIII.*, IV. iii. 2685 (*Halket to Tuller*).

[2] Cf. below, pp. 432 *f.*

[3] Cf. i. 96 *ff.*

ancestry ran in their veins—of men who could endure for
a time, but who, when roused by serious oppression, had
been accustomed to defend themselves, and to give stroke
for stroke.   It is only natural to find among the artisans
of the Flemish and Dutch towns a curious mingling of
sublime self-sacrifice for what they believed to be the
truth, of the mystical exaltation of the martyr occasionally breaking out in hysterical action, and the habit of
defending themselves against almost any odds.

So far as is known, the earliest Anabaptist martyrs
were Jan Walen and two others belonging to Waterlandt.
They were done to death in a peculiarly atrocious way at
The Hague in 1527.   Instead of being burnt alive, they
were chained to a stake at some distance from a huge fire,
and were slowly roasted to death.   This frightful punishment seems to have been reserved for the Anabaptist
martyrs.   It was repeated at Haarlem in 1532, when a
woman was drowned and her husband with two others
was roasted alive.   Some time in 1530, Jan Volkertz
founded an Anabaptist congregation in Amsterdam which
became so large as to attract the attention of the
authorities.   The head of the police (*schout*) in the city was
ordered to apprehend them.   Volkertz delivered himself
up voluntarily.   The greater part of the accused received
timely warning from the *schout's* wife.   Nine were taken
by night in their beds.   These with their pastor were
carried to The Hague and beheaded by express order of
the Emperor.   He also commanded that their heads
should be sent to Amsterdam, where they were set on
poles in a circle, the head of Volkertz being in the centre
This ghastly spectacle was so placed that it could be seen
from the ships entering and leaving the harbour.   All
these martyrs, and many others whose deaths are duly
recorded, were followers of Melchior Hoffman.   Hoffman's
views were those of the " Brethren " of the later Middle
Ages, the *Old Evangelicals* as they were called.   In a
paper of directions sent to Emden to assist in the
organisation of an Anabaptist congregation there, he says :

"God's community knows no head but Christ. No other can be endured, for it is a brother- and sisterhood. The teachers have none who rule them spiritually but Christ. Teachers and ministers are not lords. The pastors have no authority except to preach God's Word and punish sins. A bishop must be elected out of his community. Where a pastor has thus been taken, and the guidance committed to him and to his deacon, a community should provide properly for those who help to build the Lord's house. When teachers are thus found, there is no fear that the communities will suffer spiritual hunger. A true preacher would willingly see the whole community prophesy."

But the persecution, with its peculiar atrocities, had been acting in its usual way on the Anabaptists of the Netherlands. They had been tortured on the rack, scourged, imprisoned in dungeons, roasted to death before slow fires, and had seen their women drowned, buried alive, pressed into coffins too small for their bodies till their ribs were broken, others stamped into them by the feet of the executioners. It is to be wondered at that those who stood firm sometimes gave way to hysterical excesses; that their leaders began to preach another creed than that of passive resistance; that wild apocalyptic visions were reported and believed?

Melchior Hoffman had been imprisoned in Strassburg in 1533, and a new leader arose in the Netherlands—Jan Matthys, a baker of Haarlem. Under his guidance an energetic propaganda was carried on in the Dutch towns, and hundreds of converts were made. One hundred persons were baptized in one day in February (1534); before the end of March it was reported that two-thirds of the population in Monnikendam were Anabaptists; and a similar state of matters existed in many of the larger Dutch towns. Daventer, Zwolle, and Kampen were almost wholly Anabaptist. The Government made great exertions to crush the movement. Detachments of soldiers were divided into bands of fifteen or twenty, and patrolled the environs of the cities, making midnight visitations, and haling men and women to prison until the dungeons were overcrowded with captured Anabaptists.

Attempts were made by the persecuted to leave the country for some more hospitable place where they could worship God in peace in the way their consciences directed them. East Friesland had once been a haven, but was so no longer. Münster offered a refuge. Ships were chartered, —thirty of them,—and the persecuted people proposed to sail round the north of Friesland, land at the mouth of the Ems, and travel to Münster by land.[1] The Emperor's ships intercepted the little fleet, sank five of the vessels with all the emigrants on board, and compelled the rest to return. The leaders found on board were decapitated, and their heads stuck on poles to warn others. Hundreds from the provinces of Guelderland and Holland attempted the journey by land. They piled their bits of poor furniture and bundles of clothes on waggons; some rode horses, most trudged on foot, the women and children, let us hope, getting an occasional ride on the waggons. Soldiers were sent to intercept them. The leaders were beheaded, the men mostly imprisoned, and the women and children sent back to their towns and villages.

Then, and not till they had exhausted every method of passive resistance, the Anabaptists began to strike back. They wished to seize a town already containing a large Anabaptist population, and hold it as a city of refuge. Daventer, which was full of sympathisers, was their first aim. The plot failed, and the burgomaster's son Willem, one of the conspirators, was seized, and with two companions beheaded in the market-place (Dec. 25th, 1534). Their next attempt was on Leyden. It was called a plot

---

[1] Several references to the Anabaptists of the Low Countries are to be found in the *Letters and Papers, Foreign and Domestic, of the Reign of Henry VIII.* Hackett, writing to Cromwell, says that "divers places are affected by this new sect of 'rebaptisement,'" vii. p. 136. He tells about the shiploads of emigrants (pp. 165, 166), and says that they were so sympathised with, that it was difficult to enlist soldiers to fight against them; that the Regent had sent 10,000 ducats to help the Bishop of Münster to crush them (p. 167); and a wild report was current that Henry VIII. had sent money to the Anabaptists of Münster in revenge for the Pope's refusing his divorce (p. 185).

to burn the town. The magistrates got word of it, and, by ordering the great town-clock to be stopped, disconcerted the plotters. Fifteen men and five women were seized ; the men were decapitated, and the women drowned (Jan. 1535). Next month (Feb. 28th, 1535), Jan van Geelen, leading a band of three hundred refugees through Friesland, was overtaken by some troops of soldiers. The little company entrenched themselves, fought bravely for some days, until nearly all were killed. The survivors were almost all captured and put to death, the men by the sword, and the women by drowning. One hundred soldiers fell in the attack. A few months later (May 1535), an attempt was made to seize Amsterdam. It was headed by van Geelen, the only survivor of the skirmish in Friesland. He and his companions were able to get possession of the Stadthaus, and held it against the town's forces until cannon were brought to batter down their defences.

In the early days of the same year an incident occurred which shows how, under the strain of persecution, an hysterical exaltation took possession of some of these poor people. It is variously reported. According to Brandt, seven men and five women having stript off their clothes, as a sign, they said, that they spoke the naked truth, ran through the streets of Amsterdam, crying *Woe! Woe! Woe!* The Wrath of God! They were apprehended, and slaughtered in the usual way. The woman in whose house they had met was hanged at her own door.

The insurrections were made the pretext for still fiercer persecutions. The Anabaptists were hunted out, tortured and slain without any attempt being made by the authorities to discriminate between those who had and those who had not been sharers in any insurrectionary attempt. It is alleged that over thirty thousand people were put to death in the Netherlands during the reign of Charles v. Many of the victims had no connection with Anabaptism whatsoever; they were quiet followers of Luther or of Calvin. The authorities discriminated between them in their proclamations, but not in the persecution.

§ 4. *Philip of Spain and the Netherlands.*

How long the Netherlands would have stood the continual drain of money and the severity of the persecution which the foreign and religious policy of Charles enforced upon them, it is impossible to say. The people of the country were strongly attached to him, as he was to them. He had been born and had grown from childhood to manhood among them. Their languages, French and Flemish, were the only speech he could ever use with ease. He had been ruler in the Netherlands before he became King of Spain, and long before he was called to fill the imperial throne. When he resolved to act on his long meditated scheme of abdicating in favour of his son Philip, it was to the Netherlands that he came. Their nobles and people witnessed the scene with hardly less emotion than that which showed itself in the faltering speech of the Emperor.

The ceremony took place in the great Hall of the palace in Brussels (Oct. 25th, 1555), in presence of the delegates of the seventeen provinces. Mary, the widowed Queen of Hungary, who had governed the land for twenty-five years, witnessed the scene which was to end her rule. Philip, who was to ruin the work of consolidation patiently planned and executed by his father and his aunt, was present, summoned from his uncongenial task of eating roast beef and drinking English ale in order to conciliate his new subjects across the Channel, and from the embarrassing endearments of his elderly spouse. The Emperor, aged by toil rather than by years, entered the Hall leaning heavily on his favourite page and trusty counsellor, the youthful William, Prince of Orange, who was to become the leader of the revolt against Philip's rule, and to create a new Protestant State, the United Provinces.

The new lord of the Netherlands was then twenty-eight. In outward appearance he was a German like his father, but in speech he was a Spaniard. He had none of his father's external geniality, and could never stoop to win men to h:s ends. But Philip II. was much liker Charles V

than many historians seem willing to admit.   Both had
the same slow, patient industry—but in the son it was
slower; the same cynical distrust of all men; the same
belief in the divine selection of the head of the House of
Hapsburg to guide all things in State and Church irrespective
of Popes or Kings—only in the son it amounted to a sort
of gloomy mystical assurance ; the same callousness to
human suffering, and the same utter inability to comprehend
the force of strong religious conviction.   Philip was an
inferior edition of his father, succeeding to his father's
ideas, pursuing the same policy, using the same methods,
but handicapped by the fact that he had not originated but
had inherited both, and with them the troubles brought
in their train.

Philip II. spent the first four years of his reign in the
Netherlands, and during that short period of personal rule
his policy had brought into being all the more important
sources of dissatisfaction which ended in the revolt.   Yet
his policy was the same, and his methods were not different
from those of his father.   In one respect at least Charles
had never spared the Netherlands.   That country had to
pay, as no other part of his vast possessions was asked to
do, the price of his foreign policy, and Charles had wrung
unexampled sums from his people.

When Philip summoned the States General (March
12th, 1556) and asked them for a very large grant (Fl.
1,300,000), he was only following his father's example,
and on that occasion was seeking money to liquidate the
deficit which his father had bequeathed.   Was it that the
people of the Netherlands had resolved to end the practice
of making them pay for a foreign policy which had hitherto
concerned them little, or was it because they could not
endure the young Spaniard who could not speak to them
in their own language?   Would Charles have been refused
as well as Philip?   Who can say?

When Philip obtained a Bull from Pope Paul IV. for
creating a territorial episcopate in the Netherlands, he was
only carrying out the policy which his father had sketched

16**

as early as 1522, and which but for the shortness of the pontificate of Hadrian VI. would undoubtedly have been executed in 1524 without any popular opposition. Charles' scheme contemplated six bishoprics, Philip's fourteen; that was the sole difference; and from the ecclesiastical point of view Philip's was probably the better. Why then the bitter opposition to the change in 1557? Most historians seem to think that had Charles been ruling, there would have been few murmurs. Is that so certain? The people feared the institution of the bishoprics, because they dreaded and hated an Inquisition which would override their local laws, rights, and privileges; and Charles had been obliged to modify his "Placard" of 1549 against heresy, because towns and districts protested so loudly against it. During these early years Philip made no alterations on his father's proclamations against heresy. He contented himself with reissuing the "Placard" of 1549 as that had been amended in 1550 after the popular protests. The personality of Philip was no doubt objectionable to his subjects in the Netherlands, but it cannot be certainly affirmed that had Charles continued to reign there would have been no widespread revolt against his financial, ecclesiastical, and religious policy. The Regent Mary had been finding her task of ruling more and more difficult. A few weeks before the abdication, when the Emperor wished his sister to continue in the Regency, she wrote to him:

"I could not live among these people even as a private citizen, for it would be impossible to do my duty towards God and my Prince. As to governing them, I take God to witness that the task is so abhorrent to me that I would rather earn my daily bread by labour than attempt it."

In 1559 (Aug. 26th), Philip left the Netherlands never to return. He had selected Margaret of Parma, his half-sister, the illegitimate daughter of Charles V., for Regent. Margaret had been born and brought up in the country; she knew the language, and she had been so long away from her native land that she was not personally committed to any policy nor acquainted with the leaders of any of the parties.

The power of the Regent, nominally extensive, was in reality limited by secret instructions.[1] She was ordered to put in execution the edicts against heresy without any modification; and she was directed to submit to the advice given her by three Councils, a command which placed her under the supervision of the three men selected by Philip to be the presidents of these Councils. The Council of State was the most important, and was entrusted with the management of the whole foreign and home administration of the country. It consisted of the Bishop of Arras (Antoine Perronet de Granvelle, afterwards Cardinal de Granvelle);[2] the Baron de Barlaymont, who was President of the Council of Finance; Vigilius van Aytta, a learned lawyer from Friesland, "a small brisk man, with long yellow hair, glittering green eyes, fat round rosy cheeks, and flowing beard," who was President of the Privy Council, and controlled the administration of law and justice; and two of the Netherland nobles, Lamoral, Count of Egmont and Prince of Gavre, and William, Prince of Orange. The two nobles were seldom consulted or even invited to be present. The three Presidents were the *Consulta*, or secret body of confidential advisers imposed by Philip upon his Regent, without whose advice nothing was to be attempted. Of the three, the Bishop of Arras (Cardinal de

---

[1] The Royal Academy of Belgium has published (Brussels, 1877-96) the *Correspondance du Cardinal de Granvelle* in 12 volumes, and in the *Collection de documents inédits sur l'Histoire de France* there are the *Papiers d'État du Cardinal de Granvelle* in 9 vols., edited by C. Weiss (Paris, 1841-52). These volumes reveal the inner history of the revolt in the Netherlands. The documents which refer to the revolt in the *Papiers d'État* begin with p. 588 of vol. v. They show how, from the very first, Philip II. urged the extirpation of heresy as the most important work to be undertaken by his Government ; cf. *Papiers d'État*, v. 591.

[2] "Philip struck the keynote of his reign on the occasion of his first public appearance as King by presiding over one of the most splendid *auto-da-fés* that had ever been seen in Spain (Valladolid, Oct. 18th, 1559)." *Cambridge Modern History*, iii. 482. It is a singular commentary on sixteenth century Romanism, that to burn a large number of fellow-men was called "an act of faith."

Granvelle) was the most important, and the government was practically placed in his hands by his master. Behind the *Consulta* was Philip II. himself, who in his business room in the Escurial at Madrid issued his orders, repressing every tendency to treat the people with moderation and humanity, thrusting aside all suggestions of wise tolerance, and insisting that his own cold-blooded policy should be carried out in its most objectionable details. It was not until the publication of de Granvelle's State Papers and Correspondence that it came to be known how much the Bishop of Arras has been misjudged by history, how he remonstrated unavailingly with his master, how he was forced to put into execution a sanguinary policy of repression which was repugnant to himself, and how Philip compelled him to bear the obloquy of his own misdeeds. The correspondence also reveals the curiously minute information which Philip must have privately received, for he was able to send to the Regent and the Bishop the names, ages, personal appearance, occupations, residence of numbers of obscure people whom he ordered to execution for their religious opinions.[1] No rigour of persecution seemed able to prevent the spread of the Reformation.[2]

The Government—Margaret and her *Consulta*—offended grievously not merely the people, but the nobility of the Netherlands. The nobles saw their services and positions treated as things of no consequence, and the people witnessed with alarm that the local charters and privileges of the land—charters and rights which Philip at his coronation had sworn to maintain—were totally disregarded. Gradually all classes of the population were united in a silent opposition. The Prince of Orange and Count Egmont became almost insensibly the leaders.

They had been dissatisfied with their position on the Council of State; they had no real share in the business; the correspondence was not submitted to them, and they

---

[1] *Papiers d'État du Cardinal de Granvelle*, v. pp. 558, 591.
[2] Gachard, *Correspondance de Guillaume le Taciturne* (Letters from the Regent to Philip II.), i. 382–86.

knew such details only as Granvelle chose to communicate to them. Their first overt act was to resign the commissions they held in the Spanish troops stationed in the country; their second, to write to the King asking him to relieve them of their position on the Council of State, telling him that matters of great importance were continually transacted without their knowledge or concurrence, and that in the circumstances they could not conscientiously continue to sustain the responsibilities of office.[1]

The opposition took their stand on three things, all of which hung together—the presence of Spanish troops on the soil of the Netherlands, the cruelties perpetrated in the execution of the *Placards* against heresy, and the institution of the new bishoprics in accordance with the Bull of Pope Paul IV., reaffirmed by Pius IV. in 1560 (Jan.). The common fighting ground for the opposition to all the three was the invasion of the charters and privileges of the various provinces which these measures necessarily involved, and the consequent violation of the King's coronation oath.

Philip had solemnly promised to withdraw the Spanish troops within three or four months after he left the country. They had remained for fourteen, and the whole land cried out against the pillage and rapine which accompanied their presence. The people of Zeeland declared that they would rather see the ocean submerge their country—that they would rather perish, men, women, and children, in the waves—than endure longer the outrages which these mercenaries inflicted upon them. They refused to repair the Dykes. The presence of these troops had been early seen to be a degradation to his country by William of Orange.[2] At the States General held on the eve of Philip's departure, he had urged the Assembly to

---

[1] Gachard, *Correspondance de Guillaume le Taciturne*, etc. ii. 42 *f.*, 106–110, 170.
[2] He wrote to Philip about their excesses as early as Dec. 29th, 1555, Gachard, *Correspondance de Guillaume le Taciturne*, i 282, and about the exasperation of the Netherlanders in consequence (*ibid.* i. 291).

make the departure of the troops a condition of granting subsidies, and had roused Philip's wrath in consequence. He now voiced the cry of the whole country. It was so strong that Granvelle sent many an urgent request to the King to sanction their removal ; and at length he and the Regent, without waiting for orders, had the troops embarked for Madrid.

The rigorous repression of heresy compelled the Government to override the charters of the several provinces. Many of these charters contained very strong provisions, and the King had sworn to maintain them. The constitution of Brabant, known as the *joyeuse entrée* (*blyde inkomst*), provided that the clergy should not be given unusual powers ; and that no subject, nor even a foreign resident, could be prosecuted civilly or criminally except in the ordinary courts of the land, where he could answer and defend himself with the help of advocates. The charter of Holland contained similar provisions. Both charters declared that if the Prince transgressed these provisions the subjects were freed from their allegiance. The inquisitorial courts violated the charters of those and of the other provinces. The great objection taken to the increase of the episcopate, according to the provisions of the Bulls of Paul IV. and of Pius IV., was that it involved a still greater infringement of the chartered rights of the land. For example, the Bulls provided that the bishops were to appoint nine canons, who were to assist them in all inquisitorial cases, while at least one of them was to be an Inquisitor charged with ferreting out and punishing heresy. This was apparently their great charm for Philip II. He desired an instrument to extirpate heretics. He knew that the Reformation was making great progress in the Netherlands, especially in the great commercial cities. "I would lose all my States and a hundred lives if I had them," he wrote to the Pope, "rather than be the lord of heretics."

The opposition at first contented itself with protesting against the position and rule of Granvelle, and with demanding his recall. Philip came to the reluctant conclusion to dismiss his Minister, and did so with more than his usual duplicity. The nobles returned to the Council, and the Regent affected to take their advice. But they were soon to discover that the recall of the obnoxious Minister did not make any change in the policy of Philip.

The Regent read them a letter from Philip ordering the publication and enforcement of the Decrees of the Council of Trent in the Netherlands.[1] The nobles protested vehemently on the ground that this would mean a still further invasion of the privileges of the provinces. After long deliberation, it was resolved to send Count Egmont to Madrid to lay the opinions of the Council before the King. The debate was renewed on the instructions to be given to the delegate. Those suggested by the President, Vigilius, were colourless. Then William the Silent spoke out. His speech, a long one, full of suppressed passionate sympathy with his persecuted fellow-countrymen, made an extraordinary impression. It is thus summarised by Brandt:

That they ought to speak their minds freely; that there were such commotions and revolutions on account of religion in all the neighbouring countries, that it was impossible to maintain the present régime, and think to suppress disturbances by means of *Placards*, Inquisitions, and Bishops; that the King was mistaken if he proposed to maintain the Decrees of the Council of Trent in these Provinces which lay so near Germany, where all the Princes, Roman Catholics as well as Protestants, have justly rejected them; that it would be better that His Majesty should tolerate these things as other Princes were obliged to do, and annul or else moderate the punishments proclaimed in the *Placards*; that though he himself had resolved to adhere to the Catholic religion, yet he could not approve that Princes should aim at dominion over the souls of men, or deprive them of the freedom of their faith and religion.[2]

---

[1] In a letter to the Regent (March 16th, 1566), William declared that the heads of the policy of Philip which he most strongly disapproved of were: *l'entretènement du concile de Trente, favoriser les inquisiteurs ou leur office et exécuter sans nulle dissimulation les placars.* Correspondance, etc. ii. 129.

[2] Brandt, *The History of the Reformation*, etc. i. 150.

The instructions given to Egmont were accordingly both full and plain-spoken.

Count Egmont departed leisurely to Madrid, was well received by Philip, and left thoroughly deceived, perhaps self-deceived, about the King's intentions. He had a rude awakening when the sealed letter he bore was opened and read in the Council. It announced no real change in policy, and in the matter of heresy showed that the King's resolve was unaltered. A despatch to the Regent (Nov. 5th, 1565) was still more unbending. Philip would not enlarge the powers of the Council in the Netherlands; he peremptorily refused to summon the States General; and he ordered the immediate publication and enforcement of the Decrees of the Council of Trent in every town and village in the seventeen provinces. True to the policy of his house, the Decrees of Trent were to be proclaimed in *his* name, not in that of the Pope. It was the beginning of the tragedy, as William of Orange remarked.

The effect of the order was immediate and alarming. The Courts of Holland and Brabant maintained that the Decrees infringed their charters, and refused to permit their publication. Stadtholders and magistrates declared that they would rather resign office than execute decrees which would compel them to burn over sixty thousand of their fellow-countrymen. Trade ceased; industries died out; a blight fell on the land. Pamphlets full of passionate appeals to the people to put an end to the tyranny were distributed and eagerly read. In one of them, which took the form of a letter to the King, it was said:

" We are ready to die for the Gospel, but we read therein, 'Render unto Cæsar the things which are Cæsar's, and unto God the things that are God's.' We thank God that even our enemies are constrained to bear witness to our piety and innocence, for it is a common saying: 'He does not swear, for he is a Protestant. He is not an immoral man, nor a drunkard, for he belongs to the new sect'; yet we are subjected to every kind of punishment that can be invented to torment us."[1]

[1] Brandt, *The History of the Reformation*, etc. i. 160.

The year 1566 saw the origin of a new confederated opposition to Philip's mode of ruling the Netherlands. Francis Du Jon, a young Frenchman of noble birth, belonging to Bourges, had studied for the ministry at Geneva, and had been sent as a missioner to the Netherlands, where his learning and eloquence had made a deep impression on young men of the upper classes. His life was in constant peril, and he was compelled to flit secretly from the house of one sympathiser to that of another. During the festivities which accompanied the marriage of the young Alexander of Parma with Maria of Portugal, he was concealed in the house of the Count of Culemburg in Brussels. On the day of the wedding he preached and prayed with a small company of young nobles, twenty in all. There and at other meetings held afterwards it was resolved to form a confederacy of nobles, all of whom agreed to bind themselves to support principles laid down in a carefully drafted manifesto which went by the name of the *Compromise*. It was mainly directed against the Inquisition, which it calls a tribunal opposed to all laws, divine and human. Copies passed from hand to hand soon obtained over two thousand signatures among the lower nobility and landed gentry. Many substantial burghers also signed. The leading spirits in the confederacy were Louis of Nassau, the younger brother of the Prince of Orange, then a Lutheran; Philip de Marnix, lord of Sainte Aldegonde, a Calvinist; and Henry Viscount Brederode, a Roman Catholic. The confederates declared that they were loyal subjects; but pledged themselves to protect each other if any of them were attacked.

The confederates met privately at Breda and Hoogstraeten (March 1566), and resolved to present a petition to the Regent asking that the King should be recommended to abolish the *Placards* and the Inquisition, and that the Regent should suspend their operation until the King's wishes were known; also that the States General should be assembled to consider other ordinances dangerous to the country. The Regent had called an assembly of the

Notables for March 28th, and it was resolved to present the petition then. The confederation and its *Compromise* were rather dreaded by the great nobles who had been the leaders of the constitutional opposition, and there was some debate about the presentation of the *Request*. The Baron de Barlaymont went so far as to recommend a massacre of the petitioners in the audience hall; but wiser counsels prevailed. The confederates met and marshalled themselves,—two hundred young nobles,—and marched through the streets to the Palace, amid the acclamations of the populace, to present the *Request*.[1] The Regent was some-- what dismayed by the imposing demonstration, but Barlaymont reassured her with the famous words: " Madame, is your Highness afraid of these beggars (*ces gueux*)? " The deputation was dismissed with fair words, and the promise that although the Regent had no power to suspend the *Placards* or the Inquisition, there would be some moderation used until the King's pleasure was known.

Before leaving Brussels, three hundred of the confederates met in the house of the Count of Culemburg to celebrate their league at a banquet. The Viscount de Brederode presided, and during the feast he recalled to their memories the words of Barlaymont: " They call us beggars," he said; " we accept the name. We pledge ourselves to resist the Inquisition, and keep true to the King and the beggar's wallet." He then produced the leathern sack of the wandering beggars, strapped it round his shoulder, and drank prosperity to the cause from a beggar's wooden bowl. The name and the emblem were adopted with enthusiasm, and spread far beyond the circle of the confederacy.[2] Everywhere burghers, lawyers, peasants as well as nobles appeared wearing the beggar's sack. Medals,

---

[1] Gachard, *Correspondance de Guillaume le Taciturne*, ii. 434 *ff.*
[2] At meals they sang :

" *Par ce pain, par ce sel, et par cette besace,*
  Jamais les Gueux ne changeront pour chose que l'on fasse. "

William of Orange wrote to the Regent that he was met in Antwerp by crowds, shouting *Vive les Gueux* (*Correspondance*, ii. 136, etc.).

made first of wax set in a wooden cup, then of gold and silver, were adopted by the confederated nobles. On the one side was the effigies of the King, and on the obverse two hands clasped and the beggar's sack with the motto, *Fidelles au Roi jusques à porter la besace* (beggar's sack).

All these things were faithfully reported by the Regent to Philip, and she besought him either to permit her to moderate the *Placards* and the Inquisition, or to come to the Netherlands himself. He answered, promising to come, and permitted her some discretion in the matter of repression of heresy.

Meanwhile the people were greatly encouraged by the success, or appearance of success, attending the efforts of the confederates. Refugees returned from France, Germany, and Switzerland. Missioners of the Reformed faith came in great numbers. Field-preachings were held all over the country. The men came armed, planted sentinels, placed their women and children within the square, and thus listened to the services conducted by the excommunicated ministers. They heard the Scriptures read and prayers poured forth in their own tongue. They sang hymns and psalms in French, Flemish, and Dutch. The crowds were so large, the sentinels so wary, the men so well armed, that the soldiers dared not attempt to disperse them. At first the meetings were held at night in woods and desolate places, but immunity created boldness.

"On July 23rd (1566) the Reformed rendezvoused in great numbers in a large meadow not far from Ghent. There they formed a sort of camp, fortifying themselves with their waggons, and setting sentinels at all the roads. Some brought pikes, some hatchets, and others guns. In front of them were pedlars with prohibited books, which they sold to such as came. They planted several along the road whose business it was to invite people to come to the preaching and to show them the way. They made a kind of pulpit of planks, and set it upon a waggon, from which the minister preached. When the sermon was ended, all the congregation sang several psalms. They also drew water out of a well or brook near them, and a child was baptized. Two days were spent there, and then they adjourned to Deinsen, then to Ekelo near Bruges, and so through all West Flanders."[1]

Growing bolder still, the Reformed met in the environs and suburbs of the great towns. Bands of men marched through the streets singing Psalms, either the French versions of Clement Marot or Béze or the Dutch one of Peter Dathenus. It was in vain that the Regent issued a new *Placard* against the preachers and the conventicles. It remained a dead letter. In Antwerp, bands of the Reformed, armed, crowded to the preachings in defiance of the magistrates, who were afraid of fighting in the streets. In the emergency the Regent appealed to William of Orange, and he with difficulty appeased the tumults and arranged a compromise. The Calvinists agreed to disarm on the condition that they were allowed the free exercise of their worship in the suburbs although not within the towns.[2]

The confederates were so encouraged with their successes that they thought of attempting more. A great conference was held at St. Trond in the principality of Liège (July 1566), attended by nearly two thousand members. The leader was Louis of Nassau. They resolved on another deputation to the Regent, and twelve of their number were selected to present their demands. These "Twelve Apostles," as the courtiers contemptuously termed them, declared that the persecution had not been mitigated as promised, and not obscurely threatened that if some remedy were not found they might be forced to invoke foreign assistance. The threat enraged the Regent; but she was helpless; she could only urge that she had already made representations to the King, and had sent two members of Council to inform the King about the condition of the country.

It seemed as if some impression had been made on Philip. The Regent received a despatch (July 31st, 1566)

---

[1] Brandt's *History of the Reformation* . . . *in the Low Countries* (London, 1720), i. 172.

[2] Gachard, *Correspondance de Guillaume le Taciturne*, ii. 186 *ff.*

saying that he was prepared to withdraw the papal Inquisition from the Netherlands, and that he would grant what toleration was consistent with the maintenance of the Catholic religion; only he would in no way consent to a summoning of the States General.

There was great triumphing in the Netherlands at this news. Perhaps every one but the Prince of Orange was more or less deceived by Philip's duplicity. It is only since the archives of Simancas have yielded their secrets that its depth has been known. They reveal that on Aug. 9th he executed a deed in which he declared that the promise of pardon had been won from him by force, and that he did not mean to keep it, and that on Aug. 12th he wrote to the Pope that his declaration to withdraw the Inquisition was a mere blind. William only knew that the King was levying troops, and that he was blaming the great nobles of the Netherlands for the check inflicted upon him by the confederates.

Long before Philip's real intentions were unmasked, a series of iconoclastic attacks not only gave the King the pretext he needed, but did more harm to the cause of the Reformation in the Low Countries than all the persecutions under Charles v. and his son. The origin of these tumultuous proceedings is obscure. According to Brandt, who collects information from all sides :

"Some few of the vilest of the mob . . . were those who began the dance, being hallooed on by nobody knows whom. Their arms were staves, hatchets, hammers, ladders, ropes, and other tools more proper to demolish than to fight with; some few were provided with guns and swords. At first they attacked the crosses and the images that had been erected on the great roads in the country; next, those in the villages; and, lastly, those in the towns and cities. All the chapels, churches, and convents which they found shut they forced open, breaking, tearing, and destroying all the images, pictures, shrines and other consecrated things they met with; nay, some did not scruple to lay their hands upon libraries, books, writings, monuments, and even on the dead bodies in churches and churchyards."[1]

[1] Brandt, *History of the Reformation*, etc. i. 191.

According to almost all accounts, the epidemic, for the madness resembled a disease, first appeared at St. Omer's (Aug. 14th, 1566), then at Ypres, and extended rapidly to other towns. It came to a height at Antwerp (16th and 17th Aug. 1566), when the mob sacked the great cathedral and destroyed some of its richest treasures.[1] An eye-witness declared that the rioters in the cathedral did not number more than one hundred men, women, and boys, drawn from the dregs of the population, and that the attacks on the other churches were made by small parties of ten or twelve persons.

These outrages had a disastrous effect on the Reformation movement in the Netherlands, both immediately and in the future. They at once exasperated the more liberal-minded Roman Catholics and enraged the Regent: they began that gradual cleavage which ended in the separation of the Protestant North from the Romanist South. The Regent felt herself justified in practically withdrawing all the privileges she had accorded to the Reformed, and in raising German and Walloon troops to overawe the Protestants. The presence of these troops irritated some of the Calvinist nobles, and John de Marnix, elder brother of Sainte Aldegonde, attempted to seize the Island of Walcheren in order to hold it as a city of refuge for his persecuted brethren. He was unsuccessful; a fight took place not far from Antwerp itself, in which de Marnix was routed and slain (March 13th, 1567).

§ 5. *William of Orange.*

Meanwhile William of Orange had come to the conclusion that Philip was meditating the suppression of the rights and liberties of the Low Countries by Spanish troops, and was convinced that the great nobles who had hitherto headed the constitutional opposition would be the first to be attacked. He had conferences with Egmont and Hoorn at

---

[1] For this and earlier disturbances at Antwerp, cf. *Correspondance de Philip II.*, etc. i. 321, 327, 379.

Dendermonde (Oct. 3rd, 1566), and at Willebroek (April 2nd, 1567), and endeavoured to persuade them that the only course open to them was to resist by force of arms. His arguments were unavailing, and William sadly determined that he must leave the country and retire to his German estates.

His forebodings were only too correct. Philip had resolved to send the Duke of Alva to subdue the Netherlands. A force of nine thousand veteran Spanish infantry with thirteen hundred Italian cavalry had been collected from the garrisons of Lombardy and Naples, and Alva began a long, difficult march over the Mt. Cenis and through Franche Comté, Lorraine, and Luxemburg. William had escaped just in time. When the Duke arrived in Brussels and presented his credentials to the Council of State, it was seen that the King had bestowed on him such extensive powers that Margaret remained Regent in name only. One of his earliest acts was to get possession of the persons of Counts Egmont and Hoorn, with their private secretaries, and to imprison Antony van Straelen, Burgomaster of Antwerp, and a confidential friend of the Prince of Orange. Many other arrests were made; and Alva, having caught his victims, invented an instrument to help him to dispose of them.

By the mere fiat of his will he created a judicial chamber, whose decisions were to override those of any other court of law in the Netherlands, and which was to be responsible to none, not even to the Council of State. It was called the *Council of Tumults*, but is better known by its popular name, *The Bloody Tribunal*. It consisted of twelve members, among whom were Barlaymont and a few of the most violent Romanists of the Netherlands; but only two, Juan de Vargas and del Rio, both Spaniards, were permitted to vote and influence the decisions. Del Rio was a nonentity; but de Vargas was a very stern reality—a man of infamous life, equally notorious for the delight he took in slaughtering his fellow-men and the facility with which he murdered the Latin language! He

brought the whole population of the Netherlands **within**
the grip of the public executioner by his indictment:
*Hœretici fraxerunt templa, boni nihil faxerunt contra; ergo
debent omnes patibulare;* by which he meant, *The heretics
have broken open churches, the orthodox have done nothing
to hinder them; therefore they ought all of them to be hanged
together.* Alva reserved all final decisions for his own
judgment, in order that the work might be thoroughly
done. He wrote to the King, " Men of law only condemn
for crimes that are proved, whereas your Majesty knows
that affairs of State are governed by very different rules
from the laws which they have here."

At its earlier sittings this terrible tribunal defined the
crime of treason, and stated that its punishment was
death. The definition extended to eighteen articles, and
declared it to be treason—to have presented or signed
any petition against the new bishoprics, the Inquisition,
or the *Placards*; to have tolerated public preaching
under any circumstances; to have omitted to resist
iconoclasm, or field-preaching, or the presentation of the
Request; to have asserted that the King had not the
right to suspend the charters of the provinces; or to
maintain that the Council of Tumults had not a right to
override all the laws and privileges of the Netherlands.
All these things were treason, and all of them were
capital offences. Proof was not required; all that was
needed was reasonable suspicion, or rather what the
Duke of Alva believed to be so. The Council soon got
to work. It sent commissioners through every part of
the land—towns, villages, districts—to search for any
who might be suspected of having committed any act
which could be included within their definition of treason.
Informers were invited, were bribed, to come forward;
and soon shoals of denunciations and evidence flowed in
to them. The accused were brought before the Council,
tried (if the procedure could be called a trial), and
condemned in batches. The records speak of ninety-five,
eighty-four, forty-six, thirty-five at a time. Alva wrote

to Philip that no fewer than fifteen hundred had been taken in their beds early on Ash-Wednesday morning, and later he announces another batch of eight hundred. In each case he adds, " I have ordered all of them to be executed." In view of these records, the language of a contemporary chronicler does not appeared exaggerated:

"The gallows, the wheel, stakes, trees along the highways, were laden with carcasses or limbs of those who had been hanged, beheaded, or roasted ; so that the air which God made for the respiration of the living, was now become the common grave or habitation of the dead. Every day produced fresh objects of pity and of mourning, and the noise of the bloody passing-bell was continually heard, which by the martyrdom of this man's cousin, and the other's brother or friend, rang dismal peals in the hearts of the survivors." [1]

Whole families left their dwellings to shelter themselves in the woods, and, goaded by their misery, pillaged and plundered. The priests had been active as informers, and these *Wild-Beggars*, as they were called, " made excursions on them, serving themselves of the darkest nights for revenge and robbery, punishing them not only by despoiling them of their goods, but by disfiguring their faces, cutting off ears and noses." The country was in a state of anarchy.

Margaret, Duchess of Parma, the nominal Regent of the Netherlands, had found her position intolerable since the arrival of the Duke of Alva, and was permitted by Philip to resign (Oct. 6th, 1567). Alva henceforth

---

[1] Brandt, *History of the Reformation*, etc. i. 261, 266. The executions were latterly accompanied by additional atrocious cruelty. " It being perceived with what constancy and alacrity many persons went to the fire, and how they opened their mouths to make a free confession of their faith, and that the wooden balls or gags were wont to slip out, a dreadful machine was invented to hinder it for the future : they prepared two little irons, between which the tongue was screwed, which being seared at the tip with a glowing iron, would swell to such a degree as to become immovable and incapable of being drawn back ; thus fastened, the tongue would wriggle about with the pain of burning, and yield a hollow sound " (i. 275).

17**

was untrammelled by even nominal restraint. A process was begun against the Counts Egmont and Hoorn, and William of Orange was proclaimed an outlaw (Jan. 24th, 1568) unless he submitted himself for trial before the *Council of Tumults.* Some days afterwards, his eldest son, a boy of fifteen and a student in the University of Louvain, was kidnapped and carried off to Spain.[1]

William replied in his famous *Justification of the Prince of Orange against his Calumniators,* in which he declared that he, a citizen of Brabant, a Knight of the Golden Fleece, a Prince of the Holy Roman Empire, one of the sovereign Princes of Europe (in virtue of the principality of Orange), could not be summoned before an incompetent tribunal. He reviewed the events in the Netherlands since the accession of Philip II., and spoke plainly against the misgovernment caused, he said diplomatically, by the evil counsels of the King's advisers. The *Justification* was published in several languages, and was not merely an act of defiance to Philip, but a plea made on behalf of his country to the whole of civilised Europe.

The earlier months of 1568 had been spent by the Prince of Orange in military preparations for the relief of his countrymen, and in the spring his army was ready. The campaign was a failure. Hoogstraten was defeated. Louis of Nassau had a temporary success at Heiliger-Lee (May 23rd, 1568), only to be routed at Jemmingen (July 21st, 1568). After William had issued a pathetic but unavailing manifesto to Protestant Europe, a second expedition was sent forth only to meet defeat. The cause of the Netherlands seemed hopeless.

But Alva was beginning to find himself in difficulties. On the news of the repulse of his troops at Heiliger-Lee he had hastily beheaded the Counts Egmont and Hoorn. Instead of striking terror into the hearts of the Netherlanders, the execution roused them to an undying hatred of the Spaniard. He was now troubled by lack of money to pay his troops. He had promised Philip to make gold

[1] Gachard, *Correspondance de Guillaume le Taciturne,* iii. 17.

flow from the Low Countries to Spain; but his rule had destroyed the commerce and manufactures of the country, the source of its wealth. He was almost dependent on subsidies from Spain. Elizabeth of England had been assisting her fellow Protestants in the way she liked best, by seizing Spanish treasure ships; and Alva was reduced to find the money he needed within the Netherlands.

It was then that he proposed to the States General, summoned to meet him (March 20th, 1569), his notorious scheme of taxation, which finally ruined him—a tax of one per cent. (the " hundredth penny ") to be levied once for all on all property; a tax of five per cent. (the " twentieth penny) to be levied at every sale or transfer of landed property; and a tax of ten per cent. (the " tenth penny ") on all articles of commerce each time they were sold. This scheme of taxation would have completely ruined a commercial and manufacturing country. It met with universal resistance. Provinces, towns, magistrates, guilds, the bishops and the clergy—everyone protested against the taxation. Even Philip's Council at Madrid saw the impossibility of exacting such taxes from a country. Alva swore that he would have his own way. The town and district of Utrecht had been the first to protest. Alva quartered the regiment of Lombardy upon them; but not even the licence and brutality of the soldiers could force the wretched people to pay. Alva proclaimed the whole of the inhabitants to be guilty of high treason; he took from them all their charters and privileges; he declared their whole property confiscated to the King. But these were the acts of a furious madman, and were unavailing. He then postponed the collection of the hundredth and of the tenth pennies; but the need of money forced him on, and he gave definite orders for the collection of the " tenth " and the " twentieth pennies." The trade and manufactures of the country came to a sudden standstill, and Alva at last knew that he was beaten. He had to be satisfied with a payment of two millions of florins for two years.

The real fighting force among the Reformed Netherlanders was to be found, not among the landsmen, but
in the sailors and fishermen. It is said that Admiral
Coligny was the first to point this out to the Prince of
Orange. He acted upon the advice, and in 1569 he had
given letters of marque to some eighteen small vessels to
cruise in the narrow seas and attack the Spaniards. At
first they were little better than pirates,—men of various
nationalities united by a fierce hatred of Spaniards and
Papists, feared by friends and foes alike. William attempted, at first somewhat unsuccessfully, to reduce them
to discipline and order, by issuing with his letters of
marque orders limiting their indiscriminate pillage, insisting upon the maintenance of religious services on board,
and declaring that one-third of the booty was to be given
to himself for the common good of the country. In their
earlier days they were allowed to refit and sell their plunder
in English ports, but these were closed to them on strong
remonstrances from the Court of Spain. It was almost by
accident that they seized and held (April 1st, 1572)
Brill or Brielle, a strongly fortified town on Voorn,
which was then an island at the mouth of the Maas, some
twenty miles west or seaward from Rotterdam. The inhabitants were forced to take an oath of allegiance to
William as Stadtholder under the King, and the flag of
what was afterwards to become the United Provinces was
hoisted on land for the first time. It was not William,
but his brother Louis of Nassau, who was the first to see
the future possibilities in this act. He urged the seizure
of Flushing or Vlissingen, the chief stronghold in Zeeland,
situated on an island at the mouth of the Honte or western
Scheldt, and commanding the entrance to Antwerp. The
citizens rose in revolt against the Spanish garrison; the
Sea-Beggars, as they were called, hurried to assist them;
the town was taken, and the Spanish commander, Pachecho,
was captured and hanged. This gave the seamen possession
of the whole island of Walcheren save the fortified town of
Middleburg. Delfshaven and Schiedam were seized. The

news swept through Holland, Zeeland, Guelderland, Utrecht, and Friesland, and town after town declared for William of Orange the Stadtholder. The leaders were marvellously encouraged to renewed exertions.[1] Proclamations in the name of the new ruler were scattered broadcast through the country, and the people were fired by a song said to be written by Sainte Aldegonde, *Wilhelmus van Nassouwen*, which is still the national hymn of Holland. The Prince of Orange thought he might venture on another invasion, and was already near Brussels when the news of the Massacre of Saint Bartholomew reached him. His plans had been based on assistance from France, urged by Coligny and promised by Charles IX. " What a sledge-hammer blow (*coup de massue*) that has been," he wrote to his brother; " my only hope was from France." Mons, which Louis had seized in the south with his French troops, had to be abandoned; and William, after some vain efforts, had to disband his troops.

Then Alva came out from Brussels to wreak a fearful vengeance on Mons, Mechlin, Tergoes, Naarden, Haarlem, and Zutphen. The terms of the capitulation of Mons were violated. Mechlin was plundered and set on fire by the Spanish troops. The Spanish commander sent against Zutphen had orders to burn every house, and to slay men, women, and children. Haarlem was invested, resisted desperately, and then capitulated on promise of lenient treatment. When the Spaniards entered they butchered in cold blood all the Dutch soldiers and some hundreds of the citizens; and, tying the bodies two and two together, they cast them into the Haarlem lake. It seemed as if the Papists had determined to exterminate the Protestants when they found that they could not convert them.

Some towns, however, held out. Don Frederick, the son of Alva and the butcher of Haarlem, was beaten back from the little town of Alkmaar. The *Sea-Beggars* met the Spanish fleet sent to crush them, sank or scattered the

---

[1] Cf. William's letters, *Correspondance*, etc. iii. 47-73.

[2] Groen van Prinsteter, *Archives ou Correspondance inédite de la Orange Nassau* (Utrecht, 1841-61).

ships, and took the Admiral prisoner. The nation of fishermen and shopkeepers, once the scorn of Spain and of
Europe for their patient endurance of indignities, were
seen at last to be a race of heroes, determined never again
to endure the yoke of the Spaniard. Alva had soon to
face a soldiery mutinous for want of pay, and to see all
his sea approaches in the hands of Dutch sailors, whom
the strongest fleets of Spain could not subdue. The iron
pitiless man at last acknowledged that he was beaten, and
demanded his recall. He left Brussels on Dec. 18th, 1573,
and did not again see the land he had deluged with blood
during a space of six years. Like all tyrants, he had
great faith in his system, even when it had broken in his
hand. Had he been a little more severe, added a few more
drops to the sea of blood he had spilled, all would have
gone well. The only advice he could give to his successor
was, to burn down every town he could not garrison with
Spanish troops.

The new Spanish Regent was Don Louis Requesens-y-
Zuniga, a member of the higher nobility of Spain, and a
Grand Commander of the Knights of Malta. He was
high-minded, and of a generous disposition. Had he been
sent to the Netherlands ten years sooner, and allowed to
act with a free hand, the history of the Netherlands might
have been different. His earlier efforts at government
were marked by attempts to negotiate, and he was at
pains to give Philip his reasons for his conduct.

"Before my arrival," he wrote, "I could not comprehend
how the rebels contrived to maintain fleets so considerable,
while your Majesty could not maintain one. Now I see
that men who are fighting for their lives, their families,
their property, and their false religion, in short, for their own
cause, are content if they receive only rations without pay."

He immediately reversed the policy of Alva: he repealed the hated taxes; dissolved the Council of Blood,
and published a general amnesty. But he could not come
to terms with the "rebels." William of Orange refused

all negotiation which was not based on three preliminary
conditions—freedom of conscience, and liberty to preach
the Gospel according to the Word of God ; the restoration
of all the ancient charters; and the withdrawal of all
Spaniards from all posts military and civil. He would
accept no truce nor amnesty without these. " We have
heard too often," he said, " the words *Agreed* and *Eternal.*
If I have your word for it, who will guarantee that the King
will not deny it, and be absolved for his breach of faith by
the Pope ? " Requesens, hating the necessity, had to carry
on the struggle which the policy of his King and of the
Regents who preceded him had provoked.

The fortune of war seemed to be unchanged. The
patriots were always victorious at sea and tenacious in
desperate defence of their fortified towns when they were
besieged, but they went down before the veteran Spanish
infantry in almost every battle fought on land. In the
beginning of 1574 two fortresses were invested. The
patriots were besieging Middleburg, and the Spaniards
had invested Leyden. The *Sea-Beggars* routed the Spanish
fleet in a bloody fight in the mouth of the Scheldt, and
Middleburg had to surrender. Leyden had two months'
respite owing to a mutiny among the Spanish soldiers, but
the citizens neglected the opportunity thus given them
to revictual their town. It was again invested (May
26th), and hardly pressed. Louis of Nassau, leading an
army to its assistance, was totally routed at Mookerheide,
and he and his younger brother Henry were among the
slain. The fate of Leyden seemed to be sealed, when
William suggested to the Estates of Holland to cut the
dykes and let in the sea. The plan was adopted. But
the dykes took long to cut, and when they were opened
and the water began to flow in slowly, violent winds
swept it back to the sea. Within Leyden the supply of
food was melting away ; and the famished and anxious
burghers, looking over the plain from the steeples of the
town, saw help coming so slowly that it seemed as if it
could arrive only when it was too late. The Spaniards

knew also of the coming danger, and, calculating on the extremities of the townsfolk, urged on them to surrender, with promises of an honourable capitulation. "We have two arms," one of the defenders on the walls shouted back, "and when hunger forces us we will eat the one and fight you with the other." Four weary months passed amidst indescribable sufferings, when at last the sea reached the walls. With it came the patriotic fleet, sailing over buried corn fields and gardens, piloted through orchards and villages. The Spaniards fled in terror, for the *Sea-Beggars* were upon them, shouting their battle-cry, "Sooner Turks than Papists." Townsmen and sailors went to the great church to offer thanksgiving for the deliverance which had been brought them from the sea. When the vast audience was singing a psalm of deliverance, the voices suddenly ceased, and nothing was heard but low sobbing; the people, broken by long watching and famine, overcome by unexpected deliverance, could only weep.

The good news was brought to Delft by Hans Brugge, who found William in church at the afternoon service. When the sermon was ended, the deliverance of Leyden was announced from the pulpit. William, weak with illness as he was, rode off to Leyden at once to congratulate the citizens on their heroic defence and miraculous deliverance. There he proposed the foundation of what became the famous University of Leyden, which became for Holland what Wittenberg had been to Germany, Geneva to Switzerland, and Saumur to France.

The siege of Leyden was the turning-point in the war for independence. The Spanish Regent saw that a new Protestant State was slowly and almost imperceptibly forming. His troops were almost uniformly victorious in the field, but the victories did not seem to be of much value. He decided once more to attempt negotiation. The conferences came to nothing. The utmost that Philip II. would concede was that the Protestants should have time to sell their possessions and leave the country. The war was again renewed, when death came to relieve

Requesens of his difficulties (March 1575). His last months were disgraced by the recommendation he made to his master to offer a reward for the assassination of the Prince of Orange.

The history of the next few years is a tangled story which would take too long to tell. When Requesens died the treasury was empty, and no public money was forthcoming. The Spanish soldiers mutinied, clamouring for their pay. They seized on some towns and laid hold on the citadel of Antwerp. Then occurred the awful pillage of the great city, when, during three terrible November days, populous and wealthy Antwerp suffered all the horrors that could be inflicted upon it.

The sudden death of Requesens had left everything in confusion; and leading men, both Roman Catholic and Protestant, conceived that advantage should be taken of the absence of any Spanish Governor to see whether all the seventeen provinces of the Netherlands could not combine on some common programme which would unite the country in spite of their religious differences. Delegates met together at Ghent (Oct. 28th, 1576) and drafted a treaty. A meeting of States General for the southern provinces was called to assemble at Brussels in November, and the members were discussing the terms of the treaty when the news of the "Spanish Fury" at Antwerp reached them. The story of the ghastly horrors perpetrated on their countrymen doubtless hastened their decision, and the treaty was ratified both by the States General and by the Council of State. The *Pacification of Ghent* cemented an alliance between the southern provinces represented in the States General which met at Brussels and the northern provinces of Holland and Zeeland. Its chief provisions were that all should combine to drive the Spanish and other foreign troops out of the land, and that a formal meeting of delegates from all the seventeen provinces should be called to deliberate upon the religious question. In the meantime the Roman Catholic religion was to be maintained; the *Placards* were to be abolished;

the Prince of Orange was declared to be the Governor of the seventeen provinces and the Admiral-General of Holland and Zeeland; and the confiscation of the properties of the houses of Nassau and Brederode was rescinded.

Don John of Austria had been appointed by Philip Regent of the Netherlands, and was in Luxemburg early in November. His arrival there was intimated to the States General, who refused to acknowledge him as Regent unless he would approve of the *Pacification of Ghent* and swear to maintain the ancient privileges of the various provinces. Months were spent in negotiations, but the States General were unmovable. He yielded at length, and made his State entry into Brussels on May 1st, 1577. When once there he found himself overshadowed by William, who had been accepted as leader by Roman Catholics and Protestants alike. But Philip with great exertions had got together an army of twenty thousand veteran Spanish and Italian troops, and sent them to the Netherlands under the command of Alexander Farnese, the son of the former Regent, Margaret Duchess of Parma. The young Duke of Parma was a man of consummate abilities, military and diplomatic, and was by far the ablest agent Philip ever had in the Low Countries. He defeated the patriotic army at Gemblours (Jan. 31st, 1578), and several towns at once opened their gates to Parma and Don John. To increase the confusion, John Casimir, brother of the Elector Palatine, invaded the land from the east at the head of a large body of German mercenary soldiers to assist the Calvinists; the Archduke Matthias, brother of the Emperor Rudolph, was already in the country, invited by the Roman Catholics; and the Duke of Anjou had invaded the Netherlands from the south to uphold the interests of those Romanists who did not wish to tolerate Protestantism but hated the Spaniards. These foreigners represented only too well the latent divisions of the country—divisions which were skilfully taken advantage of by the Duke of Parma. After struggling in vain for a union of the whole seventeen provinces on the basis of complete religious toleration, William saw that his task was hopeless. Neither the majority of the Romanists nor the majority of the Protestants could understand toleration. Delegates of the Romanist provinces of Hainault, Douay, and Artois met at Arras (Jan. 5th, 1579) to form a league which had for its ultimate intention a reconciliation with Spain on the basis of the *Pacification of Ghent*, laying stress on the provision for the maintenance of the Roman Catholic religion. Thus challenged, the northern provinces of Holland, Zeeland, Utrecht, Guelderland, and Zutphen met at Utrecht (Jan. 29th, 1579), and formed a league to maintain themselves against all foreign Princes, including the King of Spain. These two leagues mark the definite separation of the Romanist South from the Protestant North, and the creation of a new Protestant State, the United Provinces. William did not sign the Treaty of Utrecht until May 3rd.

In 1581, Philip made a last attempt to overcome his indomitable antagonist. He published the Ban against him, denouncing him as a traitor and an enemy of the human race, and offering a reward of twenty-five thousand crowns and a patent of nobility to anyone who should deliver him to the King dead or alive. William answered in his famous *Apology*, which gives an account of his whole career, and contains a scathing exposure of Philip's misdeeds. The *Apology* was translated into several languages, and sent to all the Courts of Europe. Brabant, Flanders, Utrecht, Guelderland, Holland, and Zeeland answered Philip by the celebrated Act of Abjuration (July 26th, 1581), in which they solemnly renounced allegiance to the King of Spain, and constituted themselves an independent republic.

The date of the abjuration may be taken as the beginning of the new era, the birth of another Protestant nation. Its young life had been consecrated in a baptism of blood and fire such as no other nation in Europe had to endure. Its Declaration of Independence did not procure immediate relief. Nearly thirty years of further struggle awaited it; and it was soon to mourn the loss of its heroic leader. The rewards promised by Philip II. were a spur to the zeal of Romanist fanatics. In 1582 (March 18th), Juan Jaureguy, a Biscayan, made a desperate attempt at assassination, which for the moment was thought to be successful. The pistol was so close to the Prince that his hair and beard were set on fire, and the ball entering under the right ear, passed through the palate and out by the left jaw. Two years later (July 9th, 1584), William fell mortally wounded by Balthasar Gerard, whose heirs claimed the reward for assassination promised by Philip, and received part of it from the King. The Prince's last words were : " My God, have mercy on my soul and on these poor people."

The sixteenth century produced no nobler character than that of William, Prince of Orange. His family were Lutherans, but they permitted the lad to be brought up in the Roman Catholic religion—the condition which Charles V. had imposed before he would consent to give effect to the will of René, Prince of Orange,[1] who, dying at the early age of twenty-six, had left his large possessions to his youthful cousin, William of Nassau. In an intolerant age he stands forth as the one great leader who rose above the religious passions of the time, and who strove all his life to secure freedom of conscience and right of public worship for men of all creeds.[2] He was a consistent liberal Roman Catholic down to the close of 1555. His letter (January 24th, 1566) to Margaret of Parma

---

[1] The small principality of Orange-Chalons was situated in the south of France on the river Rhone, its south-west corner being about ten miles north of the city of Avignon. Henry of Nassau, the uncle of our William of Orange, had married Claude, the sister of Philibert, the last male of the House of Orange-Chalons ; and Philibert had bequeathed his principality to his nephew René, the son of Henry and Claude. The principality was of no great value compared with the other possessions of the House of Nassau, but as it was under no overlord, its possessor took rank among the *sovereign* princes of Europe.

[2] Putnam, *William the Silent, the Prince of Orange, the moderate man of the Sixteenth Century*, 2 vols., New York, 1895.

perhaps reveals the beginnings of a change. He called himself "a good Christian," not a "good Catholic." Before the end of that year he had said privately that he was ready to return to the faith of his childhood and subscribe the Augsburg Confession. During his exile in 1568 he had made a daily study of the Holy Scriptures, and, whatever the exact shade of his theological opinions, had become a deeply religious man, animated with the lofty idea that God had called him to do a great work for Him and for His persecuted people. His private letters, meant for no eyes but those of his wife or of his most familiar friends, are full of passages expressing a quiet faith in God and in the leadings of His Providence.[1] During the last years of his life the teachings of Calvin had more and more taken hold on his intellect and sympathy, and he publicly declared himself a Calvinist in 1573 (October 23rd). A hatred of every form of oppression was his ruling passion, and he himself has told us that it was when he learnt that the Kings of France and Spain had come to a secret understanding to extirpate heresy by fire and sword, that he made the silent resolve to drive "This vermin of Spaniards out of his country."[2]

The Protestant Netherlands might well believe themselves lost when he fell under the pistol of the assassin; but he left them a legacy in the persons of his confidential friend Johan van Oldenbarneveldt and of his son Maurice. Oldenbarneveldt's patient diplomatic genius completed the political work left unfinished by William; and Maurice,[3]

[1] Gachard, *Correspondance de Guillaume le Taciturne, Prince d'Orange*, ii. 110.

[2] It is said that William's reticence on hearing this news, which moved him so much, gained him the name of "The Silent" (*le taciturne*): it is more probable that the soubriquet was given to him by Cardinal de Granvelle.

[3] Maurice succeeded his father as Stadtholder, and became Prince of Orange in 1618 on the death of his elder brother, Philip William, who was kidnapped from Louvain and brought up as a Roman Catholic by Philip II. William was married four times:

a. In 1550, to Anne of Egmont, only child of Maximilian of Buren. Her son was Philip William; she died in March 1558.

b. In 1561, to Anne, daughter of the Elector Maurice of Saxony, and

a lad of seventeen at his father's death, was acknowledged only a few years afterwards as the greatest military leader in Europe. The older man in the politician's study, and the boy-general in the field, were able to keep the Spaniards at bay, until at length, in 1607 (October), a suspension of arms was agreed to. This resulted in a truce for twelve years (April 9th, 1609), which was afterwards prolonged indefinitely. The Dutch had won their independence, and had become a strong Protestant power whose supremacy at sea was challenged only by England.

Notwithstanding the severity of the persecutions which they endured, the Protestants of the Netherlands organised themselves into churches, and as early as 1563 the delegates from the various churches met in a synod to settle the doctrine and discipline which was to bind them together. This was not done without internal difficulties. The people of the Netherlands had received the Evangelical faith from various sources, and the converts tenaciously clung to the creed and ecclesiastical system with which they were first acquainted. The earliest Reformation preachers in the Low Countries were followers of Luther, and many of them had been trained at Wittenberg. Lutherans were numerous among the lesser nobility and the more substantial burghers. Somewhat later the opinions of Zwingli also found their way into the Netherlands, and were adopted by many very sincere believers. The French-

granddaughter of Philip of Hesse. She early developed symptoms of incipient insanity, which came to a height when she deserted her husband in 1567 and went to live a disreputable life in Cologne. She became insane, and her family seized her and imprisoned her until she died in 1573. She was the mother of Maurice.

c. In 1571, Charlotte de Bourbon, daughter of the Duc de Montpensier. She had been a nun, had embraced the Reformed faith, and fled to Germany. The marriage was a singularly happy one. She was scarcely recovered from childbirth when William was almost killed by Jaureguy, and the shock, combined with her incessant toil in nursing her husband, was too much for her strength ; she died in 1582 (May 5th).

d. In 1583, to Louise de Coligny, daughter of the celebrated Admiral Coligny. She had lost both her parents in the Massacre of Saint Bartholomew. She was a wonderful and charming woman, beloved by her stepchildren and adored by her adopted country ; she survived her husband forty years.

speaking provinces in the south had been evangelised for the most part by missioners trained under Calvin at Geneva, and they brought his theology with them. Thus Luther, Zwingli, and Calvin had all attached followers in the Low Countries. The differences found expression, not so much in matters of doctrine as in preferences for different forms of Church government; and although they were almost overcome, they reappeared later in the contest which emerged in the beginning of the seventeenth century about the relation which ought to subsist between the civil and the ecclesiastical authorities. In the end, the teaching of Geneva displaced both Lutheranism and Zwinglianism, and the Reformed in the Netherlands became Calvinist in doctrine and discipline.

Accordingly, most of the churches were early organised on the principles of the churches in France, with a minister and a consistory of elders and deacons; and when delegates from the churches met to deliberate upon an organisation which would bind all together, the system which was adopted was the Presbyterian or Conciliar. The meeting was at Emden (1569), as it was too dangerous to assemble within the jurisdiction of the Government of the Nether- lands. It was resolved that the Church should be ruled by *consistories, classes*, and *synods*. This Conciliar organisation, thus adopted at Emden in 1569, might not have met with unanimous support had not the Reformed been exposed to the full fury of Alva's persecution. The consistorial system of the Lutheran Church, and the position which Zwingli assigned to the magistracy, are possible only when the civil government is favourably disposed towards the Church within the land which it rules; but Presbyterianism, as France, Scotland, and the Netherlands have proved, is the best suited for " a Church under the Cross." Nor need this be wondered at, for the Presbyterian or Conciliar is the revival of the government of the Church of the early centuries while still under the ban of the Roman Empire.[1]

---

[1] Lindsay, *The Church and the Ministry in the Early Centuries*, 2nd ed. (London, 1903), pp. 198, 204 *f.*, 259, 330 *n.*, 339.

A synod which met at Dordrecht (Dort) in 1572 revised, enlarged, and formally adopted the articles of this Emden synod or conference.

Two pecularities of the Dutch organisation ought to be explained. The *consistory* or kirk-session is the court which rules the individual congregation in Holland as in all other Presbyterian lands; but in the Dutch Church all Church members inhabiting a city are regarded as one congregation; the ministers are the pastors of the city, preaching in turn in all its buildings set apart for public worship, and the people are not considered to be specially attached to any one of the buildings, nor to belong to the flock of any one of the ministers; and therefore there is one consistory for the whole city. This peculiarity was also seen in the early centuries. Then it must be noticed that, owing to the political organisation of the United Provinces, it was difficult to arrange for a National Synod. The civil constitution was a federation of States, in many respects independent of each other, who were bound to protect each other in war, to maintain a common army, and to contribute to a common military treasury. When William of Orange was elected Stadtholder for life, one of the laws which bound him was that he should not acknowledge any ecclesiastical assembly which had not the approval of the civil authorities of the province in which it proposed to meet. This implied that each province was entitled to regulate its own ecclesiastical affairs. There could be no meeting of a National Synod unless all the United Provinces gave their approval. Hence the tendency was to prevent corporate and united action.

According to the articles of Emden, and the revised and enlarged edition approved at Dordrecht in 1572, it was agreed that office-bearers in the Church were to sign the *Confession of Faith*. This creed had been prepared by Guido de Brès (born at Mons in 1540) in 1561, and had been revised by several of his friends. It was based on the Confession of the French Church, and was originally written in French. It was approved by a series of Synods, and was translated into Dutch, German, and Latin. It is known as the Belgic Confession. Its original title was, *A Confession of Faith, generally and unanimously maintained by Believers dispersed throughout the Low Countries who desire to live according to the purity of the Holy Gospel of our Lord Jesus Christ.*[1] The Church also adopted the *Heidelberg Catechism*[2] for the instruction of the young.

The long fight against Spain and the Inquisition had stimulated the energies of the Church and the people of the Netherlands, and their Universities and theological schools soon rivalled older seats of learning. The University of Leyden, a thank-offering for the wonderful deliverance of the town, was founded in 1575; Franecker, ten years later, in 1585; and there followed in rapid succession the Universities of Gronningen (1612), Utrecht (1636), and Harderwyk (1648). Dutch theologians and lawyers became famous during the seventeenth century for their learning and acumen.

[1] Müller, *Die Bekenntnisschriften der reformierten Kirche* (Leipzig, 1903), p. 233; Schaff, *The Creeds of the Evangelical Protestant Churches*, 383.

[2] *Ibid.* p. 682.

CHAPTER VL

THE REFORMATION IN SCOTLAND.[1]

IF civilisation means the art of living together in peace
Scotland was almost four hundred years behind the rest of
Western Europe in the beginning of the sixteenth century.

[1] SOURCES :—*Calendar of the State Papers relating to Scotland and Mary Queen of Scots, 1547-1603* (Edinburgh, 1898, etc.) ; *Calendar of State Papers, Elizabeth, Foreign* (London, 1863, etc.) ; *Acts of the Parliament of Scotland,* ii. (1814) ; *Register of the Great Seal of Scotland* (Edinburgh, 1886) ; *Register of the Privy Council of Scotland,* i. (Edinburgh, 1877) ; Labanoff, *Lettres inédites de Marie Stuart* (Paris, 1839), and *Lettres, instructions et mémoires de Marie Stuart* (London, 1844) ; Pollen, *Papal Negotiations with Mary Queen of Scots* (Scottish Historical Society, Edinburgh, 1901) ; Teulet, *Papiers d'état . . . relatifs à l'histoire de l'Écosse* (Bannatyne Club, 1851), and *Relations politiques de la France et de l'Espagne avec l'Écosse* (Paris, 1862) ; Lesley, *History of Scotland* (Scottish Text Society, Edinburgh, 1888) ; John Knox, *Works* (edited by D. Laing, Edinburgh, 1846-55) ; *The Book of the Universal Kirk* (Bannatyne Club, Edinburgh, 1839) ; *Gude and Godlie Ballatis* (edited by Mitchell for Scottish Text Society, Edinburgh, 1897) ; (Dunlop), *A Collection of Confessions of Faith,* etc. ii. (Edinburgh, 1722) ; Calderwood, *History of the Kirk of Scotland* (Woodrow Society, Edinburgh, 1842-49) ; Row, *History of the Kirk of Scotland* (Woodrow Society, Edinburgh, 1842) ; Spottiswoode, *History of the Church and State of Scotland* (Spottiswoode Society, Edinburgh, 1851) ; Scott, *Fasti Ecclesiæ Scoticanæ* (Edinburgh, 1866-71) ; Sir David Lindsay, *Poetical Works* (edited by David Laing, Edinburgh, 1879) ; *The Book of Common Order of the Church of Scotland* (edited by Sprott and Leishman, Edinburgh, 1868) ; *Rotuli Scotiæ* ; *Calvin's Letters* (*Corpus Reformatorum,* xxxviii.-xlviii.).

LATER BOOKS : D. Hay Fleming, *Mary Queen of Scots from her birth until her flight into England* (London, 1897), *The Scottish Reformation* (Edinburgh, 1904), and *The Story of the Scottish Covenants* (Edinburgh, 1904) ; P. Hume Brown, *John Knox* (London, 1895), and *George Buchanan* (Edinburgh, 1890) ; M'Crie, *Life of Knox* (Edinburgh, 1840) ; Grub, *Ecclesiastical History of Scotland* (Edinburgh, 1861) ; Cunningham, *The Church History of Scotland* (Edinburgh, 1882) ; Lorimer, *Life of Patrick Hamilton* (Edinburgh, 1857), *John Knox and the Church of England* (London, 1875).

The history of her kings is a tale of assassinations long minorities, regencies scrambled and fought for by unscrupulous barons; and kingly authority, which had been growing in other countries, was on the verge of extinction in Scotland. Her Parliament or Estates of the Realm was a mere feudal assembly, with more than the usual uncertainty regarding who were entitled to be present; while its peculiar management by a Committee of the Estates made it a facile instrument in the hands of the faction who were for the moment in power, and robbed it of any stable influence on the country as a whole. The Church, wealthy so far as acreage was concerned, had become secularised to an extent unknown elsewhere, and its benefices served to provide for the younger sons of the great feudal families in a manner which recalls the days of Charles the Hammer.[1]

Yet the country had been prepared for the Reformation by the education of the people, especially of the middle class, by constant intercourse between Scotland and France and the Low Countries, and by the sympathy which Scottish students had felt for the earlier movements towards Church reform in England and Bohemia; while the wealth and immorality of the Romish clergy, the poverty of the nobility and landed gentry, and the changing political situation, combined to give an impetus to the efforts of those who longed for a Reformation.

More than one historian has remarked that the state of education in Scotland had always been considerably in advance of what might have been expected from its backward civilisation. This has been usually traced to the enduring influence of the old Celtic Church—a Church which had maintained its hold on the country for more than seven centuries, and which had always looked upon the education of the people as a religious duty. Old Celtic ecclesiastical rules declared that it was as important to teach boys and girls to read, as to dispense the sacraments, and to take part in *soul-friendship* (confession). The

[1] Cf. *Cambridge Modern History* (Cambridge, 1903), ii. 551-58.

Celtic monastery had always been an educational centre; and when Charles the Great established the High Schools which grew to be the older Universities of northern Europe, the Celtic monasteries furnished many of the teachers. The very complete educational system of the old Church had been taken over into the Roman Church which supplanted it, under Queen Margaret and her sons. Hence it was that the Cathedral and Monastery Schools produced a number of scholars who were eager to enrich their stores of learning beyond what the mother-country could give them, and the Scotch wandering student was well known during the Middle Ages on the Continent of Europe. One Scottish bishop founded a Scots College in Paris for his countrymen; other bishops obtained from English kings safe-conducts for their students to reside at Oxford and Cambridge.

This scholastic intercourse brought Scotland in touch with the intellectual movements in Europe. Scottish students at Paris listened to the lectures of Peter Dubois and William of Ockham when they taught the theories contained in the *Defensor Pacis* of Marsiglio of Padua, who had expounded that the Church is not the hierarchy, but the Christian people, and had denied both the temporal and spiritual supremacy of the Pope. The *Rotuli Scotiæ*,[1] or collection of safe-conducts issued by English monarchs to inhabitants of the northern kingdom, show that a continuous stream of Scottish students went to the English Universities from 1357 to 1389. During the earlier years of this period—that is, up to 1364—the safe-conducts applied for and granted entitled the bearers to go to Oxford or Cambridge or any other place of learning in England; but from 1364 to 1379 Oxford seems to have been the only University frequented. During one of these years (1365) safe-conducts were given to no fewer than eighty-one Scottish students to study in Oxford. The period was that during which

[1] *Rotuli Scotiæ*, i. 808, 815, 816, 822, 825, 828, 829, 849, 851, 859, 877, 881, 886, 891, 896, ii. 8, 20, 45, 100.

the influence of Wiclif was most powerful, when Oxford seethed with Lollardy; and the teachings of the great Reformer were thus brought into Scotland.

Lollardy seems to have made great progress. In 1405, Robert, Duke of Albany, was made Governor of Scotland, and Andrew Wyntoun in his Metrical Chronicle praises him for his fidelity to the Church:

> " He wes a constant Catholike,
> All Lollard he hatyt and heretike."[1]

From this time down to the very dawn of the Reformation we find references to Lollardy in contemporary writers and in Acts of the Scots Parliament; and all the earlier histories of the Reformation movement in Scotland relate the story of the Lollards of Kyle and their interview with King James IV.[2]

The presence of Lollard opinions in Scotland must have attracted the attention of the leaders of the Hussites in Bohemia. In 1433 (July 23rd), Paul Craw or Crawar was seized, tried before the Inquisitorial court, condemned, and burnt as a heretic. He had brought letters from the Hussites of Prag, and acknowledged that he had been sent to interest the Scots in the Hussite movement—one of the many emissaries who were despatched in 1431 and 1432 by Procopius and John Rokycana into all European lands. He was found by the Inquisitor to be a man *in sacris literis et in allegatione Bibliæ promptus et exercitatus.* Knox tells us that he was condemned for denying transubstantiation, auricular confession to the priests, and prayers to saints departed. We learn also from Knox that at his burning the executioner put a ball of brass in his mouth that the people might not hear his defence. His execution did not arrest the progress of Lollardy.

---

[1] Wyntoun, *Orygynale Cronykil,* ix. c. xxvi. 2773, 2774.

[2] For a collection of these references, cf. *The Scottish Historical Review* for April 1904, pp. 266 *ff.* Purvey's revision of Wiclif's *New Testament* was translated by Murdoch Nisbet into Scots. It is being published by the Scottish Text Society, *The New Testament in Scots,* i. 1901, ii. 1903. The translation was made about 1520.

The earlier poems of Sir David Lindsay contain Lollard opinions. By the time that these were published (1529–1530), Lutheran writings had found their way into Scotland, and may have influenced the writer; but the sentiments in the *Testament and Complaynt of the Papyngo* are more Lollard than Lutheran.

The Romish Church in Scotland was comparatively wealthy, and the rude Scottish nobles managed to place their younger sons in many a fat living, with the result that the manners of the clergy did little honour to their sacred calling. Satirists began to point the moral. John Row says:

"As for the more particulare means whereby many in Scotland got some knowledge of God's trueth, in the time of great darkness, there were some books sett out, such as Sir David Lindesay his poesie upon the *Four Monarchies*, wherein many other treatises are conteined, opening up the abuses among the Clergie at that tyme; Wedderburn's Psalms and *Godlie Ballads*, changing many of the old Popish songs unto Godlie purposes; a *Complaint* given in by the halt, blinde and poore of England, aganis the prelats, preists, friers, and others such kirkmen, who prodigallie wasted all the tithes and kirk liveings upon their unlawfull pleasures, so that they could get no sustentation nor releef as God had ordained. This was printed and came into Scotland. There were also some theatricall playes, comedies, and other notable histories acted in publict; for Sir David Lindesay his Satyre was acted in the Amphitheater of St. Johnestoun (Perth), before King James the v., and a great part of the nobilitie and gentrie, fra morn to even, whilk made the people sensible of the darknes wherein they lay, of the wickednes of their kirkmen, and did let them see how God's Kirk should have bene otherwayes guyded nor it was ; all of whilk did much good for that tyme."[1]

It may be doubted, however, whether the Scottish people felt the real sting in such satires until they began to be

---

[1] Row, *History of the Kirk of Scotland from the year 1558 to August 1637* (Edinburgh, 1842), p. 6.

taught by preachers who had been to Wittenberg, or who had studied the writings of Luther and other Reformers, or who had learned from private perusal of the Scriptures what it was to be in earnest about pardon of sin and salvation of soul.

Some of the towns on the East Coast were centres of trade with the Continent, and Leith had once been an obscure member of the great Hanseatic League. Lutheran and other tracts were smuggled into Scotland from Campvere by way of Leith, Dundee, and Montrose. The authorities were on the alert, and tried to put an end to the practice. In 1525, Parliament forbade strangers bringing Lutheran books into Scotland on pain of imprisonment and forfeiture of their goods and ships ;[1] and in the same year the Government were informed that "sundry strangers and others within the diocese of Aberdeen were possessed of Luther's books, and favoured his errors and false opinions." Two years later (1527), the Act was made to include those who assisted in spreading Lutheran views. An agent of Wolsey informed the Cardinal that Scottish merchants were purchasing copies of Tindale's New Testament in the Low Countries and sending them to Scotland.[2] The efforts of the Government do not seem to have been very successful. Another Act of Parliament in 1535 declared that none but the clergy were to be allowed to purchase heretical books ; all others possessing such were required to give them up within forty days.[3] This legislation clearly shows the spread of Reformed writings among the people of Scotland.

The first Scottish martyr was Patrick Hamilton, a younger son of Sir Patrick Hamilton of Kincavel and Stanehouse. He had studied at Paris and Louvain. As he took his degree of M.A. in Paris in 1520, he had been there when the writings of Luther were being studied by all learned men, including the theological students of the

---

[1] *Act. Parl. Scot.* ii. 295.
[2] Hay Fleming, *The Scottish Reformation,* p. 12.
[3] *Act. Parl. Scot.* ii. 341.

Sorbonne (the theological faculty).[1] Hamilton must have been impressed by the principles of the German Reformer, and have made no secret of his views when he returned to Scotland; for in the beginning of 1527 he was a suspected heretic, and was ordered to be summoned and accused as such. He fled from Scotland, went to Wittenberg, was at the opening of Philip of Hesse's new Evangelical University of Marburg (May 30th, 1527), and drafted the theses for the first academic Disputation.[2] He felt constrained, however, to return to his native land to testify against the corruptions of the Roman Church, and was preaching in Scotland in the end of autumn 1527. The success attending his ministry excited the fears of the prelates. He was invited, or rather enticed, to St. Andrews; allowed for nearly a month to preach and dispute in the University; and was then arrested and tried in the cathedral. The trial took place in the forenoon, and at mid-day he was hurried to the stake (Feb. 27th, 1528). The fire by carelessness rather than with intention was slow, and death came only after lingering hours of agony.

If the ecclesiastical authorities thought to stamp out the new faith by this martyrdom, they were soon to discover their mistake. Alexander Alane (Alesius), who had undertaken to convince Patrick Hamilton of his errors, had been himself converted. He was arrested and imprisoned, but escaped to the Continent. The following years witnessed a succession of martyrs—Henry Forrest (1533), David Stratton and Norman Gourlay (1534), Duncan Simpson, Forrester, Keillor, Beverage, Forret, Russell, and Kennedy

---

[1] Luther says so himself; cf. letter to Lange of April 13th, 1519; De Wette, *Dr. Martin Luthers Briefe, Sendschreiben*, etc. (Berlin, 1825-28) i. 255; and Herminjard, *Correspondance des Réformateurs dans les pays de langue française* (Geneva and Paris, 1866-97), i. 47, 48.

[2] These theses were translated from the Latin into the vernacular by John Firth, and published under the title of *Patrick's Places*. They are printed in Fox's *Acts and Monuments*, and by Knox in his *History of the Reformation in Scotland; The Works of John Knox collected and edited by David Laing* (Edinburgh, 1846-64), i. 19 *ff*. For Patrick Hamilton, cf. Lorimer, *Patrick Hamilton, the first Preacher and Martyr of the Scottish Reformation* (Edinburgh, 1857).

(1539). The celebrated George Buchanan was imprisoned, but managed to escape.[1] The Scots Parliament and Privy Council assisted the Churchmen to extirpate the new faith in a series of enactments which themselves bear witness to its spread. In 1540, in a series of Acts (March 14th) it was declared that the Virgin Mary was "to be reverently worshipped, and prayers made to her" for the King's prosperity, for peace with all Christian princes, for the triumph of the "Faith Catholic," and that the people "may remain in the faith and conform to the statutes of Holy Kirk." Prayers were also ordered to be made to the saints. It was forbidden to argue against, or impugn, the papal authority under pain of death and confiscation of "goods movable and immovable." No one is to "cast down or otherwise treat irreverently or in any ways dishonour" the images of saints canonised by the Church. Heretics who have seen the error of their ways are not to discuss with others any matters touching "our holy faith." No one suspected of heresy, even if he has recanted, is to be eligible to hold any office, nor to be admitted to the King's Council. All who assist heretics are threatened with severe punishment. In 1543, notwithstanding all this legislation, the Lord Governor (the Earl of Arran) had to confess that heretics increase rapidly, and spread opinions contrary to the Church.[2] The terms of some of these enactments show that the new faith had been making converts among the nobility ; and they also indicate the chief points of attack on the Roman Church in Scotland.

In 1542 (Dec. 14th), James v. died, leaving an infant daughter, Mary (b. Dec. 8th), who became the Queen of Scots when barely a week old. Thus Scotland was again harassed with an infant sovereign ; and there was the usual scramble for the Regency, which this time involved questions of national policy as well as personal aggrandisement.

---

[1] Buchanan, *Rerum Scoticarum Historia,* xiv. (p. 277 in Ruddiman's edition).

[2] *Act. Parl. Scot.* ii. 871, ii. 443.

It was the settled policy of the Tudor kings to detach
Scotland from the old French alliance, and secure it for
England. The marriage of Margaret Tudor to James IV.
shows what means they thought to employ, and but for
Margaret's quarrel with the Earl of Angus, her second
husband, another wedding might have bound the nations
firmly together. The French marriages of James V., first
with Madeleine, daughter of Francis I. (1537), and on her
premature death with Mary of Guise (1538), showed the
recoil of Scotland from the English alliance. James' death
gave Henry VIII. an opportunity to renew his father's
schemes, and his idea was to betroth his boy Edward to the
baby Mary, and get the "little Queen" brought to England
for education. Many Scotsmen thought the proposal a good
one for their country, and perhaps more were induced to
think so by the money which Henry lavished upon them
to secure their support. They made the English party in
Scotland. The policy of English alliance as against French
alliance was complicated by the question of religion.
Whatever may be thought of the character of the English
Reformation at this date, Henry VIII. had broken
thoroughly with the Papacy, and union with England would
have dragged Scotland to revolt against the mediæval
Church. The leader of the French and Romanist party
in Scotland was David Beaton, certainly the ablest and
perhaps the most unscrupulous man there. He had been
made Archbishop of St. Andrews, coadjutor to his aged
uncle, in 1538. In the same month, Pope Paul III., who
needed a Churchman of the highest rank to publish his Bull
against Henry VIII. in a place as near England as was
possible to find, had sent him a Cardinal's Hat. The
Cardinal, Beaton, stood in Scotland for France *and* Rome
against England and the Reformation. The struggle for
the Regency in Scotland in 1542 carried with it an international and a religious policy. The clouds heralding the
storm which was to destroy Mary, gathered round the
cradle of the baby Queen.

At first the English faction prevailed. The claims of

the Queen Mother were scarcely considered. Beaton produced a will, said to have been fraudulently obtained from the dying King, appointing him and several of the leading nobles of Scotland, Governors of the kingdom. This arrangement was soon set aside, the Earl of Arran was appointed Governor (Jan. 3rd, 1543), and Beaton was confined in Blackness Castle.

The Governor selected John Rough for his chaplain and Thomas Williams for his preacher, both ardent Reformers. The Acts of the previous reign against heresy were modified to the extent that men suspect of heresy might enjoy office, and heretics were accorded more merciful treatment. Moreover, an Act of Parliament (March 15th, 1543) permitted the possession and reading of a good and true translation of the Old and New Testaments. But the masterful policy of Henry VIII. and the weakness of the Governor brought about a change. Beaton was released from Blackness and restored to his own Castle of St. Andrews; the Governor dismissed his Reformed preachers; the Privy Council (June 2nd, 1543) forbade on pain of death and confiscation of goods all criticism of the mediæval doctrine of the Sacraments, and forbade the possession of heretical books. In September, Arran and Beaton were reconciled; in December, the Parliament annulled the treaties with England consenting to a marriage between Edward and Mary, and the ancient league with France was renewed. This was followed by the revival of persecution, and almost all that had been gained was lost. Henry's ruthless devastation of the Borders did not mend matters. The more enlightened policy of Lord Protector Somerset could not allay the suspicions of the Scottish nation. Their "little Queen" was sent to France to be educated by the Guises, "to the end that in hir youth she should drynk of that lycour, that should remane with hir all hir lyfetyme, for a plague to this realme, and for hir finall destructioun." [1]

[1] *The Works of John Knox, collected and edited by David Laing* (Edinburgh, 1846–64), i. 218.

But if the Reformation movement was losing ground as a national policy, it was gaining strength as a spiritual quickening in the hearts of the people. George Wishart, one of the Wisharts of Pittarrow, who had fled from persecution in 1538 and had wandered in England, Germany, and Switzerland, returned to his native country about 1543, consumed with the desire to bear witness for the Gospel. He preached in Montrose, and Dundee during a visitation of the plague, and Ayrshire. Beaton's party were anxious to secure him, and after a preaching tour in the Lothians he was seized in Ormiston House and handed over to the Earl of Bothwell, who, breaking pledges he had made, delivered him to the Cardinal; he lodged him in the dungeon at St. Andrews (end of Jan. 1546), and had him tried in the cathedral, when he was condemned to the stake (March 1st, 1546).

Wishart was Knox's forerunner, and during this tour in the Lothians, Knox had been his constant companion. The Romanist party had tried to assassinate the bold preacher, and Knox carried a two-handed sword ready to cut down anyone who attempted to strike at the missionary while he was speaking. All the tenderness which lay beneath the sternness of Knox's character appears in the account he gives of Wishart in his *History*. And to Wishart, Knox was the beloved disciple. When he foresaw that the end was near, he refused to allow Knox to share his danger.[1]

Assassination was a not infrequent way of getting rid of a political opponent in the sixteenth century, and Beaton's death had long been planned, not without secret promptings from England. Three months after Wishart's martyrdom (May 29th, 1546), Norman Lesley and Kirkcaldy of Grange at the head of a small band of men broke into the Castle of St. Andrews and slew the Cardinal. They held the stronghold, and the castle became a place of refuge for men whose lives were threatened by the Government, and who sympathised with the English alliance. The Government

[1] *The Works of John Knox*, etc. i. 125–45.

laid siege to the place but were unable to take it, and their troops withdrew. John Rough, who had been Arran's Reformed chaplain, joined the company, and began to preach to the people of St. Andrews. Knox, who had become a marked man, and had thought of taking refuge in Germany, was persuaded to enter the castle, and there, sorely against his will, he was almost forced to stand forth as a preacher of the Word. His first sermon placed him at once in the foremost rank of Scottish Reformers, and men began to predict that he would share the fate of Wishart. " Master George Wishart spak never so plainelye, and yitt he was brunt: evin so will he be." [1]

Next to nothing is known about the early history of John Knox. He came into the world at or near Haddington in the year 1515,[2] but on what day or month remains hidden. He sprang from the commons of Scotland, and his forebears were followers of the Earls of Bothwell ; he was a papal notary, and in priest's orders in 1540 ; he was tutor to the sons of the lairds of Ormiston and Longniddry in 1545 ; he accompanied Wishart in December and January 1545, 1546—these are the facts known about him before he was called to stand forward as a preacher of the Reformation in Scotland. He was then thirty-two—a silent, slow ripening man, with quite a talent for keeping himself in the background.

Knox's work in the castle and town of St. Andrews was interrupted by the arrival of a French fleet (July 1547), which battered the walls with artillery until the castle was compelled to surrender. He and all the inmates were carried over to France. They had secured as terms of surrender that their lives should be spared ; that they should be safely transported to France ; and that if they could not accept the terms there offered to them by the French King, they should be allowed to depart to

---

[1] *The Works of John Knox*, etc. i. 192.
[2] Dr. Hay Fleming has settled the vexed question of the date of Knox's birth in his article in the *Bookman* for Sept. 1905, p. 193 ; cf. *Athenæum*, Nov. 5th and Dec. 3rd, 1904.

any country they might select for their sojourn, save Scotland. It was not the custom, however, for French kings to keep promises made to heretics, and Knox and his companions were made galley-slaves. For nineteen months he had to endure this living death, which for long drawn out torture can only be compared with what the Christians of the earliest centuries had to suffer when they were condemned to the mines. He had to sit chained with four or six others to the rowing benches, which were set at right angles to the side of the ship, without change of posture by day, and compelled to sleep, still chained, under the benches by night; exposed to the elements day and night alike; enduring the lash of the overseer, who paced up and down the gangway which ran between the two lines of benches; feeding on the insufficient meals of coarse biscuit and porridge of oil and beans; chained along with the vilest malefactors. The French Papists had invented this method of treating all who differed from them in religious matters. It could scarcely make Knox the more tolerant of French policy or of the French religion. He seldom refers to this terrible experience. He dismisses it with:

" How long I continewed prisoneir, what torment I susteaned in the galaies, and what war the sobbes of my harte, is now no time to receat: This onlie I can nocht conceall, which mo than one have hard me say, when the body was far absent from Scotland, that my assured houp was, in oppin audience, to preache in Sanctandrois befoir I depairted this lyeff." [1]

The prisoners were released from the galleys through the instrumentality of the English Government in the early months of 1549, and Knox reached England by the 7th of April. It was there that he began his real work as a preacher of the Reformation. He spent nearly five years as minister at Berwick, at Newcastle, and in London. He was twice offered preferment—the vacant bishopric of Rochester in 1552, and the vicarage of All Hallows in

---

[1] *Works of John Knox,* etc. i. 349.

Bread St., London, in the beginning of 1553. He refused both, and was actually summoned before the Privy Council to explain why he would not accept preferment.[1] It is probable that he had something to do with the production of *The Book of Common Prayer and Administration of the Sacraments and other Rites and Ceremonies in the Church of England, 1552*, commonly called the *Second Prayer-Book* of King Edward VI. The rubric explaining kneeling at the partaking of the Holy Supper, or at least one sentence in it, is most probably due to his remonstrances or suggestions.[2] The accession of Mary Tudor to the throne closed his career in England; but he stuck to his work long after his companion preachers had abandoned it. He was in London, and had the courage to rebuke the rejoicings of the crowd at her entry into the capital—a fearless, outspoken man, who could always be depended on for doing what no one else dared.

Knox got safely across the Channel, travelled through France by ways unknown, and reached Geneva. He spent some time with Calvin, then went on to Zurich to see Bullinger. He appears to have been meditating deeply on the condition of Scotland and England, and propounded a set of questions to these divines which show that he was trying to formulate for himself the principles he afterwards asserted on the rights of subjects to restrain tyrannical sovereigns.[3] The years 1554–58, with the exception of a brief visit to Scotland in the end of 1555, were spent on the Continent, but were important for his future work in Scotland. They witnessed the troubles in the Frankfort congregation of English exiles, where Knox's broad-minded

---

[1] Calderwood, *The History of the Kirk of Scotland* (Edinburgh, 1843–49) i. 280–81.

[2] Lorimer, *John Knox and the Church of England* (London, 1875), pp. 98 *ff.* The rubric is to be found in *The Two Liturgies with other Documents set forth by Authority in the reign of King Edward the Sixth* (Cambridge, 1842), p. 283. The volume is one of the Parker Society's publications.

[3] The questions will be found in the volumes, *Original Letters*, published by the Parker Society (Cambridge, 1847), p. 745 ; and in *The Works of John Knox*, etc. iii. 221.

toleration and straightforward action stands in noble contrast with the narrow-minded and crooked.policy of his opponents. They were the time of his peaceful and happy ministrations among the refugees at Geneva. They made him familiar with the leading Protestants of France and of Switzerland, and taught him the inner political condition of the nations of Europe. They explain Knox's constant and accurate information in later years, when he seemed to learn about the doings of continental statesmen as early as Cecil, with all the resources of the English Foreign Office behind him. Above all, they made him see that, humanly speaking, the fate of the whole Reformation movement was bound up with an alliance between a Protestant England and a Protestant Scotland.

Knox returned to Scotland for a brief visit of about ten months (Sept. 1555–July 1556). He exhorted those who visited him in his lodgings in Edinburgh, and made preaching tours, dispensing the Lord's Supper according to the Reformed rite on several occasions. He visited Dun, Calder House, Barr, Ayr, Ochiltree, and several other places, and was welcomed in the houses of many of the nobility. He left for Geneva in July, having found time to marry his first wife, Marjory Bowes,—*uxor suavissima*, and " a wife whose like is not to be found everywhere," [1] Calvin calls her,—and having put some additional force into the growing Protestantism of his native land. He tells us that most part of the gentlemen of the Mearns " band thame selfis, to the uttermost of thare poweris, to manteane the trew preaching of the Evangell of Jesus Christ, as God should offer unto thame preacheris and opportunitie "—whether by word of mouth or in writing, is not certain.[2]

In 1557 (Dec. 3rd) the Protestants of Scotland laid the foundations of a definite organisation. It took a

---

[1] Calvin to Knox (April 23rd, 1561); Calvin to Goodman (April 23rd, 1561); *The Works of John Knox*, etc. vi. 124, 125 ; cf. *Calvini Opera* (Amsterdam, 1667), ix. *Epistolæ et Responsa*, p. 150.

[2] *The Works of John Knox*, etc. i. 251 ; D. Hay Fleming, *The Story of the Scottish Covenants in Outline* (Edinburgh, 1904), p. 6.

form familiar enough in the civil history of the country, where the turbulent character of the Scottish barons and the weakness of the central authority led to constant confederations to carry out with safety enterprises some-times legal and sometimes outside the law. The confederates promised to assist each other in the work proposed, and to defend each other from the consequences following. Such agreements were often drafted in legal fashion by public notaries, and made binding by all forms of legal security known. The *Lords of the Congregation*, as they came to be called, followed a prevailing custom when they promised—

"Befoir the Majestie of God and His congregatioun, that we (be His grace) shall with all diligence continually apply our hole power, substance, and our verray lyves, to manteane, sett fordward, and establish the most blessed word of God and His Congregatioun; and shall laubour at our possibilitie to have faythfull Ministeris purely and trewlie to minister Christis Evangell and Sacramentes to His people."[1]

This "Band subscrived by the Lords" was the first (if the promise made by the gentlemen of the Mearns be excepted) of the many Covenants famous in the history of the Church of Scotland Reformed.[2] It was an old Scottish usage now impregnated with a new spiritual meaning, and become a public promise to God, after Old Testament fashion, to be faithful to His word and guidance.

This important act had immediate consequences. The confederated Lords sent letters to Knox, then at Geneva, and to Calvin, urging the return of the Scottish Reformer to his native land. They also passed two notable resolutions:

" First, It is thought expedient, devised and ordeaned that in all parochines of this Realme the Common Prayeris (prob-

---

[1] *The Works of John Knox*, etc. i. 273.
[2] For the Covenants of the Scottish Church, cf. D. Hay Fleming, *The Story of the Scottish Covenants in Outline* (Edinburgh. 1904).

19**

ably the Second Prayer-Book of Edward VI.[1]) be redd owklie (weekly) on Sounday, and other festuall dayis, publictlie in the Paroche Kirkis, with the Lessonis of the New and Old Testament, conforme to the ordour of the Book of Common Prayeris: And yf the curattis of the parochynes be qualified. to cause thame to reid the samyn; and yf thei be nott, or yf thei refuise, that the maist qualified in the parish use and read the same. Secoundly, it is thought necessare that doctrin, preacheing and interpretatioun of Scriptures be had and used privatlie in Qwyet housis, without great conventionis of the people tharto, whill afterward that God move the Prince to grant publict preacheing be faithful and trew ministeris." [2]

The Earl of Argyle set the example by maintaining John Douglas, and making him preach publicly in his mansion.

This conduct evidently alarmed the Queen Mother, who had been made Regent in 1554 (April 12th), and she attempted to stir the Primate to exercise his powers for the repression of heresy. The Archbishop wrote to Argyle urging him to dismiss Douglas, apologising at the same time for his interference by saying that the Queen wondered that he could "thole" persons with perverted doctrine within his diocese.

Another step in advance was taken some time in 1558, when it was resolved to give the *Congregation*, the whole company of those in Scotland who sincerely accepted the Evangelical Reformation, "the face of a Church," by the creation and recognition of an authority which could exercise discipline. A number of elders were chosen "by common election," to whom the whole of the brethren promised obedience. The lack of a publicly recognised ministry was supplied by laymen, who gave themselves to the work of exhortation; and at the head of them was

---

[1] Cecil, writing to Throckmorton in Paris (July 9th, 1559), says that in Scotland "they deliver the parish churches of altars, and receive the service of the Church of England according to King Edward's book" (*Calendar of State Papers, Elizabeth, Foreign, 1558–59*, p. 367).

[2] *The Works of John Knox*, etc. i. 275.

to be found Erskine of Dun. The first regularly constituted Reformed church in Scotland was in the town of Dundee.[1] The organisation gave the Protestant leaders boldness, and, through Sir James Sandilands, they petitioned the Regent to permit them to worship publicly according to the Reformed fashion, and to reform the wicked lives of the clergy. This led to the offer of a compromise, which was at once rejected, as it would have compelled the Reformed to reverence the Mass, and to approve of prayers to the saints. The Queen Mother then permitted public worship, save in Leith and Edinburgh. The Lords of the Congregation next demanded a suspension of the laws which gave the clergy power to try and punish heresy, until a General Council, lawfully assembled, should decide upon points then debated in religion; and that all suspected of heresy should have a fair trial before "temporal judges."[2] When the Regent, who gave them "amyable lookis and good wordes in aboundance," refused to allow their petition to come before the Estates, and kept it "close in hir pocket," the Reformers resolved to go to Parliament directly with another petition, in which they declared that since they had not been able to secure a reformation, they had resolved to follow their own consciences in matters of religion; that they would defend themselves and all of their way of thinking if attacked; that if tumults arose in consequence, the blame was with those who refused a just reformation; and that in forwarding this petition they had nothing in view but the reformation of abuses in religion.[3]

Knox had been invited by the Earl of Glencairn, the Lords Erskine and Lorn, and James Stewart (afterwards the Earl of Moray), to return to Scotland in 1557.[4] He reached Dieppe in October, and found letters awaiting him which told him that the times were not ripe. The

---

[1] *The Works of John Knox*, etc. i. 300.   [2] *Ibid.* etc. i. 301–12.
[3] *Ibid.* etc. i. 313.
[4] The correspondence will be found in *The Works of John Knox*, etc. i 267 *ff.*, iv. 251 *ff.*

answer he sent spurred the Reforming lords to constitute the *Band* of December 1557. It was while he was at Dieppe, chafing at the news he had received, that he composed the violent treatise, entitled *The First Blast of the Trumpet against the Monstrous Regiment of Women* [1]— a book which did more to hamper his future than anything else. The state of things was exasperating to a man who longed to be at work in Scotland or England. " Bloody " Mary in England was hounding on her officials to burn Knox's co-religionists, and the Reformation, which had made so much progress under Edward VI., seemed to be entirely overthrown ; while Mary of Guise, the Queen Mother and Regent in Scotland, was inciting the unwilling Archbishop of St. Andrews to make use of his legatine and episcopal powers to repress the believers of his native land. But as chance would have it, Mary Tudor was dead before the pamphlet was widely known, and the Queen whom of all others he desired to conciliate was seated on the throne of England, and had made William Cecil, the staunchest of Protestants, her Secretary of State. She could scarcely avoid believing that the *Blast* was meant for her ; and, even if not, it was based on such general principles that it might prove dangerous to one whose throne was still insecure. It is scarcely to be wondered at that the Queen never forgave the vehement writer, and that the *Blast* was a continual obstacle to a complete understanding between the Scottish Reformer and his English allies.[2] If Knox would never confess publicly to queens, whether to Elizabeth Tudor or to Mary Stuart, that he had done wrong, he was ready to say to a friend whom he loved :

" My rude vehemencie and inconsidered affirmations, which may rather appear to procead from coler then of zeal and reason, I do not excuse." [3]

[1] *The Works of John Knox,* etc. iv. 349.
[2] *Calendar of State Papers, Foreign Series, on the Reign of Elizabeth, 1559-60,* pp. 73, 77 ; *1558-59,* pp. 306, 310.
[3] *The Works of John Knox,* etc. v. 5.

It was the worse for Knox and for Scotland, for the reign of women had begun. Charles v., Francis I., and Henry VIII. had passed away, and the destinies of Europe were to be in the hands of Elizabeth, Catherine de' Medici, Mary Stuart, and Philip of Spain, the most felinely feminine of the four.

Events marched fast in Scotland after Knox returned in the early summer of 1559. The Queen Regent and the Lords of the Congregation were facing each other, determined on a trial of strength. Knox reached Edinburgh on May 2nd, 1559, and hurried on to Dundee, where the Reformed had gathered in some force. They had resolved to support their brethren in maintaining public worship according to the usages of the Reformed Church, and in repressing "idolatrie" in all towns where a majority of the inhabitants had declared for the Reformed religion. The Regent threw down the gauntlet by summoning the preachers to appear before her, and by inhibiting their preaching. The Lords took it up by resolving that they would answer the summons and appear along with their preachers. A letter was addressed to the Regent (May 6th, 1559) by "The professouris of Christis Evangell in the realme of Scotland." It was an admirable statement of the principles of the Scottish Reformation, and may be thus summarised:

"It records the hope, once entertained by the writers, that God would make her the instrument of setting up and maintaining his Word and true worship, of defending his congregation, and of downputting all idolatry, abomination, and superstition in the realm; it expresses their grief on learning that she was determined to do the very opposite; it warns her against crossing the bounds of her own office, and usurping a power in Christ's kingdom which did not belong to her; it distinguishes clearly between the civil jurisdiction and the spiritual; it asks her to recall her letters inhibiting God's messengers; it insists that His message ought to be received even though the speaker should lack the ordinary vocation; it claims that the ministers who had been inhibited were sent by God, and

were also called according to Scriptural order; it points out
that her commands must be disobeyed if contrary to God's,
and that the enemies were craftily inducing her to command unjust things so that the professors, when they disobeyed, might be condemned for sedition and rebellion; it
pled with her to have pity on those who were seeking the
glory of God and her true obedience; it declared that, by
God's help, they would go forward in the way they had
begun, that they would receive and assist His ministers
and Word, and that they would never join themselves again
to the abominations they had forsaken, though all the
powers on earth should command them to do so; it conveyed
their humble submission to her, in all obedience due to her
in peace, in war, in body, in goods and in lands; and it
closed with the prayer that the eternal God would instruct,
strengthen, and lead her by His Spirit in the way that was
acceptable to Him."[1]

Then began a series of trials of strength in which the
Regent had generally the better, because she was supplied
with disciplined troops from France, which were more than
a match for the feudal levies of the Lords of the Congregation.   The uprising of the people against the Regent and
the Prelates was characterised, as in France and the
Low Countries, with an outbreak of iconoclasm which did
no good to the Protestant cause.   In the three countries
the "raschall multitude" could not be restrained by the
exhortation of the preachers nor by the commandment
of the magistrates from destroying "the places of
idolatrie."[2]

From the beginning, Knox had seen that the Reformers
had small hope of ultimate success unless they were aided
from England; and he was encouraged to expect help
because he knew that the salvation of Protestant England
lay in its support of the Lords of the Congregation in
Scotland.

The years from 1559 to 1567 were the most critical
in the whole history of the Reformation.   The existence

---

[1] This summary has been taken from Dr. Hay Fleming's admirable little
book, *The Scottish Reformation* (Edinburgh, 1904), p. 44.

[2] *The Works of John Knox*, etc. i. 319.

of the Protestantism of all Europe was involved in the struggle in Scotland; and for the first and perhaps last time in her history the eyes that had the furthest vision, whether in Rome, for centuries the citadel of mediævalism, or in Geneva, the stronghold of Protestantism, were turned towards the little backward northern kingdom. They watched the birth-throes of a new nation, a British nation which was coming into being. Two peoples, long hereditary foes, were coalescing; the Romanists in England recognised the Scottish Queen as their legitimate sovereign, and the Protestants in Scotland looked for aid to their brethren in England. The question was: Would the new nation accept the Reformed religion, or would the reaction triumph? If Knox and the Congregation gained the upper hand in Scotland, and if Cecil was able to guide England in the way he meant to lead it (and the two men were necessary to each other, and knew it), then the Reformation was safe. If Scotland could be kept for France and the Roman Church, and its Romanist Queen make good her claim to the English throne, then the Reformation would be crushed not merely within Great Britain, but in Germany and the Low Countries also. So thought the politicians, secular and ecclesiastical, in Rome and Geneva, in Paris, Madrid, and in London. The European situation had been summed up by Cecil: "The Emperor is aiming at the sovereignty of Europe, which he cannot obtain without the suppression of the Reformed religion, and, unless he crushes England, he cannot crush the Reformation." In this peril a Scotland controlled by the Guises would have been fatal to the existence of the Reformation.

In 1559 the odds seemed in favour of reaction, if only its supporters were whole-hearted enough to put aside for the time national rivalries. The Treaty of Cateau-Cambrésis, concluded scarcely a month before Knox reached Scotland (April 1559), had secret clauses which bound the Kings of France and Spain to crush the Protestantism of Europe, in terms which made the young Prince of Orange, when he learned them, vow silently to devote his

life to protect his fellow-countrymen and drive the " scum
of the Spaniards" out of the Netherlands. Henry II. of
France, with his Edict of Chateaubriand and his *Chambre
Ardente*, with the Duke of Guise and the Cardinal Lorraine
to counsel him, and Diana of Poitiers to keep him up to
the mark, was doing his best to exterminate the Protestants
of France. Dr. Christopher Mundt kept reporting to
Queen Elizabeth and her Minister the symptoms of a
general combination against the Protestants of Europe—
symptoms ranging from a proposed conquest of Denmark
to the Emperor's forbidding members of his Household to
attend Protestant services.[1]   Throckmorton wrote almost
passionately from Paris urging Cecil to support the Scottish
Lords of the Congregation; and even Dr. Mundt in Strassburg saw that the struggle in Scotland was the most
important fact in the European situation.[2]

Yet it was difficult for Cecil to send the aid which
Knox and the Scottish Protestants needed sorely. It
meant that the sovereign of one country aided men of
another country who were *de jure* rebels against their own
sovereign. It seemed a hazardous policy in the case of
a Queen like Elizabeth, who was not yet freed from the
danger arising from rebellious subjects. There was France,
with which England had just made peace. Cecil had
difficulties with Elizabeth. She did not like Calvin himself. She had no sympathy with his theology, which, with
its mingled sob and hosanna, stirred the hearts of oppressed
peoples. There was Knox and his *Blast*, to say nothing
of his appealing to the commonalty of his country. "God

---

[1] *Calendar of State Papers, Foreign Series, of the Reign of Elizabeth,
1558-59*, pp. 245, 259 ; *1559-60*, p. 182. The whole of Dr. Mundt's
correspondence is interesting, and shows that after the Treaty of Cateau-
Cambrésis continual incidents occurred showing that the Romanists were
regaining the hope of repressing the whole Protestant movement.

[2] *Ibid. 1559-60*, p. 58 : "All good men hope that England, warned by
the dangers of others, will take care, by dissimulation and art, that the
nation near to itself, whose cause is the same as her own, shall not be
first deserted and then overwhelmed " (*Dr. Mundt to Cecil*, Oct. 29th,
1559).

keep us from such visitations as Knockes hath attempted
in Scotland; the people to be orderers of things!" wrote
Dr. Parker to Cecil on the 6th of November.[1] Yet Cecil
knew—no man better—that if the Lords of the Congregation failed there was little hope for a Protestant England,
and that Elizabeth's crown and Dr. Parker's mitre depended
on the victory of Knox in Scotland.

He watched the struggle across the border. He had
made up his mind as early as July 8th, 1559, that assistance must be given to the Lords of the Congregation " with
all fair promises first, next with money, and last with
arms."[2] The second stage of his programme was reached
in November; and, two days before the Archbishop of
Canterbury was piously invoking God's help to keep
Knox's influences out of England, Cecil had resolved to
send money to Scotland and to entrust its distribution to
Knox. The memorandum runs: Knox to be a counsel
with the payments, to see that they be employed to the
common action.[3]

The third stage—assistance with arms—came sooner
than might have been expected. The condition of France
became more favourable. Henry II. had died (July 10th,
1559), and the Guises ruled France through their niece
Mary and her sickly devoted husband. But the Bourbon
Princes and many of the higher nobles did not take kindly
to the sudden rise of a family which had been French for
only two generations, and the easiest way to annoy them
was to favour publicly or secretly " those of the religion."
There was unrest in France. " Beat the iron while it is
hot," Throckmorton wrote from Paris; " their fair flatter-
ings and sweet language are only to gain time."[4] Cecil
struck. He had a sore battle with his royal mistress, but
he won.[5] An arrangement was come to between England

---

[1] *Calendar of State Papers, Foreign Series, of the Reign of Elizabeth
1559-60*, p. 84.

[2] *Ibid. 1558-59*, p. 365, *Cecil to Croft*, July 8th, 1559.

[3] *Ibid. 1559-60*, p. 79.   [4] *Ibid.* p. 352.

[5] Cf. his pathetic letter offering to resign. *Ibid.* p. 186 *n.*

and the Lords of the Congregation acting on behalf 'of the second person of the realm of Scotland" (Treaty of Berwick, May 10th, 1560).[1] An English fleet entered the Firth of Forth; an English army beleaguered the French troops in Leith Fort; and the end of it was that France was obliged to let go its hold on Scotland, and never thoroughly recovered it (Treaty of Edinburgh, July 6th, 1560).[2] The great majority of the Scottish people saw in the English victory only their deliverance from French tyranny, and for the first time a conquering English army left the Scottish soil followed by blessings and not curses. The Scottish Liturgy, which had contained *Prayers used in the Churches of Scotland in the time of their persecution by the Frenchmen,* was enriched by a *Thanksgiving unto God after our deliverance from the tyranny of the Frenchmen; with prayers made for the continuance of the peace betwixt the realms of England and Scotland,* which contained the following petition:

" And seeing that when we by our owne power were altogether unable to have freed ourselves from the tyranny of strangers, and from the bondage and thraldome pretended against us, Thou of thyne especial goodnes didst move the hearts of our neighbours (of whom we deserved no such favour) to take upon them the common burthen with us, and for our deliverance not only to spend the lives of many, but also to hazarde the estate and tranquillity of their Realme and commonwealth: Grant unto us, O Lord, that with such reverence we may remember thy benefits received that after this in our defaute we never enter into hostilitie against the Realme and nation of England." [3]

The Regent had died during the course of the hostilities, and Cecil, following and improving upon the

---

[1] The Duke of Châtellerault (Earl of Arran) was next in succession after Mary and her offspring ; cf. a curious note on him and his doings, *ibid.* p. 24 n. For the Treaty, cf. *Calendar of State Papers relating to Scotland and Mary Queen of Scots,* i. 403, and *The Works of John Knox,* etc. ii. 45 ff.

[2] *Calendar of State Papers, Foreign Series, of the Reign of Elizabeth,* 1560–61, pp. 172–78.

[3] *The Works of John Knox,* etc. vi. 309, 313, 314.

wise policy of Protector Somerset, left it entirely to the Scots to settle their own affairs.[1]

Now or never was the opportunity for Knox and the Lords of the Congregation. They had not been idle during the months since Knox had arrived in Scotland. They had strengthened the ties uniting them by three additional *Bands*. At a meeting of the Congregation of the West with the Congregations of Fife, Perth, Dundee, Angus, Mearns, and Montrose, held in Perth (May 31st, 1559), they had covenanted to spare neither

"labouris, goodis, substancis, bodyis, and lives, in mantean-ing the libertie of the haill Congregatioun and everie member thairof, aganis whatsomevir power that shall intend trubill for the caus of religion."[2]

They had renewed this *Band* in Edinburgh on July 13th; and at Stirling (Aug. 1st) they had covenanted,

"that nane of us sall in tymeis cuming pas to the Quenis Grace Dowriare, to talk or commun with hir for any letter without consent of the rest and commone consultatioun."[3]

They had the bitter satisfaction of knowing that although the French troops and officers of the Regent were too strong for them in the field, the insolence and rapine of these foreigners was rousing all ranks and classes in Scotland to see that their only deliverance lay in the English alliance and the triumph of the Reformation. The *Band* of 1560 (April 27th) included, with "the nobilitie, barronis, and gentilmen professing Chryst Jesus in Scot-land . . . dyveris utheris that joyint with us, for expelling of the French army: amangis quham the Erle of Huntlie was principall."[4]

The Estates or Parliament met in Edinburgh on

---

[1] "Matters of religion to be passed over in silence" (*Calendar of State Papers*, etc. p. 178).

[2] *The Works of John Knox*, etc. i. 344.

[3] *Ibid.* i. 382.   [4] *Ibid.* ii. 61.

July 10th, 1560. Neither the French nor the English soldiers had left; so they adjourned to August 1st, and again to the 8th.[1]

Meanwhile Knox and the Congregation were busy The Reformer excelled himself in the pulpit of St. Giles', lecturing daily on the Book of the Prophet Haggai (on the building of the Temple)—" a doctrine proper for the time." [2] Randolph wrote to Cecil, Aug. 15th:

" Sermons are daylie, and greate audience; though dyvers of the nobles present ar not resolved in religion, yet do thei repayre to the prechynges, which gevethe a good hope to maynie that God wyll bowe their hartes." [3]

The Congregation held a great thanksgiving service in St. Giles'; and after it arranged for eight fully constituted churches, and appointed five superintendents in matters of religion.[4] They also prepared a petition for Parliament asking for a settlement of the religious question in the way they desired.[5] At the request of the Estates or Parliament, Knox and five companions prepared *The Confessioun of Faith professit and belevit be the Protestantis within the Realme of Scotland*, which was ratified and approved as " hailsome and sound doctrine, groundit upoun the infallible trewth of Godis Word." It was afterwards issued by the Estates as the " summe of that doctrin quhilk we professe, and for the quhilk we haif sustenit infamy and daingear." [6] Seven days later (Aug. 24th), the Estates decreed that " the Bischope of Rome have na jurisdictioun nor authoritie in this Realme in tymes cuming"; they

---

[1] Cf. *Calendar of State Papers relating to Scotland and Mary Queen of Scots*, i. 456-62.

[2] *The Works of John Knox*, etc. ii. 88.

[3] *Calendar of State Papers relating to Scotland and Mary Queen of Scots*, i. 461.

[4] Spottiswoode, *History of the Church of Scotland* (Edinburgh, 1847), i. 325.

[5] *The Works of John Knox*, etc. ii. 89.

[6] *Ibid.* ii. 95; (Dunlop's) *Collection of Confessions of Faith*, etc. (Edinburgh, 1722) ii. 17, 18.

annulled all Acts of previous Parliaments which were contrary to the Confession of Faith; and they forbade the saying, hearing, or being present at Mass, under penalty of confiscation of goods and bodily punishment at the discretion of the magistrates for the first offence, of banishment for the second, and of death for the third.[1] These severe penalties, however, were by no means rigidly enforced. Lesley (Roman Catholic Bishop of Ross) says in his *History*:

"The clemency of the heretic nobles must not be left unmentioned, since at that time they exiled few Catholic on the score of religion, imprisoned fewer, and put none to death."[2]

One thing still required to be done—to draft a constitution for the new Protestant Church. The work was committed to the same ministers who had compiled the Confession. They had been asked to prepare it as early as April 29th, and they had it ready for the Lords of the Congregation within a month. It was not approved by the Estates; but was ordered to be submitted to the next general meeting, and was meanwhile translated into Latin, to be sent to Calvin, Viret, and Beza in Geneva.[3] The delay seemed to some to arise from the unwillingness of many of the lords to see "their carnal liberty and worldly commoditie impaired";[4] but another cause was also at work. Cecil evidently wished that the Church in Scotland should be uniform with the Church in England, and had instructed Randolph to press this question of uniformity. It was a favourite idea with statesmen of both countries—pressed on Scotland by England during the reigns of James I. and Charles I., and by Scotland on England in the Solemn League and

[1] *Act. Parl. Scot.* ii. 526–35.
[2] Lesley, *De Rebus Gestis Scotorum* (Bannatyne Club, Edinburgh), p. 537.
[3] *Calendar of State Papers relating to Scotland and Mary Queen of Scots.* i. 472, in a letter from Randolph to Cecil of Aug. 25th.
[4] *The Works of John Knox*, etc. ii. 128.

Covenant. Randolph was wise enough to see that such uniformity was an impossibility.[1]

The Confession of the Faith and Doctrine, Believed and Professed by the Protestants of Scotland, was translated into Latin, and, under the title *Confessio Scoticana*, occupies an honoured place in the collections of the creeds of the Reformed Churches. It remained the symbol of the Church of Scotland during the first stormy century of its existence. It was displaced by the Westminster Confession in 1647, only on the understanding that the later document was "in nothing contrary" to the former; and continued authoritative long after that date.[2] Drawn up in haste by a small number of theologians, it is more sympathetic and human than most creeds, and has commended itself to many who object to the impersonal logic of the Westminster Confession.[3] The first sentence of the preface gives the tone to the whole :

"Lang have we thirsted, dear Brethren, to have notified to the Warld the Sum of that Doctrine quhilk we professe, and for quhilk we have susteined Infamie and Danger; Bot sik has bene the Rage of Sathane againis us, and againis Christ Jesus his eternal Veritie latlie now againe born amangst us, that to this daie na Time has been graunted unto us to cleir our Consciences as maist gladlie we wald have done."[4]

The preface also puts more clearly than any similiar document save the First Confession of Basel the reverence

---

[1] *Calendar of State Papers relating to Scotland and Mary Queen of Scots*, i. 471, 472.

[2] The Scots Confession is to be found in (Dunlop's) *Collection of Confessions of Faith, Catechisms, Directories, Books of Discipline, etc., of Public Authority in the Church of Scotland* (Edinburgh, 1722), ii. 13 *ff.*, where the Scots and the Latin versions are printed in parallel columns ; in Schaff's *Creeds of the Evangelical Protestant Churches* (London, 1877), pp. 437 *ff.* ; and the Latin version alone in Niemeyer, *Collectio Confessionum in Ecclesiis Reformatis publicatarum* (Leipzig, 1840), pp. 340 *ff.* For a statement of its characteristics, cf. Mitchell, *The Scottish Reformation* (Baird Lecture for 1899, Edinburgh 1900), pp. 99 *ff.*

[3] As Edward Irving, cf. *Collected Writings* (London, 1864), i. 601 *ff.*

[4] (Dunlop's) *Collection of Confessions*, etc. pp. 15–18.

felt by the early Reformers for the Word of God and the renunciation of any claim to infallibility of interpretation:

"Protestand that gif onie man will note in this our confessioun onie Artickle repugnand to Gods halie word, that it wald pleis him of his gentleness and for christian charities sake to admonish us of the same in writing; and we upon our honoures and fidelitie, be Gods grace do promise unto him satisfaction fra the mouth of God, that is fra his haly scriptures, or else reformation of that quhilk he sal prove to be amisse."

The Confession itself contains the truths common to the Reformed creeds of the Reformation. It contains all the Œcumenical doctrines, as they have been called—that is, the truths taught in the early Œcumenical Councils, and embodied in the Apostles' and Nicene Creeds; and adds those doctrines of grace, of pardon, and of enlightenment through Word and Spirit which were brought into special prominence by the Reformation revival of religion. The Confession is more remarkable for quaint suggestiveness of titles than for any special peculiarity of doctrine. Thus the doctrine of revelation is defined by itself, apart from the doctrine of Scripture, under the title of "The Revelation of the Promise." Election is treated according to the view of earlier Calvinism as a means of grace, and an evidence of the "invincible power" of the Godhead in salvation. The "notes by which the true Kirk is discerned from the false" are said to be the true preaching of the Word of God, the right administration of the sacraments, and ecclesiastical discipline rightly administered. The authority of Scriptures is said to come from God, and to depend neither "on man nor angels"; and the Church knows them to be true, because "the true kirk always heareth and obeyeth the voice of her own spouse and pastor."

Randolph says in a letter to Cecil (September 7th, 1560) that before the Confession was publicly read it was revised by Lethington and Lord James Stewart, who " dyd mytigate the austeritie of maynie wordes and sentences," and that a certain article which dealt with the " dysobediens that subjects owe unto their magistrates " was advised to be left out.[1] Thus amended it was read over, and then re-read article by article in the Estates, and passed without alteration,[2] — "no man present gainsaying." [3] When it was read before the Estates :

" Maynie offered to sheede ther blude in defence of the same. The old Lord of Lynsay, as grave and goodly a man as ever I sawe, said, ' I have lyved maynie yeres, I am the eldest in thys Compagnie of my sorte ; nowe that yt hathe pleased God to lett me see thys daye wher so maynie nobles and other have allowed so worthie a work, I will say with Simion, *Nunc dimittis.*'" [4]

A copy was sent to Cecil, and Maitland of Lethington assured him that if there was anything in the Confession of Faith which the English Minister misliked, " It may eyther be changed (if the mater so permit) or at least in some thyng qualifieed "; which shows the anxiety of the Scots to keep step with their English allies.[5]

The authors of the Confession were asked to draw up a short statement showing how a Reformed Church could best be governed. The result was the remarkable document which was afterwards called the *First Book of Discipline*, or *the Policie and Discipline of the Church*.[6] It provided for the government of the Church by kirk-sessions, synods, and general assemblies ; and recognised as office-bearers in the Church, ministers, teachers, elders, deacons, superintendents, and readers.

---

[1] *Calendar of State Papers relating to Scotland and Mary Queen of Scots,* i. 477, 478.

[2] *The Works of John Knox,* etc. ii. 121.

[3] *Calendar of State Papers,* etc. i. 465, *Maitland to Cecil* (August 18th).

[4] *Ibid.* i. 467, *Randolph to Cecil* (August 19th).

[5] *Ibid.* i. 479, *Maitland to Cecil* (September 13th).

[6] For a description of the *First Book of Discipline,* cf. Mitchell, *The Scottish Reformation,* etc. pp. 144 *ff.* The document itself is to be found in (Dunlop's) *Collection of Confessions,* etc. ii. 515 *ff.*

The authors of this Book of Discipline professed to go directly to Scripture for the outlines of the system of Church government which they advised their countrymen to adopt, and their profession was undoubtedly sincere and likewise just. They were, however, all of them men in sympathy with Calvin, and had had personal intercourse with the Protestants of France.' Their form of government is clearly inspired by Calvin's ideas as stated in his *Institution*, and follows closely the Ecclesiastical Ordinances of the French Church. The offices of superintendent and reader were added to the usual threefold or fourfold Presbyterian form of government. The former was due to the unsettled state of the country and the scarcity of Protestant pastors. The *Superintendents* took charge of districts corresponding not very exactly with the Episcopal dioceses, and were ordered to make annual reports to the General Assembly of the ecclesiastical and religious state of their provinces, and to preach in the various churches in their district. The *Readers* owed their existence to the small number of Protestant pastors, to the great importance attached by the early Scottish Reformers to an educated ministry, and also to the difficulty of procuring funds for the support of pastors in every parish. They were of two classes—those of a higher grade, who were permitted to deliver addresses and who were called *Exhorters*; and those of the lower grade, whose duty it was to read " distinctly " the Common Prayers and the Scriptures. Both classes were expected to teach the younger children. *Exhorters* who studied theology diligently and satisfied the synod of their learning could rise to be ministers. The Book of Discipline contains a chapter on the patrimony of the Church which urges the necessity of preserving monies possessed by the Church for the maintenance of religion, the support of education, and the help of the poor. The presence of this chapter prevented the book being accepted by the Estates in the same way as the Confession of Faith. The barons, greater and lesser, who sat there had in too many cases appropriated

20**

the "patrimony of the Kirk" to their own private uses, and were unwilling to sign a document which condemned their conduct. The Book of Discipline approved by the General Assembly, and signed by a large number of the nobles and burgesses, never received the legal sanction accorded to the Confession.

The General Assembly of the Reformed Church of Scotland met for the first time in 1560; and thereafter, in spite of the struggle in which the Church was involved, meetings were held generally twice a year, sometimes oftener, and the Church was organised for active work.

A third book, variously called *The Book of Common Order*,[1] *The Order of Geneva*, and now frequently *Knox's Liturgy*, was a directory for the public worship and services of the Church. It was usually bound up with a metrical version of the Psalms, and is often spoken of as the *Psalm Book*.

Calvin's Catechism was translated and ordered to be used for the instruction of the youth in the faith. Later, the *Heidelberg Catechism* was translated and annotated for the same purpose. They were both superseded by *Craig's Catechism*, which in its turn gave way to the *Larger* and *Shorter Catechisms* of the Westminster Divines.[2]

The democratic ideas of Presbyterianism, enforced by the practical necessity of trusting in the people, made the Scotch Reformers pay great attention to education. All the leaders of the Reformation, whether in Germany, France, or Holland, had felt the importance of enlightening the commonalty; but perhaps Scotland and Holland were the two countries where the attempt was most successful. The education of the people was no new thing in Scotland; and although in the troublous times before and during the Reformation high schools had

---

[1] For the *Book of Common Order*, cf. Mitchell's *Scottish Reformation*, pp. 133 *ff.* The Book itself is to be found in (Dunlop's) *Collection of Confessions*, ii. 383 *ff.* It has been published with learned preface and notes by Sprott and Leishman (Edinburgh, 1868)

[2] Bonar's *Catechisms of the Scottish Reformation* (London, 1866); (Dunlop's) *Collection of Confessions*, etc. ii. 139–382.

disappeared and the Universities had decayed, still the craving for learning had not altogether died out. Knox and his friend George Buchanan had a magnificent scheme of endowing schools in every parish, high schools or colleges in all important towns, and of increasing the power and influence of the Universities. Their scheme, owing to the greed of the Barons, who had seized the Church property, was little more than a devout imagination; but it laid hold on the mind of Scotland, and the lack of endowments was more than compensated by the craving of the people for education. The three Universities of St. Andrews, Glasgow, and Aberdeen took new life, and a fourth, the University of Edinburgh, was founded. Scotch students who had been trained in the continental schools of learning, and who had embraced the Reformed faith, were employed to superintend the newly-organised educational system of the country, and the whole organisation was brought into sympathy with the everyday life of the people by the preference given to day schools over boarding schools, and by a system of inspection by the most pious and learned men in each circle of parishes. Knox also was prepared to order compulsory attendance at school on the part of two classes of society, the upper and the lower—the middle class he thought might be trusted to its own natural desire for learning; and he wished to see the State so exercise power and patronage as to lay hold on all youths "of parts" and compel them to proceed to the high schools and Universities, that the commonwealth might get the greatest good of their service.

The form of Church government given in the *First Book of Discipline* represented rather an outline requiring to be filled in than a picture of what actually existed for many a year after 1560. It provided for a form of Church government by ecclesiastical councils rising from the Session of the individual congregation up to a National Assembly, and its first requisite was a fully organised church in every parish ruled by a minister

with his Session or council of Elders and his body of
Deacons. But there was a great lack of men having the
necessary amount of education to be ordained as ministers,
and consequently there were few fully equipped congregations. The first court in existence was the Kirk-
Session; it was in being in every organised congregation.
The second in order of time was the General Assembly.
Its first meeting was in Edinburgh, Dec. 20th, 1560.
Forty-two members were present, of whom only six were
ministers. These were the small beginnings from which
it grew. The Synods came into existence later. At first
they were yearly gatherings of the ministry of the
Superintendent's district, to which each congregation
within the district was asked to send an Elder and a
Deacon. The Court of the Presbytery came latest into
existence; it had its beginnings in the "weekly exercise."

The work had been rapidly done. Barely a year
had elapsed between the return of Knox to Scotland and
the establishment of the Reformed religion by the Estates.
Calvin wrote from Geneva (Nov. 8th, 1559):

"As we wonder at success incredible in so short a time,
so also we give great thanks to God, whose special blessing
here shines forth."

And Knox himself, writing from the midst of the
battle, says:[1]

"We doe nothing but goe about Jericho, blowing with
trumpets, as God giveth strength, hoping victorie by his
power alone."[2]

But dangers had been imminent; shot at through
his window, deadly ambushes set, and the man's powers
taxed almost beyond endurance:

"In twenty-four hours I have not four free to naturall
rest and ease of this wicked carcass . . . I have nead of a

[1] *The Works of John Knox,* etc. vi. 95.
[2] *Ibid.* vi. 78, *Knox to Mrs. Anna Locke* (Sept. 2nd, 1559).

good and an assured horse, for great watch is laid for my apprehension, and large money promised till any that shall kyll me." [1]

If the victory had been won, it was not secured. The sovereigns Mary and Francis had refused to ratify the Acts of their Estates; and it was not until Mary was deposed in 1567 that the Acts of the Estates of 1560 were legally placed on the Statute Book of Scotland. Francis II. died in 1560 (Dec. 5th), and Mary the young and widowed Queen returned to her native land (Aug. 19th, 1561). Her coming was looked forward to with dread by the party of the Reformation.

There was abundant reason for alarm. Mary was the Stuart Queen; she represented France, the old hereditary ally; she had been trained from childhood by a consummate politician and deadly enemy of the Reformation, her uncle the Cardinal of Lorraine, to be his instrument to win back Scotland and England to the deadliest type of Romanism. She was a lovely creature, and was, besides, gifted with a power of personal fascination greater than her physical charms, and such as no other woman of her time possessed; she had a sweet caressing voice, beautiful hands; and not least, she had a gift of tears at command. She had been brought up at a Court where women were taught to use all such charms to win men for political ends. The *Escadron volant de la Reine* had not come into existence when Mary left France, but its recruits were ready, and some of them had been her companions. She had made it clearly understood that she meant to overthrow the Reformation in Scotland.[2] Her unscrupulous character was already known to Knox and the other Protestant leaders. Nine days before her marriage she had signed deeds guaranteeing the ancient liberties and independence of

---

[1] *The Works of John Knox*, vi. 88, *Knox to Gregory Railton* (Oct. 23rd 1559).

[2] *Calendar of State Papers relating to Scotland and Mary Queen of Scots*, i. 507, 536.

Scotland; six days after her marriage she and her
husband had appended their signatures to the same
deeds; but twenty days before her wedding she had
secretly signed away these very liberties, and had made
Scotland a mere appanage of France.[1] They suspected
that the party in France whose figure-head she was,
would stick at no crime to carry out their designs, and
had shown what they were ready to do by poisoning
four of the Scotch Commissioners sent to Paris for their
young Queen's wedding, because they refused to allow
Francis to be immediately crowned King of Scotland.[2]
They knew how apt a pupil she had already shown
herself in their school, when she led her boy husband
and her ladies for a walk round the Castle of Amboise, to
see the bodies of dozens of Protestants hung from lintels
and turrets, and to contemplate " the fair clusters of
grapes which the grey stones had produced." [3]

It was scarcely wonderful that Lord James, Morton,
and Lethington, were it not for obedience' sake, " cared not
thoughe theie never saw her face," and felt that there
was no safety for them but in Elizabeth's protection.
As for Knox, we are told : " Mr. Knox is determined to
abide the uttermost, and others will not leave him till
God have taken his life and theirs together." [4] What
use might she not make of these fascinations of hers on
the vain, turbulent nobles of Scotland? Is it too much
to say that but for the passionate womanly impulse—so
like a Stuart [5]—which made her fling herself first into
the arms of Darnley and then of Bothwell, and but for

---

[1] Hay Fleming, *Mary Queen of Scots* (London, 1897), pp. 23, 24, and
210, 211.

[2] *Ibid.* pp. 25, 212.

[3] Mariéjol, *Histoire de France depuis les Origines jusqu'à la Revolution*,
VI. i. 18 (Paris, 1904).

[4] *Calendar of State Papers relating to Scotland and Mary Queen of Scots,*
i. 543.

[5] " Das Leben geliebt und die Krone geküsst,
    Und den Frauen das Herz gegeben,
    Und zuletzt einen Kuss auf das blut'ge Gerüst—
    Das ist ein Stuartleben."

Knox, she might have succeeded in re-establishing Popery in Scotland and in reducing Protestant England ?

Cecil himself was not without his fears, and urged the Protestants in Scotland to stand firm. Randolph's answer shows how much he trusted Knox's tenacity, however much he might sometimes deprecate his violence :

" Where your honour exhortethe us to stowteness, I assure you the voyce of one man is hable in one hower to put more lyf in us than five hundred trompettes contynually blusteringe in our eares."[1]

He was able to write after Mary's arrival :

" She (Mary) was four days without Mass ; the next Sunday after arrival she had it said in her chapel by a French priest. There were at it besides her uncles and her own Household, the Earle of Montrose, Lord Graham . . . the rest were at Mr. Knox sermon, as great a number as ever was any day."[2]

Mary's advisers, her uncles, knew how dangerous the state of Scotland was for their designs, and counselled her to temporise and gradually win over the leading Reforming nobles to her side. The young Queen entered on her task with some zest. She insisted on having Mass for her own household ; but she would maintain, she promised, the laws which had made the Mass illegal in Scotland ; and it says a great deal for her powers of fascination and dissimulation that there was scarcely one of the Reforming nobles that she did not win over to believe in her sincerity at one time or another, and that even the sagacious Randolph seemed for a time to credit that she meant what she said.[3] Knox alone in Scotland read her character and paid unwilling tribute to her abilities from his first interview with her.[4]

[1] *Calendar of State Papers relating to Scotland and Mary Queen of Scots,* i. 551.

[2] *Ibid.* i. 547.

[3] That is the impression which his letters give me. Cf. *Calendar,* etc. pp. 565–609.

[4] " If there be not in her a proud mind, a crafty wit, and an indurate heart

He saw that she had been thoroughly trained by her
uncles, and especially by the Cardinal of Lorraine, and that
it was hopeless to expect anything like fair dealing from
her:

" In verry dead hir hole proceadings do declayr that the
Cardinalles lessons ar so deaplie prented in hir heart, that
the substance and the qualitie ar liek to perische together.
I wold be glaid to be deceaved, but I fear I shall not. In
communication with her, I espyed such craft as I have not
found in such aige." [1]

Maitland of Lethington thought otherwise. Writing to
Cecil (Oct. 25th, 1561) he says:

" You know the vehemency of Mr. Knox spreit, which
cannot be brydled. . . . I wold wishe he shold deale with
her more gently, *being a young princess unpersuaded.*" [2]

It was thought that Mary might be led to adopt the
Reformation if she were only tenderly guided. When
Mary's private correspondence is read, when the secret
knowledge which her co-religionists abroad had of her designs
is studied and known, it can be seen how true was Knox's
reading of her character and of her intentions.[3] He stood
firm, almost alone at times among the leading men, but
faithfully supported by the commons of Scotland.[4]

Then began the struggle between the fascinating Queen,
Mary Stuart, one of the fairest flowers of the French
Renaissance, and the unbending preacher, trained in the
sternest school of the Reformation movement—a struggle
which was so picturesque, in which the two opponents had
each such strongly marked individuality, and in which the

against God and His truth, my judgment faileth me " (*The Works of John
Knox,* etc. ii. 286).

[1] *The Works of John Knox,* etc. vi. 132, *Letter from Knox to Cecil* (Oct.
7th, 1561).

[2] *Calendar of State Papers relating to Scotland and Mary Queen of Scots,*
i. 565.

[3] For summary of evidence, cf. Hay Fleming, *Mary Queen of Scots,* pp.
267–68.

[4] For summary of evidence, cf. Hay Fleming, *Mary Queen of Scots,* pp.
51–53, 263.

accessories were so dramatic, that the spectator insensibly becomes absorbed in the personal side of the conflict, and is tempted to forget that it was part of a Revolution which was convulsing the whole of middle and western Europe.

A good deal has been written about the rudeness with which Knox assailed Mary in public and in private, and his conversations with her are continually referred to but seldom quoted in full. It is forgotten that it was Mary who wished to try her gifts of fascination on the preacher, just as Catherine de' Medici tried to charm de Béze before Poissy; that Knox never sought an interview; that he never approached the Court unless he was summoned by the sovereign to her presence; that he was deferential as a subject should be; and it was only when he was compelled by Mary herself to speak on themes for which he was ready to lay down his life that he displayed a sternness which monarchs seldom experience in those to whom they give audience. What makes these interviews stand forth in history is that they exhibit the first clash of autocratic kingship and the hitherto unknown power of the people. It was an age in which sovereigns were everywhere gaining despotic power, when the might of feudal barons was being broken, when the commonalty was dumb. A young Queen, whose training from childhood had stamped indelibly on her character that kingship meant the possession of unlimited autocratic privileges before which everything must give way, who had seen that none in France had dared dispute the will of her sickly, dull boy-husband simply because he was King, was suddenly confronted by something above and beyond her comprehension:

" ' What have ye to do,' said sche, ' with my mariage ? Or what ar ye within this Commounwealth ? ' ' *A subject borne within the same,*' said he, ' Madam. And albeit I neather be Erle, Lord, nor Barroun within it, yitt hes God maid me (how abject that ever I be in your eyes) a profitable member within the same.' " [1]

---

[1] *The Works of John Knox*, etc. ii. 388.

Modern democracy came into being in that answer. It is curious to see how this conflict between autocratic power and the civil and religious rights of the people runs through all the interviews between Mary and Knox, and was, in truth, the question of questions between them.[1]

It is unnecessary to tell the story of the seven years of struggle between 1560 and 1567. In the end, Mary was imprisoned in Lochleven Castle, deposed, and her infant son, James VI., was placed on the throne. Lord James Stewart, Earl of Moray, was made Regent. The Estates or Parliament again voted the Confession of Faith, and engrossed it in their Acts. The Regent, acting for the sovereign, signed the Acts. The Confession thus became part of the law of the land, and the Reformed Church was legally recognised in Scotland.

[1] Accounts of the five interviews are to be found in *The Works of John Knox*, etc. ii. 281 *ff.*, 331 *ff.*, 371 *ff.*, 387 *ff.*, 403 *ff.*

BOOK IV.

THE REFORMATION IN ENGLAND.

CHAPTER I.

THE CHURCH OF HENRY VIII.[1]

THE Church and people of England broke away from the mediæval papal ecclesiastical system in a manner so exceptional, that the rupture had not very much in

[1] SOURCES: Læmmer, *Monumenta Vaticana historiam ecclesiasticam sæculi* 16 *illustrantia* (Freiburg, 1861); *Letters and Papers, Foreign and Domestic, of the Reign of Henry VIII.* (19 vols., London, 1860–1903); *Calendar of Venetian State Papers, 1520–26, 1527–33, 1534–54, 1555–56, 1557–58, 1558–80*; *Calendar of Spanish State Papers* (London, 1886); Furnivall, *Ballads from Manuscripts* (Ballad Society, London, 1868–72); Gee and Hardy, *Documents illustrative of English Church History* (London, 1896); Erasmus, *Opera Omnia*, ed. Le Clerc (Leyden, 1703–6); Nichols, *The Epistles of Erasmus from the earliest letters to his fifty-first year, arranged in order of time* (London, 1901–4); Pocock, *Records of the Reformation* (Oxford, 1870); Theiner, *Vetera Monumenta Hibernorum et Scotorum historiam illustrantia* (Rome, 1864); Wilkins, *Concilia*; *Chronicle of the Grey Friars of London*, (Camden Society, London, 1846); Holinshed, *Chronicles* (London, 1809); *London Chronicle in the times of Henry VII. and Henry VIII. (Camden Miscellany*, vol. iv., London, 1859); Wright, *Suppression of the Monasteries* (Camden Society, London, 1843); Foxe, *Acts and Monuments* (London, 1846); Ehses, *Römische Dokumente zur Geschichte des Heinrichs VIII. von England, 1527–34* (Paderborn, 1893); *Zurich Letters*, 2 vols. (Parker Society, Cambridge, 1846–47); *Works of Archbishop Cranmer*, 2 vols. (Parker Society, Cambridge, 1844–46).

LATER BOOKS: Dixon, *History of the Church of England* (London, 1878, etc.); Froude, *History of England* (London, 1856–70; by no means superseded, as many would have us believe); Brewer, *The Reign of Henry VIII.* (London, 1884); Gairdner, *The English Church in the Sixteenth*

315

common with the contemporary movements in France and Germany. Henry VIII. destroyed the papal supremacy, spiritual and temporal, within the land which he governed; he cut the bands which united the Church of England with the great Western Church ruled over by the Bishop of Rome; he built up what may be called a kingly papacy on the ruins of the jurisdiction of the Pope   His starting-point was a quarrel with the Pope, who refused to divorce him from Catharine of Aragon.

It would be a mistake, however, to think that Henry's eagerness to be divorced from Catharine accounts for the English Reformation. No king, however despotic, could have forced on such a revolution unless there was much in the life of the people that reconciled them to the change, and evidence of this is abundantly forthcoming.

There was a good deal of *heresy*, so called, in England long before Luther's voice had been heard in Germany. Men maintained that the tithes were exactions of covetous priests, and were not sanctioned by the law of God; they protested against the hierarchical constitution of the mediæval Church; they read the Scriptures, and attended services in the vernacular; and they scoffed at the authority of the Church and attacked some of its doctrines. Lollardy had never died out in England, and Lollardy was simply the English form of that passive protest against the mediæval Church which under various names had maintained itself in France, Germany, and Bohemia for centuries in spite of persecution. Foxe's *Acts and Monuments* show that there was a fairly active repression of so-called heresy in England before Luther's days, and his accounts are confirmed by the State Papers of the period. In 1511, Andreas Ammonius, the Latin secretary of Henry VIII., writing to Erasmus, says that wood has grown scarce and dear because so much was needed to burn heretics, " and

Century (London, 1902); Pollard, *Henry VIII.* (London, 1905), *Thomas Cranmer* (*Heroes of the Reformation Series*, New York and London, 1904); Stubbs, *Seventeen Lectures on the Study of Mediæval and Modern History*, Lectures XI. and XII. (Oxford, 1900); *Cambridge Modern History*, II. xiii.

yet their numbers grow." Yet Dr. James Gairdner declares that only a solitary pair had suffered during that year at the stake![1] Early in 1512 the Archbishop of Canterbury summoned a meeting of convocation for the express purpose of arresting the spread of heresy; [2] in that same year Erasmus was told by More that the *Epistolæ Obscurorum Virorum* were popular everywhere throughout England; [3] and a commission was given to the Bishop of Coventry and others to inquire about Lollards in Wales and other parts; [4] and as late as 1521 the Bishop of London arrested five hundred Lollards.[5] In 1530, Henry VIII. himself, always curious about theology and anxious to know about the books which interested his subjects, sent to Oxford for a copy of the Articles on which Wiclif had been condemned.[6] Anyone who scoffed at relics or pilgrimages was thought to be a Wiclifite.[7] In 1531, divinity students were required to take an oath to renounce the doctrines of Wiclif, Hus, and Luther; [8] and in 1533, More, writing to Erasmus, calls Tyndale and his sympathisers Wiclifites.[9] Henry VIII. was engaged as early as 1518 in composing a book against heresy and vindicating the claims of the Roman See, which in its first inception could scarcely be directed against Luther, and probably dealt with the views of home heretics.[10] Some modern historians are inclined to find a strong

[1] *Letters and Papers, Foreign and Domestic, of the Reign of Henry VIII.* ⁴. p. 295. There was a sudden rise in the price of wood all over Europe about that date, and it is alleged to be one of the causes why the poorer classes in Germany were obliged to give up the earlier almost universal use of the steam bath. In the fifteenth century, masters gave their workmen not *Trinkgelt*, but *Badgelt*. Nichols, *The Epistles of Erasmus*, i. 40.

[2] *Letters and Papers*, etc. i. p. 633.

[3] *Ibid.* II. i. 777 : The Oxford bookseller (1520) John Dorne had two copies in his stock of books [*Oxford Historical Society, Collectanea* (Oxford, 1885), p. 155].

[4] *Letters and Papers*, i. p. 373.

[5] Jacobs, *The Lutheran Movement in England*, p. 2.

[6] Bale, *Select Works*, p. 171.

[7] *Erasmi Colloquia* (Amsterdam, 1662), *Peregrinatio Religionis ergo* p. 376 ; *Viclevita quispiam, opinor.*

[8] *Letters and Papers*, etc. v. p. 140.

[9] *Ibid.* vi. p. 144.   [10] *Ibid.* II. ii. p. 1319.

English revolt against Rome native to the soil and borrow-ing little or nothing from Luther, which they believe to have been the initial force at work in shaping the English Reformation. Mr. Pollard points out that in many particulars this Reformation followed the lines laid down by Wiclif. Its leaders, like Wiclif, denounced the Papal Supremacy on the ground of the political injury it did to the English people; declaimed against the sloth, immorality, and wealth of the English ecclesiastics; advocated a preaching ministry; and looked to the secular power to restrain the vices and reform the manners of the clergy, and to govern the Church. He shows that

"most of the English Reformers were acquainted with Wycliffe's works: Cranmer declares that he set forth the truth of the Gospel; Hooper recalls how he resisted 'the popish doctrine of the Mass'; Ridley, how he denied tran-substantiation; and Bale, how he denounced the friars. . . . Bale records with triumph that, in spite of the efforts to suppress (the writings of Wicliffe), not one had utterly perished."[1]

And Dr. Rashdall goes the length of saying:

"It is certain that the Reformation had virtually broken out in the secret Bible-readings of the Cambridge Reformers before either the trumpet-call of Luther or the exigencies of Henry VIII.'s personal and political position set men free once more to talk openly against the Pope and the monks, and to teach a simpler and more spiritual gospel than the system against which Wycliffe had striven."[2]

Even if it be admitted that these statements are somewhat strong, they at least call attention to the fact of the vigorous Lollard leaven which permeated the English people, and are a very necessary corrective of the mislead-ing assertions of Dr. James Gairdner on the matter.

Henry VIII. had other popular forces behind him—the

---

[1] *Thomas Cranmer and the English Reformation* (New York and London 1904), p. 91.

[2] *Dictionary of National Biography*, art. " Wycliffe," lxiii. 218.

rooted dislike to the clergy which characterised a large mass of the people, the effects of the teaching of the Christian Humanists of England, and the spread of Lutheran opinions throughout the land.

The Bishop of London, writing to Wolsey about the proposal to try his Chancellor, Dr. Horsey, for complicity in the supposed murder of Richard Hunne, declared that if the Chancellor

" be tried by any twelve men in London, they be so maliciously set *in favorem hæreticæ pravitatis* that they will cast and condemn any clerk though he were as innocent as Abel."[1]

This dislike was not confined to the capital. The Parliaments showed themselves anti-clerical long before Henry had thrown off his allegiance to Rome;[2] and Englishmen could find no better term of insult to throw at the Scots than to call them " Pope's men."[3]

Nor should the work of the Christian Humanists be forgotten. The double tendency in their longings for a reformation of the abuses of superstition, of pilgrimages, of relic-worship, etc., may be seen in the lives of Sir Thomas More and of William Tyndale. When the former saw that reform meant the breaking up of the mediæval Church, he became more and more conservative. But More in 1520 (Feb. 28th) could write to Lea that if the Pope (Leo X.) should withdraw his approval of Erasmus' Greek New Testament, Luther's attacks on the Holy See were piety itself compared with such a deed.[4] Tyndale, the favourite pupil of Dean Colet, on the other hand, went forward and earned the martyr's crown. These Christian Humanists had expected much from Henry VIII., whom they looked on as imbued with the New Learning; and in the end perhaps they were not altogether mistaken. If the *Bishop's Book* and the *King's Book* be studied, it will

---

[1] *Letters and Papers*, etc. II. i. p. 1.
[2] *Ibid.* etc. I. p. 961, II. i. pp. 350, 354, 355.
[3] *Ibid.* I. p. 379.　　　　　　　　　[4] *Ibid.* III. p. 215.

be seen that in both what is insisted upon is a reformation of conduct and a study of the Bible—quite in the spirit of Colet and of Erasmus.

The writings of Luther found early entrance into England, and were read by King [1] and people. A long list of them, including six copies of his work *De potestate Papœ*, is to be found in the stock of the Oxford bookseller, John Dorne [2] (1520). Erasmus, writing to Oecolampadius (May 15th, 1521), declares that there are many of Luther's books in England, and hints that but for his exertions they would have been burnt.[3] That was before Luther's official condemnation. On May 28th, Silvester, Bishop of Worcester, wrote to Wolsey from Rome announcing that the Cardinals had agreed to declare Martin a heretic, and that a Bull was being prepared on the subject.[4] The Bull itself appeared in Rome on the 15th of June; and thereafter our information about Luther's writings in England comes from evidence of endeavours to destroy them. Warham, the Archbishop of Canterbury, wrote to Wolsey (March 8th, 1521) that he had received letters from Oxford which declared that the University was infected with Lutheranism, and that the forbidden books were in circulation there.[5] Indeed, most of the canons appointed to Wolsey's new foundation of the Cardinal College were suspect. Cambridge was as bad, if not worse. Members of the University met at the White Horse Tavern to read and discuss Luther's writings; the inn was called " Germany," and those who frequented it " the Germans." Pope Leo urged both the King and Wolsey to prevent the circulation of Lutheran literature; and they did their best to obey. We read that on May 12th, 1521, Wolsey went in great state to St. Paul's, and after various ceremonies mounted a scaffold, seated himself " under a cloth of estate," and listened to a sermon preached by Bishop Fisher against Lutheran errors.

---

[1] *Letters and Papers*, etc. III. p. 467.
[2] *Oxford Historical Society, Collectanea* (Oxford, 1885), p. 164.
[3] *Letters and Papers*, etc. III. p. 284.   [4] *Ibid.* etc. III. i. p. 293.
[5] *Ibid.* III. p. 449.

At his feet on the right side sat the Pope's ambassadors and the Archbishop of Canterbury, and on the left side the imperial ambassadors and the Bishop of Durham. While the sermon was being preached, numbers of Lutheran books were burnt in a huge bonfire kindled hard by in St. Paul's Churchyard.[1] The representatives of Pope and Emperor saw it all, and doubtless reported to their respective Courts that Wolsey was doing his duty by Church and Empire. It may be doubted whether such theatrical exhibitions hindered the spread of Luther's books in England or prevented them being read.

All these things indicated a certain preparedness in England for the Reformation, and all meant that there was a strong national force behind Henry VIII. when he at last made up his mind to defy Rome.

Nor was a national separation from Rome so formidable an affair as Dr. Gairdner would have us believe. The Papacy had secularised itself, and European monarchs were accustomed to treat the Popes as secular princes. The possibility of England breaking away from papal authority and erecting itself into a separate patriarchate under the Archbishop of Canterbury had been thought probable before the divorce was talked about.[2]

It was Henry himself who clung strenuously to the conception of papal supremacy, and who advocated it in a manner only done hitherto by canonists of the Roman Curia. Whatever be the secret reason which he gave to Sir Thomas More, and which silenced the latter's remonstrances, it is evident that the validity of Henry's marriage and the legitimacy of his children by Catharine of Aragon depended on the Pope being in possession of the very fullest powers of dispensation. Henry had been married to Catharine under very peculiar circumstances, which might well

---

[1] *Letters and Papers*, etc. III. i. p. 485.

[2] *Ibid.* IV., Preface, p. 170 : "Some are of opinion that it (the Holy See) should not continue in Rome, lest the French King should make a patriarch in his kingdom and deny obedience to the said See, and the King of England and all other Christian princes do the same."

21**

suggest doubts about the validity of the marriage ceremony.

The England of Henry VII. was almost as much a satellite of Spain as Scotland was of France, and to make the alliance still stronger a marriage was arranged between Arthur, Prince of Wales, and Catharine the youngest of the three daughters of Ferdinand and Isabella of Spain. The Spanish Princess landed at Plymouth (October 2nd, 1501), and the wedding took place in St. Paul's on November 14th. But Prince Arthur died a few months afterwards (April 2nd, 1502), and Catharine became a widow. The circumstances of the two nations appeared to require more than ever the cementing of the alliance by intermarriage, and it was proposed from the side of Spain that the young widow should marry Henry, her brother-in-law, now Prince of Wales.[1] Ferdinand brought pressure to bear on England by insisting that if this were not done Catharine should be sent back to Spain and the first instalment of her dowry (all that had been paid) returned. The two Kings then besieged the Pope, Julius II., to grant a dispensation for the marriage. At first His Holiness was very unwilling to consent. Such a marriage had been branded as sin by canonical law, and the Pope himself had great doubts whether it was competent for him to grant a dispensation in such a case.[2] In the end he was persuaded to give it. The two young people had their own scruples of conscience. Ferdinand felt called upon to reason with his proposed son-in-law.[3] The confessor of his daughter was changed.[4] The Archbishop of Canterbury, who doubted whether the Pope could grant dispensation for what was a mortal sin in his eyes, was silenced.[5] The wedding took place (June 11th, 1509).

[1] *Spanish Calendar*, i. 267.
[2] Pocock's *Records of the Reformation*, i. 1; *Letters and Papers*, etc. IV. iii. p. 2576.
[3] *Calendar of Spanish State Papers*, ii. 8.
[4] *Ibid.*, Preface, xiii.
[5] *Letters and Papers*, etc. IV. iii. p. 2579. A General Council had pronounced against such a dispensation; *ibid.* IV iii. p. 2365.

The marriage was in one sense singularly unfortunate. The first four children were either stillborn or died soon after birth; and it was rumoured in Rome as early as 1514 that Henry might ask to be divorced in order to save England from a disputed succession. Mary was born in 1516 and survived, but all the children who came afterwards were either stillborn or died in early infancy. It became evident by 1525 that if Henry did not divorce his wife he would have no male heir.

There is no doubt that the lack of a male heir troubled Henry greatly. The English people had not been accustomed to a female sovereign; it was currently, if erroneously, reported in England that the laws of the land did not permit a woman to be sovereign, and such well-informed diplomatists as the Venetian Ambassadors believed the statement;[1] and the Tudor dynasty was not so firmly settled on the throne that it could afford to look forward to a disputed succession. The King's first idea was to ask the Pope to legitimise his illegitimate son the Duke of Richmond;[2] and Cardinal Campeggio actually suggested that the Princess Mary should be married to her half-brother.[3] These projects came to an end with the death of the young Prince.

There seems to be no reason for questioning the sincerity of Henry's doubts about the legitimacy of his marriage with Catharine, or that he actually looked upon the repeated destruction of his hopes of a male heir as a divine punishment for the sin of that contract.[4] Questions of national policy and impulses of passion quicken marvellously conscientious convictions, but they do not show that the convictions are not real. In the perplexities of his position the shortest way out seemed to be to ask the Pope to declare that he had never been legally married to

---

[1] *Calendar of Venetian State Papers, 1527-33,* p. 300.

[2] *Letters and Papers,* etc. IV. ii. p. 1369; *Calendar of Spanish State Papers,* III. ii. 482, 109.

[3] *Ibid.* etc. IV. ii. p. 2113; Laemmer *Monumenta Vaticana,* p. 29.

[4] *Ibid.* etc. IV. iii. p. 2261.

Catharine. If he had scruples of conscience about his marriage with his brother's widow, this would end them; if the fears of a disputed succession haunted him, he could marry again, and might hope for a son and a lawful heir whose succession none would dispute. Cardinal Wolsey adopted his master's plans, and the Pope was to be asked for a declaration that the marriage with Catharine had been no marriage at all.

There entered, however, into all this, at what time it is not easy to determine, an element of sordidness which goes ill with asserted scruples of conscience and imperious necessities of State. Wolsey was astonished when he learned that Henry had made up his mind to marry Anne Boleyn, a lady whose station in life and personal reputation unfitted her for the position of Queen of England. It was Henry's inordinate, if not very long-lived, passion for this lady that put him in the wrong, and enabled the Pope to pose as the guardian of the public morality of Europe.

It is plain that Henry VIII. fully expected that the Pope would declare his first marriage invalid; there was many a precedent for such action—two in Henry's own family;[1] and the delay had nothing to do with the interests of public morality. The Pope was at the time practically in the power of Charles V., to whom his aunt, the injured Catharine, had appealed, and who had promised her his protection. One has only to study the phases of the protracted proceedings in the "Divorce" and compare them with the contemporary situation in Italy to see that all that the Curia cared for was the success of the papal diplomacy in the Italian peninsula. The interests of morality were so little in his mind that Clement proposed to Henry more than once that the King might take a second wife without going through the formality of having his first marriage declared null and void.[2] This had been

---

[1] For the case of Mary Tudor, cf. *Letters and Papers*, etc. IV. iii. p. 2619, cf. IV. i. p. 325; and for that of Margaret Tudor, widow of James IV., cf. IV. ii. p. 1826.

[2] *Letters and Papers*, etc. IV. iii. pp. 2987, 3023, 3189.

the papal solution of the matter in an earlier instance, and Clement VII. saw no reasons why what had been allowed to a King of Spain should be denied to the King of England.[1] He was prepared to tolerate bigamy, but not to thwart Charles, so long as the Emperor was master within Italy.[2]

It is needless to follow the intricacies of the Divorce. The protracted proceedings were an object lesson for English statesmen. They saw a grave moral question— whether a man could lawfully marry his deceased brother's widow; a matter vitally affecting the welfare of the English people—the possibility of a disputed succession; the personal wishes of a powerful, strong-willed, and choleric sovereign (for all considerations were present, not only the last)—all subjected to the shifting needs of a petty Italian prince. So far as England was concerned, the grave interest in the case ended when Campeggio adjourned the inquiry (July 23rd, 1529). Henry knew that he could not expect the Pope to give him what he wanted; and although his agents fought the case at Rome, he at once began preparing for the separation from papal jurisdiction.

The English nobles, who had long chafed under the rule of Wolsey, took advantage of the great Minister's failure in the Divorce negotiations to press forward his downfall. He was deprived of the Lord Chancellorship, which was given to Sir Thomas More, and was further indicted before the King's Bench for infringement of the law of *Præmunire*—an accusation to which he pleaded guilty.[3]

Meanwhile Henry had taken measures to summon a Parliament; and in the interval between summons and

[1] *Calendar of Spanish State Papers*, ii. 379.

[2] *Letters and Papers*, etc. IV. iii. pp. 2047, 2055.

[3] The two statutes of *Præmunire* (1353, 1393) will be found in Gee and Hardy, *Documents illustrative of English Church History* (London, 1896), pp. 103, 122. They forbid subjects taking plaints cognisable in the King's courts to courts outside the realm, and the second statute makes pointed reference to the papal courts.

assembly, it had been suggested to him that Cranmer was
of opinion that the best way to deal with the Divorce was
to take it out of the hands of the Curia and consult the
canonists of the various Universities of Europe. Cranmer
was instructed to prepare the case to be laid before them.
This was done so successfully that the two great English
Universities, the French Universities of Paris, Orleans,
Bourges, and Toulouse, decided that the King's marriage
with Catharine was not valid; the Italian Universities of
Ferrara, Padua, Pavia, and Bologna came to the same
conclusion in spite of a proclamation issued by the Pope
prohibiting all doctors from maintaining the invalid nature
of the King's marriage.[1]

Parliament met on November 3rd, 1529, and, from the
matters brought before it, received the name of the
"Parliament for the enormities of the clergy."[2] It revealed
the force of lay opinion on which Henry might count in
the struggle he was about to begin with the clergy. With
a view of strengthening his hands still further, the King
summoned an assembly of Notables,[3] which met on June
12th, 1530, and addressed the Pope in a letter in which
they prayed him to consent to the King's desire, pointed
out the evils which would follow from delaying the Divorce,
and hinted that they might be compelled to take the
matter into their own hands. This seems to have been
the general feeling among the laity of England; for a
foreigner writing to the Republic of Florence says: "Nothing else is thought of in that island every day, except of
arranging affairs in such a way that they do no longer be
in want of the Pope, neither for filling vacancies in the
Church, nor for any other purpose."[4]

---

[1] Paris and Orleans, *Letters and Papers*, etc. IV. iii. p. 2845 ; Bourges
and Bologna, *ibid.* IV. iii. p. 2895 ; Padua, *ibid.* IV. iii. pp. 2921,
2923 (it is said that the Lutherans in the city strongly opposed the King) ·
Pavia, *ibid.* IV. iii. p. 2988 ; Ferrara, *ibid.* IV. iii. 2990.

[2] A list of the matters to be brought before this Parliament is given in
Letters and Papers, etc. IV. iii. pp. 2689 *ff.*

[3] *Ibid.* IV. iii. pp. 2929, 2991.

[4] *Ibid.* IV. iii. p. 3661 (December 25th, 1530).

Having made himself sure of the great mass of the laity, Henry next set himself to force the clergy into submission. He suddenly charged them all with being guilty of *Præmunire* because they had accepted the authority of Papal Legates within the kingdom; and managed to extort a sum of £100,000, to be paid in five yearly instalments, by way of a fine from the clergy of the Province of Canterbury.[1] At the same meeting of Convocation (1531) the clergy were compelled, under threat of the law of *Præmunire*, to declare that the King was "their singular protector and only supreme lord, and, *as far as that is permitted by the law of Christ*, the Supreme Head of the Church and of the clergy." The ambiguity in the acknowledgment left a loophole for weak consciences; but the King was satisfied with the phrase, feeling confident that he could force his own interpretation of the acknowledgment on the Church. "It is all the same," Charles v.'s ambassador wrote to his master, "as far as the King is concerned, as if they had made no reservation; for no one now will be so bold as to contest with his lord the importance of this reservation."[2]

This acknowledgment was, according to the King, simply a clearer statement of what was contained in the old statutes of *Præmunire*, and in all his subsequent ecclesiastical legislation he claimed that he was only giving effect to the earlier laws of England.

The Parliament of 1532 gave the King important assistance in forcing on the submission, not only of the clergy of England, but of the Pope, to his wishes. The Commons presented a petition complaining of various grievances affecting the laity in the working of the ecclesiastical courts, which was sent with a set of demands from the King to the Convocation. The result was the important resolution of Convocation (May 15th, 1532) which is called the *Submission of the Clergy*, where it is

[1] *Letters and Papers*, etc. v. 71.
[2] *Ibid.* etc. v. p. 47. Chapuys thought that the declaration made the King "Pope of England."

promised not to make any new canons without the King's licence and ratification, and to submit all previous canons to a committee of revision, to consist of thirty-two persons, sixteen from Parliament and sixteen from the clergy, and all to be chosen by the King. This committee was to expunge all containing anything prejudicial to the King's prerogative. This Act of Convocation practically declared that the Church of England could neither make any rules for its own guidance without the King's permission, nor act according to the common law of the mediæval Church when that, in the King's opinion, invaded the royal prerogative.[1] From this Act the Church of England has never been able to free itself. The other deed of this Parliament which was destined to be of the greatest use to Henry in his dealings with the Pope was an Act dealing with the *annates, i.e.* one year's income from all ecclesiastical benefices paid to the Pope on entrance into any benefice. The Act declared that the *annates* should be withheld from the Pope and given to the King, but permitted His Majesty to suspend its operation so long as it pleased him.[2] It was the suspensory clause which enabled Henry to coerce the Pope, and he was not slow to take advantage of it.[3] Writing to Rome (March 21st, 1532), he said: " The Pope and Cardinals may gain our friendship by truth and justice. Take care that they do not hope or despair too much from this power which has been committed to us by the statute. I do not mean to deceive them, but to tell them the fact that this statute will be to their advantage, if they show themselves deserving of it; if not, otherwise. Nothing has been defined at present, which must be to their advantage if they do not despise my friendship."[4]

---

[1] Cf. Gee and Hardy, *Documents illustrative of the History of the English Church*, p. 176. Chapuys declares that "Churchmen will be of less account than shoemakers, who have the power of assembling and making their own statutes" (*Letters and Papers*, etc. v. 467 ; cf. VI. 121).

[2] *Ibid.* p. 178 ; the suspensory clause is on p. 184. *Letters and Papers*, etc. v. pp. 343, 413.

[3] *Ibid.* etc. v. p. 71.   [4] *Ibid.* etc. v. p. 415.

Archbishop Warham, who had presided at the Convocation which made the submission of the clergy, died in August 1532; and Henry resolved that Cranmer, notwithstanding his unwillingness, should succeed him as Archbishop of Canterbury. Cranmer conscientiously believed that the royal supremacy was a good thing, and would cure many of the ecclesiastical evils which no appeals to the Pope seemed able to reform; and he was also convinced that the marriage of Henry with Catharine had been one for which not even the highest ecclesiastical authority could give a dispensation. He was prepared to carry out the King's wishes in both respects. He could not be an acceptable Primate to the Roman Curia. Yet Henry, by threatening the Pope with the loss of the *annates*, actually compelled him to send Bulls to England, and that with unusual speed, ratifying the appointment to the Primacy of a man who was known to believe in the nullity of the King's marriage, and to be ready to give effect to his opinion; and this at a time when the Parliament of England had declared that the Primate's court was the supreme ecclesiastical tribunal for the English Church and people. The deed made the Curia really responsible for almost all that followed in England. For Parliament in February 1533, acting on the submission of the clergy, had passed an Act prohibiting all appeals to Rome from the Archbishop's court, and ordering that, if any appeals were taken, they must be to the King's Court of Chancery. This was the celebrated Act of Restraint of Appeals.[1]

In the beginning of 1533 (Jan. 25th), Henry VIII. was privately married to Anne Boleyn. He had taken the Pope's advice in this one particular, to get married without waiting for the Divorce; but soon afterwards (April 5th) he got from the Convocation of Canterbury a document declaring that the Pope had no power to grant a dispensation in such a case as the marriage of Henry

[1] Gee and Hardy, *Documents*, etc. p. 195; the important clause is on p. 198.

with Catharine;[1] and the Act of Restraint of Appeals had made such a decision practically final so far as England was concerned.

Cranmer was consecrated Archbishop of Canterbury on March 30th, 1533. His opinions were known. He had been one of the Cambridge " Germans "; he had freely consorted with Lutheran divines in Germany; he had begun to pray in private for the abolition of the Pope's power in England as early as 1525; and it was not without reason that Chapuys called him a " Lutheran."[2]

On April 11th, 1533, the new Primate asked the King to permit him to try the question of the Divorce before his own ecclesiastical court; and leave was granted him on the following day, as the principal minister " of our spiritual jurisdiction."[3]   The trial was begun, and the court, acting on the decisions of Convocation two months earlier, which had declared (1) that no dispensation could be given for a marriage with the widow of a brother provided the marriage had been consummated, and (2) that the marriage between Arthur and Catharine had been consummated, pronounced that the marriage between the King and Catharine of Aragon was null and void.[4]   This was followed by an inquiry about the marriage between the King and Anne Boleyn, which was pronounced valid, and preparations were made for the coronation of Queen Anne, which took place on June 1st, 1533.[5]

This act of defiance to Rome was at once resented by the Pope. The Curia declared that the marriage between Henry and Catharine was lawful, and a Bull was issued commanding Henry to restore Catharine and put away Anne within ten days on pain of excommunication; which sentence the Emperor, all Christian Princes, and Henry's own subjects were called upon to execute by force of arms.[6]

The action at Rome was answered from England by

---

[1] *Letters and Papers,* etc. VI. pp. 145, 148 ; cf. 218.
[2] *Ibid.* etc. VI. p. 35.   [3] *Ibid.* VI. p. 153.
[4] *Ibid.* VI. p. 231.   [5] *Ibid.* VI. p. 246.
[6] *Ibid.* VI. p. 413.

the passing of several strong Acts of Parliament—all in
1534. They completed the separation of the Church and
people of England from the See of Rome.

1. The Act forbidding the payment of *annates* to the
Pope was again introduced, and this time made absolute;
no *annates* were for the future to be sent to Rome as the
first-fruits of any benefice. In the same Act new provisions were made for the appointment of Bishops; they
were for the future to be elected by the Deans and Chapters
on receiving a royal letter of leave and nomination.[1]

2. An Act forbidding the payment of Peter's Pence
to the Bishop of Rome; forbidding all application to the
Pope for dispensations; and declaring that all such dispensations were to be sought for in the ecclesiastical
courts within England.[2]

3. The Act of Succession, which was followed by a
second within the same year in which the nullity of the
marriage of Henry with Catharine of Aragon was clearly
stated, and Catharine was declared to be the " Princess of
Wales," *i.e.* the widow of Arthur; which affirms the
validity of the King's marriage with Anne Boleyn, and
declares that all the issue of that marriage are legitimate;
and which affirms that, failing male succession, the crown
falls to the Princess Elizabeth.[3]

4. The Supremacy Act, which declares that the King
is rightfully the *Supreme Head of the Church of England,*
has been recognised as such by Convocation, and that it is
within his powers to make ecclesiastical visitations and to
redress ecclesiastical abuses.[4]

5. The Treasons Act must also be included, inasmuch
as one of its provisions is that it is treason to deny to the
King any of his lawful titles (the Supreme Head of the
Church of England being one), and that treason includes
calling the King a heretic or a schismatic.[5]

[1] Gee and Hardy, *Documents illustrative of the History of the English
Church*, p. 201.
[2] *Ibid.* p. 209.   [3] *Ibid.* pp. 232, 244.
[4] *Ibid.* p. 243.   [5] *Ibid.* p. 247.

To complete the list, it is necessary to mention that the two Convocations of Canterbury and of York solemnly declared that "the Roman Pontiff had no greater jurisdiction bestowed on him by God in the Holy Scriptures than any other foreign (*externus*) Bishop "—a declaration called the *Abjuration of the Papal Supremacy by the Clergy*.[1]

This separation of the Church of England from Rome really meant that instead of there being a dual control, there was to be a single one only. The Kings of England had always claimed to have some control over the Church of their realm; Henry went further, and insisted that he would share that supervision with no one. But it should be noticed that what he did claim was, to use the terms of canon law, the *potestas jurisdictionis*, not the *potestas ordinis*; he never asserted his right to ordain or to control the sacraments. Nor was there at first any change in definition of doctrines. The Church of England remained what it had been in every respect, with the exception that the Bishop of Rome was no longer recognised as the *Episcopus Universalis*, and that, if appeals were necessary from the highest ecclesiastical courts in England, they were not to be taken as formerly to Rome, but were to be settled in the King's courts within the land of England. The power of jurisdiction over the affairs of the Church could scarcely be exercised by the King personally. Appeals could be settled by his judges in the law courts, but he required a substitute to exercise his power of visitation. This duty was given to Thomas Cromwell, who was made Vicar-General,[2] and the office to some small extent may be said to resemble that of the Papal Legate; he represented the King as the Legate had represented the Pope.

It was impossible, however, for the Church of England to maintain exactly the place which it had occupied. There was some stirring of Reformation life in the land. Cranmer had been early attracted by the writings of Luther; Thomas Cromwell was not unsympathetic, and,

[1] Gee and Hardy, *Documents*, etc. p. 251.   [2] *Ibid.* p. 256.

besides, he had the idea that there would be some advantage gained politically by an approach to the German Protestants. There was soon talk about a set of Articles which would express the doctrinal beliefs of the Church of England. It was, however, no easy matter to draft them. While Cranmer, Cromwell, and such new Bishops as Latimer, had decided leanings towards the theology of the Reformation, the older Bishops held strongly by the mediæval doctrines. The result was that, after prolonged consultations, little progress was made, and very varying doctrines seem to have been taught, all of which tended to dispeace. In the end, the King himself, to use his own words, " was constrained to put his own pen to the book, and conceive certain articles which were agreed upon by Convocation as catholic and meet to be set forth by authority." [1] They were published in 1536 under the title, *Articles devised by the Kyng's Highnes Majestie to stablysh Christen quietnes*, and were ordered to be read " plainly " in the churches.[2] They came to be called the *Ten Articles*, the first doctrinal symbol of the Church of England.

According to the preface, they were meant to secure, by royal authority, unity and concord in religious beliefs, and to repress and utterly extinguish all dissent and discord. Foxe the Martyrologist describes them very accurately as meant for " weaklings newly weaned from their mother's milk of Rome." Five deal with doctrines and five with ceremonies. The Bible, the Three Creeds (Apostles', Nicene, and Athanasian), and the doctrinal decisions of the first four Œcumenical Councils, are to be regarded as the standards of orthodoxy; baptism is necessary for salvation—children dying in infancy " shall undoubtedly be saved thereby, and *else not* "; the Sacrament of Penance is retained with confession and absolution, which are declared to be expedient and necessary; the substantial, real, corporeal Presence of Christ's Body and Blood under the form of Bread and Wine in the Eucharist is taught;

[1] *Letters and Papers*, etc. XI. p. 445.   [2] *Ibid.* XI. pp. 30, 445.

faith as well as charity is necessary to salvation; images
are to remain in the churches; the saints and the Blessed
Virgin are to be reverenced as intercessors; the saints are
to be invoked; certain rites and ceremonies, such as clerical
vestments, sprinkling with holy water, carrying candles on
Candlemas Day, and sprinkling ashes on Ash-Wednesday,
are good and laudable; the doctrines of Purgatory and of
prayers for the dead were not denied, but people were
warned about them.   It should be noticed that while the
three Sacraments of Baptism, the Eucharist, and Penance
are retained, no mention is made of the other four, and
that this is not unlike what Luther taught in the *Babylonian
Captivity of the Church of Christ*; that while the Real
Presence is maintained, nothing is said about Transubstantiation; that while images are retained in churches,
all incensing, kneeling, or offering to images is forbidden;
that while saints and the Virgin may be invoked as intercessors, it is said that it is a vain superstition to believe
that any saint can be more merciful than Christ Himself;
and that the whole doctrine of Attrition and Indulgences
is paralysed by the statement that amendment of life is a
necessary part of Penance.

It is only when these Articles are read along with the
Injunctions issued in 1536 and 1538 that it can be fully
seen how much they were meant to wean the people, if
gradually, from the gross superstition which disgraced the
popular mediæval religion. If this be done, they seem
an attempt to fulfil the aspirations of Christian Humanists
like Dean Colet and Erasmus.

After warning the clergy to observe all the laws made
for the abolition of the papal supremacy, all those insisting
on the supremacy of the King as the " supreme Head of
the Church of England," and to preach against the Pope's
usurped power within the realm of England, the *Injunctions*
proceed to say that the clergy are to expound the *Ten
Articles* to their people.   In doing so they are to explain
why superfluous holy days ought not to be observed; they
are to exhort their people against such superstitions as

images, relics, and priestly miracles. They are to tell them that it is best to keep God's commandments, to fulfil His works of charity, to provide for their families, and to bestow upon the poor the money they often lavish on pilgrimages, images, and relics. They are to see that parents and teachers instruct children from their earliest years in the Lord's Prayer, the Creed, and the Ten Commandments. They are to be careful that the sacraments are duly and reverently administered within their parishes, are to set an example of moral living, and are to give themselves to the study of the Scriptures. The second set of *Injunctions* (1538) goes further. The clergy are told to provide "one whole Bible *of the largest volume* in English," which is to be set somewhere in the church where the parishioners can most easily read it; and they are to beware of discouraging any man from perusing it, "for it is the lively word of God that every Christian man is bound to embrace and follow." They are to preach a sermon at least every quarter, in which they are to declare the very gospel of Christ, and to exhort the people to the works of charity, mercy, and faith especially prescribed in the Scriptures. They are to warn them against trusting to fancies entirely outside of Scripture, such as "wandering to pilgrimages, offering of money or candles to images or relics, kissing or licking the same, and saying over a number of beads or suchlike superstitions." They are not to permit candles, tapers, or images of wax to be placed before the images in the churches, in order to avoid "that most detestable offence of idolatry."[1]

The *Ten Articles* thus authoritatively expounded are anything but "essentially Romish with the Pope left out in the cold." They are rather an attempt to construct a brief creed which a pliant Lutheran and a pliant Romanist might agree upon—a singularly successful attempt, and one which does great credit to the theological attainments of the English King.

[1] The two sets of *Injunctions* are printed in Gee and Hardy's *Documents illustrative of the History of the English Church*, pp. 269, 275.

It was thought good to have a brief manual of religious instruction to place in the hands of the lower clergy and of the people, perhaps because the *Ten Articles* were not always well received. A committee of divines, chiefly Bishops,[1] were appointed to " compile certain rudiments of Christianity and a Catechism." [2] The result was a small book, divided into four parts—an exposition of the Apostles' Creed, of the *seven* Sacraments, of the Ten Commandments, of the Lord's Prayer, and the Ave Maria. Two other parts were added from the *Ten Articles*—one on Justification, for which faith is said to be necessary; and the other on Purgatory, which is stoutly denied. Great difficulties were experienced in the compilation, owing to the "great diversity of opinions"[3] which prevailed among the compilers; and the book was a compromise between those who were stout for the old faith and those who were keen for the new; but in the end all seemed satisfied with their work. The chief difference between its teaching and that of the *Ten Articles* is that the name sacrament is given to seven and not three of the chief ceremonies of the mediæval Church; but, on the other hand, the doctrine of Purgatory is denied. It was expected that the King would revise the book before its publication,[4] but he " had no time convenient to overlook the great pains " bestowed upon it.[5] Drafts of an imprimatur by the King have been found among the State Papers,[6] but the book was finally issued in 1537 by the " Archbishops and Bishops of England," and was therefore popularly called the *Bishops' Book*. All the clergy were ordered " to read aloud from the pulpit every Sunday a portion of this book " to their people.[7] The Catechism appears to have been published at the same time, and to have been in large request.[8]

---

[1] The list of members is given in *Letters and Papers*, etc. XII. ii. p. 163.
[2] *Letters and Papers*, XII. ii. p. 165 (*Foxe of Hereford to Bucer*).
[3] *Ibid.* etc. XII. ii. p. 122.
[4] *Ibid.* XII. ii. pp. 118, 122, 162.
[5] *Ibid.* XII. ii. p. 228.   [6] *Ibid.* XII. ii. p. 228.
[7] *Ibid.* XII. ii. 252, 296.   [8] *Ibid.* XII. ii. p. 384.

Henry VIII. afterwards revised the *Bishops' Book* according to his own ideas. The revision was published in 1543, and was known as the *King's Book*.[1]

Perhaps the greatest boon bestowed on the people of England by the *Ten Articles* and the *Injunctions* which enforced them was the permission to read and hear read a version of the Bible in their own tongue. For the vernacular Scriptures had been banned in England as they had not been on the Continent, save perhaps during the Albigensian persecution. The seventh of the *Constitutions of Thomas Arundel* ordains " that no one hereafter translates into the English tongue or into any other, on his own authority, the text of Holy Scripture either by way of book, or booklet, or tract." This constitution was directed against Wiclif's translation, which had been severely proscribed. That version, like so many others during the Middle Ages, had been made from the Vulgate. But Luther's example had fired the heart of William Tyndale to give his countrymen an English version translated directly from the Hebrew and the Greek originals.

Tyndale was a distinguished scholar, trained first at Oxford and then at Cambridge. When at the former University he had belonged to that circle of learned and pious men who had encouraged Erasmus to complete his critical text of the New Testament. He knew, as did More, that Erasmus desired that the weakest woman should be able to read the Gospels and the Epistles of St. Paul ; that the husbandman should sing portions of them to himself as he followed the plough ; that the weaver should hum them to the tune of his shuttle ; and that the traveller should beguile the tedium of the road by repeating their stories ; and he did not, like More, turn his back on the ennobling enthusiasms of his youth.[2]

---

[1] Cranmer's *Miscellaneous Writings and Letters* (Parker Society, Cambridge, 1846), pp. 83–114, contains *Corrections·of the Institution of a Christian Man* (the *Bishops' Book*) by *Henry VIII.*, *with Archbishop Cranmer's Annotations.*

[2] As late as Jan. 1533 we find him writing : " Let us agitate for the use

22**

Tyndale found that he could not attempt his task in England. He went to Germany and began work in Cologne; but, betrayed to the magistrates of that centre of German Romanism, he fled to Worms. There he finished the translation of the New Testament, and printed two editions, one in octavo and the other in quarto—the latter being enriched with copious marginal notes. The ecclesiastical authorities in England had early word of this translation, and by Nov. 3rd, Archbishop Warham was exerting himself to buy and destroy as many copies as he could get hold of both in England and abroad; and, thanks to his exertions, Tyndale was supplied with funds to revise his work and print a corrected edition. This version was welcomed in England, and passed secretly from hand to hand. It was severely censured by Sir Thomas More, not because the work was badly done, but really because it was so scholarly. The faithful translation of certain words and sentences was to the reactionary More "a mischievous perversion of those writings intended to advance heretical opinion";[1] and, strange to say, Dr. James Gairdner seems to agree with him.[2] Tyndale's version had been publicly condemned in England at the Council called by the King in 1530 (May), and copies of his book had been publicly burnt in St. Paul's Churchyard, while he himself had been tracked like a wild beast by emissaries of the English Government in the Netherlands.

Cranmer induced Convocation in 1534 to petition for an English version of the Bible, and next year Cromwell persuaded Miles Coverdale to undertake his translation in 1535. It was made from the Vulgate with some assist-

of Scripture in the mother-tongue, and for learning in the Universities. . . . I never altered a syllable of God's Word myself, nor would, against my conscience " (Letters and Papers, etc. VI. p. 184).

[1] Cf. Tyndale's answer to Sir Thomas More's animadversions, Works (Day's edition), p. 118.

[2] Cf. Pollard's excellent and trenchant note, Cranmer and the English Reformation (New York and London, 1904), p. 110; Gairdner, The English Church in the Sixteenth Century, from the Accession of Henry VIII. to the Death of Mary (London, 1902), pp. 190–91.

ance from Luther's version, and was much inferior to the proscribed version of Tyndale; but it had a large private sale in England, and the King was induced to license it to enable the clergy to obey the *Injunctions* of 1536, which had ordered a copy of the English Bible to be placed in all the churches before August 1537.[1]

The Archbishop, however, had another version in view, which he sent to Cromwell (Aug. 1537), saying that he liked it better than any other translation, and hoped it would be licensed to be read freely until the Bishops could set forth a better, which he believes will not be until after Doomsday. This version was practically Tyndale's.

Tyndale had entrusted one of his friends, Rogers, with his translation of the Old Testament, finished as far as the Book of Jonah, and with his complete version of the New Testament. Rogers had taken Tyndale's New Testament, his Old Testament as far as the Book of Chronicles, borrowed the remaining portion of the Old Testament from Coverdale's version, and printed them with a dedication to the King, signed Thomas Matthew.[2] This was the edition recommended by Cranmer to Cromwell, which was licensed. The result was that Tyndale's New Testament (the same version which had been denounced as pernicious, and which had been publicly burnt only a few years before) and a large part of his Old Testament were publicly introduced into the parish churches of England, and became the foundation of all succeeding translations of the Bible into the English language.[3] On reconsideration, the translation was found to be rather too accurate for the Government, and some changes (certainly not corrections) were made in 1538–39. Thus altered, the translation was known as the *Great Bible*, and, because Cranmer wrote the preface, as Cranmer's Bible.[4] This

---

[1] *Letters and Papers*, etc. XII. ii. p. 174.

[2] *National Dictionary of Biography*, art. "Rogers."

[3] The excellence of Tyndale's version is shown by the fact that many of his renderings have been adopted in the Revised Version.

[4] Dixon, *History of the Church of England* (London, 1878, etc.), ii. 77.

was the version, the Bible "of the largest volume," which was ordered to be placed in the churches for the people to read, and portions of which were to be read from the pulpit every Sunday, according to the *Injunctions* of 1538.

From 1533 on to the middle of 1539, there was a distinct if slow advance in England towards a real Reformation; then the progress was arrested, if the movement did not become decidedly retrograde. It seems more than probable that if Henry had lived a few years longer, there would have been another attempt at an advance.

Part of the advance had been a projected political and religious treaty with the German Protestants. Neither Henry VIII. nor John Frederick of Saxony appears to have been much in earnest about an alliance, and from the English King's instructions to his envoys it would appear that his chief desire was to commit the German divines to an approval of the Divorce.[1] Luther was somewhat scornful, and seems to have penetrated Henry's design.[2] The German theologians had no doubt but that the marriage of Henry with Catharine was one which should never have taken place; but they all held that, once made, it ought not to be broken.[3] Determined efforts were made to capture the sympathies of Melanchthon. Bishop Foxe, selected as the theological ambassador, was instructed to take him presents to the value of £70.[4] His books were placed on the course of study for Cambridge at Cromwell's order.[5] Henry exchanged complimentary letters, and graciously accepted the dedication of Melanchthon's *De Locis Communibus.*[6] An embassy was despatched, consisting of Foxe, Bishop elect of Hereford; Heath, Archdeacon of Canterbury; and Dr. Barnes, an English divine, who was a pronounced Lutheran. They met the Protestant Princes at Schmalkald and had long discussions.

---

[1] *Letters and Papers*, etc. IX. p. 69.　　[2] *Ibid.* IX. 119.
[3] *Ibid.* X. p. 234 ; cf. De Wette, *Dr. Martin Luthers Briefe*, etc. iv. p. 668.
[4] *Ibid.* IX. p. 72 ; cf. p. 70.　　[5] *Ibid.* IX. p. 208.
[6] *Ibid.* IX. pp. 74, 75, 166, 311.

The confederated Princes and Henry found themselves in
agreement on many points : they would stoutly disown
the primacy of the Pope; they would declare that they
would not be bound by the decrees of any Council which
the Pope and the Emperor might assemble; and they
would pledge each other to get their Bishops and preachers
to declare them null and void. The German Princes
were quite willing to give Henry the title of "Defender
of the Schmalkald League." But they insisted as the
first articles of any alliance that the English Church and
King must accept the theology of the Augsburg Confession
and adopt the ceremonies of the Lutheran Church; and
on these rocks of doctrine and ritual the proposed alliance
was shattered.[1]   The Germans had their own private
view of the English Reformation under Henry VIII., which
was neither very flattering nor quite accurate.

" So far the King has become Lutheran, that, because
the Pope has refused to sanction his divorce, he has ordered,
on penalty of death, that every one shall believe and preach
that not the Pope but himself is the head of the universal
Church.   All other papistry, monasteries, mass, indulgences,
and intercessions for the dead, are pertinaciously adhered
to." [2]

The English embassy went from Schmalkald to
Wittenberg, where they met a number of divines, including
Luther and Melanchthon, and proceeded to discuss the
question of doctrinal agreement.   Melanchthon had gone
over the Augsburg Confession, and produced a series of
articles which presented all that the Wittenberg theologians
could concede, and Luther had revised the draft.[3]   Both
the Germans were charmed with the learning and courtesy
of Archdeacon Heath.   Bishop Foxe " had the manner
of prelates," says Melanchthon, and his learning did not

---

[1] *Letters and Papers*, etc. IX. pp. 344-48.
[2] *Ibid.* x. p. 38.
[3] These articles have been printed with a good historical introduction by
Professor Mentz of Jena, *Die Wittenberger Artikel von 1536* (Leipzig, 1905).

impress the Germans.[1]   The conference came to nothing.
Henry did not care to accept a creed ready made for him,
and thought that ecclesiastical ceremonies might differ in
different countries. He was a King " reckoned somewhat
learned, though unworthy," he said, " and having so many
learned men in his realm, he could not accept at any
creature's hand the observing of his and the realm's
faith; but he was willing to confer with learned men
sent from them." [2]

Before the conference at Wittenberg had come to an
end, Henry believed that he had no need for a German
alliance.   The ill-used Queen Catharine, who, alone of all
persons concerned in the Divorce proceedings, comes out
unstained, died on Jan. 7th, 1536. Her will contained
the touching bequest: " To my daughter, the collar of
gold which I brought out of Spain " [3]—out of Spain,
when she came a fair young bride to marry Prince Arthur
of England thirty-five years before.

There is no need to believe that Henry exhibited the
unseemly manifestations of joy which his enemies credit
him with when the news of Catharine's death was brought
to him, but it did free him from a great dread.   He read
men and circumstances shrewdly, and he knew enough of
Charles v. to believe that the Emperor, after his aunt's
death, and when he had no flagrant attack on the family
honour of his house to protest against, would not make
himself the Pope's instrument against England.

Henry had always maintained himself and England
by balancing France against the Empire, and could in
addition weaken the Empire by strengthening the German
Protestants.   But in 1539, France and the Emperor
had become allies, and Henry was feeling himself very
insecure.   It is probable that the negotiations which
led to Henry's marriage with Anne of Cleves were due
to this new danger.   On the other hand, there had
been discontent in England at many of the actions

---

[1] *Letters and Papers*, etc. x. p. 98 ; cf. 58, 97, 108,
[2] *Ibid.* ix. p. 346.   [3] *Ibid.* x. p. 15.

which were supposed to come from the advance towards
Reformation.

Henry VIII. had always spent money lavishly. His
father's immense hoards had disappeared, while England,
under Wolsey, was the paymaster of Europe, and the
King was in great need of funds. In England as elsewhere the wealth of the monasteries seemed to have been
collected for the purpose of supplying an empty royal
exchequer. A visitation of monasteries was ordered, under
the superintendence of Thomas Cromwell; and, in order to
give him a perfectly free hand, all episcopal functions
were for the time being suspended. The visitation disclosed many scandalous things. It was followed by the
Act of Parliament (1536) for *The Dissolution of the Lesser
Monasteries*.[1] The lands of all monasteries whose annual
rental was less than £200 a year were given to the
King, as well as all the ornaments, jewels, and other goods
belonging to them. The dislodged monks and nuns were
either to be taken into the larger houses or to receive
some measure of support, and the heads were to get
pensions sufficient to sustain them. The lands thus acquired
might have been formed into a great crown estate yielding
revenues large enough to permit taxation to be dispensed with; but the King was in need of ready money,
and he had courtiers to gratify. The convent lands
were for the most part sold cheaply to courtiers, and
the numbers and power of the county families were
largely increased. A new visitation of the remaining
monasteries was begun in 1538, this time accompanied
with an inquiry into superstitious practices indulged
in in various parts of the country, and notorious relics
were removed. They were of all sorts—part of St.
Peter's hair and beard; stones with which St. Stephen
was stoned; the hair shirt and bones of St. Thomas the
martyr; a crystal containing a little quantity of Our
Lady's milk, "with two other bones"; the "principal
relic in England, an angel with one wing that brought to

---

[1] The Act is printed in Gee and Hardy, *Documents*, etc. p. 257.

Caversham (near Reading) the spear's head that pierced the side of our Saviour on the cross"; the ear of Malchus, which St. Peter cut off; a foot of St. Philip at Winchester "covered with gold plate and (precious) stones"; and so forth.[1] Miraculous images were brought up to London and their mechanism exposed to the crowd, while an eloquent preacher thundered against the superstition:

"The bearded crucifix called the 'Rood of Grace' (was brought from Maidstone, and) while the Bishop of Rochester preached it turned its head, rolled its eyes, foamed at the mouth, and shed tears,—in the presence, too, of many other famous saints of wood and stone . . . the satellite saints of the Kentish image acted in the same way. It is expected that the Virgin of Walsingham, St. Thomas of Canterbury, and other images will soon perform miracles also in the same place; for the trickery was so thoroughly exposed that every one was indignant at the monks and impostors."[2]

A second Act of Parliament followed, which vested all monastic property in the King; and this gave the King

---

[1] *Letters and Papers*, etc. XIII. ii. pp. 36, 78, 147, 155. In *Letters and Papers*, etc. XIV. i. p. 153, there is an *official* account of the English Reformation under Henry VIII., in which there is the following (p. 155): "Touching images set in the churches, as books of the unlearned, though they are not necessary, but rather give occasion to Jews, Turks, and Saracens to think we are idolaters, the King tolerates them, except those about which idolatry has been committed. . . . Our Lady of Worcester, when her garments were taken off, was found to be the similitude of a bishop, like a giant, almost ten feet long; . . . the roods at Boxelegh and other places, which moved their eyes and lips when certain keys and strings were bent or pulled in secret places—images of this sort the King has caused to be voided and committed other as it was convenient, following the example of King Hezekiah, who destroyed the brazen serpent. Shrines, copses, and reliquaries, so called, have been found to be feigned things, as the blood of Christ was but a piece of red silk enclosed in a thick glass of crystalline, and in another place oil coloured of *sanguis draconis*, instead of the milk of Our Lady a piece of chalk or ceruse. Our Lady's girdle, the verges of Moses and Aaron, etc., and more of the Holy Cross than three cars may carry, the King has therefore caused to be taken away and the abusive pieces burnt, and the doubtful sort hidden away honestly for fear of idolatry."

[2] *Ibid.* XIII. i. 283–84, *Nicholas Partridge to Bullinger* (April 12th).

possession not only of huge estates, but also of an immense quantity of jewels and precious metals.[1] The shrine of St. Thomas at Canterbury, when "disgarnished," yielded, it is said, no fewer than twenty-six cartloads of gold and silver.[2]

This wholesale confiscation of monastic property, plundering of shrines, and above all the report that Henry had ordered the bones of St. Thomas of Canterbury to be burned and the ashes scattered to the winds, determined Pope Paul III. to renew (Dec. 17th, 1538) the execution of his Bull of excommunication (Aug. 30th, 1535), which had been hitherto suspended. It was declared that the Bull might be published in St. Andrews or "in oppido Calistrensi" in Scotland, at Dieppe or Boulogne in France, or at Tuam in Ireland.[3] The Pope knew that he could not get it published in England itself.

The violent destruction of shrines and pilgrimage places, which had been holiday resorts as well as places of devotion, could not fail to create some popular uneasiness, and there were other and probably deeper roots of discontent. England, like other nations, had been suffering from the economic changes which were a feature of the times. One form peculiar to England was that wool-growing had become more profitable than keeping stock or raising grain, and landed proprietors were enclosing commons for pasture land and letting much of their arable land lie fallow. The poor men could no longer graze their beasts on the commons, and the substitution of pasture for arable land threw great numbers out of employment. They had to sell the animals they could no longer feed, and did not see how a living could be earned; nor had they the compensation given to the disbanded monks. The pressure of taxation increased the prevailing distress.

[1] *The Act for the Dissolution of the Greater Monasteries* is printed in Gee and Hardy, *Documents*, etc. p. 281.

[2] *Ibid.* XIII. ii. p. 49.

[3] *Letters and Papers*, etc. XIII. ii. p. 459. "In oppido Calistrensi" is probably "at Coldstream"; Beaton had been made a Cardinal to be ready to make the publication.

Risings took place in Yorkshire, Lancashire, and Lincoln·
shire, and the insurgents marched singing:

> "Christ crucified,
> For Thy woundes wide,
> Us commons guyde,
> Which pilgrims be,
> Through Godes grace,
> For to purchache,
> Old wealth and peax
> Of the Spiritualitie."[1]

In their demands they denounced equally the contempt
shown for Holy Mother Church, the dissolution of the
monasteries, the spoliation of shrines, the contempt shown
to "Our Ladye and all the saints," new taxes, the enclosure
of commons, the doing away with use and wont in tenant
rights, the branding of the Lady Mary as illegitimate,
King's counsellors of "low birth and small estimation," and
the five reforming Bishops—Cranmer and Latimer being
considered as specially objectionable.[2]   The Yorkshire
Rising was called the Pilgrimage of Grace.

The insurgents or "pilgrims" were not more consistent
than other people, for they plundered priests to support
their "army";[3] and while they insisted on the primacy of
the Bishop of Rome, they had no wish to see his authority
re-established in England.   They asked the King to admit
the Pope to be head of spiritual things, giving spiritual
authority to the Archbishops of Canterbury and York, "so
that the said Bishop of Rome have no further meddling."[4]

The insurrections were put down, and Henry did not
cease his spoliation of shrines and monasteries in consequence of their protests; but the feelings of the people
made known by their proclamations, at the conferences held
between their leaders and the representatives of authority,
and by the examination of prisoners and suspected persons,
must have suggested to his shrewd mind whether the

---

[1] *Letters and Papers*, etc. XI. p. 305.
[2] *Ibid.* XI. pp. 238, 272, 355, 356, 477, 504, 507.
[3] *Ibid.* XI. 238.   [4] *Ibid.* XI. 477.

Reformation was not being pressed onward too hastily for the great majority of the English laity. England did not produce in the sixteenth century a great spiritual leader inspired by a prophetic conviction that he was speaking the truth of God, and able to create a like conviction in the hearts of his neighbours, while he was never so far before them that they could not easily follow him step by step. The King cried halt; and when Cromwell insisted on his plan of alliance with the Protestants of the Continent of Europe, he went the way of all the counsellors of Henry who withstood their imperious master (July 28th, 1540).

But this is to anticipate. Negotiations were still in progress with the Lords of the Schmalkald League in the spring of 1539,[1] and the King was thinking of cementing his connection with the German Lutherans by marrying Anne of Cleves,[2] the sister-in-law of John Frederick of Saxony. The Parliament of 1539 (April 28th to June 28th) saw the beginnings of the change. Six questions were introduced for discussion :

"Whether there be in the sacrament of the altar transubstantiation of the substance of bread and wine into the substance of flesh and blood or not ? Whether priests may marry by the law of God or not ? Whether the vow of chastity of men and women bindeth by the law of God or not ? Whether auricular confession be necessary by the law of God or not ? Whether private Masses may stand with the Word of God or not ? Whether it be necessary by the Word of God that the sacrament of the altar should be administered under both kinds or not ? "[3]

The opinions of the Bishops were divided ; but the lay members of the House of Lords evidently did not wish any change from the mediæval doctrines, and believed that no one could be such a wise theologian as their King when he confounded the Bishop with his stores of learning. "We of the temporalitie," wrote one who was present, "have been all of one opinion . . . all England have cause

[1] *Letters and Papers*, etc. XIV. i. p. 344.
[2] *Ibid.* XIV i. pp. 191, 192, 537.   [3] *Ibid.* XIV. i. p. 489.

to thank God and most heartily to rejoice of the King's most godly proceedings."[1]   So Parliament enacted the *Six Articles Act*,[2] a ferocious statute commonly called "the bloody whip with six strings." To deny transubstantiation or to deprave the sacraments was to be reckoned heresy, and to be punished with burning and confiscation of goods. It was made a felony, and punishable with death, to teach that it was necessary to communicate in both kinds in the Holy Supper; or that priests, monks, or nuns vowed to celibacy might marry. All clerical marriages which had been contracted were to be dissolved, and clerical incontinence was punishable by loss of property and benefice. Special commissions were issued to hold quarterly sessions in every county for the enforcement of the statute. The official title of the Act was *An Act abolishing Diversity of Opinion*. The first commission issued was for the county of London, and at the first session five hundred persons were indicted within a fortnight. The law was, however, much more severe than its enforcement. The five hundred made their submission and received the King's pardon. It was under this barbarous statute that so-called heretics were tried and condemned during the last years of the reign of Henry VIII.

The revival of mediæval doctrine did not mean any difference in the strong anti-papal policy of the English King. It rather became more emphatic, and Henry spoke of the Pope in terms of the greatest disrespect. "That most persistent idol, enemy of all truth, and usurpator of Princes, the Bishop of Rome," "that cankered and venomous serpent, Paul, Bishop of Rome," are two of his phrases.[3]

The Act of the Six Statutes made Lutherans, as previous Acts had made Papists, liable to capital punishment; but while Cromwell remained in power he evidently was able to hinder its practical execution. Cromwell, however, was soon to fall. He seemed to be higher in favour than ever.

---

[1] *Letters and Papers*, etc. XIV. i. p. 475.
[2] Gee and Hardy, *Documents*, etc. p. 303.
[3] *Letters and Papers*, etc. XIV. i. pp. 349, 438.

He had almost forced his policy on his master, and the marriage of Henry with Anne of Cleves (Jan. 6th, 1540) seemed to be his triumph. Then Henry struck suddenly and remorselessly as usual. The Minister was impeached, and condemned without trial. He was executed (July 28th); and Anne of Cleves was got rid of on the plea of pre-contract to the son of the Duke of Lorraine (July 9th). It was not the fault of Gardiner, the sleuth-hound of the reaction, that Cranmer did not share the fate of the Minister. Immediately after the execution of Cromwell (July 30th), the King gave a brutal exhibition of his position. Three clergymen of Lutheran views, Barnes, Garret, and Jerome, were burnt at Smithfield; and three Romanists were beheaded and tortured for denying the King's spiritual supremacy.

Henry had kept himself ostentatiously free from responsibility for the manual of doctrine entitled *Institution of a Christian Man*. Perhaps he believed it too advanced for his people; it was at all events too advanced for the theology of the *Six Articles*; another manual was needed, and was published in 1543 (May 19th). It was entitled *A Necessary Doctrine and Erudition for any Christian Man*; *set forth by the King's Majesty of England.*

It was essentially a revision of the former manual, and may have been of composite authorship. Cranmer was believed to have written the chapter on faith, and it was revised by Convocation. The King, who issued it himself with a preface commending it, declared it to be "a true and perfect doctrine for all people." It contains an exposition of the Creed, the Ten Commandments, the Lord's Prayer, and of some selected passages of Scripture. Its chief difference from the former manual is that it teaches unmistakably the doctrines of *Transubstantiation*, the *Invocation of Saints*, and the *Celibacy of the Clergy*. It may be said that it very accurately represented the theology of the majority of Englishmen in the year 1543. For King and people were not very far apart. They both clung to mediæval theology; and they both detested the Papacy,

and wished the clergy to be kept in due subordination.
There was a widespread and silent movement towards an
Evangelical Reformation always making itself apparent
when least expected; but probably three-fourths of the
people had not felt it during the reign of Henry. It
needed Mary's burnings in Smithfield and the fears of a
Spanish overlord, before the leaven could leaven the whole
lump.

CHAPTER IL

THE REFORMATION UNDER EDWARD VI.[1]

WHEN Henry VIII. died, in 1547 (Jan. 28th), the situation in England was difficult for those who came after
him. A religious revolution had been half accomplished; a social revolution was in progress, creating
popular ferment; evicted tenants and uncloistered monks
formed raw material for revolt; the treasury was empty,
the kingdom in debt, and the coinage debased. The kingly
authority had undermined every other, and the King was a
child. The new nobility, enriched by the spoils of the
Church, did not command hereditary respect; and the
Council which gathered round the King was torn by rival
factions.[2]

Henry VIII. had died on a Friday, but his death was

[1] SOURCES in addition to those given on p. 313 : *Calendar of State Papers,
Domestic Series, of the Reigns of Edward VI., Mary, and Elizabeth* (this
Calendar is for the most part merely an index to documents which must
be read in the Record Office); *Correspondance politique d'Odet de Selve :
Commission des Archives Politiques*, Paris, 1888); *Literary Remains of
Edward VI.* (Roxburgh Club, London, 1857); *Narratives of the Reformation*
(Camden Society, London, 1860); Wriothesley, *Chronicle* (Camden Society,
London, 1875); Weiss, *Papiers d'État du Cardinal de Granvelle (Collection
de Documents inédits*, Paris, 1841–52); Furnivall, *Ballads from Manu-
scripts* (Ballad Society, London, 1868); *Four Supplications of the Commons*,
and Thomas Starkey, *England under Henry VIII.* (Early English Text
Society, 1871); Strype, *Ecclesiastical Memorials and Life of Cranmer*
(Oxford edition, 26 vols. 1820, etc.); *Liturgies of Edward VI.* (Parker
Society, Cambridge, 1844); *Stow Annals* (London, 1631).

LATER BOOKS in addition to those given on p. 313 : Pollard, *England
under Protector Somerset* (London, 1900); Burnet, *History of the Reformation* (Oxford edition, 1865); Dixon, *History of the Church of England*
(London, 1893); Gasquet and Bishop, *Edward VI. and the Book of Common
Prayer* (London, 1890). *Cambridge Modern History*, ii. xiv.

[2] Pollard, *Cambridge Modern History*, ii. 474.

kept concealed till the Monday (Jan. 31st), when Edward VI. was brought by his uncle, the Earl of Hertford, and presented to the Council. There a will of the late King was produced, the terms of which make it almost impossible to believe that Henry did not contemplate a further advance towards a Reformation. It appointed a Council of Regency, consisting of sixteen persons who were named. Eleven belonged to the old Council, and among them were five who were well known to desire an advance, while the two most determined reactionaries were omitted—Bishop Gardiner and Thirlby. The will also mentioned by name twelve men who might be added to the Council if their services were thought to be necessary. These were added. Then the Earl of Hertford was chosen to be Lord Protector of the Realm, and was promoted to be Duke of Somerset. The coronation followed (Feb. 20th), and all the Bishops were required to take out new commissions in the name of the young King—the King's ecclesiastical supremacy being thus rigidly enforced. Wriothesley, Henry's Lord Chancellor, who had been created the Earl of Southampton, was compelled to resign the Great Seal, and with his retirement the Government was entirely in the hands of men who wished the nation to go forward in the path of Reformation.

Signs of their intention were not lacking, nor evidence that such an advance would be welcomed by the population of the capital at least. On Feb. 10th a clergyman and churchwardens had removed the images from the walls of their church, and painted instead texts of Scripture; an eloquent preacher, Dr. Barlow, denounced the presence of images in churches; images were pulled down from the churches in Portsmouth; and so on. In May it was announced that a royal visitation of the country would be made, and Bishops were inhibited from making their ordinary visitations.

In July (31st) the Council began the changes. They issued a series of *Injunctions* [1] to the clergy, in which they

---

[1] These *Injunctions*, and the *Articles of Inquiry* which interprets them, are printed in Strype, *Ecclesiastical Memorials*, etc. (Oxford, 1822) II. i. pp. 74-83.

were commanded to preach against "the Bishop of Rome's
usurped power and jurisdiction"; to see that all images
which had been "abused" as objects of pilgrimages should
be destroyed; to read the Gospels and Epistles in English
during the service; and to see that the Litany was no
longer recited or sung in processions, but said devoutly
kneeling. They next issued *Twelve Homilies*, meant to
guard the people against "rash preaching." Such a series
had been suggested as early as 1542, and a proposed draft
had been presented to Convocation by Cranmer in that year,
but had not been authorised. They were now issued on
the authority of the Council. Three of them were composed by Cranmer. These sermons contain little that is
doctrinal, and confine themselves to inciting to godly
living.[1] Along with the *Homilies*, the Council authorised
the issue of Udall's translation of the *Paraphrases* of
Erasmus, which they meant to be read in the churches.

The royal visitation seems to have extended over a
series of years, beginning in 1547. Dr. James Gairdner
discovered, and has printed with comments, an account or
report of a visitation held by Bishop Hooper in the diocese
of Gloucester in 1551. One of the intentions of the
visitation was to discover how far it was possible to expect
preaching from the English clergy. Dr. Gairdner sums up
the illiteracy exhibited in the report as follows:—Three
hundred and eleven clergymen were examined, and of these
one hundred and seventy-one were unable to repeat the
Ten Commandments, though, strangely enough, all but
thirty-four could tell the chapter (Ex. xx.) in which they
were to be found; ten were unable to repeat the Lord's
Prayer; twenty-seven could not tell who was its author;
and thirty could not tell where it was to be found. The
Report deserves study as a description of the condition of
the clergy of the Church of England before the Reformation.
These clergymen of the diocese of Gloucester were asked
nine questions—three under three separate heads: (1)

[1] Cranmer, *Miscellaneous Writings and Letters* (Parker Society, Cam
bridge, 1846), p. 128.

How many commandments are there? Where are they to be found? Repeat them. (2) What are the Articles of the Christian Faith (the Apostles' Creed)? Repeat them. Prove them from Scripture. (3) Repeat the Lord's Prayer. How do you know that it is the Lord's? Where is it to be found? Only fifty out of the three hundred and eleven answered all these simple questions, and of the fifty, nineteen are noted as having answered *mediocriter*. Eight clergymen could not answer any single one of the questions; and while one knew that the number of the Commandments was ten, he knew nothing else Two clergymen, when asked why the Lord's Prayer was so called, answered that it was because Christ had given it to His disciples when he told them to watch and pray; another said that he did not know why it was called the Lord's Prayer, but that he was quite willing to believe that it was the Lord's because the King had said so; and another answered that all he knew about it was that such was the common report. Two clergymen said that while they could not prove the articles of the Creed from Scripture, they accepted them on the authority of the King; and one said that he could not tell what was the Scripture authority for the Creed, unless it was the first chapter of Genesis, but that it did not matter, since the King had guaranteed it to be correct.[1]

There is no reason to believe that the clergy of this diocese were worse than those in other parts of England. If this report be compared with the accounts of the un-reformed clergy of central Germany given in the reports of the visitations held there between 1528 and 1535, the condition of things there which filled Luther with such despair, and induced him to write his Small Cathechism, was very much better than that of the clergy of England. Not more than three or perhaps four out of the three hundred and eleven had ever preached or could preach. These facts, extracted from the formal report of an authoritative visitation made by a Bishop, explain the

[1] *English Historical Review* for 1904 (January), pp. 98 *ff.*

constant cry of the Puritans under Elizabeth for a preaching ministry.

The Council were evidently anxious that the whole service should be conducted in the English language, and that a sermon should always be part of the public worship. The reports of the visitation showed that it was useless to make any general order, but an example was given in the services conducted in the Royal Chapel. Meanwhile (1547) Thomas Hopkins was engaged in making a version of the Psalms in metre, to be sung both in private and in the churches, and these soon became highly popular. Like corresponding versions in France and in Germany, it served to spread the Reformation among the people; and, as might have been expected, Archbishop Laud did his best to stop the singing of these Psalms in later days.

The first Parliament of Edward VI. (Nov. 4th to Dec. 24th, 1547) made large changes in the laws of England affecting treason, which had the effect of sweeping away the edifice of absolute government which had been so carefully erected by Henry VIII. and his Minister Thomas Cromwell. The kingly supremacy in matters of religion was maintained; but the *Act of the Six Articles* was erased from the Statute Book, and with it all heresy Acts which had been enacted since the days of Richard II., and treason was defined as it had been in the days of Edward III. This legislation gave an unwonted amount of freedom to the English people.

Convocation had met in November and December (1547), and, among other things, had agreed unanimously that in the Holy Supper the partakers should communicate in both *kinds*, and had passed a resolution by fifty-three votes to twelve that all canons against the marriage of the clergy should be declared void. These two resolutions were communicated to Parliament, with the result that an Act was passed ordaining that " the most blessed Sacrament be hereafter commonly administered unto the people within the Church of England and Ireland, and other the King's dominions, under both the kinds, that is to say, of bread and wine, except necessity otherwise require."[1]   An Act was also framed permitting the marriage of the clergy, which passed the Commons, but did not reach the House of Lords in time to be voted upon, and did not become law until the following year.   Other two Acts bearing on the condition of the Church of England were issued by this Parliament   According to the one, Bishops were henceforth to be appointed directly by the King, and their courts were to meet in the King's name.   According to the other, the property of all colleges, chantries, guilds, etc., with certain specified exceptions, was declared to be vested in the Crown.[2]

Communion in both kinds made necessary a new Communion Service, and as a tentative measure a new form for the celebration was issued by the Council, which is called by Strype the *Book of Communion*.[3]   It enjoined that the essential words of the Mass should still be said in Latin, but inserted seven prayers in English in the ceremony.   The Council also proceeded in their war against superstitions.   They forbade the creeping to the Cross on Good Friday, the use of ashes on Ash-Wednesday, of palms on Palm Sunday, and of candles on Candlemas ; and they ordered the removal of *all* images from the churches.   Cranmer asserted that all these measures had been intended by Henry VIII.

The next important addition to the progress of the Reformation was the preparation and introduction of a Service Book[4]—*The Boke of the Common Praier and Administration of the Sacramentes and other Rites and Ceremonies after the use of the Churche of England*

---

[1] This Act, entitled *Act against Revilers, and for receiving in both Kinds*, is printed in Gee and Hardy, *Documents*, etc. p. 322.

[2] Gee and Hardy, *Documents*, etc. p. 328.

[3] *Ecclesiastical Memorials*, etc. II. i. p. 133. It is printed in *The Two Liturgies, with other Documents set forth by Authority in the Reign of King Edward the Sixth* (Parker Society, Cambridge, 1844), p. 1.

[4] The book is printed in *The Two Liturgies*, etc., of the Parker Society, pp. 9 *ff.*

(1549), commonly called *The First Prayer-Book of King Edward VI.* It was introduced by an *Act of Uniformity*,[1] which, after relating how there had been for long time in England "divers forms of Common Prayer . . . the use of Sarum, York, Bangor, and of Lincoln," and that diversity of use caused many inconveniences, ordains the universal use of this one form, and enacts penalties on those who make use of any other. The origin of the book is somewhat obscure. There is no trace of any commission appointed to frame it, nor of any formally selected body of revisers. Cranmer had the chief charge of it, and was assisted by a number of divines—though where they met is uncertain, whether at Windsor as the King records in his diary, or at Chertsey Abbey, as is said in the Grey Friars Chronicle. About the end of October the Bishops were asked to subscribe it, and it was subjected to some revision. It was then brought before the House of Lords and discussed there. It was in this debate that Cranmer disclosed that he had definitely abandoned the theory of transubstantiation. The Prayer-Book, however, was eminently conservative, and could be subscribed to by a believer in the old theory. The giving and receiving of the *Bread* is called the *Communion of the Body of Christ*, of the *Wine*, the *Communion of the Blood of Christ*; and the practice of making the sign of the Cross is adhered to at stated points in the ceremony. An examination of its structure and contents reveals that it was borrowed largely from the old English Use of Sarum, and from a new Service Book drafted by the Cardinal Quignon and dedicated to Pope Paul III. The feeling that a new Service Book was needed was not confined to the Reformers, but was affecting all European Christians. The great innovation in this Liturgy was that all its parts were in the English language, and that every portion of the service could be followed and understood by all the worshippers.

With the publication of this *First Prayer-Book of King*

* Gee and Hardy, *Documents*, etc. pp. 358 *ff.*

Edward VI. the first stage of the Reformation during his reign comes to an end. The changes made had all been contemplated by Henry VIII. himself, if we are to believe what Cranmer affirmed. They did not content the more advanced Reformers, and they were not deemed sufficient by Cranmer himself.

The changes made in the laws of England—the repeal of the " bloody " *Statute of the Six Articles* and of the treason laws—had induced many of the English refugees who had gone to Germany and to Switzerland to return to their native land. The Emperor Charles V. had defeated the German Protestants in the battle of Mühlberg in 1547 (April), and England for a few years became a place of refuge for continental Protestants fleeing from the requirements and penalties of the *Interim.* All this gave a strong impetus to the Reformation movement in England. Martin Bucer, compelled to leave Strassburg, found refuge and taught in Cambridge, where he was for a time the regius professor of divinity. Paul Büchlin (usually known by his latinised name of Fagius), a compatriot of Bucer and a well-known Hebrew scholar, was also settled at Cambridge, where he died (Nov. 1549). Peter Martyr Vermigli and Bernardino Ochino, two illustrious Italian Protestants, came to England at the invitation of Cranmer himself, and long afterwards Queen Elizabeth confessed that she had been drawn towards their theology. Peter Alexander of Arles and John à Lasco, the Pole, also received the protection and hospitality of England.[1] The reception of these foreign

---

[1] Mr. Pollard (*Cambridge Modern History,* ii. pp. 478, 479) thinks that the influence of these foreign divines on the English Reformation has been overrated ; and he is probably correct so far as changes in worship and usages go. His idea is that the English Reformers followed the lead of Wiclif, consciously or unconsciously, rather than that of continental divines ; but if the root-thought in all Reformation theology be considered, it may be doubted whether Wiclif *could* supply what the English divines had in common with their continental contemporaries. Wiclif, with all his desire for Reformation, was essentially a mediæval thinker. The theological question which separated every mediæval Reformer from the thinkers of the Reformation was, How the benefits won by the atoning work of Christ

divines, and their appointment as teachers in the English universities, did not escape protest from the local teachers of theology, who were overruled by the Government.

Between the first and the second stage of the Reformation of the Church of England in this reign, a political change occurred which must be mentioned but need not be dwelt upon. The Duke of Somerset incurred the wrath of his colleagues, and of the new nobility who had profited by the sale of Church lands, by his active sympathy with the landless peasantry, and by his proposals to benefit them. He was driven from power, and his place was taken by the unscrupulous Earl of Warwick, who became Lord Protector, and received the Dukedom of Northumberland. The new Governor of England has been almost universally praised by the advanced Reformers because of the way in which he pushed forward the Reformation. It is well to remember in these days, when the noble character of the Duke of Somerset has received a tardy recognition,[1] that John Knox, no mean judge of men, never joined in the praise of Northumberland, and greatly preferred his predecessor, although his advance in the path of Reformation had been slower and much more cautious.

There was much in the times to encourage Northumberland and his Council to think that they might hurry on the Reformation movement.

The New Learning had made great strides in England, and was leavening all the more cultured classes, and it naturally led to the discredit of the old theology. The English advanced Reformers who had taken refuge abroad, and who now returned,—men like Ridley and Hooper,— could not fail to have had some influence on their countrymen ; they had almost all become imbued with the

were to be appropriated by men ! The universal mediæval answer was, By an imitation of Christ ; while the universal Reformation answer was, By trust in the promises of God (for that is what is meant by Justification by Faith). In their answer to this test question, the English divines are at one with the Reformers on the Continent, and not with Wiclif.

[1] Pollard, *England under Protector Somerset* (London, 1900).

Zwinglian type of theology, and Bullinger was their trusted adviser. It seemed as if the feelings of the populace were changing, for the mobs, instead of resenting the destruction of images, were rather inspired by too much iconoclastic zeal, and tried to destroy stained-glass windows and to harry priests. Cranmer's influence, always on the side of reform, had much more weight with the Council than was the case under Henry VIII. He had abandoned long ago his belief in transubstantiation, he had given up the Lutheran doctrine of consubstantiation, if he ever held it, and had now accepted a theory of a real but spiritual Presence in the communion elements which did not greatly differ from the more moderate Zwinglian view. The clergy, many of them, were making changes which went far beyond the Act of Uniformity. The removal of restrictions on printing the Bible had resulted in the publication of more than twenty editions, most of them with annotations which explained and enforced the new theology on the authority of Scripture.

In these circumstances the Council enforced the Act of Uniformity in a one-sided way—against the Romanist sympathisers. Many Romanist Bishops were deprived of their sees, and their places were filled by such men as Coverdale, Ridley, Ponet, and Scovey — all advanced Reformers. John Knox himself, freed from his slavery in the French galleys by the intervention of the English Government and made one of the King's preachers, was offered the bishopric of Rochester, which he declined. It must be remembered, however, that the Lord Protector and his *entourage* seem to have been quite as much animated by a desire to fill their own pockets as by zeal to promote the cause of the Reformation. Indeed, there came to be in England at this time something like the *tulchan* Bishops of a later period in Scotland; great nobles got possession of the episcopal revenues and allowed the new Bishops a stipend out of them.[1]

---

[1] "Tulchan is a calf skin stuffed with straw to cause the cow to give milk. The Bishop served to cause the bishoprick to yeeld commoditie to my

Then came a second revision of the Prayer-Book—*The Boke of Common Praier and Administration of the Sacramentes and other Rites and Ceremonies in the Churche of England* (1552). It is commonly called the *Second Prayer-Book of King Edward the Sixth.*[1] Cranmer had conferences with some of the Bishops as early as Jan. 1551 on the subject, and also with some of the foreign divines then resident in England; and it is more than probable that his intention was to frame such a liturgy as would bring the worship of the Church of England into harmony with that of the continental Reformers. There is no proof that the book was ever presented to Convocation for revision, or that it was subject to a debate in Parliament, as was its predecessor. The authoritative proclamation says:

" The King's most excellent majesty, with the assent of the Lords and Commons in this present Parliament assembled, and by the authority of the same, has caused the aforesaid order of common service, entitled The Book of Common Prayer, to be faithfully and godly perused, explained, and made fully perfect, and by the aforesaid authority has annexed and joined it, so explained and perfected, to this present statute."[2]

This *Book of Common Prayer* deserves special notice, because, although some important changes were made, it is largely reproduced in the Book of Common Prayer which is at present used in the Church of England. The main differences between it and the *First Prayer-Book of King Edward* appear for the most part in the communion service, and were evidently introduced to do away with all thought of a propitiatory Mass. The word *altar* is expunged, and *table* is used instead: *minister* and *priest* are used indifferently as equivalent terms. " The minister at

lord who procured it to him." Scott's *Apologetical Narration of the State and Government of the Kirk of Scotland since the Reformation* (Woodrow Society, Edinburgh, 1846), p. 25.

[1] The book is printed in *The Two Liturgies, with other Documents*, etc. (Parker Society), p. 187.

[2] Gee and Hardy, *Documents*, etc. p. 371.

the time of the communion, and at all other times in his
ministration, shall use neither Alb, Vestment, nor Cope;
but being an archbishop or bishop, he shall have or wear
a rochet: and being a priest or deacon, he shall have and
wear a surplice only." Instead of "standing humbly afore
the midst of the altar," he was to stand "at the north
side of the table"; and the communion table was ordered to
be removed from the east end of the church and to be
placed in the chancel. Ordinary instead of unleavened
bread was ordered to be used. In the older book the
prayer, *Have mercy on us, O Lord,* had been used as an
invocation of God present in the sacramental elements;
in the new it became an ordinary prayer to keep the commandments. The *Ten Commandments* were introduced for
the first time. Some rubrics—that enjoining the minister
to add a little water to the wine—were omitted. Similar
changes were made in the services for baptism and confirmation, and in the directions for ordination. One rubric was
retained which the more advanced Reformers wished done
away with. Communicants were required to receive the
elements kneeling. But the difficulties were removed by
a later rubric:

"Yet lest the same kneeling might be thought or taken
otherwise, we do declare that it is not meant thereby, that
any adoration is done, or ought to be done, either unto the
sacramental bread or wine there bodily received, or to any
real or essential presence there being of Christ's natural
flesh and blood."

This addition is said, on somewhat uncertain evidence,
to have been suggested by John Knox.

The most important change, however, was that made
in the words to be addressed to the communicant in the
act of partaking. In the *First Prayer-Book* the words
were:

"When the priest delivereth the sacrament of the Body
of Christ, he shall say to every one these words:
'*The Body of our Lord Jesus Christ, which was given for
thee, preserve thy body and soul unto everlasting life.*'

And the minister delivering the sacrament of the Blood, and giving every one once to drink and no more, shall say:
'The Blood of our Lord Jesus Christ, which was shed for thee, preserve thy body and soul unto everlasting life.' "[1]

In the *Second Prayer-Book* the rubric was altered to:

"Then the minister, when he delivereth the bread, shall say:
'Take and eat this in remembrance that Christ died for thee, and feed on Him in thy heart by faith and with thanksgiving.'
And the minister that delivereth the cup shall say:
'Drink this in remembrance that Christ's blood was shed for thee, and be thankful.'"[2]

The difference represented by the change in these words is between what *might* be the doctrine of transubstantiation and a sacramental theory distinctly lower than that of Luther or Calvin, and which *might* be pure Zwinglianism.

This *Second Prayer-Book of King Edward* was enforced by a second *Act of Uniformity*, which for the first time contained penalties against laymen as well as clergymen—against "a great number of people in divers parts of the realm, who did wilfully refuse to come to their parish churches." The penalties themselves show that many of the population refused to be dragged along the path of reformation as fast as the Council wished them to go.[3]

Soon after there followed a new creed or statement of the fundamental doctrines received by the Church of England. This was the *Forty-two Articles*, interesting because they formed the basis of the later Elizabethan *Thirty-nine Articles*. They were thrust on the Church of England in a rather disreputable way. It was expressly stated on the title-page that they had been agreed upon by the Bishops and godly divines at the last Con-

[1] Compare *The Two Liturgies*, etc. (Parker Society) p. 283.
[2] *Ibid.* pp. 92, 279.
[3] Gee and Hardy, *Documents*, etc. p. 269.

vocation in London—a statement which is not correct They were never presented to Convocation, and were issued on the authority of the King alone, and received his signature on June 12th (1553), scarcely a month before he died.

One other document belonging to the reign of Edward VI. must be mentioned—the *Reformatio Legum Ecclesiasti-carum*, drafted by Cranmer. The Archbishop had begun in 1544 to collect passages from the old Canon Law which he thought might serve to regulate the government and discipline of the Church of England. A commission of thirty-two was appointed to assist him, and from these a committee of eight were selected to " rough hew the Canon Law." When the selection was made, a Bill to legalise it was introduced into Parliament, but it failed to pass ; and the *Reformatio Legum* never became authoritative in England. It was as well, for the book enacted death penalties for various heresies, which would have made it a cruel weapon in the hands of a persecuting government.

During the reign of Edward VI. the beginnings of that Puritanism which was so prominent in the time of Elizabeth first manifested themselves. Its two principal spokesmen were the Bishops Hooper and Ridley. Hooper was an ardent follower of Zwingli, and was esteemed to be the leader of the party ; and Ridley's sentiments were not greatly different. Hooper came into contact with the Government when he was appointed to the See of Gloucester. He then objected to the oath required from Bishops at their consecration, and to the episcopal robes, which he called " Aaronic " vestments. The details of the contest are described by a Zwinglian sympathiser, Macronius, in a letter to Bullinger at Zurich [1] (Aug. 28th, 1550):

" The King, as you know, has appointed him (Hooper) to the bishopric of Gloucester, which, however, he refused to accept unless he cd. be altogether relieved from all

[1] *Original Letters relative to the English Reformation* (Parker Society, Cambridge, 1847), ii. 566.

appearance of popish superstition. Here then a question immediately arises as to the form of oath which the Bishops have ordered to be taken in the name of God, the saints, and the Gospels; which impious oath Hooper positively refused to take. So, when he appeared before the King in the presence of the Council, Hooper convinced the King by many arguments that the oath should be taken in the name of God alone, who knoweth the heart. This took place on the 20th of July. It was so agreeable to the godly King, that with his own pen he erased the clause of the oath which sanctioned swearing by any creatures; Nothing could be more godly than this act, or more worthy of a Christian king. When this was done there remained the form of episcopal consecration, wh., as lately prescribed by the Bishops in Parliament, differs but little from the popish one. Hooper therefore obtained a letter from the King to the Archbishop of Canterbury (Cranmer), that he might be consecrated without superstition. But he gained nothing by this, as he was referred from the Archbishop of Canterbury to the Bishop of London (Ridley), who refused to use any other form of consecration than that which had been subscribed by Parliament. Thus the Bishops mutually endeavour that none of their glory shall depart. A few days after, on the 30th of July, Hooper obtained leave from the King and the Council to be consecrated by the Bishop of London without any superstition. He replied that he would shortly send an answer either to the Council or to Hooper. While, therefore, Hooper was expecting the Bishop's answer, the latter went to court and alienated the minds of the Council from Hooper, making light of the use of the vestments and the like in the church, and calling them mere matters of indifference. Many were so convinced by him that they would hardly listen to Hooper's defence when he came into court shortly afterwards. He therefore requested them, that if they would not hear him speak, they would at least think it proper to hear and read his written apology. His request was granted: wherefore he delivered to the King's councillors, in writing, his opinion respecting the discontinuance of the use of vestments and the like puerilities. And if the Bishop cannot satisfy the King with other reasons, Hooper will gain the victory. We are daily expecting the termination of this controversy, which is only conducted between individuals, either by conference or by letter, for fear of any tumult being excited among the ignorant. You see in what a state of affairs the Church would be if they were left to the Bishops, even to the best of them."

In the end, Hooper allowed himself to be persuaded, and was consecrated in the usual way.

The advanced Reformers in England were probably incited to demand more freedom than the law permitted by the sight of the liberty enjoyed by men who were not Englishmen. French and German Protestants had come to England for refuge, and had been welcomed. The King had permitted them to use the Augustines' church in London, that they might "have the pure ministry of the Word and Sacraments according to the apostolic form," and they enjoyed their privileges.

"We are altogether exempted by letters patent from the King and Council from the jurisdiction of the Bishops. To each church (I mean the German and the French) are assigned two ministers of the Word (among whom is my unworthy self), over whom has been appointed superintendent the most illustrious John à Lasco; by whose aid alone, under God, we foreigners have arrived at our present state of pure religion. Some of the Bishops, and especially the Bishop of London, with certain others, are opposed to our design; but I hope their opposition will be ineffectual. The Archbishop of Canterbury, the special patron of foreigners, has been the chief support and promoter of our church, to the great astonishment of some." [1]

These foreigners, outside episcopal control and not subject to the *Acts of Uniformity*, enjoyed liberties of worship which were not granted to Englishmen. They were driven out of the country when Mary succeeded; but under Elizabeth and James they had the same privileges and were naturally envied by the English Puritans, coerced by Bishops and harried by Acts of Uniformity.

While the Reformation was being pushed forward in

---

[1] *Original Letters*, etc. (Parker Society) ii. 568, *Macronius to Bullinger* (August 28th, 1550).

England at a speed too great for the majority of the people, the King was showing the feebleness of his constitution. He died on the 6th of July 1553, and the collapse of the Reformation after his death showed the uncertainty of the foundation on which it had been built.

CHAPTER III.

THE REACTION UNDER MARY.[1]

ONE of the last acts of the dying King had been to make a will regulating the succession. It was doubtless suggested to him by the Duke of Northumberland, but, once adopted, the lad clung to it with Tudor tenacity. It set aside as illegitimate both his sisters. It also set aside the young Queen of Scotland, who, failing Mary and Elizabeth, was the legitimate heir, being the granddaughter of Margaret, the eldest sister of Henry VIII., and selected the Lady Jane Grey, the representative (eldest child of eldest child) of Mary, the younger sister of Henry VIII. Both the King and his Council seem to have thought that the nation would not submit to a Roman Catholic on the throne; and Charles V. appears to have agreed with them. He considered the chances of Mary's succession small.

The people of England, however, rallied to Mary, as the nearest in blood to their old monarch, who, notwithstanding his autocratic rule, had never lost touch with his people.

[1] SOURCES in addition to those on pp. 351: *Epistolæ Reginaldi Poli, S. R. E. Cardinalis,* 5 vols. (Brixen, 1744–57); *Chronicle of Queen Jane and of two years of Queen Mary, and especially of the Rebellion of Sir Thomas Wyat, written by a Resident in the Tower of London* (Camden Society, London, 1850); Garnett, *The Accession of Queen Mary; being the contemporary narrative of Antonio Guaras,* etc. (London, 1892).

LATER BOOKS: Stone, *History of Mary I., Queen of England* (London, 1901); Ranke, *Die römischen Päpste* (Berlin, 1854); Hume, *Visit of Philip II. (1554)* (*English Historical Review,* 1892); Leadam, *Narrative of the Pursuit of the English Refugees in Germany under Queen Mary (Transactions* of Royal Historical Society, 1896); Wiesener, *The Youth of Queen Elizabeth, 1533–58* (English translation, London, 1879); Zimmermann, *Kardinal Pole sein Leben und seine Schriften* (Regensburg, 1893).

384

The new Queen naturally turned to her cousin Charles V. for guidance. He had upheld her mother's cause and her own; and in the dark days which were past, his Ambassador Chapuys had been her indefatigable friend.

It was Mary's consuming desire to bring back the English Church and nation to obedience to Rome—to undo the work of her father, and especially of her brother. The Emperor recommended caution; he advised the Queen to be patient; to watch and accommodate her policy to the manifestations of the feelings of her people; to punish the leaders who had striven to keep her from the throne, but to treat all their followers with clemency. Above all, she was to mark carefully the attitude of her sister Elizabeth, and to reorganise the finances of the country.

Mary had released Gardiner from the Tower, and made him her trusted Minister. His advice in all matters, save that of her marriage, coincided with the Emperor's. It was thought that small difficulty would be found in restoring the Roman Catholic religion, but that difficulties might arise about the papal supremacy, and especially about the reception of a papal Legate. Much depended on the Pope. If His Holiness did not demand the restoration of the ecclesiastical property alienated during the last two reigns, and now distributed among over forty thousand proprietors, all might go well.

Signs were not wanting, however, that if the people were almost unanimous in accepting Mary as their Queen, they were not united upon religion. When Dr. Gilbert Bourne, preaching at St. Paul's Cross (Aug. 13th, 1553) praised Bishop Bonner, he was interrupted by shouts; a dagger was thrown at him; he was hustled out of the pulpit, and his life was threatened. The tumult was only appeased when Bradford, a known Protestant, appealed to the crowd. The Lord Mayor of London was authorised to declare to the people that it was not the Queen's intention to constrain men's consciences, and that she meant to trust solely to persuasion to bring them to the true faith.

24**

Five days later (August 18th), Mary issued her first *Proclamation about Religion*, in which she advised her subjects " to live together in quiet sort and Christian charity, leaving those new-found devilish terms of papist or heretic and such like." She declared that she meant to support that religion which she had always professed; but she promised " that she would not compel any of her subjects thereunto, *unto such time as further order, by common assent, may be taken therein* "—a somewhat significant threat. The proclamation prohibited unlicensed preaching and printing " any book, matter, ballad, rhyme, interlude, process, or treatise, or to play any interlude, except they have Her Grace's special licence in writing for the same," which makes it plain that from the outset Mary did not intend that any Protestant literature should be read by her subjects if she could help it.[1]

Mary was crowned with great ceremony on October 1st, and her first Parliament met four days later (Oct. 5th to Dec. 6th, 1553). It reversed a decision of a former Parliament, and declared that Henry VIII.'s marriage with Catharine of Aragon had been valid, and that Mary was the legitimate heir to the throne; and it wiped out all the religious legislation under Edward VI. The Council had wished the anti-papal laws of Henry VIII. to be rescinded ; but Parliament, especially the House of Commons, was not prepared for anything so sweeping. The Church of England was legally restored to what it had been at the death of Henry, and Mary was left in the anomalous position of being the supreme head of the Church in England while she herself devoutly believed in the supremacy of the Bishop of Rome. The title and the powers it gave were useful to restore by royal proclamation the mediæval ritual and worship, and Mass was reintroduced in this way in December.[2]

Meanwhile the marriage of the Queen was being

---

[1] Gee and Hardy, *Documents*, etc. p. 373.

[2] The Act of Parliament is printed in Gee and Hardy, *Documents*, etc. p. 377.

discussed. Mary herself decided the matter by solemnly promising the Spanish Ambassador (Oct. 19th) that she would wed Philip of Spain; the marriage treaty was signed on January 12th, 1554; the formal betrothal took place in March, and the wedding was celebrated on July 25th.[1] It was very unpopular from the first. The boys of London pelted with snowballs the servants of the Spanish embassy sent to ratify the wedding treaty (Jan. 1st, 1554); the envoys themselves were very coldly received by the populace; and Mary had to issue a proclamation commanding that all courtesy should be used to the Prince of Spain and his train coming to England to marry the Queen.[2]

In September (1553) the pronouncedly Protestant Bishops who had remained in England to face the storm, Cranmer, Ridley, Coverdale, Latimer, were ejected and imprisoned; the Protestant refugees from France and Germany and many of the eminent Protestant leaders had sought safety on the Continent; the deprived Romanist Bishops, Gardiner, Heath, Bonner, Day, had been reinstated; and the venerable Bishop Tunstall, who had acted as Wolsey's agent at the famous Diet of Worms, had been placed in the See of Durham.

Various risings, one or two of minor importance and a more formidable one under Sir Thomas Wyatt, had been crushed. Lady Jane Grey, Lord Guilford Dudley (February 12th, 1554), Sir Thomas Wyatt, Lord Suffolk, and others were executed. Charles v. strongly recommended the execution of the Princess Elizabeth, but his advice was not followed.

England was still an excommunicated land, and both Queen and King Consort were anxious to receive the papal peace. As soon as he had been informed by Mary of her succession to the throne, the Pope, Julius II., had selected

---

[1] Philip's marriages had this peculiarity about them, that his second wife (Mary) had been betrothed to his father, and his third wife had been betrothed to his son.

[2] Strype, Memorials of Queen Mary's Reign, III. ii. 215.

Cardinal Pole to be his Legate to England (early in August 1553). No one could have been more suitable. He was related to the royal house of England, a grandson of the Duke of Clarence, who was the brother of Edward IV. He had so thoroughly disapproved of the anti-papal policy of Henry VIII. that he had been compelled to live in exile. He was a Cardinal, and had almost become Pope. No one could have been more acceptable to Mary. He had protested against her mother's divorce, and had suffered for it; and he was as anxious as she to see England restored to the papal obedience. But many difficulties had to be cleared away before Pole could land in England as the Pope's Legate. The English people did not love Legates, and their susceptibilities had to be soothed. If the Pope made the restoration of the Church lands a condition of the restoration of England to the papal obedience, and if Mary insisted on securing that obedience, there would be a rebellion, and she would lose her crown. No one knew all these difficulties better than the Emperor, and he exerted himself to overcome them. The Curia was persuaded that, as it was within the Canon Law to alienate ecclesiastical property for the redemption of prisoners, the Church might give up her claims to the English abbey lands in order to win back the whole kingdom. Pole himself had doubts about this. He believed that he might be allowed to reason with the lay appropriators and persuade them to make restoration, and his enthusiasm on the subject caused many misgivings in the minds of both Charles and Philip Nor could the Cardinal land in England until his attainder as an English nobleman had been reversed by Parliament. He had been appointed Legate to England once before (February 7th, 1536), in order to compass Henry VIII.'s return to the papal obedience; he had written against the Royal Supremacy. Neither Lords nor Commons were very anxious to receive him.

At last, more than thirteen months after his appointment, the way was open for his coming to England. He landed at Dover (Nov. 20th, 1554), went on to Gravesend, and there found waiting him an Act of Parliament reversing his attainder. It had been introduced into the Lords, passed in the Upper House in two days, was read three times in the Commons in one day, and received the Royal Assent immediately thereafter (Nov. 27th, 1554). Tunstall, the Bishop of Durham, brought him letters patent, empowering him to exercise his office of Legate in England. He embarked in a royal barge with his silver cross in the prow, sailed up the Thames on a favouring tide, landed at Whitehall, and was welcomed by Mary and Philip. On the following day the two Houses of Parliament were invited to the Palace to meet him, and he explained his commission. The day after, the question was put in both Houses of Parliament whether the nation should return to the papal obedience, and was answered affirmatively. Whereupon Lords and Commons joined in a supplication to the Queen " that they might receive absolution, and be received into the body of the Holy Catholic Church, under the Pope, the Supreme Head thereof." The Supplication was presented on the 30th, and in its terms the Queen besought the Legate to absolve the realm for its disobedience and schism. Then, while the whole assembly knelt, King and Queen on their knees with the others, the Legate pronounced the absolution, and received the kingdom " again into the unity of our Mother the Holy Church."

It now remained to Parliament to pass the laws which the change required. In one comprehensive statute all the anti-papal legislation of the reigns of Henry VIII. and of Edward VI. was rescinded, and England was, so far as laws could make it,[1] what it had been in the reign of Henry VII. Two days later (Dec. 2nd, 1554), on the first Sunday in Advent, Philip and Mary, with the Legate, attended divine service in St. Paul's, and after Mass listened to an eloquent sermon from Bishop Gardiner, in the course of which he publicly abjured the teaching

[1] Gee and Hardy, *Documents*, etc. p. 335.

of his book *De vera obedientia.*[1] Convocation received a special absolution from the Legate. To show how thoroughly England had reconciled itself to Mother Church, Parliament proceeded to revive the old Acts against heresy which had been originally passed for the suppression of Lollardy, among them the notorious *De hæretico comburendo*, and England had again the privilege of burning Evangelical Christians secured to it by Act of Parliament.[2]

In March 1554 the Queen had issued a series of *Injunctions* to all Bishops, instructing them on a variety of matters, all tending to bring the Church into the condition in which it had been before the innovations of the late reign. The Bishops were to put into execution all canons and ecclesiastical laws which were not expressly contrary to the statutes of the realm. They were not to inscribe on any of their ecclesiastical documents the phrase *regia auctoritate fulcitus*; they were to see that no heretic was admitted to any ecclesiastical office; they were to remove all married priests, and to insist that every person vowed to celibacy was to be separated from his wife if he had married; they were to observe all the holy days and ceremonies which were in use in the later days of the reign of King Henry VIII.; all schoolmasters suspected of heresy were to be removed from their office. These *Injunctions* kept carefully within the lines of the Act which had rescinded the ecclesiastical legislation of the reign of Edward VI.[3] The Bishop of London, Bonner, had previously issued a list of searching questions to be put to the clergy of his diocese, which concerned the

---

[1] In the days of Henry VIII., Bishop Gardiner had published a book under this title, in which the papal jurisdiction in England was strongly repudiated. Someone, probably Bale, when Gardiner was aiding the Queen to restore that supremacy, had translated the book into English, and had printed at the bottom of the title-page, "A double-minded man is inconstant in all his ways."

[2] Gee and Hardy, *Documents*, etc. p. 384. The Act *de hæretico comburendo* will be found on p. 133.

[3] *Ibid.* p. 380.

laity as well as the clergy, and which went a good deal
further.   He asked whether there were any married
clergymen, or clergymen who had not separated themselves
from their wives or concubines ?   Whether any of the
clergy maintained doctrines contrary to the Catholic
faith ?   Whether any of the clergy had been irregularly
or schismatically ordained ?   Whether any of them had
said Mass or administered the sacraments in the English
language after the Queen's proclamation ?   Whether they
kept all the holy days and fasting days prescribed by the
Church ?   Whether any of the clergy went about in other
than full clerical dress ?   Whether any persons in the
parish spoke in favour of clerical marriage ?   These and
many other minute questions were put, with the evident
intention of restoring the mediæval ceremonies and
customs in every detail.[1]   His clergy assured the Bishop
that it was impossible to make all the changes he
demanded at once, and Bonner was obliged to give them
till the month of November to get their parishes in order.
This London visitation evidently provoked a great deal
of discontent.   In April (1554) " a dead cat was hung on
the gallows in the Cheap, habited in garments like those
of a priest.   It had a shaven crown, and held in its fore-
paws a round piece of paper to represent a wafer. . . . A
reward of twenty marks was offered for the discovery
of the author of the outrage, but it was quite ineffectual." [2]
Other graver incidents showed the smouldering discontent.

   The revival in Parliament of the old anti-heresy laws
may be taken as the time clearly foreshadowed in the
Queen's first proclamation on religious affairs when persuasion was to cease and force take its place.   The
platitudes of many modern historians about Mary's
humane and merciful disposition, about Gardiner's aversion
to shedding blood, about " the good Bishop " Bonner's

---

[1] Bonner's Articles of Inquiry are printed in Strype's *Historical
Memorials, Ecclesiastical and Civil*, etc. III. ii. p. 217.
   [2] Gairdner's *The English Church in the Sixteenth Century*, etc. (London,
1902) p. 339.

benevolent attempt to persuade his victims to recant, may be dismissed from our minds. The fact remains, that the persecutions which began in 1555 were clearly indicated in 1553, and went on with increasing severity until the Queen's death put an end to them.

The visitations had done their work, and the most eminent of the Reformed bishops and divines had been caught and secured in various prisons. " The Tower, the Fleet, the Marshalsea, the King's Bench, Newgate, and the two Counters were full of them."[1] Their treatment differed. "The prisoners in the King's Bench had tolerably fair usage, and favour sometimes shown them. There was a pleasant garden belonging thereunto, where they had liberty sometimes to walk." They had also the liberty of meeting for worship, as had the prisoners in the Marshalsea. Their sympathisers who had escaped the search kept them supplied with food, as did the early Christians their suffering brethren in the first centuries. But in some of the other prisons the confessors were not only confined in loathsome cells, but suffered terribly from lack of food. At the end of Strype's catalogue of the two hundred and eighty-eight persons who were burnt during the reign of Mary, he significantly adds, " besides those that dyed of famyne in sondry prisons."[2] Some of the imprisoned were able to draw up (May 8th, 1554) and send out for circulation a confession of their faith, meant to show that they were suffering simply for holding and proclaiming what they believed to be scriptural truth. They declared that they believed all the canonical books of Scripture to be God's very Word, and that it was to be the judge in all controversies of faith; that the Catholic Church was the Church which believed and followed the doctrines taught in Scripture; that they accepted the Apostles' Creed and the decisions of the first four Œcumenical Councils and of the Council of Toledo, as well as the teachings of Athanasius, Irenæus,

[1] Strype, *Memorials, Ecclesiastical and Civil*, etc. III. i. 221, 223.
[2] *Ibid.* III. ii. 556.

Tertullian, and Damasus ; that they believed that justification came through the mercy of God, and that it was received by none but by faith only, and that faith was not an opinion, but a persuasion wrought by the Holy Ghost; they declared that the external service of God ought to be according to God's Word, and conducted in a language which the people could understand; they confessed that God only by Jesus Christ is to be prayed to, and therefore disapproved of the invocation of the saints ; they disowned Purgatory and Masses for the dead ; they held that Baptism and the Lord's Supper were the Sacraments instituted by Christ, were to be administered according to the institution of Christ, and disallowed the mutilation of the sacrament, the theory of transubstantiation, and the adoration of the bread.[1] This was signed by Ferrar, Hooper, Coverdale (Bishops), by Rogers (the first martyr), by Bradford, Philpot, Crome, Saunders, and others. John Bradford, the single-minded, gentle scholar, was probably the author of the Confession.

Cardinal Pole, in his capacity as papal Legate, issued a commission (Jan. 28th, 1555) to Bishop Gardiner and several others to try the prisoners detained for heresy. Then followed (Feb. 4th, 1555) the burning of John Rogers, to whom Tyndale had entrusted his translation of the Scriptures, and who was the real compiler of the Bible known as Matthews'. The scenes at his execution might have warned the authorities that persecution was not going to be persuasive. Crowds cheered him as he passed to his death, " as if he were going to his wedding," the French Ambassador reported. His fate excited a strong feeling of sympathy among almost all classes in society, which was ominous. Even Simon Renard, the trusted envoy of Charles v., took the liberty of warning Philip that less extreme measures ought to be used. But the worst of a persecuting policy is that when it has once begun it is almost impossible to give it up without confession of defeat. Bishop Hooper was sent to

[1] Strype, *Memorials, Ecclesiastical and Civil*, etc. III. i. 222, III. ii. 224.

Gloucester to suffer in his cathedral town, Saunders to
Coventry, and Dr. Taylor was burnt on Aldham Common
in Suffolk. Several other martyrs suffered the same fate
of burning a few days afterwards.

Robert Ferrar, the Reformed Bishop of St. David's, was
sent to Carmarthen to be burnt in the chief town of his
diocese (March 30th, 1555). Perhaps it was his death
that gave rise to the verses in Welsh, exhorting the men
of the Principality to rise in defence of their religion
against the English who were bent on its destruction, and
calling them to extirpate image worship and the use of
the crucifix.[1]

Bishops Ridley and Latimer and Archbishop Cranmer
had been kept in confinement at Oxford since April 1554;
and they were now to be proceeded against. The two
Bishops were brought before the Court acting on a commission from Cardinal Pole, the Legate. They were condemned on Oct. 1st, 1555, and on the 16th they were
burnt at Oxford in the present Broad Street before Balliol
College. Cranmer witnessed their death from the top of
the tower in which he was confined.

In the Archbishop's case it was deemed necessary, in
order to fulfil the requirements of Canon Law, that he
should be tried by the Pope himself. He was accordingly
informed that his sovereigns had "denounced" him to the
Pope, and that His Holiness had commissioned the Cardinal
Du Puy, Prefect of the Inquisition, to act on his behalf,
and that Du Puy had delegated the duty to James Brooks,
who had succeeded Hooper as Bishop of Gloucester, to the
Dean of St. Paul's, and to the Archdeacon of Canterbury.
The trial took place in St. Mary's Church. The accusers,
Philip and Mary, were represented by Drs. Martyn and
Story. They, in the name of their sovereigns, presented
a lengthy indictment, in which the chief charges were
adultery, perjury, and heresy. The first meant that
although a priest he had been married, and had even

---

[1] *Calendar of State Papers, Domestic Series, of the Reign of Elizabeth,*
1601-3; with Addenda, 1547-65 (London, 1870), p. 483.

married a second time after he had been made an Archbishop; the second, that he had sworn obedience to the Pope and broken his oath; and the third, that he had denied the doctrine of transubstantiation.[1]

Cranmer refused to acknowledge the jurisdiction of his judges, but answered the charges brought against him to his accusers because they represented his sovereigns. He denied that the Pope had any ecclesiastical power within England; but submitted to the kingly supremacy. As Brooks had no authority from the Pope to do more than hear the case, no judgment was pronounced; it was only intimated that the proceedings would be reported to Rome. Cranmer was conducted back to his prison. There he addressed first one, then a second letter to the Queen.[2] In dignified and perfectly respectful language he expressed the degradation of the kingdom exhibited in the act of the sovereigns appealing to an "outward judge, or to an authority coming from any person out of this realm" to judge between them and one of their own subjects. Cranmer early in his career had come to the unalterable opinion that the papal supremacy was responsible for the abuses and disorders in the mediæval Church, and that reformation was impossible so long as it was maintained. In common with every thoughtful man of his generation, he repudiated the whole structure of papal claims built up by the Roman Curia during the fifteenth century, and held that it was in every way incompatible with the loyalty which every subject owed to his sovereign and to the laws of his country. He took his stand on this conviction.

"Ignorance, I know," he said, "may excuse other men; but he that knoweth how prejudicial and injurious the power and authority which the Pope challengeth everywhere is to the Crown, laws, and customs of this realm, and yet will allow the same, I cannot see in anywise how he can

---

[1] An account of Cranmer's trial is given in Foxe, *Acts and Monuments* (London, 1851), iii. 656 *ff.* The process is in Cranmer's *Miscellaneous Writings and Letters* (Parker Society), pp. 541 *ff.*

[2] Cranmer's *Works*, ii. 447 *ff.*

keep his due allegiance, fidelity, and truth to the Crown and state of this realm."

In his second letter he struck a bolder note, and declared that the oath which Mary had sworn to maintain the laws, liberties, and customs of the realm was inconsistent with the other oath she had taken to obey the Pope, to defend his person, and to maintain his authority, honour, laws, and privileges. The accusation of perjury did not touch him at all. The sovereigns—Bishop Brooks, appointed to try him—every constituted authority in the realm—when confronted by it, had to choose between the oath of allegiance to country or to Papacy; he had chosen allegiance to his fatherland; others who acted differently betrayed it. That was his position. The words he addressed to Queen Mary—" I fear me that there be contradictions in your oath "—was his justification.

At Rome, Cranmer was found guilty of contumacy, and the command went forth that he was to be deposed, degraded, and punished as a heretic. In the meantime he was burnt in effigy at Rome. When he heard his sentence, he composed an Appeal to a General Council, following, he said, the example of Luther.[1] The degradation was committed to Bonner and Thirlby, and was executed by the former with his usual brutality. This done, he was handed over to the secular authorities for execution. Then began a carefully prepared course of refined mental torture, which resulted in the " Recantations of Thomas Cranmer."[2] A series of recantations was presented to him, which he was ordered to sign by his sovereign; and, strange as it may seem now, it was the sovereign's command that made it almost impossible for Cranmer to refuse to sign the papers which, one after another, were given him. He was a man who felt the necessity of an ultimate authority. He had deliberately put aside that of the Pope, and as deliberately placed that of the sovereign in its place; and now the ultimate authority, which his con-

[1] *Works*, ii. pp. 445–56.
[2] *Miscellaneous Writings*, etc. (Parker Society) p. 563.

science approved, commanded him to sign. The first four were not real recantations; Cranmer could sign them with a good conscience; they consisted of generalities, the effect of which depended on the meaning of the terms used, and everyone knew the meanings which he had attached to the words all throughout his public life. But the fifth and the sixth soiled his conscience and occasioned his remorse. It was not enough for Mary, Pole, and Bonner that they were able to destroy by fire the bodies of English Reformers, they hoped by working partly on the conscience and partly on the weakness of the leader of the English Reformation, to show the worthlessness of the whole movement. In the end, the aged martyr redeemed his momentary weakness by a last act of heroism. He knew that his recantations had been published, and that any further declaration made would probably be suppressed by his unscrupulous antagonists. He resolved by a single action to defeat their calculations and stamp his sincerity on the memories of his countrymen. His dying speech was silenced, as he might well have expected; but he had made up his mind to something which could not be stifled.[1]

"At the moment he was taken to the stake he drew from his bosom the identical paper (the recantation), throwing it, in the presence of the multitude, with his own hands into the flames, asking pardon of God and of the people for having consented to such an act, which he excused by saying that he did it for the public benefit, as, had his life, which he sought to save, been spared him, he might at some time have still been of use to them, praying them all to persist in the doctrines believed by him, and absolutely denying the Sacrament and the supremacy of the Church. And, finally, stretching forth his arm and right hand, he said : 'This which hath sinned, having signed the writing, must be the first to suffer punishment'; and thus did he place it in the fire and burned it himself."[2]

[1] Pollard, *Cranmer*, pp. 367–81.
[2] *Calendar of State Papers and MSS. existing in the Archives and Collections of Venice, 1555–56*, p. 386.

If the martyrdoms of Ridley and Latimer lighted the torch, Cranmer's spread the conflagration which in the end burnt up the Romanist reaction and made England a Protestant nation. The very weakness of the aged Primate became a background to make the clearer his final heroism. The "common man" sympathised with him all the more. He had never been a very strong man in the usual sense of the words. The qualities which go to form the exquisite liturgist demand an amount of religious sensibility and sympathy which seldom belongs to the leader of a minority with the present against it and the future before it. His peculiar kind of courage, which enabled him to face Henry VIII. in his most truculent moods, was liker a woman's than a man's, and was especially called forth by sympathy with others in suffering. None of Henry's Ministers pleaded harder or more persistently for the Princess Mary, the woman who burnt him, than did Cranmer; and he alone of all his fellows dared to beseech the monarch for Cromwell in his fall.[1]

The death of Cranmer was followed by a long succession of martyrdoms. Cardinal Pole became the Archbishop of Canterbury, and in Philip's absence the principal adviser of the Queen. He did not manage, if he tried, to stop the burnings. Sometimes he rescued prisoners from the vindictive Bonner; at others he seems to have hounded on the persecutors. Mary's conscience, never satisfied at the confiscation of property, compelled her to restore the lands still in possession of the Crown, and to give up the "first fruits" of English benefices—the only result being to awaken the fears of thousands of proprietors, and set them against the papal claims. She attempted to restore the monastic institutions, with but scanty results; to revive pilgrimages to shrines, which were very forced affairs, and had to be kept alive by fining the parents of children who did not join them. The elevation of Pope Paul IV. (Cardinal Caraffa) to the See of Rome increased her difficulties. The new Pontiff, a Neapolitan, hated her

[1] Pollard, *Cranmer*, p. 328.

Spanish husband, and personally disliked Cardinal Pole, her chief adviser. Her last years were full of troubles.

Mary died in 1558 (Nov. 17th). "The unhappiest of queens, and wives, and women," she had been born amidst the rejoicings of a nation, her mother a princess of the haughtiest house in Europe. In her girlhood she had been the bride-elect of the Emperor—a lovely, winning young creature, all men say. In her seventeenth year, at the age when girls are most sensitive, the crushing stroke which blasted her whole life fell upon her. Her father, the Parliament, and the Church of her country called her illegitimate; and thus branded, she was sent into solitude to brood over her disgrace. When almost all England hailed her Queen in her thirty-seventh year, she was already an old woman, with sallow face, harsh voice, her dark bright eyes alone telling how beautiful she had once been. But the nation seemed to love her who had been so long yearning for affection; she married the man of her choice; and she felt herself the instrument selected by Heaven to restore an excommunicated nation to the peace of God. Her husband, whom she idolised, tired of living with her after a few years. The child she passionately longed for and pathetically believed to be coming never came.[1] The Church and the Pope she had sacrificed so much for, disregarded her entreaties, and seemed careless of her troubles. The people who had welcomed her, and whom she really loved, called her "Bloody" Mary,—a name which was, after all, so well deserved that it will

---

[1] There are few more pathetic documents among the State Papers than those thus catalogued :

"King Philip and Queen Mary to Cardinal Pole, notifying that the Queen has been delivered of a Prince."

"Passport signed by the King and Queen for Sir Henry Sydney to go over to the King of the Romans and the King of Bohemia, to announce the Queen's happy delivery of a Prince."

There are several such notifications all ready for the birth which never took place. *Calendar of State Papers, Domestic Series, of the Reigns of Edward VI., Mary, Elizabeth, 1547-80* (London, 1856), p. 67.

always remain. Each disappointment she took as a warning from Heaven that atonement had not yet been paid for England's crimes, and the fires of persecution were kept burning to appease the God of sixteenth century Romanism.

CHAPTER IV.

THE SETTLEMENT UNDER ELIZABETH.[1]

MARY TUDOR's health had long been frail, and when it was known for certain that she would leave no direct heir (*i.e.* from about June 1558), the people of England were silently coming to the conclusion that Elizabeth must be Queen, or civil war would result. It seemed also to be assumed that she would be a Protestant, and that her chief adviser would

[1] SOURCES : *Calendar of State Papers, Elizabeth, Foreign* (London, 1863, etc.) ; *Calendar of State Papers relating to Scotland and Mary Queen of Scots* (Edinburgh, 1898, etc.) ; *Calendar of State Papers, Hatfield MSS.* (London, 1883) ; *Calendar of State Papers, Venetian, 1558–80* (London, 1890) ; *Calendar of State Papers, Spanish, 1558–67* (London, 1892) ; Weiss, *Papiers d'état du Cardinal Granvelle*, vols. iv.-vi. (Paris, 1843–46) ; *Bullarium Romanum*, for two Bulls—the one of 1559 (i. 840) and the one deposing Elizabeth (ii. 324) ; *A Collection of Original Letters from the Bishops to the Privy Council, 1564* (vol. ix. of the *Camden Miscellany*, London, 1893) ; *Calvin's Letters* (vols. xxxviii.-xlviii. of the *Corpus Reformatorum*) ; *Zurich Letters* (two series) (Parker Society, Cambridge, 1853) ; *Liturgies and occasional Forms of Prayer set forth in the Reign of Queen Elizabeth* (Parker Society, Cambridge, 1847) ; Dysen, *Queene Elizabeth's Proclamation* (1618).

LATER BOOKS : Creighton, *Queen Elizabeth* (London, 1896) ; Hume, *The Courtships of Queen Elizabeth* (London, 1896) ; and *The great Lord Burghley* (London, 1898) ; Philippson, *La contre-révolution religieuse* (Brussels, 1884) ; Ruble, *Le traité de Cateau-Cambrésis* (Paris, 1889) ; Gee, *The Elizabethan Clergy* (Oxford, 1898) ; and *The Elizabethan Prayer-Book and Ornaments* (London, 1902) ; Tomlinson, *The Prayer-Book, Articles and Homilies* (London, 1897) ; Hardwick, *History of the Articles of Religion* (Cambridge, 1859) ; Lorimer, *John Knox and the Church of England* (London, 1875) ; Neal, *History of the Puritans* (London, 1754) ; Parker, *The Ornaments Rubric* (Oxford, 1881) ; Shaw, *Elizabethan Presbyterianism* (*English Historical Review*, iii. 655) ; *Cambridge Modern History*, ii. 550 *ff.* ; Frere, *History of the English Church in the Reigns of Elizabeth and James, 1558–1625* (London, 1904).

25[**]

be William Cecil, who had been trained in statecraft as
secretary to England's greatest statesman, the Lord Protector Somerset. So it fell out.

Many things contributed to create such expectations.
The young intellectual life of England was slowly becoming
Protestant. Both the Spanish ambassadors noticed this
with alarm, and reported it to their master.[1] This was
especially the case among the young ladies of the upper
classes, who were becoming students learned in Latin,
Greek, and Italian, and at the same time devout Protestants,
with a distinct leaning to what afterwards became Puritanism. Elizabeth herself, at her most impressionable age had
been the pupil of Bishop Hooper, who was accustomed to
praise her intelligence. "In religious matters she has
been saturated ever since she was born in a bitter hatred
to our faith," said the Bishop of Aquila.[2] The common
people had been showing their hatred of Romanism, and
"images and religious persons were treated disrespectfully." It was observed that Elizabeth "was very much
wedded to the people and thinks as they do," and that
"her attitude was much more gracious to the common
people than to others."[3] The burnings of the Protestant
martyrs, and especially the execution of Cranmer, had
stirred the indignation of the populace of London and the
south counties against Romanism, and the feelings were
spreading throughout the country. All classes of the
people hated the entire subjugation of English interests to
those of Spain during the late reign, just as the people of
Scotland at the same time were growing weary of French
domination under Mary of Lorraine, and Elizabeth shared
the feeling of her people.[4]

Yet there was so much in the political condition of
the times to make both Elizabeth and Cecil pause before

---

[1] *Calendar of Letters and State Papers relating to English Affairs, preserved principally in the Archives of Simancas* (London, 1892), i. p. 7.

[2] *Ibid.* p. 89. In the same letter the Bishop blames the instructions of
the "Italian heretic friars," *i.e.* Peter Martyr Vermigli and Ochino ; cf.
p. 81.

[3] *Ibid.* pp. 1, 4, 5, etc.   [4] *Ibid.* pp. 3, 77.

committing themselves to the Reformation, that it is necessary to believe that religious conviction had a great influence in determining their action. England was not the powerful nation in 1558–60 which it became after twenty years under the rule of the great Queen. The agrarian troubles which had disturbed the three reigns of Henry VIII., Edward, and Mary had not died out. The coinage was still as debased as it had been in the closing years of Henry VIII. Trade was stagnant, and the country was suffering from a two years' visitation of the plague. The war with France, into which England had been dragged by Spain, had not merely drained the country of men and money, but was bringing nothing save loss of territory and damage to prestige. Nor was there much to be hoped from foreign aid. The Romanist reaction was in full swing throughout Europe, and the fortunes of the continental Protestants were at their lowest ebb. It was part of the treaty of Cateau-Cambrésis (April 1559) that France and Spain should unite to crush the Protestantism of the whole of Europe, and the secret treaty between Philip II. and Catherine de' Medici in 1565 [1] showed that such a design was thought possible of accomplishment during the earlier years of Elizabeth. It was never wholly abandoned until the defeat of the Armada in 1588. Cecil's maxim, that the Reformation could not be crushed until England had been conquered, had for its corollary that the conquest of England must be the prime object of the Romanist sovereigns who were bent on bringing Europe back to the obedience of Rome. The determination to take the Protestant side added to the insecurity of Elizabeth's position in the earlier years of her reign. She was, in the opinion of the Pope and probably of all the European Powers, Romanist and Protestant, illegitimate; and heresy combined with bastardy was a terrible weapon in the hands of Henry II. of France, who meant to support the claims of his daughter-in-law, the young Queen of

---

[1] *Calendar of Letters and State Papers relating to English Affairs*, etc., Introduction, p. lv.

Scots,—undoubtedly the lawful heir in the eyes of all who believed that Henry VIII. had been lawfully married to Catharine of Aragon. The Spanish Ambassador, Count de Feria, tried to frighten Elizabeth by reminding her how, in consequence of a papal excommunication, Navarre had been seized by the King of Spain.[1] His statement to his master, that at her accession two-thirds of the English people were Romanists,[2] may be questioned (he made many miscalculations), but it is certain that England was anything but a united Protestant nation. Still, who knew what trouble Philip might have in the Netherlands, and the Lords of the Congregation might be encouraged enough to check French designs on England through Scotland.[3] At the worst, Philip of Spain would not like to see England wholly in the grip of France. The Queen and Cecil made up their minds to take the risk, and England was to be Protestant and defy the Pope, from "whom nothing was to be feared but evil will, cursing, and practising."

Paul IV., it was said, was prepared to receive the news of Elizabeth's succession favourably, perhaps under conditions to guarantee her legitimacy; but partly to his astonishment, and certainly to his wrath, he was not even officially informed of her accession, and the young Queen's ambassador at Rome was told that she had no need for him there.

The changes at home, however, were made with all due caution. In Elizabeth's first proclamation an " et cetera " veiled any claim to be the Head of the Church,[4] and her earliest meddling with ecclesiastical matters was to forbid all contentious preaching.[5] The statutory religion (Romanist) was to be maintained for the meantime. No

---

[1] *Calendar of Letters and State Papers relating to English Affairs*, etc. p. 62.

[2] *Ibid.* pp. 39, 67 ; cf. 83.

[3] Cf. *Device* in Gee's *Elizabethan Prayer-Book*, p. 197.

[4] Strype, *Annals of the Reformation and Establishment of Religion*, etc. (Oxford, 1824) I. ii. 389.

[5] Gee and Hardy, *Documents*, etc. p. 416.

official proclamation was made foreshadowing coming changes.

Elizabeth, however, did not need to depend on proclamations to indicate to her people the path she meant to tread. She graciously accepted the Bible presented to her on her entry into London, clasped it to her bosom, and pressed it to her lips. Her hand ostentatiously shrank from the kiss of Bonner the persecutor. The great lawyer, Goderick, pointed out ways in which Protestant feeling might find vent in a legal manner:

" In the meantime Her Majesty and all her subjects may by licence of law use the *English Litany* and suffrages used in King Henry's time, and besides Her Majesty in her closet may use the Mass without lifting up the Host according to the ancient canons, and may also have at every Mass some communicants with the ministers to be used in both kinds." [1]

The advice was acted upon, improved upon. " The affairs of religion continue as usual," says the Venetian agent (Dec. 17th, 1558), " but I hear that at Court when the Queen is present a priest officiates, who says certain prayers with the Litanies in English, after the fashion of King Edward." [2] She went to Mass, but asked the Bishop officiating not to elevate the Host for adoration ; and when he refused to comply, she and her ladies swept out of church immediately after the Gospel was read.[3] Parliament was opened in the usual manner with the performance of Mass, but the Queen did not appear until it was over ; and then her procession was preceded by a choir which sang hymns in English. When the Abbot of Westminster met her in ecclesiastical procession with the usual candles sputtering in the hands of his clergy, the

---

[1] Goderick's *Divers Points of Religion contrary to the Church of Rome* is printed by Dr. Gee in the appendix to his *Elizabethan Prayer-Book and Ornaments* (London, 1902), pp. 202 *ff.* ; the sentence quoted is on p. 205 : the document is also in Dixon's *History of the Church of England,* v. 28.

[2] *Venetian State Papers, 1558–80,* 1.

[3] *Calendar of Letters and State Papers relating to English Affairs, preserved chiefly in the Archives of Simancas,* i. 17, 25.

Queen shouted, " Away with these torches, we have light enough." [1]

She was crowned on January 15th, 1559 ; but whether with *all* the customary ceremonies, it is impossible to say ; it is most likely that she did not communicate.[2]   The Bishops swore fealty in the usual way, but were chary of taking any official part in the coronation of one so plainly a heretic.   Later in the day, Dr. Cox, who had been King Edward's tutor, and was one of the returned refugees, preached before the Queen.   As early as Dec. 14th (1558) the Spanish Ambassador could report that the Queen " is every day standing up against religion (Romanism) more openly," and that " all the heretics who had escaped are beginning to flock back again from Germany." [3]

When Convocation met it became manifest that the clergy would not help the Government in the proposed changes.   They declared in favour of transubstantiation and of the sacrifice of the Mass, and against the royal supremacy.   The Reformation, it was seen, must be carried through by the civil power exclusively ; and it was somewhat difficult to forecast what Parliament would consent to do.

What was actually done is still matter of debate, but it seems probable that the Government presented at least three Bills.   The first was withdrawn ; the second was wrecked by the Queen withholding her Royal Assent ; the third resulted in the Act of Supremacy and in the Act of Uniformity.   It is most likely that the first and second Bills, which did not become law, included in *one* proposed Act of legislation the proposals of the Government about the Queen's Supremacy and about Uniformity of Public Worship.[4]   The first was introduced into the House of

[1] *Calendar of State Papers, Domestic Series, of the Reigns of Edward VI., Mary, and Elizabeth* (London, 1856), i. 123.
[2] *Calendar of Letters and State Papers relating to English Affairs, pre-served chiefly in the Archives of Simancas,* i. 25.
[3] *Ibid.* pp. 7, 12.
[4] *English Historical Review* for July 1903, pp. 517 *ff.* ; *Dublin Review* Jan. 1903 ; *The Church Intelligencer,* Sept. 1903, pp. 134 *ff.*

Commons on Feb. 9th (1559), was discussed there Feb. 13th to 16th, and then withdrawn. A "new" Bill "for the supremacy annexed to the Crown" was introduced in the Commons on Feb. 21st, passed the third reading on the 25th, and was sent to the Lords on the 27th.[1]

The majority in the House of Commons was Protestant;[2] but the Marian Bishops had great influence in the House of Lords, and it was there that the Government proposals met with strong opposition. Dr. Jewel describes the situation in a letter to Peter Martyr (March 20th):

"The bishops are a great hindrance to us; for being, as you know, among the nobility and leading men in the Upper House, and having none there on our side to expose their artifices and confute their falsehoods, they reign as sole monarchs in the midst of ignorant and weak men, and easily overreach our little party, either by their numbers or their reputation for learning. The Queen, meanwhile, though she openly favours our cause, yet is wonderfully afraid of allowing any innovations."[3]

The Bill (Bill No. 2—the "new" Bill), which had passed the Commons on the 25th, was read for the first time in the Lords on the 28th, passed the second reading on March 13th, and was referred to a Committee consisting of the Duke of Norfolk, the Bishops of Exeter and Carlisle, and Lords Winchester, Westmoreland, Shrewsbury, Rutland, Sussex, Pembroke, Montagu, Clinton, Morley, Rich, Willoughby, and North. They evidently made such alterations on the Bill as to make that part of it at least which enforced a radical change in public worship useless for the purpose of

---

[1] Cf. Tomlinson, "Elizabethan Prayer-Book: chronological table of its enactment," in *Church Gazette* for Oct. 1906, p. 233.

[2] *Dublin Review*, Jan. 1903, p. 48 *n* : "Ad quem eundem locum (House of Commons) isti convenerunt (ut communis fertur opinio) ad numerum ducentorum virorum, et non decem catholici inter illos sunt reperti."

[3] *Zurich Letters*, i. 10 (Parker Society, Cambridge, 1842); cf. *Calendar of Letters and State Papers relating to English Affairs, preserved principally in the Archives of Simancas, 1558–67*, p. 33 : "To-morrow it (the Bill) goes to the Upper House, where the bishops and some others are ready to die rather than consent to it."

the Government. The clearest account of what the Lords did is contained in a letter of a person who signs himself " Il Schifanoya," which is preserved in the State Archives in Mantua.[1] He says :

" Parliament, which ought to have ended last Saturday, was prolonged till next Wednesday in Passion Week, and according to report they will return a week after Easter (March 26, 1559); which report I believe, because of the three principal articles the first alone passed, viz. to give the supremacy of the Anglican Church to the Queen . . . notwithstanding the opposition of the bishops, and of the chief lords and barons of this kingdom; but the Earls of Arundel and Derby, who are very good Christians, absented themselves from indisposition, feigned, as some think, to avoid consulting about such ruin of this realm.

The Earl of Pembroke, the Earl of Shrewsbury, Viscount Montague and Lord Hastings did not fail in their duty, like true soldiers of Christ, to resist the Commons, whom they compelled to modify *a book passed by the Commons forbidding the Mass to be said or the Communion to be administered (ne se communicassero) except at the table in the manner of Edward VI.*; nor were the Divine offices to be performed in church; priests likewise being allowed to marry, and the Christian religion and the Sacraments being absolutely abolished; adding thereto many extraordinary penalties against delinquents. By a majority of votes they have decided that the aforesaid things shall be expunged from the book, and that the Masses, Sacraments, and the rest of the Divine offices shall be performed as hitherto. . . . The members of the Lower House, seeing that the Lords passed this article of the Queen's supremacy of the Church, but not as the Commons drew it up,—the Lords cancelling the aforesaid clauses and modifying some others,—grew angry, and would consent to nothing, but are in very great controversy." [2]

The Lords, induced by the Marian Bishops, had wrecked the Government's plan for an alteration of religion.

The Queen then intervened. She refused her assent

---

[1] For " Il Schifanoya" and his trustworthiness, cf. *Calendar of State Papers, Venetian, 1558-80*, Preface viii.
[2] *Ibid.* p. 52.

to the Bill, on the dexterous pretext that she had doubts about the title which it proposed to confer upon her— *Supreme Head of the Church.*[1] She knew that Romanists and Calvinists both disliked it, and she adroitly managed to make both parties think that she had yielded to the arguments which each had brought forward. The Spanish Ambassador took all the credit to himself; and Sandys was convinced that Elizabeth had been persuaded by Mr. Lever, who " had put a scruple into the Queen's head that she would not take the title of Supreme Head." [2]

The refusal of Royal Assent enabled the Government to start afresh. They no longer attempted to put everything in one Bill. A new Act of Supremacy,[3] in which the Queen was declared to be " the only supreme governor of this realm . . . as well in all spiritual or ecclesiastical things or causes as temporal," was introduced into the Commons on April 10th, and was read for a third time on the 13th. Brought into the Lords on April 14th, it was read for a second time on the 17th, and finally passed on April 29th. If the obnoxious title was omitted, all the drastic powers claimed by Henry VIII. were given to Elizabeth. The Elizabethan Act revived no less than nine of the Acts of Henry VIII.,[4] and among them the statute

---

[1] Canon Dixon (*History of the Church of England*, v. 67) declares that the phrase "Supreme Head" was not in the Bill. He has overlooked the fact that Heath in his speech against it quotes the actual words used in the proposed Act: "I promised to move your honours to consider what this supremacy is which we go about by virtue of this Act to give to the Queen's Highness, and wherein it doth consist, as whether in spiritual government or in temporal. If in spiritual, like as the words of the Act do import, scilicet : *Supreme Head of the Church of England immediate and next under God*, then it would be considered whether this House hathe authority to grant them, and Her Highness to receive the same" (Strype, *Annals*, I. i. 405).

[2] *Calendar of Letters and State Papers relating to English Affairs, preserved chiefly in the Archives of Simancas, 1558–80*, pp. 37, 44, 50, 55, 66 ; *Parker's Correspondence*, p. 66 ; *Zurich Letters*, i. 33.

[3] The Act is printed in Gee and Hardy, *Documents*, etc. p. 442.

[4] The Acts of Henry VIII. which were revived were :—24 Hen. VIII. c. 12—*The Restraint of Appeals*, passed in 1533 ; 23 Hen. VIII. c. 20—*The conditional Restraint of Annates* ; 25 Hen. VIII. c. 19 - -*The Submission of the*

concerning doctors of civil law,[1] which contained these
sentences: " Most royal majesty is and hath always been,
by the Word of God, Supreme Head on earth of the
Church of England, and hath full power and authority to
correct,' punish, and repress all manner of heresies . . .
and to exercise all other manner of jurisdiction commonly
called ecclesiastical jurisdiction "; and his majesty is " the
only and undoubted Supreme Head of the Church of
England, and also of Ireland, to whom by Holy Scripture
all authority and power is wholly given to hear and
determine all manner of causes ecclesiastical." Thus the
very title Supreme Head of the Church of England was
revived and bestowed on Elizabeth by this Parliament of
1559. It may even be said that the ecclesiastical
jurisdiction bestowed upon Elizabeth was more extensive
than that given to her father, for *schisms* were added to
the list of matters subject to the Queen's correction, and
she was empowered to delegate her authority to commissioners—a provision which enabled her to exercise her
supreme governership in a way to be felt in every corner
of the land.[2] This Act of Supremacy revived an Act of
King Edward VI., enjoining that the communion should
be given in both " kinds," and declared that the revived
Act should take effect from the last day of Parliament.[3]
It contained an interesting proviso that nothing should
be judged to be heresy which was not condemned by
canonical Scripture, or by the first four General Councils
" or any of them." [4]

The same Parliament, after briefer debate (April 18th

Clergy and Restraint of Appeals of 1534 ; 25 Hen. VIII. c. 20—*The Ecclesi-
astical Appointments Act ; The absolute Restraint of Annates, Election of
Bishops, and Letters Missive Act of 1534* ; 25 Hen. VIII. c. 21—*Act forbidding
Papal Dispensations and the Payment of Peter's Pence of 1534* ; 26 Hen.
VIII. c. 14—*Suffragan Bishops' Act of 1534* ; and 28 Hen. VIII. c. 16—*Act
for the Release of such as have obtained pretended Dispensations from the See of
Rome*. These Acts are all, save the last mentioned, printed in Gee and
Hardy, *Documents*, etc. pp. 178–232, 253–56.

[1] *Ibid*. p. 445.   [2] *Ibid*. p. 447.
[3] *Ibid*. p. 446.   [4] *Ibid*. p. 455.

to 28th), passed an Act of Uniformity which took an interesting form.[1] The Act began by declaring that at the death of King Edward VI. there "remained one uniform order of common service and prayer, and of the administration of sacraments, rites, and ceremonies in the Church of England, which was set forth in one Book, entitled *The Book of Common Prayer and Administration of the Sacraments and other Rites and Ceremonies in the Church of England.*" This Book had been authorised by Act of Parliament held in the fifth and sixth years of King Edward VI., and this Act had been repealed by an Act of Parliament in the first year of the reign of Queen Mary "to the great decay of the due honour of God, and discomfort of the professors of the truth of Christ's religion." This Act of Queen Mary was solemnly repealed, and the Act of King Edward VI., with some trifling alterations, was restored. In consequence, "all and singular ministers in any cathedral or parish church" were ordered "to say and use the Matins, Evensong, celebration of the Lord's Supper, and administration of each of the sacraments, and all their common and open prayer, in such order and form as is mentioned in the said Book, so authorised by Parliament in the said fifth and sixth years of the reign of King Edward VI., with one alteration or addition of certain lessons to be used on every Sunday in the year, and the form of the Litany altered and corrected, and two sentences only added in the delivery of the sacrament to the communicants, and none other or otherwise." This meant that while there might be the fullest freedom of thought in the country and a good deal of liberty of expression, there was to be no freedom of public worship. All Englishmen, of whatever creed, were to be compelled by law to join in one common public worship according to the ritual prescribed. The Act of Parliament which compelled them to this had no specific Book of Common Prayer annexed to it and incorporated in it. It simply replaced on the Statute Book the Act of King Edward VI., and with it

[1] The Act is printed in Gee and Hardy, *Documents*, etc. pp. 458 *ff.*

the Second Prayer-Book of King Edward, which with its
rubrics had been "annexed and joined" to that Act [1]—
certain specified alterations in the Book being notified in
the Elizabethan Act.

The history of the Elizabethan Prayer-Book is confessedly obscure. If an important paper called the *Device*,[2]
probably drafted by Cecil, embodied the intentions of the
Government, their procedure may be guessed with some
probability. It enumerates carefully, after the manner of
the great Elizabethan statesman, the dangers involved in
any "alteration of religion," and shows how they can be
met or averted. France and Scotland can be treated
diplomatically. Rome may be left unheeded—it is far
away, and its opposition will not go beyond "evil will and
cursing." The important dangers were at home. They
would come from two sides—from the Romanists backed
by most of the higher clergy ; and from the advanced
Reformers, who would scoff at the alteration which is alone
possible in the condition of the kingdom, and would call it
a "cloaked papistry and a mingle-mangle." Yet both may
be overcome by judicious firmness. The Romanists may
be coerced by penal laws. The danger from the advanced
Reformers may be got over by a carefully drafted Prayer-
Book, *made as far as possible to their liking,* and enforced
by such penalties as would minimise all objections. There
is great hope that such penalties would "touch but few."
"And better it were that they did suffer than Her
Highness or Commonwealth should shake or be in danger."
The *Device* suggested that a small committee of seven
divines—all of them well-known Reformers, and most of
them refugees—should prepare a Book "which, being
approved by Her Majesty," might be laid before Parliament.
It was evidently believed that the preparation of the Book
would take some time, for suggestion is made that food,
drink, wood, and coals should be provided for their sus-

---

[1] Gee and Hardy, *Documents,* etc. p. 371.
[2] The *Device* is printed in Strype, *Annals,* etc. I. ii. 392, and in Gee's
Elizabethan Prayer Book and Ornaments (London, 1902), p. 195.

tenance and comfort. There is no direct evidence to show that the suggested committee met or was even appointed ; but evidence has been brought forward to show that most of the theologians named were in London, and were in a position to meet together and consult during the period when such a Book would naturally be prepared.[1] The whole matter is shrouded in mystery, and secrecy was probably necessary in the circumstances. No one knew exactly what was to take place ; but some change was universally expected. " There is a general expectation that all rites and ceremonies will shortly be reformed," said Richard Hilles, writing to Bullinger in the end of February (1559), " by our faithful citizens and other godly men in the afore-mentioned Parliament, either after the pattern which was lately in use in the time of King Edward the Sixth, or which is set forth by the Protestant Princes of Germany in the afore-mentioned Confession of Augsburg." [2]

The authorities kept their own counsel, and nothing definite was known to outsiders. A Book was presented to the Commons—*The Book of Common Prayer and Ministration of the Sacraments*—on Feb. 16th, at the time when the first draft of the Supremacy Bill was being discussed.[3] It must have been withdrawn along with that Bill. The second attempt at a Supremacy Act was probably accompanied with a Prayer-Book annexed to the Bill ; and this Prayer-Book was vehemently opposed in the Lords, who struck out all the clauses relating to it.[4] What this Book of Common Prayer was, cannot be exactly known. Many competent liturgist scholars are inclined

---

[1] Gee's *Elizabethan Prayer-Book and Ornaments*, pp. 76 *f.*

[2] *Zurich Letters*, ii. 17.

[3] The *Journal of the House of Commons*, i. 54 : " The Bill for the Order of Service and Ministers in the Church " (Feb. 15th) ; *The Book of Common Prayer and Ministration of Sacraments* (Feb. 16th).

[4] *Calendar of State Papers, Venetian, 1558-80*, p. 45 : " a book passed by the Commons " ; cf. above, p. 392 ; cf. also Bishop Scot's speech on the reading of the Bill which was emasculated by the Lords, in Strype's *Annals*, I. ii. 408.

to believe that it was something more drastic than the
Edwardine Prayer-Book of 1552, and that it was proposed
to enforce it by penalties more drastic than those enacted
by the Act of Uniformity which finally passed.   They find
the characteristic features of the Book in the well-known
letter of Guest (Geste) to Cecil.[1]   Such suggestions are
mere conjectures.   The Book may have been the Edwardine
Prayer-Book of 1552.

The Government had made slow progress with their
proposed "alteration of religion," and the Protestant
party were chafing at the delay.   Easter was approaching,
and its nearness made them more impatient.   Canon law
required everyone to communicate on Easter Day, which
in 1559 fell on the 26th of March, and by a long
established custom the laity of England had gone to the
Lord's Table on that one day of the year.   Men were
asking whether it was possible that a whole year was to
elapse before they could partake of the communion in a
Protestant fashion.   The House of Commons was full of
this Protestant sentiment.   The reactionary proceedings
in the House of Lords urged them to some protest.[2]   A
Bill was introduced into the Lower House declaring that
"no person shall be punished for now using the religion
used in King Edward's last year."   It was read twice and
engrossed in one day (March 15th), and was read a third
time and passed on March 18th.[3]   It does not appear to
have been before the Lords; but it was acted on in a
curious way.   A proclamation, dated March 22nd, declares
that the Queen, "with the assent of Lords and Commons,"

[1] Dr. Gee rejects the idea that Guest's letter had anything to do with the
Book passed by the Commons and rejected by the Lords ; cf. his *Elizabethan
Prayer-Book and Ornaments*, pp. 32 ff. ; and for a criticism of Dr. Gee,
Tomlinson, *The Elizabethan Prayer-Book and Ornaments ; a Review*, p. 12.
Guest's letter is printed by Dr. Gee in his *Elizabethan Prayer-Book*, etc.
p. 152, and more accurately by Mr. Tomlinson in his tract, *Why was the
First Prayer-Book of Edward VI. rejected?*

[2] "Il Schifanoya" reports the wrath of the Commons : They "grew
angry, and would consent to nothing, but are in very great controversy"
(*Calendar of State Papers, Venetian, 1558-80*, p. 52) ; cf. p. 392.

[3] *Journal of the House of Commons*, i. 57.

in the "present last session," has revived the Act of King Edward VI. touching the reception of the Communion in both "kinds," and explains that the Act cannot be ready for Easter. It proceeds : " And because the time of Easter is so at hand, and that great numbers, not only of the noblemen and gentry, but also of the common people of this realm, be certainly persuaded in conscience in such sort as they cannot be induced in any wise to communicate or receive the said holy Sacrament but under both kinds, according to the first institution, and to the common use both of the Apostles and of the Primitive Church . . . it is thought necessary to Her Majesty, by the advice of sundry of her nobility and commons lately assembled in Parliament," to declare that the statute of Edward is in force, and all and sundry are commanded to observe the provisions of the statute.[1] What is more, the Queen acted upon her proclamation. The well-informed " Schifanoya," writing on March 28th, says that the Government " during this interval (*i.e.* between March 22nd and March 28th) had ordered and printed a proclamation for every one to take the communion in both " kinds " (*sub utraque specie*). He goes on to say that on Easter Day " Her Majesty appeared in chapel, where Mass was sung in English, *according to the use of her brother, King Edward*, and the communion received in both ' kinds,' kneeling." The chaplain wore nothing " but the mere surplice " (*la semplice cotta*).[2] The news went the round of Europe.

---

[1] Professor Maitland (*English Historical Review*, July 1903, p. 527 *n.*) and Father J. H. Pollen (*Dublin Review*, January 1903) think that this proclamation of the 22nd of March was never issued ; but " Il Schifanoya " can hardly refer to any other.

[2] " On Easter Day, Her Majesty appeared in the chapel, where Mass was sung in English, according to the use of her brother, King Edward, and the communion was received in both 'kinds,' kneeling, *facendoli il sacerdote la credenza del corpo et sangue prima* ; nor did he wear anything but the mere surplice (*la semplice cotta*), having divested himself of the vestments (*li paramenti*) in which he had sung Mass ; and thus Her Majesty was followed by many Lords both of the Council and others. Since that day things have returned to their former state, though unless the Almighty stretch forth His arm a relapse is expected. These accursed preachers, who

Elizabeth had at last declared herself unmistakably on the Protestant side.

Easter had come and gone, and the religious question had not received final settlement. The authorities felt that something must be done to counteract the speeches of the Romanist partisans in the Lords.[1]   So, while Parliament was sitting, a conference was arranged between Roman Catholic and Protestant divines.   It seems to have been welcomed by both parties.   Count Feria, the Spanish Ambassador, declared that he had something to do with it. He was anxious that the disputation should be in Latin, that the arguments should be reduced to writing, and that each disputant should sign his paper.   He was overruled so far as the language was concerned.   The authorities meant that the laity should hear and understand.   The three questions debated were :—Whether a "particular Church can change rites and ceremonies ;   Whether the services of public worship must be conducted in Latin ; Whether the Mass is a propitiatory sacrifice."   The conference was held at Westminster on March 31st, in presence of the Privy Council, the Lords and Commons, and the "multitude."   Great expectations were cherished by both parties in anticipation, and when the Romanist divines withdrew on points of procedure, their cause suffered in the

have come from Germany, do not fail to preach in their own fashion, both in public and in private, in such wise that they persuaded certain rogues to forcibly enter the church of St. Mary-le-Bow, in the middle of Cheapside, and force the shrine of the most Holy Sacrament, breaking the tabernacle, and throwing the most precious consecrated body of Jesus Christ to the ground.   They also destroyed the altar and the images, with the pall (*palio*) and church linen (*tovalie*), breaking everything into a thousand pieces. This happened this very night, which is the third after Easter. . . . Many persons have taken the communion in the usual manner, and things continue as usual in the churches" (*Calendar of State Papers, Venetian, 1558-80*, p. 57).

[1] The speeches of Abbot Feckenham and Bishop Scot, reprinted in Gee's *Elizabethan Prayer-Book*, etc. pp. 228 *ff.*, represent the arguments used in the Lords.   Scot's speech was delivered on the third reading of the Act of Uniformity, quite a month after the Westminster conference, and Feckenham's *may* have been made at the same time ; still they show the arguments of the Romanists.

popular estimation. Two of the Bishops were sent to the Tower "for open contempt and contumacy"; and others seem to have been threatened.[1]

Parliament reassembled after the Easter recess and passed the Act of Supremacy in its third form, and the Act of Uniformity, which re-enacted, as has been said, the revised Prayer-Book—that is, the Second Book of King Edward VI. with the distinctly specified alterations. The most important of these changes were the two sentences added to the words to be used by the officiating minister when giving the communion. The clauses had been in the First Prayer-Book of Edward VI.

While in the Second Prayer-Book of King Edward the officiating minister was commanded to say while giving the Bread:

" *Take and eat this, in remembrance that Christ died for thee, and feed on Him in thy heart by faith with thanksgiving,*"

and while giving the Cup, to say:

" *Drink this in remembrance that Christ's blood was shed for thee, and be thankful ;* "

the words were altered in the Elizabethan book to:

" *The Body of our Lord Jesus Christ, which was given for thee, preserve thy body and soul unto everlasting life. Take and eat this in remembrance that Christ died for thee, and feed on Him in thy heart by faith with thanksgiving ;* "

" *The Blood of our Lord Jesus Christ, which was shed for thee, preserve thy body and soul unto everlasting life. Drink this in remembrance that Christ's Blood was shed for thee, and be thankful.*"

The additions in no way detracted from the Evangelical doctrine of the Sacrament. They rather brought the

---

[1] *Calendar of Letters and State Papers relating to English Affairs, preserved principally in the Archives of Simancas, 1558–67*, pp. 45, 46–48 ; *Zurich Letters*, i. 13 *ff.*; Strype's *Annals*, etc. I. i. 128–40, I. ii. 466 ; *Calendar of State Papers, Venetian, 1558–80*, pp. 64, 65.

26**

underlying thought into greater harmony with the doctrine of the Reformed Churches. But they have had the effect of enabling men who hold different views about the nature of the rite to join in its common use.

When the Act of Uniformity was passed by Parliament, the advanced Reformers, who had chafed at what appeared to them to be a long delay, were contented. They, one and all, believed that the Church of England had been restored to what it had been during the last year of the reign of Edward VI. ; and this was the end for which they had been striving, the goal placed before them by their friend and adviser, Henry Bullinger of Zurich.[1] Their letters are full of jubilation.[2]

Yet there were some things about this Elizabethan

---

[1] "King Edward's reformation satisfieth the godly" : Bullinger to Utenhovius (*Zurich Letters*, 2nd series, p. 17 *n.* ; Strype, *Annals*, I. i. 259).

[2] May 20th, Cox to Weidner : "The sincere religion of Christ is therefore established among us in all parts of the kingdom, just in the same manner as it was formerly promulgated under our Edward of blessed memory " (*Zurich Letters*, i. 28).

May 21st, Parkhurst to Bullinger : " The Book of Common Prayer, set forth in the time of King Edward, is now again in general use throughout England, and will be everywhere, in spite of the struggles and opposition of the pseudo-bishops " (*Zurich Letters*, i. 29).

May 22nd, Jewel to Bullinger : "Religion is again placed on the same footing on which it stood in King Edward's time ; to which event I doubt not but that your own letters and those of your republic have powerfully contributed " (*Zurich Letters*, i. 33).

May 23rd, Grindal to Conrad Hubert : " But now at last, by the blessing of God, during the prorogation of Parliament, there has been published a proclamation to banish the Pope and his jurisdiction altogether, and to restore religion to that form which we had in the time of Edward VI." (*Zurich Letters*, ii. 19).

Dr. Gee seems to beg an important historical question when he says that these letters *must* have been written before the writers knew that the Prayer-Book had been actually altered in more than the three points mentioned in the Act of Uniformity. Grindal, writing again to Hubert on July 14th, when he must have known everything, says : "The state of our Church (to come to that subject) is pretty much the same as when I last wrote to you, except only that what had heretofore been settled by proclamations and laws with respect to the reformation of the churches is now daily being carried into effect." Cf. Gee's *Elizabethan Prayer Book*, etc. p. 104 *n.*, for the actual differences between the Edwardine Book of 1552 and the Elizabethan Book of 1559.

settlement which, *if* interpreted as they have been by some ecclesiastical historians, make it very difficult to understand the contentment of such men as Grindal, Jewel, and Sandys. "Of what was done in the matter of *ornaments*," says Professor Maitland, "by statute, by the rubrics of the Book, and by *Injunctions* that the Queen promptly issued, it would be impossible to speak fairly without lengthy quotation of documents, the import of which became in the nineteenth century a theme of prolonged and inconclusive disputation." [1] All that can be attempted here is to mention the principal documents involved in the later controversy, and to show how they were interpreted in the life and conduct of contemporaries.

The Act of Uniformity had restored, with some trifling differences clearly and definitely stated, Edward VI.'s Prayer-Book of 1552, and therefore its rubrics. [2] It had

[1] *Cambridge Modern History*, ii. 570.

[2] The rubric explaining kneeling at the communion had not the authority of Parliament, but only of the Privy Council, and was not included.

The rubric of 1552 regarding *ornaments*, which had the authority of Parliament and was re-enacted by the Act of Uniformity of 1559, was : "And here is to be noted that the minister at the time of communion, and at all other times in his ministration, shall use *neither alb, vestment, nor cope ; but being archbishop or bishop, he shall have and wear a rochet : and being priest or deacon, he shall have and wear a surplice only.*"

This is the real *ornaments* rubric of the Elizabethan settlement, and appears to be such in the use and wont of the Church of England from 1559 to 1566, save that *copes* were used occasionally.

The proviso in the Act of Uniformity (1559) was : "Such ornaments of the Church and of the ministers thereof shall be retained and be in use as was in this Church of England by authority of Parliament in the *second* year of the reign of King Edward VI., until other order shall be therein taken by the authority of the Queen's Majesty, with the advice of her commissioners appointed and authorised under the Great Seal of England for causes ecclesiastical, or of the metropolitan of this realm."

The ornaments in use in the second year of Edward VI. are stated in the rubrics of the first Prayer-Book of King Edward (1549) :

"Upon the day, and at the time appointed for the ministration of the Holy Communion, the Priest that shall execute the holy ministry shall put upon him the vesture appointed for that ministration, that is to say : a white Albe plain, with a vestment or Cope. And where there be many Priests or Deacons, there so many shall be ready to help the Priest in the ministration as shall be requisite : and shall have upon them likewise the vestures appointed for their ministry, that is to say, Albes with tunicles." At the end there

at the same time contained a proviso saying that the
ornaments sanctioned by the authority of Parliament in
the second year of Edward VI. were " to be retained and
be in use " " until further order shall therein be taken."

Men like Grindal and Jewel took no exception to this
proviso, which they certainly would have done had they
believed that it ordained the actual use in time of public
worship, of the ornaments used in the second year of King
Edward.   The interpretation they gave to the proviso is
seen from a letter from Sandys to Parker (afterwards
Archbishop of Canterbury), written two days after the Act
of Uniformity had passed the Lords.   He says :

"The last book of service has gone through with a
proviso to retain the ornaments which were used in the
first and second year of King Edward, until it please the
Queen to take other order for them.   Our gloss upon the
text is that we shall not be enforced to use them, but that
others in the meantime shall not convey them away, but
that they may remain for the Queen."[1]

Sandys and others understood the proviso to mean
that recalcitrant clergy like the Warden of Manchester,
who carried his consecrated vestments to Ireland, were not
to make off with the ornaments, and that churchwardens
or patrons were not to confiscate them for their private
use.   They were property belonging to the Queen, and to
be retained until Her Majesty's pleasure was known.   The
whole history of the visitations goes to prove that Sandys'
interpretation of the proviso was that of its framers.

When the Prayer-Book was actually printed it was
found to contain some differences from the Edwardine

is another rubric : " Upon Wednesdays and Fridays, the English Litany shall
be said or sung in all places after such form as is appointed by the King's
Majesty's Injunctions ; or as is or shall be otherwise appointed by His Highness.   And though there be none to communicate with the Priest, yet these
days (after the Litany ended) the Priest shall put upon him a plain Albe or
surplice, with a cope, and say all things at the Altar appointed to be said at
the celebration of the Lord's Supper, until after the offertory."

[1] *Parker Correspondence,* p. 65.

Book of 1552 besides those mentioned in the Act as the only ones to be admitted; and early editions have not always the same changes. But the one thing of importance was a rubric which, on what seems to be the only possible interpretation, enjoins the use in public worship of the ornaments (*i.e.* the vestments) in use in the second year of King Edward.[1] How this rubric got into the Prayer-Book it is impossible to say. It certainly was not enacted by the Queen "with assent of Lords and Commons." We have no proof that it was issued by the Privy Council.[2]

[1] The rubric is: "And here it is to be noted that the minister at the time of communion and at all other times in his ministrations, shall use such ornaments in the church as were in use by authority of Parliament in the second year of the reign of King Edward VI., according to the Act of Parliament set in the beginning of this Book."

[2] Dr. Gee (*Elizabethan Ornaments*, etc. p. 131) thinks that there can be no reasonable doubt that the rubric was recorded on the authority of the Privy Council. "The Privy Council had certainly inserted the Black Rubric in 1552, as their published Acts attest, but all the records of the Privy Council from 13th May 1559 until 28th May 1562 have disappeared." The precedent cited is scarcely a parallel case. The Black Rubric was an explanation; the Rubric of 1559 is almost a contradiction in terms of the Act which restores the Prayer-Book of 1552. If I may venture to express an opinion, it seems to me most likely that the rubric was added by the Queen herself, and that she inserted it in order to be able to "hedge." It is too often forgotten that the danger which overshadowed the earlier years of Elizabeth was the issue of a papal Bull proclaiming her a heretic and a bastard, and inviting Henry II. of France to undertake its execution. The Emperor would never permit such a Bull if Elizabeth could show reasonable pretext that she and her kingdom held by the Lutheran type of Protestantism. An excommunication pronounced in such a case would have invalidated his own position, which he owed to the votes of Lutheran Electors. In the middle of the sixteenth century the difference between the different sections of Christianity was always estimated in the *popular* mind by differences in public worship, and especially in the celebration of the Lord's Supper. All over Germany the Protestant was distinguished from the Romanist by the fact that he partook of the communion in both "kinds." Elizabeth had definitely ranged herself on the Protestant side from Easter Day 1559; and a more or less ornate ritual could never explain away the significance of this fact. The great difference between the Lutherans and the Calvinists to the popular mind was that the former retained and the latter discarded most of the old ceremonial. Luther says expressly: "Da lassen wyr die Messgewand, altar, liechter noch bleyben" (Daniel, *Codex Liturgicus Ecclesiæ Lutheranæ*, p. 105); and crosses, vestments, lights, and an altar appear in regular Lutheran fashion

The use and wont of the Church of England during the period of the Elizabethan settlement was as if this rubric had never existed. It is directly contradicted by the thirtieth Injunction issued for the Royal Visitation of 1559.[1] It was not merely contemptuously ignored by the Elizabethan Bishops; they compelled their clergy, if compulsion was needed, to act in defiance of it.

Contemporary sources abundantly testify that in the earlier years of the reign of Queen Elizabeth the English clergy in their ministrations scarcely ever wore any ecclesiastical garment but the surplice; and sometimes not even that. The *Advertisements*[2] of 1566, which almost all contemporary notices speak of as prescribing what had been enjoined in the Injunctions of 1559, were drafted for the purpose of coercing clergymen who were in the habit of refusing to wear even the surplice, and they enjoined the surplice only, and the cope[3] in cathedrals. In the

whenever the Queen wished to place herself and her land under the shield of the Augsburg Peace. This rubric was a remarkably good card to play in the diplomatic game.

[1] *XXXth Injunction of 1559* : "Item, Her Majesty being desirous to have the prelacy and clergy of this realm to be had as well in outward reverence, as otherwise regarded for the worthiness of their ministries, and thinking it necessary to have them known to the people in all places and assemblies, *both in the church* and without, and thereby to receive the honour and estimation due to the special messengers and ministers of Almighty God, wills and commands that all archbishops and bishops, and all other that be called or admitted to preaching or ministry of the sacraments, or that be admitted into any vocation ecclesiastical, or into any society of learning in either of the Universities or elsewhere, shall use and wear such seemly habits, garments, and such square caps as were most commonly and orderly received *in the latter year of the reign of King Edward VI.* ; not meaning thereby to attribute any holiness or special worthiness to the said garments, but as St. Paul writeth : ' *Omnia decenter et secundum ordinem fiant* ' (1 Cor. xiv. cap.)." Cf. Gee's *Elizabethan Prayer Book and Ornaments* (London, 1902) ; Tomlinson, *The Prayer Book, Articles and Homilies* (London, 1897) ; Parker, *The Ornaments Rubric* (Oxford, 1881).

[2] The *Advertisements* are printed in Gee and Hardy, *Documents*, etc. p. 467 ; the *Injunctions*, at p. 417.

[3] *Copes* were used in the cathedrals and sometimes in collegiate churches in the years between 1559 and 1566, when it was desired to add some magnificence to the service ; but it ought to be remembered that the *cope*

Visitation carried out in accordance with the directions in the Injunctions, a clean sweep was made of almost all the *ornaments* which were not merely permitted but ordered in the proviso of the Act of Uniformity and the Rubric of 1559 on the ordinary ritualistic interpretation of these clauses. The visitors proceeded on a uniform plan, and what we hear was done in one place may be inferred as the common practice. The Spanish Ambassador (July or August 1559) wrote to his master: " They are now carrying out the law of Parliament respecting religion with great rigour, and have appointed six visitors. . . . They have just taken the crosses, images, and altars from St. Paul's and all the other London churches." [1] A citizen of London noted in his diary : " The time before Bartholomew tide and after, were all the roods and Maries and Johns, and many other of the church goods, both copes, crosses, censers, altar cloth, rood cloths, books, banners, banner stays, wainscot and much other gear about London, burnt in Smithfield." [2] What took place in London was done in the provinces. At Grantham, " the vestments, copes, albs, tunicles, and all other such baggages were defaced and openly sold by the general consent of the whole corporation, and the money employed in setting up desks in the church, and making of a decent communion table, and the remnant to the poor." [3]

It is true that we find complaints on the part of men like Jewel of ritualistic practices which they do not like ; but these in almost every case refer to worship in the royal chapel. The services there were well known, and both friends and foes of the Reformation seemed to take it for granted that what was the fashion in the royal

was never a sacrificial vestment. It was originally the *cappa* of the earlier Middle Ages—the mediæval greatcoat. Large churches were cold places, the clergy naturally wore their greatcoats when officiating, and the homely garment grew in magnificence. It never had a doctrinal significance like the *chasuble* or *casula*.

[1] *Calendar of State Papers, Spanish, 1558–67*, p. 89.
[2] Machyn's *Diary* (Camden Society, London, 1844), p. 108.
[3] Peacock's *Church Furniture*, p. 87.

chapel would soon extend to the rest of the realm.[1]
Historians have usually attributed the presence of crosses,
vestments, lights on the altar, to the desire of the Queen
to conciliate her Romanist subjects, or to stand well with
the great Roman Catholic Powers of Europe.   It is quite
likely that the Queen had this thought in her mind.
Elizabeth was a thrifty lady, and liked to bring down
many birds with the one stone.   But the one abiding
thought in the mind of the astute Queen was to stand well
with the Lutherans, and to be able, when threatened with
papal excommunication, to take shelter under the ægis of
the Peace of Augsburg.

When the Government had secured the passing of the
Acts of Supremacy and Uniformity, they were in a position
to deal with the recalcitrant clergy.   Eleven of the
English Episcopal Sees had been vacant at the accession of
Elizabeth, among them that of the Primate ; for Cardinal
Pole had died a few hours after Mary.   In the summer
and autumn of 1559 the sixteen Bishops were called upon
to sign the Oath of Supremacy, in which the papal rule
over the Church of England was abjured, and the Queen
declared to be the Supreme Governor of the Church.   All
the Bishops, more or less definitely, refused to take the
oath ; although three were at first doubtful.   They were
deprived, and the English Church was practically without
Bishops.[2]   Some of the deprived Bishops of King Edward's
time survived, and they were restored.   Then came discussion about the manner of appointing new ones.   Some
would have preferred a simple royal nomination, as in
Edward's time ; but in the end it was resolved that the

---

[1] *Calendar of State Papers, Spanish, 1558-67*, p. 105 : "The crucifixes
and vestments that were burnt a month ago publicly are now set up again
in the royal chapel, as they soon will be all over the kingdom, unless,
which God forbid, there is another change next week.   They are doing it
out of sheer fear to pacify the Catholics ; but as forced favours are no sign
of affection, they often do more harm than good."   Cf. *Zurich Letters*, i.
63, etc.

[2] *Calendar of Letters and State Papers relating to English Affairs, preserved principally in the Archives of Simancas*, i. pp. 76, 79.

appointment should be nominally in the hands of the Deans and Chapters according to mediæval rule, with the proviso, however, that the royal permission to elect had first to be given, and that the person named in the "leave to elect" should be chosen. Then the question of consecration gave rise to some difficulties; but these were got over in ways which were deemed to be sufficient. Matthew Parker, after more than one refusal, was nominated and consecrated Archbishop of Canterbury. Lists of clerical persons suitable for promotion were prepared for the Queen,[1] and the other Sees were gradually filled. The Elizabethan episcopate, with the exception of the few Edwardine Bishops, was an entirely new creation. A large number of the Deans and members of the Cathedral Chapters had also refused to sign the Oath of Supremacy; they were deprived, and others who were on the lists were appointed in their place. The inferior clergy proved to be much more amenable, and only about two hundred were in the end deprived. The others all accepted the "alteration of religion"; and the change was brought about quietly and without the riotings which had accompanied the alterations made in the days of Edward, or the wholesale deprivations which had followed upon those made by Queen Mary—when almost one-third of the beneficed clergy of the Church of England had been removed from their benefices. A similar passive acquiescence was seen in the introduction of the new Book of Common Prayer, and in the fulfilment of the various orders for the removal of images, etc. The great altars and crucifixes were taken away, and the pictures covered with whitewash, without any disturbances to speak of.

The comparative ease with which the "alteration of religion" was effected was no doubt largely due to the increased Protestant feeling of the country; but the tact and forbearance of those who were appointed to see the changes carried out counted for something; and perhaps

[1] *Calendar of State Papers, Domestic Series, Edward VI., Mary, Elizabeth*, l. 130.

the acquiescence of the Roman Catholics was due to the fact that they had no great leader, that they did not expect the Elizabethan settlement to last long, and that they waited in expectation that one or other of the two Romanist Powers, France or Spain, would interfere in their behalf. The religious revolution in Scotland in 1560 saved the Elizabethan settlement for the time; and Philip of Spain trifled away his opportunities until a united England overthrew his Armada, which came thirty years too late.

The change was given effect to by a Royal Visitation. England was divided into six districts, and lists of visitors were drawn up which included the Lords Lieutenants of the counties, the chief men of the districts, and some lawyers and clergymen known to be well affected to the Reformation. They had to assist them a set of Injunctions, modelled largely, not entirely, on those of Edward VI., drafted and issued by royal command.[1] The members of the clergy were dealt with very patiently, and explanations, public and private, were given of the Act of Supremacy which made it easier for them to accept it. The Elizabethan Bishops were also evidently warned to deal tenderly with stubborn parish clergymen; they would have been less patient with them if left to themselves. One, Bishop Best, Bishop of Carlisle, is found writing to Cecil about his clergy, that "the priests are wicked impes of Antichrist," for the most part very ignorant and stubborn; another, Pilkington, the Bishop of Durham, in describing the disordered state of his diocese, declared that "like St. Paul, he has to fight with beasts at Ephesus"; and a third, Scory, Bishop of Winchester, wrote that he was much hindered by justices of the peace who were Roman Catholics, and that when certain priests who had refused to take the oath were driven out of Exeter and elsewhere, they were received and feasted in the streets with torchlights.[2]

---

[1] The *Injunctions* are printed in Gee and Hardy, *Documents*, etc. p. 417.
[2] *Calendar of State Papers, Domestic Series, of the Reigns of Edward VI., Mary, and Elizabeth*, i. pp. 180. 183, 187.

Elizabeth's second Parliament was very much more Protestant than the first, and insisted that the Oath of Supremacy must be taken by all the members of the House of Commons, by all lawyers, and by all school-masters. The Convocation of 1563 proved that the clergy desired to go much further in the path of Reformation than the Queen thought desirable.

They clearly wished for some doctrinal standard, and Archbishop Parker had prepared and laid before Convocation a revised edition of the *Forty-two Articles* which had defined the theology of the Church of England in the last year of King Edward VI.[1] The way had been prepared for the issue of some authoritative exposition of the doctrinal position of the Elizabethan Church by the *Declaration of the Principal Articles of Religion*—a series of eleven articles framed by the Bishops and published in 1561 (March), which repudiates strongly the Romanist doctrines of the Papacy, private Masses, and the propitiatory sacrifice in the Holy Supper. The Spanish Ambassador, who had heard of the meetings of the Bishops for this purpose, imagined that they were preparing articles to be presented to the Council of Trent on behalf of the Church of England.[2] The Archbishop's draft was revised by Convocation, and was " diligently read and sifted " by the Queen herself before she gave her consent to the authoritative publication of the Articles.

These *Thirty-nine Articles* expressed the doctrine of the Reformed or Calvinist as distinguished from the Evangelical or Lutheran form of Protestant doctrine, and the distinction lay mainly in the views which the respective Confessions of the two Churches held about the Presence of Christ in the Sacrament of the Holy Supper. By this time (1562) Zwinglianism, as a doctrinal system, not as

---

[1] For the history of these Articles, see Hardwick, *A History of the Articles of Religion; to which is added a Series of Documents from A.D. 1536 to A.D. 1615*, etc. (Cambridge, 1859).

[2] *Calendar of Letters and State Papers relating to English Affairs, preserved principally in the Archives of Simancas*, i. 190.

an ecclesiastical policy, had disappeared;[1] and the three theories of the Presence of Christ in the Sacrament had all to do with the Presence of the Body of Christ and not with a spiritual Presence simply. The Romanist theory, transubstantiation, was based on the mediæval conception of a substance existing apart from all accidents of smell, shape, colour, etc., and declared that the "substance" of the Bread and of the Wine was changed into the "substance" of the Body and Blood of Christ, while the accidents or qualities remained the same—the change being miraculously effected by the priest in consecrating the communion elements. The Lutheran explanation was based upon a mediæval theory also—on that of the ubiquity or natural omnipresence of the "glorified" Body of Christ. The Body of Christ, in virtue of its ubiquity, was present everywhere, in chairs, tables, stones flung through the air (to use Luther's illustrations), and therefore in the Bread and in the Wine as everywhere else. This ordinary presence became an efficacious sacramental Presence owing to the promise of God. Calvin had discarded both mediæval theories, and started by asking what was meant by *substance* and what by *presence*; he answered that the substance of anything is its power (*vis*), and its presence is the immediate application of its power. Thus the substance of the crucified Body of Christ is its power, and the Presence of the crucified Body of Christ is the immediate application of its power; and the guarantee of the application of the power is the promise of God received by the believing communicant. By discarding the Lutheran thought that the substance of the Body of Christ is something extended in space, and accepting the thought that the main thing in substance is power, Calvin was able to think of the substance of the Body of Christ in a way somewhat similar to the mediæval conception of "substance without accidents," and was able to show that the Presence of Christ's Body in the sacrament could be accepted and understood without the priestly

[1] The *Consensus Tigurinus* (1549) dates the disappearance.

miracle, which he and all Protestants rejected. Hence it came to pass that Calvin could teach the Real Presence of Christ's Body in the Sacrament of the Supper without having recourse to the mediæval doctrine of "ubiquity," which was the basis of the Lutheran theory. They both (Calvin and Luther) insisted on the Presence of the Body of Christ; but the one (Luther) needed the theory of "ubiquity" to explain the Presence, while the other (Calvin) did not need it. But as both discarded the priestly miracle while insisting on the Presence of the Body, the two doctrines might be stated in almost the same words, provided all mention of "ubiquity" was omitted. Calvin could and did sign the Augsburg Confession; but he did not read into it what a Lutheran would have done, the theory of "ubiquity"; and a Calvinist statement of the doctrine, provided only "ubiquity" was not denied, might be accepted by a Lutheran as not differing greatly from his own. Bishop Jewel asserts again and again in his correspondence, that the Elizabethan divines did not believe in the theory of "ubiquity," [1] and many of them probably desired to say so in their articles of religion. Hence in the first draft of the Thirty-nine Articles presented to Convocation by Archbishop Parker, Article XXVIII. contained a strong repudiation of the doctrine of "ubiquity," which, if retained, would have made the Articles of the Church of England more anti-Lutheran than even the second Helvetic Confession. The clause was struck out in Convocation, probably because it was thought to be needlessly offensive to the German Protestants.[2] The Queen, however, was not satisfied with

---

[1] The *Zurich Letters, 1558–79, First Series* (Parker Society, Cambridge, 1842), pp. 123, 127, 135, 100, 139. Bishop Jewel, writing to Peter Martyr (p. 100), says : "*As to matters of doctrine, we have pared everything away to the very quick, and do not differ from your doctrine by a nail's breadth*" (Feb. 7th, 1562) ; and Bishop Horn, writing to Bullinger (Dec. 13th, 1563, *i.e. after* the Queen's alterations), says, : "*We have throughout England the same ecclesiastical doctrine as yourselves*" (*ibid.* p. 135).

[2] The deleted clause was : "*Christus in cœlum ascendens, corpori suo immortalitatem dedit, naturam non abstulit, humanæ enim naturæ veritatem*

what her divines had done, and two important interferences with the Articles as they came from Convocation are attributed to her. The first was the addition of the words : *and authoritie in controversies of fayth,* in Article XX., which deals with the authority possessed by the Church. The second was the complete suppression for the time being of Article XXIX., which is entitled, *Of the wicked which do not eate the Body of Christe in the use of the Lordes Supper,* and is expressed in terms which most Lutherans would have been loath to use.

The Queen's action was probably due to political reasons. It was important in international politics for a Protestant Queen not yet securely seated on her throne to shelter herself under the shield which a profession of Lutheranism would give. The German Lutherans had won legal recognition within the Empire at the Diet of Augsburg in 1555 ; the votes of two Lutheran Electors had helped to place the Emperor on his throne ; and the Pope dared not excommunicate Lutheran Princes save at the risk of offending the Emperor and invalidating all his acts. This had been somewhat sternly pointed out to him when he first threatened to excommunicate Elizabeth, and the Queen knew all the difficulties of the papal position. One has only to read an account of a long conversation with her, reported by the Spanish Ambassador to his master (April 29th, 1559), to see what use the " wise Queen with the eyes that could flash "[1] made of the situation. The Ambassador had not obscurely threatened her with a papal Bull declaring her a bastard and a heretic, and had brought home its effects by citing the case of the King of Navarre, whose kingdom was taken

(juxta Scripturas), perpetuo retinet, quam uno et definito loco esse, et non in multa, vel omnia simul loca diffundi oportet. Quum igitur Christus in cœlum sublatus, ibi usque ad finem seculi permansurus, atque inde, non aliunde (ut loquitur Augustinus) venturus sit, ad judicandum vivos et mortos, non debet quisquam fidelium, et carnis eius, et sanguinis, realem et corporealem (ut loquuntur) presentiam in Eucharistia vel credere, vel profiteri."

[1] " Cette reine est extremement sage, et a des yeux terribles." *Calendar of State Papers, Domestic Series, of the Reign of Elizabeth, 1595-97,* p. xxi.

from him by Ferdinand of Spain acting as the Pope's agent, and Elizabeth had played with him in her usual way. She had remarked casually " that she wished the Augsburg Confession to be maintained in her realm, whereat," says the Count de Feria, " I was much surprised, and found fault with it all I could, adducing the arguments I thought might dissuade her from it. She then told me it would not be the Augsburg Confession, but something else like it, and that she differed very little from us, as she believed that *God was in the Sacrament of the Eucharist*, and only dissented from three or four things in the Mass. After this she told me that she did not wish to argue about religious matters." [1] She did not need to argue ; the hint had been enough for the baffled Ambassador.

Article XXIX. was suppressed, and only *Thirty-eight Articles* were acknowledged publicly. The papal Bull of excommunication was delayed until 1570, when its publication could harm no one but Elizabeth's own Romanist subjects, and the dangerous period was tided over safely. When it came at last, the Queen was not anathematised in terms which could apply to Lutherans, but because she personally acknowledged and observed " the impious constitutions and atrocious mysteries of Calvin," and had commanded that they should be observed by her subjects.[2] Then, when the need for politic suppression was past, Article XXIX. was published, and the *Thirty-nine Articles* became the recognised doctrinal standard of the Church of England (1571).

What the Queen's own doctrinal beliefs were no one can tell ; and she herself gave the most contrary descriptions when it suited her policy. The disappearance and reappearance of crosses and candles on the altar of the royal chapel were due as much to the wish to keep in touch with the Lutherans as to any desire to conciliate the Queen's Romanist subjects.

[1] *Calendar of Letters and State Papers relating to English Affairs, preserved principally in the Archives of Simancas*, i. 61, 62.
[2] *Calendar of State Papers, Venetian, 1558-80*, p. 449,

The Convocation of 1563 had other important matters before it. Its proceedings showed that the new Elizabethan clergy contained a large number who were in favour of some drastic changes in the Prayer-Book and in the Act of Uniformity. Many of them had become acquainted with and had come to like the simplicity of the Swiss worship, thoroughly purified from what they called " the dregs of Popery "; and others envied the Scots, " who," wrote Parkhurst to Bullinger (Aug. 23rd, 1559), " have made greater progress in true religion in a few months than we have done in many years." [1]

Such men were dissatisfied with much in the Prayer-Book, or rather in its rubrics, and brought forward proposals for simplifying the worship, which received a large measure of support. It was thought that all organs should be done away with; that the ceremony of " crossing " in baptism should be omitted; that all festival days save the Sundays and the " principal feasts of the Church " should be abolished;—this proposal was lost by a majority of one in the Lower House. Another motion, leaving it to the option of communicants to receive the Holy Supper either standing, sitting, or kneeling, as it pleased them, was lost by a very small majority. Many of the Bishops themselves were in favour of simplifying the rites of the Church; and five Deans and twelve Archdeacons petitioned against the use of the surplice. The movement was so strong that Convocation, if left to itself, would probably have purified the Church in the Puritan sense of the word. But the Queen had all the Tudor liking for a stately ceremonial, and she had political reasons, national and international, to prevent her allowing any drastic changes. She was bent on welding her nation together into one, and she had to capture for her Church the large mass of people who were either neutral or who had leanings to Romanism, or at least to the old mediæval service. The Council of Trent was sitting; Papal excommunication was always threatened, and, as above explained, Lutheran protection

[1] The *Zurich Letters*, etc., First Series, p. **91**.

and sympathy were useful. The ceremonies were retained, the crucifixes and lights on the altars were paraded in the chapel royal to show the Lutheran sympathies of the Queen and of the Church of England. The Reforming Bishops, with many an inward qualm,[1] had to give way ; and gradually, as the Queen had hoped, a strong Conservative instinct gathered round the Prayer-Book and its rubrics. The Convocation of 1563 witnessed the last determined attempt to propose any substantial alteration in the public worship of the English people.

At the same Convocation a good deal of time was spent upon a proposed Book of Discipline, or an authoritative statement of the English canon law. It is probable that its contents are to be found in certain " *Articles for government and order in the Church, exhibited to be permitted by authority ; but not allowed,*" which are printed by Strype [2] from Archbishop Parker's MSS. Such a book would have required parliamentary authority, and the Parliament of 1563 was too much occupied with the vanishing protection of Spain and with the threatening aspect of France and Scotland. The marriage of the Queen of Scots with Darnley had given additional weight to her claims on the English throne; and it was feared that the English Romanists might rise in support of the legitimate heir. Parliament almost in a panic passed severe laws against all recusants, and increased the penalties against all who refused the oath of allegiance or who spoke in support of the authority of the Bishop of Rome. The discipline of the Church was left to be regulated by the old statute of Henry VIII., which declared that as much of the mediæval canon law as was not at variance with the Scriptures and the Acts of the English Parliament was to form the basis of law for the ecclesiastical courts. This gave the Bishop's

---

[1] The *Zurich Letters*, etc., First Series, p. 74 ; cf. 55, 63, 64, 66, 68, 100, 129, 135. Bishop Jewel called clerical dress the "relics of the Amorites" (p. 52), and wished that he could get rid of the surplice (p. 100) ; and "the little silver cross" in the Queen's chapel was to him an ill-omened thing (p. 55); cf. Strype, *Annals*, etc. I. i. 260.

[2] *Annals*, etc. I. ii. 562.

27 **

officials who presided over the ecclesiastical courts a very free hand ; and under their manipulation there was soon very little left of the canon law—less, in fact, than in the ecclesiastical courts of any other Protestant Churches. For these officials were lawyers trained in civil law and imbued with its principles, and predisposed to apply them whenever it was possible to do so.

The formulation of the *Thirty-nine Articles* in the Convocation of 1563 may be taken as marking the time when the " alteration of religion " was completed. The result, arrived at during a period of exceptional storm and strain, has had the qualities of endurance, and the Church of England is at present what the Queen made it. It was the Royal Supremacy which secured for High Church Anglicans the position they have to-day. The chief features of the settlement of religion were :

1. The complete repudiation within the realm and Church of England of the authority of the Bishop of Rome. All the clergy and everyone holding office under the Crown had to swear to this repudiation. If they refused, or were recusants in the language of the day, they lost their offices and benefices ; if they persisted in their refusal, they were liable to forfeit all their personal property ; if they declined to take the oath for a third time, they could be proclaimed traitors, and were liable to the hideous punishments which the age inflicted for that crime. But Elizabeth, with all her sternness, was never cruel, and no religious revolution was effected with less bloodshed.

2. The sovereign was made the supreme Governor of the Church of England ; and that the title differed in name only from that assumed by Henry VIII. was made plain in the following ways :

(a) Convocation was stript of all independent legislative action, and its power to make ecclesiastical laws and regulations was placed under strict royal control.[1]

---

[1] The *Advertisements* of Archbishop Parker, issued and enforced on the authority of the Primate, to which the royal imprimatur was more than once refused, may be looked on as an exception. For these rules, meant

(b) Appeals from all ecclesiastical courts, which were themselves actually, if not nominally, under the presidency of civil lawyers, could be made to royal delegates who might be laymen ; and these delegates were given very full powers, and could inflict civil punishments in a way which had not been permitted to the old mediæval ecclesiastical courts. These powers raised a grave constitutional question in the following reigns. The royal delegates became a Court of High Commission, which may have been modelled on the Consistories of the German Princes, and had somewhat the same powers.

3. One uniform ritual of public worship was prescribed for all Englishmen in the Book of Common Prayer with its rubrics, enforced by the Act of Uniformity. No liberty of worship was permitted. Any clergyman who deviated from this prescribed form of worship was liable to be treated as a criminal, and so also were all those who abetted him. No one could, under penalties, seek to avoid this public worship. Every subject was bound to attend church on Sunday, and to bide the prayers and the preaching, or else forfeit the sum of twelvepence to the poor. Obstinate recusants or nonconformists might be excommunicated, and all excommunicated persons were liable to imprisonment.

4. Although it was said, and was largely true, that there was freedom of opinion, still obstinate heretics were liable to be held guilty of a capital offence. On the other hand, the Bishops had little power to force heretics to stand a trial, and, unless Parliament or Convocation ordered it otherwise, only the wilder sectaries were in any danger.[1]

Protestant England grew stronger year by year. The debased copper and brass coinage was replaced gradually by honest gold and silver.[2] Manufactures were encouraged.

to control the Church in the vestiarian controversy, see Gee and Hardy, *Documents*, etc. p. 467 ; and for the vexed question of their authority, Moore, *History of the Reformation*, p. 266.

[1] Maitland, *Cambridge Modern History*, ii. 569 ff.

[2] *Calendar of State Papers, Domestic Series, of the Reigns of Edward VI., Mary, and Elizabeth, 1547–80*, p. 159.

Merchant adventurers, hiring the Queen's ships, took an increasing share in the world-trade with Elizabeth as a partner.[1] Persecuted Huguenots and Flemings settled in great numbers in the country, and brought with them their thrift and knowledge of mechanical trades to enrich the land of their adoption;[2] and the oppressed Protestants of France and of the Low Countries learnt that there was a land beyond the sea ruled by a "wise young Queen" which might be their city of refuge, and which was ready to aid them, if not openly, at least stealthily. England, formerly unarmed, became supplied "more abundantly than any other country with arms, munitions, and artillery." Sound money, enlarged trade, growing wealth, and an increasing sense of security, were excellent allies to the cause of the Protestant Religion.

So long as Mary of Scotland was in Holyrood and able to command the sympathy, if not the allegiance, of the English Roman Catholics, the throne of Elizabeth was never perfectly secure; but the danger from Scotland was minimised by the jealousy between Catherine de' Medici and her daughter-in-law, and the Scottish Protestant Lords could always be secretly helped. When Philip II. of Spain, in his slow, hesitating way, which made him always miss the turn of the tide, at length resolved to aid Mary to crush her rebels at home and to prosecute her claims on England, his interference had no further consequences than to afford Elizabeth an honourable pretext for giving effectual assistance in the conflict which drove Mary from her throne, and made Scotland completely and permanently Protestant.[3]

---

[1] *Calendar of State Papers, Domestic Series*, etc. p. 247.

[2] *Ibid.* p. 177; *Calendar of Letters and State Papers relating to English Affairs, preserved principally in the Archives of Simancas*, i. 77, 118, 119.

[3] The story of Francis Yaxley, Mary's agent, of his dealings with Philip II., of Philip's subsidy to Scotland of 20,000 crowns, of its loss by shipwreck, and how the money was claimed as treasure-trove by the Duke of Northumberland, Roman Catholic and a pledged supporter of Mary as he was, may be traced in the *Calendar of Letters and State Papers relating to English Affairs, preserved principally in the Archives of Simancas*, pp. lix, 499, 506, 516, 523, 546, 557; and how the Pope also gave aid in money, p. 559.

BOOK V.

ANABAPTISM AND SOCINIANISM

CHAPTER I.

REVIVAL OF MEDIÆVAL ANTI-ECCLESIASTICAL MOVEMENTS.

The revolt of Luther was the occasion for the appearance—the outbreak, it might be called—of a large amount of irregular independent thinking upon religion and theology which had expressed itself sporadically during the whole course of the Middle Ages. The great difference between the thinkers and their intellectual ancestors who were at war with the mediæval Church life and doctrine, did not consist in the expression of anything essentially new, but in the fact that the Renaissance had introduced a profound contempt for the intellectual structure of ecclesiastical dogma, and that the whole of the sixteenth century was instinct with the feeling of individuality and the pride of personal existence. The old thoughts were less careful to accommodate themselves to the recognised modes of theological statement, they took bolder forms of expression, presented sharper outlines, and appeared in more definite statements.

Part of this thinking scarcely belongs to ecclesiastical history at all. It never became the intellectual basis of an institution; it neither stirred nor moulded the lives of masses of men. The leaders of thought remained solitary thinkers, surrounded by a loose fringe of followers. But

as there is always something immortal in the forcible expression of human thought, their opinions have not died
altogether, but have affected powerfully all the various
branches of the Christian Church at different periods and
in divers ways.   The old conceptions, somewhat disguised,
perhaps, but still the same, reappear in most systems of
speculative theology.   It therefore demands a brief notice.

The greater portion of this intellectual effervescence,
however, did not share the same fate.   Menno Simons,
aided, no doubt, by the winnowing fan of persecution, was
able to introduce order into the wild fermenting elements
of Anabaptism, and to form the Baptist Church which has
had such an honourable history in Europe and America.
Fausto Sozzini did the same for the heterogeneous mass of
anti-Trinitarian thinking, and out of the confusion brought
the orderly unity of an institutional life.

This great mass of crude independent thought may be
roughly classified as Mystic, or perhaps Pantheist Mystic,
Anabaptist, and anti-Trinitarian ; but the division, so far
as the earlier thinkers go, is very artificial.   The groups
continually overlap ; many of the leaders of thought might
be placed in two or in all three of these divisions.   What
characterised them all was that they had little sense of
historical continuity, cared nothing for it, and so broke
with the past completely ; that they despaired of seeing
any good in the historical Church, and believed that it
must be ended, as it was impossible to mend it ; and that
they all possessed a strong sense of individuality, believing
the human soul to be imprisoned when it accepted the confinement of a common creed, institution, or form of service
unless of the very simplest kind.

Pantheistic Mysticism was no new thing in Christianity.
As early as the sixth century at least, schools of thought
may be found which interpreted such doctrines as the
Trinity and the Person of Christ in ways which led to
what must be called Pantheism ; and if such modes of dis-
solving Christian doctrines had not a continuous succession
within the Christian Church, they were always appearing.

They were generally accompanied with a theory of aj
"inner light" which claimed either to supersede the Scrip
tures as the Rule of Faith, or at least to interpret them. The
Scriptures were the husk which might be thrown away
when its kernel, discovered by the "inner light," was once
revealed. The Schwenkfelds, Weigels, Giordano Brunos of
the sixteenth century, who used what they called the
"inner light" in somewhat the same way as the Council oi
Trent employed dogmatic tradition, had a long line ot
ancestry in the mediæval Church, and their appearance at
the time of the Reformation was only the recrudescence
of certain phases of mediæval thought. But, as has been
said, such thinkers were never able, nor perhaps did they
wish, to form their followers into a Church ; and they belong much more to the history of philosophy than to an
ecclesiastical narrative. They had no conception whatever
of religion in the Reformation sense of the word. Their
idea of faith was purely intellectual—something to be fed
on metaphysics more or less refined.

By far the most numerous of those sixteenth century
representatives of mediæval nonconformists were classed
by contemporaries under the common name of Anabaptists
or Katabaptists, because, from 1526 onwards, they all, or
most of them, insisted on *re*-baptism as the sign of belonging to the brotherhood of believers. They were scattered
over the greater part of Europe, from Sweden in the north
to Venice in the south, from England in the west to
Poland in the east. The Netherlands, Germany,—southern,
north-western, and the Rhineland,—Switzerland, the Tyrol,
Moravia, and Livonia were scenes of bloody persecution
endured with heroic constancy. Their leaders flit across
the pages of history, courageous, much-enduring men, to
whom the world was nothing, whose eyes were fixed on
the eternal throne of God, and who lived in the calm consciousness that in a few hours they might be fastened to
the stake or called upon to endure more dreadful and
more prolonged tortures,—men of every varying type of
character, from the gentle and pious young Humanist Hans

Denck to Jan Matthys the forerunner of the stern Cami-
sard and Covenanter. No statement of doctrine can
include the beliefs held in all their innumerable groups.
Some maintained the distinctive doctrines of the mediæval
Church (the special conceptions of a priestly hierarchy, and
of the Sacraments being always excluded); others were
Lutherans, Calvinists, or Zwinglians; some were Unitarians,
and denied the usual doctrine of the Person of Christ; [1] a
few must be classed among the Pantheists. All held some
doctrine of an " inner light "; but while some sat very loose
to the letter of Scripture, others insisted on the most
literal reading and application of Biblical phraseology.
They all united in maintaining that true Christians ought
to live separate from the world (*i.e.* from those who were
not rebaptized), in communities whose lives were to be
modelled on the accounts given in the New Testament of
the primitive Christians, and that the true Church had
nothing whatever to do with the State.

Curiously enough, the leaders in the third group, the
anti-Trinitarians, were almost all Italians.

The most outstanding man among them, distinguished
alike by his learning, his pure moral life, a distinct vein of
piety, and the calm courage with which he faced every
danger to secure the propagation of his opinions, was the
Spaniard Miguel Servede (Servetus), [2] who was burnt at

---

[1] For example, the *Nikolsburger Articles* say : "Cristus sei in der erb-
sunden entphangen ; Cristus sei nit Got sunder ein prophet, dem das
gesprech oder wort Gottes bevollen worden " (Cornelius, *Geschichte des Münsterischen Aufruhrs*, ii. 279, 280).

[2] Servede was born in 1511, in the small town of Tudela, which then
belonged to Aragon. He came from an ancient family of jurists, and was
at first destined to the profession of law. His family came originally
from the township of Villanova, which probably accounts for the fact that
Servede sometimes assumed that name. He was in correspondence with
Oecolampadius (Heusgen) in 1530 ; and from the former's letters to and
about Servede, it is evident that the young Spaniard was then fully persuaded about his anti-Trinitarian opinions. No publisher in Basel would
print his book, and he travelled to Strassburg. When his first theological
book became known, its sale was generally interdicted by the secular authorities. His great book, which contains his whole theological thinking, was
published in 1553 without name of place or author. Its full title is:

Geneva in 1553. He was very much a man by himself. His whole line of thought separated him from the rest of the anti-Trinitarian group associated with the names of the Sozzini. He reached his position through a mystical Pantheism—a course of thought which one might have expected from a Spaniard. He made few or no disciples, and did not exert any permanent influence.

The other anti-Trinitarians of the first rank were all cultured Italians, whom the spirit of the Renaissance prompted to criticise and reconstruct theology as they found it. They were all men who had been driven to reject the Roman Church because of its corruptions and immoralities, and who had no conception of any other universal Christian society. Men of pure lives, pious after their own fashion, they never had any idea of what lay at the root of the Reformation thought of what real religion was. It never dawned upon them that the sum of Christianity is the God of Grace, manifest in Christ, accessible to every believing soul, and unwavering trust on man's part. Their interest in religion was almost exclusively intellectual. The Reformers had defined the Church as the fellowship of believers, and they had said that the marks of that fellowship were the preaching of

Christianismi Restitutio, Totius ecclesiæ apostolicæ ad sua limina vocatio, in integrum restituta cognitione Dei, fidei Christi, justificationis nostræ, regenerationis baptisimi et cœnæ domini manducationis, Restituto denique nobis regno cælesti, Babylonis impiæ captivitate soluta, et Antichristo cum suis penitus destructo. He entered into correspondence with Calvin, offered to come to Geneva to explain his position ; but the Reformer plainly indicated that he had no time to bestow upon him. The account of his trial, condemnation, and burning at Geneva is to be found in the *Corpus Reformatorum,* xxxvi. 720 *ff.* The sentence is found on p. 825 : " Icy est este parle du proces de Michiel Servet prisonnier et veu le sommairre dycelluy, le raport de ceux esquelz lon a consulte et considere les grands erreurs et blaffemes—est este arreste Il soit condampne a estre mene en Champel et la estre brusle tout vyfz et soit exequente a demain et ses livres brusles." This trial and execution is the one black blot on the character of Calvin. He was by no means omnipotent in Geneva at the time ; but he thoroughly approved of what was done, and had expressed the opinion that if Servede came to Geneva, he would not leave it alive . " Nam si venerit modo valeat mea auctoritas, virum exire nunquam patiar" (*Corpus Ref.* xi. 283).

the Word and the right use of the sacraments—the means through which God manifests Himself to men, and men. manifest their faith in God. These men never apprehended this; the only idea which they seemed able to have of the Church was a school of definite and correct opinions. Compelled to flee from their native land, they naturally took refuge in Switzerland or in the Grisons. It is almost pathetic to see how they utterly failed to understand the men among whom they found themselves. Reformation to them was a criticism and reconstruction of theology; they were simply carrying the criticism a little further than their new neighbours. They never perceived the real gulf fixed between them and the adherents of the Reformation.

They were all highly educated and cultivated men—individual units from all parts of Italy. Camillo Renato, who proclaimed himself an Anabaptist, was a Sicilian. Gentili came from Calabria; Gribaldo from Padua; Bernardino Occhino, who in his later days joined the band, and the two Sozzini from Siena. Alciato was a Piedmontese. Blandrata (Biandrata), the most energetic member of the group save Fausto Sozzini, belonged to a noble family in Saluzzo which had long been noted for the protection it had afforded to poor people persecuted by the Church. They were physicians or lawyers; one, Gentili, was a schoolmaster.

The strong sense of individuality, which seems the birthright of every Italian, fostered by their life within their small city republics, had been accentuated by the Renaissance. The historical past of Italy, and its political and social condition in the sixteenth century, made it impossible for the impulse towards reform to take any other shape than that of individual action. The strength and the impetus which comes from the thought of fellow-man, fellow-believer, and which was so apparent in the Reformation movements beyond the Alps and in the Jesuit reaction, was entirely lacking among these Reformers in Italy. In that land the Empire had never

regained its power lost under the great Popes, Gregory
VII. and Innocent III. The Romish Church presented
itself to all Italians as the only possible form under
which a wide-spreading Christian *Society* could be
organised. If men rejected it, personal Christian life alone
remained. The Church dominated the masses unprepared
by any such conception of ecclesiastical reform as influenced the people in Germany and Switzerland. Only
men who had received some literary education were
susceptible to the influences making for Reformation.
They were always prevented by the unbroken power of
the agencies of the Church from organising themselves
publicly into congregations, and could only meet to exchange confidences privately and on rare occasions.[1] We
hear of several such assemblies, which invariably took the
form of conferences, in which the members discussed and
communicated to each other the criticisms of the mediæval
theology which solitary meditation had suggested to them.
They were much more like debating societies than the
beginnings of a Church. Thus we hear of one at
Vincenza,[2] in 1546, where about forty friends met,
among whom was Lelio Sozzini, where they debated such
doctrines as the Satisfaction of Christ, the Trinity, etc.,
and expressed doubts about their truth. It was inevitable
that such men could not hope to create a popular movement towards Reformation in their native land, and also
that they should be compelled to seek safety beyond the
bounds of Italy. They fled, one by one, across the Alps.
In the Grisons and in Reformed Switzerland they found
little communities of their countrymen who had sought

[1] Ritschl, *A critical History of the Christian Doctrine of Justification and
Reconciliation* (Eng. trans., Edin. 1872), p. 295.

[2] "Circa annum 1546 instituerat (Lælius Socinus) cum sociis suis
iisdem Italis, quorum numerus quadragenarium excedebat, in Veneta ditione
(apud Vincentiam) collegia colloquiaque de religione, in quibus potissimum
dogmata vulgaria de Trinitate ac Christi Satisfactione hisque similia in
dubium revocabant" (*Bibl. Antit.* p. 19—I have taken the quotation from
Fock, *Der Socinianismus nach seiner Stellang in der Gesammtentwicklung
des christlichen Geistes,* etc., Kiel, 1847, i. 132).

shelter there, and their presence was always followed by dissensions and by difficulties with the native Protestants.

Their whole habits of life and thought were not of the kind calculated to produce a lasting Christian fellowship. Their theological opinions, which were not the outcome of a new and living Christian experience, but had been the result of an intellectual criticism of the mediæval theology, had little stability, and did not tend to produce unity. The execution of Servede and the jealousy which all the Reformed cantons of Switzerland manifested towards opinions in any way similar to those of the learned Spaniard, made life in Switzerland as unsafe as it had been in Italy. They migrated to Poland and Transylvania, attracted by the freedom of thought existing in both lands.

Poland, besides, had special attractions for refugees from Italy. The two countries had long been in intimate relationship. Italian architects had designed the stately buildings in Crakau and other Polish cities, and the commercial intercourse between the two countries was great. The independence and the privileges of the Polish nobles secured them from ecclesiastical interference, and both Calvinism and Lutheranism had found many adherents among the aristocracy. They, like the Roman patricians of the early centuries, gave the security of their halls to their co-religionists, and the heads of the Romanist Church chafed at their impotence to prevent the spread of opinions and usages which they deemed heretical. In Transylvania the absence of a strong central government permitted the same freedom to the expression of every variety of religious opinion.

The views held by the group of anti-Trinitarians were by no means the same. They reproduced in Poland the same medley of views we find existing in the end of the third century. Some were Sabellians, others Adoptianists, a few were Arians. Perhaps most of them believed in the miraculous birth of our Lord, and held as a consequence that He ought to be adored; but a strong minority, under the leadership of Francis Davidis, repudiated the miraculous birth, and refused to worship Christ (*non-adorantes*). For a time they seem to have lived in a certain amount of accord with the members of the Reformed communities. A crisis came at the Polish Diet of 1564, and the anti-Trinitarians were recognised then to be a separate religious community, or *ecclesia minor*. This was the field in which Fausto Sozzini exercised his commanding intellect, his genius for organisation, and his eminently strong will. He created out of these jarring elements the Socinian Church.

The Anabaptist and the Socinian movements require, however, a more detailed description.

CHAPTER II.

ANABAPTISM.[1]

THE old monotonous mode of describing Anabaptism has almost entirely disappeared with the modern careful examination of sources. It is no longer possible to sum up the

[1] SOURCES : *Magna Bibliotheca Veterum Patrum* (Coloniæ Agrippinæ, 1618), xiii. 299–307 ; Sebastian Franck, *Chronica, Zeitbuch und Geschichtbibel* (Augsburg, 1565), pt. iii. ; Hans Denck, *Von der waren Lieb*, etc. (1527—republished by the *Menonitische Verlagsbuchhandlung*, Elkhart, Indiana, U.S.A.) ; Bouterwek, *Zur Literatur und Geschichte der Wiedertäufer* (Bonn, 1864—gives extracts from the rarer Anabaptist writings such as the works of Hübmaier) ; *Ausbund etlicher schöner christlicher geseng*, etc. (1583) ; Liliencron, "Zur Liederdichtung der Wiedertäufer" (in the *Abhandlungen der könig. Bair. Akad. der Wissenschaften Philosophische Klasse*, 1878) ; von Zezschwitz, *Die Katachismen der Waldenser und Bömischen Bruder* (Erlangen, 1863) ; Beck, *Geschichtsbücher der Wiedertäufer in Oestreich-Ungern, 1526 bis 1785* (Vienna, 1883), printed in the *Fontes Rer. Austr. Diplom. et Acta*, xliii. ; Kessler, *Sabbata*, ed. by Egli and Schoch (St. Gall, 1902) ; Bullinger, *Der Wiedertäuferen Ursprung, Secten*, etc. (Zurich, 1560) ; Egli, *Actensammlung zur Geschichte der Züricher Reformation* (Zurich, 1879), *Die Züricher Wiedertäufer* (Zurich, 1878) ; Leopold Dickius, *Adversus impios Anabaptistarum errores* (1533) ; Cornelius, *Berichte der Augenzeugen über das Münsterische Wiedertäuferreich*, forming the 2nd vol. of the *Geschichtsquellen des Bisthums Münster* (Münster, 1853) and the Beilage in his *Geschichte des Münsterischen Aufruhrs* (Leipzig, 1855) ; Detmer's edition of Kerssenbroch, *Anabaptistici furoris Monasterium inclitam Westphaliæ metropolim evertentis historica narratio*, forming vols. v. and vi. of the *Geschichtsquellen des Bisthums Münster* (Münster, 1899, 1900) ; *Chroniken der deutschen Städte, Nurnberg Chronik*, vols. i. and iv.

LATER BOOKS : Keller, *Geschichte der Wiedertäufer und ihres Reichs zu Münster* (Münster, 1880), *Ein Apostel der Wiedertäufer, Hans Denck* (Leipzig, 1882), and *Die Reformation und die älteren Reformparteien* (Leipzig, 1885—Keller is apt to make inferences beyond his facts) ; Heath, *Anabaptism, from its rise at Zwickau to its fall at Münster, 1521–1536* (London, 1895) ; Belfort Bax, *Rise and Fall of the Anabaptists* (London,

movement in four stages, beginning with the Zwickau
prophets and ending with the catastrophe in Münster, or
to explain its origin by calling it the radical side of
the Reformation movement.[1] It is acknowledged by
careful students to have been a very complicated affair,
to have had roots buried in the previous centuries, and to
have had men among its leaders who were distinguished
Humanists. It is now known that it spread over Europe
with great rapidity, and attracted to itself an enormously
larger number of adherents than had been imagined.

It is impossible within the limits of one brief chapter
to state and criticise the various theories of the origin and
roots of the movement which modern investigation has
1903) ; Rörich, "Die Gottesfreunde und die Winkeler am Oberrhein" (in
Zeitschrift für hist. Theol. i. 118 ff., 1840) ; Zur Geschichte der strassburg-
ischen Wiedertäufer (Zeitschrift für. hist. Theol. xxx. 1860) ; S.B. ten Cate,
Geschiedenis der doopgezinden in Groningen, etc., 2 vols. (Leewarden, 1843) ;
Geschiedenis der doopgezinden in Friesland (Leewarden, 1839) ; Geschiedenis
der doopgezinden in Holland en Guelderland, 2 vols. (Amsterdam, 1847) ;
Tileman van Braght, Het bloedig Toeneel of Martelaars Spiegel der
doopgesinde (Amsterdam, 1685) ; E. B. Underhill, Martyrology of the
Churches of Christ commonly called Baptist (translated from Van Braght) ;
H. S. Burrage, A History of the Anabaptists in Switzerland (founded on
Egli's researches, Philadelphia, 1881) ; Newman, A History of Anti-
Pedobaptism (Philadelphia, 1897) ; Detmer, Bilder aus den religiösen und
sozialen Unruhen in Münster während des 16 Jahrhunderts : i. Johann von
Leiden (Münster, 1903), ii. Bernhard Rothmann (1904), iii. Ueber die
Auffassung von der Ehe und die Durchführung der Vielweiberei in Münster
während der Taüferherrschaft (1904) ; Heath, Contemporary Review, lix.
389 ("The Anabaptists and their English Descendants"), lxii. 880
("Hans Denck the Baptist), lxvii. 578 (Early Anabaptism, what it meant,
and what we owe to it), lxx. 247 ("Living in Community—a sketch of
Moravian Anabaptism"), 541 ("The Archetype of the Pilgrim's
Progress"), lxxii. 105 ("The Archetype of the Holy War").

[1] The difference in treatment may be seen at a glance by comparing the
articles on Anabaptism in the second (1877) and in the third (1896)
edition of Herzog's Realencyclopädie für protestantische Theologie und
Kirche. Some eminent historians, however, still cling to old ideas ; for
example, Edward Armstrong, The Emperor Charles V. (London, 1902), who
justifies the treatment his hero meted out to the Anabaptists—roasting
them to death before slow fires—by saying that "whenever they
momentarily gained the upper hand, they applied the practical methods
of modern Anarchism or Nihilism to the professed principles of
Communism" (ii. 342). No one who has examined the original sources
could have penned such a sentence.

suggested. All that can be done is to set down succinctly the conclusions reached after a tolerably wide examination of the sources—admitting at the same time that more information must be obtained ere the history of the movement advances beyond the controversial stage.

It is neither safe nor easy to make abrupt general statements about the causes or character of great popular movements. The elements which combine to bring them into being and keep them in existence are commonly as innumerable as the hues which blend in the colour of a mountain side. Anabaptism was such a complicated movement that it presents peculiar difficulties. As has been said, it had a distinct relation to two different streams of mediæval life, the one social and the other religious—the revolts of peasants and artisans, and the successions of the *Brethren.*

From the third quarter of the fifteenth century social uprisings had taken place almost every decade, all of them more or less impregnated with crude religious beliefs. They were part of the intellectual and moral atmosphere that the " common man," whether in town or country district, continuously breathed, and their power over him must not be lost sight of. The Reformation movement quickened and strengthened these influences simply because it set all things in motion. It is not possible, therefore, to draw a rigid line of separation between some sides of the Anabaptist movement and the social revolt ; and hence it is that there is at least a grain of truth in the conception that the Anabaptists were the revolutionaries of the times of the Reformation.

On the other hand, there are good reasons for asserting that the distinctively religious side of Anabaptism had little to do with the anarchic outbreaks. It comes in direct succession from those communities of pious Christians who, on the testimony of their enemies, lived quiet God-fearing lives, and believed all the articles in the Apostles' Creed ; but who were strongly anti-clerical. They lived unobtrusively, and rarely appear in history save when the chronicle of some town makes casual mention of their existence, or when an Inquisitor ferreted them out and records their so-called heresies. Their objections to the constitution and ceremonies of the mediæval Church were exactly those of the Anabaptists of the sixteenth century; and if we do not find a universal repudiation of infant baptism, there are traces that some did not approve of it. They insisted that the service ought to be in the vulgar tongue; they objected to all the Church festivals; to all blessing of buildings, crosses, and candles; they alleged that Christ did not give His Apostles stoles or chasubles; they scoffed at excommunications, Indulgences, and dispensations; they declared that there was no regenerative efficacy in infant baptism; and they were keenly alive to all the injunctions of Christian charity—it was better, they said, to clothe the poor than to expend money on costly vestments or to adorn the walls of Churches, and they kept up schools and hospitals for lepers. They met in each other's houses for public worship, which took the form of reading and commenting upon the Holy Scriptures.[1]

As we are dependent on very casual sources of information, it is not surprising that we cannot trace their *continuous* descent down to the period of the Reformation; but we do find in the earlier decades of the sixteenth century notices of the existence of small praying communities, which have all the characteristics of those recorded in the Inquisitors' reports belonging to the end of the fourteenth or beginning of the fifteenth centuries. They appeared in Basel in 1514, in Switzerland in 1515, in Mainz in 1518, and in Augsburg somewhat earlier.[2] By the year 1524 similar "praying circles" were recorded as existing in France, in the Netherlands, in Italy, in Saxony, in Franconia, at Strassburg, and in Bohemia. They used a common catechism for the instruction of their young

---

[1] *Magna Bibliotheca Veterum Patrum* (Coloniæ Agrippinæ, 1618), xiii. 299, 300, 307 (the *Summa* of Raiverus Sacchonus). Cf. i. 152.

[2] These are the dates at which town chronicles incidentally show that such communities existed, not the dates of their origin.

28**

people which was printed in French, German, Bohemian,
and perhaps Italian. In Germany, the Bible was the
German Vulgate—a version retained among the Anabaptists
long after the publication of Luther's. They exhibited
great zeal in printing and distributing the pious literature
of the *Friends of God* of the fourteenth and fifteenth
centuries. Many of them taught Baptist views, though
the tenets were not universally accepted, and they were
already called Anabaptists or Katabaptists—a term of
reproach. Some of their more distinguished leaders were
pious Humanists, and *their* influence may perhaps be seen
in the efforts made by the *Brethren* to print and distri-
bute the *Defensor Pacis* of Marsiglio of Padua.

This quiet Evangelical movement assumed a more
definite form in 1524. Before that date the associations
of pious people acted like the Pietists of the seventeenth
or like the Wesleyans of the eighteenth century. They
associated together for mutual edification ; they did not
obtrusively separate themselves from the corrupt or slothful Church. But in June 1524, delegates representing a
very wide circle of "praying assemblies" or *Readings* met
at Waldshut, in the house of Balthasar Hübmaier,[1] bringing
their Bibles with them, to consult how to organise their
Christian living on the lines laid down in the New Testament. No regular ecclesiastical organisation was formed.
The Brethren resolved to separate from the Papal Church ;
they published a Directory for Christian living, and drew
up a statement of principles in which they believed.
Amongst other things, they protested against any miraculous
efficacy in the Sacraments in general, and held that Baptism
is efficacious only when it is received in faith. This led
afterwards to the adoption of Baptist views. A second
conference was held at Augsburg in 1526, which probably
dates the time when adult-baptism became a distinctive
belief among all the *Brethren*. This conference suggested
a General Synod which met at Augsburg in 1527 (Aug.),
and included among its members, delegates from Munich,

---

[1] Vedder, *Balthazar Hübmaier* (New York, 1905).

Franconia, Ingolstadt, Upper Austria, Styria, and Switzerland. There they drew up a statement of doctrinal truth, which is very simple, and corresponds intimately with what is now taught among the Moravian Brethren. Their Hymnbook [1] does not bear any traces of the errors in doctrine usually attributed to them. Its chief theme is the love of God awakening our love to God and to our fellow-men. Instead of infant baptism they had a ceremony in which the children were consecrated to God. Baptism was regarded as the sign of conversion and of definite resolve to give one's self up to the worship and service of God. It was administered by *sprinkling*; the recipient knelt to receive it in the presence of the congregation. The Holy Supper was administered at stated times, and always after one or two days of solemn preparation. Their officebearers were deacons, elders, masters and teachers, or pastors. They distinguished between pastors who were wandering evangelists and those who were attached to single congregations. The latter, who were ordained by the laying on of hands, alone had the right to dispense the Sacraments. All the deacons, elders, and pastors belonging to communities within a prescribed district, selected from among themselves delegates who formed their ecclesiastical council for the district, and this council elected one of the pastors to act as Bishop or Superintendent. It was the Superintendent who ordained by laying on of hands. The whole of the *Brethren* were governed ecclesiastically by a series of Synods corresponding to those in the Presbyterian Churches. This organisation enabled the Anabaptists to endure the frightful persecution which they were soon to experience at the hands of the papal and Lutheran State Churches.

The chief leaders were Balthasar Hübmaier and Hans Denck. Hübmaier was a distinguished scholar. He became, at an unusnally early age, Professor of theology at

---

[1] Liliencron, "Zur Liederdichtung der Wiedertaüfer," in the *Transactions of the Königl. Bair. Akad. der Wissenschaften, Philosophisch-historische Klasse*, 1877.

Ingolstadt (1512); he was Rector of the famous High
School in that city (1515); and Cathedral preacher at
Regensburg (Ratisbon) (1516). In 1519, feeling that he
could no longer conscientiously occupy such positions, he
retired to the little town of Waldshut. Hans Denck was
a noted Humanist, a member of the "Erasmus circle" at
Basel, and esteemed the most accurate Greek scholar in the
learned community. Conrad Grebel, another well-known
Anabaptist leader, also belonged to the "Erasmus circle,"
and was a member of one of the patrician families of Zurich.
Like Hübmaier and Denck, he gave up all to become an
evangelist, and spent his life on long preaching tours.
These facts are sufficient to refute the common statement
that the Anabaptists were ignorant fanatics.

Perhaps Denck was the most widely known and highly
esteemed. In the summer of 1523 he was appointed
Rector of the celebrated Sebaldus School in Nürnberg.
In the end of 1524 he was charged with heresy, and
along with him Jörg Penz, the artist, the favourite pupil
of Albert Dürer, and four others. Denck was banished
from the city, and his name became well known. This
trial and sentence was the occasion of his beginning that
life of wandering evangelist which had among other
results the conferences in 1526 and 1527, and the
organisation above described. Denck had drunk deeply
at the well of the fourteenth and fifteenth century Mystics,
and his teaching was tinged by many of their ideas. He
believed that there was a spark of the divine nature in man,
an Inner Word, which urged man to walk in the ways of
God, and that man could always keep true to the inward
monitor, who was none else than Christ. The accounts
given of some of his addresses seem to be echoes of Tauler's
famous sermon on the Bridegroom and the Bride, for he
taught that the sufferings of the faithful are to be looked
upon as the love-gifts of the Saviour, and are neither to
be mourned nor resisted. We are told in the quaint
Chronicle of Sebastian Franck, that the Baptist current
swept swiftly through the whole land; many thousands were

baptized, and many hearts drawn to them. "For they taught nothing but love, faith, and crucifixion of the flesh, manifesting patience and humility under many sufferings, breaking bread with one another in sign of unity and love, helping one another with true helpfulness, lending, borrowing, giving, learning to have all things in common, calling each other ' brother.' "[1] He adds that they were accused of many things of which they were innocent, and were treated very tyrannically.

The Anabaptists, like the earlier Mystics, displayed a strong individuality; and this makes it impossible to classify their tenets in a body of doctrine which can be held to express the system of intellectual belief which lay at the basis of the whole movement. We have three contemporary accounts which show the divergence of opinion among them—two from hostile and one from a sympathetic historian. Bullinger[2] attempts a classification of their different divisions, and mentions thirteen distinct sects within the Anabaptist circle; but they manifestly overlap in such a way as to suggest a very large amount of difference which cannot be distinctly tabulated. Sebastian Franck[3] notes all the varieties of views which Bullinger mentions, but refrains from any classification. "There are," he says, "more sects and opinions, which I do not know and cannot describe, but it appears to me that there are not two to be found who agree with each other on all points." Kessler,[4] who recounts the story of the Anabaptists of St. Gallen, notes the same great variety of opinions.

It is quite possible to describe the leading ideas taught by a few noted men and approved of by their immediate circle of followers, and so to arrive with some accuracy at the popularity of certain leading principles among different parties, but it must be remembered that no great

---

[1] *Chronica* (Augsburg edition, 1565), f. 164.
[2] *Der Wiedertäuferen Ursprung, Furgang, Secten*, etc. (Zurich, 1560).
[3] *Chronica* (3 pts., Strassburg, 1531).
[4] *Sabbata* (ed. by Egli and Schoch, St. Gall, 1902)

leader imposed his opinions on the whole Anabaptist circle, and that the views held at different times by prominent men were not invariably the sentiments which lay at the basis of the whole movement.

The doctrine of passive resistance was held by almost all the earlier Anabaptists, but it was taught and practised in such a great variety of ways that a merely general statement gives a misleading idea. All the earlier Anabaptists believed that it was unchristian to return evil for evil, and that they should take the persecutions which came to them without attempting to retaliate. Some, like the young Humanist, Hans Denck, pushed the theory so far that they believed that no real Christian could be either a magistrate or a soldier. A small band of Anabaptists, to whom one of the Counts of Lichtenstein had given shelter at Nikolsburg, told their protector plainly that they utterly disapproved of his threatening the Austrian Commissary with armed resistance if he entered the Nikolsburg territory to seize them. In short, what is called " passive resistance " took any number of forms, from the ordinary Christian maxim to be patient under tribulation, to that inculcated and practised by the modern sect of Dunkhers.

The followers of Melchior Hoffmann, called " Melchiorites," held apocalyptic or millenarian views, and expected in tbe near future the return of Christ to reign over His saints ; but there is no reason to suppose that this conception was very widely adopted, still less that it can be called a tenet of Anabaptism in general. All the Anabaptists inculcated the duty of charity and the claims of the poor on the richer members of the community ; but that is a common Christian precept, and does not necessarily imply communistic theories or practices. All that can be definitely said of the whole Anabaptist circle was that they did keep very clearly before them the obligations of Christian love. The so-called Communism in Münster will be described later.

When we examine carefully the incidental records of contemporary witnesses observing their Anabaptist neighbours, we reach the general conclusion that their main thought was to reproduce in their own lives what seemed to them to be the beliefs, usages, and social practices of the primitive Christians. Translations of the Bible and of parts of it had been common enough in Germany before Luther's days. The "common man," especially the artisan of the towns, knew a great deal about the Bible. It was the one book he read, re-read, and pondered over. Fired with the thoughts created in his mind by its perusal, simple men felt impelled to become itinerant preachers. The "call" came to them, and they responded at once to what they believed to be the divine voice. Witness Hans Ber of Alten-Erlangen, a poor peasant. He rose from his bed one night and suddenly began to put on his clothes. "Whither goest thou?" asked his poor wife. "I know not; God knoweth," he answered. "What evil have I done thee? Stay and help me to bring up my little children." "Dear wife," he answered, "trouble me not with the things of time. I must away, that I may learn the will of the Lord."[1] Such men wandered about in rude homespun garments, often barefooted, their heads covered with rough felt hats. They craved hospitality in houses, and after supper produced their portions of the Bible, read and expounded, then vanished in the early morning. We are told how Hans Hut came to the house of Franz Strigel at Weier in Franconia, produced his Bible, read and expounded, explained the necessity of adult baptism, convinced Strigel, the house father, and eight others, and baptized them there and then. He wandered forth the same night. None of the baptized saw him again; but the little community remained—a small band of Anabaptists.[2]

These wandering preachers, "prophets" they may be called if we give them the early Christian name, were not drilled in any common set of opinions. Each conceived

[1] C. A. Cornelius, *Geschichte des Münsterischen Aufruhrs* (Leipzig, 1855), ii. 49.

[2] *Ibid.* ii. 49.

the primitive teaching and social life as he seemed to see it reflected in the New Testament ; and no two conceptions were exactly the same. The circumstances and surroundings produced an infinite variety of thought about the doctrines and usages which ought to be accepted and practised. Yet they had traditional modes of interpretation handed down to them from the praying circles of the " Brethren." Compare what the Austrian Inquisitor says of the "Brethren" in the thirteenth century, with what Johann Kessler tells about the Anabaptists of St. Gallen, and the resemblance is striking so far as external appearance goes. " Hæretici cognoscuntur per mores et verba," says the Inquisitor. "Sunt enim in moribus compositi et modesti ; superbiam in vestibus non habent, nec pretiosis, nec multum abjectis utuntur. . . . Doctores etiam ipsorum sunt sutores et textores. Divitias non multiplicant, sed necessariis sunt contenti. Casti etiam sunt. . . . Temperati etiam in cibo et potu. Ad tabernas non eunt, nec ad choreas, nec ad alias vanitates. Ab ira se cohibent ; semper operantur, discunt vel docent, et ideo parum orant. . . . Cognoscuntur etiam in verbis præcisis et modestis. Cavent etiam a scurrilitate et detractione, et verborum levitate, et mendacio, et juramento." [1] Kessler tells us that the walk and conversation of these Anabaptists was " throughout pious, holy, and blameless " ; that they refrained from wearing costly apparel, despised luxurious eating and drinking, clothed themselves in rough cloth, wore slouch hats on their heads. Franck relates that they refused to frequent wine-shops and the " gild " rooms where dances were held.

As they lived again the life of these mediæval sectaries, so they reproduced their opinions in the same sporadic way. Some of them objected to all war even in self-defence, as did some of the earlier Lollards. Their Lord had said to His first disciples : " Go your ways : behold, I send you forth as lambs in the midst of wolves." They flung

---

[1] *Magna Bibliotheca Veterum Patrum* (Coloniæ Agrippinæ, 1618), Rainerii Socchoni, *Summa*, c. vii.

from them the sword, with which peasant and artisan were then alike girt, and went about as the apostles were ordered to do, with staves in their hands—the *Stäbler* or *staffmen* who would have nothing to do with the weapons of wolves. Others, also like some of the Lollards, would not enter the " huge stone houses with great glass windows which men called ' churches.' " The early Christians had preached and " broken bread " in houses ; and they would follow their example ; and in private rooms, in the streets, in the market-places, they proclaimed their gospel of peace and contentment. The infinitesimal number who taught something like " free love," and who were repudiated by the others, were reproducing the vagaries of the mediæval *Brethren and Sisters of the Free Spirit*, who gave Meister Eckhart so much trouble centuries before in the Rhineland. All the more extravagant ideas and practices which appear among small sections of these Anabaptists of the sixteenth century can be found among the sectaries of the Middle Ages. For the whole Anabaptist movement was mediæval to the core ; and, like most of the mediæval religious awakenings, produced an infinite variety of opinions and practices. The one idea common to all was, that the Christians of the sixteenth century were called to reproduce in thought and life the intellectual beliefs and usages of the primitive Christians. It is simply impossible to give any account of opinions and practices which were *universally* prevalent among them. Even the most widely spread usages, adult baptism and the " breaking of bread," were not adopted in all the divisions of the Anabaptists.

What is more, they were modern enough, at least in the earlier stages of the movement, to be conscious of this (which the Mystics were not), and to give it expression. All felt and thought as did a " simple man," Hans Müller of Medikon, when brought before the Zurich magistrates : " Do not lay a burden on my conscience, for faith is a gift given freely by God, and is not common property. The mystery of God lies hidden, like the treasure in the field, which no one can find but he to whom the Spirit shows it.

So I beg you, ye servants of God, let my faith stand free." [1]
And the Anabaptists, alone of all the religious parties in
those strenuous times, seem to have recognised that what
they claimed for themselves they were bound to grant to
others. Great differences in opinion did not prevent the
strictest brotherly fellowship. Hans Denck held a doctrine
of non-resistance as thoroughgoing as that of Count Tolstoy,
and fully recognised the practical consequences to which it
led. But this did not prevent the ardent and gifted young
Humanist working loyally with Hübmaier, who did not share
his extreme opinions. The divergences among the leaders
appeared in their followers without destroying the sense of
brotherhood. Franck tells us in his *Chronicle* [2] that some,
but very few, held that no Christian could enter the
magistracy, for Christians had nothing to do with the sword,
but only with spiritual excommunication, and that no
Christian should fight and slay. The others, he says, including the very great majority, believed that Christians
might become magistrates, and that in case of dire necessity
and when they clearly saw the leading of God, might take
their share in fighting as soldiers.

Melchior Hoffmann, while he believed in the incarnation, held that Jesus received His flesh directly from God,
and did not owe His body to the Virgin Mother, through
whom He passed " as light through a pane of glass."
He also held that the whole history of the world, down
to the last days, was revealed in Scripture, and could be
discovered through prayer and meditation. He was an
eloquent and persuasive preacher, and his views were
accepted by many; but it would be a great mistake to
assume that they were shared in by the Anabaptists as a
community. Yet even contemporaries, who were opponents,
usually attribute the extreme opinions of a few to the entire
body.

It ought to be observed that this tolerance of different
opinions within the one society did not extend to those

---

[1] Egli, *Die Züricher Wiedertäufer* (Zurich, 1878), p. 96.
[2] Folio 158^b of the Augsburg edition of 1565.

who remained true to the State Churches, whether Romanist
or Reformed. The Anabaptists would have nothing to do
with a State Church; and this was the main point in their
separation from the Lutherans, Zwinglians, and Calvinists.
It was perhaps the *one* conception on which all parties
among them were in absolute accord. The real Church,
which might be small or great, was for them an association
of believing people; and the great ecclesiastical institutions
into which unconscious infants were admitted by a ceremony
called baptism long before they could have or exercise faith,
represented to them an idea subversive of true Christianity.
They had no wish to persecute men who differed widely
from them, but they would not associate with them. This
enforced " separation," like everything else connected with
Anabaptism, differed considerably in the way in which it
was carried into practice. In some of the smaller sections it
appeared in very extravagant forms. Wives and husbands,
Anabaptists whose partners belonged to the State Churches,
were in some small sections advised to refuse cohabita-
tion. It is more than probable that some recorded sayings
on which opponents have founded charges of encouraging
sexual irregularities,—that it was better for women to have
connection irregularly with members of the brotherhood
than to cohabit with unbelieving husbands,—were simply
extravagant ways of expressing this duty of separation.

It is also true that as time went on and sects of extreme opinions multiplied, the excommunication of members
for their views came to be a common practice. It was as
frequent among some of the smaller divisions as it is among
modern Plymouth Brethren; but the occasion was, as a rule,
difference of opinion about the way to express and exercise
the duty of not returning evil for evil—was it permitted
to pay taxes or not? was it lawful to see without protest
their protectors using force to prevent their enemies from
attacking them, etc.?

The earlier ideas of non-resistance, whatever practical
shape they might take, gave way before the continuous and
terrible persecution which the Anabaptists had to endure

They were first definitely condemned by Melchior Hoffmann and his followers. They believed in the speedy establishment on earth of the millennial kingdom of Christ, and they declared that they were ready to fight for it when it appeared. With them the conception was simply a pious opinion, and they had no occasion to reduce it to action. The Anabaptists, however, who followed the teaching of Jan Matthys and of his disciple Jan Bockelson, repudiated passive resistance both in theory and in practice.

Of course, there are many things about some, perhaps all, great religious awakenings which critics can lay hold of to their disparagement; and it was so with the Anabaptist movement. Everything, from the scientific frame of mind to the religious sensibility, has the defects of its qualities. When a man is seized and possessed by a new spiritual emotion which seems to lift him above all previous experience of life or of thought, all things are new to him, and all things seem possible. His old life with its limitations has departed. He is embarked on a sea which has no imprisoning shores. He is carried along on a great current of emotion, and others are borne with him. Human deep calleth unto deep when they exchange confidences. He and his fellows have become new creatures; and that is almost all that they know about themselves. Such experiences are quite consistent with soundness of mind and clearness of vision of God and Divine things—that is usual; but sometimes they are too powerful for the imperfect mind which holds them. The converts are " puffed up," as St. Paul said. Then arise morbid states, distorted vision, sometimes actual shipwreck of mental faculties, not seldom acute religious mania. Leaders in a great religious awakening have always to reckon with such developments—St. Paul, Francis of Assisi, Eckhart, Tauler, to say nothing of modern instances. The Apostle addressed morbid souls with severe sarcasm. Did any man really think, he asked, that to commit incest, to take to wife his father's widow, was an example of the freedom with which Christ had made them free ?

The Anabaptist movement had its share of such cases, like other religious movements; they grew more frequent as the unfortunate people were maddened by persecution; and these exceptional incidents are invariably retailed at length by historians hostile to the movement.

The Anabaptists, as a whole, were subjected to persecutions, especially from the Romanists and the Lutherans, much more harsh than befell any of the religious parties of the sixteenth century. Their treatment in Zurich may be taken as an example of how they came in contact with the civil authorities, and how their treatment grew in severity.[1]

The Swiss Anabaptists were in no sense disciples of Zwingli. They had held their distinctive principles and were a recognised community long before Zwingli came from Einsiedeln, and were the lineal descendants of the mediæval Waldenses. They welcomed the Reformer; some of them were in the company who challenged the authorities by eating meat during Lent in 1522; but a fundamental difference soon emerged. After the Public Disputation of 1523, when it became clear that Zurich meant to accept the Reformation, a deputation of the *Brethren* appeared before the Council to urge their idea of what a Reformed Church should be. Their statement of principles is an exposition of the fundamental conceptions which lay at the basis of the whole Anabaptist movement, and explains why they could not join either the Lutheran or the Reformed branch of the Reformation Church. They insisted that an Evangelical Church must differ from the Roman Church in this among other things, that it should consist of members who had made a personal profession of faith in their Saviour, and who had vowed to live in obedience to

---

[1] The Swiss Anabaptists have been selected because we have very full contemporary documentary evidence in their case. Cf. Egli, *Actensammlung zur Geschichte der Züricher Reformation* (Zurich, 1879); *Die Zuricher Wiedertäufer* (Zurich, 1878); *Die St. Galler Wiedertäufer* (Zurich).

The documentary evidence given in Egli's works has been condensed and summarised by H. S. Burrage, *A History of the Anabaptists in Switzerland* (Philadelphia, 1881).

Jesus Christ their *Hauptmann*. It could not be like a State Church, whether Romanist or other, to which people belonged without any individual profession of faith. They insisted that the Church, thus formed, should be free from all civil control, to decide for itself what doctrines and ceremonies of worship were founded on the Word of God, and agreeable thereto, and should make this decision according to the opinions of a majority of the members. They further asked that the Church should be free to exercise, by brotherly admonition and, as a last resort, by excommunication, discipline on such of its members as offended against the moral law. They also declared that the Church which thus rejected State control ought to refuse State support, and proposed that the tithes should be secularised. The New Testament, they said, knew nothing about interest and usury, tithes, livings, and prebends.

These views were quite opposed to the ideas of the Zurich Council, who contemplated a State Church reformed from Romanist abuses, but strictly under the control of the State, and supported by the tithes, as the mediæval Church had been. They refused to adopt the ideas of the Anabaptists; and this was the beginning of the antagonism. The Council found that the great majority of the petitioners had doubts about infant baptism, and were inclined to what are now called Baptist views; and they brought matters to a crisis by ordering a Public Disputation on Baptism (Jan. 17th, 1525). Among the Anabaptists who appeared to defend their principles, were young Conrad Grebel the Humanist, Felix Manz, and Brother Jörg from Jacob's House, a conventual establishment near Chur, who is always called " Blaurock " (Blue-coat). They were opposed by Zwingli, who insisted that infant baptism must be maintained, because it took the place of circumcision. The Council decided that Zwingli's contention was right, and they made it a *law* that *all children must be baptized*, and added that all persons who refused to have their children baptized after Feb. 1st, 1525, were to be arrested. The Anabaptists were not slow to answer the challenge thus given. They met, and after deliberation and prayer Blaurock asked Conrad Grebel to baptize him in a truly Christian fashion, " there being no ordained person present," and Grebel did so. " When this had been done the others entreated Blaurock to baptize them, which he did; and in deep fear of the Lord they gave themselves to God." They resolved to preach and baptize, because in this they ought to obey God rather than men.[1]

When the Council heard that adult baptism had begun, they enacted that all who had been rebaptized after Feb. 8th (1525) were to be fined a silver mark, and that whoever was baptized after the issue of their decree should be banished. They also imprisoned the leaders. When they found that neither fines, nor threats, nor imprisonment, nor banishment had any effect on the Anabaptists, the Town Council thought to terrify them by a death sentence. Two were selected, Manz and Blaurock. The latter was not a citizen, and the sentence of death was commuted to one of public scourging and being thrust out of the town; but Felix Manz, a townsman, was put to death by drowning (1527). Zwingli insisted that this judicial murder was not done because of baptism, but because of rebellion!

What was done in Reformed Switzerland was seen all over Roman Catholic and Lutheran Germany. It is only fair to say that the persecution was more murderous within the Romanist districts; but the only Lutheran Prince who refused to permit a death penalty on Anabaptism was Philip of Hesse. He was afterwards joined by the Elector of Saxony.

In 1527 (Aug. 26th), the Archduke Ferdinand of Austria published an imperial mandate threatening all Anabaptists with the punishment of death. Two months later, two thousand copies of this proclamation were sent to the provinces of the German Empire, calling on the authorities to extirpate these unfortunate people. The

---

[1] The scene is described in Beck, *Die Geschichts-Bücher der Wiedertäufer in Ostreich-Ungern von 1526 bis 1785* (Vienna, 1883).

rulers in Salzburg and in the Tyrol obeyed the ordei at once, and a fierce persecution soon raged. The minds of the population were inflamed by infamous calumnies. It was said in Salzburg that the Anabaptists had planned to massacre all the priests and monks within the principality. The well-known dislike of the brethren to war was tortured into the accusation that on a Turkish invasion they would side with the enemy against all loyal Germans. A certain Leopold Dickius, who wrote an atrocious book against the Anabaptists, demanded that all the men should be slain and the women and children suffered to perish from starvation; in this way only, he said, could their errors be stamped out.

The Salzburg chronicler, Kilian Leib, a Romanist, gives details of the persecution. He tells us that men, women, and young maidens suffered death by fire, beheading, and drowning, not only uncomplainingly, but with solemn joy. He dwells on the case of " a beautiful young girl " of sixteen, whose gentle innocence excited universal compassion, and who utterly refused to recant. The executioner pinned her hands to her sides, plunged her head downwards into a horse trough, held her there till she was suffocated, and then took her body away to burn it. The official lists show that the victims came from all classes in society. Noblemen, girdle-makers, wallet-makers, shoemakers, a town clerk, and ex-priests.

The persecution in the Tyrol was severe and thorough. A large number of the miners of the district were Anabaptists, and it was resolved to root out the so-called heresy. Descriptions were published of prominent Anabaptists, who wandered from place to place encouraging their brethren to steadfastness. " One named Mayerhofer has a long brown beard and wears a grey soldier's coat; a companion, tall and pale, wears a long black coat with trimming; a third is shorter; a fourth, thin and of a ruddy complexion, is known as a cutler." Conrad Braun, an assessor to the imperial Chamber and an eye-witness to the persecutions, wrote,—" I have seen with my own eyes that nothing has been able to bring back the Anabaptists from their errors or to make them recant. The hardest imprisonment, hunger, fire, water, the sword, all sorts of frightful executions, have not been able to shake them. I have seen young people, men, women, go to the stake singing, filled with joy; and I can say that in the course of my whole life nothing has moved me more."[1] In the Tyrol and Görz the number of executions by the year 1531 amounted to a thousand, according to the chronicler Kirchmayr. Sebastian Franck reckons the number in Enisheim, within the government of Upper Austria, at six hundred. Seventy-three martyrs suffered in Linz within six weeks. The persecution in Bavaria was particularly severe; Duke William ordered that those who recanted were to be beheaded, and those who refused were to be burned. The general practice, made a law by Ferdinand of Austria in 1529 (April 23rd), was that only preachers, baptizers, Baptists who refused to recant, and those who had relapsed after recantation, were to be punished with death.[2]

In these bloody persecutions, which raged over almost all Europe, most of the earlier leaders of the Anabaptists perished; but the great body of their followers were neither intimidated nor disposed to abjure their teaching. Persecution did not come unexpectedly. No one was admitted into an Anabaptist community without being warned of the probable fate which lay before him. Baptism was a vow that he would be constant unto death; the "breaking of bread" strengthened his faith; the sermon was full of exhortations to endurance unto the end. Their whole service of worship was a preparation for and an expectation of martyrdom.

The strain of Christian song seemed to rise higher with the fires of persecution. Most of the Anabaptist

---

[1] The history of the persecution in the Tyrol is to be found in J. Loserth, *Anabaptismus in Tirol*; and in Kirchmayr, *Denkwürdigkeiten seiner Zeit, 1519–53*, pt. i. in *Fontes Rerum Austriacarum*, i. 417–534.

[2] Cornelius, *Geschichte des Münsterischen Aufruhrs* (Leipzig, 1855), ii. 58.

29**

hymns belong to the time when their sufferings were greatest. Some are simply histories of a martyrdom, as of Jörg Wagner at Munich, or of the "Seven Brethren at Gemünd." They are all echoes of endurance where the notes of the sob, the trust, the warning, the hosanna of a time of martyrdom, blend in rough heroic strains. They sing of Christ, who in these last days has manifested Himself that the pure word of His Gospel may again run through the earth as it did in the days of the early Church. They tell how the arch-enemy of souls seeks to protect himself against the advancing host of Jesus by exciting bloody persecutions. They utter warnings against false prophets, ravening wolves in sheep's clothing, who beset all the paths of life leading towards the true fold, who pour forth threats and curses against the people of God, and urge on the rulers of this world to torture and to slay. They depict how the evil world storms against the true Church, shrieks out lies against the true followers of Jesus, and threatens them with burnings and all manner of cruel deaths. They mourn that the disciples of Jesus are slaughtered like sheep who have lost their shepherd; that they wander in wildernesses full of thorns that tear; that they have their homes like the night-birds among the cliffs or in the clefts of the rocks; that they are snared in the nets of the fowler; that they are hunted with hounds like the hares. Others, inspired by the internal hope which lives undying in every Christian heart, tell how Christ the Bridegroom seeks the love of the soul His bride, and how He wins her to Himself by His love-gifts of trial and of suffering, till at last the marriage feast is held, and the soul becomes wholly united to her Lord. The thoughts and phrases of the old Hebrew prophets, of the Psalmist, of the hymns of the Apocalypse, which have fed the fears and the hopes of longing, suffering, trusting generations of Christian people, reappear in those Anabaptist hymns. Life is for them a continuous Holy War, a Pilgrim's Progress through an evil world full of snares, of dangers, of temptations, until at last the weary feet tread the Delectable Mountains, the River of Death is passed, and the open gates of the heavenly Jerusalem receive the wayfarer who has persevered to the end.

These poor persecuted people naturally sought for some city of refuge, *i.e.* a municipality or district where baptism of children was not enforced under penalties, and where the re-baptism of adults was not punished by imprisonment, torture, and death. For a time they found many such asylums. The Anabaptists were for the most part good workmen, and patient and provident cultivators of the soil, ready to pay all dues but the unscriptural war-tax. They were a source of wealth to many a great landed proprietor who was willing to allow them to live their lives in peace. Moravia, East Friesland, and, among the municipalities, Augsburg, Worms, and Strassburg gave shelter until the slow determined pressure of the higher authorities of the Empire compelled them to act otherwise. All that the Anabaptists desired was to be allowed to live in peace, and we hear of no great disturbances caused by their presence in any of these " cities of refuge."

This brings us to what has been called " The Kingdom of God in Münster," and to the behaviour of the Anabaptists there—the communism, polygamy, and so forth, which are described in all histories of the times.

Münster was the capital of the large and important ecclesiastical principality which bears the same name. The bishop was a Prince of the German Empire, and ruled his principality with all the rights of a secular prince. Clergy filled almost all the important posts of government; they levied taxes on imports and exports; the rich canonries of the cathedral were reserved for the sons of the landed gentry; the townspeople had no share in the richer benefices, and chafed under their clerical rulers. The citizens lived in a state of almost permanent disaffection, and their discontent had frequently taken the form of civic insurrections. They rose in 1525, in 1527 (in which year the name of a wealthy burgher, Bernard Knipperdolling, first appears as a leader of his fellow-citizens), and in 1529, the dreadful year of famine and plague.[1] Many have been disposed to see in these *emeutes*, anticipations of the struggle which followed; but nothing in the sources warrants the conclusion. They were simply examples of the discontent of the unprivileged classes which had been common enough in Germany for at least a century.

The city of Münster had been slow to receive the religious Reformation, but in 1529 the people began to listen to the preaching of an obscure young chaplain attached to the Church of St. Maurice, built outside the walls of the town.[2] Bernhard Rothmann was a scholar, imbued with Humanist culture, gifted with the power of clear reasoning, and with natural eloquence. It is probable that he had early been attracted by the teaching of Luther;[3] but while he dwelt upon justification by faith, his sermons were full of that sympathy for the down-trodden toiling masses of the community which was a permanent note in all Anabaptist teaching. His sermons were greatly appreciated by the townsfolk, especially by the artisans, who streamed out of the gate to hear the

---

[1] The disease was known as the English plague or the sweating sickness. It is thus described by Hecker (*Epidemics of the Middle Ages*, p. 181): "It was violent inflammatory fever, which, after a short rigour, prostrated the powers as with a blow; and amidst painful oppression at the stomach, headache, and lethargic stupor, suffused the whole body with foetid perspiration. All this took place within the course of a few hours, and the crisis was always over within the space of a day and a night. The internal heat that the patient suffered was intolerable, yet every refrigerant was death."

[2] Rothmann was born at Stadtlohn, and received the rudiments of education in the village school there; a relation sent him to the Gymnasium at Münster; he studied afterwards at Mainz, where he received the degree of M.A.; he was made chaplain in the St. Maurice church at Münster about 1525.

[3] His confession of faith, published in Latin and German in 1532, shows this. I know it only by the summary in Detmer (*Bernhard Rothmann*, Münster, 1904, pp. 41 f.). Detmer says that he knows of only one printed copy, which is in the University Library at Münster.

young chaplain of St. Maurice. Was he not one of themselves, the son of a poor smith! The cathedral Canons, who, in the absence of the Bishop, had the oversight of all ecclesiastical affairs, grew alarmed at his popularity. Their opportunity for interference came when the mob, excited, they said, by Rothmann's denunciations of relic and image worship, profaned the altars, tore the pictures, and destroyed the decorations in St. Maurice on the eve of Good Friday, 1531. Rothmann's influence with the townsmen might have enabled him to defy the Canons, especially as the Prince Bishop, Friedrich von Wied, showed no inclination to molest the chaplain, and was himself suspected of Evangelical sympathies. But he quietly·left the town and spent a year in travelling. He visited Wittenberg, where he made the acquaintance of Luther, Melanchthon, and Bugenhagen ; went to Marburg, Speyer, and Strassburg. At Strassburg he had long intercourse with Capito and with Schwenkfeld the Mystic, who is frequently classed with the Anabaptists. An irresistible impulse seems to have drawn him back to Münster, where he was welcomed by the people, and the church of St. Maurice became henceforth the centre of a movement for religious Reformation; the preacher was supported by the "gilds" of artisans and by most of the citizens, among whom the most noted was Bernhard Knipperdolling.

An energetic protest by the Canons induced the Bishop to inhibit Rothmann from preaching in St. Maurice. He continued his addresses in the churchyard of St. Lambert (Feb. 18th, 1532), and a few days later he was placed in possession of the church itself. St. Lambert's had been built by the municipality, and was the property of the town. Rothmann was appointed by the Town Council Evangelical preacher to the town, and was given one of the town's "gild" houses for a parsonage.

Two months later the Bishop resigned, and was succeeded by Duke Erich of Brunswick-Grubenhagen, already Bishop of Osnabrück and Paderborn. The new

Bishop determined to get rid of Rothmann. He made representations to Hesse and Electoral Saxony and other Evangelical Powers, and persuaded them to induce the more moderate of the reforming party in Münster to abandon Rothmann; and, this done, the preacher was ordered to leave the city. The "gilds" of artisans refused to let their preacher depart, and, under the leadership of Knipperdolling,[1] drafted a letter to the authorities declaring their determination to retain him at all hazards. The democracy of Münster and the religious movement for the first time openly combined against the authorities of the city.

While things were at this pass, the Bishop died (May 13th, 1532). The Chapter elected (June 1st) Count Franz von Waldeck, already in possession of Minden, and made Bishop of Osnabrück a few days later (June 11th)—a pluralist of the first rank. The reforming party in Münster expected the worst from their new ruler. A full assembly of the "gilds" of the town was held, and by an overwhelming majority the members pledged themselves to defend their pastor and his Gospel with body and goods while life lasted. A committee of thirty-six burghers was elected to watch the course of events and to take counsel with the civic rulers and the presidents of the "gilds." Rothmann published *theses* explaining his teaching, and challenging objectors to a public disputation. Public meetings were held; the Town Council was formally requested to hand over all the parochial churches to Evangelical preachers; which was done— the Cathedral alone remaining for Roman Catholic worship.

These proceedings produced unavailing remonstrances from the Bishop. The nobles in the neighbourhood tried to interfere, but to no purpose. In October (1532) the

---

[1] Bernard Knipperdolling or Knipperdollinck (both forms are found) was a wealthy cloth merchant, an able and fervent speaker, a man of strong convictions, who had early espoused the people's cause, and had become the trusted leader of the democracy of Münster.

Bishop's party within the town began to take action. They attempted to sequester the goods of the more prominent disaffected citizens; chains were placed across the principal streets to prevent communication between the different quarters; an attempt was made to isolate the town itself. These things meant war. The "gilds," always a military organisation in mediæval cities, armed. A party of knights sent to invade the town retired before the armed citizens. While the Bishop sought to strengthen himself by alliances and to beguile the townsmen by negotiation, a thousand armed burghers marched by night to the little township of Telgte, where a large number of the ecclesiastical and secular nobles were encamped, surrounded it, captured the Bishop's partisans, and returned to hold them as hostages. This act afforded the occasion for the intervention of Philip of Hesse. An arrangement was come to by which Münster was declared to be an Evangelical city and enrolled within the Schmalkald League. The history of Münster up to this time (Feb. 14th, 1533) did not differ from that of many towns which had adopted the Reformation. Rothmann had been the leader in Münster, like Brenz in Hall, Alber in Reutlingen, or Lachmann at Heilbron.

It is usually assumed that up to this time Rothmann was a Lutheran in his teaching, that he had won Münster for the great Lutheran party, and that his future aberrations from the Evangelical theology were due to his weakness before the Anabaptist mob who later invaded the city. This seems to be a mere assumption. He had certainly taught justification by faith; but that did not make him a Lutheran. The dividing line between the various classes of objectors to the Roman Catholic theology in the sixteenth century was drawn at the meaning of the Sacraments, and especially of the Lord's Supper. There is absolutely no evidence to show that Rothmann was ever a follower of Luther in his theory of the Holy Supper. He had visited Luther and Melanchthon during his year

of absence from Münster, but they had never been quite
sure of him. He has confessed that it was at Strassburg
and not at Wittenberg that he got most help for his
future work and received it from Capito, who was no
Lutheran, and from Schwenkfeld, who was an Anabaptist
Mystic. It was Strassburg and not Wittenberg that he
called " the crown of all Christian cities and Churches ! "
In his confession of faith he says that the Mass is no
sacrifice, but only a sign of the true Sacrifice ; and that
the Mass and the Lord's Supper have *no other meaning*
than to remind us of the death of Christ, and to awaken
in our hearts a certainty of the freely given grace of
God. That is not Lutheran doctrine, it is not even
Zwinglian ; it is much nearer the Anabaptist. It is also
pretty clear that he held the doctrine of the " inner light "
in the sense of many Anabaptists. It may be safely
said that if Rothmann was not an Anabaptist from the
beginning, his was a mind prepared to accept their doctrines
almost as soon as they were clearly presented to him.
Heinrich Roll, a fugitive from Jülich who sought refuge
in Münster, convinced Rothmann of the unlawfulness of
infant baptism. No sooner had this conviction laid hold
on him than he refused to baptize infants—for Rothmann
was always straightforward. His views annoyed a large
number of the leading citizens, prominent among whom
was Van der Wieck, the syndic of the town. These men,
all Lutherans, besieged their pastor with remonstrances,
and finally brought him before the Town Council. The
matter came to a head on Sept. 7th (1533), when
Staprade, the assistant preacher at St. Lambert's, refused
to baptize the children of two Lutheran members of the
Town Council who had been brought to the church for
the purpose. When the preachers were brought before
the Council, they were informed that such things would
not be allowed. Staprade, the chief offender and a
non-burgher, was banished, and Rothmann with the other
clergy who agreed with him were threatened with the
same fate if they persisted in declining to baptize infants.

They refused to obey the Council; they were promptly deposed, and their churches were closed against them. But the mass of the citizens were attached to Rothmann, and their attitude became too threatening for the Magistrates to maintain their uncompromising position. Rothmann was permitted to remain, and was allowed to preach in the Church of St. Servetius. The Lutheran Magistrates brought preachers into the town to occupy the other places of worship.

The Magistrates, Van der Wieck being the leading spirit among them, resolved to hold a public disputation on the subject of Baptism. They had brought to Münster the famous Humanist, Hermann von dem Busche, now a professor in Marburg and a distinguished defender of the Lutheran Reformation, and they counted on his known learning and eloquence to convince their fellow-citizens that the views of Rothmann were unscriptural. The conference was to be perfectly free. Roman Catholic theologians were invited, and took part. Rothmann appeared to defend his position. The invitations had been signed not only by the Magistrates, but by the heads of the "gilds" of the town.[1] Van der Wieck confessed that the result of the disputation was not what he expected. So far as the great mass of the people were concerned, Rothmann appeared to have the best of the argument, and he stood higher than ever in the estimation of the citizens. Rothmann, whose whole career shows that opposition made him more and more advanced, now began to dwell upon the wrongs of the commonalty and the duty of the rich to do much more for their poorer brethren than they did. He taught by precept as well as example. He lived an openly ascetic life, that he might abound in charity. His sermons and his life had an extraordinary effect on the rich as well as on the poor. Creditors forgave debtors, men placed sums of money in the hands of Rothmann for distribution. There was no enforced communism, but the example of the

---

[1] The details of this Disputation have been published by Detmer in the *Monatshefte der Commenius-Gesellschaft* (Berlin, 1900), ix. 273 *ff*.

primitive Church in Jerusalem was followed as far as possible. Among these thoroughgoing followers of Rothmann, a wealthy lady, the mother-in-law of Bernard Knipperdolling, was conspicuous.

The Magistrates became seriously alarmed at the condition of things. They knew that so long as they remained a Lutheran municipality, even nominally, the great Lutheran Princes, like Philip of Hesse and the Elector of Saxony, would protect them against their Romanist Bishop; but Lutherans and Romanists alike disliked and distrusted Anabaptists, and the imperial edict would surely be enforced against them sooner or later. Rothmann's preaching, which they could not control, and the power he exercised through the " gilds," made it impossible for them to maintain that Münster was a member of the confederacy of Lutheran cities. On the other hand, the news that Münster had practically become Anabaptist, spread far and wide among these persecuted people, who began to think that it was destined to be a conspicuous city of refuge, perhaps the Zion or New Jerusalem whose establishment Melchior Hoffmann had predicted. They gathered from all parts to place themselves under the protection of its walls. The great majority naturally came from the Netherlands, where the persecution was hottest. The refugees were almost all *Melchiorites*—men who looked for a speedy termination of their sufferings in the establishment of the kingdom of God upon the earth; and the majority of them were Dutch *Melchiorites*, men to whom freedom was a tradition, ready to fight for it, disciples of Jan Matthys, who had taught them to abandon the doctrine of passive resistance so universally held by all sections of the earlier Anabaptists.[1] Rothmann had long been acquainted with the books and tracts of Hoffmann, and had great sympathy with them. He as well as the Magistrates foresaw trouble for himself and for the city. He went the length of advising friends who did not share his opinions to leave the town; for himself, his manifest duty appeared to be

---

[1] Cf., above, ii. 235 *ff*.

to risk all on behalf of the poor people whom God had given into his hand.

The last months of 1532 saw Rothmann and the Lutheran Town Council facing each other with growing mutual suspicion. On Dec. 8th, a journeyman smith, Johann Schröder, began preaching Anabaptist doctrines in the churchyard of St. Lambert's, and challenged the Lutheran pastor, Fabricius, to a disputation. This was more than the Town Council could endure. They prohibited Rothmann preaching, and declared that they withdrew their protection—a sentence of virtual outlawry (Dec. 11th). He calmly told the messenger of the Council that he depended on the help of higher powers than his masters, and preached publicly in the Church of St. Servatius. Schröder had begun to preach again, and was apprehended. The " gild " of the smiths rose, and, headed by their officials, forced the Council to release their comrade. The Anabaptists and Rothmann had won a notable triumph, which was soon widely known. Banished Anabaptist pastors returned to the town.

Events marched quickly thereafter. Bartholomaeus Boekbinder and Willem de Kuiper, sent by Jan Matthys, appeared in Münster (Jan. 5th, 1533). We can infer what their message was from what followed. Rothmann denounced the Council and its Lutheran preachers. Riots were the consequence, many of the rioters being women, among whom the nuns of the Überwasser convent were conspicuous. It was declared that all believers ought to be rebaptized, and that a list of the faithful ought to be made. The document contained fourteen hundred names within eight days. The mass of the people enthusiastically believed in the near approach of the Day of the Lord.

Soon afterwards (Jan. 13th, 1533), Jan Bockelson (John of Leyden) entered the town. He was the favourite disciple and *alter ego* of Jan Matthys. He brought with him the famous Twenty-one Articles, and called upon the faithful to unite themselves into a compact organisation pledged to carry them out. He was received with enthusiasm.

The Council, feeling their helplessness, appealed to the Bishop, who contented himself with ordering them to execute the imperial mandate against Anabaptists. He was as much incensed against the Lutherans as against the Anabaptists, and hoped that the two parties would destroy themselves. Within the town, Anabaptists fought with the combined Evangelicals and Romanists, and on two occasions the tumults were succeeded by truces which guaranteed full liberty of worship to all persons (Jan. 28th and Feb. 9th). Then the Council abandoned the struggle. The principal Burgomaster, Tylbeck, was baptized, and Van der Wieck, with many of the principal citizens, left the town. Van der Wieck fell into the hands of the Bishop, who slaughtered him barbarously.

A new Council, entirely Anabaptist, was elected, with Bernard Knipperdolling and Gerhard Kibbenbroick, a leading merchant, as Burgomasters (Feb. 28th). The complete rule of the Anabaptists had begun. This date also marks the beginning of the investment of the city by the Bishop's troops. It should never be forgotten, as it frequently is, that during the *whole* period of Anabaptist domination in Münster the town was undergoing the perils of a siege, and that military considerations *had* to be largely kept in mind. Nor should it be forgotten that during its existence the Bishop's troops were murdering in cold blood every Anabaptist they could lay their hands on.

Jan Matthys himself had come to Münster some time in February, urged thereto by a letter from Bockelson, and the citizens had become accustomed to see the long lean figure of the prophet, with his piercing eyes and flowing black beard, pass to and fro in their streets. They had learned to hang breathless on his words as his sonorous voice repeated the message which the Lord had given him to utter, or described the visions which had been vouchsafed to him. When an Anabaptist Council ruled the city they were but the mouthpiece of the prophet. His reign was brief, but while it lasted he issued command after command.

Separation from the world was one of the ideas he dwelt upon in his addresses; and to him this meant that no unbelievers, no unbaptized, could remain within the walls of an Anabaptist city. The command went forth that all adults must be baptized or leave the town. It is scarcely to be wondered that, with the great likelihood of falling into the hands of the Bishop's soldiers as soon as they got beyond the walls, the great majority of those who had not yet received the seal of the new communion submitted to the ceremony. They were marched to the market-place, where they found "three or more" Anabaptist preachers, each with a great vessel full of water before them. The neophytes knelt down, received the usual admonition, and a dish of water was thrice emptied on their heads in the name of the Father, the Son, and the Holy Ghost. This done, they went to the Burgomaster's house and had their names entered on the roll.[1]

It was also by Matthys' orders that what is called the communism of Münster was begun. The duty of systematic and brotherly charity had from the first been an outstanding one among the Anabaptists. Like all other principles which find immediate outcome in action, this one of brotherly love had found many ways of taking actual shape. In a few of the smaller sections of the brethren it had appeared in the form of communism so far as food and raiment went. In some of the communities in Moravia the Brethren subscribed to a common fund out of which common meals were provided; and these payments were compulsory. We have seen how Rothmann's sermons had produced an extraordinary outburst of benevolence in Münster before the coming of the prophets.

[1] *Meister Heinrich Gresbeck's Bericht von der Wiedertaufe in Münster*, p. 29 (edited by Cornelius for *Die Geschichtsquellen des Bisthums Münster*, vol. ii., Münster, 1853).

It does not appear that Matthys' commands went further than the exhortations of Rothmann. Münster was a beleaguered city. When the siege began it contained about seventeen hundred men, between five and six thousand women, besides thousands of children. The largest proportion of these were refugees. It is evident that numbers could not support themselves, but were absolutely dependent upon the charity of their neighbours. The preachers invited the faithful to give up their money, and what provisions they could spare to feed the poverty striken. Large numbers thus appealed to brought all their portable property; others gave part; some refused, and were denounced publicly. The provisions stored in the monasteries or in private houses abandoned by their proprietors—were taken for the common good. When the siege had lasted long, and the enemy were deliberately starving the inhabitants into surrender, the communism in food became stricter, as is the case in any beleaguered fortress. No attempt was ever made to institute a thoroughgoing communism. What existed at first was simply an abundant Christian charity enforced by public opinion,[1] and latterly a requisitioning of everything that could be used to support the whole population of a besieged city.

Jan Matthys did not long survive his coming to Münster. On the evening of the 4th of April, as he sat at supper in a friend's house, he was observed to spend long minutes in brooding. At last, sighing heavily, he was heard to ejaculate, "Loved Father, not my will but Thine be done." He rose quietly from his seat, shook hands with all his companions, solemnly kissed each one; then left the house in silence, accompanied by his wife. Next day with about twenty companions he went out by one of the gates of the city, fell fiercely on the enemy, was overpowered by numbers, and received his death-stroke.

---

[1] Cf. *Die Münsterische Apologie*, printed by Cornelius in his *Berichte der Augenzeugen über das münsterische Wiedertäuferreich*, p. 457 (*Geschichts- quellen des Bisthums Münster*, vol. ii.).

A religious enthusiast and a singularly straightforward and courageous man!

His death depressed the defenders of Münster greatly; but they were rallied by the persuasive eloquence of Jan Bockelson, the favourite disciple of the dead prophet. It was under the leadership of Bockelson—Jan of Leyden he was called—that the Town Council of Münster was abolished; that twelve elders were chosen to rule the people; that Jan himself became king, and had his Court; that the old miracle plays were revived, etc. The only one of the many actions of this highly talented and eloquent young Dutchman which need concern us was the institution of polygamy, for which he seems to have been almost solely responsible.

Polygamy is the one dark stain on the Anabaptists of Münster, and one that is ineffaceable. Not unnaturally, yet quite unjustly, the fact of its institution has been used continually to blacken the character of the whole movement. It was an episode, a lamentable one, in the history of Anabaptism in Münster; it had nothing to do with the brethren outside the town. The whole question presents difficulties which, with our present information, cannot be removed. That men whose whole past lives had been examples of the most correct moral behaviour, and who had been influenced by deep and earnest religious feelings, should suddenly (for it was sudden) have given the lie to their own previous teaching and to the tenets of every separate section of Anabaptism, that they should have sullied the last few months of an heroic and desperate defence within a doomed city by the institution of polygamy, is an insoluble puzzle.[1]

We are not now dependent for our knowledge of

---

[1] By far the best and most impartial discussion of the institution of polygamy in Münster—one that is based on the very widest examination of contemporary documentary evidence—is that of Dr. Detmer, *Ueber die Auffassung von der Ehe und die Durchführung der Vielweiberei in Münster während der Täuferherrschaft* (Münster, 1904). It forms the third of his *Bilder aus den religiösen und sozialen Unruhen in Münster während des 16 Jahrhunderts.*

the Anabaptist movement on the writings of embitteied
opponents, or upon such tainted sources as confessions of
martyrs wrung from them under torture. The diligence
of archæologists has exhumed a long list of writings of
the leaders in the rising. They give us trustworthy
accounts of the opinions and teachings of almost every
sect classed under the common name. We know what
they thought about all the more important matters which
were in controversy during the sixteenth century—what
they taught about Free Will, Original Sin, Justification,
the Trinity, the Person of Christ, and so on. We have
clear glimpses of the kind of lives they led—a genuinely
pious, self-denying, Christian walk and conversation. Their
teaching was often at variance with the Romanist and
the Lutheran doctrinal confessions; but they never varied
from the moral life which all Christians are called upon
to live. Their writings seldom refer to marriage; but
when they do it is always to bear witness to the universal
and deeply rooted Christian sentiment that marriage is a
sacred and unbreakable union of one man with one
woman. Nay more, one document has descended to us
which bears testimony to the teaching of the Anabaptists
within the beleaguered city only a few weeks before the
proclamation of polygamy. It is entitled *Bekentones des
globens und lebens der gemein Criste zu Monster*,[1] and was
meant to be an answer to calumnies circulated by their
enemies. It contains a paragraph on Marriage which is
a clear and distinct assertion that the only Christian
marriage is the unbreakable union of one man with one
woman.[2]

---

[1] The tract is to be found in Cornelius, *Berichte der Augenzeugen über
das münsterische Wiedertäuferreich*, which forms the second volume of
Die Geschichtsquellen des Bisthums Münster (pp. 445 ff.).

[2] "Die ehe, sagen wir und halten mit der Schrift, das sie ist eins mans
und weips vorgaderong und vorpflichtong in dem Herrn . . . Got hot den
menchen von anfanck geschaffen, ein man und weip hat Er sie geschaffen,
di peide in den heiligen estant (ehestat) voreiniget, dos di peide zwo sellen
und ein fleische solen sein. Und mage also kein mensche scheiden selche
voreinigong" (pp. 457, 458).

It is true that the Anabaptist thought of " separation,"
when carried out in its most extreme way and to its
utmost logical consequences, struck a blow at the sanctity
of the marriage tie.   All taught that the " believer," *i.e*
he or she who had been rebaptized, ought to keep
themselves separate from the " world," *i.e.* those who had
not submitted to rebaptism; and in the more extreme
sects it was alleged that this meant that spouses ought
not to cohabit with " unbelieving " partners.   This was
held and practised among the *Melchiorites,* and was stated
in its extremest form in the Twenty-one Rules sent to
Münster by Jan Matthys by the hand of Bockelson.   They
contained two prescriptions—one for the unmarried,
which exhorted them only to marry in the Lord ; another
for the married, which implies that marriage contracted
between husband and wife before rebaptism ought to be
repeated.   This meant that marriages contracted by
persons yet " in the world " were not valid, and, of course,
destroyed the sanctity of all marriages outside the circle
of the brethren.   But when a *Melchiorite* at Strassburg,
Klaus Frey, whose wife was not an Anabaptist, carried
out the principle to its logical consequences and married
an Anabaptist woman, his " unbelieving" wife being alive,
he was promptly excommunicated.

When the information to be gathered from the various
sources is combined, what took place in Münster seems to
have been as follows.   Sometime in July (1534), John
Bockelson summoned the preachers, Rothmann at their
head, and the twelve elders to meet him in the *Rathaus.*
There he propounded to them his proposal to inaugurate
polygamy, and argued the matter with them for eight
successive days.   We are told that Rothmann and the
preachers opposed the scheme in a determined manner.
The arguments used by the prophet—arguments of the
flimsiest nature—have also been recorded.   He dwelt on
the necessity of accepting certain biblical expressions in
their most literal sense, and in giving them their widest
application.   He insisted especially on the command of

30**

God, *Be fruitful, and multiply, and replenish the earth*, he brought forward the example of the patriarchs and other examples of polygamy from the Old Testament; he went the length of saying that when St. Paul insisted that bishops must be husbands of one wife, the phrase implied that all who were not bishops were free to take more than one; he dwelt on the special conditions existing among the population within the town,—the number of male refugees, either unmarried or who had left their wives behind them in the places from which they had fled; the disproportionate number of women (more than three women for every man),—and the difficulties thereby created to prevent them from obeying the command of God to be fruitful and increase; and he urged that in their present condition the command of God could only be obeyed by means of polygamy.

In the end he brought preachers and elders round to his opinion; and in spite of opportunities given them for revolt, they remained steadfast to it. They preached upon its advantages for three days to the people in the Cathedral square; and it was Rothmann who proclaimed the decree commanding polygamy to the people. How were the preachers persuaded to forego their opposition? What one of the threadbare arguments used by the prophet convinced them? Had he proclaimed polygamy as a divine command received by him as a prophet, we might imagine the preachers and people, such was the exalted state of their minds, receiving it with reverence; but the prophet did not announce that he had received any such message. He relied solely upon his arguments. They did not convince all the people. The proclamation of polygamy awoke violent protests upon the part of the native townsmen, who, headed by a " master-smith " named Möllenbecke, felt that they would rather hand over the city to the Bishop's forces than live in a polygamist society, and the revolt was almost successful; but the preachers stood firm in their support of the prophet and of his polygamy; and it was the women who were mainly instrumental in causing the revolt to be a failure.

If we are to judge by the use made of it in Rothmann's *Restitution*,[1] which defends the introduction of the new marriage laws, the preachers seem to have been most impressed by the argument which dwelt on the condition of the city—the large proportion of men whose wives were in the towns they had abandoned to take refuge in Münster, and the great multitude of women. It is just possible that it was this economic argument that affected both them and the prophet himself. This is the view taken by such writers as Kautsky, Belfort Bax, and Heath. The explanation is confirmed by the fact that the decree was more than a proclamation of polygamy. It provided that *all* marriageable men must take wives, and that *all* women must be under the care of a husband. The laws against sexual irregularity were as strong during the reign of polygamy as before its introduction. But there is this to be said against it, that the town of Münster, notwithstanding its abnormal conditions, was singularly pure in life, and that polygamy, so far from improving the moral condition, made it distinctly worse.

Detmer, whose opinions are always worthy of respect, believes than Jan of Leyden had fallen violently in love with the young, beautiful, and intellectual Divara, the widow of Jan Matthys, and that, as he could not marry her apart from polygamy, he persuaded his preachers and elders to consent to his proposals. His wonderful magnetic influence overbore their better judgment.

What is evident is that the decree of polygamy was suddenly conceived and forced upon the people. If Jan of Leyden [2] took no share in its proclamation, he set the

---

[1] The *Restitution*, written by Rothmann and Kloprys in conjunction with Jan of Leyden and the elders, is published in Bouterwek, *Literatur und Geschichte der Wiedertäufer*; marriage and polygamy are treated in sections 14–16.

[2] Jan Bockelson, commonly called Jan van Leyden, was the illegitimate son of a village magistrate, and was born near Leyden in 1510. After a brief time of education at a village school he was apprenticed to a tailor,

people an example of obedience. He promptly married
Divara as soon as it was lawful to do so. He used the
ordinance to strengthen his position. His other wives—
he had sixteen in all—were the daughters or near relations
of the leaders in Münster. There is evidence to show
that his own character deteriorated rapidly under the new
conditions of life.

The siege of Münster went on during all these
months. The Bishop's soldiers attempted several assaults,
and were always beaten back. They seem latterly to
have relied on the power of hunger. The sufferings of
the citizens during the later weeks were terrible. At
length Heinrich Gresbeck, deserting to the besiegers' camp,
offered to betray the city to its enemies. He showed
them, by plans and models in clay, how to get through the
defences, and himself prepared the way for the Bishop's
soldiers to enter. The Anabaptists gathered for one last
desperate defence in the market-place, under the leadership
of Bernard Knipperdolling and Bernard Krechting, with
Rothmann by their side. When the band was reduced to
three hundred men, they capitulated on promise of safe-
conduct to leave the town. It is needless to say that the
bargain was not kept. Rothmann was believed to have
perished in the market-place. The city was given over
to pillage, and the streets were soon strewn with dead
bodies. Then a court was established to try the Anabaptist prisoners. The first woman to suffer was the

and in his leisure hours diligently educated himself. He travelled more
widely than artisans usually did during their year of wandering—visiting
England as well as most parts of Flanders. On his return home he
married the widow of a shipmaster, and started business as a merchant.
He was a prominent member of the literary "gilds" of his town, and had
a local fame as a poet and an actor. His conversion through Jan Matthys
changed his whole life; there is not the slightest reason to suppose that he
was not an earnest and honest adherent of the Anabaptist doctrines as
taught by Matthys. He is described as strikingly handsome, with a fine
sonorous voice. He had remarkable powers of organisation. His whole
brief life reveals him to be a very remarkable man. He was barely
twenty-five when he was tortured to death by the Bishop of Münster after
the capture of the town.

fair young Divara. She steadfastly refused to abjure, and met her fate in her own queenly way. No man who had been in any way prominent during the siege was allowed to escape death. Jan Bockelson, Bernard Knipperdolling, and Bernard Krechting were reserved to suffer the most terrible tortures that the diabolical ingenuity of mediæval executioners could devise. It was long believed that Rothmann had escaped, and that he had got away to Rostock or to Lübeck ; more than one person was arrested on the suspicion of being the famous preacher of Münster —" a short, dark man, with straight brown hair," was his description in the Lübeck handbills.

The horrible fate of Münster did not destroy the indomitable Anabaptists. Menno Simons (b. 1496 or 1505 at Witmarsum, a village near Franecker), " a man of integrity, mild, accommodating, patient of injuries, and so ardent in his piety as to exemplify in his own life the precepts he gave to others," spent twenty-five laborious years in visiting the scattered Anabaptist communities and uniting them in a simple brotherly association. He purged their minds of the apocalyptic fancies taught by many of their later leaders under the influence of persecution, inculcated the old ideas of non-resistance, of the evils of State control over the Church, of the need of personal conversion, and of adult baptism as its sign and seal. From his labours have come all the modern Baptist Churches.

CHAPTER III.

SOCINIANISM.[1]

THE fathers of the Socinian Church were the two Sozzini, uncle and nephew, Lelio and Fausto, both natives of the town of Siena.

The uncle, Lelio Sozzini (b. 1525), was by profession a lawyer. He was a man of irreproachable moral life, a Humanist by training, a student of the classics and also of theology. He was thoroughly dissatisfied with the condition of the Romish Church, and early began to entertain grave doubts about some of its leading doctrinal positions. He communicated his views to a select circle of friends. Notwithstanding the precautions he had taken, he became suspected. Cardinal Caraffa had persuaded Pope Paul III. to consent to the reorganisation of the Inquisition in 1542, and Italy soon became a very unsafe place for any suspected person. Lelio left Siena in 1547, and spent the remaining portion of his life in travelling in those lands which had accepted the Lutheran or the Reformed faith. He made the acquaintance of all the leading Protestant theologians, including Melanchthon and Calvin. He kept up an extensive correspondence

---

[1] SOURCES : *Bibliotheca Fratrum Polonorum* (Amsterdam, 1656) i. ii. *Racovian Catechism* (London, 1818).

LATER BOOKS : Fock, *Der Socinianismus nach seiner Stellung in der Gesammtentwicklung des christlichen Geistes, nach seinem historischen Verlauf und nach seinem Lehrbegriff dargestellt* (Kiel, 1847) ; A Ritschl, *Jahrbücher f. deutsche Theologie*, xiii. 268 *ff.*, 283 *ff.* ; *A critical History of the Christian Doctrine of Justification and Reconciliation* (Edinburgh, 1872) ; Dilthey, *Archiv f. Geschichte d. Philos.* vi. ; Harnack, *History of Dogma*, vii. 118 *ff.* (London, 1899).

with them, representing his own personal theological opinions in the form of questions which he desired to have solved for him. From Calvin's letters we can learn that the great theologian had grave doubts about the moral earnestness of his Italian correspondent, and repeatedly warned him that he was losing hold on the saving facts of heart religion.

All the while Sozzini seems to have made up his mind already on all the topics introduced into his correspondence, and to have been communicating his views, on pledge of secrecy, to the small communities of Italian refugees who were settled in Switzerland. He can scarcely be blamed for this secretiveness; toleration, as the sad example of the burning of Servede had shown, was not recognised to be a Christian principle among the Churches of the Reformation. Lelio died at Zurich in 1562 without having published his opinions, and without his neighbours and hosts being aware of his real theological position.

He bequeathed all his property, including his books and his manuscripts, to his nephew, Fausto, who had remained at Siena. This nephew was the founder of the Socinian Church.

Fausto Sozzini (b. 1539) was, like his uncle, a man of irreproachable life, a lawyer, a diligent and earnest student, fond of theology, and of great force of character. How early he had come to think as his uncle had done, is unknown. Report affirms that after he had received his uncle's books and papers, and had given sufficient time to their study, he left Italy, visited the places where Lelio had gathered small companies of secret sympathisers, to confirm them in the faith. His uncle had visited Poland twice, and Fausto went there in 1579. He found that the anti-Trinitarians there had no need to conceal their opinions. The Transylvanian Prince, Stephen Báthory, protected them, and they had in the town of Krakau their own church, school, and printing-press. But the sect as a whole was torn by internal divisions. Fausto bent his whole energies to overcome these differences.

Before his arrival in Poland he had published two books, which are interesting because they show the pathway by which Fausto arrived at his theological conclusions. He started not with the doctrines of the Trinity or of the Person of Christ, but with the doctrine of the Atonement —a fact to be kept in mind when the whole Socinian system of theology is examined.

He believed that the real cause of the divisions which wasted the sect was that the Polish Unitarians were largely Anabaptists. They insisted that no one could be a recognised member of the community unless he was rebaptized. They refused to enroll Fausto Sozzini himself, and excluded him from the Sacrament of the Supper, because he would not submit to rebaptism. They declared that no member of their communities could enter the magistracy, or sue in a civil court, or pay a war tax. They disagreed on many small points of doctrine, and used the ban very freely against each other. Sozzini saw that he could not hope to make any progress in his attempts to unite the Unitarians unless he was able to purge out this Anabaptist leaven. His troubles can be seen in his correspondence, and in some of his smaller tracts in the first volume of the *Bibliotheca Fratrum Polonorum*.[1] In spite of the rebuffs he met with, he devoted all his energies to the thankless task of furthering union, and in the end of his days he had the satisfaction of seeing that he had not laboured in vain. Shortly before his death, a synod held at Krakau (1603) declared that rebaptism was not necessary for entrance into a Unitarian community. Many of the lesser differences had been got rid of earlier. The literary activity of Sozzini was enormous: books and pamphlets flowed from his untiring pen, all devoted to the enforcing or explaining the Socinian theology. It is not too much to say that the inner history of the Unitarian communities in Poland from 1579 until his death in 1604 is contained in his voluminous correspondence. The united Unitarians of

[1] Pp. 397 *ff.*

Poland took the name of the *Polish Brethren*; and from this society what was known as Socinian theology spread through Germany (especially the Rhineland), Switzerland, and England. Its principles were not formulated in a creed until 1642, when the *Racovian Catechism* was published. It was never formally declared to be the standard of the Unitarian Church, but its statements are universally held to represent the views of the older Socinians.

Socinianism, unlike the great religious movement under the guidance of Luther, had its distinct and definite beginning in a criticism of doctrines, and this must never be forgotten if its true character is to be understood. We have already seen [1] that there is no trace of any intellectual difficulties about doctrines or statement of doctrines in Luther's mind during the supreme crisis in his spiritual history. Its whole course, from the time he entered the Erfurt convent down to the publication of the Augsburg Confession, shows that the spiritual revolt of which he was the soul and centre took its rise from something much deeper than any mere criticism of the doctrines of the mediæval Church, and that it resulted in something very much greater than a reconstruction of doctrinal conceptions. The central thing about the Protestant Reformation was that it meant a rediscovery of religion as *faith*, " as a relation between person and person, higher therefore, than all reason, and living not upon commands and hopes, but on the power of God, and apprehending in Jesus Christ the Lord of heaven and earth as Father." [2] The Reformation started from this living experience of the believing Christian, which it proclaimed to be the one fundamental fact in Christianity—something which could never be proved by argument, and could never be dissolved away by speculation.

On the contrary, the earliest glimpse that we have of Lelio Sozzini is his meeting with friends to discuss and cast doubts upon such doctrines as the Satisfaction of

[1] Cf. i. 426 *ff*.   [2] Harnack, *History of Dogma*, vii. 167.

Christ, the Trinity, and others like them.[1] Socinianism maintained to the end the character with which it came into being. It was from first to last a criticism and attempted reconstruction of doctrines.

This is sufficient of itself to discount the usual accounts which Romanist controversialists give of the Socinian movement, and of its relation to the Protestant Reformation. They, and many Anglicans who have no sympathy with the great Reformation movement, are accustomed to say that the Socinian system of doctrines is the legitimate deduction from the principles of the Reformation, and courageously carries out the rationalist conceptions lurking in all Protestant theology. They point to the fact that many of the early Presbyterians of England and Puritans of America have furnished a large number of recruits to the Unitarian or Socinian ranks. They assert that the central point in the Socinian theology is the denial of the Divinity of our Lord, which they allege is the logical outcome of refusing to accept the Romanist doctrine of the Mass and the principle of ecclesiastical tradition.

The question is purely historical, and can only be answered by examining the sources of Socinian theology and tracing it to its roots. The result of such an examination seems to show that, while Socinianism did undoubtedly owe much to Humanism, and to the spirit of critical inquiry and keen sense of the value of the individual which it fostered, most of its distinguishing theological conceptions are mediæval. It laid hold on the leading principles of the Scotist-Pelagian theology, which were extremely popular in the fifteenth and beginning of the sixteenth centuries, and carried them out to their logical consequences. In fact, most of the theological principles of Socinian theology are more akin to those of the Jesuit dogmatic— which is the prolongation of Scotism into modern times— than they are to the theology of Luther or of Calvin. It is, of course, to be remembered that by discarding the authority of the Church the Socinians are widely separated

[1] Cf. p. 427.

from both Scotists and Jesuits. Still the roots of Socinian theology are to be found in the Scotist doctrines of God and of the Atonement, and these two doctrines are their starting-point, and not the mere negation of the Divinity of Christ.

In three most important conceptions the Socinian thought is distinctly mediæval, and mediæval in the Scotist way.

Their idea of *faith* is intellectual. It is *assensus* and not *fiducia*. "In Scripture," says the Racovian Catechism, " the *faith* is most perfectly *taught*, that God exists and that He recompenses. This, however, and nothing else, is the faith that is to be directed to God and Christ." It is afterwards described as the way in which one must adjust himself to the known commands and promises of God ; and there is added that this faith " both makes our obedience more acceptable and well-pleasing to God, and supplies the defects of our obedience, provided it be sincere and earnest, and brings it about that we are justified by God." This is good Scotist doctrine. These theologians were accustomed to declare that all that the Christian needs is to have faith in God as the recompenser (*i.e.* to assent to the truth that God does recompense), and that with regard to all the other doctrines of the Church implicit faith (*i.e.* submission to the Church's teaching) is enough. Of course the extreme individualism of the Socinians coloured their conception of faith ; they cannot accept an implicit faith ; their assent to truth must always be explicit ; what they assent to must recommend itself to their individual reason. They cannot assent to a round of truths which are presented to them by the Church, and receive them implicitly on the principle of obedience to authority. But what is to be observed here is that the Socinian type of faith is always assent to truths which can be stated in propositional form ; they have no idea of that faith which, to use Luther's phrase, throws itself upon God. They further declare, quite in accordance with Scotist teaching, that men are justified because of their *actual* obedience to the *known* commands and promises of

God. There is not a trace of the Evangelical attitude. The accordance with Scotist theology descends to very minute particulars, did space permit to trace it.

The Socinian conception of *Scripture* corresponds to their idea of faith. The two thoughts of Scripture and saving faith, as has been already said,[1] always correspond in mediæval theology they are primarily intellectual and propositional; in Reformation thinking they are, in the first instance, experimental and personal. The Socinian conception allies itself with the mediæval, and discards the Reformation way of regarding both faith and Scripture. With the Socinians as with mediæval theologians, Scripture is the divine source of information about doctrines and morals; they have no idea of Scripture as a means of grace, as the channel of a personal communion between God and His trusting people. But here as elsewhere the new individualism of the Socinians compels them to establish both the authority and the dogmatic contents of Scripture in a way different from their mediæval predecessors. They had rejected altogether the authority of the Church, and they could not make use of the thought to warrant either the authority of Scripture or a correct interpretation of its contents. In the place of it they put what they called *reason*. " The use of right reason (*rectæ rationis*) is great in things which pertain to salvation, since without it, it is impossible either to grasp with certainty the authority of Scripture, or to understand those things that are contained in it, or to deduce some things from other things, or, finally, to recall them to put them to use (*ad usum revocari*)." The *certitudo sacrarum litterarum* is accordingly established, or attempted to be proved, by a series of external proofs which appeal to the ordinary reasoning faculties of man. The Reformation conception of the Witness of the Spirit, an essential part of its doctrine of Scripture, finds no place in Socinian theology. They try to establish the authority of Scripture without any appeal to faith; the Confessions of the Reformation

[1] Cf. i. 461.

do not recognise any infallibility or divine authority which is otherwise apprehended than by faith. The Reformation and the Socinian doctrines are miles apart; but the Socinian and the mediæval approach each other closely. It is somewhat difficult to know what books the older Socinians recognise as their rule of faith. They did not accept the Canon of the mediæval Church. They had no difficulty about the New Testament; but the references to the Old Testament in the Racovian Catechism are very slight: its authority is guaranteed for them by the references to it in the New Testament.

When we turn to the Socinian statements about *God*, and to their assertions about the *nature and meaning of the Work of Christ*, we find the clearest proof of their mediæval origin. The Scotist theology is simply reproduced, and cleared of its limitations.

A fundamental conception of God lay at the basis of the whole Scotist theology. God, it maintained, could best be defined as *Dominium Absolutum*; man as set over against God they described as an individual free will. If God be conceived as simply *Dominium Absolutum*, we can never affirm that God *must* act in any given way; we may not even say that He is bound to act according to moral considerations. He is high above all considerations of any kind. He does not will to act in any way because it is right; and action is right because God wills to act in that way. There can be neither metaphysical nor moral necessity in any of God's actions or purposes. This Scotist idea, that God is the absolutely arbitrary one, is expresssd in the strongest language in the Racovian Catechism. " It belongs to the nature of God that He has the right and supreme power to decree whatsoever He wills concerning all things and concerning us, even in those matters with which no other power has to do; for example, He can give laws, and appoint rewards and penalties according to His own judgment, to our thoughts, hidden as these may be in the innermost recesses of our hearts."

If this thought, that God is simply *Dominium Absolutum*, be applied to explain the nature and meaning of the work of Christ, of the Atonement, it follows at once that there can be no real necessity for that work; for all necessity, metaphysical or moral, is derogatory to the *Dominium Absolutum*, which is God. If the Atonement has merit in it, that is only because God has announced that He means to accept the work of Christ as meritorious, and that He will therefore free men from the burden of sin on account of what Christ, the Saviour, has done. It is the announced *acceptation* of God which makes the work of Christ meritorious. A *meritorious* work has nothing in its nature which makes it so. To be meritorious simply means that the work so described will be followed by God's doing something in return for its being done, and this only because God has made this announcement. God could have freed men from the guilt and punishment due for sin without the work of Christ; He could have appointed a human mediator if He had so willed it; He might have pardoned and accepted man as righteous in His sight without any mediator at all. He could have simply pardoned man without anything coming between His act of pardon and man's sin. This being the case, the Scotist theologians argued that it might seem that the work of Christ, called the Atonement, was entirely superfluous; it is, indeed, superfluous as far as reason is concerned; it can never be justified on rational grounds. But, according to the dogmatic tradition of the Church, confirmed by the circle of the Sacraments, God has selected this mode of getting rid of the sin and guilt of man. He has announced that He will *accept* this work of Christ, Atonement, and therefore the Scotist theologians declared the Atonement must be believed in and seen to be the divinely appointed way of salvation. Erasmus satirised the long arguments and hypotheses of the Scotist theologians when he enumerated among the questions which were highly interesting to them: "Could God have taken the form of a woman, a devil, an ass, a gourd, or a stone? How could a gourd have preached, done miracles, hung on the Cross ? " [1]

It is manifest that this idea of *Dominium Absolutum* is simply the conception of the extremest individualism applied to God instead of being used to describe man. If we treat it anthropomorphically, it comes to this, that the relation of God to man is that of an infinite Individual Will set over against a number of finite individual wills. If this view be taken of the relations between God and man, then God can never be thought of as the Moral Ruler in a moral commonwealth, but only as a private individual face to face with other individuals; and the relations between God and man must be discussed from the standpoint of private and not of public law. When wrong-doing is regarded under the scheme of public law, the ruler can never treat it as an injury done to himself, and which he can forgive because he is of a kindly nature; he must consider it an offence against the whole community of which he is the public guardian. On the other hand, when offences are considered under a scheme of private law, they are simply wrongs done to a private person who, as an individual, may forgive what is merely a debt due to himself. In such a case the wrong-doer may be forgiven without infringing any general moral principle.

The Socinians, following the mediæval Scotist theologians, invariably applied the principles of private law to the relations between God and man. God, the *Dominium Absolutum*, the Supreme Arbitrary Will, was never regarded as the Moral Ruler in a moral commonwealth where subjects and rulers are constrained by the same moral laws. Sins are simply private debts due by the individual finite wills to the One Infinite Will. From such premises the Scotists deduced the conclusion that the Atonement was unnecessary; there they stopped, they could not say that there was no such thing as Atonement, for the dogmatic tradition of the Church prevented them. The Socinians had thrown overboard the

[1] Erasmus, *Opera Omnia*, iv. 465.

thought of a dogmatic tradition which had to be respected even when it appeared to be irrational. If the Atonement was not necessary, that meant to them that it did not exist; they simply carried out the theological premises of the Scotist-Pelagian mediæval theologians to their legitimate consequences.

In these three important conceptions—faith, Scripture, the nature of God, involving the character of His relations to man—the Socinians belong to a mediæval school of thought, and have no sympathy whatever with the general principles which inspired Reformation theological thinking.

But the Socinians were not exclusively mediæval; they owed much to the Renaissance. This appears in a very marked manner in the way in which they conceived the very important religious conception of the *Church*. It is a characteristic of Socinian theology, that the individual believer is considered without much, if any, reference to the Church or community of the saved. This separates the Socinians not only from mediæval Christians, but from all who belonged to the great Protestant Evangelical movement.

The mediæval Church always regarded itself, and taught men to look to it, as a religious community which came logically and really before the individual believer. It presented itself to men as a great society founded on a dogmatic tradition, possessing the Sacraments, and governed by an officially holy caste. The pious layman of the Middle Ages found himself within it as he might have done within one of its great cathedrals. The dogmatic tradition did not trouble him much, nor did the worldliness and insincerity often manifested by its official guardians. What they required of him was implicit faith, which really meant a decorous external obedience. That once rendered, he was comparatively free to worship within what was for him a great house of prayer. The hymns, the prayers, many of the sermons of the mediæval Church, make us feel that the Institution was for the mediæval Christian the visible symbol of a wide purpose of God, which embraced his individual life and guaranteed a repose which he could use in resting on the promises of God. The records of mediæval piety continually show us that the Church was etherealised into an assured and historical fellowship of believers into which the individual entered, and within which he found the assuring sense of fellowship. He left all else to the professional guardians of this ecclesiastical edifice. Probably such are the unspoken thoughts of thousands of devout men and women in the Roman and Greek communions to-day. They value the Church because it represents to them in a visible and historical way a fellowship with Christ and His saints which is the result of His redeeming work.

This thought is as deeply rooted in Reformation as in mediæval piety. The Reformers felt compelled to protest against the political form which the mediæval Church had assumed. They conceived that to be a degradation from its ideal. They saw the manifold abuses which the degradation had given rise to. But they always regarded visible Christendom as a religious community called into being by the work of Christ. They had always before them the thought of the Church of Christ as the fellowship which logically and really comes *before* the individual believer, the society into which the believer is brought; and this conception stood with them in close and reciprocal connection with the thought that Jesus, by His work of Atonement, had reconciled men with God, had founded the Church on that work of His, and, *within* it had opened for sinners the way to God. They protested against the political form which the Church had assumed; they never ceased to cling to the thought of the Catholic Church Visible which is founded on the redeeming work of Christ, and within which man finds the way of salvation. They described this Church in all their creeds and testimonies; they gave the marks which characterised it and manifested its divine origin; the thought was an essential part of their theology.

The Socinians never felt the need of any such con-

31**

ception. Jesus was for them only the teacher of a
superior kind of morality detailed in the commands and
promises of God; they looked to Him for that guidance
and impulse towards a moral self-culture which each man
can appropriate for himself without first coming into a
society which is the fellowship of the redeemed. Had
they ever felt the burden of sin as the Reformers felt it,
had they ever yearned for such a fellowship with Christ
as whole-hearted personal trust gives, or even for such as
comes in the sense of bodily contact in the Sacrament, had
they ever felt the craving to get in touch with their Lord
somehow or *anyhow*, they would never have been able to do
without this conception of a Church Catholic of some kind
or other. They never seemed to feel the need of it. The
Racovian Catechism was compelled to make some reference
to the kingly and priestly offices of Christ. It owed so
much to the New Testament. Its perfunctory sentences
show that our Lord was for the Socinians simply a
Prophet sent from God to proclaim a superior kind of
morality. His highest function was to communicate
knowledge to men, and perhaps to teach them by example
how to make use of it. They had no conception that
Jesus came to *do* something for His people, and that what
He *did* was much more valuable than what He said, however precious that might be. They were content to become
His scholars, the scholars of a teacher sent from God, and
to become members of His school, where His opinions were
known and could be learned. They had no idea that they
needed to be saved in the deeper sense of that word. They
have no need, therefore, for the conception of the Church;
what they did need and what they have is the thought of
a school of opinions to which they could belong.[1]

In this one thought they were equally far apart from

---

[1] A very full analysis of the contents of the Racovian Catechism is given
in Harnack's *History of Dogma*, vii. 137 ff., also in Fock, *Der Socinianismus*,
etc. ii. A. Ritschl has shown that the Unitarianism of the Socinians is simply
the legitimate conclusion from their theory of the nature of God and of the
work of Christ, in his two essays in the *Jahrbücher f. deutsche Theol.* xiii.
268 ff., 283 ff.

the circle of mediæval and of Reformation theological thinking. In most of their other theological conceptions their opinions were inherited from mediæval theology. They had little or no connection with Reformation theology or with what that represents—the piety of the mediæval Church.

BOOK VI.

THE COUNTER-REFORMATION.

CHAPTER I.

THE NECESSITY OF A REFORMATION OF SOME SORT UNIVERSALLY ADMITTED.[1]

In the end of the fifteenth and beginning of the sixteenth centuries the urgent need for a Reformation of the Church was recognised by all thoughtful men everywhere throughout western Europe, and was loudly expressed by almost everyone outside the circle of the influence of the Roman Curia. Statesmen and men of letters, nobles and burghers, great Churchmen as well as monks and parish priests—all bewailed the condition of the organised Christian life, and most of them recognised that the unreformed Papacy was

---

[1] SOURCES : Læmmer, *Monumenta Vaticana historiam ecclesiasticam seculi 16 illustrantia* (Freiburg i. B. 1861) ; Weiss, *Papiers d'État du Cardinal Perronet de Granvelle* (in the *Collection des documents inédits de l'Histoire de France, 1835–49*) ; Fiedler, *Relationen Venetianischer Botschaften über Deutschland und Oesterreich im 16ten Jahrhunderte* (in the *Fontes Rerum Austriacarum, Diplomatica et Acta*, xxx., Vienna, 1870) ; Friedenburg, *Nuntiaturberichte aus Deutschland, 1533–39* (Gotha, 1892–93) ; *Carteggio di Vittoria Colonna* (Rome, 1889).

LATER BOOKS : Marrenbrecher, *Geschichte der katholischen Reformation* (Nördlingen, 1880—only one volume published, which ends with 1534) ; also *Karl V. und die deutschen Protestanten* (Düsseldorf, 1865) ; Ranke, *Die römischen Päpste, ihre Kirche und ihr Staat im sechszehnten und siebzehenten Jahrhundert* ; Gothein, *Ignatius von Loyola und die Gegenreformation* (Halle, 1895) ; Philippson, *La Contre-Revolution religieuse du 16e siècle* (Brussels, 1884) ; Ward, *The Counter-Reformation* (London, 1889) ; Dupin, *Histoire de l'Église du 16e siècle* (Paris, 1701–13) ; Jerrold, *Vittoria Colonna* (London, 1906).

the running sore of Europe. The protest against the state of religion was not confined to individual outcries; it found expression in the States-General of France, in the Diet of Germany, and in the Parliament of England.

The complaints took many forms. One of the most universal was that the clergy, especially those of higher rank, busied themselves with everything save the one thing which specially belonged to them—the cure of souls. They took undue share in the government of the countries of Europe, and ousted the nobles from their legitimate places of rule. Clerical law-courts interfered constantly with the lives of burghers; and the clergy protested that they were not bound to obey the ordinary laws of the land. A brawling priest could plead the " benefit of clergy "; but a layman who struck a priest, no matter what the provocation, was liable to the dread penalty of excommunication. Their "right of sanctuary" was a perpetual encouragement to crime.[1] They and their claims menaced the quiet life of civilised towns and States. Constitutional lawyers, trained by Humanism to know the old imperial law codes of Theodosius and Justinian, traced these evils back to the interference of Canon Law with Civil, and that to the universal and absolute dominion of a papal absolutism. The Reformation desired, floated before the minds of statesmen as a reduction more or less thorough of the papal absolutism, and of the control exercised by the Pope and the clergy over the internal affairs of the State, even its national ecclesiastical regulations. The historical fact that the loosely formed kingdoms of the Middle Ages were being slowly transformed into modern States, perhaps furnished unconsciously the basis for this idea of a Reformation.

The same thought took another and more purely ecclesiastical form. The papal absolutism meant frequently that Italians received preferments all over western Europe, and supplanted the native clergy in the more important and richer benefices. Why should the Churches of Spain,

---

[1] Cf. *A Relation . . . of the Island of England . . . about the year 1500* (Camden Society, London, 1847), pp. 34–36, 86–89.

England, or France be ruled by Italian prelates, whether
resident or non-resident ? It was universally felt that
Roman rule meant a lack of spirituality, and was a source
of religious as well as of national degradation. Men
longed for a change, clergy as well as laity ; and the
thought of National Churches really independent of Rome,
if still nominally under the Western Obedience, filled the
minds of many Reformers.[1]

The early mediæval Church had been a stern preacher
of righteousness, had taught the barbarous invaders of
Europe lessons of pure living, honesty, sobriety ; it had
insisted that the clergy ought to be examples as well as
preachers ; Canon Law was full of penalties ordained to
check clerical vices. But it was notorious that the higher
clergy, whose duty it was to put the laws in execution,
were themselves the worst offenders. How could English
Bishops enforce laws against incontinence, when Wolsey,
Archbishop, Cardinal, and Legate, had made his illegitimate
daughter the Abbess of Salisbury ? What hope was there
for strict discipline when no inconsiderable portion of a
Bishop's annual income came from money paid in order
to practise clerical incontinence in security ? Reformers
demanded a reformation of clerical morals, beginning with
the Bishops and descending through all grades to monks
and nuns.[2]

[1] Cf. i. 36.

[2] This had been protested against for a century and a half, not merely by
individual moralists, but by such conventions of notables as the English
Parliament ; cf. *Rolls of Parliament,* ii. 313–14 ; *Item,* "prie la Commune que
comme autre foithz au Parlement tenuz a Wyncestre, supplie y fuist par la
Commune de remedie de ce que les Prelatz et Ordinares de Seint Esglise
pristrent sommes pecuniers de gentz de Seint Esglise et autres pur redemption de lour pecche de jour en jour, et an en an, de ce que ils tiendrent
overtement lours concubines ; et pur autres pecches et offenses a eux surmys,
dount peyne pecunier ne serroit pris de droit : Quele chose est cause, mein-
tenance et norisement de lour pecche, en overte desclandre, et mal ensample
de tut la Commune ; quele chose issint continue nient duement puny, est
desesploit au Roi et a tout le Roialme. Qe pleise a nostre Seigneur le Roi
ent ordeiner que touz tiels redemptions soient de tut ousteiz ; et que si nul
viegne encontre ceste Ordeinance, que le prenour encourge la somme del
double issint pris devers la Roi et cely que le paie eit mesme la peyne."

Humanism brought forward yet another conception of reform. It demanded either a thorough repudiation of the whole of Scholastic Theology and a return to the pure and simple " Christian Philosophy " of the Church of the first six centuries, or such a relaxation of that Scholastic as would afford room for the encouragement of the New Learning.

Lastly, a few pious souls, with the clear vision of God which purity and simplicity of heart and mind give declared that the Church had lost religion itself, and that the one reformation needed was the rediscovery of religion and the gracious enlightenment of the individual heart and conscience.[1]

The first conception of a reformation which looked for a cure of the evils which all acknowledged to the supremacy of the secular over ecclesiastical rule, may be seen in the reformation of the local Churches of Brandenburg and Saxony under Frederick of Brandenburg and William of Saxony. Archbishop Cranmer believed that the only way of removing the evils under which the Church of the later Middle Ages was groaning was to subordinate the ecclesiastical to the secular powers. The reformation of the Church of England under Henry VIII. carried out this idea to practical issue, but involved with it a nominal as well as a real destruction of the political unity of the mediæval Church. His actions were carefully watched and admired by many of the German Romanist Princes, who made more than one attempt, about the year 1540, to create a National Church in Germany under secular guidance, and remaining true to mediæval doctrine, hierarchy, and ritual.[2] The thought of a reformation of this kind was so familiar to men of the sixteenth century, that the probability of Henry VIII.'s separation from Rome was matter of discussion long before it had entered into the mind of that monarch.[3]

[1] Cf. i. 166, 213.   [2] Cf. vol. i. 140, 141, 378 ; vol. ii.

[3] *Letters and Papers, Foreign and Domestic, of the Reign of Henry VIII.*, iv., Preface, p. 485. Cf. Brown, *Fasciculus rerum expectendarum et fugiendarum* (1690), pp. 19, 20, for the speech of an English Bishop at Rome (Nov. 27th, 1425), saying that if the Curia does not speedily undertake the work of Reformation, the secular powers must interfere,

CHAPTER II.

THE SPANISH CONCEPTION OF A REFORMATION.[1]

§ 1. *The Religious Condition of Spain.*

THE country, however, where all these various conceptions of what was meant by a reformation of the Church were combined in one definite scheme of reform which was carried through successfully, was Spain. It is to that country one must turn to see what mediævalists, who were at the same time reformers, wished to effect, and what they meant by a reformation of the Church. It included a measure of secular control, a revival and enforcement of all canonical laws framed to purify the morals of the clergy, a measured accommodation with Humanism, a steady adherence to the main doctrines of the Scholastic Theology, the preservation in their entirety of the hierarchy, the rites and the usages of the mediæval Church, and a ruthless suppression of heresy. Spain furnishes the example of what has been called the Catholic Reformation.

In Spain, as nowhere else in mediæval Europe, the firm maintenance of the Christian religion and patriotism had been felt to be one and the same thing. The seven hundred years' war, which the Christians of Spain had waged with the Moors, had given strength and tenacity to their religious sentiments, and their experience as

---

[1] Lea, *Chapters from the Religious History of Spain* (Philadelphia, 1890); Prescott, *Ferdinand and Isabella* (London, 1887); V. de la Fuente, *Historia eclesiastica en Espana* (Madrid, 1873, etc.); Menendezy Palayo, *Los Heterodoxos Espanoles* (Madrid, 1880); Hefele, *The Cardinal Ximenes* (London, 1860); Paul Rousselot, *Les Mystiques Espagnols* (Paris, 1867).

Christians in daily battle with an enemy of alien race and alien faith, left to themselves in their Peninsula, cut off from the rest of Europe, had made them cling all the more closely to that visible solidarity of all Christian people which found expression in the mediæval conception of the mediæval Catholic Church. Spain had given birth to the great missionary monastic order of the Dominicans, —the leaders of an intellectual crusade against the penetrating influence of a Moslem pantheism (Averroism), —and to the great repressive agency of the Inquisition in its sternest and most savage form. It was Spain that was to furnish the Counter-Reformation, with its most devoted leader, Ignatius Loyola, and with its strongest body of combatants, the Society of Jesus which he founded.

It need scarcely be wondered at that it was in Spain that we find the earliest systematic attempts made to save the Church from the blindness and perversity of its rulers by the interposition of the secular authority to combat the deteriorating influence of the Roman Curia upon the local Church, and to restore discipline among the clergy. The Cortes of the various small kingdoms of the Spanish Peninsula repeatedly interfered to limit the overgrowth of clerical privileges, to insist on the submission of the clergy to the common law of the land, and to prevent the too great preponderance of clerical influence in secular administration. The ordinances of their Kings were used, time after time, to counteract the influence of harmful papal Bulls, and to prevent the interference of Italian ecclesiastics in the affairs of the Spanish Church. In the end of the fifteenth century the Spanish Bishops had been reduced to a state of dependence on the Crown ; all exercise of ecclesiastical authority was carefully watched ; the extent of ecclesiastical jurisdiction was specifically limited, and clerical courts were made to feel their dependence on the secular tribunals. The Crown wrung from the Papacy the right to see that piety and a zeal for religion were to be indispensable qualifications for clerical promotion. All this regulative zeal was preserved from being simply the attempts of politicians to control a rival power by certain fundamental elements in the national religious character, which expressed themselves in rulers as well as in the mass of their subjects. In Spain, more than in any other land, asceticism and mystical raptures were recognised to be the truest expression of genuine religious sentiment. Kings and commonalty alike shared in the firm belief that a real imitation of Christ meant to follow in the footsteps of the Man of Sorrows, who wandered about not knowing where to lay His head, and who was enabled to endure what was given Him to do and to suffer by continuous and rapt communion with the Unseen.

The ecclesiastical Reformer of Spain had all these elements to work upon, and they made his task comparatively easy.

§ 2. *Reformation under Ximenes.*

The consolidation of the Peninsula under Ferdinand and Isabella suggested a thorough reorganisation of the Spanish Church. The Crown extorted from the Papacy extraordinary powers to deal with the secular clergy and with the monasteries. The great Queen was determined to purge the Church of her realm of all that she deemed to be evil. She called to her councils three famous Churchmen in whom she had thorough confidence—the great Spanish Cardinal, Mendoza, her confessor, Fernando de Talavera, and Francesco Ximenes. It was Ximenes who sketched the plan and who carried through the reformation.

Francesco Ximenes de Cisneros, as he is called, had been a Franciscan monk devoted to the ideals of his order. He belonged to a poor family, and had somehow or other attracted the attention of Cardinal Mendoza, at whose instigation the Queen had made him her father-confessor (1492). She insisted on his accepting the dignity of Archbishop of Toledo (1495), and had selected him to carry out her plans for the organisation and purification of the Spanish Church. After his elevation to the arch-episcopal chair he gave the example of what he believed to be the true clerical life by following in the most literal way the maxims of St. Francis about self-denial, devotion, and ascetic life. He made these the ideal for the Spanish clergy; they followed where he led.

The Concordat of 1482 gave the Spanish Crown the right of "visitation" (held to involve the power to dismiss from office) and of nomination to benefices. Ximenes used these powers to the full. He "visited" the monasteries personally, and received full reports about the condition of the convents. He re-established in all of them monastic discipline of the strictest kind. The secular clergy were put to like proof. The secular power was invoked to sweep all opponents to reform from his path. His Queen protected him when the vacillations of the papal policy threatened to hinder his work. In the end, the Church in Spain secured a devoted clergy whose personal life was free from the reproaches justly levelled at the higher clergy of other lands.

Ximenes, having purified the morals of the Spanish clergy, next set himself to overcome their ignorance and lack of culture. In every Chapter within Castile and Aragon, two prebends were set apart for scholars, one of them for a student in Canon Law, and the other for an expert theologian. A special "visitation" of the clergy removed from their places all utterly ignorant persons. New schools of theology were instituted. In addition to the mediæval Universities of Salamanca and Valladolid, Ximenes founded one in Alcala, another in Seville, a third at Toledo. Alcala and Valladolid were the principal theological schools, and there, in addition to the older studies of Dogmatic Theology and Ethics, courses of lectures were given in Biblical Exegesis. The theology taught was that of Thomas Aquinas, to the exclusion of the later developments of Scholastic under John Duns Scotus and William of Occam. The Augustinian elements in Thomas were specially dwelt upon; and soon there arose a school of theologians who were called the New Thomists, who became very powerful, and were later the leading opponents of the Jesuit teachers. There was also an attempt to make use of the New Learning in the interest of the old theology. Ximenes collected at Alcala the band of scholars who under his superintendence prepared the celebrated Complutensian Polyglot.

The labours of Erasmus were sympathised with by the leaders of this Spanish movement. The Princes of the Church delighted to call themselves his friends. They prevented the Spanish monks from attacking him even when he struck hardest at the follies of the monastic life. He was esteemed at Court. The most prominent statesmen who surrounded Charles, the young Prince of the Netherlands, the King of Spain, called themselves Erasmians. Erasmus, if we are to believe what he wrote to them,—which is scarcely possible,—declared that the work in Spain under Ximenes followed the best type of a reformation in the Church.

But there was another and terrible side to this Spanish purification of the Church and of the clergy The Inquisition had been reorganised, and every opinion and practice strange to the mediæval Church was relentlessly crushed out of existence. This stern repression was a very real part of the Spanish idea of a reformation.

The Spanish policy for the renovation of the Church was not a reformation in the sense of providing room for anything new in the religious experience. Its sole aim was to requicken religious life within the limits which had been laid down during the Middle Ages. The hierarchy was to remain, the mediæval conceptions of priesthood and sacraments; the Pope was to continue to be the acknowledged and revered Head of the Church; "the sacred ceremonies, decrees, ordinances, and sacred usages" [1] were to be left untouched; the dogmatic theology of the

---

[1] Cf. paper read by Charles v. to the Estates of Germany at Worms —Wrede, *Deutsche Reichstagsakten unter Kaiser Karl v.* (Gotha, 1896) ii. 595.

mediæval Church was to remain in all essentials the same as before. The only novelty, the only sign of appreciation of new ideas which were in the air, was that the papal interference in the affairs of national Churches was greatly limited, and that at a time when the Papacy had become so thoroughly secularised as to forget its real duties as a spiritual authority. The sole recognition of the new era, with its new modes of thought, was the proposal that the secular authorities of the countries of Europe should undertake duties which the Papacy was plainly neglecting. Perhaps it might be added that the slight homage paid to the New Learning, the appreciation of the need of an exact text of the original Scriptures, its guarded approval of the laity's acquaintance with Holy Writ, introduced something of the new spirit; but these things did not really imply anything at variance with what a devoted adherent of the mediæval Church might readily acquiesce in.

§ 3. *The Spaniards and Luther.*

Devout Spaniards were able to appreciate much in Luther's earlier work. They could sympathise with his attack on Indulgences, provided they did not inquire too closely into the principles implied in the *Theses*—principles which Luther himself scarcely recognised till the Leipzig Disputation. Their hearts responded to the intense religious earnestness and high moral tone of his earlier writings. They could welcome his appearance, even when they could not wholly agree with all that he said, in the hope that his utterances would create an impetus towards the *kind* of reformation they desired to see. The reformation of the Spanish Church under Cardinal Ximenes enables us to understand both the almost universal welcome which greeted Luther's earlier appearances and the opposition which he afterwards encountered from many of his earlier supporters. Some light is also cast on that opposition when we remember that the Emperor Charles himself fully accepted the principles underlying the Spanish Reformation, and that they had been instilled into his youthful mind by his revered tutor whom he managed to seat in the chair of St. Peter—Adrian VI., whose short-lived pontificate was an attempt to force the Spanish Reformation on the whole of the Western Obedience.

If it be possible to accept the statements made by Glapion, the Emperor's confessor, to Dr. Brück, the Saxon Chancellor in the days before Luther's appearance at Worms, as a truthful account of the disposition and intentions of Charles V., it may be said that an attempt was made to see whether Luther himself might be made to act as a means of forcing the Spanish Reformation on the whole German Church. Glapion professed to speak for the Emperor as well as for himself. Luther's earlier writings, he said, had given him great pleasure ; he believed him to be a " plant of renown," able to produce splendid fruit for the Church. But the book on the *Babylonian Captivity* had shocked him ; he did not believe it to be Luther's ; it was not in his usual style ; if Luther had written it, it must have been because he was momentarily indignant at the papal Bull, and as it was anonymous, it could easily be repudiated ; or if not repudiated, it might be explained, and its sentences shown to be capable of a catholic interpretation. If this were done, and if Luther withdrew his violent writings against the Pope, there was no reason why an amicable arrangement should not be come to. The papal Bull could easily be got over, it could be withdrawn on the ground that Luther had never had a fair trial. It was a mistake to suppose that the Emperor was not keenly alive to the need for a Reformation of the Church ; there were limits to his devotion to the Pope ; the Emperor believed that he would deserve the wrath of God if he did not try to amend the deplorable condition of the Church of Christ. Such was Glapion's statement. It is a question how far he was sincere, and if so, whether he really did express what was in the mind of the Emperor. Frederick of

Saxony did not believe either in his sincerity or in his representation of the Emperor's real opinions; and Luther himself refused all private conference with Glapion. Yet it is almost certain that Glapion did express what many an earnest Spanish ecclesiastic thoroughly believed. We have an interesting confirmation of this in the conversation which Conrad Pellican had with Francisco de los Angeles, the Provincial of the Spanish Franciscans at Basel. The Franciscan expressed himself in almost the very same terms as Glapion.[1]

Three forces met at the Diet of Worms in 1521— the German movement for Reform inspired by Luther, the Spanish Reformation represented by Charles v., and the stolid inertia of the Roman Curia speaking by the Nuncio Aleander. The first and the second could unite only if Luther retraced his steps and stood where he did before the Leipzig Disputation. If he refused, the inevitable result was that the Emperor and the Curia would combine to crush him before preparing to measure their strength against each other. The two different conceptions of reform may be distinguished from each other by saying that the Spanish conception sought to awaken the benumbed and formalist mediæval Church to a new religious life, leaving unchanged its characteristics of a sacerdotal ministry, an external visible unity under a hierarchy culminating in the Papacy, and a body of doctrine guaranteed by the decisions of Œcumenical Councils. The other wished to free the human spirit from the fetters of merely ecclesiastical authority, and to requicken the life of the Church through the spiritual priesthood of all believers. The former sought the aid of the secular

---

[1] "Is Cæsaris consanguineus, legatus missus a Wormacia, festinando ad Hispanos pro sedando quodam tumultu. Is in profesto vigiliæ natalicii dominici superveniens eques, cum ministris, biduo manens integro et tribus noctibus, mihi multum loquebatur de causa Lutherana, quæ magna ex parte arridebat viro bono et docto, præter librum de captivitate Babel, quem legerat Wormatiæ cum mœrore et displicentia, quem ego nondum videram" (Riggenbach, Das Chronikon des Konrad Pellikan, p. 77 (Basel, 1877).

power to purge national Churches and restore ecclesiastical discipline, but always under a decorous air of submission to the Bishop of Rome, and with a very real belief in the supremacy and infallibility of a General Council. The latter was prepared to deny the authority of the Bishop of Rome altogether, and to see the Church of the Middle Ages broken up into territorial or National Churches, each of which, it was contended, was a portion of the one Visible Catholic Church. But as separate tendencies may be represented by a single contrast, it may be said that Charles would have forgiven Luther much had the Reformer been able to acknowledge the infallibility of a General Council. The dramatic wave of the hand by which Charles ended the altercation between Official Eck and Luther, when the latter insisted that General Councils had erred, and that he could prove it, ended the dream that the movement in Germany could be used to aid in the universal introduction of the Spanish Reformation. If the ideas of reforming Spanish ecclesiastics and states-men were to requicken the whole mediæval Church, some other way of forcing their acceptance had to be found.

§ 4. *Pope Adrian VI. and the Spanish Reformation.*

The opportunity seemed to come when, owing to the rivalries of powerful Cardinals and the steady pressure of Charles V on the Conclave, Adrian of Utrecht was elected Pope. The new Pontiff had a long reputation for learning and piety. His courage had been manifested in his fearless denunciation of prevailing clerical abuses, and in the way he had dealt with difficult questions in mediæval theology. He had no sympathy with the new curialist ideas of papal inerrancy and infallibility, nor with the repeated assertions of Italian canonists that the Pope was superior to all ecclesiastical law. He rather believed that such ideas were responsible for the degrada-tion of the Church, and that no amendment was possible until the whole system of papal reservations, exemptions, and other ways in which the Papacy had evaded the plain declarations of Canon Law, was swept away. The public confidence in his piety, integrity, and learning was so great that the Netherlands had entrusted him with the religious education of their young Prince, and none of his instructors so stamped themselves on the mind of Charles.

Adrian was a Dutch Ximenes. He had the same passionate desire for the Reformation of the Church, and the same ideas of how such Reformation could be brought about. He prized the ascetic life; he longed to see the monastic orders and the secular clergy disciplined in the strictest way; he had a profound admiration for Thomas Aquinas, and especially for that side of the great School-man's teaching which represented the ideas of St. Augustine. He so exactly reproduced in his own aspirations the desires of the Spanish Reformers, that Cardinal Carvajal, who with the grave enthusiasm of his nation was engaged in the quixotic task of commending the Spanish Reforma-tion to the authorities in Rome, desired to take him there as an indispensable assistant. He was also in full sympathy with the darker side of the Spanish Reforma-tion. During his sojourn in Spain he had become one of the heads of the Inquisition, and was firmly opposed to any relaxation of the rigours of the Holy Office. With Adrian in the chair of St. Peter, the Emperor and the leaders of the Spanish Church might hope to see their type of a reformation adopted to cure the ills under which the Church was suffering.

The new Pope did not lack sympathisers in Italy when he began his task of cleansing the Augean stables without turning the torrent of revolution through them. Cardinal Carvajal welcomed him in a speech which ex-pressed his own ideas if it displeased his colleagues in whose name he was supposed to speak. A memorial drafted by Egidio, General of the Augustinian Eremites, was presented to him, which practically embodied the

32**

reforms the new Pope wished to see accomplished.[1]   His programme was as extensive as it was thorough.   A large part of it may be compared with the reforms sketched in Luther's *Address to the Nobility of the German Nation.* He disapproved of the way in which *prebends* were taken from foundations within national Churches to swell the incomes of Roman Cardinals.   He disliked the whole system of papal *reservations, indults,*[2] *exemptions, expectances,* which under the fostering care of Pope John XXII. had converted the Curia into a great machine for raking in money from every corner of western Europe.[3]   He disapproved of the system of encouraging complainants to pass over the episcopal courts of their own lands and bring their cases at once before the papal court.   But every one of these reforms would cut off a source of revenue.   It meant that hundreds of hungry Italian Humanists would lose their pensions, and that as many pens would lampoon the Holy Father who was intent on taking bread from his children.   It meant that hundreds of ecclesiastical lawyers who had invested their savings in purchasing places in the Curia, would find themselves reduced to penury.   It meant that the incomes of the Princes of the Church would shrink in an incalculable manner.   Adrian set himself to show such men how to meet the changes in prospect.   He brought his old Flemish peasant housekeeper with him to Rome, contented himself with the simple dishes she cooked for him, and lived the life of an anchorite in a corner of his vast palace on the Vatican hill; but in this case example did not seem better than precept.   It had seemed so easy to the simple-minded Dutch scholar to

---

[1] Carvajal's speech and Egidio's memoir are given in Höfler, "Analecten z. Geschich. Deutschlands und Italiens" (*Abhandlungen der Münch. Akad.* IV. iii. 57–89).

[2] An *indult* can be best explained by an example : according to the Council of Bourges (1438), the selection of French Bishops was left exclusively in the hands of the Chapters of the Cathedrals ; but Pope Eugenius IV. permitted Charles VII. the right to appoint to several specified bishoprics ; such a papal grant was called an *indult.*

[3] Cf. vol. i. 12 *f.*

reform the Church; everything was provided for in the Canon Law, whose regulations had only to be put in force. His Spanish experience had confirmed him in the possibility of the task. But at Rome he found a system of Rules of Chancery which could not be set aside all at once; there was no convenient Inquisition so organised that it could clear all objectors out of his path; no secular power always ready to support a reforming Churchman.

Where was he to begin? The whole practice of Indulgences appeared to be what was most in need of reform. Its abuses had kindled the storm in Germany. To purge them away would show how much in earnest he was. He knew the subject well. He had written upon it, and therefore had studied it from all sides. Rightly understood, Indulgences were precious things. They showed how a merciful God had empowered His Church to declare that He pardoned sins freely; and, besides, they proclaimed, as no other usage of the Church did, the brotherhood of all believers, within which the stronger could help the weaker, and the holier the more sinful, and all could fulfil the law of Christ by bearing each other's burdens. Only it was to be remembered that every pardon required a heart unfeignedly penitent, and the sordid taint of money must be got rid of. But—there was always a "but" for poor Adrian—it was shown to him that the papal court could not possibly pay its way without the money which came in so easily from the sale of Indulgences. He was baffled at the very start; checks, for the most part quite unexpected, thwarted every effort. He was like a man in a nightmare, set in a thicket of thorns, where no hewing could set him free, clothes torn, limbs bleeding, till at last he sank exhausted, welcoming the death which freed him from his impossible task. Adrian was the distinguished martyr of the Spanish Reformation. History has dwelt upon his failures; they were only too manifest. It has derided his simplicity in sending Chieregati to Germany with the confession that the Curia was the source of most of the evils which beset the mediæval Church, and at the same time demanding the death of Luther, who had been the first to show the fact in such a way that all men could see it. It has said little of the success that came in due time. Chieregati was unable to overcome the deeply rooted Evangelical Reformation in Germany. But his mission and the honest statement that the Curia was the seat of evil in the Church, date the beginnings of a reaction, of a genuine Romanist party with a vague idea of reforms on mediæval lines. It must be taken as the starting-point of the Counter-Reformation in Germany. Adrian's example, too, did much to encourage the few spiritually minded Churchmen in Italy, and its effects can be seen in the revival of a zeal to purify the Church which arose during the pontificate of Paul III.

CHAPTER III.

ITALIAN LIBERAL ROMAN CATHOLICS AND THEIR CONCEPTION OF A REFORMATION.[1]

§ 1. *The Religious Condition of Italy.*

ITALY is the land which next to Spain is the most important for the Counter-Reformation. While we can trace in Spain and in Germany a certain solidarity of religious movement, the spiritual conditions of Italy during the first half of the sixteenth century were as manifold as its political conditions. It is impossible to speak of the Italians as a whole. Italy had been the land of the Renaissance, but that great intellectual movement had never rooted itself deeply in the people as it had done in Germany, France, or England.

The Italian peasantry were a class apart from the burghers as they were nowhere else. Their religion was usually a thinly veiled paganism, a belief in the omnipresence of spirits, good and bad, to be thanked, propitiated, coaxed or compelled by use of charms, amulets, spells, and

---

[1] SOURCES : Contarini, *Opera* (Paris, 1571) ; *Correspondenz Contarinis*, ed. by L. Pastor (1880) ; Cortese, *Epistolarum familiarum liber* (Venice, 1573) ; Ghiberti, *Opera* (Verona, 1740) ; Sadoleto, *Epistolarum libri sexdecim* (Lyons, 1560) ; Pole, *Epistolæ, et aliorum ad ipsum* (Brescia, 1744–57), *Carteggio di Vittoria Colonna* (Turin, 1889) ; Vergerio, *Briefwechsel* (edited for the *Bibliothek des literarischen Vereins*, Stuttgart, 1875).

LATER BOOKS : Jacob Burckhardt, *The Civilisation of the Period of the Renaissance* (Eng. trans., London, 1892) ; Symonds, *Renaissance in Italy*. *The Catholic Reaction* (London, 1886) ; Cantù, *Gli Eretici d'Italia* (Turin, 1865–67) ; Braun, *Cardinal Gasparo Contarini* (1903) ; Dittrich, *Gasparo Contarini* (Braunsberg, 1883) ; Duruy, *Le Cardinal Carlo Caraffa* (Paris, 1882) ; Gothein, *Ignatius Loyola und die Gegenreformation*, pp. 77–207 (Halle, 1895) ; v. Reumont, *Vittoria Colonna* (Freiburg i. B. 1881).

ceremonies. The gods of their pagan ancestors had been replaced by local saints, and received the same kind of worship. To fight for their faith had never been a tradition with them as with the Spaniards; they were not troubled by any continuous sense of sin as were the people of the northern nations; but they had an intense fear of the supernatural, and their faith in the priest, who could stand between them and the terrors of the unseen, was boundless. Goodness touched them as it does all men. But the immorality of their religious guides did not embarrass them; a bad priest had as powerful spells as a good one. The only kind of Christianity which seemed able to impress them and hold them was that of Francis of Assisi. He was the highest embodiment of the Christian spirit for the Italian peasantry; the impression he had made upon the people of the Peninsula was enduring; the wandering revivalist preacher who lived as Francis had done always made the deepest impression. John of Capistrano owed much of his power to the fact that he remained always the Abruzzi peasant. During the whole of the period of the Renaissance the peasantry and the clergy who served the village chapels were regarded by those above them with a scorn that degenerated into hatred. We may search in vain through the whole of the literature of the time for the thought that any attempt ought to be made to lead them to a deeper faith and a purer life. The whole of the peasant population of Italy were believed to be beneath the level of desire for something better than what the religious life of the times gave.[1]

[1] Mediæval songs tell us that this hatred of the peasantry is much older than the Renaissance:

> " Si quis scire vult naturam,
> Maledictam et obscuram
> Rusticorum genituram
> Infelicem et non puram
> Denotent sequentia," etc.

Carmina Medii Ævi (Florence, 1883), p. 34; the song belongs to the thirteenth century.

The towns presented an entirely different picture. There was a solidarity binding together all the civic population. The ordinary division of ranks, made by greater or less possession of wealth or by social standing, existed, but it did not prevent a common mode of thinking. We can trace the same thoughts among artisans, small shopkeepers, rich merchants, and the patricians of the towns. No country presented so many varieties of local character as Italy; but the inhabitants of Venice or Florence, Milan, Naples, however else they might differ, were all on the same spiritual level. They thought much about religion; they took the moral degradation of the Church and of the clergy to heart; they longed to see some improvement, if it was only within their own city. They were clearsighted enough to trace the mischief to the influence of the Roman Curia, and their belief in the hopelessness of reforming the evil Court gives a settled despondency to their thought which appears in most of the Chronicles. The external side of religion was inextricably interwoven with their city life. The civic rulers had always something to do with the churches, monasteries, and other ecclesiastical foundations within their walls. They had no great interest in doctrine; what they wanted was a real improvement in the moral living of clergy and of people. When an Italian town was blessed with a good and pious Bishop, it is touching to see how the whole population rallied round him.

When we turn to the outstanding men of the Italian peninsula, whose opinions have been preserved in their writings or correspondence, we find, to begin with, a great variety of religious opinions whose common note is unconstrained hostility to the Church as it was then constituted. The institution was a necessary evil, very important as a factor in the game of politics, useless for the religious life. This sentiment existed almost universally, both among those who merely maintained a decorous relation towards the existing ecclesiastical institutions, and among those who really believed in Christianity, and acknowledged its power over their mind and life. The papal Curia oppressed them ; they were hopeless of its reformation, and yet there was little hope of a revival of religion, with its social worship and its sacraments, unless it was reformed. The feeling of hopelessness is everywhere apparent ; the deepest spiritual longings and experiences were to be treasured as sacred secrets of the heart, and not to be spoken about. Yet the work of Savonarola had not been entirely consumed in the fire that burnt the martyr, and the earlier message of Luther had found an echo in many Italian hearts.

§ 2. *The Italian Roman Catholic Reformers.*

There is no evidence of any widespread acceptance of the whole of Luther's teaching, little appreciation of the thought that the Church may be conceived as a fellowship of God with man depending on the inscrutable purpose of God and independent of all visible outward organisation, none of the idea that the Visible Church Catholic exists one and indivisible in the many forms in which men combine to listen to the Word and to manifest their faith. The Catholic Church was always to these pious Italians the great historical and external institution with its hierarchy, and its visible head in the Bishop of Rome. A reform of the Church meant for them the reformation of that institution. So long as this was denied them they could always worship within the sanctuary of their own souls, and they could enjoy the converse of likeminded friends. So there came into existence coteries of pious Italians who met to encourage each other, and to plan the restoration of religion within the Church. Humanism had left its mark on all of them, and their reunions were called academies, after the Platonic academies of the earlier Renaissance. The first had come into being before the death of Leo. x.—a society of pious laymen and prelates, who met in the little church of Santi Silvestro et Dorotea in the Trastevere in Rome. The associates were more than fifty in number, and they were all distinguished by their love of the New Learning, the strict purity of their lives, and their devotion to the theology of St. Augustine. The members were scattered after the sack of Rome (1527), but this *Oratory of Divine Love* gave rise to many kindred associations within which the original members found a congenial society.

The most important found a home in Venice. Its most prominent members were Gasparo Contarini, a distinguished Senator, who afterwards was induced to become a Cardinal. With him were Cardinal Caraffa, already meditating upon taking another path, and Gregorio Cortese, then Abbot of San Giorgio Maggiore. The friends met in the beautiful garden of the convent. All shades of opinion were represented in this circle, where Humanists and Churchmen met to exchange views about a reformation of the Church. To share in such intercourse, Reginald Pole willingly spent his days far from his native England. Cardinal Fregoso, Archbishop of Salerno, gathered a similar company around him at Genoa ; and Ghiberti, Bishop of Verona, collected likeminded friends to talk about the possibilities of reformation. Modena and Padua had their Christian academies also. Nor must the influence of well-born, cultured and pious ladies be forgotten.

Renée, Duchess of Ferrara and daughter of Louis xii. of France, had accepted the Reformation in its entirety, and had surrendered herself to the guidance of Calvin. She corresponded with the great Frenchman and with Bullinger. She sheltered persecuted Italian Protestants, or had them safely conveyed to Switzerland.[1] But she saw good wherever it was to be found. Her letters, instinct with Christian graciousness, remind the reader of those of her kinswoman Marguerite of Navarre. She was full of sympathy with the circle of men and women who longed for a regeneration of Italy ; and it is interesting to notice how the far more highly gifted Vittoria Colonna leant on the woman whose spiritual insight was deeper, and whose heart was purified

[1] Herminjard, *Correspondance*, etc. viii. 161.

by the trials which her decision in religious matters made her pass through.

Caterina Cybó, a niece of Pope Clement, Princess of Camerino, Eleonore Gonzaga, Duchess of Urbino, Julia Gonzaga at Naples, and Vittoria Colonna at Viterbo and at Rome, formed a circle of highly intellectual and deeply pious women, who by their letters and intercourse inspired men who were working for the regeneration of the Church in Italy.

The network of their correspondence covered Italy from Venice to Naples and from Genoa to Camerino, and the letters exchanged between Marguerite of Navarre and Vittoria Colonna extended the influence of the association beyond the peninsula. The correspondents, men and women, regarded themselves as a band of companions pledged to each other to work together for the Reformation of the Church and of society. It is not easy to describe their aims, for they contented themselves for the most part with vague aspirations ; and they all had their favourite likes and dislikes. It is impossible to doubt their earnestness, but it was of the high-bred placid kind. It had nothing of the Spanish exaltation of Teresa, of the German vehemence of Luther, of the French passion scarcely veiled by the logical precision of Calvin. They all admired St. Francis, but in a way out of sympathy with the common people, for they looked on asceticism with a mild wonder, and had no eagerness for *that* type of the imitation of Christ. Vittoria Colonna indeed found the convent at Viterbo a pleasant retreat for a few weeks at a time. A sigh sometimes escaped her that perhaps the nuns were all Marys who had chosen the better part, but that was only when she was we j with the perversities of the incomprehensible world. Their correspondence suggests an academy of the earlier Italian Renaissance, where the theory of Ideas had given way to doctrines of Justification, and the Epistles of St. Paul had taken the place of the Dialogues of Plato. There is a touch of dilettantism in their habits of thought, and a savour of the eighteenth century Salon in their intercourse. They longed to mediate between contending parties in the religious strife which was convulsing Europe beyond the Alps and might invade Italy ; but they were unfit for the task. A true *via media* can only be found by men who see both sides of the controversy in the clear vision of thought, not by men who perceive neither distinctly. Sadoleto, to take one example, declared that he could see much to admire in the German Reformation, but what he approved were only the external portions which came from Humanism, not those elements which made the movement a religious revival. He disliked Luther, but had a great esteem for Bucer and Melanchthon. Indeed, the Italian Cardinal may be called the Melanchthon of Romanism. Melanchthon, rooted in Protestantism, felt compelled by his intellectual sympathy and humility to believe that there was some good in Romanism and to try to find it; Sadoleto, rooted in Romanism, was impelled to some sympathy with the Protestant theology. He had, however, a fatal lack of precision of thought. One doctrine tended to slide insensibly into another, into its opposite even, under the touch of his analysis. The man who could defend and commend auricular confession because it was an example of Christian humility, and saint-worship because it was a testimony to the immortality of the soul, ran the risk of being regarded as a trifler by Protestants and a traitor by Romanists. Such was his fate.

Contemporary with these offshoots from the *Oratory of Divine Love* was a revival among some of the monastic orders in Italy which had distinct connection with some of the members of the associations above mentioned.

The most important for its influence on the religious life of the people was the Order of the Capucins. It took its rise from Matteo de Grassis, a man of no intellectual powers, but endowed with more than the usual obstinacy of the Italian peasant. He was an Umbrian, like Francis himself. He belonged to a district where traditions of the great mediæval revivalist had been handed down from parents to children for generations, and one of these insisted

that St. Francis had worn a hood with its peak pointed
and not rounded, as the fashion among the monks then
was. He declared that St. Francis had appeared to him
in a vision, and had said that the brethren of the order
ought to obey his rules " to the letter, to the letter, to the
letter." He for one resolved to obey. He threw away his
rounded hood and wore one with pointed peak. The
peasants refused to recognise the novelty, and drove him off
with stones ; his brethren argued with him, and belaboured
him with their fists ; but Matteo stuck to his pointed hood.
The shape was nothing, but the Founder's commands were
everything ; Matteo would die before he would wear the
rounded thing which had never been hallowed by St.
Francis. The Princess Caterina Cybó took compassion on
the hunted man, and gave him an asylum within her little
principality of Camerino, where he wore his pointed *capuze*
in peace. He soon sank back into the obscurity from
which he had for a moment emerged. But new life was
stirring among the Franciscans. Many were dissatisfied
with the laxity of the order, and were longing for a
monastic Reformation. All down the Middle Ages the
watchword of every monastic revival had been, " Back to
the Founder's rules." The pointed hood was a trifle, but it
was the symbol of a return to the rigid discipline of
Francis. Men heard that Camerino was an asylum for
Franciscans discontented with the laxity of the superiors
of the order, and gradually they flocked to the little
principality. Vittoria Colonna had long mourned over the
decadence of the genuine monastic life ; she encouraged
her friend the Princess Caterina to beseech her uncle the
Pope to permit the pointed hood, and gradually there
came into being a new fresh offshoot of the Franciscans,
called the Capucins, who revived the traditions of St.
Francis, and went preaching among the villages after the
fashion of his earlier followers. Francis had told his
disciples to beware of books when making their sermons ;
he had advised them to talk to the women as they washed,
Italian fashion, by the side of streams, to masons while

they were hewing, to artisans at their work, to find out what their religious difficulties were, what prevented them becoming really Christians in their lives, and then to discourse on the things they had heard. This old Franciscan preaching was restored by the Capucins, and they did more than any others to bring the people of Italy back to the discredited Church. They were accused of heresy. What " reformation " of the Franciscans was not ? They were called Lutherans ; and a good deal of Luther's Evangelical teaching was unconsciously presented in their sermons ; but they could always quote St. Francis for what they said ; and who could gainsay what Francis had taught ?

This monastic revival affected the commonalty; another spoke to the educated classes. As early as 1504 an attempt had been made to reorganise the great Benedictine order, and a number of Benedictine abbeys had united to form a Congregation, which soon after its institution took the name of the Benedictine Mother-Cloister, Monte Cassino. Gregorio Cortese, one of the members of the *Oratory of Divine Love*, entered into the movement, and as Abbot of the Benedictine convent on the Island of Lerina on the Riviera, and afterwards in the convent of San Giorgio Maggiore at Venice, led his monks to show that their convents were the centres of learning dedicated to the service of the Church. He interested himself more especially in historical studies with a view of maintaining the historic traditions of the Church, which were beginning to be shaken by historical criticism, then in its infancy.

The improvement of the secular clergy was more important for the Church in Italy than any reforms of the monastic orders. An attempt to do this was begun by two members of the *Oratory of Divine Love*, Giovanni Pietro Caraffa and Gætano da Thiene. Their idea was that in every diocese there ought to be a small band of men doing the work of secular clergy but bound by monastic vows. Their idea was taken from Augustine's practice of living

monastically with some of his clergy; and fulfilled itself in
the order of the Theatines. The name was derived from
Theate (Chieti), the small See of which Caraffa was Bishop.
These picked clergy were to be to the Bishop what his
staff is to a general. The Theatines were not to be
numerous, still less to include the whole secular clergy of a
diocese; but they were to incite by precept, and above all
by example, to a truly clerical life. The idea spread, and
similar associations arose all over Italy.[1]

Such were the preparations in Italy for the Counter-
Reformation. There was no prospect of any attempt to set
the Church in order while Pope Clement VII. lived. He
exhausted all his energies in preventing the summoning of
a General Council—a measure on which Charles V. was
growing more and more set as the only means of ending the
religious dispute in Germany.

The accession of Paul III. (1534) seemed to inaugurate
a new era full of hopes for the advocates of reform at the
centre of the Roman Church. The new Pope made Gasparo
Contarini, Caraffa, Sadoleto, and Pole Cardinals. A Bull,
which remained unpublished, was read in the Consistory
(January 1536), sketching the possibility of reforming the
Curia. The Pope appointed a commission of nine members
to report upon the needful reforms, and the commission was
everywhere regarded as a sort of preliminary Council, a
body of men who were appointed to investigate and tabulate
a programme of necessary reforms to be laid before a
General Council. The Commissioners were Contarini,
Caraffa, Ghiberti, Sadoleto, Pole, Fregoso, all of whom had
been members of the *Oratory of Divine Love*, Aleander who
had been Nuncio at the Diet of Worms, and Tomaso Badia,
Master of the Sacred Palace. They met and drafted a
report which was presented to the Pope in 1537, and is
known as the *Consilium delectorum cardinalium et aliorum
prælatorum de emendanda ecclesia*. A more scathing
indictment of the condition of the Roman Church could

---

[1] The name went beyond the original foundation. The Jesuits were
sometimes called *Theatines* both in Spain and in France.

scarcely be imagined, nor one which spoke more urgently of the need of radical reformation. Its very thoroughness was disconcerting. It revealed so many scandals connected with the Papacy that it was resolved not to make it known. But it had been printed as a private document; a copy somehow or other reached Germany; it was at once republished there, with comments showing how a papal commission itself had justified all the German demands for a reformation of the Church. At Rome the appearance of reforming activity was maintained. Contarini, Caraffa, Aleander, and Badia were appointed to investigate the workings of those departments of the Curia which had most to do with the abuses detailed in the report of the Commission of Nine—the *Chancery*, the *Datary*, and the *Penitentiary*, where reservations, dispensations, exemptions, etc., were given and registered. They presented their report in the autumn of 1537. It was entitled *Consilium quattuor delectorum a Paulo III. super reformatione sanctæ Romanæ Ecclesiæ*. But Contarini evidently felt that the Pope needed pressing. When the Commission of Nine had been appointed, the Pope had summoned a General Council to meet at Mantua in May 1537, in a Bull published on May 29th, 1536, and had also published a Bull of Reformation in September of that year. The Council never met—the war between Charles v. and Francis I preventing. The Council was then summoned to meet at Vicenza, but was again postponed. The Emperor had no wish for a General Council in Italy, and the Pope was determined not to call one to meet in Germany. In these circumstances Contarini published his *Epistola de potestate Pontificis in usu clavium*, and his *De potestate Pontificis in Compositionibus*.[1]

---

[1] They are to be found in *Bibliotheca Maxima Pontificia* (Rome, 1790), pp. 178 *ff*. The contents of the second letter are condensed in the phrase which occurs near the end : " in legibus voluntas non debet regula esse " (p. 183). The first letter urges the Pope to make an end of the scandals caused by the sale of dispensations : " Dispensator non potest vendere id quod non suum est sed Domini. Neque etiam potest transgredi in dispensatione mandatum Domini. . . . Expresse Christus in Evangelio præcipit : Gratis accepistis,

Historians differ about the sincerity of Pope Paul III. in
the matter of reform, and there is room for two opinions.
His Italian policy was anti-Hapsburg, and the German
Romanist Princes, at all events, had little belief in his
sincerity, and were seriously meditating on following the
example of Henry VIII. Cardinal Morone, the Nuncio in
Germany, made no concealment of the difficulties attending
the position of the Romanist Church there, and urged
continually substantial reforms in Italy, and the necessity
of a General Council. Perhaps these energetic messages
stirred the Pope to renewed activity in Rome, and also to
the necessity of formulating a definite policy with regard
to the Lutherans beyond the Alps. In April (1540)
commissions were appointed to reform certain offices in the
Curia—the Rota, the Chancery, and the Penitentiary.
Consultations were held about how to deal with the state
of affairs in Germany. For the moment the ideas of the
more liberal-minded Italian Reformers were in the ascendant.
Charles had determined to find out whether it was not
possible to reunite the broken Church in Germany.
Conferences were to be held with the leading Lutheran
theologians. The Pope determined to reject the advice of
Faber, the Bishop of Vienna, and to refrain from pro-
nouncing judgment on a series of Lutheran propositions
sent to him for condemnation. Cardinal Contarini, whose
presence had been urgently required by the Emperor, was
permitted to cross the Alps to see, in conference with
distinguished Lutherans, whether some common terms of
agreement might be arrived at which would serve as
a programme to be set before the General Council,
which all were agreed must be summoned sometime
soon.

Gratis date " (p. 79). It closes with an urgent appeal : " Pater Sanctissime
ingressus es viam Christi, audacter age. . . . Deus omnipotens diriget
gressus tuos, et tuorum omnium. Familiæ tuæ Protector erit, et super
omnia bona sua constituet te, ut ipse in Evangelio pollicetur servo fideli,
quem constituit super familiam suam. Dominus diu nobis servet Sanctitatem
tuam incolumem."

§ 3. *Cardinals Contarini and Caraffa.*

This mission of Contarini's to Germany dates the separation between two different ways of proposing to deal with the Reformation movement. The two methods were embodied in two men, Cardinals Contarini and Caraffa. They had both belonged to the *Oratory of Divine Love*; they were both zealous to see the Church reformed in the sense of reviving its moral and spiritual life; they both longed to see the rent which had made itself apparent repaired, and the Church again reunited. They differed entirely about the means to be adopted to bring about the desirable end. The differences originated in the separate characters and training of the two leaders.

Gasparo Contarini belonged to an ancient patrician family of Venice, and spent the greater portion of his life in the service of the Republic. He was looked on as the ablest and most upright of its statesmen. He had drunk deeply of the well of the New Learning, and yet can hardly be called a Humanist. He had been a student at Padua, and had there studied and learned to appreciate Scholastic Theology. He had been trained as a Venetian statesman, and clung to the political ideas of the mediæval jurisprudence. The whole round of mediæval thought encircled and possessed him. Christendom was one great commonwealth, and embodied three great imperialist ideas—a world King, the Emperor; a world priest, the Pope; a realm of sanctified science, the Scholastic Philosophy under Theology, the Queen of the Sciences. He held these three conceptions in a broad-minded and liberal way. There was room under the Emperor for a community of Christian States, under the Pope for a brotherhood of national Churches, under Scholastic for the New Learning and what it brought to enrich the mind of mankind.

Erasmus had ridiculed Scholastic; Contarini's friend Cortese called it a farrago of words; Luther had maintained

23**

that it sounded hollow because at its centre was the vague eternal Something of Pagan Philosophy and not the Father who had revealed His heart in Jesus Christ; but Contarini saw the grandeur of the imposing edifice, believed in its solidity, and would do nothing to destroy it. But this did not prevent him sympathising strongly with Luther's doctrine of Justification by Faith, nor from believing that room might be found for it and other Protestant conceptions within the circle of mediæval theological thought. He had little sympathy with the enthusiasm which some of his friends—Cardinal Pole for example—expressed for Plato. Aristotle was for him the great master-builder of human systematic thinking; but the Aristotle he recognised as the Master was not the sage revealed in the Greek text or commentaries (although he studied both), but the Aristotle who had cast his spell over Thomas Aquinas and Albertus Magnus. He was firmly persuaded that the Bishop of Rome was the Head of the Church, and as such had his place in the political system of Christendom from which he could not be removed without serious danger to the whole existing framework of society; but he looked on the Pope as a constitutional monarch bound to observe in his own person the ecclesiastical laws imposed by his authority on the Christian world. Luther, he believed, had recognised this in his earlier writings, and in this recognition lay the possibilities of a readjustment which would bring Christendom together again. On the other hand, Calvin's *Institutio* filled him with mingled admiration and dread. He recognised it to be the ablest book which the Protestant movement had produced; but the thought of a Christian democracy with which it was permeated, the stress it laid on the procession of the divine purpose down through the ages, and the manner in which it taught the prevenience of divine grace, were conceptions whose acceptance, he thought, would be dangerous to the political governance of mankind.

He dwelt with complacency on the thought that he had never longed for ecclesiastical place or power. The

Pope had persuaded him to permit himself to be made Cardinal because the Holy See had need of his service. He was conscious with a sort of proud humility that he was generally esteemed the foremost Italian of his generation, that enthusiastic friends spoke of his learning and virtue as "more divine than human." He thought much more of his position as a Venetian Senator and the trusted counsellor of the Republic, whose constitution he believed to be the embodiment of the best political principles of the time, than he did of his place in the Roman Court. "I for my part, to tell the truth, do not think that the Red Hat is my highest honour," he was accustomed to say. Such was the leader of the liberal-minded Roman Catholics of Italy, who was asked by the Pope and urgently entreated by the Emperor to visit Germany and end the schism by his persuasions.

Giovanni Pietro Caraffa, the intimate, the rival and the supplanter of Contarini, belonged to one of the oldest noble families of Naples. His house was intimately allied to the Church, and for more than one hundred years its members had been Archbishops of Naples, and several had been made Cardinals. The boy was destined for the Church. As a child he had longed to enter a cloister, and had once set out to join the Dominicans. His family, however, had other views for him. He was sent when eighteen years of age to the papal court, and was soon almost burdened with marks of distinction and with offices. He had been highly educated while at Naples, and had steeped himself in the New Learning. At the Humanist Courts of Alexander VI. and Julius II. he studied Greek and Hebrew, and became an accomplished theologian besides. In 1504, much against his will, he had been consecrated Bishop of the small diocese of Chieti (Theate), lying in the wild Abruzzi district, almost due east of Rome, on the slopes from the highest spurs of the Apennines to the Adriatic. He found his people demoralised by constant feuds, and the priests worse than their parishioners. Caraffa, determined to reduce his

unruly diocese to order, began with persuasion ; and finding
this of small avail, flogged people and clergy into something like decency by repeated spiritual censures and
rigidly enforced excommunications.   His methods revealed
the man.   His talents were of too high an order and
his family influence too great to permit him to linger
in his uncivilised diocese.   He was sent as Nuncio to
England and thence to Spain.   His visit to the latter
country made an indelible impression on his strong nature.
His earnest petitions for the independence of his native
Naples were contemptuously refused by the young King
Charles, and the fierce Neapolitan pursued the Emperor
with an undying hatred.   But what was more important,
his stay in Spain imbued him with the ideas of the
Spanish Reformation.   He was too much an Italian and
too strong a believer in the papal supremacy to adopt the
thought of secular interference in the affairs of the Church,
but with that exception the Spanish method of renovating
the Church took possession of him heart and soul.   The
germs of fanaticism, hitherto sleeping within him, were
awakened to life, and never afterwards slumbered.   He
sympathised with the projects of Adrian VI., and was a
power during his brief pontificate.   During the reign of
Clement VII. he took little part in public affairs, but all
the attempts to put new life into the monastic orders
were assisted by him.   He viewed with some suspicion
the attempt to conciliate the Germans; and the results
of Contarini's dealing with the Protestants at Regensburg
filled him with alarm.

Contarini's attempt to reunite the Church by reconciliation was twenty years too late.   It is doubtful whether
anyone in Germany save the Emperor had much faith in
the uniting influences of a conference.   Morone, who had
for years represented the Vatican at the Court of Ferdinand
of Austria, and who was perpetually urging the Pope to
summon a General Council, was afraid ever since Hagenau
that conferences benefited the Protestants more than the
Romanists.   Contarini himself had said that what was

needed to overcome the German movement was neither conferences nor discussions about doctrine, but a Reformation in morals. The Curia regarded his mission as a dangerous experiment. They tied his hands as firmly as they could by his letter of instructions: He was to inform the Emperor that no Legate, not even the Pope himself until he had consulted the other nations, could modify the doctrines of the Church for the sake of the Germans; he was to do his utmost to prevent the assembly of a National Council for Germany. He heard from Paris that the French Romanists believed that he was about to betray the Church to the heretics. No one encouraged him except his own circle of immediate friends. The men with whom he was to work, Cardinal de Granvelle and Dr. Eck, were suspicious of him and of his antecedents. Nevertheless his natural and confirmed optimism urged him to the task.

The situation, looked at broadly and from the point of view taken by a contemporary who had made himself acquainted with the theology and constitution of the mediæval Church, was not so hopeless as it must seem to us with the history of what followed to enlighten us. The great mass of mediæval doctrines lay uncodified. They were not codified until the Council of Trent. The extreme claims made by the supporters of a papal absolutism—claims which may be briefly expressed by the sentence: The Church Universal is condensed in the Roman Church, and the Roman Church is represented by the Pope—which had been used to crush the Lutheran movement in its earliest stages, were of recent origin. Curialism could be represented to be almost as much opposed to the mediæval theory of the Church as anything that Luther had brought forward. There was a real *via media*, if it could only be discovered and defined. The commonplace opinions of men who were sincerely attached to the mediæval conception of the Church, with its claims to catholicity, with its doctrines, usages, ceremonies and hierarchy, could scarcely be better represented than in the declaration said to have been made by Charles v. to his sister Maria his governor in the Netherlands:

"It happened that on the Vigil of St. John the Baptist the Emperor held a banquet in the garden. Now, when Queen Maria asked him what he thought of doing with the people and with the Confession (the Augsburg) that had been presented, he made reply: 'Dear Sister, when I was made chief of the Holy Roman Empire, the great complaint reached me that the people who profess this doctrine were more wicked than the devil. But the Bishop of Seville gave me the advice that I should not think of acting tyrannically, but should ascertain whether the doctrine is at variance with the articles of the Christian faith (the Apostles' Creed). This advice pleased me, and so I find that the people are not so devilish as had been represented; nor is the subject of dispute the Twelve Articles, but a matter lying outside them, which I have therefore handed over to the scholars. If their doctrine had been in conflict with the Twelve Articles I should have been disposed to apply the edge of the sword.'"[1]

The Twelve Articles, as the Apostles' Creed was called, always occupied a peculiar position in the Western Church. They were believed to contain the *whole* of the *theologia revelata*. The great Schoolmen of the most opposite parties (Thomas Aquinas and John Duns Scotus alike) were accustomed to deduce from the Apostles' Creed fourteen propositions, seven on God and seven on the Incarnation, and to declare that they contained the sum of revealed theology; everything else was natural theology on which men might differ without being considered to have abandoned the essentials of the Christian faith. Charles v. had been taught at first, probably by Aleander's insistent reiterations, that Luther had denied some portion of this revealed theology; he had come to learn that he had been wrongly informed; therefore conference and adjustment were possible.

Men like Charles v. and Contarini could honestly believe that so far as doctrine was concerned a compromise might be effected.

[1] Kawerau, *Johann Agricola* (1881), p. 100.

§ 4. *The Conference at Regensburg.*

The Diet was opened at Regensburg in February 1541
The Emperor explained his position and intentions. He
declared that the most important duty before them was to
try to heal the division in religion which was separating
Germany into two opposing parties. The one duty of the
hour was to endeavour to come to a unanimous decision
on religious matters, and to bring about this he proposed
to name some peace-loving men who could confer together
upon the points in debate. Count Frederick of the
Palatinate, brother of the Elector, and Cardinal de Granvelle
were nominated presidents : three pronounced Protestants,
two pronounced Romanists, and one whose opinions were
doubtful, were the assessors ; Eck, Gropper, and Pflug
were to support the Romanist side, Melanchthon, Bucer,
and Pistorius were the speakers for the Protestants.
Perhaps the only name that could be objected to was that
of Eck; it was impossible to think of him as a man of
peace. The Legate Contarini guided everything.

During preliminary conferences an understanding was
come to on some practical questions which served to
preserve an appearance of unanimity. It was thought
that marriage might be permitted to the clergy and the
cup to the laity within Germany; that the Pope might
be honoured as the Primate of the Church, provided it
was clearly understood that his position did not give him
the power of perpetual interference in the affairs of the
national Churches; that the hierarchy might be maintained
if the episcopal jurisdiction were exercised conjointly by
a vicar appointed by the Bishop and a learned layman
appointed by the secular authority.

It was the business of the conference to discuss the
deeper theological differences which were supposed to
separate the two parties. So in the opening meetings
the delegates began to consider those questions which
gathered round the thought of Justification.

It was agreed that there was no distinction between

the ordinances of grace and those of nature in the original condition of man. This declaration involved the denial of the distinction between the *dona supernaturalia* and the *dona naturalia* made so much of in Scholastic Theology, and the basis of a great deal of its Pelagian tendencies. It was expressly conceded by the Romanist theologians that man had lost his original freedom of will by the Fall—a concession directly at variance with the future declaration of the Council of Trent.[1] The statement agreed upon about the origin of sin was given almost in the words of the Augsburg Confession, and agrees with them. The doctrine of the tenacity of original sin scarcely differs from a statement of Luther's which had been condemned in the Bull *Exurge Domine* of Pope Leo X.[2] In the discussions and conclusions about this first head of doctrine the conclusions of Protestant theology had been amply vindicated.

There was more difficulty on the matter of Justification. Two definitions suggested by the Romanist theologians and by Melanchthon were successively rejected, and one brought forward, it is said by Contarini himself, was accepted after some discussion. It was couched in language which the Lutheran theologians had not been accustomed to use. It embodied phrases which Pole, Contarini, and other liberal Italian Roman Catholics had made their own. The Protestants of Germany, however, saw nothing in it to contradict their cherished ideas upon Justification, and they gladly accepted the definition. The statement, repeated more than once, that grace is the free gift of God and is not merited by our works, expressed their deepest thought, and completely excluded the

---

[1] The Regensburg article said : *Creata libertas per hominis lapsum est amissa* ; the decree of Trent declared : *Si quis liberum hominis arbitrium post Adæ peccatum amissum et extinctum esse dixerit, anathema sit* (Denzinger, *Enchiridion Symbolorum et Definitionum*, etc., 9th ed. p. 192).

[2] The Regensburg article says : *Etsi post baptismum negare remanens materiale peccatum*, etc., the second heresy of Luther condemned in the Bull is : *In puero post baptismum negare remanens peccatum, est Paulum et Christum simul conculcare* (*ibid.* p. 176).

meritorious character of ecclesiastical good works. They seemed rather pleased than otherwise that their thoughts could be expressed in language suggested by Romanist theologians.[1] It appears that Eck, while consenting to the definition, wished to avoid signing it, but was compelled by Granvelle to fix his name to the document.[2]

The fact that the Romanist and Protestant members of the conference could agree upon an article on Justification caused great rejoicings among Contarini's friends in Italy. Cardinal Pole was convinced that every obstacle in the way of reunion had been removed, and the most extravagant expectations were cherished.[3] The Protestant members of the conference were entirely satisfied with the results so far as they had gone.

The conference then turned to questions affecting the organisation and worship of the Church.

Somewhat to their surprise, the Protestants found that their opponents were willing to accept their general theory of what was meant by the Church and what were its

---

[1] Calvin, who was present at the conference, sums up the results so far in a letter to Farel as follows : *Delecti nostri de peccato originali non difficulter transegerunt : sequuta est disputatio de libero arbitrio, quæ ex Augustini sententia composita fuit : nihil in utroque nobis decessit. De justificatione acriores fuerunt contentiones. Tandem conscripta est formula, quam adhibitis certis correctionibus utrinque receperunt. Miraberis, scio, adversarios tantum concessisse, quum legeris exemplar, ita ut postrema manu correctum fuit, quod literis inclusum reperies. Retinuerunt enim nostri doctrinæ veræ summam : ut nihil illic comprehensum sit, quod non exstet in scriptis nostris : scio, desiderabis clariorem explicationem, et in ea re me tibi assentientem habebis. Verum, si reputes quibuscum hominibus negotium nobis sit, agnosces multum esse effectum (Corpus Reformatorum,* xxxix. 215). Calvin had been somewhat suspicious of Contarini at the outset : *Contarenus sine sanguine subigere nos cupit ; proinde tentat omnes vias conficiendi ex sua utilitate negotii citra arma (ibid.* xxxix. 176).

[2] In the dedication of the fourth portion of Melanchthon's Works to Joachim II. of Brandenburg, the editor Peucer says : *Granvellus.* . . . *Eccium, cum descriptæ formulæ testimonium chirographi addendum esset, tergiversantem et astute renuentem facere id coegit.* Eck with his great coarse body, his loud harsh voice, his bullying habits, and his insincerity, was universally disliked ; *ista bestia, gehobelter Eck,* he had been nicknamed by Pirkheimer of Nürnberg.

[3] *Epistolarum Reginaldi Poli, S. R. E. Cardinalis* (Brixiæ, 1744-57), iii. 25-30.

distinguishing characteristics. The Christian Society was defined without any reference to the Pope as its permanent Head on earth. This provoked strong dissents from Rome when the definition was known there. Differences emerged when the power of the Church was discussed, and as there was no prospect of agreement it was resolved for the meanwhile to omit the article.[1]

The question of the Sacrament of the Holy Supper evoked differences which were felt to be almost insuperable. It was inevitable. For here the one fundamental divergence between the new Evangelical faith and mediæval religion came to practical expression. Nothing could reconcile the Evangelical thought of a spiritual priesthood of all believers with the belief in a mediating priesthood who could give and could withhold God. Doctrines might be stated in terms which hid this fundamental difference; a definition of Justification by Faith alone might be conceded to the Protestants; but any thought of a priestly miracle in the Sacrament of the Holy Supper had to be repudiated by the one party and clung to by the other.

At first things went smoothly enough; it was conceded that special ways of dispensing the Sacraments were matters indifferent, but whenever the question of Transubstantiation emerged, things came to a deadlock. It was perhaps characteristic of Contarini's somewhat surface way of dealing with the whole question at stake between the two parties, that he never probed the deeper question. He rested his plea for Transubstantiation on the ground that an important article of faith which had been assented to for so long must not be questioned.[2] The Protestants held a private conference, at which all the theologians present were asked to give their opinions in turn. There Calvin

---

[1] Calvin says : *Ventum est deinde ad ecclesiam : in definitione congruebant sententiæ : in potestate dissidere cœperunt. Quum nullo modo possent conciliari, visum est articulum illum omittere.*

[2] *Nunquam Legatum assensurum, ut conspicua fidei decreta tot sæculis culta in dubium adducerentur.*

spoke, dwelling on the thought that Transubstantiation implied adoration, which could never be conceded. His firmness produced unanimity. Melanchthon drafted their common opinion, which was given in writing to Granvelle who refused in strong language to accept it, and the conference came to an end. The more difficult practical subjects of the sacrificial character of the Mass and of private Masses were not discussed.[1]

This conference at Regensburg may almost be said to be the parting of the ways. Up to 1525 the movement under Luther had the appearance of a Reformation of the whole Church in Germany. From 1525 to the date of this conference there was always the expectation that the Lutherans who had formed territorial Churches might yet be included in a general Reformation of the whole German Church. Joachim II. of Brandenburg cherished the idea long after 1541; and Charles V. still believed that what could not be effected by mutual compromise might be done by a mediating creed imposed upon all by the authority of

---

[1] The proceedings of the conference are given in full in the *Acta Ratisbonensia*. By far the most succinct account is to be found in Calvin's letter to Farel of date 11th May 1541. He says of the discussion about the sacraments : *In sacramentis rixati sunt nonnihil : sed quum nostri suas illis cæremonias, ut res medias, permitterent, usque ad cænam progressi sunt. Illic fuit insuperabilis scopulus. Repudiata transubstantiatio, repositio, circumgestatio, et reliqui superstitiosi cultus. Hæc adversariis nequaquam tolerabilia. Collega meus (Bucer), qui totus ardet studio concordiæ, fremere et indignari, quod intempestive fuissent motæ eiusmodi quæstiones, Philippus (Melanchthon) in adversam partem magis tendere, ut rebus exulceratis omnem pacificationis spem præcideret. Nostri habita consultatione, nos convocarunt. Jussi sumus omnes ordine dicere sententias : fuit una omnium vox, transubstantiationem rem esse fictitiam, repositionem superstitiosam, idololatricam esse adorationem, vel saltem periculosam, quum fiat sine verbo Dei. Me quoque exponere latine oportuit quid sentirem. Tametsi neminem ex aliis intellexeram* (because they spoke in German), *libere tamen sine timore offensionis, illam localem præsentiam damnavi : adorationem asserui mihi esse intolerabilem. Crede mihi, in eiusmodi actionibus opus est fortibus animis, qui alios confirment. . . . Scriptum deinde a Philippo compositum, quod ubi Granvellano oblatum est, asperis verbis repudiavit, quod illi tres delecti ad nos retulissent. Hæc quum fiant in ipso limine, cogita quantum adhuc supersit difficultatis, in missa privata, sacrificio, in communicatione calicis. Quid si ad apertam præsentiæ confessionem veniretur ? quanti tumultus effervescerent ?* (*Corpus Reformatorum*, xxxix. 215, 216).

the Emperor. But compromise failed at Ratisbon, and there was no further hope of its succeeding.

The decisive character of the Regensburg conference was seen in Italy almost at once. Its failure involved the destruction of the party of Italian Romanists who hoped to end the religious strife by a compromise. When Contarini returned to Italy he found that his influence was gone. He was rewarded with the Government of Bologna, which removed him from the centre of things. He died soon after (Aug. 24th, 1542), leaving none behind him to fill his place. Ghiberti survived him only sixteen months. Caraffa had become more and more alienated from his early friends. Sadoleto, Pole, and Morone remained, all of them men of intellect, but lacking the qualities which fit men to be leaders in trying times. Pole lived to make atonement for his liberalism by hounding on the persecutions in England, and Morone by becoming the champion of ultramontanism at the close of the Council of Trent. The conception of a Catholic Reformation disappeared; the idea of a Counter-Reformation took its place.

CHAPTER IV.

IGNATIUS LOYOLA AND THE COMPANY OF JESUS.[1]

§ 1. At Manresa.

THE little mountainous province of Guipuzcoa, lying at the corner of the Bay of Biscay, bordering on France, was the district of Spain which produced one of the greatest of her sons, Iñigo de Recalde de Loyola, the founder of the Society of Jesus. The tower which was the family seat still stands, rough and windowless as a Scottish border keep, adorned with one ornament only, a stone above the doorway, on which are carved the arms of the family—two wolves in quest of prey. Guipuzcoa had never been conquered by the Moors, and its nobles, poor in their barren highlands, boasted that the bluest Gothic blood ran in their veins. The Recaldes belonged to the very oldest nobility of the district, and possessed the highly valued privilege of the

[1] SOURCES : *Monumenta historica Societatis Jesu, nunc primum edita a Patribus ejusdem Societatis* (Madrid, 1894, etc.) ; *Cartas de San Ignacio de Loyola, fundador de la Compania de Jesus* (Madrid, 1874, etc.) ; G. P Maffei, *De vita et moribus Ignatii Loyolæ, qui Societatem Jesu fundavit* (Cologne, 1585) ; Ribadeneyra, *Vida del P. Ignacio de Loyola* (Madrid, 1594) ; Orlandino, *Historia Societatis Jesu, pars prima sive Ignatius*, etc. (Rome, 1615) ; Braunsberger, *Petri Canisii Epistolæ et Acta* (Freiburg i. B. 1896) ; *Decreta, etc., Societatis Jesu* (Avignon, 1827) ; *Constitutiones Societatis Jesu* (Rome, 1558).

LATER BOOKS : Huber, *Der Jesuit-Orden nach seiner Verfassung und Doctrin, Wirksamkeit und Geschichte characterisirt* (Berlin, 1873) ; Gothein, *Ignatius von Loyola und die Gegenreformation* (Halle, 1895) ; Symonds, *Renaissance in Italy, The Catholic Reaction* (London, 1886) ; Cretinau-Joly, *Histoire religieuse politique et littéraire de la Compagnie de Jésus* (Paris, 1845–46) ; Maurice Martel, *Ignace de Loyola, Essai de psychologie religieuse* (Paris).

right of personal summons to the coronation of the Kings of Leon. Their younger sons were welcomed at Court as pages, and then as soldiers; and the young Iñigo was a page at the Court of Ferdinand. He was well educated for a Spanish noble; could read and write; composed ballads; and could illuminate manuscripts with miniatures. Most of his spare time was employed in reading those romances of chivalry then very popular. When older he became a soldier like his elder brothers.

In 1521, when twenty-eight years of age (b. 1493), he was the youngest officer in command of the garrison of Pampeluna, ordered to withstand a combined force of invading French troops and some revolting Spaniards. The enemy appeared before the place in such overwhelming numbers that all but the youngest officer wished to surrender without a struggle. Iñigo's eloquence persuaded the garrison to attempt a desperate defence. No priest was among the soldiers; the Spaniards, according to their custom, confessed each other, and were ready to die at their posts. A bullet struck the young officer as he stood in the breach encouraging his men. His fall gave the victory to the besiegers.

The conspicuous bravery of Iñigo had won the respect of his enemies. They extricated him from the heap of dead under which he was buried, and conveyed him to the old family castle. There his shattered leg was so badly set as to unfit him for a soldier's career. He had it twice broken and twice reset. The prolonged torture was useless; he had to believe that he would never fight on horseback again. The dream of taking a man's part in the conquests which all Spaniards of that age believed lay before their country, had to be abandoned. His body was a useless log.

But Iñigo was a noble of the Basque provinces, and possessed, in a superlative degree it was to be discovered, the characteristics of his race — at once taciturn and enthusiastic, wildly imaginative, and sternly practical. He has himself recorded that, as soon as he was convinced that he could never become a distinguished soldier, he asked

himself whether he might not become a famous saint like
Dominic or Francis, and that the question arose from no
spiritual promptings, but simply from the determination to
win fame before his death. As he lay bedridden, thinking
much and dreaming more, it suddenly occurred to him
that no one could become a saint unless he lived very near
God, and that his life had not been of such a kind. He at
once resolved that he would change; he would feed on
herbs like a holy hermit; he would go to Jerusalem as a
devout pilgrim. This vow, he tells us, was the earliest
conscious movement of his soul towards God. His reward
came soon in the shape of his first revelation. The blessed
Virgin, with the Child Jesus in her arms, appeared to him
in a dream. He awoke, hustled out of bed, dragged himself to the small window of his turret-room, and looked
out. The earth was dark, an obscure mingling of black
shadows; the heavens were a great vault of deepest blue
strewn with innumerable stars. The sight was a parable
and an inspiration. "How dull earth is," he cried, "how
glorious heaven!" He felt that he must *do* something to
get nearer God. He must be alone in some holy place to
think things out with his own soul. His brother's servants
hoisted the maimed body of the once brilliant soldier on
an ass, one foot in a boot, the wounded leg still swathed
in bandages and its foot in a large soft slipper, and Iñigo
left the old castle determined to live a hermit's life on
Montserrat, the holy hill of Aragon.

There in the church of Our Lady of Montserrat he
resolved to dedicate himself to her service with all the
ceremonies prescribed in that masterbook of mediæval
chivalry, Amadis of Gaul. He hung his arms on her
altar, and throughout the long night, standing or kneeling,
he kept his watch, consecrating his knightly service to the
Blessed Virgin. At daybreak he donned an anchorite's
dress, gave his knightly robes to the first beggar he met.
and, mounted on his ass, betook himself to the Dominican
convent of Manresa, no longer Iñigo Recalde de Loyola,
but simply Ignatius.

At Manresa he practised the strictest asceticism, hoping to become in heart and soul fitted for the saint life he wished to live. Then began a time of unexpected, sore and prolonged spiritual conflict, not unlike what Luther experienced in the Erfurt convent. Who was he and what had been his past life that he should presumptuously think that God would ever accept him and number him among His saints? He made unwearied use of all the mediæval means of grace; he exhausted the resources of the confessional; he consulted one spiritual guide after another without experiencing any relief to the doubts which were gnawing at his soul. The whole machinery of the Church helped him as little as it had Luther: it could not give peace of conscience. He has placed on record that the only real help he received during this prolonged period of mental agony came from an old woman. Confession, instead of soothing him, rather plunged him into a sea of intolerable doubt. To make his penitence thorough, to know himself as he really was, he wrote out his confession that he might see his sins staring at him from the written page. He fasted till his life was in danger; he prayed seven times and scourged himself thrice daily, but found no peace. He tells us that he often shrieked aloud to God, crying that He must Himself help him, for no creature could bring him comfort. No task would be too great for him, he exclaimed, if he could only see God. "Show me, O Lord, where I can find Thee; I will follow like a dog, if I can only learn the way of salvation." His anguish prompted him to suicide. More than once, he says, he opened his window with the intention of casting himself down headlong and ending his life then and there; but the fear of his sins and their consequences restrained him. He had read of a saint who had vowed to fast until he had been vouchsafed the Beatific Vision, so he communicated at the altar and fasted for a whole week; but all ended in vanity and vexation of spirit.

Then, with the sudden certainty of a revelation, he resolved to throw himself on the mercy of God, whose long-

suffering pity would pardon his sins. **This was the crisis.**
Peace came at last, and his new spiritual life began. He
thought no longer about his past; he no longer mentioned
former sins in his confessions; the certainty of pardon had
begun a new life within him; he could start afresh. It is
impossible to read his statements without being struck with
the similarity between the spiritual experience of Ignatius
and what Luther calls Justification by Faith; the words
used by the two great religious leaders were different, but
the experience of pardon won by throwing one's self upon
the mercy of God was the same.

This new spiritual life was, as in Luther's case, one of
overflowing gladness. Meditation and introspection, once
a source of anguish, became the spring of overpowering joy.
Ignatius felt that he was making progress. "God," he
says, "dealt with me as a teacher with a scholar; I cannot
doubt that He had always been with me." Many
historical critics from Ranke downwards have been struck
with the likeness of the experience gone through by Luther
and Ignatius. One great contrast manifested itself at
once. The humble-minded and quiet German, when the
new life awoke in him, set himself unostentatiously to do
the common tasks which daily life brought; the fiery and
ambitious Spaniard at once tried to conquer all mysteries,
to take them by assault as if they were a beleaguered
fortress.

He had his visions as before, but they were no longer
temptations of Satan, the source of doubt and torture. He
believed that he could actually see with bodily eyes divine
mysteries which the intelligence could not comprehend.
After lengthened prayer, every faculty concentrated in one
prolonged gaze, he felt assured that he could *see* the
mystery of Transubstantiation actually taking place. At
the supreme moment he saw Christ in the form of a white
ray pass into the consecrated bread and transform it into
the Divine Victim (Host). He declared that in moods of
exaltation the most impenetrable mysteries of theology, the
Incarnation of our Lord, the Holy Trinity, the personality

34**

of Satan, were translated into visible symbols which made them plainly understood. These visions so fascinated him, that he began to write them down in simple fashion for his own satisfaction and edification.

In all this the student of the religious life of Spain during the sixteenth century will recognise the mystical devotion which was then characteristic of the people of the Peninsula. The Spanish character, whether we study it in the romances of chivalry which the land produced, or in the writing of her religious guides, was impregnated by enthusiasm. It was passionate, exalted, entirely penetrated and possessed by the emotion which for the time dominated it. In no country were the national and religious sentiment so thoroughly fused and united. The long wars with the Moors, and their successful issue in the conquest of Grenada, had made religion and patriotism one and the same thing. Priests invariably accompanied troops on the march, and went into battle with them. St. James of Compostella was believed to traverse the country to bring continual succour to the soldiers who charged the Moors invoking his name. A victory was celebrated by a solemn procession in honour of God and of the Virgin, who had delivered the enemy into the hands of the faithful. This intensity of the Spanish character, this temperament distinguished by force rather than moderation, easily gave birth to superstition and burning devotion, and both furnished a fruitful soil for the extravagances of Mysticism, which affected every class in society. Statesmen like Ximenes, no less than the common people, were influenced by the exhortations or predictions of the *Beatæ*,—women who had devoted themselves to a religious life without formally entering into a convent,—and changed their policy in consequence. It was universally believed that such devotees, men and women, could be illuminated divinely, and could attain to a state of familiar intercourse with God, if not to an actual union with Him, by giving themselves to prayer, by abstinence from all worldly thoughts and actions, and by practising the most rigid asceticism. It was held that those who had attained to this state of mystical union received in dreams, trances, and ecstasies, visions of the divine mysteries.

The heads of the Spanish Inquisition viewed this Mysticism, so characteristic of the Peninsula, with grave anxiety. The thought that ardent believers could by any personal process attain direct intercourse, even union with God, apart from the ordinary machinery of the Church, cut at the roots of the mediæval penitential system, which always presupposed that a priestly mediation was required. If God can be met in the silence of the believer's soul, where is the need for the priest, who, according to mediæval ideas, must always stand between the penitent and God, and by his action take the hand of faith and lay it in the hand of the divine omnipotence? Other dangers appeared. The Mystic professed to draw his knowledge of divine things directly from the same source as the Church, and his revelations had the same authority. It is true that most of the Spanish Mystics, like St. Teresa, had humility enough to place themselves under ecclesiastical direction, but this was not the case with all. Some prophets and prophetesses declared themselves to be independent, and these *illuminati*, as they were called, spread disaffection and heresy. Hence the attitude of the Inquisition towards Mystics of all kinds was one of suspicious watchfulness. St. Teresa, St. Juan de la Cruz, Ignatius himself, were all objects of distrust, and did not win ecclesiastical approbation until after long series of tribulations.

It is necessary to insist on the fact that Ignatius had a deeply rooted connection with the Spanish Mystics. His visions, his methods, the *Spiritual Exercises* themselves, cannot be understood apart from their intimate relations to that Mysticism which was characteristic of the religion of his land and of his age.

Ignatius was no ordinary Mystic, however. What seemed the whole or the end to Teresa or Osuna was to him only a part, or the means to something better. While he received and rejoiced in the visions vouchsafed to him, he practised the keenest introspection. He observed and analysed the moods and states of mind in which the visions came most readily or the reverse, and made a note of them all. He noted the postures and gestures of the body which helped or hindered the reception of visions or profitable meditation on what had been revealed. He saw that he could reproduce or at least facilitate the return of his visions by training and mastering his mind and body, and by subjecting them to a spiritual drill which might be compared with the exercises used to train a soldier in the art of war. Out of these visions, introspections, comparisons, experiments experienced in solitude at Manresa, came by long process of gradual growth and elaboration the famous *Spiritual Exercises*, which may be called the soul of the Counter-Reformation, as Luther's book on *The Liberty of the Christian Man* contains the essence of Protestantism.

Ignatius spent nearly a year at Manresa. He had accomplished his object—to find himself at peace with God. It remained to fulfil his vow of pilgrimage. He laid aside his hermit's garb, and with it his ascetic practices; but he believed it to be his duty to renounce all property and live absolutely poor. He left all the money he possessed upon a bench and walked to Barcelona, supporting himself by begging. There he was given a passage to Venice, and thence he sailed for the Holy Land. His enthusiasm, and above all his project for beginning a mission among the Turks, alarmed the chief of the Franciscans in Jerusalem, who insisted on shipping him back to Italy. He reached Barcelona determined to pursue such studies as would enable him to know theology. He had never learned Latin, the gateway to all theological learning, and the man of thirty entered school, and seated himself on the bench with boys. Thence he went to Alcala and to Salamanca, and attended classes in these towns. Before he had quitted Manresa he had begun to speak to others about his visions, and to persuade them to

submit themselves to the spiritual drill of his *Exercises.*
Some ladies in Barcelona had become his devoted disciples.
At Alcala and Salamanca he had tried to make converts
to his system. The ecclesiastical authorities of the districts,
fearing that this was a new kind of dangerous Mysticism,
seized him, and he was twice incarcerated in the episcopal
Inquisition. It would probably have fared ill with him
had it not been for the intercession of some of the
distinguished ladies who had been his disciples. His
imprisonment in both cases was short, but he was forbidden to discriminate between mortal and venial sins (a
thing essential if he acted as a spiritual director) until
he had studied theology for four years.

§ 2. *Ignatius at Paris.*

With prompt military obedience Ignatius decided to
study at Paris. He reached the city in the beginning of
1528, driving an ass laden with his books and clothes. He
went naturally to the College Montaigu, which under its
Principal, Noel Beda, was the most orthodox in Paris ; but
with his well known determination to see and judge
everything for himself, he soon afterwards obtained
leave to reside in the College Ste. Barbe, one of the
most liberal, in which George Buchanan was then a
Regent.[1]

---

[1] "The residence of Ignatius Loyola in the College of Ste. Barbe is
connected with an incident which is at once illustrative of his own spirit
and of the manners of the time. He had come to Paris for the purpose of
study ; but he could not resist the temptation to make converts to his
great mission. Among these converts was a Spaniard named Amador, a
promising student in philosophy in Ste. Barbe. This Amador, Loyola had
transformed from a diligent student into a visionary as wild as himself,
to the intense indignation of the University, and especially of his own
countrymen. About the same time Loyola craved permission to attend Ste.
Barbe as a student of philosophy. He was admitted on the express condition
that he should make no attempt on the consciences of his fellows. Loyola
kept his word as far as Amador was concerned, but he could not resist
the temptation to communicate his visions to others. The Regent thrice
warned him of what would be the result, and at length made his complaint

His sojourn in Paris could not fail to make a deep impression on the middle-aged Spaniard, consumed with zeal to maintain in its minutest details the old religion, and to destroy heresy and disobedience. Two passions possessed him, both eminently Spanish. He could say with St. Teresa that he suffered so much to see the Lutherans, whose baptism had rendered them members of the Church, lose themselves unhappily, that had he several lives he would willingly give them to deliver only one of them from the horrible torments which awaited them; but he also believed that it was for God a point of honour to avenge Himself on those who despised His word, and that it belonged to all the faithful to be instruments of the vengeance of the Almighty.

His keen practical nature grasped the religious situation in Paris (City and University), and suggested his lifework. He saw the strength of the Roman Catholic democracy face to face with the Reformation, and to what power it might grow if it were only organised and subjected to a more than military discipline. Ignatius was in Paris during the years when partisan feelings ran riot.

Francis I. was by taste and training a man of the Renaissance. It pleased him to be called and to imagine himself to be the patron of men of letters. He was as devoted as his selfish, sensual nature permitted him to be, to his sister Marguerite d'Angoulême, and for her sake

to the Principal (Jacques de Gouvéa). Gouvéa was furious, and gave orders that next day Loyola should be subjected to the most disgraceful punishment the College could inflict. This running of the gauntlet, known as *la salle*, was administered in the following manner. After dinner, when all the scholars were present, the masters, each with his ferule in his hand, ranged themselves in a double row. The delinquent, stripped to the waist, was then made to pass between them, receiving a blow across the shoulders from each. This was the ignominious punishment to which Loyola, then in his fortieth year, as a member of the College, was bound to submit. The tidings of what was in store for him reached his ears, and in a private interview he contrived to turn away Gouvéa's wrath. . . . This was in 1529, the year of Buchanan's entrance into Ste. Barbe" (P. Hume Brown, *George Buchanan, Humanist and Reformer*, Edinburgh, 1890, pp. 62 f.).

countenanced such Reformers as Lefévre and the "group of Meaux." He had a grudge against the Sorbonne and the *Parlement* of Paris for their attempts to baffle the Concordat of 1516; while he recognised the power which these two formidable associations possessed. He was an anti-Sorbonnist, who feared the Sorbonne (the great theological faculty of the University of Paris), and could not help displaying his dread. He had long dreamed of instituting a *Collége de France*, a free association of learned teachers, men who could introduce the New Learning and form a counterpoise to the Sorbonne which dominated the University. The project took many forms, and never came to full fruition until long after the days of Francis; but the beginnings were sufficient to encourage Reformers and to irritate to fury the supporters of the Sorbonne. The theological faculty of the University was then ruled by Noel Beda, a man of no great intellectual capacity, who hated everything which seemed to menace mediævalism. Beda, by his dogged courage, by his unflinching determination, by his intense conviction that he was in the right, was able to wage a pitiless warfare against the New Learning and every appearance of religious reform. He was able to thwart the King repeatedly, and more than once to attack him through Marguerite, his sister. His whole attitude and activity made him a forerunner of the Romanist League of two generations later, and, like the Leaguers, he based his power on organising the Romanist fanaticism lying in the populace of Paris and among the students of the Sorbonne. All this Loyola saw under his eyes during his stay in Paris. He heard the students of the Sorbonne singing their ferocious song:

> " Prions tous le Roi de gloire
> Qu'il confonde ces chiens mauldicts,
> Afin qu'il n'en soit plus mémoire,
> Non plus que de vielz os pourris.
> Au feu, au feu ! c'est leur repère
> Fais-en justice ! Dieu l'a permys " ;

and the defiant answer:

> " La Sorbonne, la bigotte,
> La Sorbonne se taira !
> Son grand hoste, l'Aristote,
> De la bande s'ostera !
> Et son escot, quoi qu'il coste,
> Jamais ne la soûlera !
> La Sorbonne, la bigotte,
> La Sorbonne se taira !
>
> . . . . .
>
> La saincte Escriture toute
> Purement se preschera,
> Et toute doctrine sotte
> Des hommes on oublîra !
> La Sorbonne, la bigotte,
> La Sorbonne se taira ! " [1]

Amidst this seething crowd of warring students and teachers, Ignatius went, silent, watchful, observing everything. He cared little for theological speculation, being a true and typical Spaniard. The doctrines of the mediæval theology were simply military commands to his disciplined mind; things to be submitted to whether understood or not. Heresy was mutiny in the ranks. He had a marvellous natural capacity for penetrating the souls of others, and had cultivated and strengthened it by his habits of daily introspection and of writing down whatever, good or bad, passed through his own soul. It is told of him that in company he talked little, but quietly noted what others said, and that he had infinite genius for observing and storing details.[2] He sought to learn the conditions of life and thought outside Paris and France, and made journeys to the Low Countries and to England, saying little, thinking much, observing more. All the time he was winning the confidence of fellow-students, and

---

[1] *Bulletin de la Société de l'Histoire de Protestantisme Français*, xii. 129.

[2] One of Loyola's earliest biographers, Ribadeneyra, dwells on the eagerness with which Ignatius welcomed the slightest details of the life of his disciples in the Indies, and how he one day said : " I would assuredly like to know, if it were possible, how many fleas bit them each night."

taking infinite pains to do so—weighing and testing their character and gifts. He played billiards with some, paid the college expenses of others, and was slowly, patiently making his selection of the young men whom he thought fit to be the confidants of his plans for the regeneration of Christendom, and to be associates with him in the discipline which the *Exercises* gave to his own soul.[1]

He finally chose a little band of nine disciples—Peter Faber, Diego Lainez, Francis Xavier, Alonzo Salmeron, Nicholas Boabdilla, Simon Rodriguez, Paul Broet, Claude Jay, and Jean Codure. Codure died early. Faber, the first selected, was a Savoyard, the son of a poor peasant, with the unbending will and fervent spiritual imagination of a highlander. No one of the band was more devoted to his leader. Francis Xavier belonged, like Loyola himself, to an ancient Basque family; none was harder to win than this proud young Spaniard. Lainez and Salmeron were Castilians, who had been fellow-students with Ignatius at Alcala. Lainez had always been a prodigy of learning, "a young man with the brain of an ancient sage." He, too, had been hard to win, for his was not a nature to kindle easily; but once subdued he was the most important member of the band. Salmeron, his early companion, was as impetuous and fiery as Lainez was cool and logical. He was the eloquent preacher of the company. Boabdilla, also a Spaniard, was a man of restless energy, who needed the strictest discipline to make him keep touch with his brothers. Rodriguez, a Portuguese, and Jay, from Geneva, were young men of insinuating manners, and were the destined diplomatists of the little company. Broet, a phlegmatic Netherlander among these fiery southerners, endeared himself to all of them by his sweet purity of soul.

Such were the men whom Ignatius gathered together on the Feast of the Ascension of Mary in 1534 in the

[1] Loyola had long abandoned the vow of poverty; his faithful disciples, the circle of Barcelona ladies, sent him supplies of money, and he received sums from Spanish merchants in France and the Low Countries.

Church of St. Mary of Montmartre, then outside the walls of Paris. There they vowed that if no insuperable difficulty prevented, they would go together to Palestine to work for the good of mankind. If this became impossible, they would ask the Pope to absolve them from their vow and betake themselves to whatever work for the good of souls His Holiness directed them to do. No Order was founded; no vows of poverty and obedience were taken; the young men were a band of students who looked on each other as brothers, and who promised to leave family and friends, and, " without superfluous money," work together for a regeneration of the Church. Faber, already in priest's orders, celebrated Mass; the company dined together at St. Denys. Such was the quiet beginning of what grew to be the Society of Jesus.

The companions parted for a season to meet again at Venice.

§ 3. *The Spiritual Exercises.*

All the nine associates had submitted themselves to the spiritual guidance of Ignatius, and had all been subjected to the training contained in the *Exercitia Spiritualia.* It is probable that this manual of military drill for the soul had not been perfected at the date of the meeting at Montmartre (1534), for we know that Loyola worked at it from 1522 on to 1548, when it was approved by Pope Paul III.; but it may be well at this stage to give some account of this marvellous book, which was destined to have such important results for the Counter-Reformation.[1]

The thought that the spiritual senses and faculties might be strengthened and stimulated by the continuous repetition of a prescribed course of prayer and meditation,

---

[1] The *Exercitia Spiritualia S. P. Ignatii Loyolæ, Fundatoris Ordinis Societatis Jesu,* and their indispensable companion the *Directorium in Exercitia Spiritualia B. P. N. Ignatii,* are to be found in vol. iv. of the *Insti. Soc. Jesu.* The editions used here are, of the *Exercises,* that of Antwerp, 1676, and of the *Directory,* that of Rome, 1615.

was not a new one. The German Mystics of the fourteenth century, to name no others, had put their converts through such a discipline, and the practice was not unusual among the Dominicans. It is most likely that a book of this kind, the *Exercitatorio dela vida spirital* of Garcia de Cisneros, Abbot of the Monastery of Montserrat (1500), had been studied by Ignatius while he was at Manresa. But this detracts nothing from the striking and unique originality of the *Exercitia Spiritualia*; they stand alone in plan, contents, and intended result.[1] They were the outcome of Loyola's protracted spiritual struggles, and of his cool introspection of his own soul during these months of doubt and anguish. Their evident intention is to guide the soul through the long series of experiences which Loyola had endured unaided, and to lead it to the peace which he had found.

It is universally admitted that Ignatius had always before him the conception of military drill. He wished to discipline the soul as the drill-sergeant moulds the body. The *Exercises* are not closet-rules for solitary believers seeking to rise to communion with God by a ladder of meditation. A guide was indispensable, *the Master of the Exercises*, who had himself conquered all the intricacies of the method, and who, besides, must have as intimate a knowledge as it was possible to acquire of the details of the spiritual strength and weakness of his pupil. It was the easier to have this knowledge, as the disciple must be

---

[1] A careful study of the *Exercises*, of the *Directory*, of Loyola's correspondence, and of his sayings recorded by early and contemporary biographers, has convinced me that the book was mainly constructed out of the abundant notes which Loyola took of his own inward experiences at Manresa, and that the only book he used in compiling it was the *De Imitatione Christi* of Thomas à Kempis—a book which Ignatius believed to have been written by Gerson. We know otherwise how highly Ignatius prized the *De Imitatione*. When he visited the Abbey of Monte Casino he took with him as many copies as there were monks in the monastery ; it was the one volume which he kept on the small table at his bedside ; and it was the only book which the neophyte was permitted to read during the first week of the *Exercises* : " si tamen instru tori videbitur, posset in prima hebdomada legere librum Gersonis de Imitatione Christi " (*Directory*, iii. 2).

more than half won before he is invited to pass through
the drill. He must have submitted to one of the fathers
in confession; he must be made to understand the absolute
necessity of abandoning himself to the exercises with his
whole heart and soul; he must promise absolute submission
to the orders of the director; he must by frequent confession reveal the recesses of his soul, and describe the
most trivial thoughts which flit through it; above all, he
must enter on his prolonged task in a state of the liveliest
expectation of the benefits to be derived from his faithful
performance of the prescribed exercises.[1] A large, though
strictly limited, discretion is permitted to the *Master of the
Exercises* in the details of the training he insists upon.

The course of drill extends over four weeks [2] (twenty-
five days). It includes prolonged and detailed meditations
on four great subjects:—sin and conscience; the earthly
Kingdom of Christ; the Passion of Jesus; and the Love
of God with the Glory of the Risen Lord.[3] During all
this time the pupil must live in absolute solitude. Neither
sight nor sound from the world of life and action must be
allowed to enter and disturb him. He is exhorted to purge
his mind of every thought but the meditation on which he
is engaged; to exert all his strength to make his introspection vivid and his converse with the Deity unimpeded.

[1] Cf. *Directory*, i. ii. v.

[2] It is explained that by "week" is meant not a space of time, sever.
days, but a distinct subject of meditation. The drill may be finished within
seven or eight days; it may have to be prolonged beyond the twenty-five.
The first meditation is the basis of all, and it may have to be repeated over
and over again until the soul is sufficiently bruised (*Directory*, xi. 1).

[3] "Prima continet considerationem peccatorum, ut eorum fœditatem
cognoscamus, vereque detestemur cum dolore, et satisfactione convenienti.
Secunda proponit vitam Christi ad excitandum in nobis desiderium ac
studium eam imitandi. Quam imitationem ut melius perficiamus, pro-
ponitur etiam modus eligendi vel vitæ statum, qui sit maxime ex voluntate
Dei; vel si jam eligi non possit, dantur quædam monita ad eum in quo
quisque sit, reformandum. Tertia continet Passionem Christi, qua miseratio,
dolor, confusio generatur, et illud imitationis desiderium una cum Dei amore
vehementius inflammatur. Quarta demum est de Resurrectione Christi,
ejusque gloriosis apparitionibus, et de beneficiis, et similibus, quæ pertinent
ad Dei amorem in nobis excitandum " (*Directory*, xi. 2).

True meditation, according to Ignatius, ought to include four things—a preparatory prayer; *prœludia*, or the ways of attuning the mind and sense in order to bring methodically and vividly some past historical scene or embodiment of doctrine before the soul of the pupil; *puncta*, or definite heads of each meditation on which the thoughts are to be concentrated, and on which memory, intellect, and will are to be individually exercised; *colloquia*, or ecstatic converse with God, without which no meditation is supposed to be complete, and in which the pupil, having placed the crucifix before him, talks to God and hears His voice answering him.

When the soul's progress on the long spiritual journey in which it is led during these meditations is studied, one can scarcely fail to note the crass materialism which envelops it at every step. The pupil is required to *see* in the mirror of his imagination the boundless flames of hell, and souls encased in burning bodies; to *hear* the shrieks, howlings, and blasphemies; to *smell* the sulphur and intolerable stench; to *taste* the saltness of the tears, and to *feel* the scorching touch of the flames.[1] When the scene in the Garden of Gethsemane is the subject of meditation, he must have in the *camera obscura* of his imagination a garden, large or small, see its enclosing walls, gaze and gaze till he discerns where Christ is, where the Apostles sleep, perceive the drops of sweat, touch the clothes of our Lord.[2] When he thinks of the Nativity, he must conjure up the figures of Joseph, Mary, the Child, *and a maidservant*, hear their homely family talk, see them going

[1] "Punctum primum est, spectare per imaginationem vasta inferorum incendia, et animas igneis quibusdam corporibus, velut ergastulis inclusas. Secundum, audire imaginarie, planctus, ejulatus, vociferationes, atque blasphemias in Christum et Sanctos ejus illinc erumpentes. Tertium, imaginario etiam olfactu fumum, sulphur, et sentinæ cujusdam seu fæcis atque putredinis graveolentiam persentire. Quartum, gustare similiter res amarissimas, ut lachrymas, rancorem, conscientiæque vermem. Quintum, tangere quodammodo ignes illos, quorum tactu animæ ipsæ amburuntur" (*Exercitia Spiritualia, Quintum Exercitium* (pp. 105, 106 in Antwerp edition of 1676)).

[2] *Exercitia, Tertia Hebdomada*, ii. *Contemplatio* (p. 157).

about their ordinary work.[1]   The same crass materialism
envelops the meditations about doctrinal mysteries.
Thinking upon the Incarnation is almost childishly limited
to picturing the Three Persons of the Trinity contemplating
the broad surface of the earth and men hurrying to destruction, then resolving that the Second is to descend to
save ; and to the interview between the angel Gabriel and
the Virgin.[2]

A second characteristic of this scheme of meditation
is the extremely limited extent of its sphere.   The attention is confined to a few scenes in the life of our Lord and
of the Virgin.   No lessons from the Old Testament are
admitted.   All theological speculation is strictly excluded.
What is aimed at is to produce an intense and concentrated
impression which can never be effaced while life lasts.
The soul is alternately torn by terror and soothed by the
vision of heavenly delights.   " The designed effect was to
produce a vivid and varied hypnotic dream of twenty-five
days, from the influence of which a man should never
wholly free himself." [3]

The outstanding feature, however, of the *Exercises* and
of the *Directory* is the minute knowledge they display of
the bodily conditions and accompaniments of states of
spiritual ecstasy, and the continuous, not to say unscrupulous, use they make of physical means to create spiritual
abandon.   They master the soul by manipulating the body.
Not that self-examination, honest and careful recognition of
sins and weaknesses in presence of temptation, have no
place in the prolonged course of discipline.   This is
inculcated with instructions which serve to make it
detailed, intense, almost scientific.   The pupil is ordered to
examine himself twice a day, in the afternoon and in the
evening, and to make clear to himself every sin and failure
that has marked his day's life.   He is taught to enter them
all, day by day, in a register, which will show him and his

---

[1] *Exercitia, Tertia Hebdomada,* ii. *Contemplatio,* pp. 125, 126.
[2] *Ibid.* p. 121.
[3] J. A. Symonds, *The Renaissance in Italy, The Catholic Reaction,* i. 289.

confessor his moral condition with arithmetical accuracy
But during his own period of spiritual struggle and depression
at Manresa, Ignatius, in spite of the mental anguish which
tore his soul, had been noting the bodily accompaniments
of his spiritual states; and he pursued the same course of
introspection when rejoicing in the later visions of God and
of His grace. The *Exercises* and the *Directory* are full of
minute directions about the physical conditions which
Ignatius had found by experience to be the most suitable
for the different subjects of meditation. The old Buddhist
devotee was instructed to set himself in a spiritual trance
by the simple hypnotic process of gazing at his own navel;
the Ignatian directions are much more complex. The
glare of day, the uncertainty of twilight, the darkness of
night are all pressed into service; some subjects are to be
pondered standing upright motionless, others while walking
to and fro in the cell, when seated, when kneeling, when
stretched prone on the floor; some ought to be meditated
upon while the body is weak with fasting, others soon after
meals; special hours, the morning, the evening, the middle
of the night, are noted as the most profitable times for
different meditations, and these vary with the age and sex
of the disciple. Ignatius recognises the infinite variety
that there is in man, and says expressly that general rules
will not fit every case. The *Master of Exercises* is therefore
enjoined to study the various idiosyncrasies of his patients,
and vary his discipline to suit their mental and physical
conditions.

It is due chiefly to this use of the conditions of the
body acting upon the mind that Ignatius was able to
promise to his followers that the ecstasies which had been
hitherto the peculiar privilege of a few favoured saints
should become theirs. The Reformation had made the
world democratic ; and the Counter-Reformation invited the
mob to share the raptures and the visions of a St. Catherine
or a St. Teresa.

The combination of a clear recognition of the fact that
physical condition may account for much in so-called

spiritual moods with the use made of it to create or
stimulate these moods, cannot fail to suggest questions.   It
is easy to understand the Mystic, who, ignorant of the
mysterious ways in which the soul is acted upon by the
body, may rejoice in ecstasies and trances which have been
stimulated by sleepless nights and a prolonged course of
fasting.   It is not difficult to understand the man who,
when he has been taught, casts aside with disdain all this
juggling with the soul through the body.   But it is hard
to see how anyone who perceived with fatal clearness the
working of the machinery should ever come to think that
real piety could be created in such mechanical ways.   To
believe with some that the object Ignatius had was simply
to enslave mankind, to conquer their souls as a great
military leader might master their lives, is both impossible
and intolerable.   No one can read the correspondence of
Loyola without seeing that the man was a devout and
earnest-minded Christian, and that he longed to bring
about a real moral reformation among his contemporaries.
Perhaps the key to the difficulty is given when it is
remembered that Ignatius never thought that the raptures
and the terrors his course of exercises produced were an
end in themselves, as did the earlier Mystics.   They were
only a means to what followed.   Ignatius believed with
heart and soul that the essence of all true religion was the
blindest submission to what he called the "true Spouse
of Christ and our Holy Mother, which is the orthodox,
catholic, and hierarchical Church."   We have heard him
during his time of anguish at Manresa exclaim, "Show me,
O Lord, where I can find Thee; I will follow like a dog,
if I only learn the way of salvation!"   He fulfilled his
vow to the letter.   He never entered into the meaning of
our Lord's saying, "Henceforth I call you not servants . . .
but friends"; he had no understanding of what St. Paul
calls "reasonable service" (λογικὴ λατρεία).   The only
obedience he knew was unreasoning submission, the
obedience of a dog.   His most imperative duty, he believed,
lay in the resignation of his intelligence and will to

ecclesiastical guidance in blind obedience to the Church. It is sometimes forgotten how far Ignatius carried this. It is not that he lays upon all Christians the duty of upholding every portion of the mediæval creed, of mediæval customs, institutions, and superstitions; or that the philosophy of St. Thomas of Bonaventura, of the Master of the Sentences, and of "other recent theologians," is to be held as authoritative as that of Holy Writ;[1] but "if the Church pronounces a thing which seems to us white to be black, we must immediately say that it is black."[2] This was for him the end of all perfection; and he found no better instrument to produce it than the prolonged hypnotic trance which the *Exercises* caused.

§ 4. *Ignatius in Italy.*

In the beginning of 1537 the ten associates found themselves together at Venice. A war between that Republic and the Turks made it difficult for them to think of embarking for Palestine; and they remained, finding solace in intercourse with men who were longing for a moral regeneration of the Church. Contarini did much for them; Vittoria Colonna had the greatest sympathy with their projects; Caraffa only looked at them coldly. The mind of Ignatius was then full of schemes for improving the moral tone of society and of the Church—daily prayer in the village churches, games of chance forbidden by law; priests' concubines forbidden to dress as honest women did, etc.;—all of which things Contarini and Vittoria had at heart.

After a brief stay in Venice, Ignatius, Lainez, and Faber travelled to Rome, and were joined there by the others in Easter week (1538). No Pontiff was so

[1] These and other declarations of a like kind are to be found in the last chapter of the *Exercitia Spiritualia*, entitled *Regulæ aliquot servandæ ut cum orthodoxa Ecclesia vere sentiamus.*

[2] *Ibid.* "Si quid, quod oculis nostris apparet album, nigrum illa (ecclesia catholica) esse definierit, debemus itidem, quod nigrum sit, pronuntiare" (*Regula*, 13, p. 267).

35**.

accessible as Paul III., and the three had an audience, in which they explained their missionary projects. But this journey through Italy had evidently given Ignatius and his companions new ideas. The pilgrimage to Palestine was definitely abandoned, the money which had been collected for the voyage was returned to the donors, and the associates took possession of a deserted convent near Vicenza to talk over their future. This conference may be called the second stage in the formation of the Order. They all agreed to adopt a few simple rules of life—they were to support themselves by begging; they were to go two by two, and one was always to act as the servant for the time being of the other; they were to lodge in public hospitals in order to be ready to care for the sick; and they pledged themselves that their chief work would be to preach to those who did not go to church, and to teach the young.

The Italian towns speedily saw in their midst a new kind of preachers, who had caught the habits of the well-known popular *improvisatori*. They stood on the kerb-stones at the corners of streets; they waved their hats; they called aloud to the passers-by. When a small crowd was gathered they began their sermons. They did not preach theology. They spoke of the simple commands of God set forth in the Ten Commandments, and insisted that all sins were followed by punishment here or hereafter. They set forth the prescriptions of the Church. They described the pains of hell and the joys of heaven. The crowds who gathered could only partially understand the quaint mixture of Italian and Spanish which they heard. But throughout the Middle Ages the Italian populace had always been easily affected by impassioned religious appeals, and the companions created something like a revival among the masses of the towns.

It war this experience which made Ignatius decide upon founding a *Company of Jesus*. It was the age of military companies in Italy, and the mind of Ignatius always resphnded to anything which suggested a soldier's life.

Other Orders might take the names of their founders; he resolved that his personality should be absorbed in that of his Crucified Lord. The thought of a new Order commended itself to his nine companions. They left their preaching, journeyed by various paths to Rome, each of them meditating on the Constitution which was to be drafted and presented to the Pope.

The associates speedily settled the outlines of their Constitution. Cardinal Contarini, ever the friend of Loyola, formally introduced them to the Pope. In audience, Ignatius explained his projects, presented the draft Constitution of the proposed new Order, showed how it was to be a militia vowed to perpetual warfare against all the enemies of the Papacy, and that one of the vows to be taken was: " That the members will consecrate their lives to the continual service of Christ and of the Popes, will fight under the banner of the Cross, and will serve the Lord and the Roman Pontiff as God's Vicar upon earth, in such wise that they shall be bound to execute immediately and without hesitation or excuse all that the reigning Pontiff or his successors may enjoin upon them for the profit of souls or for the propagation of the faith, and shall do so in all provinces whithersoever he may send them, among Turks or any other infidels, to the farthest Ind, as well as in the region of heretics, schismatics, or unbelievers of any kind." Paul III. was impressed with the support that the proposed Order would bring to the Papacy in its time of stress. He is reported to have said that he recognised the Spirit of God in the proposals laid before him, and he knew that the associates were popular all over Italy and among the people of Rome. But all such schemes had to be referred to a commission of three Cardinals to report before formal sanction could be given.

Then Loyola's troubles began. The astute politicians who guided the counsels of the Vatican were suspicious of the movement. They had no great liking for Spanish Mysticism organised as a fighting force; they disliked the enormous powers to be placed in the hands of the General of the "Company"; they believed that the Church had suffered from the multiplication of Orders; eight months elapsed before all these difficulties were got rid of. Ignatius has placed on record that they were the hardest months in his life.

During their prolonged audience Paul III. had recognised the splendid erudition of Lainez and Faber. He engaged them, and somewhat later Salmeron, as teachers of theology in the Roman University, where they won golden opinions. Ignatius meanwhile busied himself in perfecting his *Exercises*, in explaining them to influential persons, and in inducing many to try their effect upon their own souls. Contarini begged for and received a MS. copy. Dr. Ortiz, the Ambassador of Charles V. at Rome, submitted himself to the discipline, and became an enthusiastic supporter. "It was then," says Ignatius, "that I first won the favour and respect of learned and influential men." But the opposition was strong. The old accusations of heresy were revived. Ignatius demanded and was admitted to a private audience of the Pope. He has described the interview in one of his letters.[1] He spoke with His Holiness for more than an hour in his private room; he explained the views and intentions of himself and of his companions; he told how he had been accused of heresy several times in Spain and at Paris, how he had even been imprisoned at Alcala and Salamanca, and that in each case careful inquiry had established his innocence; he said he knew that men who wished to preach incurred a great responsibility before God and man, and that they must be free from every taint of erroneous doctrine; and he besought the Pope to examine and test him thoroughly.[2]   On Sept. 27th, 1540, the Bull

---

[1] *Cartas de San Ignacio de Loyola, fundador de la Compañia de Jesus* (Madrid, 1874, etc.), No. 14.

[2] Ignatius was fond of recalling these accusations and acquittals. In a celebrated letter to the King of Portugal he said that he had been eight times accused of heresy and as often acquitted, and that these accusations

Regimini militantis ecclesiæ was published, and the *Company of Jesus* was founded. The student band of Montmartre, the association of revivalist preachers of Vicenza, became a new Order, a holy militia pledged to fight for the Papacy against all its assailants everywhere and at all costs. In the Bull the members of the Company were limited to sixty, whether as a concession to opponents or in accordance with the wishes of Ignatius, is unknown. It might have been from the latter cause. In times of its greatest popularity the number of members of full standing has never been very large—not more than one per cent. of those who bear the name.[1] The limitation, from whatever motive it was inserted, was removed in a second Bull, *Injunctum nobis*, dated March 14th, 1543.

§ 5. *The Society of Jesus.*

On April 4th, 1541, six out of the ten original members of the Order (four were absent from Rome) met to elect their General; three of those at a distance sent their votes in writing; Ignatius was chosen unanimously. He declined the honour, and was again elected on April 7th. He gave way, and on April 22nd (1541) he received the vows of his associates in the church of *San Paolo fuori le mura.*

The new Order became famous at once; numbers sought to join it; and Ignatius found himself compelled to admit more members than he liked. He felt that the more his Society increased in numbers and the wider its sphere of activity, the greater the need for a strict system of laws to govern it. All other Orders of monks had their rules, which stated the duties of the members, the

had really arisen, not from any associations he had ever had with schismatics, Lutherans, or *Alumbrados* (heretical Mystics), but from the astonishment caused by the fact that he, an unlearned man, should presume to speak about things divine (*Cartas de San Ignacio*, etc., No. 52).

[1] At the time of Ignatius' death (1556), "the Professed of the Four Vows," who were the Society in the strictest sense, and who alone had any share in its government, numbered only thirty-five.

mode of their living together, and expressed the common sentiment which bound them to each other. The Company of Jesus, which from the first was intended to have a strict military discipline, and whose members were meant to be simply dependent units in a great machine moved by the man chosen to be their General, required such rules even more than any other. Ignatius therefore set himself to work on a Constitution. All we know of the first Constitution presented by the ten original members when they had their audience with Pope Paul III., is contained in the Bull of Foundation, and it is evident that it was somewhat vague. It did contain, however, four features, perhaps five, if the fourth vow of special obedience to the Pope be included, which were new. The Company was to be a fighting Order, a holy militia; it was to work for the propagation of the faith, especially by the education of the young; the members were not to wear any special or distinctive dress; and the power placed in the hands of the General was much greater than that permitted to the heads of any other of the monastic Orders. At the same time, constitutional limitations, resembling those in other Orders, were placed on the power of the General. There was to be a council, consisting of a majority of the members, whom the General was ordered to consult on all important occasions; and in less weighty matters he was bound to take the advice of the brethren near him. Proposed changes tending to free the General from these limitations were given effect to in the Bulls, *Licet debitum pastoralis officii* (Oct. 18th, 1549) and *Exposcit pastoralis officii* (July 21st, 1550); but the Bulls themselves make it clear that the Constitution had not taken final form even then. It is probable that the completed Constitution drafted by Ignatius was not given to the Society until after his death.

The way in which he went to work was characteristic of the man, at once sternly practical and wildly visionary. He first busied himself with arrangements for starting the educational work which the Company had undertaken

to do; he assorted the members of his Society into
various classes;[1] and then he turned to the Constitution.
He asked four of his original companions, Lainez, Salmeron,
Broet, and Jay, all of whom were in Rome, to go carefully
over all the promises which had been made to the Pope,
or what might be implied in them, and from this material
to form a draft Constitution. He gave them one direction
only to guide them in their work: they were to see that
nothing was set down which might imply that it was a
deadly sin to alter the rules of the Company in time to come.
The fundamental aim of his Company was different from
that of all other Orders. It was not to consist of societies
of men who lived out of the world to save their own souls,
as did the Benedictines; nor was it established merely to
be a preaching association, like the Dominicans; it was
more than a fraternity of love, like the Franciscans. It
was destined to aid fellow-men in every way possible; and
by fellow-men Ignatius meant the obedient children of the
catholic hierarchical Church. It was to fight the enemies
of God's Vicar upon earth with every weapon available.
The rules of other Orders could not help him much. He
had to think all out for himself. During these months
and years Ignatius kept a diary, in which he entered as in
a ledger his moods of mind, the thoughts that passed
through it, the visions he saw, and the hours at which
they came to him.[2] Every possible problem connected
with the Constitution of his Company was pondered
painfully. It took him a month's meditation ere he saw

---

[1] The Society came to consist of (1) *Novices* who had been carefully
selected (a) for the priesthood, or (b) for secular work, or (c) whose special
vocation was yet undetermined—the *Indifferents*; (2) the *Scholastics*, who
had passed through a noviciate of two years, and who had to spend five
years in study, then five years as teachers of junior classes; (3) *Coadjutors*,
spiritual or temporal—the one set sharing in all the missionary work of
the Society, preaching or teaching, the other in the corresponding temporal
duties; (4) *the Professed of the Four Vows*, who were the élite of the Society,
and who alone had a share in its government. Heads of Colleges and
Residences were taken from the third class.

[2] This diary was used by Vigilio Nolarci in his *Compendio della Vita
di S. Ignatio di Loiola* (Venice, 2nd ed., 1687), pp. 197-211.

how to define the relation of the Society to property. Every solution came to him in a flash with the effect of a revelation, usually in the short hour before Mass. Once, he records, it took place " on the street as I returned from Cardinal Carpi." It was in this way that the Constitution grew under his hands, and he believed that both it and the *Exercises* were founded on direct revelations from God.

This was the Constitution which was presented by Lainez to the assembly which elected him the successor of Loyola (July 2nd, 1558). The new General added a commentary or *Directorium* of his own, which was also accepted. It received papal sanction under Pius IV.

In this Constitution the Society of Jesus was revealed as an elaborate hierarchy rising from Novices through Scholastics, Coadjutors, Professed of Four Vows, with the General at its head, an autocrat, controlling every part, even the minutest, of the great machine. Nominally, he was bound by the Constitution, but the inner principle of this elaborate system of laws was apparent fixity of type qualified by the utmost laxity in practice. The most stable principles of the Constitution were explained or explained away in the *Directorium*, and by such an elaborate labyrinth of exceptions that it proved no barrier to the will of the General. He stood with his hand on the lever, and could do as he pleased with the vast machine, which responded in all its parts to his slightest touch. He had almost unlimited power of " dispensing with formalities, freeing from obligations, shortening and lengthening the periods of initiation, retarding or advancing a member in his career." Every member of the Society was bound to obey his immediate superiors as if they stood for him in the place of Christ, and that to the extent of doing what he considered wrong, of believing that black was white if the General so willed it. The General resided at Rome, holding all the threads of the complicated affairs of the Society in his hands, receiving minute reports of the secret and personal history of every one of its members.

dealing as he pleased with the highest as well as the lowest of his subordinates.

"Yet the General of the Jesuits, like the Doge of Venice, had his hands tied by subtly powerful though almost invisible fetters. He was subjected at every hour of the day and night to the surveillance of five sworn spies, especially appointed to prevent him from altering the type or neglecting the concerns of the Order. The first of these functionaries, named the Administrator, who was frequently also the confessor of the General, exhorted him to obedience, and reminded him that he must do all things for the glory of God. Obedience and the glory of God, in Jesuit phraseology, meant the maintenance of the Company. The other four were styled Assistants. They had under their charge the affairs of the chief provinces; one overseeing the Indies, another Portugal and Spain, a third France and Germany, a fourth Italy and Sicily. Together with the Administrator, the Assistants were nominated by the General Congregation (an assembly of the Professed of the Four Vows), and could not be removed or replaced without its sanction. It was their duty to regulate the daily life of the General, to control his private expenditure on the scale which they determined, to prescribe what he should eat and drink, to appoint his hours for sleep, and religious exercises, and the transaction of public business. . . . The Company of Jesus was thus based upon a system of mutual and pervasive espionage. The novice on entering had all his acts, habits, and personal qualities registered. As he advanced in his career, he was surrounded by jealous brethren, who felt it their duty to report his slightest weakness to a superior. The superiors were watched by one another and by their inferiors. Masses of secret information poured into the secret cabinet of the General; and the General himself ate, slept, prayed, worked, and moved beneath the fixed gaze of ten vigilant eyes."[1]

Historians have not been slow to point out the evils which this Society has wrought in the world, its purely political aims, the worldliness which deadened its spiritual life, and its degradation of morals, which had so much to

[1] Symonds, *The Renaissance in Italy*, *The Catholic Reaction* (London, 1886), i. 293, 294.

do with sapping the ethical life of the seventeenth and eighteenth centuries.   It is frequently said that the cool-headed
Lainez is responsible for most of the evil, and that a change
may be dated from his Generalship.   There seems to be a
wide gulf fixed between the Mystic of Manresa, the revival
preacher of Vicenza, the genuine home mission work in
Rome, and the astute, ruthless worldly political work of
the Society.   Yet almost all the changes may be traced
back to one root, the conception which Ignatius held of
what was meant by true religion.   It was for him, from
first to last, an unreasoning, blind obedience to the
dictates of the catholic hierarchic Church.   It was this
which poisoned the very virtues which gave Loyola's
intentions their strength, and introduced an inhuman
element from the start.

He set out with the noble thought that he would
work for the good of his fellow-men; but his idea of
religion narrowed his horizon.   His idea of "neighbour"
never went beyond the thought of one who owed entire
obedience to the Roman Pontiff—all others were as much
outside the sphere of the brotherhood of mankind as the
followers of Mahomet were for the earliest Crusaders.
Godfrey of Bouillon was both devout and tender-hearted,
yet when he rode, a conqueror, into Jerusalem up the
street filled with the corpses of slaughtered Moslems, he
saw a babe wriggling on the breast of its dead mother,
and, stooping in his saddle, he seized it by the ankle and
dashed its head against the wall.   For Ignatius, as for
Godfrey, all outside the catholic and hierarchic Church
were not men, but wolves.

He was filled with the heroic conception that his
Company was to aid their fellow-men in every department
of earthly life, and the political drove out all other
considerations; for it contained the spheres within which
the whole human life is lived.   Thus, while he preferred for
himself the society of learned and devout men, his acute
Basque brain soon perceived their limitations, and the
Jesuit historian Orlandino tells us that Ignatius selected

the members of his Company from men who knew the world, and were of good social position. He forbade very rightly the follies of ascetic piety, when the discipline of the *Exercises* had been accomplished ; it was only repeated when energies flagged or symptoms of insubordination appeared. Then the General ordered a second course, as a physician sends a patient to the cure at some watering-place. The Constitution directs that novices were to be sought among those who had a comely presence, with good memories, manageable tempers, quick observation, and free from all indiscreet devotion. The Society formed to fight the Renaissance as well as Protestantism, borrowed from its enemy the thought of general culture, training every part of the mind and body, and rendering the possessor a man of the world.

No one can read the letters of Ignatius without seeing the fund of native tenderness that there was in the stern Spanish soldier. That it was no mere sentiment appears in many ways, and in none more so than in his infinite pity for the crowds of fallen women in Rome, and in his wise methods of rescue work. It was this tenderness which led him to his greatest mistake. He held that no one could be saved who was not brought to a state of abject obedience to the hierarchic Church ; that such obedience was the only soil in which true virtues could be planted and grow. He believed, moreover, that the way in which the " common man" could be thoroughly broken to this obedience was through the confessional and the directorate, and therefore that no one should be scared from confession or from trust in his director by undue severity. In his eagerness to secure these inestimable benefits for the largest number of men, he over and over again enjoined the members of his Society to be very cautious in coming to the conclusion that any of their penitents was guilty of a mortal sin. Such was the almost innocent beginning of that Jesuit casuistry which in the end almost wiped out the possibility of anyone who professed obedience commit-ting a mortal sin, and occasioned the profane description of Father Bauny, the famous French director—" Bauny qui tollit peccata mundi per definitionem."

The Society thus organised became powerful almost at once. It made rapid progress in Italy. Lainez was sent to Venice, and fought the slumbering Protestantism there, at Brescia, and in the Val Tellina. Jay was sent to Ferrara to counteract the influence of Renée of France, its Duchess. Salmeron went to Naples and Sicily. The chief Italian towns welcomed the members of the new Order. Noble and devout ladies gave their aid. Colleges were opened; schools, where the education was not merely free, but superior to what was usually given, were soon crowded with pupils. Rome remained the centre and stronghold of the Company.

Portugal was won at once. Xavier and Rodriguez were sent there. They won over King John, and he speedily became their obedient pupil. He delivered into their hands his new University at Coimbra, and the Humanist teachers, George Buchanan among them, were persecuted and dispersed, and replaced by Jesuit professors.

Spain was more difficult to win. The land was the stronghold of the Dominicans, and had been so for generations; and they were unwilling to admit any intruders. But the new Order soon gained ground. It was native to the soil. It had its roots in that Mysticism which pervaded the whole Peninsula. Ignatius gained one distinguished convert, Francis Borgia, Duke of Candia and Viceroy of Catalonia. He placed the University he had founded in their hands. He joined the Order, and became the third General. His influence counterbalanced the suspicions of Charles v., who had no liking for sworn bondmen of the Vatican, and they soon laid firm hold on the people.

In France their progress was slow. The University and the *Parlement* of Paris opposed them, and the Sorbonne made solemn pronouncement against their doctrine. Still they were able to found Colleges at St. Omer, Douai, and Rheims.

Ignatius had his eye on Germany from the first. He

longed to combat heresy in the land of its birth.   Boabdilla, Faber, and Jay were sent there at once.   Boabdilla won the confidence of William, Duke of Bavaria; Jay insinuated himself into the counsels of Ferdinand of Austria, and Faber did the most important work of the three by winning for the Society, Petrus Canisius.   He was the son of a patrician of Nymwegen, trained in Humanist lore, drawn by inner sympathy to the Christian Mysticism of Tauler, and yet steadfast in his adherence to the theology of the mediæval Church.   Faber soon became conscious of his own deficiencies for the work to be done in Germany. His first appearance was at the Religious Conference at Worms, where he found himself face to face with Calvin and Melanchthon, and where his colleagues, Eck and Cochlæus, were rather ashamed of him.   The enthusiastic Savoyard lacked almost everything for the position into which, at the bidding of his General, he had thrust himself. Since then he had been wandering through those portions of Germany which had remained faithful to Rome, seeking individual converts to the principles of the Society, and above all some one who had the gifts for the work Ignatius hoped to do in that country.   It is somewhat interesting to note that almost all the German Roman Catholics who were attracted by him to the new Order were men who had leanings towards the fourteenth century Mystics—men like Gerard Hammond, Prior of the Carthusians of Köln.   Faber caught Canisius by means of his Mysticism.   He met him at Mainz, explained the *Exercitia Spiritualia* to him, induced the young man to undergo the course of discipline which they prescribed, and won him for Loyola and the Company.   "He is the man," wrote Faber to Ignatius, "whom I have been seeking—if he is a man, and not rather an angel of the Lord."

Ignatius speedily recognised the value of the new recruit.   He saw that he was not a man to be kept long in the lower ranks of the Company, and gave him more liberty of action than he allowed to his oldest associates.   Faber had sent him grievous reports about the condition of affairs in Germany. "It is not misinterpretation of Scripture," he wrote, "not specious arguments, not the Lutherans with their preaching and persuasions, that have lost so many provinces and towns to the Roman Church, but the scandalous lives of the ministers of religion." He felt his helplessness. He was a foreigner, and the Germans did not like strangers. He could not speak their language, and his Latin gave him a very limited audience. People and priests looked on him as a spy sent to report their weaknesses to Rome. When he discoursed about the *Exercitia,* and endeavoured to induce men to try them, he was accused of urging a "new religion." When he attempted to form student associations in connection with the Company, it was said that he was urging the formation of "conventicles" outside the Church's ordinances. But the adhesion of Canisius changed all that. He was a German, one of themselves; his orthodoxy was undisputed; he was an eminent scholar, the most distinguished of the young masters of the University of Köln, a leader among its most promising students. Under his guidance the student associations grew strong; after his example young men offered themselves for the discipline of the *Exercises.* Loyola saw that he had gained a powerful assistant. He longed to see him personally at Rome; but he was so convinced of his practical wisdom that he left it to himself either to come to Italy or to remain in Germany. Canisius decided to remain. Affairs at Köln were then in a critical state. The Archbishop-Elector, Hermann von Wied, favoured the Reformation. He had thoughts of secularising his Electorate, and if he succeeded in his design his example might be followed in another ecclesiastical Electorate, with the result that the next Emperor would be a Protestant. Canisius organised the people, the clergy, the University authorities against this, and succeeded in defeating the designs of the Archbishop. When his work at Köln was done, he went to Vienna. There he became the confessor and private adviser of Ferdinand of Austria, administered the affairs of the diocese of Vienna during a long episcopal interregnum, helped to found its Jesuit College, and another at Ingolstadt. These Colleges became the centres of Jesuit influence in Germany, and helped to spread the power of the Society. But with all this activity it can scarcely be said that the Company was very powerful in that country until years after the Council of Trent.

The foreign mission activity of the Jesuits has been often described, and much of the early progress of the Company has been attributed to the admiration created by the work of Francis Xavier and his companions. This was undoubtedly true; but in the earliest times it was the home mission successes that drew most attention and sympathy; and these have been too often left unmentioned.

Nothing lay nearer the hearts of devout persons who refused to accept the Reformation than the condition of the great proportion of the Roman Catholic priests in all countries, and the depravity of morals among laity and clergy alike. Ignatius was deeply affected by both scandals, and had resolved from the first to do his best to cure them. It was this resolve and the accompanying strenuous endeavours which won Ignatius the respect and sympathy of all those in Italy who were sighing for a reform in the moral life of people and clergy, and brought the Company of Jesus into line with Italian Reformers like Contarini, Ghiberti, and Vittoria Colonna. His system of Colleges and the whole use he made of education could have only one result—to give an educated clergy to the Roman Church. It was a democratic extension of the work of Caraffa and Gætano da Thiene. Ignatius had also clear views about the way to produce a reformation of morals in Rome. Like Luther, he insisted that it must begin in the individual life, and could not be produced by stringent legislation; " it must start in the individual, spread to the family, and then permeate the metropolis." But meanwhile something might be done to heal the worst running sores of society. Like Luther, Ignatius fastened on three —the waste of child life, the plague of begging, and what is called the "social evil"; if his measure of success in dealing with the evils fell far short of Luther's, the more corrupted condition of Italy had something to do with his failure.

His first measure of social reform was to gather Roman children, either orphans or deserted by their parents. They were gratuitously housed, fed, and taught in a simple fashion, and were instructed in the various mechanical arts which could enable them to earn a living. In a brief time, Ignatius had over two hundred boys and girls in his two industrial schools.

How to cure the plague of beggars which infested all Roman Catholic countries, a curse for which the teaching of the mediæval Church was largely responsible,[1] had been a problem studied by Ignatius ever since his brief visit to his native place in 1535. There he had attempted to get the town council of Azpeitia to forbid begging within the bounds of the city, and to support the deserving and helpless poor at the town's cost. He urged the same policy on the chief men in Rome. When he failed in his large and public schemes, he attempted to work them out by means of charitable associations connected with and fostered by his Society.

Nothing, however, excited the sympathy of Loyola so much as the numbers and condition of fallen women in all the larger Italian towns. He was first struck with it in Venice, where he declared that he would willingly give his life to hinder a day's sin of one of these unfortunates. The magnitude of the evil in Rome appalled him. He felt that it was too great for him to meddle with as a whole. Something, however, he could attempt, and did. In Rome, which swarmed with men vowed to celibacy simply because they had something to do with the Church, prostitution was frequently concealed under the cloak of marriage. Husbands lived by the sinful life of their wives. Deserted wives also swelled the ranks of unfortunates. Loyola provided homes for any such as might wish to leave their

[1] Cf. vol. i. p. 142.

degrading life. At first they were simply taken into families whom Ignatius persuaded to receive them. The numbers of the rescued grew so rapidly that special houses were needed. Ignatius called them " Martha-Houses." They were in no sense convents. There was, of course, oversight, but the idea was to provide a bright home where these women could earn their own living or the greater part of it. The scheme spread to many of the large Italian towns, and many ladies were enlisted in the plans to help their fallen sisters.

Loyola's associations to provide ransom for Christian captives among the Moslems, his attempts to discredit duelling, his institutions for loans to the poor, can only be alluded to. It was these works of Christian charity which undoubtedly gained the immediate sympathy for the Company which awaited it in most lands south of the Alps.

Almost all earlier monastic Orders provided a place for women among their organisation. An Order of Nuns corresponded to the Order of Monks. Few founders of monastic Orders have owed so much to women as Ignatius did. A few ladies of Barcelona were his earliest disciples, were the first to undergo the discipline of the *Exercises*, then in an imperfect shape, and encouraged him when he needed it most by their faith in him and his plans.[1] One of them, Isabella Roser (Rosel, Rosell), a noble matron, wife of Juan Roser, heard Ignatius deliver one of his first sermons, and was so impressed by it, that she and her husband invited him to stay in their house, which he did. She paid all his expenses while he went to school and college in Spain. She and her friends sent him large sums of money when he was in Paris. Ignatius could never have carried out his plans but for her sympathy and assistance. In spite of all this, Ignatius came early to the conclusion that his Company should have as little as

---

[1] Many of Loyola's letters are addressed to these ladies : *Cartas*, i. pp. 1, 4, 23, to Inés Pascual ; pp. 16, 63, 112, 279, to Isabella Roser ; pp. 34, 44, 177, to Teresa Rejadella de St. Clara, a nun.

36**

possible to do with the direction of women's souls (it took
so much time, he complained); that women were too
emotional to endure the whole discipline of the *Exercises*;
and that there must never be Jesuit nuns. The work he
meant his Company to do demanded such constant and
strained activity—a Jesuit must stand with only one foot
on the ground, he said, the other must be raised ready to
start wherever he was despatched—that women were unfit
for it. That was his firm resolve, and he was to suffer
for it.

In 1539 he had written to Isabella Roser that he
hoped God would forget him if he ever forgot all that she
had done for him ; and it is probable that some sentences
nonintentional on the part of the writer) had made the
lady, now a widow, believe that she was destined to play
the part of Clara to this Francis. At all events (1543)
she came to Rome, accompanied by two friends bringing
with them a large sum of money, sorely needed by Ignatius
to erect his house in Rome for the Professed of the Four
Vows. In return, they asked him to give some time to
advise them in spiritual things. This Ignatius did, but
not with the minuteness nor at the length expected. He
declared that the guidance of the souls of the three ladies
for three days cost him more than the oversight of his
whole Society for a month. Then it appeared that Isabella
Roser wanted more. She was a woman of noble gifts, no
weak sentimental enthusiast. She had studied theology
widely and profoundly. Her learning and abilities impressed the Cardinals whom she met and with whom she
talked. She desired Ignatius to create an Order of Jesuit
nuns of whom she should be the head. When he refused
there was a great quarrel. She demanded back the money
she had given ; and when this was refused, she raised an
action in the Roman courts. She lost her case, and
returned indignant to Spain.[1] Poor Isabella Roser—she
was not a derelict, and so less interesting to a physician of
souls ; but she needed comforting like other people. She

[1] Cf. *Cartas*, i. pp. 291, 470, 471.

forgave her old friend, and their correspondence was renewed. She died the year before Ignatius.

When the Society of Jesus was at the height of its power in the seventeenth century, another and equally unsuccessful attempt was made to introduce an Order of Jesuit nuns.

Ignatius died at the age of sixty-five, thirty-five years after his conversion, and sixteen after his Order had received the apostolic benediction. His Company had become the most powerful force within the reanimated Roman Church; it had largely moulded the theology of Trent; and it seemed to be winning back Germany. It had spread in the swiftest fashion. Ignatius had seen established twelve Provinces—Portugal, Castile, Aragon, Andalusia, Italy (Lombardy and Tuscany), Naples, Sicily, **Germany, Flanders, France, Brazil, and the East Indies.**

CHAPTER V.

THE COUNCIL OF TRENT.[1]

§ 1. *The Assembling of the Council.*

THE General Council, the subject of many negotiations between the Emperor and the Pope, was at last finally fixed to meet at Trent in 1545.[2] The city was the

[1] SOURCES : *The Canons and Decrees of the Council of Trent* (London, 1851) ; Theiner, *Acta genuina Concilii Tridentini* (1875) ; Döllinger, *Ungedruckte Berichte und Tagebücher zur Geschichte des Concils von Trient* (Nördlingen, 1876) ; Grisar, *Iacobi Lainez Disputationes Tridentinæ* (Innsbruck, 1886) ; Le Plat, *Monumentorum ad historiam Concilii Tridentini potissimum illustrandum spectantium amplissima collectio* (Louvain, 1781–87) ; Paleotto, *Acta Concilii Tridentini, 1562–63* ; Planck, *Anecdota ad Historiam concilii Tridentini pertinentia* (Göttingen, 1791–1818) ; Sickel, "Das Reformations-Libell Ferdinands I." (in *Archiv für österreichische Geschichte*, xiv., Vienna, 1871), *Catechismus Romanus* (Paris, 1635) ; Denzinger, *Enchiridion* (Würzburg, 1900).

LATER BOOKS : Maurenbrecher, "Tridentiner Concil, Vorspiel und Einleitung" (in the *Historisches Taschensbuch*, sechste Folge, 1886, pp. 147–256), "Begründung der katholischen Glaubenslehre" (in the *Hist. Tasch.* 1888, pp. 305–28), and "Die Lehre von der Erbsünde und der Rechtfertigung" (in the *Hist. Tasch.* 1890, pp. 237–330) ; Harnack, *History of Dogma*, vii. (London, 1899) ; Loofs, *Leitfaden zum studium der Dogmengeschichte* (Halle, 1893) ; R. C. Jenkins, *Pre-Tridentine Doctrine* (London, 1891) ; Froude, *Lectures on the Council of Trent* (London, 1896) ; Sickel, *Zur Geschichte des Concils von Trient* (Vienna, 1872), and *Die Geschäfts-ordnung des Concils von Trient* (Vienna, 1871) ; Milledonne, *Journal de Concile de Trente* (Paris, 1870) ; Braunsberger *Entstehung und erste Entwicklung der Katechismen des Petrus Canisius* (Freiburg i. B. 1893) ; Dejob, *De l'influence du Concile de Trente* (Paris, 1884) ; Paolo Sarpi, *History of the Council of Trent* (London, 1619) ; *Lettere di Fra Paolo Sarpi* (Florence, 1863).

[2] For an account of these negotiations, and for the false start made on Nov. 1st, 1542, see W. Maurenbrecher, "Tridentiner Concil, Vorspiel und Einleitung," *Historisches Taschenbuch*, Sechste Folge, 1886, pp. 147–256 ;

capital of a small episcopal principality, its secular over-lord was the Count of the Tyrol, whose deputy resided in the town. It was a frontier place with about a thousand houses, including four or five fine buildings and a large palace of the Prince Bishop. It contained several churches, one of which, Santa Maria Maggiore, was reserved for the meetings of the Council.[1] Its inhabitants were partly Italian and partly German—the two nationalities living in separate quarters and retaining their distinctive customs and dress. It was a small place for such an assembly, and could not furnish adequate accommodation for the crowd of visitors a General Council always involved.

The Papal Legates entered Trent in state on the 13th of March (1545). Heavy showers of rain marred the impressive display. They were received by the local clergy with enthusiasm, and by the populace with an absolute indifference. Months passed before the Council was opened. Few delegates were present when the papal Legates arrived. The representatives of the Emperor and those of Venice came early; Bishops arrived in straggling groups during April and May and the months that followed. The necessary papal Brief did not reach the town till the 11th of December, and the Council was formally opened on the 13th. The long leisurely opening was symptomatic of the history of the Council. Its proceedings were spread over a period of eighteen years:—under Pope Paul III., 1545–47, including Sessions i. to x.; under Pope Julius III., 1551–52, including Sessions xi. to xvi.; under Pope Pius IV., 1562–1563, including Sessions xvii. to xxv.[2]

---

also *Cambridge Modern History*, ii. 660 *ff.* It seems to be pretty certain that the fear that the Germans might hold a National Council and the possibility that there might result a National German Church independent of Rome on the lines laid down by Henry VIII. of England, was the motive which finally compelled Pope Paul III. to decide on summoning a General Council; cf. i. pp. 378, 379.

[1] The church now contains a picture on the north wall of the choir of the group of theologians who were members of the Council.

[2] The Council sat at Trent from the 13th Dec. 1545 to the 11th March 1547 (Sessions i.–viii.); at Bologna from the 21st of April to the 2nd of

The Papal Legates were Gian Maria Giocchi, Cardinal del Monte, a Tuscan who had early entered the service of the Roman Curia, a profound jurist and a choleric man of fifty-seven (*first* President); Marcello Cervini, Cardinal da Sante Croce; and Cardinal Reginald Pole, the Englishman. The three represented the three tendencies which were apparent in ecclesiastical Italy. The first belonged to the party which stood by the old unreformed Curia, and wished no change. Cervini represented the growing section of the Church, which regarded Cardinal Caraffa as their leader. They sought eagerly and earnestly a reform in life and character, especially among the clergy; but refused to make any concessions in doctrines, ceremonies, or institutions to the Protestants. They differed from the more reforming Spanish and French ecclesiastical leaders in their dislike of secular interference, and believed that the Popes should have more rather than less power. Reginald Pole was one of those liberal Roman Catholics of whom Cardinal Contarini was the distinguished leader. He was made a Legate probably to conciliate his associates. He was a man whom most people liked and nobody feared—a harmless, pliant tool in the hands of a diplomatist like Cervini. The new Society of Jesus was represented by Lainez and Salmeron, who went to the Council with the dignity of papal theologians—a title which gave them a special standing and influence.

According to the arrangement come to between the Emperor and the Pope, the Bull summoning the Council declared that it was called for the three purposes of overcoming the religious schism; of reforming the Church; and of calling a united Christendom to a crusade against unbelievers. By general consent the work of the Council was limited to the first two objects. They were stated in terms vague enough to cover real diversity of opinion about the work the Council was expected to do.

June 1547 (Sessions ix.-x.); at Trent from the 1st of May 1551 to the 28th of April 1552 (Session xi-xvi.); and at Trent from the 18th of Jan. 1562 to the 3rd of Dec. 1563 (Sessions xvii.-xxv.).

Almost all believed that the questions of reforming the Church and dealing with the religious revolt were inseparably connected ; but the differences at once emerged when the method of treating the schism was discussed.

Many pious Roman Catholics believed that the Lutheran movement was a divine punishment for the sins of the Church, and that it would disappear if the Church was thoroughly reformed in life and morals. They differed about the agency to be employed to effect the reformation. The Italian party, who followed Cardinal Caraffa, maintained that full powers should be in the hands of the Pope; non-Italians, especially the Spaniards, thought it vain to look for any such reformation so long as the Curia, itself the seat of the greatest corruption, remained unreformed, and contended that the secular authority ought to be allowed more power to put down ecclesiastical scandals.

The Emperor, Charles v., had come to believe that there were no insuperable differences of doctrine between the Lutherans and the Roman Catholics, and that mutual explanations and a real desire to give and take, combined with the removal of scandals which all alike deplored, would heal the schism. He had never seen the gulf which the Lutheran principle of the spiritual priesthood of all believers had created between the Protestants and mediæval doctrines and ceremonies.[1] He persisted in this belief long after the proceedings at Trent had left him hopeless of seeing the reconciliation he had expected brought about by the Council he had done so much to get summoned. The Augsburg Interim (1548) shows what he thought might have been done.[2] He was badly seconded at Trent. The only Bishop who supported his views heartily was Madruzzo, the Prince Bishop of Trent; his representative, Diego de Mendoza, fell ill shortly after the opening of the Council, and his substitute, Francisco de Toledo, did not reach Trent until March 1546.

[1] It was enough for him that the Protestants held the Twelve Articles (the *Apostles' Creed*) ; cf. i. 264 *n.* ; and ii. 517, 518.
[2] Cf. i. 390.

§ 2. *Procedure at the Council.*

The ablest of the three Legates, Cervini, had a definite plan of procedure before him. He knew thoroughly the need for drastic reforms in the life and morals of the clergy and for purifying the Roman Curia; but, with the memories of Basel and Constance before him, he dreaded above all things a conflict between the Pope and the Council, and he believed that such a quarrel was imminent if the Council itself undertook to reform the Curia. His idea was that the Council ought to employ itself in the useful, even necessary task of codifying the doctrines of the Church, so that all men might discern easily what was the true Catholic faith. While this was being done, opportunity would be given to the Pope himself to reform the Curia—a task which would be rendered easier by the consciousness that he had the sympathy of the Council behind him. He scarcely concealed his opinion that such codification should make no concessions to the Protestants, but would rather show them to be in hopeless antagonism to the Catholic faith. He did not propose any general condemnation of what he thought to be Lutheran errors; but he wished the separate points of doctrine which the Lutherans had raised—Justification, the authority of Holy Scripture, the Sacraments—to be examined carefully and authoritatively defined. In this way heretics would be taught the error of their ways without mentioning names, and without the specific condemnation of individuals. He expounded his plan of procedure to the Council.

His suggestions were by no means universally well received by the delegates. The proposal to leave reforms to the Pope provoked many speeches from the Spanish Bishops, full of bitter reproaches against the Curia; and his conception of codifying the doctrines of the Church with the avowed intention of irrevocably excluding the Lutherans was by no means liked by many.

A great debate took place on Jan. 18th, which revealed to the Legate that probably the majority of the delegates did not favour his proposed course of procedure. Madruzzo, the eloquent Prince Bishop of Trent, and a Cardinal, made a long speech, in which he asserted that the Council should not rashly take for granted that the Lutherans were irreconcilable. They ought to acknowledge frankly that the corrupt morals of the mediæval clergy had done much to cause dissatisfaction and to justify revolt. Let them therefore assume that these evils for which the Church was responsible had produced the schism. Let them invite the Protestants to come among them as brethren. Let them show to those men, who had no doubt erred in doctrine, that the Catholic Church was sincerely anxious to reform the abounding evils in life and morals, and, with this fraternal bond between them, let them reason amicably together about the doctrinal differences which now separated them. The eloquent and large-minded Cardinal condensed the recommendations in his speech in one sentence : " Cum corrupti mores ecclesiasticorum dederint occasionem Lutheranis confingendi falsa dogmata, sublata causa, facilius tolletur effectus ; subdens optimum fore, si protestantes ipsos amicabiliter et fraterne literis invitaremus, ut ipsi quoque ad synodum venirent, et se etiam reformari paterentur." [1] We are told that this speech raised great enthusiasm among the delegates, and that the Legates had some difficulty in preventing its proposal from being universally accepted. At the most they were able to prevent any definite conclusion being come to about the procedure at the close of the sitting. Cervini saw that he could not get his way adopted. He agreed that proposals for reform and for the codification of doctrine should be discussed simultaneously, his knowledge of theological nature telling him that if he once got so many divines engaged in doctrinal discussions two things would surely follow : their eagerness would make them neglect everything else, and their polemical instincts would carry them beyond the point where a conciliation of the Protestants required them to come to a halt. So it happened. The

---

[1] (Theiner) *Acta genuina ss. œcumenici concilii Tridentini*, p. 40.

Council found itself committed to a codification and definition of Catholic doctrine. The suggestion of the Bishop of Feltre (Thomas Campeggio) was adopted, that the discussion of doctrines and the proposals for reform should be discussed by two separate Commissions, whose reports should come before the Synod alternately. The Legates obtained a large majority for this course, and the protest of Madruzzo was unavailing.

The decision to attack the question of reform was very unacceptable to the Pope. He went so far as to ask the Legates to get it rescinded; but that was impossible, and he had to content himself with the assurances of Cervini that no real harm would come of it.

This important question being settled, the Council decided upon the details of procedure. The whole Synod was divided into three divisions or Commissions, to each of which allotted work was given. Each question was first of all to be prepared for the section by theologians and canonists, then discussed in the special Commission to which it had been entrusted. If approved there, it was to be brought before a general Congregation of the whole Synod for discussion. If it passed this scrutiny, it was to be promulgated in a solemn session of the Council.

§ 3. *Restatement of Doctrines.*

It ought to be said, before describing the doctrinal labours of the Council, that the work done at Trent was not to give Conciliar sanction to the whole mass of mediæval doctrinal tradition. There was a thorough revision of doctrinal positions in which a great deal of theology which had been current during the later Middle Ages was verbally rejected, and the rejection was most apparent in that Scotist theology which had been popular before the Reformation, and which had been most strongly attacked by Luther. The Scotist theology, with its theological scepticism, was largely repudiated in name at least—whether its spirit was banished is another question which has to be discussed later. A great many influences unknown during the later Middle Ages pressed consciously and unconsciously upon the divines assembled at Trent and coloured their dogmatic work. Although the avowed intention of the theologians there was to defeat both Humanism and the Reformation, they could not avoid being influenced by both movements. Humanism had led many of them to study the earlier Church Fathers, and they could not escape Augustine in doing so. They were led to him by many paths. The Dominican theologians had begun, quite independently of the Reformation, to study the great theologian of their Order, and Thomas had led them back to Augustine. The Reformation had laid stress on the doctrines of sin, of justification, and of predestination, and had therefore awakened a new interest in them and consequently in Augustine. The New Thomism, with Augustinianism behind it, was a feature of the times, and was the strongest influence at work among the theologians who assembled at Trent. It could not fail to make their doctrinal results take a very different form from the theology which Luther was taught by John Nathin in the Erfurt convent. Christian Mysticism, too, had its revival, especially in Spain and in Italy, and among some of the reconstructed monastic orders. If it had small influence on the doctrines, it worked for a more spiritual conception of the Church. What has been called Curialism, the theory of the omnipotence of the Pope in all things connected with the Church's life, practice, and beliefs, was also a potent factor with some of the assembled fathers. But above all things the theologians who met at Trent were influenced by the thought and fact of the Lutheran Reformation. This is apparent in the order in which they discussed theological questions, in the subjects they selected and in those they omitted. All these things help us to understand how the theology of the Council of Trent was something peculiar, something by itself, and different both from what may be vaguely called mediæval theology and from that of the modern Church of Rome.[1]

The Council, in its third session, laid the basis of its doctrinal work by reaffirming the Niceo-Constantinopolitan Creed with the *filioque* clause added, and significantly called it: Symbolum fidei quo sancta ecclesia *Romana* utitur. This done, it was ready to proceed with the codification and definition of doctrines.

On the 18th of April 1546, the Commission which had to do with the preparation of the subject reported, and the Council proceeded to discuss the sources of theological knowledge or the Rule of Faith. The influence of the Reformation is clearly seen not merely in the priority assigned to this subject, but also in the statement that the "purity of the Gospel" is involved in the decision come to. The opposition to Protestantism was made emphatic by the Council declaring these four things:

It accepted as canonical all the books contained in the Alexandrine Canon (the Septuagint), and therefore the Apocrypha of the Old Testament, and did so heedless of the fact that the editor of the Vulgate (afterwards pronounced authoritative), Jerome, had thought very little of the Apocrypha. The Reformers, in their desire to go back to the earliest and purest sources, had pronounced in favour of the Hebrew Canon; the Council, in spite of Jerome, accepted the common mediæval tradition.

It declared that in addition to the books of Holy

---

[1] Loofs in his *Leitfaden zum studium der Dogmengeschichte* (Halle a. S. 1893) declares that the following tendencies within the Roman Catholic Church of the sixteenth century have all to be taken into account as influencing the decisions come to at the Council of Trent: The reorganisation of the Spanish Church in strict mediæval spirit *by the Crown* under Isabella and Ferdinand; the revival of Thomist theology, especially in the Dominican Order; the fostering of mystical piety, especially in new and in reconstructed Orders; the ennobling of theology by Humanism, and its influence, direct and indirect, in leading theologians back to Augustine; the strengthening of the Papacy in the rise of Curialism; and, lastly, the ecclesiastical interests of temporal sovereigns generally opposed to this Curialism. He declares that the newly-founded Order of the Jesuits served as a meeting-place for the first, third, fourth, and fifth of these tendencies (pp. 333-34).

Scripture, it "receives with an equal feeling of piety and reverence the traditions, whether relating to faith or to morals, dictated either orally by Christ or by the Holy Spirit, and preserved in continuous succession within the Catholic Church." [1] The practical effect of this declaration, something entirely novel, was to assert that there was within the Church an infallibly correct mode of interpreting Scripture, and to give the ecclesiastical authorities (whoever they might be) the means of warding off any Protestant attack based upon Holy Scripture alone. The Council were careful to avoid stating who were the guardians of this dogmatic tradition, but in the end it led by easily traced steps to the declaration of Pope Pius IX. : *Io sono la tradizione,* and placed a decision of a Pope speaking *ex cathedra* on a level with the Word of God.

It proclaimed that the Vulgate version contained the authoritative text of Holy Scripture. This was also new, and, moreover, in violent opposition to the best usages of the mediæval Church. It cast aside as worse than useless the whole scholarship of the Renaissance both within and outside of the mediæval Church, and, on pretence of consecrating a text of Holy Scripture, reduced it to the state of a mummy, lifeless and unfruitful.[2]

It asserted that every faithful believer must accept the sense of Scripture which the Church teaches, that no one was to oppose the unanimous consensus of the Fathers— and this without defining what the Church is, or who are

---

[1] "Nec non traditiones ipsas, tum ad fidem, tum ad mores pertinentes, tanquam vel oretenus a Christo, vel a Spiritu Sancto dictatas, et continua successione in Ecclesia catholica conservatas, *pari* pietatis affectu ac reverentia suscipit et veneratur." The references to the decisions of Trent have been taken from Denzinger, *Enchiridion Symbolorum et Definitionum quæ de rebus fidei et morum a conciliis œcumenicis et summis Pontificibus emanarunt* (Würzburg, 1900), p. 179.

[2] "Statuit et declarat, ut hæc ipsa vetus et vulgata editio, quæ longo tot sæculorum usu in ipsa Ecclesia probata est, in publicis lectionibus, disputationibus, prædicationibus pro authentica habeatur ; et ut nemo illam rejicere quovis prætextu audeat vel præsumat" (Denzinger, *Enchiridion,* etc. p. 179).

the Fathers.[1] The whole trend of this decision was to place the authoritative exposition of the Scriptures in the hands of the Pope, although at the time the Council lacked the courage to say so.

It must not be supposed that these decisions were reached without a good deal of discussion. Some members of the Council would have preferred the Hebrew Canon. Nacchianti, Bishop of Chioggia, protested against placing traditions on the same level as Holy Scripture;[2] some wished to distinguish between apostolical traditions and others; but the final decision of the Council was carried by a large majority. The most serious conflict of opinion, however, arose about the clause which declared that the Vulgate version was the only authoritative one. It was held that such a decision entailed the prohibition of using translations of the Scripture in the mother tongue. The Spanish Bishops, in spite of the fact that translations of the Scriptures into Spanish had once been commonly used and their use encouraged, would have had all Bible reading in the mother tongue prohibited. The Germans protested. The debate waxed hot. Madruzzo, of Trent, eloquently declared that to prohibit the translation of the Scriptures into German would be a public scandal. Were children not to be taught the Lord's Prayer in a language they could understand? A Bull of Pope Paul II. was cited against him. He replied that Popes had erred and were liable to err; but that the Apostle Paul had not erred, and that he had commanded the Scriptures to be read by every one, and that this could not be done unless they were translated. A compromise was suggested, that each country should decide for itself whether it would have translations of the Scriptures or not. In the end, however, the Vulgate was proclaimed the only authentic Word of God.

[1] "Nemo . . . contra eum sensum, quem tenuit et tenet sancta mater Ecclesia, cujus est judicare de vero sensu et interpretatione Scripturarum Sanctarum, aut etiam contra unanimem consensum Patrum, ipsam Scripturam Sacram interpretari audeat" (ibid. p. 180).

[2] "Non possum pati synodum pari pietatis affectu suscipere traditiones et libros sanctos : hoc enim, ut vere dicam quod sentio, impium est."

In the fifth session (June 17th, 1546) and in the sixth session (Jan. 13th, 1547) the Council attacked the subjects of Original Sin and Justification. The Reformation had challenged the Roman Church to say whether it had any *spiritual* religion at all, or was simply an institution claiming to possess a secret science of salvation through ceremonies which required little or no spiritual life on the part of priests or recipients. The challenge had to be met not merely on account of the Protestants, but because devout Romanists had declared that it must be done. The answer was given in the two doctrines of Original Sin and Justification, as defined at the Council of Trent. They both deserve a much more detailed examination than space permits.

The Legates had felt that the Council as constituted might come to decisions giving room for Protestant doctrine, and pled with the Pope to send them more Italian Bishops, whose votes might counteract the weight of northern opinion (June 2nd, 1546). They were extremely anxious about the way in which the Council might deal with those two doctrines.

The first, the definition of Original Sin, *seems* to reject strongly that Pelagianism or Semi-Pelagianism which had marked the later Scholasticism which Luther had been taught in the Erfurt convent. It appears to rest on and to express the evangelical thoughts of Augustine. But a careful examination shows that it is full of ambiguities—intentional loop-holes provided for the retention of the Semi-Pelagian modes of thought. Space forbids our going over them all, but one example may be selected from the first chapter. It is there said that Adam lost the holiness and righteousness *in which he had been constituted.* Why not *created?* The phrase may mean created, and all the New Thomists at the Council doubtless read it in that way. By the Fall man lost what Thomas, following Augustine, had called increased righteousness. But the phrase *in qua constitutus fuerat* could easily be interpreted to mean that what man did lose were the superadded *dona supernaturalia* whose loss in no way impaired human nature; and, if so interpreted, room is provided for Pelagianism.[1]   Again, while the Augustinian doctrine of the Fall seems to be taught, it is added that by Original Sin *liberum arbitrium* is *minime extinctum viribus licet attenuatum*, which is Semi-Pelagian.[2]   The whole definition closes with a statement that it is not to be applied to the Blessed Virgin, the doctrine about whom has been expressed in the Constitutions of Pope Sixtus IV. of happy memory.[3]

The statement of the Doctrine of Justification is a masterpiece of theological dexterity, and deserves much more consideration than can be given it.   The whole treatment of the subject was the cause of considerable anxiety outside the Council.   On the one hand, the Emperor Charles v., who was greatly disappointed at the course taken by the Council, and saw the chance of conciliating the Protestants diminishing daily, wished to defer all discussion; while the Pope, bent on making it impossible for the Protestants to return, desired the Council to define this important doctrine in such a way that none of the Reformed could possibly accept it.   The Emperor's wishes were speedily overruled; but it was by no means easy for the Legates to carry out the desires of the Pope.   There was a great deal of Evangelical doctrine in the Roman Church which had to be reckoned with.   So much existed that at one time it had actually been proposed at the Vatican to approve of the first part of the Augsburg Confession in order to win the Protestants over.

[1] "Si quis non confitetur, primum hominem Adam, cum mandatum Dei in paradiso fuisset transgressus, statim sanctificationem et justitiam, in qua constitutus fuerat, amisisse. . . . Anathema sit" (Denzigner, *Enchiridion*, etc. p. 180).

[2] "Tametsi in eis liberum arbitrium minime extinctum esset, viribus licet attenuatum et inclinatum"; in the first paragraph of the decree on Justification (*ibid.* p. 182).

[3] "Declarat tamen hæc ipsa sancta Synodus, non esse suæ intentionis comprehendere in hoc decreto, ubi de peccato originali agitur, beatam et immaculatam Virginem Mariam, Dei genitricem; sed observandas constitutiones felicis recordationis Sixti Papæ IV. sub pœnis in eis constitutionibus contentis, quas innovat" (*ibid.* p. 182).

The day for such proposals was past; but the New Thomism was a power in the Church, and perhaps the strongest *theological* force at the Council of Trent, and had to be reckoned with. If the Protestant conception of Justification be treated merely as a doctrine,—which it is not, being really an experience deeper and wider than any form of words can contain,—if it be stated scholastically, then it is possible to express it in propositions which do not perceptibly differ from the doctrine of Justification in the New Thomist theology. At the conference at Regensburg (Ratisbon) in 1541, Contarini was able to draft a statement of the doctrine which commended itself to such opponents as Calvin and Eck.[1] Harnack has remarked that the real difference between the two doctrines appeared in this, that "just on account of the doctrine of Justification the Protestants combated as heretical the *usages* of the Roman Church, while the Augustinian Thomists could not understand why it should be impossible to unite the two."[2] But the similarity of statement shows the difficulty of the Legates in guiding the Council to frame a decree which would content the Pope. They were able to accomplish this mainly through the dexterity of the Jesuit Lainez.

The discussion showed how deeply the division ran. Some theologians were prepared to accept the purely Lutheran view that Justification was by Faith alone. They were in a small minority, and were noisily interrupted. One of them, Thomas de San Felicio, Bishop of La Cava, and a Neapolitan, came to blows with a Greek Bishop. The debate then centred round the mediating view of the doctrine, which Contarini had advocated in his *Tractatus de Justificatione*, and which may be said to represent the position of the New Thomists. It seemed to commend itself to a majority of the delegates. The leader of the party was Girolamo Seripando (1493–1553), since 1539 the General of the Augustinian Eremites, the Order to

---

[1] Cf. above, pp. 520, 521.
[2] *History of Dogma* (English translation), vii. 57.

37**

which Luther had belonged.[1] He distinguished between
an imputed and an inherent righteousness, a distinction
corresponding to that between prevenient and co-operating
grace, and to some extent not unlike that between Justification and Sanctification in later Protestant theology.   In
the former, the imputed righteousness of Christ, lay the
only hope for man ; inherent righteousness was based upon
the imputed, and was useless without it.   The learning
and candour of Seripando were conspicuous ; his pleading
seemed about to carry the Council with him, when Lainez
intervened to save the situation for the strictly papal
party.   The Jesuit theologian accepted the distinction
made between imputed and inherent righteousness ; he
even admitted that the former was alone efficacious in
Justification ; but he alleged that in practice at least the
two kinds of righteousness touched each other, and that
it would be dangerous to practical theology to consider
them as wholly distinct.   His clear plausible reasoning had
great effect, and the ambiguities of his address are reflected
in the looseness of the definitions in the decree.

The definition of the doctrine of Justification which
was adopted by the Council is very lengthy.   It contains
sixteen chapters followed by thirty-three canons.   It
naturally divides into three divisions — chapters i.–ix.
describing what Justification is ; chapters x.–xiii. the
increase of Justification ; and chapters xiv.–xvi. the
restoration of Justification when it is lost.   Almost every
chapter includes grave ambiguities.

The first section is the most important.   It begins
with statements which are in themselves evangelical.   All
men have come under the power of sin, and are unable to
deliver themselves either by their strength of nature or
by the aid of the letter of the law of Moses.[2]   Our

---

[1] Seripando was made a Cardinal in 1561 by Pope Pius IV., who also
sent him to the Council of Trent in that year as one of his Legates.

[2] " Cum omnes homines in prævaricatione Adæ innocentiam perdi dissent
facti immundi . . . ut non modo gentes per vim naturæ, sed ne Judæi
quidem per ipsam etiam litteram legis Moysi, inde liberari aut surgere
possent " (Denzinger, *Enchiridion*, etc. 182).

Heavenly Father sent His Son and set Him forth as the propitiator through faith in His blood for our sins.[1] It is then said that all do not accept the benefits of Christ's death, although He died for all, but only those to whom the merit of His passion is communicated; and this statement is followed by a rather confused sentence which suggests but commits no one to the Augustinian doctrine of election.[2] This is followed up by saying that Justification is the translation from that condition in which man is born into a condition of grace through Jesus Christ our Saviour; and it is added that this translation, in the Gospel dispensation, does not happen apart from Baptism or *the wish to be baptized*.[3] In spite of some ambiguities, these first four chapters have quite an Evangelical ring about them; but with the fifth a change begins. While some sentences seem to maintain the Evangelical ideas previously stated, room is distinctly made for Pelagian work-righteousness. It is said, for example, that Justification is wrought through the *gratia præveniens* or *vocatio* in which adults are called apart from any merit of their own; but then it is added that the end of this calling is that sinners may be *disposed*, by God's inciting and aiding grace, to *convert themselves* in order to their own justification by freely assenting to and co-operating with the grace of God.[4] This was the suggestion of Lainez. The good disposition into which sinners are to be brought is said to

[1] "Hunc proposuit Deus propitiatorem *per fidem* in sanguine ipsius pro peccatis nostris" (Denzinger, *Enchiridion*, etc. p. 183).

[2] "Ita nisi in Christo renascerentur, nunquam justificarentur, cum ea renascentia per meritum passionis ejus gratia, qua justi fiunt, illis tribuatur; pro hoc beneficio Apostolus gratias nos semper agere hortatur Patri, qui dignos nos fecit in partem sortis sanctorum in lumine, et eripuit de potestate tenebrarum, transtulitque in regnum Filii dilectionis suæ, in quo habemus redemptionem et remissionem peccatorum" (*ibid.* 183).

[3] "Translatio ab eo statu in quo homo nascitur . . . in statum gratiæ et adoptionis filiorum Dei per . . . Jesum Christum, salvatorem nostrum; quæ quidem translatio post Evangelium promulgatum sine lavacro regenerationis, aut ejus voto, fieri non potest" (*ibid.* p. 183).

[4] "Ut, qui per peccata a Deo aversi erant, per ejus excitantem atque adjuvantem gratiam ad convertendum se ad suam ipsorum justificationem eidem gratiæ libere assentiendo et co-operando, disponantur . . ."

consist of several things, of which the first is faith—defined to be a belief that the contents of the divine revelation are true. In the two successive chapters faith is declared to be only the beginning of Justification; and Justification itself, in flat contradiction to what had been said previously, is no longer a translation from one state to another; it becomes the actual and gradual conversion of a sinner into a righteous man. It is scarcely necessary to pursue the definitions further. It is sufficient to say that the theologians of Trent do not seem to have the faintest idea of what the Reformers meant by faith, and never appear to see that there is such a thing as religious experience.

The second and third sections of the decree treating of the increase of Justification and of its renewal in the Sacrament of Penance, were drafted still more emphatically in an anti-evangelical spirit, though here and there they show concessions to the Augustinian feeling in the Church. The result was that the Pope obtained what he wanted, a definition which made reconciliation with the Protestants impossible. The New Thomists were able to secure a sufficient amount of Augustinian theology in the decree to render Jansenism possible in the future; while the prevailing Pelagianism or Semi-Pelagianism foreshadowed its overthrow by Jesuit theology.

While these theological definitions were being discussed and framed, the Council also occupied itself with matters of reform. They began to make regulations about preaching and catechising, and this led them insensibly to the question of exemptions from episcopal control. The Popes had for some centuries been trying to weaken the authority of the Bishops, by placing the *regular* clergy or monks beyond the control of the Bishops within whose diocese their convents stood, and this exemption had been the occasion of many ecclesiastical disorders. The discussion was long and excited. It ended in a compromise.

When the decree on Justification was settled, the Council, guided by the Legates, proceeded to discuss the doctrine of the Sacraments, with the intention of still more thoroughly preventing any doctrinal reconciliation with the Protestants. This action called forth remonstrances from the Emperor, whose successes at the time in Germany were alarming the Pope, and making him anxious to withdraw the Council from Germany altogether. He sent orders to the Legates to endeavour to persuade the members at Trent to vote for a transfer to Bologna, where the papal influence would be stronger, and where it would be easier to pack the Synod with a pliant Italian majority. A pretext was found in the appearance of the plague at Trent; and although a strong minority, headed by Madruzzo of Trent, opposed the scheme, the majority (38 to 14) decided that they must leave Trent and establish themselves at the Italian city. The Spanish Bishops, however, remained at Trent awaiting the Emperor's orders.

Charles V. had suffered many disappointments from the Council he had laboured to summon, and this action made him lose all patience. He ordered the Spanish Bishops not to leave Trent; the Diet of Augsburg refused to recognise the prelates who had gone to Bologna as the General Council. After much hesitation, Pope Paul III. felt compelled to suspend the proceedings of the Council at Bologna (September 17th, 1549). This ended the first part of the sittings of the Council.

§ 4. *Second Meeting of the Council.*

Pope Paul III. died November 10th, 1549. At the Conclave which followed, the Cardinal del Monte, the senior Legate of the Council, was chosen Pope, and took the title of Julius III. (February 7th, 1550). He and the Emperor soon came to an agreement that the Council should return to Trent. It accordingly reopened there on May 1st, 1551. The Cardinal Marcello Crescenzio was appointed sole Legate, and two assistants, the Archbishop of Siponto and the Bishop of Verona, were entitled Nuncios. The second meeting of the Council did not promise well.

The Pope had agreed that something was to be done to conciliate the Protestants, and that it should be left an open question whether the preceding decisions of the Council might not be revised.   But before its assembly the policy of the Pope again ran counter to that of the Emperor, and the Protestants had ceased to expect much.   The delegates themselves showed little eagerness to come to the place of meeting.   The Council was forced to adjourn, and it was not until the 1st of September that it began its work.

The earlier proceedings showed that there was little hope of conciliatory measures.   There was no attempt to revise these former decisions, and the Council began its work of codifying doctrine and reformation at the place where it had dropped it.

During the later months of the first meeting, the question of the Sacraments had been under discussion, and so far as the second meeting is concerned it may be said that the whole of its theological work was confined to this subject.

Little pains were taken to conciliate the Protestants. The decisions arrived at pass over in contemptuous silence all the Protestant contendings.   The relations of the Sacraments to the Word and Promises of God, and to the faith of the recipient, are not explained.   The thirteen Canons which sum up the doctrine of the Sacraments in general, and the anathemas with which they conclude, are the protest of the Council against the whole Protestant movement.

This did not prevent the Council being confronted with great difficulties in their definitions—difficulties which arose from the opposition between the earlier and more Evangelical Thomist and the later Scotist and Nominalist theology.   It would almost appear that the fathers of Trent despaired of harmonising the multitude of Scholastic theories on the nature of the Sacraments in general.   They did not venture on constructing a decree, but contented themselves for the most part with merely negative definitions.   They declare

that there are seven Sacraments, neither more nor fewer, all
positively instituted by Christ. They sever the intimate
connection between faith and the Sacraments, attributing
to them a secret and mysterious power. They practically
deny the universal priesthood of believers (Can. 10).
Perhaps the most important Canon is the last: "If any
one shall say that the received and approved rites of the
Catholic Church, commonly used in the solemn administration of the Sacraments, may be contemned, or without sin
omitted at pleasure by the ministrants, or be changed by
any pastor of the churches into other new ones: let him be
anathema" (Can. 13). It enables us to see how, while not
going beyond the verbal limits of the definitions of the
Thomist theology, the Council provided room for subsequent
aberrations of doctrine by raising the use and wont of the
Roman Church to the level of dogma.

In their definitions of the single Sacraments the
Council could and did found on the *Decretum pro Armenis*
of the Council of Florence (1439), incorporated in the Bull
Exultate Deo of Pope Eugenius IV. The real substance of
the definition of Baptism is found in that Canon (3), which
declares that "the Roman Church, which is the mother and
mistress of all Churches, has the true doctrine of the
Sacrament of Baptism." The common practice for the
Bishop to confirm, an historical testimony to the original
position of Bishops as pastors of congregations, is elevated
to the rank of a dogma. The decree and canons on the
Eucharist are a dexterous dove-tailing of sentences making
a mosaic of differing scholastic theories. One detail only
need concern us. Most of the theologians present wished
the denial of the cup to the laity to be elevated into a
dogma, and a decree was actually prepared. But the
secular princes and a widespread public opinion made the
theologians hesitate, and the question was settled in a late
meeting (Session xxi., July 16th, 1562) in a dexterously
ambiguous way. It was declared that "from the beginning
of the Christian religion the use of both *species* has not been
unfrequent," but it was added that no one of the laity was

permitted to demand the cup *ex Dei præcepto*, or to believe that the Church was not acting according to just and weighty reasons when it was refused, or that the " whole and entire Christ " was not received " under either species alone." Few statements have been made in such defiance of history as this decree, with its corresponding canons, when one and another practice of the mediæval Church are said to have existed from the beginning.

The decree on Penance is one of the most carefully constructed and least ambiguous. It is a real codification of Scholastic doctrine. On one portion only was there need for dexterous manipulation, and it received it. The immoral conception of *attrition* was verbally abandoned and really retained. *Contrition,* which is godly sorrow, is declared to be necessary ; and *attrition* is declared to be only a salutary preparation. But the real distinction thus established is at once cancelled by calling *attrition* an *imperfect contrition,* by distinguishing between *contrition* itself and a more perfect *contrition*—contrition perfected by love ; and place is provided for the reintroduction of the immoral conceptions of the later Scotist theologians.[1]

When the theological decrees and canons of the Council of Trent are read carefully in the light of past Scholastic controversies and of varying principles at work in the Roman Catholic Church of the sixteenth century, it is scarcely possible to avoid the conclusion that while the older and more Evangelical Thomist theology gained a verbal recognition, the real victory lay with the Scotist party now represented by the Jesuits. On one side of its activity, the general tendency of Scotist theology had been to produce what was called " theological Scepticism "—a state of mind which was compelled to dissent intellectually from most of the great doctrines of the mediæval Church, and at the same time to accept them on the external authority of the Church—to show that there were no really permanent principles in dogmatic, and that there was need everywhere for reference to a permanent and external source

[1] Cf. i. 222*f.*

of authority who could be no other than the Roman Pontiff.

The Curialist position, that the Universal Church was represented by the Roman Church, and that the Roman Church was, as it were, condensed in the Pope, was not confined to the sphere of jurisdiction only. It had its theological side. Scripture, it was held, was to be interpreted according to the tradition of the Church, and the Pope alone was able to determine what that tradition really was. Hence, the more indefinite theology was, the fewer permanent principles it contained, the more indispensable became the papal authority, and the more thoroughly religion could be identified with a blind unreasoning submission to the Church identified as the Pope. This had been the thought of Ignatius Loyola ; the training of the mind to such a state of absolute submission had been the motive in his *Spiritual Exercises*; and the Jesuit theologians at the Council, Lainez and Salmeron, did very much to secure the practical victory won by Scotist theology, in spite of the fact that the phrases of the decrees came from the theology of their opponents.

The second meeting of the Council of Trent ended on April 28th, 1552. The Peace of Augsburg (1555) showed that the Protestants had acquired a separate legal standing within the Empire, and most people thought that the work of the Council had been wasted. Things were as if it had never been in existence. Pope Paul III. died on March 24th, 1555, and the Conclave elected Cervini, who took the title of Marcellus II. The new Pope survived his elevation only three weeks. He was succeeded by Cardinal Caraffa, Paul IV., and the Counter-Reformation began in earnest.

Paul IV., hater of Spaniards as he was, was the embodiment of the Spanish idea of what a reformation should be. He believed that the work of reform could be done better by the Pope himself than by any Council, and he set to work with the thoroughness which characterised him. There was to be no tampering with the doctrines, usages, or institutions of the mediæval Church. Heresy and Schism were to be crushed by the Inquisition, and the spread of new ideas was to be prevented by the strict examination of all books, and the destruction of those which contained what the Pope conceived to be unwholesome for the minds or morals of mankind. But the Church needed to be reformed thoroughly; the lives of the clergy, and especially of the higher clergy, had to be amended; and abuses which had crept into administration had to be set right.

For some time any real reformation was retarded by the influence of his nephews, who played on the old Pontiff's hatred of the Spaniards, and easily persuaded him that his first duty was to expel the Spaniards from the Italian peninsula. But the evil deeds of these near kinsmen gradually reached his ears. In an assembly of the Inquisition, held in 1559, he was told by Cardinal Pacheco that " reform must begin with *us.*" The old man retired to his apartments, instituted a searching inquiry into the conduct of his nephews, and within a month had deprived them of all their offices and emoluments, and banished them from Rome. Free from this family embarrasment, the Pope prosecuted vigorously his plans for reformation. The secular administration of the States of the Church was thoroughly purified. A Congregation was appointed to examine, classify, and remedy ecclesiastical abuses. Many of the abuses of the Curia were swept away. The Jesuits taught him, although he had no great love for the Order, that spiritual services should not be sold for money. He prohibited taking fees for marriage dispensations. He was a stern censor of the morals of the higher clergy. Under his brief rule Rome became respectable if not virtuous. He restored some of the privileges of the Bishops which had been absorbed by the Papacy. All the while his zeal for purity of doctrine made him urge on the Inquisition and the Index to use their terrible powers. He spared no one. Cardinal Morone, one of the few survivals of the liberal Roman Catholics, was imprisoned, and the suppression of all liberal ideas was ster ly prosecuted.[1]

§ 5. *Third Meeting of the Council.*

Paul IV. died on the 18th of August 1559. He was succeeded by Giovanni de' Medici (Dec. 26th, 1559), a man of a very different type of character, who took the title of Pius IV. The new Pope was by training a lawyer rather than a theologian, and a man skilled in diplomacy. He recognised, as none of his predecessors had done, the difficulties which confronted the Church of Rome. The Lutheran Church had won political recognition in Germany. Scandinavia and Denmark were hopelessly lost. England had become Protestant, and Scotland was almost sure to follow the example of her more powerful neighbour. The Low Countries could not be coerced by Philip and Alva. More than half of German Switzerland had declared for the Reformation. Geneva had become a Protestant fortress, and Calvin's opinions were gaining ground all over French Switzerland. France was hopelessly divided. Bohemia, Hungary, and Poland were alienated from Rome, and might soon revolt altogether. The Pope was convinced that a General Council was necessary to reunite the forces still on the side of the Roman Catholic Church. He saw that it was vain to expect to do this without coming to terms with the Romanist sovereigns. It was the age of autocracy. He pleaded for an alliance of autocrats to confront and withstand the Protestant revolution. He tried to persuade the Emperor (now Ferdinand), Francis II. of France, and Philip of Spain that the independent rule of Bishops was one side of the feudalism which was hostile to monarchy, and that the Pope and the Kings

---

[1] He classed Cardinal Pole among heretics ; Vittoria Colonna became suspect because she was "filia spiritualis et discipula Cardinalis Poli, hæretici" ; and the nuns of St. Catherine at Viterbo were noted as "suspectæ" from their intimacy with Vittoria (*Carteggio di Vittoria Colonna,* pp. 433 *ff.* ; Turin, 1889).

ought to work together. His representations had some
effect as time went on.

A papal Bull (Nov. 29th, 1560) summoned a Council
at Trent on April 6th, 1561. Five Legates were appointed
to preside, at their head Ercole di Gonzaga, Cardinal of
Mantua. They reached Trent on the 16th of April (1561),
and were received by Ludovico Madruzzo, who had succeeded
his uncle, the Cardinal, in the bishopric. The delegates
came slowly. The first session (xvii[th]) was not held till
Jan. 18th, 1562, and was unimportant. The real work
began at the second session (xviii[th]), held on Feb. 26th
(1562).

The Protestants had been invited to attend, but it
was well known that they would not; the assembly represented the Roman Catholic Powers, and them alone. Its
object was not to conciliate the Protestants, but to organise
the Romanist Church. The various Roman Catholic Powers,
however, had different ideas of what ought to be involved
in such a reorganisation.

The Emperor knew that there were many lukewarm
Protestants on the one hand and many disaffected Romanists
on the other. He believed that the former could be won
back and the latter confirmed by some serious modifications
in the usages of the Church. His scheme of reform, set
down in his instructions to his Ambassadors, was very
extensive. It included the permission to give the cup to
the laity, marriage of the priests, mitigation of the prescribed fasts, the use of some of the ecclesiastical revenues
to provide schools for the poor, a revision of the service
books in the sense of purging them of many of their legends,
singing German hymns in public worship, the publication
of a good and simple catechism for the instruction of the
young, a reformation of the cloisters, and a reduction of
the powers of the Roman Pontiff according to the ideas of
the Council of Constance. These reforms, earnestly pressed
by the Emperor in letters, had the support of almost all the
German Roman Catholics.

The French Bishops, headed by the Cardinal Lorraine,

supported the German demands. They were especially anxious for the granting the cup to the laity, the administration of the Sacraments in French, French hymns sung in public worship, and that the celebration of the Mass should always be accompanied by instruction and a sermon. They also pressed for a limitation of the powers of the Pope, according to the decisions of the Council of Basel.

The Spanish Bishops, on the other hand, were thoroughly opposed to any change in ecclesiastical doctrine or usages. They did not wish the cup given to the laity; they abhorred clerical marriage; they protested against the idea of the services or any part of them in the mother tongue. But they desired a thorough reformation of the Curia, of the whole system of dispensations; they wished a limitation of the powers of the Pope, and to see the Bishops of the Church restored to their ancient privileges.

France and Germany desired that the Council should be considered a new Synod; Spain and the Pope meant it to be simply a continuation of the former sessions at Trent.

These difficulties might well have daunted the Pope; but the suave diplomatist faced the situation, trusting mainly to his own abilities to carry matters through to a successful issue. He knew that he must have command of the Council, and to that end several resolutions were passed mainly by the adroit generalship of the Legates. It was practically, if not formally, resolved that the Synod should be simply a continuation of that Council which had begun at Trent in 1545. This got rid at once of a great deal of difficult doctrinal discussion, and provided that all dogmas had to be discussed on the lines laid down in previous sessions. It was decreed that no proxies should be allowed. This enabled the Pope to keep up a constant majority of Italian Bishops, who outnumbered those of all other nations put together. By a clever ruse the Council was induced to vote that the papal Legates alone should have the privilege of proposing resolutions to the Council.

This made it impossible to bring before the Council any matter to which the Pope had objection.

The Pope knew well, however, that it mattered little what conclusions the Council came to, if its decisions were to be repudiated by the Roman Catholic Powers. He therefore carried on elaborate negotiations with the Emperor and the Kings of Spain and France while the Council was sitting, and arranged with them the wording of the decrees to be adopted. His tactics, which never varied during the whole period of the Council, and which were finally crowned with success, were simple. He maintained at all costs a numerical majority in the Synod ready to vote as he directed. This was done by systematic drafts of Italian Bishops to Trent. Many of the poorer ones were subsidised through Cardinal Simonetta, whose business it was to see that the mechanical majority was kept up, and to direct it how to vote. His Legates had the exclusive right of proposing resolutions ; couriers took the proposals drafted by the various Congregations to Rome, and the Pope revised them there before they were laid before the whole Council to be voted upon ; spies informed him what were the objections of the French, Spanish, or German Bishops, and the Pope was diligent to bring all manner of influences to bear upon them to incline them to his mind ; if he failed, he prevented the proposals being laid before the Council until he had consulted and bargained with the monarchs through special agents. The papal post-bags, containing proposed decrees or canons, went the round of the European Courts before they were presented to the Council, and the Bishops spoke and voted upon what had been already settled behind their backs and without their knowledge.

In spite of all this dexterous manipulation, the Council, composed of so many jarring elements, did not work very smoothly. The papal diplomacy sometimes increased the disturbances. Men chafed under the thought that they were only puppets, and that the matters they had been called together to discuss were already irrevocably settled.

" Better never to have come here at all," said a Spanish
Bishop, "than to be reduced to mere spectators." Few
ecclesiastical assemblies have seen stormier scenes than
took place during these later sittings of the Council of
Trent.

In the end, the papal diplomacy prevailed. His
conciliatory manner helped Pius through difficulties in
which another would have failed. No man was readier
to give way in things which he did not consider essential,
and what he promised he scrupulously performed. The
success of the last meeting of the Council was due to
bargaining and dexterous persuasion. When the critical
point arrived, and it seemed as if the Council must fall to
pieces, his agents, Morone and Peter Canisius, the great
German Jesuit, won Ferdinand over to the Pope's side.
Similar persuasive diplomacy secured the influence of
the Cardinal of Lorraine. Even Philip of Spain was
brought to see that the Spanish Bishops were asking
too much.

It must also be remembered that while Pius IV. refused
to tolerate any loss of papal rights or privileges, he consented
to and did his best to carry out numberless salutary
reforms ; and that the Council of Trent not only reorganised, but greatly purified the Roman Church. Almost
all that was good in the reformation wrought by his
predecessor Paul IV. was made part of the Tridentine
regulations.

The special matter in dispute between the Pope and
the great majority of non-Italian Bishops concerned the
relations in which the Bishops of the Catholic Church
stood to the Bishop of Rome, whom all acknowledged as
their head. The Spanish, French, and German Bishops
were strongly opposed to that doctrine of papal supremacy
which had been assiduously taught by the canonists of the
Roman Curia for at least two centuries, and which was
called *curialism*. Curialism taught that the Pope was
lord of the Church in the sense that all the clergy were
his servants, and that Bishops in particular were mer

assistants whom he had appointed for the purpose of oversight to act as his vicars. Whatever powers of jurisdiction they possessed came from him, and from him alone. The opposite conception, that insisted on at Trent by the northern and Spanish Bishops, that maintained at the great Councils of Constance and Basel, was that every Bishop had his power directly from Christ, and that the Pope, while he was the representative of the unity of the Church, and therefore to be recognised as its head, was only a *primus inter pares*, and subject to the episcopate as a whole in Council assembled. The question kept cropping up in almost all the discussions in the Council which turned on reform. It began as early as the fifth session (June 17th, 1546) and went on intermittently; but it positively raged in the later sessions.

The question was raised on its practical side. One of the standing abuses in the mediæval Church was the non-residence of Bishops. The Council was passionately called upon by the Spanish and northern Bishops to declare that residence was a necessary thing, and unanimously responded that it was. Their function was the oversight of their dioceses, and this could only be done when they were resident. But how was this to be enforced? To compel the Bishops to reside within their dioceses would depopulate the Court of Rome, and make it very much poorer. Bishops from every country in Europe were attached to the Roman Court, and their stipends, drawn from the countries in which their Sees lay, were spent in Rome, and aided the magnificence of the papal entourage. The reformers felt that a theoretical question lay behind the practical, and insisted that the oversight and therefore the residence of Bishops was *de jure divino* and not merely *de lege ecclesiastica*—something enjoined by God, and therefore beyond alteration by the Pope. Behind this lay the thought, first introduced by Cyprian, that every Bishop was within his congregation or diocese the Vicar of Christ, and in the last resort responsible to Him alone. Thus the old conciliar conception, maintained at Constance and at

Basel, faced the curial at Trent; and both were too powerful to give way entirely. In spite of his Italian majority, the Pope could not get a majority for a direct negative denying the *de jure divino* theory. At the final vote, sixty-six fathers declared for the *de jure divino* theory, while seventy-one either rejected it altogether or voted for remitting it to the decision of the Pope. The Pope dared not make use of the liberty of decision thus accorded to him by a majority of five. If he did he would then be left to face the European Roman Catholic Courts of Germany, France, and Spain—all of whom supported the conciliar view. Thus the theoretical question was left undecided at Trent, but the papal diplomacy prevailed to the extent of creating a bias in favour of curialist ideas, which left the Pope in a stronger position as regards the episcopate than any other General Council had ever placed him in.

The prominence given to the *Roman* (*i.e.* the papal) Church throughout the decisions of the Council, beginning with the way in which the Constantinopolitan (Nicene) Creed was affirmed ; [1] the insertion of the phrase *His own Vicar upon earth* ; [2] the injunction that Patriarchs, Primates, Archbishops, Bishops, and all others who of right and custom ought to be present at a provincial council . . . *promise and profess true obedience to the Sovereign Roman Pontiff* ; [3] the 10th clause in the *Professio Fidei Tridentinæ*: "I acknowledge the holy Catholic Apostolic Roman Church for the mother and mistress of all Churches; and I promise and swear true obedience to the Bishop of Rome, successor to St. Peter, Prince of Apostles, and Vicar of Jesus Christ"; the way in which the Council at its last session (Dec. 4th, 1563) left entirely in the Pope's hands the confirmation of its decrees and the measures to be used for carrying them out; and

---

[1] "Symbolum fidei quo sancta *Romana* Ecclesia utitur."

[2] "Through the mercy of God and the provident care of *His own Vicar upon earth.*" Session vi. de reform. c. 1.

[3] Session xxv. de reform. c. 2.

38**

above all its calm acquiescence in the Bull *Benedictus Deus* (Jan. 24th, 1564), in which Pope Pius IV. reserved the exposition of its decrees to himself [1]—all testify to the triumph of curialist ideas at the Council of Trent. The Roman Catholic Church had become, in a sense never before universally accepted, the " Pope's House."

This Council, so eagerly demanded, so greatly protracted, twice dissolved, buffeted by storms in the political world, exposed, even in its later sessions, to many a danger, ended in the general contentment of the Roman Catholic peoples. When the prelates met together for the last time on the 4th of December 1563, ancient opponents embraced, and traces of tears were seen in many of the old eyes.

It had done three things for the Roman Catholic Church. It had provided a compact system of doctrine, stript of many of the vagaries of Scholasticism, and yet opposed to Protestant teaching. Romanism had an intellectual basis of its own to rest on. It had rebuilt the hierarchy on what may be called almost a new foundation, and made it symmetrical. It had laid down a scheme of reformation which, if only carried out by succeeding Pontiffs, would free the Church from many of the crying evils which had given such strength to the Protestant movement. It had insisted on and made provisions for an educated clergy — perhaps the greatest need of the Roman Church in the middle of the sixteenth century.

All this was largely due to the man who ruled in Rome. Pope Pius IV., sprung from the shrewd Italian middle-class,

---

[1] ꞌꞋ We by apostolic authority forbid all persons . . . that they presume without our authority to publish in any form any commentaries, glosses, annotations, scholia, or any kind of interpretation whatsoever touching the decrees of the said Council ; or to settle anything in regard thereof under any plea whatsoever. . . . But if anything therein shall seem to any one to have been expressed and ordained obscurely . . . and to stand in need of interpretation or decision, let him go up to the place which the Lord hath chosen, to wit, to the Apostolic See, the mistress of all the faithful, whose authority the Holy Synod also has reverently acknowledged."

caring little for theology, by no means distinguished for piety, had seen what the Church needed, and by deft diplomacy had obtained it. A stronger man would have snapped the threads which tied all parties together; one more zealous would have lacked his infinite patience; a deeply pious man could scarcely have employed the means he continually used. He was magnificently assisted by the new Company of Jesus. No theologians had so much influence at Trent as Lainez and Salmeron; the Council would have broken down altogether but for the aid given by Canisius to Morone in his negotiations with the Emperor.

Pius IV. was not slow to fulfil the promises he had made to sovereigns and Council. The Breviary and the Missal were revised, as Ferdinand had requested. Ecclesiastical music was purified. Exertions were made to establish colleges and theological seminaries. But a sterner Pontiff was needed to guide the battle against the growing Protestantism. He was found in the next, Pope Pius V.

The influence of Cardinal Borromeo, the pious nephew of Pius IV., was powerful in the Conclave, and was exerted to procure the election of Michele Ghislieri, Cardinal of Alessandria, who took the name of Pius V. The new Pontiff had entered a Dominican convent when fourteen years of age, and had given himself up heart and soul to the strictest life his Order enjoined. He had all the zeal for strict orthodoxy which characterised the Dominicans, an asceticism which never spared himself, and a detestation of the immoralities and irregularities which too often disgraced the lives of ecclesiastics. He carried the habits of the cloister with him into the Vatican. He never missed attendance at the prescribed services of the Church, and in his devotion there was no trace of hypocrisy. He was a Pope to lead the new Romanism, with its intense hatred of heresy, its determination to reform the moral life, and its contempt for the Renaissance and all its works. Philip II. of Spain sent a special letter of congratulation to

Cardinal Borromeo to thank him for his efforts in the Conclave.

The new Pontiff believed, heart and soul, in repression. He meant to fight the Reformation by the Inquisition and the Index; and these two instruments were unsparingly used.

CHAPTER VI.

§ 1. *The Inquisition in Spain.*

THE idea conveyed in the term Inquisition is the punishment of spiritual or ecclesiastical offences by physical pains and penalties. It was no new conception in the Christian Church. It had existed from the days of Constantine. So far as the mediæval Church is concerned, historians roughly distinguish between the Episcopal, the Papal, and the Spanish Inquisitions. In the half-barbarous Church of the early Middle Ages, in which a curious give-and-take policy existed between the secular and civil powers, a seemingly consistent understanding was arrived at between Church and State, which may be summed up by saying that it was recognised to be the Church's duty to point out heretics, and that of the State to punish them —the Church being represented by the Bishops. This episcopal Inquisition took many forms, and was never a very effective instrument in the suppression of heresy.

In 1203, Pope Innocent III., alarmed at the spread of heresies through southern France and northern Italy, published a Bull censuring the indifference of the Bishops, appointing the Abbot of Citeaux his delegate in matters of heresy, and giving him power to judge and *punish*

---

[1] Llorente, *Histoire critique de l'Inquisition d'Espagne* (Paris, 1818) ; Lea, *A History of the Inquisition of the Middle Ages* (London, 1888) ; Reusch, *Der Index der Verbotener Bücher* (Bonn, 1885) ; Lea, *The Spanish Inquisition* (London, 1906) ; Symonds, *Renaissance in Italy, The Catholic Reaction* (London, 1886).

heresy. This was the beginning of the Inquisition as a separate institution. It was an act of papal centralisation, and a distinct encroachment on the episcopal jurisdiction. The papal Inquisition, thus started, took root. It did not displace the old episcopal Inquisition; the two existed side by side; but the "Apostolic Tribunal for the suppression of heresy" was by far the more effective weapon. It was usually managed by the Dominican and Franciscan Orders.

The Spanish Inquisition took its rise in the closing decades of the fifteenth century. The Popes had frequently desired to see the papal Inquisition introduced into Spain, and leave had always been refused by the sovereigns, jealous of papal interference. Pope Sixtus IV. had gone the length of granting to his Legate, Nicolo Franco, "full inquisitorial powers to prosecute and punish false Christians who after baptism persisted in the observance of Jewish rites," but Isabella and Ferdinand did not allow him to exercise them. But the power and wealth of the *Conversos*—Jews who had nominally embraced Christianity—had made them detested by the Spanish people, and a large section of the clergy were clamouring for their overthrow. Thomas de Torquemada, the Queen's confessor, eagerly pressed the Inquisition upon his royal penitent, and at last the sovereigns applied to the Pope for a Bull to enable them to establish in Spain an Inquisition of a peculiar kind. It was to differ from the ordinary papal Inquisition in this, that it was to be strictly under royal control, that the sovereigns were to have the appointment of the Inquisitors, and that the fines and confiscations were to flow into the royal treasury. The Bull was granted (November 1st, 1478), but the sovereigns hesitated to use the rights it conveyed. After a year's delay, two royal Inquisitors were appointed (September 17th, 1480), and the first *auto-da-fé*, at which six persons were burnt, took place on February 6th, 1481. The succeeding years saw various modifications in the constitution of the Holy Office; but at last it was organised with a council, presided over by an Inquisitor-General, Thomas de Torquemada. He was a man of pitiless zeal, stern, relentless, and autocratic ; and he stamped his nature on the institution over which he presided. The Holy Office was permitted to frame its own rules. The permission made it practically independent, while all the resources of the State were placed at its command. When an Inquisitor came to assume his functions, the officials took an oath to assist him to exterminate all whom he might designate as heretics, and to observe, and compel the observance by all, of the decretals *Ad abolendum, Excommunicamus, Ut officium Inquisitionis,* and *Ut Inquisitionis negotium*—the papal legislation of the thirteenth century, which made the State wholly subservient to the Holy Office, and rendered incapable of official position any one suspect in the faith or who favoured heretics. Besides this, all the population was assembled to listen to a sermon by the Inquisitor, after which all were required to swear on the cross and the Gospels to help the Holy Office, and not to impede it in any manner or on any pretext. The methods of work and procedure were also taken from the papal Inquisition. The Inquisitors were furnished with letters patent. They travelled from town to town, attended by guards and notaries public. Their expenses were defrayed by taxes laid on the towns and districts through which they passed. Spies and informers, guaranteed State protection, brought forward their information. The Court was opened ; witnesses were examined ; and the accused were acquitted or found guilty. The sentence was pronounced ; the secular assessor gave a formal assent ; and the accused was handed over to the civil authorities for punishment. When Torquemada reorganised the Spanish Inquisition, a series of rules were framed for its procedure which enforced secrecy to the extent of depriving the accused of any rational means of defence ; which elaborated the judicial method so as to leave no loop-hole even for those who expressed a wish to recant ; and which multiplied the charges under which suspected heretics, even after death, might be treated as impenitent and their property confiscated. The Spanish Inquisition differed from the papal in its close relation to the civil authorities, its terrible secrecy, its relentlessness, and its exclusion of Bishops from even a nominal participation in its work. Thus organised, it became the most terrible of curses to unhappy Spain. During the first hundred and thirty-nine years of its existence the country was depopulated to the extent of three millions of people. It had become strong enough to overawe the monarchy, to insult the episcopate, and to defy the Pope. The number of its victims can only be conjectured. Llorente has calculated that during the eighteen years of Torquemada's presidency 114,000 persons were accused, of whom 10,220 were burnt alive, and 97,000 were condemned to perpetual imprisonment or to public penitence. This was the terrible instrument used relentlessly to bring the Spanish people into conformity with the Spanish Reformation, and to crush the growing Protestantism of the Low Countries. It was extended to Corsica and Sardinia ; but the people of Naples and Sicily successfully resisted its introduction when proposed by the Spanish Viceroys.

§ 2. *The Inquisition in Italy.*

Cardinal Caraffa (afterwards Pope Paul IV.), the relentless enemy of the Reformation, seeing the success of this Spanish Inquisition in its extermination of heretics, induced Pope Paul III. to consent to a reorganisation of the papal Inquisition in Italy on the Spanish model, in 1542. The Curia had become alarmed at the progress of the Reformation in Italy. They had received information that small Protestant communities had been formed in several of the Italian towns, and that heresy was spreading in an alarming fashion. Caraffa declared that " the whole of Italy was infected with the Lutheran heresy, which had been extensively embraced both by statesmen and ecclesiastics." Ignatius Loyola and the Jesuits highly approved of the suggestion, and they were all-powerful with the Cardinal

Borromeo, the pious and trusted nephew of the Pope. In 1542 the Congregation of the Holy Office was founded at Rome, and six Cardinals, among them Cardinals Caraffa and Toledo, were named Inquisitors-General, with authority on both sides of the Alps to try all cases of heresy, to apprehend and imprison suspected persons, and to appoint inferior tribunals with the same or more limited powers. The intention was to introduce into this remodelled papal Inquisition most of the features which marked the thoroughness of the Spanish institution. But the jealousy of the Popes prevented the Holy Office from exercising the same independent action in Italy as in Spain. The new institution began its work at once within the States of the Church, and was introduced after some negotiations into most of the Italian principalities. Venice refused, until it was arranged that the Holy Office there should be strictly subject to the civil authorities.

Although modelled on the Spanish institution, the work of the Holy Office in Italy never exhibited the same murderous activity; nor was there the same need. The Italians have never showed the stern consistency in faith which characterised the Spaniards. It was generally found sufficient to strike at the leaders in order to cause the relapse of their followers. Still the records of the Office and contemporary witnesses recount continuous trials and burnings in Rome and in other cities. In Venice, death by drowning was substituted for burning. The victims were placed on a board supported by two gondolas ; the boats were rowed apart, and the unfortunate martyrs perished in the waters. The Protestant congregations which had been formed in Bologna, Faenza, Ferrara, Lucca, Modena, Naples, Siena, Venice, and Vicenza were dispersed with little or no bloodshed. A colony of Waldenses, settled near the town of Cosenza in the north-central part of Calabria, were made of sterner stuff. Nothing would induce them to relapse, and they were exterminated by sword, by hurling from the summits of cliffs, by prolonged confinement in deadly prisons, at the stake, in the mines,

in the Spanish galleys.   One hundred elderly women were
first tortured and then slaughtered at Montalto.   The
survivors among the women and children were sold into
slavery   Such was the work of the Counter-Reformation
in Italy, and the measures to which it owed much of its
success.

§ 3. *The Index.*

Leaders of the Counter-Reformation in Italy like
Popes Paul IV. and Pius V. were determined on much more
than the dispersion of Protestant communities and the
banishment or martyrdom of the missionaries of Evangelical
thought.   They resolved to destroy what they rightly
enough believed to be its seed and seed-bed——the cultiva-
tion of independent thinking and of impartial scholarship.
They wished to extirpate all traces of the Renaissance.   In
the fifteenth and first half of the sixteenth centuries, Italy
had been " the workshop of ideas," the *officina scientiarum*
for the rest of Europe.   The Inquisition, in Italy as in Spain,
attacked the Academies, the schools of learning, above all
the libraries in which the learning of the past was stored,
and the printing-presses which disseminated ideas day by
day.   They had the example of Torquemada before them,
who had burnt six thousand volumes at Salamanca in
1490 on pretence that they taught sorcery.

It was no new thing to order the burning of heretical
writings.   This had been done continuously throughout
the Middle Ages.   The episcopal Inquisition, the Universities, the papal Inquisition, had all endeavoured to
discover and destroy writings which they deemed to be
dangerous to the dogmas of the Church.   After the
invention of printing such a method of slaying ideas was
not so easy ; but the ecclesiastical authorities had tried
their best.   The celebrated edict of the Archbishop of
Mainz of 1486, prompted by the number of Bibles printed
in the vernacular, and trying to establish a censorship of
books, may be taken as an example.[1]

[1] It is to be found in Gudenus, *Codex Diplomaticus.* iv. 469.

Pope Sixtus IV. in 1547 had ordered the University of Köln to see that no books (*libri, tractatus aut scripturæ qualescunque*) were printed without previous licence, and had empowered the authorities to inflict penalties on the printers, purchasers, and readers of all unlicensed books. Alexander VI. had sent the same order to the Archbishops of Köln, Mainz, Trier, and Magdeburg (1501). In a *Constitution* of Leo X., approved by the Lateran Council of 1515, it was declared that no book could be printed in Rome which had not been expressly sanctioned by the *Master of the Palace,* and in other lands by the Bishop of the diocese or the Inquisitor of the district ; and this had been homologated by the Council of Trent.[1] From its reorganisation in 1543 the papal Inquisition in Rome had undertaken this work of censorship.

Outside the States of the Church the suppression of books and the requirement of ecclesiastical licence could only be carried out through the co-operation of the secular authorities ; and they naturally demanded some uniformity in the books condemned. This led to lists of prohibited books being drawn up—as at Louvain (1546 and 1550), at Köln (1549), and by the Sorbonne, who managed the Inquisition for the north of France (1544 and 1551). Pope Paul IV. drafted the first papal Index in 1559. It was very drastic, and its very severity prevented its success.[2] It was this *Index Librorum Prohibitorum* which

---

[1] "Wishing also to impose a restraint . . . upon printers . . . who print without licence of ecclesiastical superiors, the said books of Sacred Scripture, and the annotations and expositions upon them of all persons indifferently . . . (this Synod) ordains and decrees, that, henceforth, the Sacred Scripture, and especially the aforesaid old and Vulgate edition, be printed in the most correct manner possible ; and that it shall not be lawful for anyone to print, or cause to be printed, *any books whatever on sacred matters,* without the name of the author ; nor to sell them in future or even to keep them by them, *unless they shall have been first examined and approved by the ordinary* ; under pain of anathema and fine imposed in a canon of the last Lateran Council " (Sess. iv.)

[2] The original Index of Pope Paul IV. contained a list of no less than sixty-one *printers,* and prohibited the reading of *any book printed by them.* He afterwards withdrew this clause. But his Index gives a long catalogue of authors *all* of whose writings are prohibited. It is, with one dis-

was discussed by the Commission appointed at the Council of Trent.[1]

The Commission drafted a set of ten rules to be followed in constructing a list of prohibited books, and left the actual formation of the Index to the Pope. This new Index (the Tridentine Index) was published by Pope Pius IV. in 1564. His successor, Pius V., appointed a special Commission of Cardinals to deal with the question of prohibited books. It was called the Congregation of the Index, and although distinct from the Inquisition, worked along with it. Its work was done very thoroughly. Italian scholarship was slain so far as the peninsula was concerned. The scholarship of Spain and Portugal was also destroyed. Learning had to take shelter north of the Alps and the Pyrenees. So thoroughly was the work of prohibition carried out, so many difficulties beset even Roman Catholic authors, that Paleario called the whole system "a dagger drawn from the scabbard to assassinate all men of letters"; Paul Sarpi dubbed it "the finest secret which has ever been discovered for applying religion to the purpose of making men idiots"; and Latini, a champion of the Papacy, declared it to be a "peril which threatened the very existence of books."

The rules for framing the Index, drafted by the commission of the Council of Trent, are curious reading. The writings of noted Reformers, of Zwingli, Luther, and especially of Calvin, were absolutely prohibited. The Vulgate was to be the only authorised version of the Scriptures, and the only one to be quoted as an inspired text. Scholars might, by special permission of their ecclesiastical superiors, possess another version, but they were never to quote it as authoritative. Versions in the vernacular were never to be quoted. Bible Dictionaries,

tinguished exception, a mere list of names; but it contains : "Desiderius Erasmus Roterodamus cum universis commentariis, annotationibus, scholiis, dialogis, epistolis, censuris, versionibus, libris et scriptis suis, etiam si nil penitus contra religionem vel de religione contineant."

[1] Session xviii.—Decree anent the choice of books ; Session xxv.—Anent the Index of books, the Catechism, Breviary, and Missal.

Concordances, books on controversial theology, had to pass the strictest examination at the hands of the censors before publication. The censors were directed to examine with the utmost care not merely the text, but all summaries, notes, indexes, prefaces, and dedications, searching for any heretical phrases or for sentences which the unwary might be tempted to think heretical, for all criticisms on any ecclesiastical action, for any satire on the clergy or on religious rites. All such passages were to be expunged.

North of the Alps the Index had small effect. It was impotent in lands where the Reformation was firmly established; and in France, papal Germany, and north Italy a class of daring colporteurs carried the prohibited tracts, Bibles, and religious literature throughout the lands.

The tremendous powers of suppression set forth in the Tridentine rules could not avoid doing infinite mischief to thought and scholarship, even if placed in the hands of qualified and well-intentioned men. But the censors were neither capable nor high-minded. Scholars refused the odious task. Commentaries on the Fathers were read by men who knew little Latin, less Greek, and no Hebrew. They were discovered extorting money from unfortunate authors, levying blackmail on booksellers, listening to the whispers of jealous rivals.

So effectually was learning slain in Italy, that when the Popes at the close of the sixteenth century strove to revive the scholarship of the Church and to gather together at Rome a band of men able to defend the Papacy with their pens, these scholars had to work under immense disabilities. Baronius wrote his *Annals*, and Latini edited the Latin Fathers, both of them ignorant of Greek, and both harassed by the censorship.

Some of the more distinguished leaders of the Counter-Reformation saw the dangers which lurked in this system of pure suppression. The great German Jesuit, Canisius, who did more than any other man for the maintenance and revival of the Roman Catholic Church in Germany, pointed out that destruction was powerless to effect permanent good. The people must have books, and the Church ought to supply them. He laboured somewhat successfully to that end.

§ 4. *The Society of Jesus and the Counter-Reformation.*

Neither the Inquisition nor the Index account for the Counter-Reformation. Repression might stamp out Reformers in southern Europe; but faith, enthusiasm, unselfish and self-denying work were needed to enable the Roman Church to assume the offensive. These were supplied to a large extent by the devoted followers of Ignatius Loyola.

Roman Catholicism reached its ebb during the pontificate of Pius IV. It stood everywhere on the defensive, seeing one stronghold after another pass into the hands of a victorious Protestantism. Pius V., his successor, was the first fighting Pope of the new Roman Catholicism. He had behind him the reorganisation effected by the Council of Trent; the Roman Catholic revival of mediæval piety of which Carlo Borromeo, Philip Neri, and Francis de Sales were distinguished types; the Inquisition and Congregation of the Index; and, above all, the Company of Jesus. Romanism under his leadership boldly assumed the offensive.

In 1564 it seemed as if all Germany might become Protestant. The States which still acknowledged the Papacy were honeycombed with Protestant communities. Bavaria, the Rhine Provinces, the Duchy of Austria itself, were, according to contemporary accounts, more than half-Protestant. Nearly all the seats of learning were Protestant. The Romanist Universities of Vienna and Ingolstadt were almost deserted by students. Under the skilful and enthusiastic leadership of Peter Canisius, the Jesuits were mainly instrumental in changing this state of things. They entered Bavaria and Austria. They appeared there as the heralds and givers of education, and took possession of the rising generation. They established their schools in all the principal centres of population. They were good teachers; they produced school-books of a modern type; the catechism written by Canisius himself was used in all their schools (it transplanted into Romanism the Lutheran system of catechising); they charged no fees; they soon had the instruction of the Roman Catholic children in their hands. The astonished people of town and country districts began to see pilgrimages of boys and girls, conducted like modern Sunday-school treats, led by the good fathers, to visit famous churches, shrines, holy crosses, miraculous wells, etc. The parents were induced to visit the teachers; visits led to the confessional, and the confessional to the directorate. Then followed the discipline of the *Spiritual Exercises*, usually shortened to suit the capacities of the penitents. Whole districts were led back to the confessional—the parents following the children.

The higher education was not neglected. Jesuit colleges founded at Vienna and Ingolstadt peopled the decaying universities with students, and gave them new life. Student associations, on the model of that founded by Canisius at Köln, were formed, and were affiliated to the Company of Jesus. Pilgrimages of students wended their way to famous shrines; talented young men submitted their souls to the direction of the Jesuit fathers, and shared in the hypnotic trance given by the course of the *Spiritual Exercises*. A generation of ardent souls was trained for the active service of the Roman Church, and vowed to combat Protestantism to the death.

The Company had another, not less important, field of work. The Peace of Augsburg had left the management of the religion of town or principality in the hands of the ruling secular authority. The maxim, *Cujus regio ejus religio*, placed the religious convictions of the population of many districts at the mercy of one man. Many Romanist Princes had no wish to persecute, still less to see their principalities depopulated by banishment. Some of them had given guarantees for freedom of conscience and limited rights of worship to their Protestant subjects. The Jesuits set themselves to change this condition of things. They could be charming confessors and still more delightful directors for the obedient sons and daughters of the Papacy. They were invited to take charge of the souls of many of the Princes and especially of the Princesses of Germany. They set themselves to charm, to command, and, lastly, to threaten their penitents. Toleration of Protestants they represented to be the unpardonable sin. They succeeded in many cases in inducing Romanist rulers to withdraw the protection they had hitherto accorded to their Protestant subjects, who, if they stood firm in their faith, had to leave their homes and seek refuge within a Protestant district.

Thus openly and stealthily the wave of Romanist reaction rolled northwards over Germany, and district after district was won back for the Papacy. This first period of the Counter-Reformation may be said to end with the sixteenth century ; the second, which included the Thirty Years' War, lies beyond our limit.

The savage struggle in France, culminating in the Massacre of St. Bartholomew, did not belong to the New Roman Catholicism, and lay outside of what may be called the Counter-Reformation proper. The force of this new aggressive movement was first felt in the formation of the Holy League, which had for its object to prevent Henry of Navarre from ascending the throne of France. The League was the symbol in France of this Counter-Reformation. The Jesuits never attained a preponderating influence in that country until the days of Marie de Medici ; but they were the restless and ruthless organisers of the Holy League. The Jesuit fathers, Auger, Henri Saumier, and, above all, Claude Matthieu, called the *Courrier de la Ligue*, worked energetically on its behalf. The Company issued tracts from their printing-presses asserting the inalienable rights of the people to govern and therefore to choose their rulers. They taught that while God had given spiritual power into the hands of one man, the Pope,

He had bestowed the secular power on the many. Kings, they asserted, do not reign by any divine right of hereditary succession, but by the will of the people and of the Pope. Hence all Romanist France was justified in setting aside the King of Navarre and putting in his place the Cardinal of Bourbon, his uncle.

The arguments they laid before the English people were based on principles altogether different, even contradictory. There they extolled hereditary and legitimate succession. Elizabeth was illegitimate, and Mary of Scotland had divine rights to the throne of England. It is needless to relate the efforts made by the leaders of the Counter-Reformation to bring England back to the Papacy —the College at Douai, the English College at Rome, both erected to train missionaries for service against the heretical Queen; the mission of the Jesuits, Parsons and Campion. The student of history can scarcely fail to note one thing,—that the sailing of the Spanish Armada marks the flood-tide of the first period of the Counter-Reformation. After the ruin of the great fleet the first wave of the reaction seems to have spent itself. The League failed in France, and Henry IV. secured the rights of his Protestant subjects in the Edict of Nantes. The Hollanders emerged triumphant from their long war of liberation. Even in Germany the defeat of the Armada dates in a rough way the end of the impetus of the Romanist reaction. The German Protestants assumed the offensive again, and an energetic and aggressive Calvinism redeemed the halting character of the Lutheran Reformation.

Mr. Symonds, in his brilliant sketches of the forces at work to make the Romanist reaction, thinks that the part of the Jesuits in the Counter-Reformation has rather been exaggerated than insufficiently recognised. "Without the ecclesiastical reform which originated in the Tridentine Council; without the gold and sword of Spain; without the stakes and prisons of the Inquisition; without the warfare against thought conducted by the Congregation of the Index,—the Jesuits alone could not have masterfully

39**

governed the Catholic revival." [1]   This is perhaps true ;
but what would all these things have come to apart from
the activity of the Company of Jesus ?   They were little
better than the mechanism to which the enthusiasm and
the indomitable work bred from enthusiasm gave the soul.
Stern, relentless, savage repression can do much.   It can
make a desert and call it peace ; but it cannot requicken
with renewed life.   The gentle piety of Carlo Borromeo,
the sweet languishing tenderness of Francis de Sales, the
revived mediæval mysticism discernible in the Romanist
reaction, had neither the religious depth nor the endurance
needed for the times.   Ignatius breathed the Spanish
spirit, at once wildly visionary and intensely practical,
into his Company, and they transfused it throughout the
Church of the Counter-Reformation—the exalted devotion,
the tenacity which no reverses could wear out, and the
unquenchable religious hope.   They ruled it as the soul
governs the body.

It was the time of Spanish domination.   Spain grasped
the New World and hoped to subdue the Old.   Her
soldiers were the best in Europe.   They dreamed of
nothing but conquests.   The Jesuits brought the Spanish
spirit into the Church.   Others might scheme, and wish,
and wonder.   They worked.   They reaped the harvest
which hard and unremitting labour gathers in every field.
It was not for nothing that Adrian and other papal
statesmen dubbed Luther another Mahomet ; the word
kindled in every Spanish breast the memory of their
centuries of war with the Moslems and its victorious
ending.   If the gold and sword of Spain were at the
service of the Counter-Reformation, it was the Spanish
spirit incarnate in the Company of Jesus that made such
dry bones live.

We must remember that in the first period of the
Romanist reaction we have to do with the Jesuits of the
sixteenth century, and must banish from our minds the history
of the Order in the two centuries that follow.   Its worst

---

[1] Symonds, *The Renaissance in Italy : The Catholic Reaction*, i. 301.

side had scarcely appeared. Its theory of Probabilism, by which directors were trained to transform all deadly sins, even murder, adultery, and theft, into venial offences, and casuistry became a method for the entire guidance of souls, belonged to a later period. It was not till the seventeenth century that the forgiveness of sins had been reduced by them to a highly refined art. Their shameless neglect of religion and morality, when the political interests of the Church and of the Society seemed to require it, was also later. What the depressed Romanists of the sixteenth century saw was a body of men whom no difficulties daunted, who spent themselves in training boys and girls and in animating them with religious principles; who persuaded boys and youths to attend daily Mass, to resort to monthly confession, to study the articles of their faith; who elevated that obedience, which for generations they had been taught was due to the earthly head of the Church, into a sublime religious principle.

All this the Romanism of the Counter-Reformation owed to those three unknown men, who crept into Rome through the Porto del Popolo during Easter 1538 to beg Pope Paul III. to permit them and their companions to enroll themselves in a new Order for the defence of the faith.

It is true that men can never get rid of their personal responsibility in spiritual things, but multitudes will always attempt to cast the burden upon others. In all such souls the spirit of the Counter-Reformation lives and moves and has its being, and they are sustained, consciously or unconsciously, by that principle of blind obedience which its preachers taught. It is enough for us to remember that no weakened sense of personal responsibility and no amount of superstitious practice can utterly quench the conscience that seeks its God, or can hinder that upward glance to the Father in heaven which carries with it a living faith.

INDEX.

40**